WITH SO MANY FIRSTS, NO WONDER WE'VE CALLED OUR NEW TRUCK THE MAGNUM.

RENAULT Trucks

At Renault Trucks we believe in putting the customer first. That's why we were the first to offer a free 3 year Driveline warranty. The first to bring trucks into the 1990's, with 5 new product ranges from 3.5 to 38 tonne GVW in just 18 months. And the first to introduce a truck that breaks the 500 bhp barrier. No wonder we've built up quite a thirst. If you want to talk trucks, call 0582 479100. First.

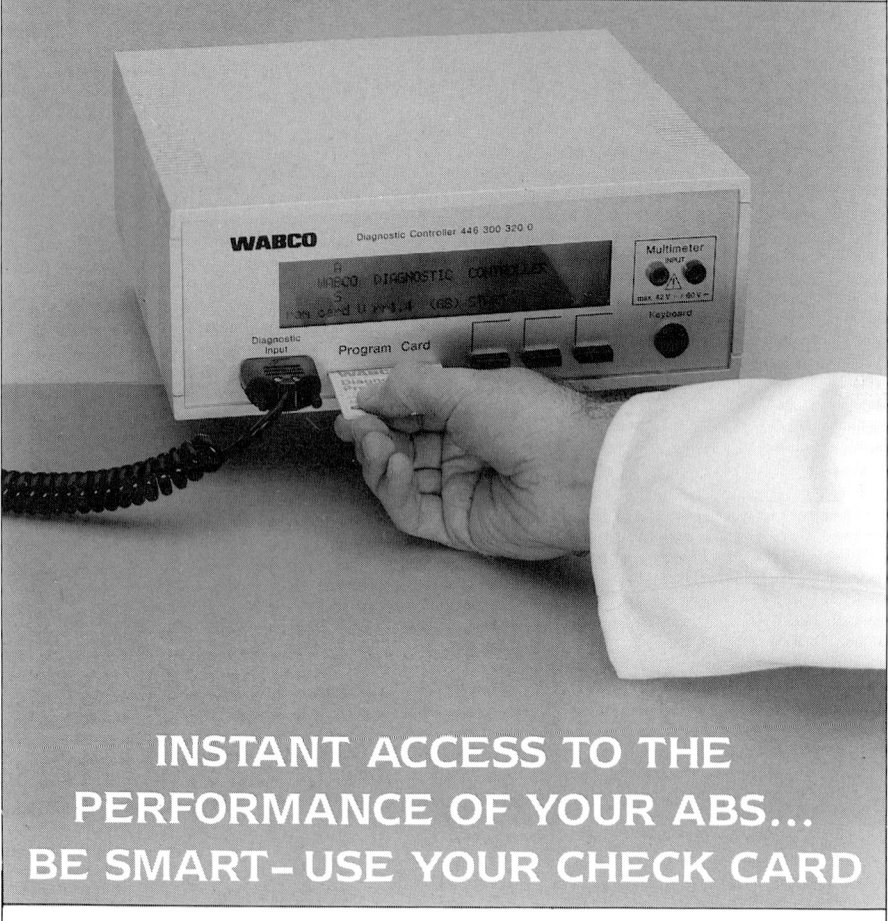

The new WABCO 'Smart Card' and Diagnostic Controller checks your ABS system in no time and indicates any problem areas immediately.

By simply connecting up to the ECU of the system and inserting the dedicated card, you can read your system's performance and check out the source of any problems.

'Smart Card' diagnostics reduce downtime, helping to keep your vehicle where it should be – on the road, earning money.

Get smart, and check out WABCO diagnostics.

INSTANT ACCESS TO THE PERFORMANCE OF YOUR ABS... BE SMART – USE YOUR CHECK CARD

WABCO ABS

A WORLD OF AUTOMOTIVE EXCELLENCE

WABCO Automotive
Clayton Dewandre Aftermarket Ltd
Mill Road
Rugby
Warwickshire CV21 1BZ
Telephone: 0788 571371
Telex: 31308
Facsimile: 0788 561048

The TRANSPORT MANAGER'S & OPERATOR'S Handbook 1991

Formerly published as *The Transport Manager's Handbook*

This twenty-first edition first published in 1991

Apart from any fair dealing for the purposes of research or private study, or criticism or review, as permitted under the Copyright, Designs and Patents Act, 1988, this publication may only be reproduced, stored or transmitted, in any form or by any means, with the prior permission in writing of the publishers, or in the case of reprographic reproduction in accordance with the terms of licences issued by the Copyright Licensing Agency. Enquiries concerning reproduction outside those terms should be sent to the publishers at the undermentioned address:

Kogan Page Limited
120 Pentonville Road,
London N1 9JN

© David Lowe 1991

British Library Cataloguing in Publication Data
A CIP record for this book is available from the British Library.

ISBN 0 7494 0276 8

Typeset from author's disk by Saxon Printing Ltd., Derby
Printed and bound in Great Britain by
Biddles Ltd, Guildford and King's Lynn

The TRANSPORT MANAGER'S & OPERATOR'S Handbook 1991

21st Edition

David Lowe
FILDM, MCIT, MInstTA

KOGAN PAGE

ONE CALL AND YOU'RE HOOKED!

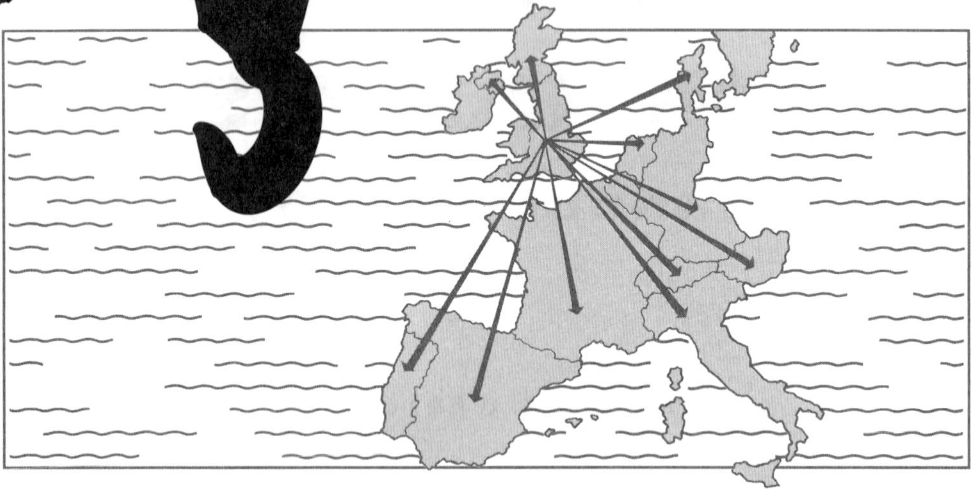

It takes just one telephone call to appreciate the full benefits of AA-BRS Fleet Rescue membership. A telephone call that will guarantee **the fastest possible response, the highest quality of service** and **unbeatable value for money**. Not just in the UK, but throughout the major countries in Western Europe as well.

Only AA-BRS Fleet Rescue **has the resources** and expertise to ensure this level of assistance for all your HGVs - whatever the make - day and night, all year round. Wherever your drivers break down in Great Britain and Western Europe, they can call for help from a **network of selected agents** co-ordinated by our English-speaking Control Centre in the UK.

One low annual membership registration fee covers your entire fleet for the full range of services. From then on, you only pay for the services you use - if you don't break down, you won't be charged.

If you would like to know more about AA-BRS Fleet Rescue and its European service, ring us now on **021-622 6841** or complete and post the coupon today. By return, we'll send you a free copy of our brochure and details of our highly competitive breakdown rates.

AA-BRS Fleet Rescue Monaco House, Bristol Street, Birmingham B5 7AS

Contents

Preface to the Twenty-first Edition	7
Acknowledgements	9
Introduction	11
1: Operators' Licensing	15
2: Professional Competence	49
3: Goods Vehicle Drivers' Hours	59
4: Goods Vehicle Drivers' Records	75
5: Tachographs	81
6: Ordinary Driving Licences	97
7: HGV Drivers' Licences	111
8: Driving Tests (Ordinary – HGV – Advanced)	125
9: Vehicle Weights and Dimensions	139
10: Construction and Use of Vehicles	155
11: Type Approval	189
12: Vehicle Lighting and Marking	193
13: HGV Plating, Annual Testing and Vehicle Inspections	207
14: Light Vehicle Testing	233
15: Vehicle Maintenance	237
16: Maintenance Records	249
17: Safety – Vehicle, Loads and at Work	255
18: Loads – General	273
19: Loads – Abnormal and Projecting	281
20: Loads – Dangerous and Explosive	291
21: Vehicle Excise Duty	315
22: Insurance – Vehicle, Premises and Business	327
23: Road Traffic Regulations	349
24: Fleet Car and Light Vehicle Operations	371
25: Northern Ireland Operations	381
26: International Transport Operations	393
27: Rental, Hiring and Leasing of Vehicles	421
28: Vehicle Fuel Economy	427
29: Mobile Communications	435
Appendices	
I Licensing Authorities and Areas Covered	445
II FTA Regional Offices	447
III RHA Regional Offices	448
IV Organisations Connected with Transport	449
V Approved Tachograph Centres	452
Directory of Transport Support Services	479
Index of Advertisers	489
Index	491

Preface to the Twenty-first Edition

The Transport Manager's and Operator's Handbook continues, as in previous years, to record new legislation, update existing provisions and explain new interpretations resulting mainly from published decisions of the courts in appeal cases. In particular this year's edition contains details of the new articulated vehicle lengths (ie up to 16.5 metres) and the complicated related provisions on turning circles. The new legislation on driver licensing, brought in to enable the UK to comply with EC Directives, is explained together with the proposed new arrangements for driver testing. While there have been no changes in either the EC drivers' hours rules or tachograph requirements, additional text has been provided to expand further on the explanations given and to emphasise the significant change of interpretation of the break period requirements after four and a half hours of driving.

The new syllabus for the professional competence examinations which takes effect in time for the March 1991 examinations is included, and so too are the changes in vehicle lighting regulations whereby front and rear position lights on vehicles must now be illuminated between sunset and sunrise rather than 'during the hours of darkness' as before. Additionally, a large number of minor changes have been made throughout the *Handbook* in order to improve the information given and to assist understanding of the text. The intention as always is to provide the reader with the best and simplest possible explanations of complex legal requirements to help him run his business, or manage his department, with the maximum of efficiency and within the law.

It is an important responsibility of goods vehicle management to comply with legal requirements. Failure to conform to the law can have very serious and very expensive consequences as many vehicle operators, and heavy goods drivers, regularly find to their dismay. Regular scanning of the transport trade press will indicate the severe penalties imposed on hgv drivers, managers and vehicle operators by the courts or the Licensing Authorities following their misdemeanours.

The purpose of this *Handbook*, as it has been from the very outset in 1969, is to help operators, managers and others responsible for road transport operations to avoid the risks of financial penalty and worse, penalty against their operator's licence. I sincerely hope its contents provide interesting and intelligible reading and prove to be a useful and ready source of reference to the many and complex legal requirements relating to goods vehicle ownership and use. More importantly, I hope it helps readers to avoid problems with the enforcement authorities and the courts, to keep their operators' (and hgv drivers') licences and to protect their own livelihoods and the many others which may depend on these licences.

Acknowledgements

I am grateful to all the many individuals and organisations who have provided helpful information for inclusion in this *Handbook*. Over the years I have been writing the *Handbook* I have approached so many people for information, guidance and assistance that it really is impossible to thank them all individually. Some people are consulted regularly year after year; some have been newly sought out for guidance. There is no doubt that without such help the *Handbook* would not have achieved its prominence as the so-called 'bible' for transport managers and others. To all these people, once again, I express my sincere thanks for their help.

Reference has been made to many sources for information – to the legislation itself, both British and EC; published guides and notes; the Department of Transport, the Licensing Authorities and their Traffic Area Office staff and the enforcement authorities. Many other relevant bodies have been consulted and both the national press and the transport trade press have provided a continuous reminder of changing legislation and developments in the industry. Similarly, a constant flow of comments and questions from clients and seminar delegates has provided the source of many leads for inclusion of information and the inspiration to continue revising the contents of the *Handbook* to include more and more legislative detail. To all these nameless people I am greatly indebted.

Acknowledgement is made to the controller of Her Majesty's Stationery Office for permission to reproduce forms and diagrams from Statutory Instruments and from the Highway Code.

I must thank especially my wife Patricia and many friends in the industry who are a constant source of encouragement. And finally, my thanks are due, as always, to the editorial staff of Kogan Page whose help and kindly cajoling ensure yet another edition of the *Handbook*.

Every effort has been made to ensure that the material contained in this book is as correct and as up to date as possible. While I accept full responsibility for any errors which may be found, I cannot stem the progress of legislation which inevitably occurs during the life of the current edition of this annual publication.

David Lowe
July 1990

Introduction

Historically, the road transport industry in Great Britain has had to contend with a mass of legislation which has imposed considerable restriction on operations, to say nothing of the burdens of high cost and considerable worry for the owners, operators and managers of goods vehicle fleets.

The past 20 or so years in particular have seen more than their fair share of such legislation. Looking back to the days when the Road Safety Act 1967 (now defunct) and the Transport Act 1968 were about to be introduced, it would have been difficult then to foresee the mass of legal requirements which would have to be faced over the years ahead.

In 1970 we had changes in drivers' hours and records which were eventually understood and accepted; and in place of carriers' licensing, a new system of operators' licensing was also introduced in 1970 bringing own-account operators and professional hauliers under one common scheme for the control of goods vehicle operations. This, too, was accepted and largely appreciated by the industry which recognised the need for increased road safety measures.

By 1978, however, many changes in these items alone, as respective chapters in the book show, had taken place and in 1984 further significant changes were made. The hours regulations have become those of Europe; the records requirements changed to meet EC law late in 1976 and subsequently have been largely replaced by tachographs on a mandatory basis from 1981; and the one-for-all system of 'O' licensing was torn apart to satisfy the demands for establishing standards of professional competence. In 1986 major changes were made to both the EC and the British drivers' hours rules and the EC tachograph rules, with the object of making the law simpler and more flexible for operators to apply.

Besides these particular items of legislation there have been many more changes which earlier editions of this book have charted year by year. In fact, each year has seen something new in legal responsibilities for the vehicle operator and transport manager to digest. If it has not always been significant in transport terms it has been significant in other terms, significant Acts being the ill-fated Industrial Relations Act, the Equal Pay Act, the Health and Safety at Work, etc Act, the Employment Protection Act and the Employment Protection (Consolidation) Act 1978, then the Employment Act 1980 and the Employment Act 1982, and others since then.

In previous years this introduction has referred to the great difficulty which confronts those engaged in the industry, no matter what their capacity or title, in keeping track of what must, and must not, be done (and the penalties involved for non-compliance). The pile of transport, social and environmental legislation is constantly mounting, and as it does so the problems of keeping up to date with it all – and putting it into practice – become increasingly complex and time-consuming. Now, the industry has to look towards the effects of 1992 and the Single European Market with all that this entails by way of changing administrative and operational practices as well as the increased competition. From a legislative viewpoint, international transport operators may find the way eased as barriers are removed and restrictive measures, such as the requirement for road haulage permits and certain customs procedures, are eliminated. On the other hand, the domestic road haulage industry may find such steps as the legalisation of cabotage presenting them with unwelcome competition on their own doorsteps from marauding Euro-hauliers looking to pay their running costs home after delivering international loads into Britain.

So it seems that the tide of legislation cannot, and will not, be stemmed even for a brief period to allow the industry some respite from pressure and change, from new restrictions and new burdens.

The purpose of this handbook, therefore, is to gather as much of this legislative material together as can be reasonably squeezed between the covers, to explain what it is all about in lay terms which are both easy to read and to understand and apply, and thereby to provide the hard-pressed vehicle operator or transport manager with one accessible, intelligible source of information on the responsibilities laid on him by law emanating from both the British governments and the EC. The handbook is intended for the fleet operator (whatever the size of his fleet – large or very small), the transport manager, the owner-driver haulier or anybody else, whatever his or her title, whose responsibilities include the day-to-day control, administration or operation of goods vehicles, and the small operator who has found that there is a lot more to running a goods vehicle besides just taxing and insuring it. In addition to its function as a ready source of reference for the main legal requirements affecting goods vehicle operation and other useful information, the book may also be found, by those studying for transport examinations, to be an additional means of acquiring a detailed knowledge of the relevant legislation currently applicable to the UK road freight industry.

The major items of legislation affecting the operator and driver of goods vehicles have been covered, together with some of the other legal requirements which are not necessarily new but which it is important for him to know about. Besides transport legislation the owner or manager has been increasingly confronted with social and environmental legislation which affects him both as an employer of staff and as the occupier of premises.

Apart from this there is still a great deal more information that the operator and manager should have at his fingertips. Some of it concerns particular branches of the transport industry; the carriage of dangerous goods, abnormal loads, food or livestock, for example. The person responsible for these specialised traffics should have acquired, through experience, some knowledge of the regulations concerning his particular field. The newcomer to such operations will need to obtain the appropriate regulations direct from Her Majesty's Stationery Office (HMSO), or from a bookseller who stocks Stationery Office publications, and study them carefully.

The principal Acts of Parliament which form the basis of the legislation explained in this book are supported by, and their provisions brought into effect by, a much larger number of regulations, orders and amendments. These are the means by which the Secretary of State for Transport puts into effect the legal requirements laid down in principle in an Act of

INTRODUCTION

Parliament. Legislation contained in an Act is not of itself effective until brought into force by regulations or orders made by the Secretary of State, for which purpose he is given the necessary powers in the Act. Many provisions contained in such Acts may, in fact, never be brought into use but they do not automatically become extinct by lack of use. They remain dormant on the statute book unless repealed by a further Act.

EC legislation arises as the result of draft proposals, similar to British government white papers, which are circulated among interested parties (the trade unions, trade associations, and so on) for comment prior to legislative action being taken, and are then enforced by means of directives and regulations of the Council of the European Communities.

It is most important for transport people to be aware of the regulations affecting both their own special type of operations and transport in general. To keep up with all the individual acts, regulations, amendments and modifications which Her Majesty's Stationery Office publishes on behalf of the government in connection with transport and the statutory publications of the European Communities is no mean task. A more convenient method of keeping up to date on all that is new affecting the industry is to read the trade press regularly.

The principal journals covering the road goods transport field are *Transport Week, Motor Transport* and *Commercial Motor* published weekly, *Headlight* and *Trucking International* published monthly. Contents include the latest industry news, new regulations with simple explanations and articles on subjects of special interest such as insurance, vehicle maintenance, road tests of new vehicles, costing, education and training and management topics. *Headlight* in particular is of special interest, because of its extensive reporting of both Court and Tribunal cases, which give the reader a good indication of how the law is applied, how the enforcement agencies, and subsequently the courts, interpret legal provisions and the levels of penalties imposed on offenders and those who lose out in Tribunal cases.

It must be emphasised that the fleet operator and transport manager should keep abreast of what is happening in the industry if he wants to be efficient, progressive and stay on the right side of the law. To concentrate on the job in hand to the exclusion of all that is happening in the industry at large is an attitude adopted by many operators and many of them have already suffered the consequences of not being prepared to meet some of the drastic changes that have taken place in recent years.

A valuable aid to the operator is membership of one or other of the trade associations, the Freight Transport Association – which represents the own-account operator, and the Road Haulage Association – looking after the interests of the hire and reward professional haulier, provide a number of services to their members as well as keeping them informed about what is happening in the industry through their respective journals, *Freight Transport* and *Roadway*. Both organisations hold open meetings and training sessions, addressed by specialists on various topics of importance, at which members can hear first-hand details of current and new legislation, ask questions and air their views.

Additionally, for the operator or manager who wants to keep abreast of current legislation and practices in the industry there are commercial seminars and training sessions ranging from one day to over a week in duration. These provide an excellent means of keeping up to date with what is going on, and of meeting and talking to other people in the industry with similar interests and problems.

The road transport industry plays an important part in the life of Great Britain. Its safe operation is essential for the well-being of the people and its efficient operation is vital to the economy. Higher standards of management and control within the industry with a far greater awareness and understanding of the legal requirements, the operational demands and the economic considerations are necessary if these essential criteria of safety and efficient operation are to be achieved and upheld.

Special Note
It should be pointed out that this book is intended purely as a practical interpretation of legal matters for the lay reader and is intended only as a guide to matters current at the time of writing. It is not a definitive legal work of reference and should not be used as such. Readers are advised to check the legislation itself before committing time or expenditure to any particular course of action and any operator needing detailed legal advice is recommended to seek it through normal legal channels. The author and publishers can accept no responsibility whatsoever for decisions taken or other irrevocable actions based on the contents herein.

1: Operators' Licensing

Operators' licensing is the main regulatory control system imposed to ensure the safe and legal operation of most goods vehicles in Great Britain. While other individual aspects of legislation also apply to such vehicles, the 'O' licensing system provides the overriding control of road freight transport operations. Failure to observe this other legislation can result in appropriate penalties as set out in respective statutes and, subsequently, will involve penalties against the operators' licence itself. Similar licensing controls apply to goods vehicle operations in Northern Ireland under the Road Freight Operator's Licence scheme operated in the Province and in other EC member states where common standards for entry into the haulage industry are applied.

Under the British licensing scheme commercial (ie trade or business) users of most goods vehicles over 35 tonnes maximum permissible weight must hold an 'O' licence for such vehicles, whether they are used for carrying goods in connection with the operator's trade or business as an own-account operator (ie a trade or business other than that of carrying goods for hire or reward) or are used for hire or reward haulage operations. Certain goods vehicles, including those used exclusively for private purposes, are exempt from the licensing requirements. Details of the exempt vehicles to which 'O' licensing does not apply are given on pp 16–18.

The original system of operators' licensing was established by the Transport Act 1968. Section 60 of that Act states that no person may use a goods vehicle on a road for hire or reward or in connection with any trade or business carried on by him except under an operator's licence. The basis of the present revised regulations remains in this statute.

Regulations which took effect on 1 January 1978 made substantial changes to the 'O' licensing system which had existed from 1970 to the end of 1977. These regulations, the Goods Vehicle (Operators' Licences) Regulations 1977, introduced a three-tier system of 'O' licensing in contrast to the previous single-tier system which applied similarly to both professional hauliers and own-account operators. From 1 June 1984 further significant changes to the system were introduced by the Goods Vehicles (Operators' Licences, Qualifications and Fees) Regulations 1984 (as amended 1986 and 1987) which, principally, gave Licensing Authorities powers to consider representations to 'O' licence applications on the grounds that environmental nuisance or discomfort would be caused to local residents by the presence of goods vehicles at or operating from particular locations.

The 'O' licensing system, which is based on the concept of ensuring legal and safe operation and thus is a system of 'quality' as opposed to 'quantity' licensing, is administered on a regional (ie Traffic Area) basis throughout Great Britain. Northern Ireland's Road Freight Operators' Licensing system is dealt with separately by the Department of the Environment in Belfast. There are nine Traffic Areas (see Appendix I for list) each controlled by a

Licensing Authority (LA) – although currently there are only eight LAs, one holding the post in two Traffic Areas – which has the statutory power to grant or refuse operators' licences, to place environmental conditions or restrictions on such licences where necessary, and subsequently to impose penalties against licences in the event of the holder being convicted for goods vehicle related offences. Approximately 400,000 vehicles are specified on 'O' licences in Great Britain on about 130,000 licences of which some 60,000 are restricted licences, 56,000 are standard national licences and 14,000 are standard international licences.

Exemptions from 'O' Licensing

There are a number of categories of vehicle which are exempt from 'O' licensing requirements.

Small Vehicles

The principal exemption applies to 'small' vehicles identified as follows.

Rigid vehicles are 'small' if:
(a) they are plated and the gross plated (ie maximum permissible) weight is not more than 3.5 tonnes;
(b) they are unplated and have an unladen weight of not more than 1525kg.

A combination of a rigid vehicle and a draw-bar trailer is 'small' if:
(a) both the vehicle and the trailer are plated, and the total of the gross *plated* weights is not more than 3.5 tonnes;
(b) either the vehicle or the trailer is not plated, and the total of the *unladen* weights is not more than 1525kg.

However, if the unladen weight of an unplated trailer is not more than 1020kg this does not have to be added to the unladen weight of the drawing vehicle for the purposes of deciding if the combination is 'small' for 'O' licensing purposes.

Articulated vehicles are 'small' if:
(a) the semi-trailer is plated, and the total of the *unladen* weight of the tractive unit and the plated weight of the semi-trailer is not more than 3.5 tonnes;
(b) the semi-trailer is not plated, and the total of the *unladen* weights of the tractive unit and the semi-trailer is not more than 1525kg.

Also included in the exemptions are pre-1 January 1977 vehicles which have an unladen weight not exceeding 1525kg and a gross weight greater than 3.5 tonnes but not exceeding 3.5 tons (NB: 3.5 tonnes equals 3.44 tons approx).

Other Exemptions:

Regulations list the following further specific exemptions from 'O' licensing requirements.
1. Vehicles licensed as agricultural machines used solely for handling specified goods, and any trailer drawn by them.

1: OPERATORS' LICENSING

2. Dual-purpose vehicles and any trailer drawn by them.
3. Vehicles used on roads only for the purpose of passing between private premises in the immediate neighbourhood and belonging to the same person (except in the case of a vehicle used only in connection with excavation or demolition) provided that the distance travelled on the road in any one week does not exceed six miles.
4. Motor vehicles constructed or adapted primarily for the carriage of passengers and their effects and any trailer drawn by them while being so used.
5. Vehicles used for the purpose of funerals.
6. Vehicles used for police, fire brigade and ambulance service purposes.
7. Vehicles used for fire fighting or rescue work at mines.
8. Vehicles on which a permanent body has not yet been built carrying goods for trial or for use in building the body.
9. Vehicles used under a trade licence.
10. Vehicles in the service of a visiting force or headquarters.
11. Vehicles used for naval, military or air force purposes.
12. Trailers not constructed for the carriage of goods but which are used incidentally for that purpose in connection with the construction, maintenance or repair of roads.
13. Road rollers or any trailer drawn by them.
14. Vehicles used by HM Coastguards or the Royal National Lifeboat Institution for the carriage of lifeboats, life saving appliances or crew.
15. Vehicles fitted with permanent equipment (ie machines or appliances) so that the only goods carried are:
    (a) for use in connection with the equipment;
    (b) for thrashing, grading, cleaning or chemically treating grain or for mixing by the equipment with other goods not carried on the vehicle to make animal fodder; or
    (c) mud or other matter swept up from the road by the equipment.
16. Vehicles used by a local authority for road cleansing and watering, snow clearing, refuse collection, night soil, septic tank and cesspool clearing, and for purposes of enactments relating to weights and measures or the sale of food and drugs or for the distribution of grit, salt or other materials on frosted, icebound or snow-covered roads.
17. Vehicles used by a local authority under the Civil Defence Act 1948.
18. Steam-propelled vehicles.
19. Tower wagons or any trailer drawn by them.
20. Vehicles used on airports under the Air Authority Act 1948.
21. Electrically propelled vehicles.
22. Showmen's goods vehicles and any trailer drawn by such vehicles.
23. Vehicles plated for more than 3.5 tonnes but not more than 3.5 tons and which are not over 1525kg unladen weight and which were first registered prior to 1977.
24. Vehicles used by a highway authority in connection with weighbridges.
25. Vehicles fitted with machines, appliances or apparatus or other contrivance, provided the only goods carried on the vehicle are to be mixed by the machine, appliance, apparatus or other contrivance with other goods not carried on the vehicle on a road in order to thrash, grade, clean or chemically treat grain.
26. Minibuses and any trailer drawn.
27. Hackney carriages.
28. Vehicles used for emergency operations by the water, electricity, gas and telephone services.

Exemptions also apply to vehicles used privately (ie for carrying goods for solely private purposes and not in any way connected with a business activity) and by voluntary organisations and to foreign vehicles entering Britain from countries with which road haulage agreements are in force, vehicles entering the country carrying goods for delivery within 25 kilometres of the port, vehicles of not more than 6 tonnes gross weight operating between EC countries and Britain and vehicles operating on EC and ECMT permits.

All other goods-carrying vehicles over 3.5 tonnes gross weight, including Post Office vehicles and public and local authority vehicles (the work of such authorities is deemed to be the carrying on of a business for 'O' licensing purposes), must be covered by an 'O' licence. This includes such vehicles only temporarily in the operator's possession, hired or borrowed on a short-term basis, where they are used in connection with a business (even a part-time business).

The Vehicle User

An 'O' licence must be obtained by the 'user' of the vehicle for all the vehicles he operates to which the regulations apply. The 'user' may be the owner of the vehicle or he may have hired it. If the vehicle was hired without a driver, the hirer is the 'user'. There is considerable importance attached to the word 'user', and its exact meaning, both for the purposes of 'O' licensing and in other regulations. It may be explained simply as follows:
1. An owner-driver who uses his vehicle in connection with his own business is the 'user' of his own vehicle.
2. If the owner of a vehicle employs a driver to drive it for him and he pays the driver's wages then the owner is the 'user' because he is the employer of the driver.
3. If a vehicle is borrowed, leased or hired without a driver and the borrower or hirer drives it himself or pays the wages of a driver he employs to drive it then the borrower or hirer is the 'user'.

From this it can be seen that, in general, the person who pays the driver's wages is the 'user' of a vehicle, and it is this person (or company) who is responsible for holding an 'O' licence and for the safe condition of the vehicle on the road and for ensuring that it is operated in accordance with the law. However, it must be remembered that the driver himself, although an employee, is still also the user of the vehicle in the context of certain legislation (eg the Road Vehicles [Construction and Use] Regulations 1986, as amended) and he, too, is responsible for its safe condition on the road and is liable to prosecution if it is not in safe and legal condition.

A situation has arisen in recent times where owner-drivers of goods vehicles who cannot themselves obtain the professional competence qualification have had their vehicles specified on the 'O' licence of another operator but have nevertheless been paid as self-employed contractors to the other operator. This practice is illegal because if the driver owns the vehicle then by virtue of the regulations he is the 'user' and is therefore responsible for holding the 'O' licence for it.

Agency Drivers

Dependence on agencies for the supply of temporary drivers to provide relief manpower when regular drivers are not available has caused difficulty in interpretation of the term 'user' and in deciding who should hold the 'O' licence; the vehicle owner or the agency which employs the driver. It can be seen from item 2 above that the person who pays the driver's wages is the 'user', and is therefore the person who should hold the 'O' licence.

However, the status of the vehicle 'user' in these circumstances has been determined by the agencies getting operators to sign agreements whereby the vehicle operator technically becomes the employer of the driver rather than the agency being the employer and consequently the operator remains the legal 'user' of the vehicle. Usually the agency asks the hirer to sign an agreement whereby the agency becomes the 'agent' of the operator for these purposes in paying the driver's wages. This practice has been proved in court to be legally acceptable on the grounds that the Transport Act 1968 s92(2) states that '... the person whose servant or agent the driver is, shall be deemed to be the person using the vehicle'. The driver is considered to be the servant of the hirer because the hirer gives instructions and directs the activities of the driver who is temporarily in his employ.

The great danger with agency drivers is that the operator has no sound means of establishing whether the driver is legally qualified to drive or whether he has already exceeded his permitted driving times on previous days and whether he has had adequate rest periods. Reputable agencies usually go to considerable lengths to ensure that drivers provided by them for their clients are properly licensed and have complied with the driving hours rules in all respects. It is worth also remembering that the use of casually hired or temporary drivers (whose backgrounds and previous experiences may not be fully known) can result in jeopardy of the contract of insurance covering the use of vehicles and there could also be serious security risks as well as possible 'O' licence penalties for infringements of the law. For this reason the operator should confine himself to obtaining drivers from reputable agencies who are known to have vetted drivers satisfactorily.

Restricted and Standard 'O' Licences

The system of 'O' licensing is as follows:
1. **Restricted licences**: available only to own-account operators who carry nothing other than goods in connection with their own trade or business, which is a business other than that of carrying goods for hire or reward. These licences cover both national and international transport operations with own-account goods. Restricted 'O' licence holders must not use their vehicles to carry goods on behalf of customers' businesses – even if it is done only as a favour or is seen as being part of the service provided to a customer and even if no charges are raised (see below) – such activities are illegal and could result in penalties.
2. **Standard licences (national operations)**: for hire or reward (ie professional) hauliers, or own-account operators who also engage in hire or reward operations, but restricted solely to national transport (ie operations exclusively within the UK) except that own-account holders of such licences may also carry their own goods (but not goods for hire or reward) on international journeys.

3. **Standard licences (national and international operations)**: for hire or reward (ie professional) hauliers, or own-account operators who also engage in hire or reward carrying, on both national and international transport operations.

National transport operations in this context includes journeys to and from ports with loaded trailers which were previously considered to be international journeys.

Standard Licences for Own-account Operators

Own-account operators may voluntarily choose to hold a standard 'O' licence for national or both national and international transport operations instead of a restricted licence provided they are prepared to meet the necessary additional qualifying requirements (principally the professional competence qualification – see Chapter 2). Among the reasons which may influence them to take this step is the desire to carry goods for hire or reward to utilise spare capacity on their vehicles, especially on return trips. Such a requirement may arise because a firm is involved in carrying goods for associate companies on a reciprocal or integrated working basis which does not come within the scope of activities which are permitted between subsidiary companies and holding companies (see p 39) or firms may find themselves in the position where they carry goods in connection with their customer's, as opposed to their own, businesses. Firms holding restricted 'O' licences may not carry on their vehicles goods on behalf of customers (ie in connection with the trade or business of the customer rather than in connection with their own business) or other firms even if such operations are described as being a 'favour' or 'part of the service' to the customer and involve no payment whatsoever. This may occur, for example, when a vehicle delivers goods to a customer and the customer then asks the driver to drop off items on his return journey because he is 'going past the door' and their own vehicle is not available. Such activities would be illegal under the terms of a restricted 'O' licence and if two convictions for such an offence are made within five years, the licence must be revoked by the LA.

Requirements for 'O' Licensing

In order to obtain an 'O' licence, applicants must satisfy certain conditions specified in regulations.

Restricted Licences

Applicants must be:
1. Fit and proper persons.
2. Of appropriate financial standing.

Standard Licences (national transport operations)

Applicants must be:
1. Of good repute.
2. Of appropriate financial standing.

1: OPERATORS' LICENSING

3. Professionally competent, or must employ on a full-time basis a person who is professionally competent, in national transport operations.

Standard Licences (national and international transport operations)

Applicants must be:
1. Of good repute.
2. Of appropriate financial standing.
3. Professionally competent, or must employ on a full-time basis a person who is professionally competent, in both national and international transport operations.

Other Legal Requirements

Besides the specific requirements mentioned above, licence applicants and holders have to satisfy further legal requirements relating to the suitability and environmental acceptability of their vehicle operating centres, the suitability of their vehicle maintenance facilities or arrangements and, overall, their ability and willingness to comply with the law in regard to vehicle operating as demonstrated by signing the declaration of intent on the 'O' licence application form. These matters are dealt with in detail in this chapter.

Good Repute

The term 'good repute' for the purposes of the standard 'O' licensing scheme means that the applicant for a licence does not have a past record of convictions during the previous five years (excluding those which are 'spent' – see below) relating to the the roadworthiness of goods vehicles on an 'O' licence. Similarly, to be a fit and proper person in order to obtain a restricted 'O' licence means that there should not be a past record of such offences. It should be noted that the LA will not necessarily refuse to grant a licence to an applicant who has had such convictions but he will consider the number and seriousness of the convictions before making a grant. He may, for example, issue a licence for a shorter period to see if the applicant has 'mended his ways', or grant a licence for fewer vehicles than the number requested. If, during the currency of a licence, an 'O' licence holder is convicted of offences related to goods vehicle operations, the LA may call the operator to a public inquiry and determine whether he is still a fit and proper person or of good repute and whether he should be allowed to continue holding an 'O' licence (see also pp 40–41).

The relevant offences which lead to conviction in this case are those specified in the Transport Act 1968 S69(4) and include matters relating to:
- unlawful use of vehicles;
- unroadworthiness of vehicles, maintenance and maintenance records;
- plating and testing;
- speed limits;
- weight limits, safe loading and overloading of vehicles;
- licensing of drivers;
- drivers' hours and record keeping (including tachographs);
- certain traffic offences (eg parking);
- illegal use of rebated fuel oil;

- forgery;
- international road haulage permits.

Spent Convictions

Spent convictions, which are referred to above in the context of good repute, are those which *do not* have to be declared on the licence application form, because they were incurred sufficiently long ago to be legally considered invalid for determining a person's past record. Under the Rehabilitation of Offenders Act 1974 a person who was convicted of an offence for which they were fined by a court need not disclose that conviction after five years (or two and a half years if aged under 17 at the time), or if a prison sentence of six months or less was imposed it need not be disclosed after seven years (or three and a half years if aged under 17 at the time). In the case of a prison sentence of between six months and two and a half years the rehabilitation period (after which no disclosure is necessary) is ten years, or five years if aged under 17 at the time. A table showing the full range of rehabilitation periods is given below:

(i) Fixed rehabilitation periods:

Sentence	Rehabilitation period
For a prison sentence between 6 months and 2½ years	10 years (5 years if aged under 17 years at the time)
For a prison sentence of 6 months or less	7 years (3½ years if aged under 17 years at the time)
For a fine or a community service order	5 years (2½ years if aged under 17 years at the time)
For an absolute discharge	6 months
For Borstal	7 years
For a detention centre	3 years

(ii) Variable rehabilitation periods:

Sentence	Rehabilitation period
A probation order, conditional discharge or bind over	1 year or until the order expires (whichever is longer)
A care order or supervision order	1 year or until the order expires (whichever is longer)
An order for custody in a remand home, an approved school or an attendance centre order	A period ending 1 year after the order expires
A hospital order (with or without a restriction order)	5 years or a period ending 2 years after the order expires (whichever is longer)

In Scotland, supervision requirements made by children's hearings attract similar rehabilitation periods to those for care or supervision orders.

Appropriate Financial Standing

This means the applicant being able to prove to, or assure, the Licensing

Authority that he has sufficient funds (ie money) readily available to maintain the vehicles for which he has applied for a licence to the standards of fitness and safety required by law. An additional questionnaire relating to the applicant's financial resources is sometimes required to be completed in addition to the normal 'O' licence application form (see p 28) when making a new application or renewal application for a standard licence. The LA has considerable powers to inquire into the finances of applicants including the right to ask for the production of proof of financial standing by means of audited accounts and bank statements or bank references, savings or deposit account books or other evidence of funds stated to be available for the maintenance of vehicles.

Professional Competence

Details of the professional competence requirements for standard 'O' licence holders are given in Chapter 2.

Wrong Licences

Applicants are required to specify which type of licence they require and those who specify restricted licences will be subject to severe penalties if they subsequently carry goods for hire or reward. Operators who specify standard licences covering only national operations and who engage in international operations will be similarly penalised.

Operating Centres

Under the 1984 regulations referred to earlier, a definition is given for the vehicle operating centre. It is the place where the vehicle is 'normally kept'. This is commonly taken to mean the place where the vehicle is regularly parked when it is not in use. Thus if operators regularly permit drivers to take vehicles home with them at night and at weekends then the place where the drivers park near to their home becomes the vehicle operating centre. This place then must be declared on the 'O' licence application form.

In these circumstances an operator could have to declare a number of separate operating centres in addition to his normal depot or base and he could face environmental representation against each of these places and have restrictive environmental conditions placed on his licence in respect of their use. Alternatively, he could lose his licence if he fails to declare such places as operating centres. Failure to notify the LA of new or additional operating centres is an offence.

Advertising of Applications

Applicants for 'O' licences who are seeking a new licence, renewal of an existing licence (technically a new licence application – licences are not 'renewable') or variation of an existing licence are required to arrange for publication of an advertisement (following a specified format to contain the necessary information for potential environmental representors – see Figure 1.1) in a local newspaper circulating in the area where the operating centre is located. If more than one operating centre is specified in the application separate advertisements must be placed for each such centre in the respective local newspapers serving those locations.

THE TRANSPORT MANAGER'S AND OPERATOR'S HANDBOOK

How to fill in advert	Goods Vehicles Operator's Licence
Full name(s) of Company, Partners, or Sole Trader applying for licence	[ ] Trading as
Put your trading name here if different *(cross out if it does not apply)*	[ ] of
Address where you normally receive letters including postcode	[ ] [ ]
Choose the one you are applying for *(cross out the others)*	is applying for a licence to use is applying to renew without change a licence to use is applying to renew with change a licence to use is applying to change an existing licence to use
Put in the address of your operating centre including postcode *(Each newspaper advert must only contain a list of the operating centres within the distribution area of that paper)*	[ ] [ ] as an operating centre for
Put the maximum number of vehicles/trailers you want including your margin of spares *(Cross out trailers if you do not have any)*	[ ] goods vehicle(s) and [ ] trailer(s) instead of
Put the number of vehicles/trailers you have now *(Cross out trailers if you do not have any)*	[ ] goods vehicle(s) and [ ] trailer(s) with the following environmental conditions applying
Put in the new conditions you want on the licence *(Cross out if you do not want this type of change)*	[ ] [ ] instead of
Put in the old conditions *(cross out if you do not want this type of change)*	[ ] [ ] by removing the following environmental conditions from the licence
Put in existing conditions *(cross out if you do not want this type of change)*	[ ] [ ] Owners of occupiers of land (including buildings) in the vicinity of the operating centre who believe the use or enjoyment of the land will be prejudicially affected, may make written representation to the Licensing Authority at
Put in the address of the Traffic Area Office you are sending your application to.	[ ] [ ] [ ] within 21 days following the publication of this notice. Representors must at the same time send a copy of their representation to the applicant at the address given in this notice.

Figure 1.1 *Format which must be used for 'O' licence newspaper advertisement*

1: OPERATORS' LICENSING

The advertisement need appear only once but it must be published during a period extending from not more than 21 days before and not more than 21 days after the licence application is made. There is no specified minimum or maximum size requirement for the advertisement but the LAs advise that it 'should not be too small and should be easy to read'. Normally the advertisement will appear in the public or official notices section of the newspaper. Proof that the advertisement has appeared must be given to the LA before he considers the application and failure to produce this proof (usually achieved by sending in the appropriate page torn from the newspaper showing the advertisement itself and the name and date of the paper) will mean that the LA, by law, must refuse to consider the application. Normally this would mean making a fresh application which, of course, delays the whole matter and could mean vehicles having to stand until the licence or variation is granted.

The purpose of the advertisement is to give local residents an opportunity (given to them under the regulations) to make representations against the licence but only on environmental grounds (see p 32).

Licence Application

Applications for 'O' licences must be made to the LA for each Traffic Area in which the operator has vehicles based. These bases will be the operating centres (see p 23 for definition) for the vehicles. One 'O' licence will be sufficient to cover any number of vehicles operating at one centre and any number of operating centres in any one Traffic Area. If operating centres are in different Traffic Areas then separate 'O' licences will be required for each Traffic Area. (A list of the Traffic Area offices is to be found in Appendix 1.)

Form GV79

Application for a licence has to be made on the appropriate form – form GV79 obtainable from the Traffic Area office – which is straightforward and simple to answer. This form incorporates questions relating to vehicle operating centres, the previous history of licence applicants during the past five years and the type of licence required.

There are questions to be answered on the form relating to the name and address of the business, its partners or directors; details are requested of the applicant's previous experience in operating goods vehicles; information regarding vehicles currently owned and those which it is planned to acquire is also required and the address of their respective operating centres. Questions ask if the applicant company or individual or any partners of the business have convictions which are not 'spent' (under the Rehabilitation of Offenders Act 1974 a person is relieved of the obligation to disclose information about a conviction which is 'spent' – see p 22). Details are required of any such convictions including the date of the conviction, the nature of the offence, the name of the Court and the penalty imposed.

Further questions require information about vehicle maintenance – who is to do it, when and where is it to be done, and what facilities there are at that place. Questions are asked about the financial status of the business proprietor, his partners or the directors of the business, in particular asking whether during the past three years any of them have been made bankrupt, been involved with a company which has gone into insolvent liquidation, or been disqualified from acting as a director or taking part in the management of a company. Details about the professionally competent person supporting the application are required, where that person lives, their actual place of work and the address of the operating centre for which they are responsible.

Declaration of Intent

When the applicant signs the form he is not only declaring that the statements of fact made on the form are true but also, in effect, he is making a legally binding promise – a declaration of intent – that statements of what he intends to do will be fulfilled. The declaration of intent relates to the observation of certain aspects of the law concerned with goods vehicle operation and the maintenance of vehicles included in the licence application. If at some time during the currency of the licence the LA finds that these intentions have not been fulfilled, as evidenced by any convictions for relevant offences, he may use his powers to revoke, suspend or curtail the licence. The basis on which the applicant makes the declaration of intent is that he promises the following:

I will make proper arrangements so that:
- the rules on drivers' hours are observed and proper records are kept;
- vehicles are not overloaded;
- vehicles are kept fit and serviceable;
- drivers will report safety faults in vehicles as soon as possible;
- records are kept (for 15 months) of all safety inspections, routine maintenance and repairs to vehicles and make these available on request;

I will:
- have adequate financial resources to maintain the vehicles covered by the licence;
- tell the Licensing Authority of any changes or convictions which affect the licence;
- maintain adequate financial resources for the administration of the business (applies to standard licence applicants only).

As already stated, the application form is straightforward and simple to answer and extensive explanatory notes are provided for guidance. The Traffic Area office also sends applicants a free booklet *A Guide to Goods Vehicle Operators' Licensing* (GV74) to provide further help. This does not, however, mean that the form should not be carefully studied or that any answer will do in an attempt to gain a licence. While it is obvious that to get an 'O' licence the statement of intent must be signed, it should be remembered that the consequences of not fulfilling the stated intentions can lead to penalties so severe as to put a small operator out of business and even to cause hardship to a large one. A warning about this in the following terms is included in the explanatory notes on the form so that applicants are left in no doubt as to the consequences of making false statements or not fulfilling statements:

'I declare that the statements made in this application are true. I understand that the licence may be revoked if any of the statements are false or I do not fulfil the statement of intent made ...'

1: OPERATORS' LICENSING

It is also worth remembering that the earlier warning in the following terms is still valid:

Under Section 69(1)(c) of the Transport Act 1968, the Licensing Authority has the power to revoke, suspend, or curtail any licence he has granted if it comes to his notice that any statement of fact made is false or that any statement of intention or expectation has not been fulfilled. He may also prohibit you from holding any operator's licence for as long as he thinks fit (S.69 [5]).

There are plans to extend the declaration of intent to secure a promise from operators that they will make proper arrangements to ensure that their vehicles are driven within the speed limits. This follows both the action of certain LAs in imposing penalties against operators and their hgv drivers for regularly exceeding speed limits as evidenced by tachograph chart recordings and the purge by police on speeding offenders generally.

Form GV79A

Another form is involved in making an application for an 'O' licence. This is form GV79A which is a supplementary sheet used for supplying details of vehicles for example, registration number, maximum gross weight body type – flat or sided including skeletals, box body or van, tanker or other type such as cement mixer or livestock carrier – and whether the vehicle is articulated, a tipper or refrigerated. Certain designation letters and numbers are used to indicate body and vehicle type as follows:
1. Flat or sided including skeletals
2. Box body or van
3. Tanker
4. Other type (such as cement mixer, livestock carrier).

> T Tipper
> R Refrigerated
> A Articulated

Additional Application Forms

Two supplementary application forms are used in connection with certain licence applications. These forms are GV79E (pale green in colour) dealing with environmental information and GV79F (beige in colour) dealing with financial information. The forms are used only when the LA requires further information following the initial application on form GV79 on either or both of the relevant matters (ie environmental issues or finance).

Environmental Information
Form GV79E is sent to licence applicants if the LA receives representations from local residents following publication of details of the applicant's proposals regarding his vehicle operating centre in the local newspaper. The form must be completed and returned to the LA who will then consider the application in the light of this further information, the information given by those making the environmental representations, and as a result of making his own enquiries.

The form requires details of the applicant's name and address, and the address of his proposed operating centre (see p 23 for definition). It then requires information about the vehicles to be normally kept at the centre and the number and types of trailer to be kept there. Information must be given about any other parking place in the vicinity of the operating centre which is to be used for parking authorised vehicles (ie those authorised on the licence). If the applicant is not the owner of the premises he must send evidence to show that he has permission or authority to use the place for parking vehicles.

A number of further questions must be answered on the form about the operating times of authorised vehicles. In particular, what time lorries will arrive at and leave the centre, whether they will use the centre on Saturdays or Sundays, what times they will arrive and leave on these days, whether maintenance work will be carried out there and between what hours, and whether any of this work will take place on Saturdays or Sundays and if so between what hours? The LA also wants to know whether there are any covered buildings at the centre in which this work is carried out.

A plan showing the parking positions for authorised vehicles must be sent when returning the completed form. This should show entry and exit points, main buildings, surrounding roads with names and the normal parking area for the vehicles. The scale of the plan must be indicated and this is suggested as being 1:500 which is 1 centimetre to 5 metres or 1 inch to 35 feet. A larger scale of 1 inch to 100 feet can be used if this is more convenient when the operating centre is large. If the proposed operating centre has not previously been used as such the LA must be given information about any application for or planning permission granted for the proposed use of the site as a goods vehicle operating centre.

Financial Information
Form GV79F is sometimes sent to new standard licence applicants when the LA requires additional information to enable him to consider whether the applicant meets the financial requirements for this type of licence. An application will be refused unless the LA is satisfied that the applicant has sufficient financial resources to set up and run his business both legally and safely. This fact is pointed out clearly on the form. Answers have to be given to questions about the vehicles, their average annual mileage and the estimated running cost for each individual type of vehicle.

Details must be given about the funds available to start up the business and where these are held (eg in the bank, in savings or as agreed bank overdraft or loan facilities or in the form of share capital), and about the start-up costs for the business including the purchase price or amount of down payments on vehicles and on premises and the sum to be held in reserve as working capital. The applicant is required to give a forecast of the annual expenditure and income for his road haulage operations for a financial year. The LA expects this information to give a clear indication of the business finances for the year ahead. In certain cases the LA may ask for monthly information.

NB: Not all Licensing Authorities currently use this form, some prefer to rely on supporting financial information in other forms – bank references for example.

1: OPERATORS' LICENSING

Date for Applications

Application for an 'O' licence should be made at least nine weeks before the day on which it is desired to take effect. In some Traffic Areas the time taken to process applications is much longer than nine weeks so new operators should be aware of the fact that it is illegal to start operating vehicles until their licence has actually been granted. Where there is an urgent need to start operations before a licence is granted through the normal processes, application can be made to the LA for an interim licence (see below). Where an application is made to renew an existing licence prior to its expiry date, the old licence will continue in force until the LA makes his decision on the new application. Where an existing licence expires without a renewal application being made, the old licence ceases to be valid immediately following the expiry date and it becomes illegal to continue operating vehicles on that licence. In such circumstances a fresh application has to be made and vehicles cannot be operated until a new licence is granted.

Offences while Applications are Pending

Applicants for licences have a duty to advise the LA if, in the interval between the application being submitted and it being dealt with by the LA, they are convicted of a relevant offence (see p 21) which they would have had to include on the application form had the conviction been made before the application was made. Failure to notify the LA is an offence and it could jeopardise any licence subsequently granted.

Interim Licences

In certain circumstances the LA may grant an interim licence pending his decision on the full licence application. The circumstances under which such a licence may be granted are not specified but they may be connected with some urgent need to move goods quickly because they are perishable or for some other urgent reason. A grant of an interim licence should not be taken as a guarantee that a full-term licence will be granted by the LA. An interim licence will not be granted in any case where the main requirements for 'O' licensing appear not to be met. For example, such a licence would not be granted to an applicant for a standard 'O' licence if he has not yet passed the CPC examination nor, indeed, while examination results are being awaited, nor on the assumption that the candidate will have passed. Neither will a grant of an interim licence be considered before the statutory 21-day waiting period for environmental representations and objections has expired.

Duration of Licences

Operators' licences will normally be granted for five years although in some instances, where operators have had past convictions for offences relating to the operation of goods vehicles or where the LA is not fully satisfied as to the ability or intention of the applicant to operate satisfactorily within the law, licences for a shorter period may be granted to enable the LA to consider the applicant's record over such shorter period before granting a full-term licence. Licenses may continue in force beyond their expiry date pending the LA's decision on a renewal application but only where the new application was submitted prior to the expiry date of the old licence.

Licence Fees and Discs

The fee for an 'O' licence is £60.00, plus £20.00 per vehicle specified on the licence (Form OL1) per year payable on issue. On receipt of the fee the licence itself will be issued together with windscreen discs for each of the vehicles specified on the licence. There is no fee for additional trailers. For a licence variation which requires publication in *Applications and Decisions* (see p 34) a fee of £60.00 is charged. The fee for an interim licence or direction is £10.00 per authorised vehicle.

'O' licence discs must be displayed on the vehicle (normally in the windscreen) in a clearly visible position near to the excise duty disc and in a waterproof container. Licence discs are coloured as follows to differentiate between restricted and standard licences and between standard national and standard international licences:
1. Restricted Licence – orange
2. Standard Licence, National – blue
3. Standard Licence, International – green
4. Interim Licence – yellow
5. Copy Discs – word 'COPY' in red across face of disc.

Licence Surrender/Termination

In the case of licence surrender, vehicle fees are proportionately refunded but only on a full year basis. The £60.00 licence (or variation) fee itself is not refundable. If a licence is prematurely terminated by the LA by way of penalty for contraventions of the law there is no refund of licence fees for the outstanding period on the licence but vehicle fees will be refunded proportionately on a full-year basis. The licence itself and all the vehicle windscreen discs must be returned to the LA on surrender or termination of an 'O' licence.

The LA's Considerations

When an application for an 'O' licence is made, the LA will have certain points to take into consideration before deciding whether or not to grant any licence. Mainly he has to ensure that the basic legal requirements as described previously have been met and particularly that those relating to vehicle operation and maintenance will be complied with. These points are dealt with here.

Fit Persons and Good Repute

The first point, and one of the fundamental requirements for 'O' licensing (as already described on p 20 – but a repeat here is useful), is whether the applicant is a fit person or is of good repute and is therefore fit to hold a licence. Basically, being a fit person and being of good repute are the same but the former relates to restricted 'O' licences over which the EC has no influence while the latter is the term used by the EC in setting its

1: OPERATORS' LICENSING

requirements for the holding of a licence to carry goods for hire or reward (ie the UK system of standard 'O' licences). The LA, when deciding this, will take into account any previous record which the applicant (or the partners or directors of the applicant's business) might have had as an operator in terms of their ability or willingness to comply with the law in respect of vehicle operations and particularly maintenance, drivers' hours and records, overloading and the like, also any previous convictions they may have for offences relating to the roadworthiness of vehicles and for other relevant offences.

Maintenance Facilities/Arrangements

The next point that the LA will consider, and one of the most important since it is at the very foundation of the 'O' licensing system, is whether the applicant has suitable facilities or has made satisfactory arrangements for the maintenance of vehicles to be specified on the licence in a safe and legal condition and for keeping suitable maintenance records (this is dealt with in more detail in Chapter 15). In particular the LA will be concerned to know that vehicles are being subjected to safety inspections at regular intervals of time or mileage.

The Licensing Authority for the West Midland and South Wales Traffic Areas, for example, currently suggests that for operators in his area inspections should be based on a time interval only with no mileage alternative and that a period of six weeks between inspections is the maximum that he would find acceptable. He also seeks assurances that operators are using a *written* driver defect reporting system and wall charts for planning inspection and maintenance schedules. Other LA's seek similar assurances.

Drivers' Hours and Records

The LA will consider whether there are satisfactory arrangements for ensuring that the law relating to drivers' hours and records (including tachographs) will be complied with.

Overloading

Similarly, the LA will want to be sure that arrangements are made to prevent the overloading of vehicles and that vehicle weight limits in general will be observed.

Professional Competence Requirements

The LA will want to know details of the nominated professionally competent person, who may be the applicant himself or a full-time employee who holds a certificate of competence covering national or both national and international transport operations (or a person who qualifies by exemption or by having passed the appropriate Royal Society of Arts examination) as appropriate to the type of standard 'O' licence applied for (see Chapter 2).

Number of Qualified Persons

There is no restriction under the regulations (see Chapter 2) on the number of people in a transport department or organisation who may be professionally competent and consequently hold certificates of competence. Further, although restricted 'O' licence holders have no need to specify the name of a professionally competent person in order to obtain a licence there is no restriction on such licence holders or their employees being professionally competent if they qualify personally.

In determining how many qualified persons must be named on a standard 'O' licence the LA will take account of the management structure of applicant firms, but generally there will need to be a minimum of one qualified person per 'O' licence. The LA may require the names of more qualified persons to be specified if he considers it appropriate in view of a division of responsibilities for the operation of vehicles under the licence or if vehicles specified on the licence are located at different operating centres within the Traffic Area. The current normal requirement of at least one CPC holder at each vehicle operating centre is to be abandoned in new legislation and so too is the present need for nominated CPC holders to be 'full-time' employees of the licence holder.

Financial Standing

In addition to these points the LA is required under the regulations (as already stated) to establish details of the applicant's financial standing (a bank statement or a bank manager's letter of reference or an accountant's certificate of solvency may be requested, for example, or other evidence of the availability of funds) because this has a bearing on the applicant's ability to operate and maintain vehicles in a safe condition and in compliance with the law (see also p 28). While considering an applicant's financial status for this purpose the LA has authority to call for the services of an assessor from a panel of persons appointed by the Secretary of State for Transport if this is appropriate due to the complexity of the financial structure of the applicant's business or affairs. According to recent press reports, at least one LA is watching for 'O' licence holders who ask for time to pay fines or request the opportunity to make payment in instalments following conviction for offences by the courts and taking this as good cause for investigating their financial position.

Representations by Local Residents

Opportunities are given to local residents individually to make representations against 'O' licence applications and variations on environmental grounds. Local residents are more carefully defined in the regulations as 'owners or occupiers of land within the vicinity' (ie of the operating centre). Those residents who wish to make representation must do so individually because group action is not permitted (although a group of individual representors may appoint a joint spokesperson to put forward their case) nor is representation by any environmental pressure group, political or other campaigning body. The grounds on which such owners or occupiers can make their representations are confined purely to environmental matters such as noise, vibration, fumes and visual intrusion but could include obstruction. The grounds are specified in the legislation in the following terms, 'that place (ie the operating centre) is unsuitable on environmental grounds for ...(such use and)...any adverse effects on environmental conditions arising from that use would be capable of prejudicially affecting the use or enjoyment of the land' (ie the land owned or occupied by the person making the representation).

One of the facts that has been difficult to establish in connection with this is a definition of the term 'within the vicinity'. It has been shown that residents living along an access road to a vehicle operating centre can be considered to be in the vicinity and adverse environmental effects of vehicles travelling along the road could be taken account of by the LA in his consideration of any environmental representations against a licence application.

There is no opportunity for people living near an operating centre to make representations on grounds other than environmental matters or to use the opportunity to vent long-standing grudges against the vehicle operator. The LAs will not consider any representation which falls outside the terms described above or which is vexatious, frivolous or irrelevant.

Local residents will normally become aware of their opportunity to make representations against the grant of a licence or licence variation through the local newspaper advertisement placed by the applicant (see p 23). Those people wishing to make a representation must do so in writing (or have their solicitor do so on their behalf), within a period of 21 days from the date of publication of the advertisement, to the LA at the Traffic Area office address given in the advertisement. They must also send a copy of their representation (ie letter to the LA) to the licence applicant at his address which is also given in the advertisement. Failure to do this, or to do so within the specified time scale, will automatically disqualify their case. These rights of representation are not to be confused with the rights of objection described later. Representors have no right of appeal should their case against use of the operating centre fail.

Suitability of Premises

Licensing Authorities must inquire into and be satisfied that the place or places to be used as vehicle operating centres are both suitable and environmentally acceptable. Local residents have rights (as described above) to make representations about the environmental consequences of the use of places for transport depots or vehicle operating centres and the LAs are bound to listen to these representations and make appropriate decisions about the application depending on the weight of the argument on either side – residents or operator. In particular the LA, when considering the suitability of premises, will take account of the following:
- the nature or use of any other land in the vicinity of the operating centre and the effect which the granting of the licence would be likely to have on the environment of that land;
- how much granting a licence which is to materially change the use of an existing (or previously used) operating centre, would harm the environment of the land in the vicinity of the operating centre;
- for a new operating centre, any planning permission (or planning application) relating to the operating centre or the land in its vicinity;
- the number, type and size of the authorised vehicles (including trailers) which will use the operating centre;
- the parking arrangements for authorised vehicles within and near to the operating centre;
- nature and times of use of the operating centre ;
- nature and times of use of equipment at the operating centre;
- how many vehicles would be entering or leaving the operating centre, and how often.

Applications and Decisions

When an application for a new 'O' licence, a variation of an existing licence or a renewal (ie a new licence to replace an existing licence) of an existing licence is received by the LA, details of the application (ie the name of the applicant and the number of vehicles and trailers included in the application) will be published in a Traffic Area notice called *Applications and Decisions (As & Ds)*. As its name implies, this notice will also contain details of licences granted by the LA and details of public inquiries to be held. The notice is published weekly or fortnightly by all Traffic Areas and may be inspected at Traffic Area offices or purchased on an individual copy or regular basis. It is by means of this notice that statutory objectors (see below) are able to know when applications have been made against which they may wish to object which they can do within 21 days of publication of the relevant As&Ds notice.

Objections to the Application

Applications for 'O' licences are open to statutory objection by certain bodies listed below (and only by the listed bodies — no other individual or organisation has this statutory right). Potential objectors to 'O' licences become aware of pending applications for new licences or variations to existing licences through the publication *Applications and Decisions* mentioned above.

Objections to applications can only be made by the bodies mentioned on the grounds that the applicant does not meet the essential qualifying criteria for the grant of a licence, namely that the applicant is not of good repute, is not of adequate financial standing or does not meet the professional competence requirements (where appropriate), that the law in respect of those matters which the LA will be considering when he is deciding whether or not to grant a licence is not likely to be complied with, namely that the drivers' hours and records regulations will not be observed, that vehicles will be overloaded and that there are not satisfactory arrangements or facilities for maintaining the vehicles. The bodies may also object on environmental grounds (for example that the operating centre is environmentally unsuitable).

The list of bodies who may make a statutory objection to an 'O' licence application are as follows:
- A chief officer of police
- A local authority
- A planning authority
- The British Association of Removers
- The Freight Transport Association
- The Road Haulage Association
- The General and Municipal Workers' Union
- The National Union of Railwaymen
- The Transport and General Workers' Union
- The Union of Shop, Distributive and Allied Workers
- The United Road Transport Union.

These are the only sources of objection (not to be confused with an environmental representation) to an application for an 'O' licence. If any of these bodies do make a statutory objection they are required to send a

1: OPERATORS' LICENSING

copy of their objection to the applicant at his published address at the same time as sending one to the LA and this must be within 21 days of the publication of details of the application in *Applications and Decisions*. Failure to send a copy to the applicant renders the objection invalid.

Grant or Refusal of a Licence

The LA has power to grant an 'O' licence to applicants if he considers that they meet all the necessary requirements. Alternatively, he may refuse to grant a licence or he may grant a licence for a shorter period, as previously mentioned (see p 29) or he may grant a licence for fewer vehicles than the number applied for if he doubts the ability of the applicant to be able to comply with the law with more vehicles, to be able properly to maintain more vehicles or to be able adequately to finance the operation of more vehicles. He can impose environmental conditions on any licence granted and can also refuse to accept the name put forward for the professionally competent person (in the case of standard licence applications) if he believes that the person is not of good repute. The LA may be influenced in his decision by the points made by any statutory objectors or environmental representors.

Licence Grant with Conditions

The case made by those making valid environmental representations may influence the LA to either refuse the application on the grounds that the operating centre is not environmentally suitable or alternatively to grant the licence but with environmental conditions attached. Thus to prevent or minimise any adverse effects on the environment he may place conditions or restrictions on the licence granted under the following headings:
- the number, type and size of authorised vehicles (including trailers) at the operating centre for maintenance or parking;
- parking arrangements for authorised vehicles (including trailers) at or in the vicinity of the centre;
- the times when the centre may be used for maintenance or movement of any authorised vehicle; and
- how authorised vehicles enter and leave the operating centre.

As an alternative to placing environmental conditions on the licence, the LA may seek undertakings from the operator that he will or will not follow certain practices in order to reduce environmental disturbance of local residents (eg control the number of vehicle movements into and out of the centre). The licence holder should be aware that any such undertakings he may voluntarily give to the LA become legally binding upon him and could result in penalty against his licence if he subsequently fails to observe them.

Licence holders who find they have breached environmental conditions on their licence through unforeseen circumstances must notify the LA. Failure to comply with any of these conditions during the currency of a licence may result in the LA imposing penalties on the licence such as suspension or curtailment. In serious cases the licence may be totally revoked.

Additional Vehicles

Seeking a Margin

At the time of making an application for an 'O' licence the applicant is given the opportunity to request authorisation for any additional vehicles which he may need to acquire or hire during the currency of the licence. By taking this opportunity the operator saves the problems of making a fresh application when wanting to add or hire-in vehicles on a temporary basis to meet trading peaks. It also saves facing any further environmental representations or statutory objections because once the original application is granted with additional vehicles specified, extra vehicles can be added within the number authorised by completion of form GV80 when they are acquired and sent to the LA within one month. There will be no need for the details to be advertised in a local newspaper or published in *Applications and Decisions*.

If additional vehicles were requested and the request was granted at the time of making the original application, the operator will have a 'margin' for extra vehicles on the licence. As described above, the LA will need to be notified within one month of actually putting the additional vehicles into service (by submitting form GV80) so that a windscreen disc can be issued for the vehicle and the appropriate fee charged (ie £20 per vehicle per year of the remaining duration of the licence).

It is useful here to clarify the terms used in connection with the numbers of vehicles for 'O' licensing purposes:

- Authorised vehicles — the maximum number of vehicles/trailers which the licence is actually granted to cover (it is illegal to operate more than this number of vehicles at any time)
- Specified vehicles — the actual vehicles which the operator has in possession and which are specified on the licence by registration number
- Margin — the difference between the number of authorised and specified vehicles on the licence, in other words the vehicles still to be acquired by the operator whether on a permanent or a temporary basis.

Hired Vehicles

If an operator plans to hire extra vehicles without drivers (ie where he intends to have his own driver to drive the vehicle/s) during the currency of his licence, whether for a short period (a day, a few days or even one or two weeks) or on a long-term contract, they must be covered by his 'O' licence and he will need to have applied for a sufficient margin of additional vehicles on his licence to cover these. If vehicles are hired, within the margin, for less than one month there will be no need to notify the LA but details of vehicles hired for more than one month must be sent to the LA and an 'O' licence disc obtained for display on the vehicle.

It is illegal to operate (ie to have employed drivers to drive) more vehicles (ie of over 3.5 tonnes gross weight) than are authorised on the 'O' licence even for a temporary period or reason (eg when an authorised vehicle is off the road for service or repairs or to cover additional delivery requirements).

Number of Extra Vehicles

When making the request for additional vehicles on the initial application for an 'O' licence, the number which may be requested is not limited in any way but it is recommended that it should be in reasonable proportion to the number of vehicles already operated (or initially required) and, most important, it should only be of a number which the applicant can maintain, and prove he can maintain (both physically and financially) on the same basis as the remainder of his fleet. If the request for additional vehicles relates to vehicles which are to be hired rather than owned it must be remembered that the person who hires a self-drive vehicle is fully responsible for the mechanical condition of the vehicle in so far as safety and legal requirements are concerned.

An applicant specifying additional vehicles on the original application should give some careful thought to the exact number of vehicles which may be needed and the reasons for needing them because the LA will ask questions about this if he calls the applicant to a public inquiry. Evidence in the form of business forecasts and trends in trade would be most useful as would figures to indicate past growth of the business; evidence also to show the financial prospects of the applicant during the currency of the licence period will help towards convincing the LA that he would be justified in granting a licence for the additional vehicles requested.

Replacement Vehicles

If for some reason an authorised vehicle ceases to be used the LA must be advised of the fact, but if at that time or later another vehicle is acquired to replace it the operator must advise the LA on form GV80 within one month of acquiring the replacement vehicle. Vehicles which are not removed from the licence (even when standing smashed or cannibalised in a yard or workshop) are still counted as specified vehicles and cannot be replaced by others within the authorised number on the licence until they are removed by notifying the LA and the windscreen discs returned to the Traffic Area office.

Licence Variation

If the holder of a restricted 'O' licence wishes to change the licence to a standard 'O' licence it is necessary to make application on form GV81 and satisfy the legal requirements for standard licences, national or international. A standard national licence holder who wishes to change to a licence covering international operations must satisfy the LA that they, or an employee, are professionally competent in international transport operations (apply on form GV81).

Where the licence holder finds, during the currency of the licence, a need to add vehicles to the fleet that were not specified on the original application then an application must be made to the LA by completing form GV81 and submitting this well in advance (minimum nine weeks). This will necessitate placing an advertisement in a local newspaper as with the original application (see p 23).

Unless the variation is only of a trivial nature the LA will publish details of it in *Applications and Decisions* and it may attract objectors in the same way as a new application and the public inquiry procedure will be the same as that already described.

The licence holder must never operate more vehicles or trailers than the total number specified on his licence. When extra vehicles are required the operator must wait until the application for an increase in the licence is granted before actually putting the vehicles on the road. This can take at least nine weeks – which is the minimum application period required – and as many as 12 to 15 weeks in some Traffic Areas.

Form GV81

Form GV81 is a five-page document called *Application to Change a Goods Vehicle Operator's Licence* and must be used by applicants who wish to:
1. Change the number of vehicles authorised.
2. Change the operating centre, add another centre or stop using a centre.
3. Change the type of licence (eg restricted to standard).
4. Change or remove a condition attached to the licence (including conditions on the use of operating centres).

Most of the changes involve the need to advertise the application in local newspapers (see p 23) and where this is necessary the fact is pointed out on the form. The applicant must send a copy of the published advertisement with the form or state the expected date of publication and the name of the newspaper in which it is to be published. The usual information regarding name and address, addresses of operating centres and the number of vehicles to be based there which are in possession now or to be acquired has to be given. Also required is similar information about vehicle maintenance arrangements to that required on the original GV79 application (see p 25).

Section 3 of the form deals with any addition or deletion to the specified operating centres and section 4 is completed if the applicant wishes to change the type of licence (for example from restricted to standard or from standard national to standard international licence). Details of the professionally competent person must be given where appropriate, so too must details of any convictions (other than those which are 'spent' – see p 22) of the applicant or the partners or co-directors.

Section 5 of the form has to be completed if the applicant wishes to change or remove any of the environmental conditions attached to the use of the operating centres. Reasons must be given as to why this change or removal is wanted and details given of any alternative proposals if the applicant has any.

The form has to be signed and the applicant is warned that the licence may be revoked if any of the statements given are false.

Transfer of Vehicles

If a vehicle is transferred from the Traffic Area in which it is licensed to a base in another Traffic Area for a period of more than three months, it must be removed from the original licence and specified on a licence in the new Traffic Area. Transfers for periods of less than three months are permitted with no need for notification to the LA provided an 'O' licence with a sufficient margin to cover the transferred vehicles is already held for that Traffic Area.

If the operator does not hold an 'O' licence in the other Traffic Area, or holds a licence in the area but it does not have a sufficient margin to accommodate the transferred vehicles, then an application for a new licence or a variation of the existing licence must be made to the LA for that Traffic Area. It is illegal to operate vehicles (ie over 3.5 tonnes gvw) from a base in a Traffic Area unless a licence is held in that area.

Notification of Changes

Licence holders should notify the LA in writing, within *one month* of any changes in the legal entity of their business such as a change of name, address, ownership, if a new partnership has been formed, a limited company formed or the constitution of the partnership has been changed, as this makes a material difference to the information given in answer to questions on the original GV79 licence application. The LA must also be informed if the proprietor or persons concerned in the business die or if the business becomes bankrupt or goes into liquidation.

A change of operating address as given in the original licence application must be notified to the LA within *3 weeks.* A change of operating centre (or the use of an additional operating centre) also requires a variation application using form GV81 and the need to follow the newspaper advertisement procedure.

Other changes which must be notified in writing are those in maintenance facilities or arrangements and any breach of environmental conditions which the LA placed on the licence. Failure to notify the LA of such changes can have the same result as making false statements or failing to fulfil intentions stated in the original application, namely the risk of licence suspension, curtailment or revocation. The offender could also be prosecuted with the consequent penalties which can be imposed by the courts.

Subsidiary Companies

A holding company can include in its application for an 'O' licence vehicles belonging to any subsidiary company in which it owns more than a 50 per cent shareholding. But associate companies (ie where the shareholding arrangement is less than 50 per cent), owned by the same holding company, cannot have vehicles specified on each other's licences and separate divisions of a company are not permitted to hold separate licences unless they are separate entities in law.

The vehicles of any subsidiary company acquired during the currency of the holding company's 'O' licence can, if desired, be included in the holding company's licence either within its existing licence margin or by making application to the LA, on form GV81, to vary the licence. It is not generally likely that an application to include a subsidiary company's vehicles on the holding company's licence would be published in *Applications and Decisions* or that it would attract any objections.

Under the regulations, for the purposes of determining whether goods are carried for hire or reward in order to choose between a restricted or a standard 'O' licence, goods belonging to, or in the possession of, a subsidiary company are considered to belong to, or be in the possession of, the holding company and vice versa, so that in such cases a restricted 'O' licence would be adequate even if charges for the movement of the goods were made between the holding company and its subsidiary.

Renewals

When existing 'O' licences expire, whether at the end of the full five-year period or, if the original licence was for a shorter period, at the end of that period, a fresh application will have to be made for a new licence using the same forms GV79 (the application) and GV79A. This application will be considered by the LA in the same way as a new application and it will be published and liable to attract objectors and environmental representations in the same way. The LA will, of course, by this time have information from his staff about the conduct of the applicant during the currency of the previous licence and this will have a bearing on the LA's consideration of the renewal (ie new licence) application.

Farmers' 'O' Licenses

Farmers' goods vehicles over 3.5 tonnes gross weight must be specified on an 'O' licence in the same way as already described for other goods vehicles.

Goods vehicles owned by farmers which are taxed at the full goods vehicle excise duty rate and specified on an 'O' licence may be used with complete freedom to carry any goods for any person to any destination. If, however, vehicles owned by farmers are taxed at the concessionary 'F' licence excise duty rate (see Chapter 21) they will still need an 'O' licence but may only be used for the purposes which enable them to claim the concessionary 'F' licence rate. The conditions applicable to an 'O' licence application from a farmer are the same as those applying to other haulage and own-account operators.

Penalties against 'O' Licences

The LAs, as the issuing authorities for goods vehicles licenses, are also given considerable legal powers to revoke, suspend or curtail an 'O' licence for a large number of reasons, of which the following are a few of the important examples:

1. Contravention by the licence holder of the provision, in the case of standard 'O' licences, regarding professional competence requirements.
2. Failure to notify the LA of changes in the business.
3. Convictions for failure to maintain vehicles in a fit and serviceable condition.
4. Contravention of speed limits, overloading or offences in connection with loading or unloading vehicles in restricted parking or waiting areas.

1: OPERATORS' LICENSING

5. Failure to ensure that drivers are correctly licensed.
6. Convictions relating to the use of rebated (duty free) fuel oil in vehicles (see Chapter 18).
7. Failure to keep records relating to vehicle inspections and repairs and driver defect reports.
8. For falsely stating facts on applications for 'O' licences and for not fulfilling statements of intent or environmental conditions placed on the licence.
9. If the licence holder becomes bankrupt or, in the case of a company, goes into liquidation.
10. If a place not listed on the licence is used as a vehicle operating centre.

Usually, the offending licence holder will be called to public inquiry by the LA and be required to explain why the offences occurred and what action is being taken to put matters right or to ensure they will not happen again. Depending on his reaction to such explanations the LA may initially give a warning about future conduct and the likely consequences if there is any repetition of the contraventions of the law or he will decide that an appropriate penalty should be imposed. This will be suspension, curtailment or premature termination of the licence or revocation. If the licence holder is found no longer to comply with the basic requirements for 'O' licensing, namely good repute, financial standing or professional competence then the LA must revoke the licence (except in the latter case where a period of temporary derogation is permitted – see p 42). If a restricted 'O' licence holder is convicted twice in a period of five years of operating outside the terms of the licence his licence must be revoked.

Curtailment is the most commonly imposed penalty and this implies removal of one or more authorised vehicles from the licence for any period up to the expiry of the licence. Suspension involves suspension of the whole licence and this may be combined with premature termination so the LA can review the whole operation under the provisions for consideration of a new licence application. As with premature termination of an existing licence, the need to apply for a new licence places the operator at risk of objection and environmental representation. The LA can direct that a vehicle on a licence which has been suspended or limited may not be used by another operator for a maximum of six months during the period of suspension.

When the LA revokes an 'O' licence he may order the holder to be disqualified, for a certain period or indefinitely, from holding or obtaining an 'O' licence and the order may be limited to one or may apply to more Traffic Areas. Following an order to revoke a licence, the LA may allow the licence holder to request a 'stay' to enable the operation to continue until an appeal to the Transport Tribunal is heard.

Offences are committed, for which prosecution and a court appearance may follow, if:
1. A windscreen licence disc is not displayed.
2. A change of address is not notified.
3. A licence is not produced for examination on request.
4. A duplicate windscreen disc is not returned if the original is found.
5. A disc is not returned when a vehicle is disposed of.
6. A subsidiary company featured on a holding company licence is disposed of and the LA is not advised.

In recent times the LAs have been active in preventing speeding by hgv drivers, firstly by imposing a penalty of suspension on the hgv driving licences of offending drivers and then by penalising the 'O' licences of firms whose drivers persistently and wilfully exceed speed limits. Evidence of such matters is mainly obtained during routine enforcement checking of tachograph charts where recordings showing frequent instances of driving above 100kph is clear evidence of breach of the 60mph maximum speed limit for vehicles exceeding 7.5 tonnes maximum laden weight.

Temporary Derogation

There are provisions in the regulations to enable a standard 'O' licence to remain in force for up to one year initially and a further six months (maximum derogation is 18 months) if the LA feels it is appropriate if the specified professionally competent person named on the licence dies or becomes legally incapacitated (ie unable to carry out his duties due to reasons of mental disorder) in order to allow a replacement person to be found and specified.

The regulations enable the LA to defer revocation of or refusal to grant a standard 'O' licence in the event of the death or incapacity of the holder of the licence, a transport manager, or a partner whose professional competence is relied upon. Further, in the event of the death or incapacity of the licence holder the LA is empowered to authorise another person to carry on the business during the changeover period as though that person was the licence holder. Also, the LA may allow time for a transport business to be transferred to another person licensed to carry it on or for a transport manager or new partner to be appointed.

Where a person who was carrying on a business as a licence holder dies, becomes mentally incapacitated, bankrupt or goes into liquidation or where a partnership is disolved the LA must be notified within two months. The person carrying on the business will be considered by the LA to be the holder of the licence if a new licence application is made within one month in the case of restricted 'O' licences and within four months in the case of standard 'O' licences.

Production of 'O' Licences

Operator's licence holders must produce their 'O' licence (form OL 1 plus forms OL 1(R) or OL 1(S) where appropriate) for examination when required to do so by the police, DTp examiners (ie certifying officers) or by the LA or a person with his authority. The holder has 14 days in which to present the licence either at one of the operating centres authorised on the licence or at his principal place of business in the Traffic Area. In the case of production to the police this can be at a police station of the holder's choice also within 14 days.

Licensing Courts/Transport Tribunal

Inquiries and Appeals

Licensing Authorities regularly hold public inquiries to which 'O' licence

1: OPERATORS' LICENSING

applicants are called to explain the basis of their operations and to enable the LA to seek more information prior to determining whether he should grant a licence or not. In the event of a representation on environmental grounds or an objection being made to a licence application the LA will hold a public inquiry at which the parties (applicant, objectors or those making representations) will have an opportunity to state their case further. If the application is refused in whole or in part or if environmental conditions are attached to a licence the applicant has rights of appeal against the LA's decision to the Transport Tribunal. Normally an existing licence will remain in force while an appeal is being heard and the LA may allow a revoked or suspended licence to continue during this time. If the LA refuses this the Tribunal can be asked to allow it to do so.

Statutory objectors also have a right of appeal to the Transport Tribunal if an application for a licence is granted and they still feel that their objection is valid. Those individuals making representations on environmental grounds have *no* similar right of appeal if their case fails.

It should be noted that the Transport Tribunal is the *only* source of appeal in regard to 'O' licensing matters.

Besides public inquiries conducted for the purposes of determining 'O' licence applications, such inquiries are also held at the LA's behest where it is necessary for him to examine the conduct of a licence holder for disciplinary purposes under the powers given him by the Transport Act 1968. Section 69 of this Act empowers him to conduct such inquiries (hence reference to 'section 69 inquiries') and impose penalties of suspension, curtailment or revocation of a licence (further details of this matter are given on p 41).

Appeals are heard only in London whereas public inquiries are usually held in the town or city in which the LA's office (ie the Traffic Area office – see Appendix I for addresses) is situated.

Public Inquiries

It is useful here to mention the way in which a public inquiry is conducted. It is presided over by the LA or his deputy and is open to members of the general public, other operators and interested persons who may sit in and listen, and to the press, who may report all that is said. Verbal evidence is given to the LA by the applicant (or by his legal representative if he has one) in answer to the LA's questions, and the same applies to objectors and those making representations. The evidence, unlike at criminal or civil courts, is not given under oath and statements made at a public inquiry that are defamatory or libellous of other people do not have protection by privilege. The offended person can take civil action if such statements or comments come to his notice. Evidence in some instances may be provided in writing and the LA may ask for certain supporting documents, in which case the applicant should have these to hand with extra copies for the objectors to examine. When he has heard all the evidence the LA will normally make a decision without conferring with anybody else. He may announce this at the time or defer his decision to be given later in writing. The entire proceedings of the inquiry will be recorded and transcripts can be obtained by interested parties.

Appeals to the Transport Tribunal

The Transport Tribunal, which is now under the control of the Lord

Chancellor, is a completely independent body comprising at least three sitting members, one of whom is the president, and must be a lawyer. At least two of the other members must also be legally qualified and have experience in the transport industry.

An appeal may be made against an LA's decision to refuse to grant an 'O' licence, if he attaches environmental conditions to an 'O' licence, if a licence is granted authorising fewer vehicles than the number applied for, if a licence is granted for a shorter period than that applied for, or where an existing licence is withdrawn, suspended or prematurely terminated by the LA.

A time limit of 28 days is allowed in which to make an appeal to the Transport Tribunal following an LA's decision, counting from the date of publication of the issue of *Applications and Decisions* in which the decision is published. Where the LA's decision is not published within 21 days an appeal can be made within 49 days of notification of the decision by the LA.

Where an LA makes a disciplinary decision against an 'O' licence (ie suspension, curtailment or revocation) and the licence holder wishes to appeal, he can apply for a 'stay' of the decision until the appeal is heard in order to keep his vehicles operating. Otherwise he would have to observe the decision irrespective of the consequences (financial and operational) on his business. An initial request for a 'stay' of the decision is made direct to the LA, but failing this an application must be made immediately to the Tribunal giving details of the decision and the reason for requesting the 'stay'. Application for a 'stay' of the decision cannot be made if there is no intention to appeal.

Appeals to the Transport Tribunal must be in writing and six copies should be sent to the Tribunal stating the decision against which the appeal is made, the grounds for the appeal, and the names and addresses of every person to whom a copy of the appeal has been sent.

Copies of the appeal must be sent to the LA and to all objectors if the appeal is being made by a licence applicant, or to the applicant if the appeal is being made by an objector to the decision.

Although the Tribunal has the powers and status of the High Court, its proceedings are conducted informally and appellants may represent themselves or be represented by any person they choose (there are no wigs and gowns even for barristers present). However, in the best interests of the applicant he should be legally represented at an appeal by a solicitor or barrister experienced in transport law to ensure that his case is fully and correctly made.

When an appeal is heard, the Tribunal examines the transcript of the public inquiry or the LA's statement of his reasons for the decision against which the appeal is lodged and then may ask further questions of the applicant or his advocate. No oath has to be taken and there is no protection by privilege. The proceedings are open to the public and the press. Tribunal appeal decisions may be announced at the hearing or later. All parties will be sent a full statement of the decision usually within three weeks of the hearing.

Generally, Tribunal decisions will fall into one of three categories. Either to uphold the LA's decision, to change the decision or to refer the matter back to the LA with a direction that he should reconsider his decision but taking account of legal guidance from the Tribunal. In exceptional circumstances the Tribunal may review its decision subject to a request to do so made within 14 days of the appeal hearing. Decisions of the Tribunal are binding from the date they are given, in other words they have immediate effect.

Further appeals against decisions of the Tribunal may be made to the Court of Appeal or the Court of Sessions in Scotland but only on points of law, not on the original decision of the LA or the subsequent ruling of the Transport Tribunal.

Further details of the appeals procedure can be found in booklet GV251A available free from Traffic Area offices. The address of the Tribunal is: 48–49 Chancery Lane, London WC2A 1JR. Telephone 071-936 7494.

No fees are payable in respect of appeals but costs may be awarded against frivolous, vexatious, improper or unreasonable appeals.

Northern Ireland

Northern Ireland has its own scheme of Road Freight Operator's Licensing administered in the Province by the department of the Environment. This is described fully in Chapter 25.

Goods vehicle operators in NI no longer need to obtain a short-term 'O' licence prior to entry into Great Britain. Similarly, there is no longer any need for GB operators to obtain a short-term licence prior to entry into Northern Ireland. A goods vehicle operating on a current 'O' licence issued in Great Britain or a Road Freight 'O' licence issued in Northern Ireland will be permitted to carry goods throughout the UK. However, cabotage (ie picking up and delivering a load within one country) is not permitted in either case.

Goods vehicles from Northern Ireland engaging in own-account operations for which a Road Freight Operator's licence is not required in the Province must, while operating in Great Britain, carry a document showing details of their load and route in Great Britain.

Use of Light Goods Vehicles

Many existing transport operators and new entrants to the industry have sought to avoid the problems and pitfalls of 'O' licensing by using vehicles defined as 'small' vehicles – those vehicles not exceeding 3.5 tonnes maximum permissible weight. With such vehicles there is no need to obtain an 'O' licence and consequently no need to face the LA and satisfy all the conditions previously explained. The operator is also free from the legal requirements under other legislation for his drivers to operate tachographs or to keep other written records of their hours of work and to hold hgv driving licences.

Despite this apparent freedom the operator of such vehicles does have certain obligations and responsibilities. First, if he tows a trailer with such a vehicle the combined weight of both vehicle and trailer (if over 1020kg unladen) could exceed the 3.5 tonne weight threshold above which an 'O' licence would be needed and the provisions of the EC or British driver's hours law and the relevant record keeping or tachograph requirements may apply (see Chapters 3, 4 and 5). Second, if he also operates, or plans to operate in the future, larger vehicles which are within the scope of 'O' licensing, his conduct as an operator of small vehicles will be taken into account by the LA when deciding whether to grant or renew his 'O' licence.

The LAs have made the point that when an operator applies to renew an 'O' licence they (the LAs) would take notice of any relevant convictions in respect of smaller vehicles belonging to the operator and could call the operator to public inquiry to show cause why the 'O' licence should not be revoked or curtailed. The operator of small vehicles still has to ensure that his vehicles are not overloaded and that they are kept in a safe mechanical order under other regulations; they must be tested annually after they become three years old. Drivers of these vehicles are required to observe the drivers' hours regulations with certain exceptions. All these individual legal exemptions and requirements are discussed in later chapters.

Foreign Vehicles in the UK

Vehicles entering Great Britain from countries with which the UK has concluded a bilateral agreement do not need an 'O' licence; they may, however, require other documents (ie permits – or own-account documents). Vehicles from countries where no such agreement exists must be covered by an 'O' licence which will be issued for a period of not more than 90 days. Such an 'O' licence does not permit the holder to engage in internal transport in Great Britain – cabotage operations may however be permitted under appropriate permits issued to the operator in his own EC member state.

Foreign vehicles entering Great Britain under an EC or ECMT permit do not need an 'O' licence provided the permit is being carried on the vehicle.

Proposed Changes to 'O' Licensing

A number of proposals for changes to the present 'O' licensing system have been publicised during recent times. There have been suggestions that own-account vehicle operation would become exempted from the licensing system – as is the case in Northern Ireland (part of the UK) and in most European Community member states – and that all vehicles not exceeding 6 tonnes maximum permissible weight would be exempted.

Proposed EC requirements include a suggestion that financial guarantees may have to be given by new entrants to the road haulage industry – figures such as 10 per cent of the vehicle fleet replacement value and up to £4000 per vehicle have been reported for those seeking standard 'O' licences covering international transport operations.

A government review of 'O' licensing is reported to have considered replacing present fixed-term 'O' licences (normally valid for five years) with lifetime licences, an annual fee instead of advance payment of full-term fees, elimination of vehicle identity (ie windscreen) discs and a facility to increase fleet size by up to 10 per cent without further application.

There are proposals to reorganise Traffic Areas (closing three Traffic Area offices, namely Metropolitan, Newcastle and Nottingham) and the role of Licensing Authorities. Principally the suggestion is for Traffic Areas to become an executive agency (as has already happened with the Vehicle

Inspectorate Executive Agency – which has taken over running of the DTp heavy goods vehicle testing stations). Also proposed are fewer LAs dealing with disciplinary and environmental 'O' licensing public inquiries under one 'supremo' (now appointed as Senior Traffic Commissioner is Major General John Carpenter, LA for the Western Traffic Area) with no responsibility for hgv or psv driver licensing (which is being switched to the DVLC at Swansea under the driver licensing scheme – see Chapter 6).

Looking to 1992

The advent of a single European free market from 1992 when the last of the trading barriers between EC member states are finally demolished will have an effect on road transport operations. From 1993 the liberalisation of community transport will mean the scrapping of road haulage permits to allow unrestricted movement of vehicles throughout the community and the likelihood that cabotage operations (which are currently illegal) will be legalised. There are also proposals to implement much stricter industry entry qualifications to add safety and environmental provisions to the current good repute, financial standing and professional competence requirements, to introduce 'Community Licences' and to harmonise road tax (ie vehicle excise duty).

NB: A more detailed examination of the effects of 1992 on the UK road transport industry is provided in David Lowe's book The Transport and Distribution Manager's Guide to 1992 *also published by Kogan Page.*

IMPORTANT NEWS FOR COMMERCIAL FLEET MANAGERS!

As any driver or Commercial Fleet operator will know, a breakdown on the road can spell disaster: perishable loads rotting, goods undelivered, and valuable time wasted. Setbacks that won't increase your popularity amongst clients!

And no driver anywhere can guarantee that his vehicle *won't* break down.

Moreover, when you consider that there's a breakdown on British roads every 5 seconds, the next casualty could easily be you. Or one of your colleagues.

So to avoid such a disaster, it makes sense to take out breakdown cover, and that's where we come in.

National Breakdown have been getting drivers' loads back onto the road for years. And 'TRUCKLINK' is a special scheme whereby a nominal registration fee covers your vehicle

TRUCKLINK GETS YOUR LOAD BACK ON THE ROAD. FAST!

Put yourself in the driving seat with the "Pay-As-You-Break Down" Plan!

and trailer against breakdowns. You then only *pay* for the service you *use* (call-out, parts, labour, etc).

So if you never break down, we won't charge you for service you don't need... a very sensible idea you'll agree, by any vehicle operator's standards!

YOU INSTRUCT US WHAT TO DO AND WE'LL DO IT!

Of course we'll do our very best to repair your vehicle there and then at the roadside. However, if this is not possible you can choose whether to be recovered to your destination, or to your base... your vehicle put into secure storage... or not. Whatever we do it's entirely up to you!

So with such flexible cover you can see why we have over 1,000,000 members, including some of the UK's largest companies! (In fact no less than 70% of all new heavy commercial

vehicles are covered by National Breakdown).

You'll find us highly efficient, and fast. (Just what you need to get you and your load right back on the road in today's competitive commercial environment). Moreover, if your driver *does* break down we can let you know at base what's happened.

Reassuring?

Certainly. What's more there's just one number to National Breakdown's Control Centre should you break down. And we're on call 24 hours a day, 365 days a year.

So to find out more about the cover that could save you money *and* save your bacon (or fresh fruit, or whatever you're carrying) send for your FREE Information Pack (post-free) to: **National Breakdown, Commercial Sales, FREEPOST, Leeds LS99 2NB.**

NATIONAL BREAKDOWN

TRUCK*LINK*

OR CALL BRIAN HADWIN, COMMERCIAL SALES MANAGER, ON

☎ 0532 393666

CUT CORNERS ON THE COST, NOT THE COVER!

To: National Breakdown, Commercial Sales, FREEPOST, Leeds LS99 2NB.
Please send me my free information pack today.

Name _____
Position _____
Company Address _____
_____
_____
_____ Postcode ___
Telephone _____ Ext. _____
Fleet Size: Trucks _____ Cars/Light Vans _____
Please send me details of your tailor made Fleetcall scheme for cars. ☐ PLEASE TICK

TMN 11/90

REPLY TODAY FOR YOUR FREE INFORMATION PACK

2: Professional Competence

The legal requirement for certain people employed in road transport (ie road freight and road passenger) operations to be professionally competent came into effect in Britain on 1 January 1978.

On the road goods side of the industry, this scheme was the final outcome of many years' work on the development of a plan to make individuals more responsible for the safe operation of vehicle fleets in their charge and better qualified to understand the legal, economic and operational requirements for safe and efficient goods vehicle operation. Previous proposals (in the Transport Act 1968) were based on a licensing system which would require transport managers to hold a 'transport manager's licence'. As a result of EC influence via EC Directive 74/561 'On Admission to the Occupation of Road Haulage Operator in National and International Operations', the proposed British transport manager's licensing scheme was abandoned in favour of one which provides all those people who qualify, not just those fulfilling the role of transport manager, with either a certificate of professional competence or a professional competence qualification by exemption or by examination.

Under the Goods Vehicles (Operators' Licences, Qualifications and Fees) Regulations 1984 (as amended), road haulage operators (including own-account operators who wish to carry goods for hire or to reward or in connection with a business which is not their own) are required to meet the professional competence requirement in order to obtain a standard operator's licence or renew (ie apply for a new licence to replace the expired licence) an existing standard 'O' licence.

Own-account transport operators who have no desire to or intention of carrying goods for hire or reward or for any purpose which is not in connection with their own trade or business (including not doing favours for customers by carrying their goods also) can apply for a restricted 'O' licence for which there is no need to meet the professional competence requirement.

The important point for road hauliers and others who carry goods for hire or reward is that in order to obtain a new or to renew an existing operator's licence they must request a standard 'O' licence covering either national or both national and international operations and specify in their application the name of a person who is professionally competent and who is responsible for the operation of the vehicles authorised on the licence. This person may be the applicant himself, if suitably qualified, or it may be a person holding the title of transport manager (or some other person – the law is not concerned as to the person's actual job-title only that they should be the person who is responsible for the vehicle operations on a day-to-day basis) who is professionally competent and is employed by the applicant.

Employment in this context normally means full-time employment with the licence holder. Part-time or casual employment of a professionally competent person would not previously have met the requirements of the regulations but a proposed change likely in 1990/91 will enable a part-time qualified employee to be nominated in support of a licence application. Also, whereas a professionally competent person in one firm could not previously be specified in support of the licence held by another, non-related firm, this situation may change when the proposed new rules take effect.

There has been a Licensing Authority's decision which indicates that a self-employed transport manager may be acceptable as the professionally competent person specified on an 'O' licence. While the 'full-time employment' requirement continues to exist this does not necessarily mean that the person concerned must devote all of their working time to the transport management function, they may have other duties and responsibilities in the firm (eg such as administration manager, works manager, company secretary etc).

Who may become Professionally Competent?

Professional competence is available and applicable only to individuals. Under the regulations, a firm or a corporate body cannot be classed as being professionally competent. Any individual, male or female, whether employed with the title of 'transport manager' or not, may become professionally competent if they meet the necessary qualifying conditions or otherwise pass the official examination. There is no pre-qualifying standard and no requirement that the person should have any previous experience of or is, has been or plans to actually work in the transport industry in any capacity whatsoever. It is open to absolutely anybody to become professionally competent if they so wish.

However, only those who are actually responsible for the operation of goods vehicles on a day-to-day basis will need to be 'nominated' as the professionally competent 'transport manager' in support of an application for a standard 'O' licence. Such individuals must themselves be of good repute and of appropriate financial standing (as well as the applicant – see Chapter 1) otherwise their name may not be acceptable to the LA despite the fact that they are qualified as being professionally competent (see below).

Proof of Professional Competence

Proof that a person is professionally competent and is therefore able to satisfy the requirements of the 'O' licence system is dependent on holding a certificate of professional competence (CPC) issued by a Licensing Authority (Form GV 203) or confirmatory evidence provided by any other body approved by the Secretary of State for Transport, namely a Royal Society of Arts examination pass certificate or a membership certificate from one of the recognised professional institutes which confers exemption (see p 52). No other document provides evidence of professional competence for these purposes.

Classes of Competence

Professional competence in road freight operations falls into two classes covering national operations only or both national and international operations. A parallel scheme covers road passenger operations.

All certificates of professional competence (CPCs – Form GV 203) granted under the original Grandfather Rights scheme (see below) cover both national and international operations (although it does not specifically say so on them).

In cases where people qualify for professional competence under the exemption arrangements, the level at which they qualify determines whether they are entitled to be classed as professionally competent in national transport operations only or in both national and international transport operations (see p 53).

Candidates who achieve professional competence by examination will obtain appropriate documentary evidence (ie a Royal Society of Arts examination pass certificate) indicating that they have passed the modular examinations covering national operations only (modules A and B freight – or C passenger) or the additional examination covering international operations (module D freight – or E passenger).

Those qualified for professional competence in national operations only will be permitted to engage in or be responsible for operations conducted on standard 'O' licences solely within the UK (ie covering national transport operations).

Holders of certificates of professional competence (Form GV 203) or those qualifying for professional competence in both national and international operations, by exemption or examination, will be permitted to engage in or be responsible for the operation of goods vehicles on standard 'O' licences covering national operations within the UK and international operations outside the UK.

National and International Transport Operations

Following legal decisions made in the EC the definition of what constitutes an international journey has been changed in Britain. So, for example, where loaded trailers are taken to a port for onward movement outside the UK, while the tractive unit and driver do not leave the UK, such journeys constitute national operations (previously, these were international operations), and a standard 'O' licence covering national transport operations only is needed for such operations (and the employed manager will need to be professionally competent only in national operations).

Qualifications for Professional Competence

The qualifications needed to obtain professional competence fall into three categories as follows:
1. By experience in the industry prior to 1 January 1975 (known as Grandfather Rights).
2. By exemption.
3. By examination.

Each of these three qualifying methods is described below.

Grandfather Rights

(NB: The issue of certificates of competence (Form GV 203 – known as

CPCs) under this scheme ended on 31 December 1979, since which date the only means of qualifying for professional competence is by exemption or examination. However, since many people continue to ask about the scheme it was felt useful to continue to include an explanation in the current edition of the Handbook).

Transport managers and other people employed in 'responsible road transport employment' prior to 1 January 1975 were able to obtain the grant of a so-called 'Grandfather Rights' certificate of competence, without examination, as of right. Once granted, the certificate will continue to remain valid for as long as the scheme is in force.

For the purposes of the (now extinct) Grandfather Rights scheme, responsible road transport employment was defined as employment in the service of a person or a firm carrying on a road transport undertaking and was employed in a position where the individual had responsibility for the operation of goods vehicles used under an operator's licence.

Similar conditions applied to any person who was the holder of an 'O' licence prior to 1 January 1975. In other words any owner-driver or small fleet operator who held an 'O' licence in his own name or under a business name qualified, having been a licence holder. In the case of an 'O' licence held by a partnership prior to this date, all the partners qualified under the Grandfather Rights arrangements. Where a licence was held by a limited company, the person responsible for the day-to-day operation of the vehicles under the licence (eg the transport manager) qualified for the Grandfather Rights grant of a CPC.

In order to obtain a certificate under this arrangement, application had to be made to the Licensing Authorities no later than 30 November 1979. Since that date, the opportunity to obtain a CPC other than by examination or exemption has ceased.

Issue of CPC Certificates
Certificates of professional competence (Form GV 203) issued under the Grandfather Rights scheme were obtainable from the Traffic Area offices on application provided that the necessary form and certification of appropriate qualifying experience by an employer was supplied. Although certificates carry the name of the issuing Traffic Area, they are valid for operations in all Traffic Areas and individuals had no need to obtain separate certificates for each area in which they were responsible for the operation of vehicles.

There was no fee for the issue of a certificate of competence (CPC), and certificates thus granted remain valid for the life of the scheme. There is no system for revocation or disqualification of CPC holders but where the holder is also the 'O' licence holder, or is the nominated professionally competent transport manager employed by an 'O' licence holder, then there is a requirement that he must be of good repute (see pp 21 and 56) and of adequate financial standing; otherwise the 'O' licence will be subject to penalty (see p 40). Grandfather Rights CPCs issued on the basis of information provided which is subsequently found to be false may be withdrawn by the Licensing Authority.

Exemption

People who did not qualify for a CPC based on previous experience in road transport operations as described above and new entrants to the industry may obtain the professional competence qualification if they satisfy certain exemption criteria.

The exemption qualifications are based on holding current and valid membership of one or more of a number of professional bodies at certain levels. There are two levels of qualification; one covering both international and national operations and the other covering national operations only. The exemption qualifications are as follows:

For both national and international operations
1. Membership of the Chartered Institute of Transport in the grade of Fellow or Member (engaged in the road transport sector).
2. Membership of the Institute of Transport Administration in the grade of Fellow, Member, Associate Member or Associate (by examination) (engaged in the road transport sector).
3. Membership of the Institute of Road Transport Engineers in the grade of Member or Associate Member.
4. Membership of the Institute of the Furniture Warehousing and Removing Industry in the grade of Fellow or Associate.

For national operations only
1. Membership of the Chartered Institute of Transport in the grade of Associate Member (engaged in the road transport sector).
2. Membership of the Institute of Road Transport Engineers in the grade of Associate (by examination).
3. Membership of the Institute of Transport Administration in the grade of Graduate or Associate (must be at least 21 years old, have 3 years' practical experience and be a holder of the NEBSS Certificate) (engaged in the road transport sector).
4. Holder of the General Certificate in Removals Management issued by the Institute of the Furniture Warehousing and Removing Industry.
5. Holder of the Royal Society of Arts Certificate in Road Goods transport gained by examination since May 1984.

There are no grounds for obtaining professional competence by exemption other than those detailed above. Valid membership of the relevant body (ie subscription paid etc) is sufficient to confirm professional competence but, if required, the institutes will issue a confirmatory certificate or statement (ie not a certificate of competence of the type issued under Grandfather Rights).

Examination

A system of examinations has been established to enable new entrants to the transport (ie road freight and road passenger) industry and those people who do not qualify under the previously mentioned Grandfather Rights or exemption arrangements to study for and obtain professional competence by examination. The examination scheme is organised and conducted on behalf of the Department of Transport by the Royal Society of Arts and examinations for both goods and passenger vehicle operations are held at main centres throughout the country four times each year.

In 1991 the examinations are to be held on the following *provisional** dates: Friday 22 March 1991, Friday 21 June 1991, Friday 4 October 1991 and Friday 6 December 1991.

* *Potential examination candidates should check these dates with the Royal Society of Arts or their local examination centre.*

For the national examination a modular system is adopted with a common 'core' for both goods (ie road freight) and passenger subjects and then the individual modal (freight – module B or passenger – module C) sections. The 'core' (module A) comprises 20 questions to be answered in 30 minutes and the remaining freight modal section (module B) comprises 40 questions to be completed in one hour. Candidates who pass either module A alone, or the freight module B, or passenger module C sections alone, will be issued with a 'credit' pending their achievement of the full certificate, which they can gain having re-sat and passed the remainder of the examination. Thus, 'failed' examinees do not have to study for and sit the whole examination again, but only the module in which they failed.

This split modular system does not apply to the international examinations (freight module D or passenger module E) which remains unchanged with the candidate taking the one hour examination at a single sitting during which 30 questions have to be answered.

The examinations can be taken at individual sittings or all at the same examination centre on the same day (providing the local centre is offering all examinations at one sitting – this usually depends on there being a sufficient number of candidate entries), the choice is open to the candidate.

Fees for the 1990/91 year examinations are £15.00 for both modules (ie A and freight B or passenger C) of the national examinations and £28.50 if both modules of the national (A and B) and the international (modules D or E) examinations are taken on the same day. Module A taken alone is £5.00 and module B or C taken alone is £10.00. These fees are payable to the Royal Society of Arts. Additional charges may be made by examining centres for the facilities they provide. Candidates who fail examinations may apply to the RSA for details of their performance. They should state where and when they sat the examination and should enclose a remittance of £2.50.

Note: Fees are reviewed for each examination year commencing in October, so prospective candidates should check the latest fees when making application to sit the examinations.

The address of the Royal Society of Arts is as follows: RSA Examinations Board, Westwood Way, Westwood Business Park, Coventry CV4 8HS (Tel: 0203 470033. Fax: 0203 468080).

Examination Method

Examinations conducted for the purpose of providing the qualification for professional competence are based on the 'objective testing' or multiple choice method. This means that the candidate is faced with either a number of questions, each of which is provided with a choice of possible answers (usually four), only one of which is correct, or alternatively statements to which a 'True' or 'False' answer must be indicated. The candidate must select and mark the correct answer to each question or statement.

With this method of examination, the need for high standards of literacy is removed and it ensures uniform standards of marking for all candidates.

The examinations are designed to be within the grasp of candidates whose educational standard corresponds to the level normally reached at school leaving age.

Examination Syllabus

Candidates for the examination are not compelled to study beforehand but a study syllabus covering the examination subjects has been formulated and is available from the Royal Society of Arts. Study may be undertaken at courses organised by a number of bodies including the RTITB, group training associations, trade associations or commercial organisations. Some local technical colleges and other teaching establishments also offer part-time, usually evening, classes on the subject. The study may involve full-time or part-time attendance at such courses or it may be by correspondence course or by training or home learning package (ie notes and cassette tapes) or with the aid of teaching manuals. David Lowe's *Study Manual of Professional Competence in Road Transport Management* (Kogan Page Ltd, 120 Pentonville Road, London N1 9JN. Tel: 071-278 0433 covering both the freight national and international examinations, ie *not* the PSV syllabus) has been used successfully by many candidates, and in some cases without resorting to attendance at study courses or evening classes.

The newly published – and expanded – RSA syllabus for road freight operations effective from the March 1991 examinations onwards is detailed here:

Syllabus for National Transport Operations
  MODULE A
   1. Law
      1.1 Structure of Law
      1.2 Business and Company Law
      1.3 Social Legislation
   2. Business and Financial Management
      2.1 Financial Management Techniques
      2.2 Commercial Conduct of the Business
      2.3 General Insurance
   3. Technical Standards and Aspects of Operations
      3.1 Mechanical Conditions – Vehicle Maintenance
   4. Road Safety
      4.1 General Traffic Regulations

  MODULE B
   1. Law
      1.1 Taxation
   2. Business and Financial Management
      2.1 Marketing
      2.2 Commercial Conduct of the Business
      2.3 Methods of Operating
   3. Access to the Market
      3.1 Operator Licensing
   4. Technical Standards and Aspects of Operation
      4.1 Weights and Dimensions of Vehicles and Loads
      4.2 Vehicle Selection
      4.3 Safe Loading of Vehicle and Transit of Goods
      4.4 Mechanical Conditions

5. Road Safety
   5.1 Drivers' Hours and Records
   5.2 Vocational Driving Licences
   5.3 Speed Limits
   5.4 Procedure in Case of Traffic Accidents
   5.5 Vehicle and Goods Insurances

Syllabus for International Transport Operations
   MODULE D
   1. Law
   2. **Control of Road Haulage Operations**
   3. **Customs, Insurance and other Formalities**
   4. **Operations, Technical Standards and Road Safety**

The RSA states that new legislative measures will not be included in the examination for at least three months from the date of implementation.

Those wishing to study for the examination should ensure that they have an up-to-date syllabus, which covers both goods and passenger vehicle operations, from the Royal Society of Arts (see p 54 for address).

Note: A separate syllabus is published to cover Northern Ireland requirements.

Length of Study Course

The Royal Society of Arts recommends that the study course for the national examination should involve 72 hours of direct teaching and for the international examination a further 30 hours of direct teaching. Candidates starting from 'scratch', and particularly those without any assisted tuition, may find that they need considerably more than this amount of time which, in any case, does not include time needed for private study outside the tuition periods.

Transfer of Qualifications

Provisions are made to allow an interchange of professional competence qualifications and recognition of professional competence qualification certificates between the United Kingdom, Northern Ireland and other EC member states. Thus the UK Licensing Authorities are required to take into account any certificate of professional competence or any alternative to such a certificate showing relevant experience in the road haulage industry issued either in Northern Ireland or in other member states when considering an application for an 'O' licence.

Similarly, the Licensing Authorities in the UK will issue a Certificate of Qualification (fee £2 – payable to the Traffic Area) confirming the good repute, professional competence and, where relevant, the financial standing of persons or companies from the UK who wish to be admitted to the occupation of road haulage operator, or to be employed to manage the transport operations of a goods haulage undertaking in Northern Ireland or in any other EC member state.

Good Repute

A great deal of attention has been focused on the 'good repute' aspect of professionally competent persons. The good repute of such persons is only called into question when their name is put forward in support of a standard 'O' licence application. At that time the Licensing Authority will want to know if the person has previous convictions for offences relating to the operation of goods vehicles (see below).

Following on from the previous explanation of the interchange of qualifications between the UK and other EC member states, the Licensing Authorities, in considering an application for an 'O' licence and the good repute of the nominated professionally competent person, are required to take into account any convictions incurred by the person in Northern Ireland or in a country or territory outside the UK.

The relevant convictions are those which correspond to the relevant convictions under the British regulations, namely: offences relating to vehicle roadworthiness, speeding, overloading, safe loading, drivers' hours and record keeping, drivers' licensing, maintenance, illegal use of rebated fuel, certain traffic offences and to the International Road Haulage Permits Act 1975.

Further, the Transport Tribunal has ruled that the Licensing Authority can consider other convictions when considering a professionally competent person's good repute. The Tribunal ruled that the LA does not have to regard only those convictions mentioned above (as identified in the 1968 Transport Act) in deciding good repute.

In another instance a Licensing Authority has said that a nominated professionally competent person must be clear of past financial difficulties. This followed a case where a nominated person was shown to be an adjudged bankrupt and the Licensing Authority refused to accept the person's name on this account.

Under proposed new regulations to be introduced in 1990/1 LAs will not be permitted to examine and rule upon a transport manager's good repute or professional competence unless the individual has been notified in advance that this is to happen and has had an opportunity to make personal representation to the LA (at a public inquiry if necessary and represented by a solicitor if he so wishes) concerning any allegations made about him.

TRANSPORT RECORDS

From stock or...
printed to your specifications

- Maintenance — Costing — Wages etc.

Specialists in Stationery for the Transport Industry

LETTERHEADS — INVOICES — JOB SHEETS

Send for list and specimens

Charnwood Publishing Co. Ltd.

Vaughan Street, Coalville, Leicester LE6 2DG
Telephone Coalville 0530 32288
Fax: 0530 510390

3: Goods Vehicle Drivers' Hours

Any person who drives a goods vehicle which is being used for commercial or business purposes (ie not including those used for purely private purposes and other vehicles specifically exempted – see pp 16–17) irrespective of the vehicle weight must conform to strict rules on the amount of time they may spend driving. For most goods vehicle drivers the rules also include requirements relating to minimum breaks to be taken during the driving day and both daily and weekly rest periods.

The driving hours rules are applied for reasons of public safety, to protect road users from the dangers of having overworked and tired drivers at the wheel of heavy vehicles. They are enforced vigorously by both the police and Department of Transport enforcement officers and offenders are being dealt with very severely by the courts to emphasise the importance with which these road safety measures are viewed.

Drivers found to be in contravention of the rules as set out in this chapter can expect to be prosecuted and fined heavily on conviction – the most serious of such offences can result in imprisonment – and those who hold hgv driving licences may find they have placed their licence, and thus possibly their job, in jeopardy.

Employers of such drivers also risk prosecution and heavy fines on conviction for similar offences. Additionally they may have penalties imposed on their 'O' licences by the LAs since they promised in the declaration of intent at the time of their 'O' licence application that they would make arrangements to ensure the drivers' hours law would be observed. It is also a specific requirement of the EC rules that employers must make periodic checks to ensure the rules are observed and must take appropriate action if they discover breaches of the law to ensure there is no repetition of offences. On the Continent, breaches of the rules may result in drivers incurring heavy on-the-spot fines which must be paid immediately, otherwise the vehicle may be impounded and the driver held until the fine is paid.

Goods vehicle driver employers and drivers themselves need to understand the hours rules clearly and especially which particular set of rules applies to them depending on the vehicle being driven or the nature of the transport operation on which they are engaged. Three main sets of rules apply, the EC rules, the British domestic rules and what are known as the AETR rules for international journeys outside the EC. The specific requirements under each of these sets of rules are explained in the following pages.

European Community Rules

The currently applied EC rules, contained in EC Regulation 3820/85, came into effect in the UK on 29 September 1986. British regulations as follows implementing these rules and modifying previous provisions came into

effect on the same date:
1. The Community Drivers' Hours and Recording Equipment (Exemptions and Supplementary Provisions) Regulations 1986 – which implement the EC Regulations in the UK and the derogations (ie exemptions) from them.
2. The Community Drivers' Hours and Recording Equipment Regulations 1985 – which make consequential changes to the 1968 Transport Act provisions.
3. The Drivers' Hours (Goods Vehicles) (Modifications) Order 1985 – which implements changes to national and domestic driving under the 1986 Act.
4. The Drivers' Hours (Harmonisation with Community Rules) Regulations 1986 – which harmonise the rules for those who drive under both the EC Regulations and the revised 1968 Act rules.

Vehicles Covered

EC rules always take precedence over national rules. Therefore since all goods vehicles used in connection with business activities as stated above are covered by one or other of the sets of drivers' hours rules (ie EC, British or AETR) the requirements of specific EC legislation must be considered first. Mainly, this involves examination of the list of EC rules exemptions (see below) to determine whether the vehicle or the transport operation falls within scope of the rules or outside.

Where a vehicle has a maximum permissible weight not exceeding 3.5 tonnes it is exempt from the EC rules or if it is one identified on the EC exemption list or is used for a purpose which is shown in the list as exempt as mentioned above (eg vehicles used by the public utilities and local authorities etc) it automatically comes within the scope of the British domestic rules set out in the 1968 Transport Act rules as described in detail on pp 67–9.

Where vehicles are over 3.5 tonnes permissible maximum weight, including the weight of any trailer drawn, and are not exempt as shown by the list or used for an exempt purpose, the EC hours law applies.

Exemptions to EC Rules

The EC regulations list a number of exemptions and national governments (eg the British government) are permitted to make certain other exemptions (derogations) if they so wish, as shown below.

International Exemptions (under EC regulations)
1. Vehicles not exceeding 3.5 tonnes gross weight including the weight of any trailer drawn.
2. Passenger vehicles constructed to carry not more than nine persons including driver.
3. Vehicles on regular passenger services on routes not exceeding 50 kilometres.
4. Vehicles with legal maximum speed not exceeding 30kph (approx 18.6 mph).
5. Vehicles used by armed services, civil defence, fire services, forces responsible for maintaining public order (ie police).

3: GOODS VEHICLE DRIVERS' HOURS

6. Vehicles used in connection with sewerage; flood protection; water, gas and electricity services; highway maintenance and control; refuse collection and disposal; telephone and telegraph services; carriage of postal articles; radio and television broadcasting; detection of radio or television transmitters or receivers.
7. Vehicles used in emergencies or rescue operations.
8. Specialised vehicles used for medical purposes.
9. Vehicles transporting circus and funfair equipment.
10. Specialised breakdown vehicles.
11. Vehicles undergoing road tests for technical development, repair or maintenance purposes, and new or rebuilt vehicles which have not yet been put into service.
12. Vehicles used for non-commercial carriage of goods for personal use (ie private use).
13. Vehicles used for milk containers or milk products intended for animal feed.

National Exemptions (under British derogations)
1. Passenger vehicles constructed to carry not more than 17 persons including driver.
2. Vehicles used by public authorities to provide public services which are not in competition with professional road hauliers.
3. Vehicles used by agricultural, horticultural, forestry or fishery* undertakings, for carrying goods within a 50-km radius of the place where the vehicle is normally based, including local administrative areas the centres of which are situated within that radius.
   • *to gain this exemption the vehicle must be used to carry live fish or to carry a catch of fish which has not been subjected to any process or treatment (other than freezing) from the place of landing to a place where it is to be processed or treated.*
4. Vehicles used for carrying animal waste or carcasses not intended for human consumption.
5. Vehicles used for carrying live animals from farms to local markets and vice versa, or from markets to local slaughterhouses.
6. Vehicles specially fitted for and used:
   – as shops at local markets and for door-to-door selling
   – for mobile banking, exchange or savings transactions
   – for worship
   – for the lending of books, records or cassettes
   – for cultural events or exhibitions.
7. Vehicles (not exceeding 7.5 tonnes gvw) carrying materials or equipment for the driver's use in the course of his work within 50-km radius of base provided the driving does not constitute the driver's main activity and does not prejudice the objectives of the regulations.
8. Vehicles operating exclusively on islands not exceeding 2300 sq km not linked to the mainland by bridge, ford or tunnel for use by motor vehicles (excludes Isle of Wight).
9. Vehicles (not exceeding 7.5 tonnes gvw) used for the carriage of goods propelled by gas produced on the vehicle or by electricity.
10. Vehicles used for driving instruction (but not if carrying goods for hire or reward).
11. Tractors used after 1 January 1990 exclusively for agricultural and forestry work.

12. Vehicles used by the RNLI for hauling lifeboats.
13. Vehicles manufactured before 1 January 1947.
14. Steam propelled vehicles.

Note: In exemption 2 above relating to vehicles used by public authorities, the exemption applies only if the vehicle is being used by:
(a) a health authority in England and Wales or a health board in Scotland
   – to provide ambulance services in pursuance of its duty under the NHS Act 1977 or NHS (Scotland) Act 1978; or
   – to carry staff, patients, medical supplies or equipment in pursuance of its general duties under the Act;
(b) a local authority to fulfil social services functions, such as services for old persons or for physically and mentally handicapped persons;
(c) HM Coastguard or lighthouse authorities;
(d) harbour authorities within harbour limits;
(e) airports authority within airport perimeters;
(f) British Rail, London Regional Transport, a Passenger Transport Executive or local authority for maintaining railways;
(g) British Waterways Board for maintaining navigable waterways.

EC Regulations 3820/85

These regulations, introduced on 29 September 1986 throughout the EC repealed previous regulations (EC 543/69 as amended). To apply the rules as required and appreciate their implications it is necessary to understand the definitions of certain words and phrases used as follows:

Driver
The regulations apply specifically to the 'driver' of the vehicle. For these purposes a 'driver' is any person who drives the vehicle, even for a short period, or who is carried on the vehicle in order to be available for driving if necessary. They do not apply to persons carried as mates (ie to help load and unload only) or statutory attendants.

Driving
Driving is time spent behind the wheel actually driving the vehicle and relates to an accumulation of periods spent driving before a break is needed or a daily rest period is commenced. The maximum limit for driving before a break is taken is four and a half hours.

Vehicle Categories
Drivers of all types and weight categories of vehicles within the scope of the regulations are treated equally in regard to driving, break and rest periods.

A Day
For the purposes of the regulations a day is any period of 24 hours, in other words a rolling period. If a driver drives a vehicle to which the EC

3: GOODS VEHICLE DRIVERS' HOURS

regulations apply on any day (no mattter how short the actual time spent driving or how short the journey on the road – for example, a ten-minute drive down the road would still bring the driver within scope of the rules) then the legal requirements apply to him for the whole of that day and the week in which that day falls.

Fixed Week
The definition of a 'week' for the purpose of the regulations is a fixed week from 00.00 hours Monday to 24.00 hours on the following Sunday. All references in the rules to weeks and weekly limits must be considered against this fixed week. Reference to 'fortnight' means two consecutive fixed weeks as described above.

Driving Limits
Goods vehicle drivers are restricted in the amount of time they can spend driving before taking a break and the amount of driving they can do in a day, in a week and in a fortnight. The maximum limits are as follows:

Maximum aggregated driving before a break:		4½ hours
Maximum daily driving:	normally:	9 hours
	extension:	10 hours on 2 days in the week
Maximum weekly driving:		6 daily driving shifts*
Maximum fortnightly driving:		90 hours

* NB: The High Court ruled in 1988 that drivers can exceed the maximum of six daily driving shifts within six days as specified in the EC rules provided they do not exceed the maximum number of hours permitted in six consecutive driving periods. It should be noted that where a driver spends the maximum amount of driving time behind the wheel in one week (ie 4 x 9 hours plus 2 x 10 hours = 56 hours), during the following fixed week he may drive for a maximum of only 34 hours.

Break Periods

Drivers are required by law to take a break or breaks if in a day the aggregate of their driving time amounts to 4½ hours or more. If the driver does not drive for periods amounting in aggregate to 4½ hours in the day there is no legal requirement for him to take a break during that day.

Break periods must not be regarded as parts of a daily rest period and during breaks the driver must not carry out any 'other work'. However, waiting time, time spent riding as passenger in a vehicle or time spent on a ferry or train are not counted as 'other work' for these purposes.

The requirement for taking a break is that immediately the four and a half hour driving limit is reached a break of 45 minutes must be taken. This break may be replaced by a number of other breaks of *at least* 15 minutes each distributed over the driving period or taken during and immediately after this period, so as to equal at least 45 minutes and taken in such a way that the $4\frac{1}{2}$ hour limit is not exceeded. A break period which was otherwise due in accordance with this requirement does not have to be taken if immediately following the driving period the driver commences a daily or weekly rest period, so long as the four and a half hours' aggregated driving is not exceeded.

Following a highly publicised court case brought by the Lancashire police (DPP v Mayfield Chicks Ltd), it has been established, after a Crown Court appeal against the original conviction, that the $4\frac{1}{2}$ hour period should be looked upon as a rolling period so that at no time during the day must the driver have exceeded an aggregate of $4\frac{1}{2}$ hours' driving without having had 45 minutes break in respect of that driving. The previous 'wipe the slate clean' interpretation of the break period requirement has now been shown to be incorrect and must not be followed.

Example of New Interpretation
It would be illegal under the new interpretation for a driver to drive for one hour, then take 15 minutes break, drive for a further three hours and take a 30-minute break and then drive for a further $4\frac{1}{2}$ hours which was acceptable under the previous understanding of the rules.

According to DTp examples the driver could, however, legally operate the following procedures:

1. Drive one hour, 15 minutes break, drive $3\frac{1}{2}$ hours, 30 minutes break, drive one hour, 15 minutes break, drive $3\frac{1}{2}$ hours, commence daily rest period.
2. Drive one hour, 15 minutes break, drive one hour, 15 minutes break, drive $2\frac{1}{2}$ hours, 15 minutes break, drive two hours, 30 minutes break, drive $2\frac{1}{2}$ hours, commence daily rest period.
3. Drive three hours, 15 minutes break, drive $1\frac{1}{2}$ hours, 30 minutes break, drive three hours, 15 minutes break, drive $1\frac{1}{2}$ hours, commence daily rest period.

NB: It is important to note that break periods (ie especially the 45 minute period as well as the alternative minimum 15 minute periods) should not be curtailed even by a minute or two. Prosecutions have been brought for break periods which are alleged not to conform to the law even though they have been only a matter of minutes below the minimum specified in the regulations.

Rest periods

Rest periods are defined as uninterrupted periods of at least one hour during which the driver 'may freely dispose of his time'. Daily rest periods, and particularly rest periods which are compensating for previously reduced rest periods, should not be confused with, or combined with, statutory break periods required to be taken during the driving day as described above.

Daily Rest Periods
Once each day drivers are required to observe either a normal, a reduced or a split daily rest period during which time they must be free to dispose of

3: GOODS VEHICLE DRIVERS' HOURS

their time as they wish. Thus in each 24-hour period one or other of the following daily rest periods must be taken:

Normal daily rest: 11 hours

or alternatively,

Reduced rest: 9 hours – may be taken three times in a week but the reduced time must be compensated by an equal amount of additional rest taken with other rest periods before the end of the next following fixed week

Split rest: Where the daily rest period is not reduced (as above) the rest may be split and taken in two or three separate periods during the 24 hours, provided:
(a) one continuous period is of at least eight hours' duration;
(b) other periods are of at least one hour's duration;
(c) the total daily rest period is increased to 12 hours.

Double-manned Vehicles
Where a vehicle is operated by a two-man crew, the daily rest period requirement is that each man must have had a minimum of eight hours' rest in each period of 30 hours.

Daily Rest on Vehicles
Daily rest periods may be taken on a vehicle provided:
(a) the vehicle has a bunk so the driver can lie down
(b) the vehicle is stationary for the whole of the rest period.

It follows from this that a driver on a double-manned vehicle cannot be taking part of his daily rest period on the bunk while his co-driver continues to drive the vehicle. He could, however, be taking a break at this time while the vehicle is moving or he could merely spend his time lying on the bunk with his tachograph chart recording other work.

Daily Rest on Ferries/Trains
Daily rest periods which are taken when a vehicle is carried for part of its journey on a ferry crossing or by rail may be interrupted, but *once* only, provided:
(a) part of the rest is taken on land before or after the ferry crossing/rail journey;
(b) the interruption must be 'as short as possible' and in any event must not be more than one hour before embarkation or after disembarkation and this time *must* include dealing with customs formalities;
(c) during both parts of the rest (ie in the terminal and on board the ferry/train) the driver must have access to a bunk or couchette;

(d) when such interruptions to daily rest occur, the total daily rest period must be extended by two hours.

Weekly Rest Period
Once each fixed week (and after six driving shifts) a daily rest period must be combined with a weekly rest period to provide a weekly rest period totalling 45 hours. A weekly rest period which begins in one fixed week and continues into the following week may be attached to either of these weeks.

While the normal weekly rest period is 45 hours as described above, this may be reduced to:
(a) 36 hours when the rest is taken at the place where the vehicle or the driver is based; or
(b) 24 hours when taken the rest period is taken elsewhere.

Reduced weekly rest periods must be compensated (ie made up) by an equivalent amount of rest period time taken *en bloc* and added to another rest period of at least eight hours' duration before the end of the third week following the week in which the reduced weekly rest period is taken.

Compensated Rest Periods
When reduced daily and/or weekly rest periods are taken, the compensated time must be attached to another rest period of at least eight hours' duration and must be granted, at the request of the driver, at the vehicle parking place or at the driver's base. Compensation in this respect *does not* mean compensation by means of payment; it means the provision of an equivalent amount of rest time taken on a later occasion but within the specified limits (ie by the end of the next week for compensated daily rest and by the end of the third following week in the case of compensated weekly rest periods and in each case added to other rest periods).

Summary of EC Rules

The following table summarises the EC rules applicable to both national and international goods vehicle operations:

Maximum daily driving:	9 hours 10 hours on 2 days in week
Maximum weekly driving:	6 daily driving periods (see p 63)
Maximum fortnightly driving:	90 hours
Maximum driving before a break:	4½ hours
Minimum breaks after driving:	45 minutes or other breaks of at least 15 minutes each to equal 45 minutes
Minimum daily rest (normally):	11 hours
Reduced daily rest:	9 hours on up to 3 days per week (must be made up by end of next following week)

Split daily rest:	The 11-hour daily rest period may be split into 2 or 3 periods – one at least 8 hours, the others at least one hour each: total rest must be increased to 12 hours
Minimum weekly rest (normally):	45 hours once each fixed week
Reduced weekly rest:	36 hours at base – 24 hours elsewhere (any reduction must be made up *en bloc* by end of 3rd following week)
Rest on ferries/trains:	Daily rest may be interrupted once only if: – part taken on land – no more than 1 hour between parts – drivers must have bunk/couchette – total rest must increase by 2 hours

Emergencies

It is permitted for the driver to depart from the EC rules as specified above to the extent necessary to enable him to reach a suitable stopping place when emergencies arise where he needs to ensure the safety of persons, the vehicle or its load, providing road safety is not jeopardised. The nature of and reasons for departing from the rules in these circumstances must be shown on the tachograph chart.

Prohibition on Certain Payments

The EC rules prohibit any payment to wage-earning drivers in the form of bonuses or wage supplements related to distances travelled and/or the amount of goods carried unless such payments do not endanger road safety.

British Domestic Rules

The current British drivers' hours rules contained in the 1968 Transport Act (as amended) came into effect on 29 September 1986. They apply to goods vehicle drivers whose activities are outside the scope of the EC requirements as described above (ie which are specified as exempt from the EC rules) and comprise only limits on daily driving and daily duty.

NB Detailed provisions which previously applied in regard to daily and weekly duty, daily spreadover and daily and weekly rest period limits were completely abolished when these rules' changes were introduced.

It is important to emphasise that drivers who are exempt from the EC rules, either because their vehicle does not exceed 3.5 tonnes permissible maximum weight or because the activity in which they are engaged falls within the scope of the EC exemptions list (see p 60), must observe the British rules.

NB: It should be noted that:
1. *Although no records of driving or working times are required to be kept, drivers of light goods vehicles (ie not exceeding 3.5 tonnes maximum permissible weight) must still conform to the legal limits on maximum daily driving and maximum daily duty.*

2. If a trailer is attached to a vehicle not exceeding 3.5 tonnes maximum permissible weight (which itself is exempt from the EC rules on account of its weight) thereby taking the combined weight to over 3.5 tonnes then the EC rules must be followed as described in the foregoing text (unless it is exempt for other reasons – namely the nature of the operations on which it is engaged) and a tachograph must be fitted to the vehicle and used by the driver for record-keeping purposes (see Chapter 5).

Exemptions and Concessions

The British Domestic rules apply to drivers of all goods vehicles which are exempt from the EC regulations as described earlier but with the following further exceptions which are totally exempt from all hours rules control:
1. Armed forces
2. Police and fire brigade services
3. Driving off the public road system
4. Driving for purely private purposes (ie not in connection with any trade or business).

The British Domestic rules do not apply to a driver who on any day does not drive a relevant vehicle or to a driver who on each day of the week does not drive a vehicle within these rules for more than four hours (Note: this exemption *does not* apply to a driver whose activities fall within scope of the EC rules).

Driving and Duty Definitions

For the purposes of the British Domestic rules, driving means time spent behind the wheel actually driving a goods vehicle and the specified maximum limit applies to such time spent driving on public roads. Driving on off-road sites and premises such as quarries, civil engineering and building sites and on agricultural and forestry land is counted as duty time, not driving time. Duty time is the time a driver spends working for his employer and includes any work undertaken including the driving of private motor cars, for example and non-driving work which is not driving time for the purposes of the regulations. The daily duty limit does not apply on any day when a driver does not drive a goods vehicle.

Summary of British Domestic Rules

Maximum daily driving:	10 hours
Maximum daily duty:	11 hours
Continuous duty:	no specified limit
Daily spreadover:	no specified limit
Weekly duty:	no specified limit
Breaks during day:	no requirement specified
Daily rest:	no specified requirement (but obviously minimum 13 hours so as not to exceed the daily 11-hour duty limit)
Weekly rest:	no specified requirement

Emergencies

The daily driving and duty limits specified above may be suspended when an emergency situation arises. This is defined as an event requiring immediate action to avoid danger to life or health of one or more individuals or animals, serious interruption in the maintenance of essential public services for the supply of gas, water, electricity, drainage, or of telecommunications and postal services, or in the use of roads, railways, ports or airports, or damage to property. Details of the emergency should be entered by the driver on his record sheet when the limits are exceeded.

Light Vehicle Driving

As explained above, drivers of light goods vehicles not exceeding 3.5 tonnes permissible maximum weight – as with drivers of other goods vehicles which fall within scope of these rules – must observe the daily limits on driving (10 hours) and duty (11 hours). However, in the case of such vehicles used for the following purposes only the 10-hour daily driving limit applies. Vehicles used:
1. By doctors, dentists, nurses, midwives or vets.
2. For any service of inspection, cleaning, maintenance, repair, installation or fitting.
3. By a commercial traveller and carrying only goods used for soliciting orders.
4. By an employee of the AA, the RAC or the RSAC.
5. For the business of cinematography or of radio or television broadcasting.

Mixed EC and British Driving

It is possible that a goods vehicle driver may be engaged in transport operations which come within both the EC drivers' hours rules and the British Domestic hours' rules on the same day or within the same week. When such a situation arises he may conform strictly to the EC rules throughout the whole of the working period or he may take advantage of the more liberal Domestic rules where appropriate. If he decides on this course of action and thereby combines both British and EC rules he must beware of the following points:
1. time spent driving under the EC rules cannot count as an off-duty period for the British rules;
2. time spent driving or on duty under the British rules cannot count as a break or rest period under the EC rules;
3. driving under the EC rules counts towards the driving and duty limits for the British rules;
4. if any EC rules' driving is done in a week the driver must observe the EC daily and weekly rest period requirements for the whole of that week.

AETR Rules

Drivers on international journeys beyond the EC which take them to or through the list of countries given below are required to observe The European Agreement Concerning the Work of Crews of Vehicles Engaged in International Road Transport – 1971 (commonly known and referred to as AETR). When on such journeys the driver must observe the AETR rules for the whole of the outward and return journey including the portion travelled in Britain and through other EC member states. These rules are basically similar to the old (ie pre-September 1986) EC rules.

The countries beyond the EC referred to above where the AETR rules apply (ie on journeys to or through) are as follows:

Austria
Czechoslovakia
East Germany (GDR)
Norway
Sweden
USSR
Yugoslavia

Summary of AETR Rules

Maximum daily driving:	8 hours This may be increased to 9 hours on two occasions in the week by drivers of rigid vehicles and those with trailers exceeding 20 tonnes maximum permissible weight.
Maximum continuous driving:	4 hours This may be extended to 4½ hours to enable a journey to be completed or a suitable stopping place reached – the daily total must not be exceeded.
Break periods:	½ hour after 4 hours' driving or two breaks of 20 minutes each or three breaks of 15 minutes each taken during or during and after the driving period. In the case of vehicles with trailers exceeding 20 tonnes maximum permissible weight the minimum break is one hour or two breaks of 30 minutes each spread throughout the day so the continuous driving limit is not exceeded.
Maximum weekly driving:	48 hours
Maximum two-weekly driving:	92 hours
Minimum daily rest:	Normally 11 hours May be reduced to 9 hours on two occasions in the week if the driver is at base or 8 hours on two occasions in the week if he is away from base. Any reduction from the normal daily rest period must be made up.
Minimum weekly rest:	Normally 24 hours plus a daily rest period (ie 11 hours or 9 hours or 8 hours) to make 35/33/32 hours.

For the purposes of these regulations a 'day' is any period of 24 hours and a week is seven consecutive days (ie a rolling week). Two weeks means two consecutive rolling weeks (ie 14 days consecutively).

Double-manned Vehicles

Where a vehicle is manned by two drivers the normal daily rest period requirement stated above is modified as follows:

1. If the vehicle is fitted with a bunk, each driver must have 8 hours' daily rest in a 30-hour period;
2. If the vehicle is not fitted with a bunk, each driver must have 10 hours' daily rest in a 27-hour period.

Break and Rest Periods

Drivers may take daily rest periods in their vehicle provided it is fitted with a bunk and is stationary at the time. Break periods may be taken while riding passenger in a moving vehicle.

The Future of AETR

Discussions are taking place in Europe in an attempt to align the AETR rules as described above with the current EC rules contained in EC Regulation 3820/85. The last occasion when the two sets of rules were aligned was in 1971. Changes in the EC rules since that time have caused the present divergence of provisions.

Tax Relief

Sleeper-cab allowances

The Inland Revenue has agreed that hgv drivers can be paid night-out allowances amounting to £16.00 per night before the employer is required to deduct tax. This applies where the driver has used overnight accommodation and is intended to reflect the actual costs likely to have been incurred. A new national sleeper-cab rate has been agreed whereby the IR will allow payments of £16.00 and £12.45 to cover day and sleeper-cab payments to drivers on a tax-free basis.

Meal Expenses

With regard to repayment to drivers of meal expenses incurred while away from base, the Inland Revenue has issued a Statement of Practice as follows but it should be noted that the Statement 'has no binding force and does not affect a taxpayer's rights of appeal on points concerning his liability to tax'.

1. Employees Absent from Home and Normal Place of Employment – General

An employer is allowed to make reimbursement of certain expenses payments without deduction of tax to an employee working temporarily away from home and his normal place of employment. The payments are those which are intended to cover the extra cost of travelling and subsistence which the employee incurs because he is away on duty – but not the cost of his travelling from home to his normal place of work or his usual expenses on food or meals taken when at his normal place of work. Similarly, where the employee is not reimbursed, a deduction for expenses may be allowed where the extra expenses of the absence are incurred wholly, exclusively and necessarily in the performance of the employee's duties.

2. Travelling Appointments

Where travelling itself is an essential feature of an employee's duties, with the result that he has to spend money on meals in restaurants or cafes above what he would spend if he had a fixed place or area of work or were able to get home for meals, a deduction may be allowed for the extra expenses necessarily incurred in the performance of the duties. Drivers who qualify for consideration under this heading are those who are engaged full time in travelling in the performance of their duties. By this is meant employment as a driver throughout the full normal working hours of each day, except those days when the employee is precluded from working by reason of sickness or other reasonable cause, or which are holidays or rest days. Employees whose jobs entail only incidental travelling would not be regarded as holding travelling appointments. Even full-time drivers are excluded from consideration if they travel only in a limited area. This is because they incur no additional expenses when at work from one day to the next, as they have an established pattern of expenditure on meals in the same way as any other employee who has to work at a distance from home and who cannot return home for lunch.

Inspectors of Taxes require claimants to give full details of the nature of their duties in addition to providing evidence of the expenditure actually incurred, as described in the following paragraph. In practice, relief is not restricted by reference to amounts of expenditure saved by not having meals at home or a fixed place of work.

3. Evidence of Expenditure

The amount of relief which can be allowed depends mainly on the bills and vouchers which can be supplied by a driver in support of his claims. Employees who consider that they may have a potential claim should ensure that bills, receipts, etc are available in support of any claim for relief for the current tax year and future years; but if exceptionally they are unable on any occasion to obtain bills or receipts, they must make a note at the time of the date, place and amount spent. (Where the employer makes a contribution in cash or otherwise towards the cost of meals this must be specified and the amount received set off against the expense in arriving at the net amount for which relief is claimed.) An expenses deduction cannot be given in the absence of evidence of expenditure and Tax Districts will not accept estimated figures of outgoings.

Copies of this statement may be obtained by calling at or writing to the Public Enquiry Room, New Wing, Somerset House, Strand, London WC2R 1LB.

There have been recent reports about tax inspectors querying payment of night-out allowances where drivers have stayed only a few miles from base. Currently there is an agreement with the Inland Revenue for night-out payments of up to £14.40 (1988 figure) per night without receipts except where alternative figures have been agreed in which case an annual increase of 3.7 per cent on the previously agreed figure is acceptable.

These payments should only be made where the employee does actually spend the night away and incurs extra expense. If he uses the bunk in a sleeper cab the allowable amount is only that required to meet the expenses he incurs, not the full night-out allowance. Where expense payments to drivers or other staff for nights away exceed the amount stated above the employer should be prepared to bear the tax on the extra amount or, alternatively, he should include it as part of the wages within PAYE.

There have been many reports in the past year of the Inland Revenue refusing claims for tax-free payments of night-out allowances above £8.00. Employers who have paid in excess of this amount (or a locally agreed rate) without deduction of tax may find themselves liable to meet the tax due on the additional amounts paid except where it can be proved that the expense was genuinely incurred (by production of a valid receipt).

Revision of EC Rules

The European Council of Transport Ministers have been discussing proposals for amendment to the current EC regulation (EC 3820/85) which came into force on 29 September 1986. At the time of this 1991 edition of the *Handbook* going to press there is still no further news of the matter other than the fact that a draft amending regulation has been published as has a draft directive aimed at standardising enforcement of the hours law provisions throughout the member states.

Truck Drivers!

The complete handbook for total professionalism on the road

"An invaluable quick reference book"
TRUCK AND DRIVER

"Packed with invaluable facts and easy to follow advice"
TRANSPORT NEWS

Extensively illustrated with figures and diagrams, this fully updated edition covers all the latest legislation.

The Handbook's contents include:

▶ **The HGV licence**, including how to get one, the different types available and how an offence affects the licence.

▶ **Driving Safely**, including coupling and uncoupling trailers, an illustrated guide to roping and sheeting, wide and long loads.

▶ **Useful Information**, including addresses, telephone numbers and maps and an up-to-date list of commercial recovery services countrywide.

PLUS a special guide to driving in London, including details of tunnels, parking and specific height, weight and length restrictions.

Only £7.99 Paperback   ISBN 0 7494 0205 9   240 pages

Available from good bookshops or direct from the publisher:
120 Pentonville Road, London N1 9JN Tel: 071 278 0433
Fax: 071 837 6348

KOGAN PAGE

4: Goods Vehicle Drivers' Records

Drivers of goods vehicles over 3.5 tonnes gross weight must keep records of the time they spend driving such vehicles and their working times. Most drivers are also required to record breaks taken during driving periods and their daily and weekly rest periods. Where vehicles fall within the scope of the EC drivers' hours law as described in Chapter 3 (ie unless they are specifically exempt as shown in the relevant exemptions list) the record-keeping requirement is based on the mandatory use of tachographs as described in Chapter 5.

Where a vehicle is outside the scope of the EC rules then the British Domestic (ie 1968 Transport Act – as amended) driving hours rules apply (see Chapter 3) and the driver of such a vehicle is required to keep written records by means of a 'log-book' system.

To summarise the main record-keeping requirements, these are as follows:
1. Goods vehicles not exceeding 3.5 tonnes maximum permissible weight – NO RECORDS.
2. Goods vehicles over 3.5 tonnes maximum permissible weight (including the weight of any trailer drawn) operating within EC rules – TACHOGRAPH RECORDS.
3. Goods vehicles over 3.5 tonnes maximum permissible weight exempt from EC rules – WRITTEN 'LOG-BOOK' RECORDS (but subject to further exemption in certain cases).
4. Goods vehicles over 3.5 tonnes maximum permissible weight exempt from both EC and British domestic rules (eg military vehicles) – NO RECORDS.

This chapter describes the record-keeping requirements applying to drivers falling within item 3 above, namely, those operating under the British Domestic rules who must keep written 'log-book' records.

Prior to 29 September 1986 when the EC rules and British Domestic hours rules changed, the written record-keeping requirement related to the use of the EC diagrammatic-type International Control Book (ICB). From this date there was a transitional arrangement for phasing out the use of this record book and the introduction of a new-style of simplified British record which relates specifically to the British Domestic driving hours rules. Regulations brought the 'simplified' record book into use from 2 November 1987 with the old type EEC diagrammatic control book ceasing to have any further legal standing from that date.

Record-Keeping System

Record Books

Ready-printed record books can be purchased 'off the shelf' or firms can have their own version pre-printed with their own name and logo if desired. In the latter case it is important that the specific requirements of the regulations are observed in both the format and the printing of the book. The book must be a standard A6 format (105mm x 148mm) or it may be larger if preferred. It must comprise a front sheet on which is entered relevant information, a set of instructions for the use of the book, and a number of individual weekly record sheets with facilities for completing these in duplicate (ie with carbon paper or carbonless copy paper) and for the duplicate sheet to be detached for return to the employer when completed.

There is no legal requirement for the numbering of record books or for their issue against an entry in a register of record book issues as previously required.

Weekly record sheets in the book must follow the format set out in the regulations with appropriate spaces for entries to be made under the following headings:
1. Driver's name.
2. Period covered by sheet week commencing ...week ending...
3. Registration number of vehicle(s).
4. Place where vehicle(s) based.
5. Time of going on duty.
6. Time of going off duty.
7. Time spent driving.
8. Time spent on duty.
9. Signature of driver.
10. Certification by employer (ie signature and position held).

Issue and Return of Record Books

Employers must issue their drivers with record books when they are required to drive vehicles to which the British Domestic driving hours regulations apply and where records must be kept. Before issuing the book the employer must complete the front cover to show the firm's name, address and telephone number preferably with a rubber stamp if he has one.

When a record book is issued to the driver he should complete the front cover with his surname, first name(s), date of birth and home address and the date he first used the book. When the book is completed he should also enter the date of the last entry (ie date of last use). There is space to record the name and address of a second employer.

Books issued by an employer to an employee-driver must be returned to that employer when complete (subject to the requirement for the driver to retain it for two weeks after use) or when the employee leaves that employment. He must not take it with him to his new employer. Any unused weekly sheets and all duplicates must be included when the book is returned.

Two Employers
Where a driver has two employers who employ him to drive goods vehicles to which the British Domestic hours rules apply, the first employer must issue the record book as described, and the second employer must write or

stamp his firm's name and address on the front cover of the record book with a statement that the holder is also a driver in his employment. When the driver does part-time driving work for another employer he must disclose to each employer, if requested, details of his working and driving times with the other employer. Similarly, when a driver changes to a new employer the former employer must give the new employer details of the driver's previous driving and working times if requested.

Retention and Production of Record Books

The driver should have his record book with him at all times when working and must produce it for inspection at the request of an authorised examiner. The book should be shown to the employer at the end of every week or as soon as possible after the week so he can examine and countersign the entries. Following completion of the book the driver must continue to keep it with him for a further two weeks (available for inspection by the enforcement authorities) before returning it to his employer.

Completed record books must be retained by the employer, available for inspection, for not less than 12 months.

Record Book Entries

The driver must make entries on the weekly sheet for each day on which a record is required (instructions on the correct use of the book are printed inside the cover). All entries must be made in ink or by ball-point pen. Care must be taken to ensure that an exact duplicate of the entry is made simultaneously (ie two separately written repeat entries are *not* acceptable even if no carbon paper is available). When completing a daily sheet he must enter all the required details under each of the headings. If he changes vehicles during the day he must write in the registration number for each vehicle. He must then sign the sheet before returning it to his employer.

Completion of the record is straightforward, the driver having to enter the vehicle registration number, the time of coming on duty, and at the end of the day he must enter the time at which he went off duty and he must sign the sheet. He may enter any remarks concerning his entries, or point out corrections which should be made, in the appropriate box at the foot of the record. The employer may also use this space if required for making comments regarding the record. This space may also be used for recording the name of a second driver.

Corrections
Entries in the record book must be in ink or made by a ball-point pen and there must be no erasures, corrections or additions. Mistakes may only be corrected by writing an explanation or showing the correct information in the remarks space. Sheets must not be mutilated or destroyed.

Return and Signing of Record Sheets

On completion of the weekly sheet and after it has been signed by the driver, the duplicate copy must be detached from the book and handed to the employer within seven days of the date of the last entry on the sheet, and then within a further seven days the employer must have examined and signed the duplicate sheet. However, if in either case it is not reasonably practicable to do so within this time, these actions must be carried out as soon as it is possible to do so.

Exemptions from Record Keeping

Written records do not have to be kept in the following cases:
1. By drivers of vehicles which are exempt from 'O' licensing except that the exemption does not apply to drivers of Crown vehicles which would have needed an 'O' licence if the vehicle had not been Crown property.
2. By drivers of goods vehicles on any day when they drive for four hours or less and within 50 kilometres of the vehicle's base (NB this exemption is applicable only in the case of domestic operations – it does not apply to tachograph use – see pp 67–8).
3. By drivers using an EC tachograph for record-keeping purposes which has been calibrated and sealed at a DTp-approved tachograph centre.

4: GOODS VEHICLE DRIVERS' RECORDS

WEEKLY RECORD SHEETS

WEEKLY SHEETS

1. DRIVER'S NAME ....

2. PERIOD COVERED BY SHEET
   WEEK COMMENCING (DATE) ....
   TO WEEK ENDING (DATE) ....

DAY ON WHICH DUTY COMMENCED	REGISTRATION NO. OF VEHICLE(S) 3	PLACE WHERE VEHICLE(S) BASED 4	TIME OF GOING ON DUTY 5	TIME OF GOING OFF DUTY 6	TIME SPENT DRIVING 7	TIME SPENT ON DUTY 8	SIGNATURE OF DRIVER 9
MONDAY							
TUESDAY							
WEDNESDAY							
THURSDAY							
FRIDAY							
SATURDAY							
SUNDAY							

10. CERTIFICATION BY EMPLOYER

I HAVE EXAMINED THE ENTRIES IN THIS SHEET
SIGNATURE ....
POSITION HELD ....

Figure 4.1 *New simplified record sheet for British Domestic transport operations*

79

5: Tachographs

Tachograph instruments installed in goods and passenger vehicles provide a means of recording time and the speed and distance travelled by the vehicle. This record enables drivers' working activities and driving practices to be monitored to ensure that legal requirements – especially observance of the driver's hours rules – have been met.

The fitment of tachographs and their use in relevant vehicles (ie those operating within the scope of the EC driving hours rules – see Chapter 3) for record-keeping purposes, originally became a legal requirement in the United Kingdom on 31 December 1981. EC regulations (EC 3821/85) which came into effect on 29 September 1986 amended some of the original requirements.

The legislation requires the fitment and use of tachographs in most goods vehicles over 3.5 tonnes maximum permissible weight with certain EC-approved exemptions which are listed at the end of this chapter (see p 89). Since the list of exemptions is limited, many categories of goods vehicle which may be thought to be exempt are not so. It should be stressed that the law applies to *any* goods vehicle over 3.5 tonnes gvw (or a combination of a goods vehicle and goods-carrying trailer which together exceed 3.5 tonnes maximum permissible weight) when used for business purposes unless it is specifically exempted as shown by the exemption list.

In particular, it should be noted that there is no exemption for short distance operations, infrequent-use vehicles or occasional drivers – once a relevant vehicle is on the highway the law applies in full.

This means that tachograph instruments must be installed in the vehicle and that whosoever drives it must keep a tachograph record and observe the EC driver's hours law in full for both the day on which the driving takes place and the week in which that day falls. It should also be noted that vehicles which are exempt from the tachograph rules are not necessarily exempt from record-keeping requirements (for example, those operating under the British Domestic hours rules). See Chapter 4 for details of activities where written records must be kept.

Under the EC regulations a number of specific basic requirements relating to tachograph use must be met as follows:
1. The tachograph instrument must conform to the technical specification laid down in the EC regulations (EC 3821/85 Annex I – see p 83).
2. The instrument must be calibrated and officially sealed at a DTp-approved calibration centre in order to ensure that accurate records are made (see p 83).
3. The instrument must be used in accordance with the regulations, with individual responsibilities being observed by both employer and driver.

Employer's Responsibilities

The regulations place specific responsibilities on the employer of a driver who drives within the EC rules as follows:

1. The employer must organise the driver's work in such a way that he is able to comply with both the driver's hours and tachograph rules.
2. The employer must supply drivers with sufficient numbers of the correct type of tachograph charts (ie one chart for the day, one spare in case the first is impounded by an enforcement officer, plus any further spares which are necessary to account for any charts which become too dirty or damaged to use), and he must ensure that completed charts are collected from drivers no later than 21 days after use.
3. The employer must periodically check completed charts to ensure that the law has been complied with (ie that the driver has made a chart for the day, that he has completed it fully and properly and that he has observed the driving hours rules). If breaches of the law are found the employer must take appropriate steps to prevent their repetition.
4. The employer must retain completed charts for 12 months for inspection by DTp examiners, if required.
5. The employer must give copies of the record to drivers concerned who request them.

Drivers' Responsibilities

Drivers of vehicles operating within the EC rules must observe the tachograph requirements. In particular this means understanding what the law requires and how to comply with it. The specific responsibilities of the driver in regard to the law are as follows:

1. Drivers using tachograph charts must ensure that a proper record is made by the instrument:
   (a) that it is a continuous record
   (b) that it is a 'time right' record (ie recordings are in the correct 12-hour section of the chart – daytime or night-time hours).
2. In the event of instrument failure or in circumstances where no vehicle is available when the driver is working he must make manual recordings of his activities on the chart 'legibly and without dirtying' it.
3. Drivers must produce for inspection on request by an authorised inspecting officer a current chart for that day plus the charts relating to the current week and for the last day of the previous week in which he drove.
4. Drivers must return completed charts to their employer no later than 21 days after use.
5. Drivers must allow any authorised inspecting officer to inspect the tachograph calibration plaque which is usually fixed inside the body of the instrument.

Two-Crew Operation

Reference above to a driver also includes any other driver who is carried on the vehicle to assist with the driving. In this case a two-man tachograph must be fitted and both drivers must use it to produce records. The person who is driving must have his chart located in the uppermost (ie number 1) position in the instrument and use the number 1 activity mode switch to enable both his activities and the vehicle speed and distance recordings to be made on the chart as appropriate. The person who is riding passenger must have his chart in the rearmost (ie number 2) position and must use the number 2 activity mode switch to record his other work activities, or break or rest periods. Only time group recordings are made on this chart; driving, speed and distance traces are *not* produced on the second-man chart.

Tachograph Calibration, Sealing and Inspection

To make legally acceptable records tachograph installations in vehicles must be calibrated initially at DTp-approved tachograph centres (see Appendix V) and subsequently must be inspected every two years and fully re-calibrated every six years or after repair at an approved centre.

The DTp specifies and approves the premises (and the display of approved signs), equipment, staff (including their training) and procedures for the installation, repair, inspection, calibration and sealing of tachographs. Such centres must be approved to the BS 5750 Part 2 quality standard before they can gain DTp approval. No other workshops or individuals are permitted to carry out such work and any work carried out by unauthorised agents would render the installation incapable of producing legally acceptable records. It is an offence for any unauthorised person to carry out work on tachograph installations. It is also an offence for a vehicle operator (maximum fine £2000) to obtain and use a tachograph instrument repaired by a firm which is not BS 5750 approved.

The calibration process requires the vehicle to be presented to an approved tachograph centre in normal road-going trim, complete with body and all fixtures, unladen and with tyres complying with legal limits as to tread wear and inflated to manufacturer's recommended pressures. At the centre, the necessary work on the installation is carried out to within specified tolerances.

The regulations specify a range of tolerances within which the tachograph installation must operate and valid for temperatures between 0° and 40° C as follows:

	On bench test	**On installation**	**In use**
Speed	± 3kph	± 4kph	± 6kph
Distance	± 1/ (ie per cent)	± 2/ (ie p/c)	± 4/ (ie p/c)
Time	in all cases, ± 2 minutes per day with a maximum of 10 minutes per seven days		

In the case of both speed and distance figures shown above the tolerance is measured relative to the real speed and to the real distance of at least one kilometre.

Calibration and Periodic Inspection Fees

The DTp specifies the official fees to be charged in connection with tachograph calibration and periodic inspections. Calibration currently costs £28.11 plus VAT and the official time for the task is one and a half hours. The two-yearly inspection costs £17.93 plus VAT (*increased* from £13.82). These prices are exclusive of any replacement parts used.

Sealing of Tachographs

Approved centres seal tachograph installations after calibration or two-yearly inspections with their own official seals (each of which is coded differently) and details of all seals are maintained on a register by the DTp. The seals are of the customs type whereby a piece of wire is passed through each of the connecting points between the vehicle and the tachograph itself and then a lead seal is squeezed tight on to the wire with special pliers which imprint the centre code number in the metal. Attempts to remove any of the seals or their actual removal will show and need to be accounted for.

The purpose of sealing is to ensure that there is no tampering with the equipment or any of its drive mechanism or cables which could either vary the recordings of time, speed or distance or inhibit the recording in any way. Such tampering is illegal and once seals are broken the installation no longer complies with the law and legally acceptable records cannot be made.

Besides the seals inside the body of the instrument head, the following points are sealed:
1. the installation plaque;
2. the two ends of the link between the recording equipment and the vehicle;
3. the adaptor itself and the point of its insertion into the circuit;
4. the switch mechanism for vehicles with two or more axle ratios;
5. the links joining the adaptor and the switch mechanism to the rest of the equipment;
6. the casings of the instrument.

Seal Breakage
Obviously, there are occasions when certain of the seals have to be broken of necessity to carry out repairs to the vehicle and replacement of defective parts (eg the vehicle clutch or gearbox). The only seals which may be broken in these circumstances are as follows:
1. those at the two ends of the link between the tachograph equipment and the vehicle;
2. those between the adaptor (ie the tachograph drive gearbox) and the point of its insertion into the circuit;
3. those at the links joining the adaptor and the switch mechanism (ie where the vehicle has a two-speed rear axle) to the rest of the equipment.

While it is permitted to break these particular seals, a written record must be kept of the seal breakage and the reason for doing so. The installation must be inspected or re-calibrated and fully sealed following repair or seal breakage as soon as 'circumstances permit' and before the vehicle is used again.

Calibration Plaques

When a tachograph has been installed in a vehicle and calibrated, the approved centre must fix, either inside the tachograph head or near to it on the vehicle dashboard in a visible position, a plaque giving details of the centre, the 'turns count', and the calibration date. The plaque is sealed and must not be tampered with or the sealing tape removed. When an instrument is subjected to a two-year inspection or re-calibration a new plaque must be fitted. If a vehicle is found on the road with an 'out-of-date' plaque an offence will have been committed and prosecution may follow.

The normal sequence for plaques is that one will show the initial calibration date, the next (two years later), which is fitted alongside the first plaque, will show the date of the two-year inspection and a third plaque will show the second two-year inspection. After a further two years a six-year re-calibration of the installation will be due and at this time all the previous plaques will be removed, the new calibration plaque will be fitted and the procedure described above starts again. In between times, following certain repairs, a 'minor work' plaque may be fitted but this does not alter the sequence of dates for two-year inspection and re-calibration plaques.

The two-year and six-year periods referred to above for inspections and calibrations are counted to the day/date, *not* to the end of the month in which that day/date falls.

Tachograph Breakdown

If tachograph equipment becomes defective (or the seals are broken for whatever reason including authorised breakage, as described above, to carry out mechanical repairs to the vehicle, or unauthorised interference) it must be repaired at an approved centre as soon as 'circumstances permit', but in the meantime the driver must continue to record manually on the chart all necessary information regarding his working, driving, breaks and rest times which are no longer being recorded by the instrument. There is *no* requirement to attempt to record speed or distance.

Once a vehicle has returned to base with a defective tachograph, it should not leave again until the instrument is in working order and it has been re-calibrated (if necessary) and the seals replaced. If it cannot be repaired immediately, the vehicle can be used so long as the operator has taken positive steps (which he can satisfactorily prove later if challenged by the enforcement authorities – see paragraph below) to have the installation repaired as soon as reasonably practicable.

If a vehicle is unable to return to base within *one week* (ie seven days) counting from the day of the breakdown, arrangements must be made to have the defective instrument repaired and re-calibrated as necessary at an approved centre *en route* within that time.

Defence

There is a defence in the regulations against conviction (ie not against prosecution) for an offence of using a vehicle with a defective tachograph. This has the effect of allowing subsequent use of the vehicle with a defective tachograph provided steps have been taken to have the installation restored to a legal condition as soon as circumstances permit and provided the driver continues to record his driving, working and break period times manually on a tachograph chart. In such circumstances it will be necessary to satisfactorily prove to the enforcement authorities – and to the court if they proceed with prosecution – that a definite booking for the repair had already been made at the time the vehicle was apprehended and that this appointment was for the repair to be carried out at the earliest possible opportunity. It is also a defence to show that at the time it was examined by an enforcement officer the vehicle was on its way to an approved tachograph centre to have necessary repairs carried out.

Use of Tachographs

Drivers are responsible for ensuring that the tachograph instrument in their vehicle functions correctly throughout the whole of their working shift in order that a full and proper recording for a full 24 hours can be produced. They must also ensure that they have sufficient quantities of the right type of charts (see below) on which to make recordings.

Time Changes

Drivers must ensure that the time at which the instrument clock is set and consequently recordings are made on the chart agrees with the official time in the country of registration of the vehicle. This is a significant point for British drivers travelling in Europe who may be tempted to change the clock in the instrument to the correct local European time rather than, for example, having it indicate and record the time in Britain. To re-emphasise the point, this means that for British drivers in British-registered vehicles the tachograph chart recording must accord with the official time in Britain regardless of the country in which that recording was made – the tachograph clock must *not* be re-set to show local time when travelling abroad.

Dirty or Damaged Charts

If a chart becomes dirty or damaged in use, it must be replaced and the old chart should be securely attached to the new chart which is used to replace it.

Completion of Centre Field

Before starting work with a vehicle in which tachograph charts are used the driver must enter on the centre field of the chart the following details:
1. His surname and first name (not initials).
2. The date and place where use of the chart begins.
3. Vehicle registration number.
4. The distance recorder (odometer) reading at the start of the day.

At the end of a working day, the driver should then record the following information on the chart:
1. The place and date where the chart is completed.
2. The closing odometer reading.
3. By subtraction, the total distance driven – in kilometres.

Making Recordings

When the centre field has been completed the chart should be inserted in the tachograph instrument ensuring that it is the right way up (it should be impossible to fit it wrongly) and that the recording will commence on the correct part of the 24-hour chart (day or night). The instrument face should be securely closed. The activity mode switch (number 1) should be turned as necessary throughout the work period to indicate the driver's relevant activities, namely driving, other work, break or rest periods. While some drivers find difficulty in getting into the habit of turning the switch to coincide with each change of activity, nevertheless this is what the law requires and it is an offence to fail to do so (ie not keep proper records).

Overnight Recordings
At the end of his shift the driver can leave the chart in the instrument overnight to record the daily rest period or alternatively it can be removed and the rest period recorded manually on the chart. Generally, enforcement staffs prefer an automatic recording of daily rest made by the instrument but this is not always practicable where the vehicle may be used on night-shift work, may be driven for road testing or other purposes by workshop staff or moved around the premises by others when the driver is at home having the rest period. Also, if the driver is scheduled to start work much later on the following day there will be an overlap recording on the chart which is illegal.

Vehicle Changes

If the driver changes to another vehicle during the working day he must take the existing chart with him and record details of the time of change, the registration number of the further vehicle(s) and distance recordings in the appropriate spaces on the chart. He then uses that chart in the next vehicle to record his continuing driving, working activities and break periods. This procedure is repeated no matter how many different vehicles (except those not driven on the public highway) are driven during the day so the one chart shows all of the driver's daily activity.

Mixed Tachographs
It is important to note that the various makes and models of tachograph currently available in the UK have different charts and they cannot all be interchanged. So the driver who switches from a vehicle with one make of instrument to a vehicle with a different make during the working day will have to make fresh entries on a second or even third chart. At the end of the day all the charts used should be clipped together to present a comprehensive (and legal) record for the whole day. However, there are some charts now available on the market suitable for dual use in different makes of tachograph. It is the employer's duty to issue drivers with the correct charts (ie with matching type approval numbers to those on the tachograph instrument in use) in sufficient numbers for the schedule which the driver has to operate.

Note: Where instruments are standardised in a fleet, one chart will suffice for the whole day and the driver must take this with him from one vehicle to the next, recording changes as previously described.

Manual Records

Drivers are responsible for ensuring that the instrument is kept running while they are in charge of the vehicle and should it fail or otherwise cease making proper records they should remove the chart and continue to record their activities manually on it as previously described. They must also make manual recordings on the chart of work done or time spent away from the vehicle (for example, periods during the day spent working in the yard, warehouse or workshop). Manual recordings must be made legibly and in making them the sheet must not be 'dirtied'.

Records for Part-Time Drivers

The rules on the use of tachographs described in the foregoing text apply equally to part-time or occasional drivers such as yard and warehouse staff, office people and even the transport manager. The rules also apply fully even if the driving on the road is for a very short distance or period of time — a five-minute drive without a tachograph chart in use would be sufficient to break the law and risk prosecution. Vehicle fitters and other workshops staff who drive vehicles on the road for testing in connection with repair or maintenance are specifically exempt from the need to keep tachograph records when undertaking such activities (see exemption list on p 89) but this exemption *does not* apply to them when using vehicles for other purposes (eg collecting spare parts, ferrying vehicles back and forth, taking replacement vehicles out to on-road breakdowns, taking and collecting vehicles to and from hgv test stations etc).

Retention, Return and Checking of Tachograph Charts

Drivers must retain and be able to produce, on request by authorised examiners (including the police), completed tachograph charts for each driving day of the current week and for the last day of the previous week on which they drove. Remember, charts do not have to be made for non-driving days or rest days and therefore cannot be asked for by the police or others in respect of such days.

Charts must be returned by drivers to their employer no later than 21 days after use and, on receiving the charts, the employer must periodically check them to ensure that the drivers' hours and record-keeping regulations have been complied with. They must then be retained, available for inspection if required, for a period of one year.

Official Inspection of Charts

An authorised inspecting officer may require any person to produce for inspection any tachograph chart on which recordings have been made. Further, he may enter a vehicle to inspect a chart or a tachograph instrument (he should be able to read the recordings relating to the nine hours prior to the time of his inspection) and the calibration plaques and detain a vehicle for this purpose. At any reasonable time he may enter premises on which he believes vehicles or tachograph charts are kept and inspect the instruments in such vehicles and the completed charts. He can require (by serving a notice in writing) charts to be produced at a Traffic Area office at any time on giving at least 10 days' notice in which to do so. Where a chart is suspected as showing a false entry he may 'seize' the chart and retain it for a maximum period of six months after which time, if no charges for offences have been made, the chart should have been returned.

If not, the person from whom it was taken can apply to a magistrate's court to seek an order for its return.

In practice, Licensing Authorities regularly ask operators to provide batches of tachograph charts covering one or more of their vehicles for a short period or possibly some months either on a routine basis or following investigations into, or leads about, hours' law or tachograph infringements. These charts are then analysed for contraventions of the law.

It is an offence to fail to produce records for inspection as required or to obstruct an enforcement officer in his request to inspect records or tachograph installations in vehicles.

Offences

Some tachograph related offences have already been mentioned in connection with specific requirements of the law but there are other overriding, and very serious, offences to be considered. In particular, it is an offence to use, cause or permit the use of a vehicle which does not have a fully calibrated tachograph installed; for the driver to fail to keep records by means of a tachograph (or manually if the instrument is defective) and to make false recordings. Further, it is an offence for the driver to fail to return used charts to his employer within 21 days after use or to fail to notify his first employer of any other employer for whom he drives vehicles to which the regulations apply. Penalties on summary conviction for offences under these regulations can be a fine of up to £2000 and conviction for such offences can jeopardise both the employers' 'O' licence and the driver's hgv driving licence.

Exemptions

There is no requirement for the fitment and use of tachographs in the following vehicles or in vehicles used in connection with the particular transport operations specified in the exemption list.

NB: It should be noted that this is the same list of exemptions as that for the EC hours law under EC 3820/85 (see p 60):

International Exemptions
1. Vehicles not exceeding 3.5 tonnes gross weight including the weight of any trailer drawn.
2. Passenger vehicles constructed to carry not more than nine persons including driver.
3. Vehicles on regular passenger services on routes not exceeding 50 kilometres.
4. Vehicles with legal maximum speed not exceeding 30kph (approx 18.6 mph).
5. Vehicles used by armed services, civil defence, fire services, forces responsible for maintaining public order (ie police).
6. Vehicles used in connection with sewerage; flood protection; water, gas and electricity services; highway maintenance and control; refuse collection and disposal; telephone and telegraph services; carriage of postal articles; radio and television broadcasting; detection of radio or television transmitters or receivers.

7. Vehicles used in emergencies or rescue operations.
8. Specialised vehicles used for medical purposes.
9. Vehicles transporting circus and funfair equipment.
10. Specialised breakdown vehicles.
11. Vehicles undergoing road tests for technical development, repair or maintenance purposes, and new or rebuilt vehicles which have not yet been put into service.
12. Vehicles used for non-commercial carriage of goods for personal use (ie private use).
13. Vehicles used for milk containers or milk products intended for animal feed.

National Exemptions
14. Passenger vehicles constructed to carry not more than 17 persons including driver.
15. Vehicles used by public authorities to provide public services which are not in competition with professional road hauliers.
16. Vehicles used by agricultural, horticultural, forestry or fishery* undertakings, for carrying goods within a 50-km radius of the place where the vehicle is normally based, including local administrative areas the centres of which are situated within that radius.

* to gain this exemption the vehicle must be used to carry live fish or to carry a catch of fish which has not been subjected to any process or treatment (other than freezing) from the place of landing to a place where it is to be processed or treated.

17. Vehicles used for carrying animal waste or carcasses not intended for human consumption.
18. Vehicles used for carrying live animals from farms to local markets and vice versa, or from markets to local slaughterhouses.
19. Vehicles specially fitted for and used:

    – as shops at local markets and for door-to-door selling
    – for mobile banking, exchange or savings transactions
    – for worship
    – for the lending of books, records or cassettes
    – for cultural events or exhibitions.
20. Vehicles (not exceeding 7.5 tonnes gvw) carrying materials or equipment for the driver's use in the course of his work within 50-km radius of base provided the driving does not constitute the driver's main activity and does not prejudice the objectives of the regulations.
21. Vehicles operating exclusively on islands not exceeding 2300 sq km not linked to the mainland by bridge, ford or tunnel for use by motor vehicles (excludes Isle of Wight).
22. Vehicles (not exceeding 7.5 tonnes gvw) used for the carriage of goods propelled by gas produced on the vehicle or by electricity.
23. Vehicles used for driving instruction (but not if carrying goods for hire or reward).

24. Tractors used after 1 January 1990 exclusively for agricultural and forestry work.
25. Vehicles used by the RNLI for hauling lifeboats.
26. Vehicles manufactured before 1 January 1947.
27. Steam propelled vehicles.

Note: In the exemption above relating to vehicles used by public authorities, the exemption applies only if the vehicle is being used by:
   (a) a health authority in England and Wales or a health board in Scotland
   - *to provide ambulance services in pursuance of its duty under the NHS Act 1977 or NHS (Scotland) Act 1978; or*
   - *to carry staff, patients, medical supplies or equipment in pursuance of its general duties under the Act;*
   (b) a local authority to fulfil social services functions, such as services for old persons or for physically and mentally handicapped persons;
   (c) HM Coastguard or lighthouse authorities;
   (d) harbour authorities within harbour limits;
   (e) airports authority within airport perimeters;
   (f) British Rail, London Regional Transport, a Passenger Transport Executive or local authority for maintaining railways;
   (g) British Waterways Board for maintaining navigable waterways.

Item 4 above includes certain works trucks and industrial tractors which have a statutory 30 kilometres per hour speed limit imposed upon them but this does not include fork lift trucks which may come within the scope of the rules.

Declaration of Exemption

When presenting a vehicle for the hgv annual test which the operator believes is exempt from the tachograph regulations in accordance with the list above , a 'Declaration of Exemption' form has to be completed.

The Tachograph Instrument

A tachograph is a cable or electronically driven speedometer incorporating an integral electric clock and a chart recording mechanism. It is fitted into the vehicle dashboard or in some other convenient visible position in the driving cab. The instrument indicates time, speed and distance and permanently records this information on the chart as well as the driver's working activities. Thus, the following factors can be determined from a chart:
1. The varying speeds (and the highest speed) at which the vehicle was driven.
2. The total distance travelled and distances between individual stops.

3. The times when the vehicle was being driven and the total amount of driving time.
4. The times when the vehicle was standing and whether the driver was indicating other work, break or rest period during this time.

Recordings

Recordings are made on special circular charts, each of which covers a period of 24 hours (Figure 5.1), by three styli. One stylus records distance, another records speed and the third records time-group activities as determined by the driver turning the activity mode switch on the head of the instrument (ie driving, other work, breaks and rest periods). The styli press through a wax recording layer on the chart, revealing the carbonated layer (usually black) between the top surface and the backing paper (some charts are made of Melanex and have no carbonated layer – recordings expose the translucent backing sheet). The charts are accurately pre-marked with time, distance and speed reference radials and when the styli have marked the chart with the appropriate recordings these can be easily identified and interpreted against the printed reference marks.

Movement of the vehicle creates a broad running line on the time radial, indicating when the vehicle started running and when it stopped. After the vehicle has stopped, the time-group stylus continues to mark the chart but with an easily distinguishable thin line. The speed trace gives an accurate recording of the speeds attained at all times throughout the journey, continuing to record on the speed base line when the vehicle is stationary to provide an unbroken trace except when the instrument is opened. The distance recording is made by the stylus moving up and down over a short stroke, each movement representing five kilometres travelled; thus, every five kilometres the stylus reverses direction, forming a 'V' for every ten kilometres of distance travelled. To calculate the total distance covered the 'V's are counted and multiplied by ten and any 'tail ends' are added in, the total being expressed in kilometres.

When a second chart is located in the rear position of a two-man tachograph, only a time recording of the second man's activities (ie other work, break or rest) is shown. Traces showing driving, vehicle speed or distance cannot be recorded on this chart.

Precautions against interference with the readings are incorporated in the instrument. It is opened with a key and a security mark is made on the chart every time the instrument is opened.* When checking the chart it can be easily established at what time the instrument was opened and thus whether this was for an authorised reason or not. Interference with the recording mechanism to give false readings, particularly of speed, can be determined quite simply by an experienced chart analyst.

NB: Changes to the EC tachograph specification to reduce the possibility of fraudulent recordings are to be introduced in due course to apply to new instruments receiving type approval from 1991. These will include a provision for the chart to be marked at every interruption of the power supply (eg when a fuse is removed).

Faults
Tachographs are generally robust instruments, but listed below are some

5: TACHOGRAPHS

of the faults which may occur:
1. failure of the cable drive at the vehicle gearbox;
2. failure of the cable drive at the tachograph head;
3. failure of the adaptor/corrector/triplex gearbox;
4. cable braking or seizure;
5. electrical faults affecting lights in the instrument or the clock;
6. incorrect time showing on the 24-hour clock (eg day-shift work becomes shown against night hours on the charts);
7. failure of the tachograph head;
8. damage to the recording styli;
9. failure of the distance recorder;
10. damage to charts because of incorrect insertion.

Fiddles
A key feature of tachograph recordings is that careful observation will show results of the majority of faults in recordings as well as fiddles and attempts at falsification of recordings by drivers. The main faults likely to be encountered will show as follows.
1. Clock stops – recordings continue in a single vertical line until the styli penetrate the chart.
2. Styli jam/seize up – recordings continue around the chart with no vertical movement.
3. Cable or electronic drive failure – chart continues to rotate and speed and distance styli continue to record on base line and where last positioned respectively. Time-group recordings can still be made but no driving trace will appear.

Attempts at falsification of charts will appear as follows.
1. Opening the instrument face will result in a gap in recordings.
2. Winding the clock backwards or forwards will leave either a gap in the recording or an overlap. In either case the distance recording will not match up if the vehicle is moved.
3. Stopping the clock will stop the rotation of the chart so all speed and distance recordings will be on one vertical line (see item 1 above about how faults in instruments show on charts).
4. Restricting the speed stylus to give indications of lower than actual speed will result in flat-topped speed recordings while bending the stylus down to achieve the same effect will result in recordings below the speed base line when the vehicle is stationary.
5. Written or marked-in recordings with pens or sharp pointed objects are readily identifiable by even a relatively unskilled chart analyst.

NB: This is only an outline list of a large number of possible faults and attempts at falsification likely to be encountered. Some driver fiddles are one-off attempts, crudely and clumsily executed and obvious; others are much more sophisticated in their execution, often as part of an on-going violation of legal requirements. These are more difficult, but not impossible, for the transport manager or fleet operator to detect and would certainly be picked up quickly by an experienced chart analyst.

EC Instruments and Charts

Tachographs may only be used for legal record-keeping purposes if they

are type-approved and comply with the detailed EC specification. Such instruments have provision for indicating to the driver, without the instrument being opened, that a chart has been inserted and that a continuous recording is being made. They also provide for the driver to select, by an activity mode switch on the instrument, the type of recording which is being made. In the UK this must be one of the following:
1. Driving time.
2. Other work time.
3. Break and rest periods.

Two-man instruments are also provided with a means of simultaneously recording the activities of a second crew member on a separate chart located in the rear position in the instrument.

The charts used for legal purposes must also be type-approved as indicated by the appropriate 'e' markings printed on them. It is illegal to use non-approved charts or charts which are not approved for the specific type of instrument being used. Care should be taken that charts used have accurate time registration – cheap and non-type approved versions, which are illegal anyway, have been found in the past to be significantly inaccurate in the way they are printed thus producing inaccurate and worthless records.

The chart must have facilities for the driver to record the following information:
1. Surname and first name.
2. Date and place where use of the chart began.
3. Date and place where use of the chart ended.
4. Vehicle registration number.
5. Odometer reading at point of departure.
6. Odometer reading on completion of the day's work.
7. By subtraction, the total distance travelled in the day (in kilometres).

Chart Analysis

Analysis of the information recorded on tachograph charts can provide valuable data for determining whether drivers have complied with the law on driving, working, break and rest period times and have conformed to statutory speed limits. The data can also be extremely useful as a basis for finding means of increasing the efficiency of vehicle operation and for establishing productivity monitoring and payment schemes for drivers.

Tachograph manufacturers supply accessories to enable detailed chart analysis to be carried out. A chart analyser magnifies the used chart to the extent that detailed analysis beyond the scope of a normal visual examination can be made of the vehicle's minute-by-minute and kilometre-by-kilometre progress. Journey times, average running times and speeds, delivery times, route miles, traffic delays and many other relevant factors can be readily established. With the aid of a fixed hairline cursor on the magnifier to allow precise definition of the time and speed scales and recordings on the chart even vehicle's rates of acceleration and deceleration can be determined.

The German company, Mannesman Kienzle GmbH (and its British counterpart Lucas Kienzle Instruments Limited of Birmingham), which is

5: TACHOGRAPHS

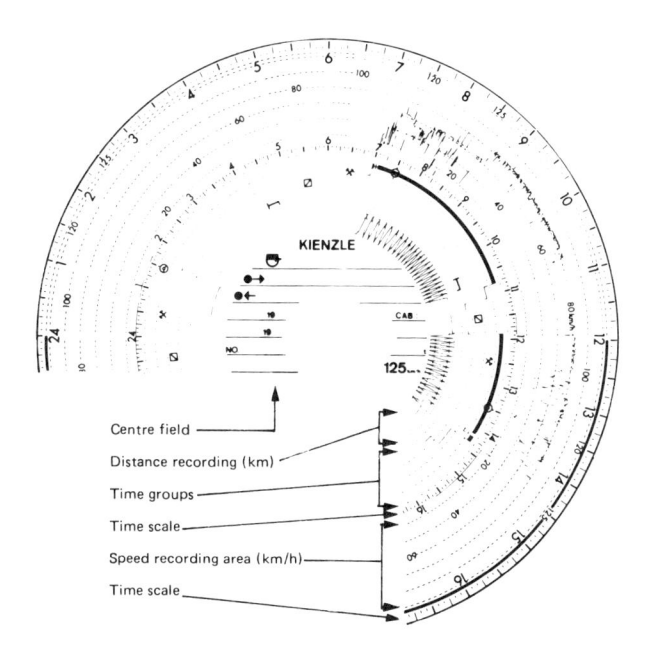

Figure 5.1 *A typical tachograph chart showing recordings of time, distance and speed*

the leading tachograph manufacturer, has undertaken considerable research into chart analysis and is able to offer users the service of its analysis experts both in West Germany and the UK as well as in other countries to determine the activities of vehicles and particularly the progress of a vehicle immediately prior to an accident and at the point of impact. In some instances such analysis has shown that witnesses' accounts of the speed of the vehicle and its braking force just before the accident have been far from correct.

It is also claimed that by detailed analysis of the charts and by keeping drivers aware of the information obtained, driving methods can be improved, thus saving fuel and cutting down on the wear and tear on vehicle brakes, tyres, transmission and other components.

Comprehensive information on tachographs and their use including information on carrying out detailed chart analysis is contained in The Tachograph Manual *by David Lowe and published by Kogan Page Limited.*

6: Ordinary Driving Licences

Major changes to Britain's ordinary and hgv driving licence schemes have been introduced to enable the UK to harmonise with EC requirements. These changes started to take effect from 1 June 1990. However, for a large proportion of ordinary driving licence holders, currently holding 'licences-for-life', the changes will not be noticed unless or until they apply to make a change of the details on their licence (eg to record a new address or in the case of a woman applying, for a new licence after marriage) when they will be issued with the new style Euro-licence. Holders of hgv/psv vocational licences will first become involved in the new scheme when they apply for renewal of their present licences and are issued with a single 'unified' pink Euro-licence. For the purposes of this book, both the pre-existing British and the new EC-based schemes are described, but the reader should be sure to read the correct material when trying to determine information about licences required and the procedures for licensing.

Any person wishing to drive a motor (ie mechanically propelled) vehicle on a public road in Great Britain must hold a driving licence covering the type of vehicle being driven. It is the responsibility of an employer to ensure that employee drivers are correctly licensed to drive company vehicles irrespective of their function, status or seniority – and this includes very senior executives up to the company chairman. The fact that the driver may have 'lost' his licence or allowed it to lapse without the employer being aware of the fact has been held to be no excuse against prosecution for allowing an unlicensed person to drive a vehicle. Driving without a current and valid driving licence to cover the type of vehicle being driven can invalidate insurance cover and result in accident and damage claims being refused.

Special Note: It has come to light that a number of licence holders with three-year licences issued prior to 1976 have not exchanged these for 'for life' licence. It appears that a number of people slipped through the DVLC net at the time of the changeover and with no subsequent need to produce their licences have continued to drive on them quite unaware that they are expired and therefore invalid. This situation will not apply to hgv/psv licence holders who will have had to produce their ordinary licences to obtain or renew their vocational licences, but could apply to other drivers. Any person having such an expired licence may have to take the driving test before a new licence can be issued – they should stop driving immediately and contact the DVLA at Swansea. Transport managers should examine the ordinary driving licences of company employees before permitting them to drive company vehicles to avoid any risk of insurance invalidation resulting from the use of vehicles by unlicensed or incorrectly licensed drivers.

Towed Vehicles

Following a High Court ruling it is clear that a person who steers a vehicle being towed (whether it has broken down or even has vital parts missing, such as the engine) is 'driving' the vehicle and therefore needs to hold a current and appropriate class of driving licence covering that class of vehicle.

Learner Drivers

Learner drivers must hold a provisional driving licence to cover them while under tuition and they must be accompanied, when driving on public roads, by the holder of a full licence covering the class of vehicle being driven (see below). Learner drivers are not allowed to drive on motorways (this does not apply to learner hgv drivers who already hold a full ordinary driving licence). An 'L' plate of the approved dimensions must be displayed on the front and rear of a vehicle being driven by a learner driver. Such drivers must not drive a vehicle drawing a trailer except in the case of articulated vehicles or agricultural trailers.

New regulations are to be made requiring those persons supervising learner drivers to be at least 21 years old and to have held a full driving licence for at least three years.

New applicants for provisional driving licences are now issued with the new-type licence showing the EC vehicle categories (see page 107) rather than the old British groups listed below.

Full Licences (Pre-existing Type)

Existing full British-type driving licences cover one or more of the following vehicle groups:

Group	Class of vehicle	Additional groups covered
A	A vehicle without automatic transmission, of any class not included in any other group	B, C, E, F, K and L
B	A vehicle with automatic transmission, of any class not included in any other group	E, F, K and L
C	Motor tricycle weighing not more than 425kg unladen, but excluding any vehicle included in group E, J, K or L	E, K and L
D	Motor bicycle (with or without side-car) but excluding any vehicle included in group E, K or L	C, E and motor cycles in group L
E	Moped	–
F	Agricultural tractor, but excluding any vehicle included in group H	K
G	Road roller	–
H	Track-laying vehicle steered by its tracks	–
J	Invalid carriage	–
K	Mowing machine or pedestrian controlled vehicle	–
L	Vehicle propelled by electrical power, but excluding any vehicle included in group J or K	K
M	Trolley vehicle	–
N	Vehicle exempted from duty under section 7(1) of the Vehicles (Excise) Act 1971	

Age of Drivers

Certain minimum ages are specified for drivers of various classes of vehicle

6: ORDINARY DRIVING LICENCES

as follows:
1. Invalid carriage or moped*   16 years
2. Motor cycle other than a moped* (ie over 50cc engine
   capacity)   17 years
3. Small passenger vehicle or small goods vehicle (ie not
   exceeding 3.5 tonnes gross weight and not adapted to
   carry more than nine people including the driver)   17 years
4. Agricultural tractor   17 years
5. Medium-sized goods vehicle (ie exceeding 3.5 tonnes
   gross weight but not exceeding 7.5 tonnes gross weight)   18 years
6. Other goods vehicles (ie over 7.5 tonnes gross weight)   21 years

*Note: The definition of moped is as follows:
1. In the case of a vehicle first registered before 1 August 1977 a motor cycle with an engine cylinder capacity not exceeding 50cc which is equipped with pedals by means of which it can be propelled.
2. In the case of a vehicle first registered on or after 1 August 1977 a motor cycle which does not exceed the following limits:
   (a) maximum design speed 30mph
   (b) kerbside weight 250kg
   (c) cylinder capacity (if applicable) 50cc.

If a vehicle and trailer combination exceeds 3.5 tonnes maximum permissible weight the driver must be at least 18 years of age; if the combination exceeds 7.5 tonnes the driver must be at least 21 years of age (and will need to also hold an hgv driving licence).

Members of the armed forces are exempt from the 21 years age limit for driving heavy goods vehicles when such driving is in aid of the civil community.

Disabled young people who receive a mobility allowance may drive cars at 16 years of age provided they can do so safely.

Road Rollers

A person under 21 but not less than 17 years old may drive a road roller if it is either a motor car for purposes of the 1972 Road Traffic Act or if it:
- is propelled by means other than steam
- has an unladen weight of not more than 11.5 tonnes
- is fitted with hard tyres or rollers
- is not constructed or adapted to carry a load other than water, fuel, accumulators and other equipment used for the purpose of propulsion, loose tools, loose equipment and any object which is specially constructed for attachment to the vehicle so as to increase, temporarily, its unladen weight.

Agricultural Tractors

A person under 17 but over 16 may drive an agricultural tractor only if it is:
- of the wheeled type
- not more than eight feet wide including the width of any fitted implement
- specially licensed at the £16.00 vehicle excise duty rate or is exempt from duty because it travels less than six miles on a road in a week

- not drawing a trailer other than one of the two-wheeled or close coupled four-wheeled type which is not more than eight feet wide.

A 16-year-old must not drive an agricultural tractor on a road unless he has passed the appropriate test.

Licence Application

The ordinary and in future the combined (ie unified) ordinary and vocational driving licence scheme is administered by the Driver and Vehicle Licensing Agency – DVLA – previously the DVLC but now one of the government's new executive agencies, at Swansea. Application for driving licences, either full or provisional, has to be made to Swansea on form D1 (obtainable from Swansea, Local Vehicle Registration Offices or main post offices).

Medical Condition

In completing the application form, details of any physical disabilities must be given and the applicant must certify that certain eyesight requirements are met. It is also a legal requirement that existing licence holders must advise the Licensing Authority (ie the DVLC at Swansea) of the onset or worsening of any health condition likely to cause them to be a source of danger when driving. Examples of such conditions are giddiness, fainting, blackouts, epilepsy, diabetes, strokes, multiple sclerosis, Parkinson's disease, heart disease, angina, 'coronaries', high blood pressure, arthritis, disorders of vision, mental illness, alcoholism, drug-taking and the loss or loss of use of a limb (temporary loss of use such as fractures or sprains do not have to be advised). Licences may be granted to persons who have had cardiac pacemakers fitted provided they have regular medical checkups and are not likely to be a source of danger when driving, and to those suffering from epilepsy who have been free from attacks for more than two years and where they may be considered to be able to drive safely. Where the attacks have occurred only while sleeping the person will need to establish a clear pattern of such attacks over a period of more than three years otherwise a licence will not be granted.

A recent DTp statement (July 1989) on diabetes and driving says that this condition and its treatment may lead to complications which can affect safe driving. Drivers who are diagnosed as diabetic, no matter how well controlled, must inform the DVLC so that medical enquiries can be made. If the enquiries reveal satisfactory control of the condition and there are no significant complications, a licence may be issued for one, two or three years to allow the driver's fitness to drive to be reviewed at regular intervals.

Vision Requirements

The eyesight requirement is that licence applicants and holders should have the ability to read in good daylight (with glasses or contact lenses if worn) a motor vehicle number plate at a distance of 75 feet if the symbols are $3^{1}/_{2}$ inches high or 67 feet if the symbols are $3^{1}/_{8}$ inches high. In the case of vehicles in Group K (ie mowing machines or pedestrian controlled vehicles) lower levels of sight requirement apply as follows: symbols $3^{1}/_{2}$ inches high at 45 feet and symbols $3^{1}/_{8}$ inches high at 40 feet.

6: ORDINARY DRIVING LICENCES

If glasses or contact lenses are needed to reach these vision standards they must be worn at all times while driving. It is an offence to drive with impaired eyesight. A proposal in the Road Traffic Bill currently before parliament requires drivers to undergo regular eye tests.

Licence Fees and Validity

The fee for a 'first' or provisional ordinary driving licence is £17.00 and it is valid until the holder's 70th birthday. The fee also covers the conversion of the provisional licence to a full licence after passing the driving test. Licences are valid from the date of issue until the applicant's 70th birthday, after which a new application must be made and, if granted, each subsequent licence will be valid for three years. No additional fee is payable for these licences. A fee of £5.00 is payable for the issue of a new licence to drivers who have been disqualified.

Duplicate and exchange licences cost £5.00 each except for those due to a change of name or address, which are made free of charge. A £5.00 fee applies to the issue of a British licence in exchange for one issued in Northern Ireland, the Isle of Man, the Channel Islands or the EC.

Note: Since 1 October 1982 no new licences have been issued for trolleybuses, as these vehicles are no longer in service.

Licence Examination

A police officer can ask to see a driver's licence and if it cannot be produced at the time, the driver can nominate a police station at which he or she will produce it in person within *seven* days. The police officer will give the driver a small form (HO/RT 1) to hand in to the nominated police station when producing the licence.

Police officers also have authorisation to ask a driver to state their date of birth and in the event of a prosecution this question will be asked by the court – proof of the date may be requested. British driving licences carry a coded number which indicates the holder's name and date of birth as part of the licence number. The first five letters are the first five letters of the holder's surname. If the name has less than five letters the remaining spaces are filled with the figure 9. Thus SMITH shows as SMITH, SMYTHE as SMYTH, and LEE as LEE 99. The next panel contains numbers the first and last of which show the year of birth, the fourth and fifth the day of the month and the second and third the month of the year with, in the case of female holders, a figure 5 added to the second figure. Thus a licence number 411027 indicates a male holder born on 2 November 1947, while 555217 indicates a female holder born on 21 May 1957.

Northern Ireland driving licences do not carry this number but they do carry a photograph of the holder.

Licence holders apprehended for endorseable fixed penalty offences are required to produce their driving licence to the police officer at the time or later (ie within seven days) to a selected police station and surrender the licence for which they will be given a receipt. Vehicle drivers prosecuted and summoned to appear in court for driving and road traffic offences must produce their driving licence to the court on at least the day before the hearing.

Endorsement Codes

Employers examining licences need to be aware of the endorsement codes shown on licences following conviction for road traffic and driving offences. These are listed below:

Code	Accident offences
AC 10	Failing to stop and/or give particulars after an accident.
AC 20	Failing to report an accident within 24 hours.
AC 30	Undefended accident offence.

Disqualified driver (banned)
BA 10   Driving while disqualified.
BA 20   Disqualification on age grounds.

Careless driving
CD 10   Driving without due care and attention.
CD 20   Driving without reasonable consideration for other road users.
CD 30   Driving without due care and attention or without reasonable consideration for other road users.

Construction and use offences
CU 10   Using a vehicle with defective brakes.
CU 20   Causing or likely to cause danger by reason of unsuitable vehicle or using a vehicle with parts or accessories (excluding brakes, steering or tyres) in a dangerous condition.
CU 30   Using a vehicle with defective tyres.
CU 40   Using a vehicle with defective steering.
CU 50   Causing or likely to cause danger by reason of load or passengers.
CU 60   Undefined failure to comply with Construction and Use Regulations.

Dangerous driving
DD 10   Driving in a dangerous manner.
DD 20   Driving at a dangerous speed.
DD 30   Reckless driving.
DD 40   Driving in a dangerous manner, at a dangerous speed or recklessly.
DD 50   Causing death by dangerous driving.
DD 60   Culpable homicide while driving a vehicle.

Drink or drugs
DR 10   Driving or attempting to drive with blood alcohol level above limit.
DR 20   Driving or attempting to drive while unfit through drink or drugs.
DR 30   Driving or attempting to drive then refusing to supply a specimen of blood or urine for laboratory testing.
DR 40   In charge of a vehicle while blood alcohol level above limit.
DR 50   In charge of a vehicle while unfit through drink or drugs.
DR 60   In charge of a vehicle then refusing to supply a specimen of blood or urine for laboratory testing.

Insurance offences
IN 10   Using a vehicle uninsured against third-party risks.

Licence offences
LC 10   Driving without a licence.
LC 20   Driving while under age.

Miscellaneous offences
MS 10   Leaving a vehicle in a dangerous position.
MS 20   Unlawful pillion riding.

6: ORDINARY DRIVING LICENCES

MS 30   Playstreet offences.
MS 40   Driving with uncorrected defective eyesight or refusing to submit to a test.
MS 50   Motor racing on the highway.

Motorway offences
MW 10   Contravention of Special Roads Regulations (excluding speed limits).

Pedestrian crossings
PC 10   Undefined contravention of Pedestrian Crossing Regulations.
PC 20   Contravention of Pedestrian Crossing Regulations with moving vehicle.
PC 30   Contravention of Pedestrian Crossing Regulations with stationary vehicle.

Provisional licence offences
PL 10   Driving without 'L' plates.
PL 20   Not accompanied by a qualified person.
PL 30   Carrying a person not qualified.
PL 40   Drawing an unauthorised trailer.
PL 50   Undefined failure to comply with conditions of a Provisional Licence.

Speed limits
SP 10   Exceeding goods vehicle speed limit.
SP 20   Exceeding speed limit for type of vehicle (excluding goods or passenger vehicles).
SP 30   Exceeding statutory speed limit on a public road.
SP 40   Exceeding passenger vehicle speed limit.
SP 50   Exceeding speed limit on a motorway.
SP 60   Undefined speed limit offence.

Traffic directions and signs
TS 10   Failing to comply with traffic light signals.
TS 20   Failing to comply with double white lines.
TS 30   Failing to comply with a 'Stop' sign.
TS 40   Failing to comply with directions of a traffic constable.
TS 50   Failing to comply with a traffic sign (excluding 'Stop' signs, traffic lights or double white lines).
TS 60   Failing to comply with a school crossing patrol sign.
TS 70   Undefined failure to comply with a traffic direction or sign.

Theft or unauthorised taking
UT 10   Taking and driving away a vehicle without consent or an attempt thereat.
UT 20   Stealing or attempting to steal a vehicle.
UT 30   Going equipped for stealing or taking a vehicle.
UT 40   Taking or attempting to take a vehicle without consent; driving or attempting to drive a vehicle knowing it to have been taken without consent; allowing oneself to be carried in or on a vehicle knowing it to have been taken without consent.

Special code
XX 99   To signify a disqualification under 'totting-up' procedure.

Where the offence is one of aiding or abetting, causing or permitting or inciting, the codes are modified as follows:

Aiding, abetting, counselling or procuring
Offences as coded, but with zero changed to 2, eg UT 10 becomes UT 12.

Causing or permitting
Offences as coded, but with zero changed to 4, eg LC 20 becomes LC 24.

Inciting
Offences as coded, but with zero changed to 6, eg DD 30 becomes DD 36.

The length of time for periods of disqualification are shown by use of the letters D = days, M = months and Y = years. Consecutive periods of disqualification are signified by an asterisk (*) against the time period.

Driving Licence Penalty Points and Disqualification

The system of driving licence endorsement of penalty points following conviction for motoring offences was introduced by the Transport Act 1981 and came into effect on 1 November 1982. These provisions are now incorporated into the Road Traffic Offenders Act 1988.

The concept is to grade traffic offences according to their seriousness by a number or range of penalty points, between 2 and 10 points. Once a maximum of 12 penalty points has been accumulated within a three-year period counting from the date of the first offence to the current offence (not from the date of conviction), disqualification for at least six months will follow.

Most offences rate a fixed number of penalty points to ensure consistency and simplify the administration; but a discretionary range applies to a few offences where the gravity may vary considerably from one case to another. For example, failing to stop after an accident which only involved minor vehicle damage is obviously less serious than a case where an accident results in injury.

Penalty Points on Conviction and Disqualification

When a driver is convicted of more than one offence at the same court hearing, only the points relative to the most serious of the offences will be endorsed on the licence. The points relative to each individual offence will not be aggregated. Once sufficient points (ie 12) have been endorsed on the driving licence and a period of disqualification has been imposed (six months for the first totting-up of points), the driver will have his 'slate' wiped clean and those points will not be counted again. Twelve more points would have to be accumulated before a further disqualification would follow, but to discourage repeated offences the courts will impose progressively longer disqualification periods in further instances (minimum 12 months for subsequent disqualifications within three years and 24 months for a third disqualification within three years).

6: ORDINARY DRIVING LICENCES

The grading of offences for penalty points contained in Schedule 2 of the 1988 Act is as follows:

Description	Number of penalty points
Reckless driving	10
Careless or inconsiderate driving	3-9*
Being in charge of motor vehicle when unfit through drink or drugs	10
Being in charge of motor vehicle with alcohol above prescribed limit	10
Failing to provide specimen for breath test	4
Failing to provide specimen for analysis	10
Carrying passenger on motor cycle contrary to section 16	1
Failing to comply with traffic directions	3
Leaving vehicle in dangerous position	3
Failing to stop after accident	8-10*
Failing to give particulars or report accident	8-10*
Contravention of Construction and Use regulations	3
Driving without licence	2
Failing to comply with conditions of licence	2
Driving with uncorrected defective eyesight	2
Refusing to submit to test of eyesight	2
Driving while disqualified as under age	2
Driving while disqualified by order of court	6
Using, or causing or permitting use of, motor vehicle uninsured and unsecured against third-party risks	6-8*
Taking in Scotland a motor vehicle without consent or lawful authority or driving, or allowing oneself to be carried in, a motor vehicle so taken	8
Contravention of pedestrian crossing regulations	3
Failure to obey sign exhibited by school crossing patrol	3
Contravention of order prohibiting or restricting use of street playground by vehicles	2
Exceeding a speed limit	3
Taking or attempting to take conveyance without consent or lawful authority or driving or attempting to drive a motor vehicle so taken or allowing oneself to be carried in a motor vehicle so taken	8
Going equipped for stealing with reference to theft or taking of motor vehicle	8

*Note: The ranges of penalty points for these offences were increased to the levels shown in March 1989 in order to stress the importance of stopping and reporting accidents, to deter people from driving without adequate insurance cover and to deter careless and inconsiderate driving behaviour.

Disqualification Offences

The endorsing of penalty points will arise in respect of offences where disqualification is discretionary and where the court has decided that immediate disqualification is not appropriate. In this case the offender's driving licence will be endorsed with four points (see also below). The courts are still free to disqualify immediately if the circumstances justify this.

Offences carrying obligatory disqualification, are shown in the following list:
1. Causing death by reckless driving and manslaughter.
2. Reckless driving within three years of a similar conviction.
3. Driving while unfit through drink or drugs.
4. Driving or attempting to drive with more than the permitted breath-alcohol level.

5. Failure to provide a breath, blood or urine specimen.
6. Racing on the highway.

Drink-Driving Disqualification

Conviction for a first drink-driving offence will result in a minimum one-year period of disqualification and for a second or subsequent offence of driving or attempting to drive under the influence of drink or drugs longer periods of disqualification will be imposed by the court. If the previous such conviction took place within ten years of the current offence the disqualification must be for at least three years. See pp 361–2 for details of the breathalyser system.

Drivers convicted twice for drink-driving offences may have their driving licence revoked altogether. Offenders found to have an exceptionally high level of alcohol in the breath (ie more than $2\frac{1}{2}$ times over the limit or twice refusing to provide a specimen) will be classified as High Risk Offenders (HROs) by the Driver and Vehicle Licensing Agency. They will be required to show that they no longer have an 'alcohol problem' and be subject to an additional medical examination by a DTp-approved doctor (fee £33.40) before their licence will be restored to them.

Special Reasons for Non-Disqualification

The courts have discretion in exceptional mitigating circumstances (ie when there are 'special reasons') not to impose a disqualification. The mitigating circumstance must not be one which makes the offence less serious and no account will be taken of hardship other than exceptional hardship. Pleading that you have a wife and children to support or that you will lose your job is not generally considered to be exceptional hardship for determining whether or not disqualification should be imposed.

If account has previously been taken of circumstances in mitigation of a disqualification, the same circumstances cannot be considered again within three years.

Where a court decides, in exceptional circumstances as described above, not to disqualify a convicted driver, four penalty points will be added to the driver's licence in lieu of the disqualification.

Other Penalties

In addition to the penalties of disqualification and the endorsement of penalty points on driving licences, courts may impose fines and, for certain offences, imprisonment. The maximum fine for most offences is in the range of £100 to £400, but a special case has been made of the offence of failing to stop after an accident or failure to report an accident and drink/driving offences, which now carry maximum fines of £2000, as do certain vehicle construction and use offences (eg overloading and insecure loads).

Removal of Penalty Points and Disqualifications

Penalty points endorsed on driving licences can be removed (by application to DVLC Swansea on form D1 and on payment of a fee of £3.00).

6: ORDINARY DRIVING LICENCES

The waiting period before which no such application would be accepted are four years from the date of the offence, except in the case of reckless driving convictions when the four years is taken from the date of conviction. Endorsements for alcohol-related offences must remain on a licence for 11 years (see below).

Licences returned after disqualification will show no penalty points but previous disqualifications (within four years) will remain and if a previous alcohol/drugs driving offence disqualification has been incurred, this will remain on the licence for 11 years.

Application may be made by disqualified drivers for reinstatement of their licence after varying periods of time depending on the duration of the disqualifying period as follows:
1. Less than two years – no prior application time.
2. Less than four years – after two years have elapsed.
3. Between four years and ten years – after half the time has elapsed.
4. In other cases – after five years have elapsed.

The fee charged for replacement licences following disqualification is £5, but where the disqualification was for drink-driving-type offences the fee for a replacement is £20.

New Driver Licensing Scheme

From 1 June 1990 the new European scheme for 'unified' driver licensing came into effect in the UK. New regulations, the Motor Vehicles (Driving Licence) (Amendment) Regulations 1990 brought these changes into effect and particularly introduction of the European categorisation of vehicles to replace the existing British system of vehicle groups (as listed on page 98).

EC Vehicle Categories

The new vehicle categories are as follows:

Category	Vehicle type	Other categories covered
A	Motorcycle (with or without sidecar) – excluding vehicles in categories K, P.	B1, P
B	Motor vehicle not exceeding 3.5 tonnes and not more than 8 seats (excl driver's), not included in any other category (incl drawing trailer not exceeding 750kg mass).	B+E, B1, C1, C1+E, D1, D1+E, F, K, L, N, P
B1	Motor tricycle not exceeding 500kg mass and engine over 50cc – excluding vehicles in categories K, L, P.	
C1	Goods vehicles exceeding 3.5 tonnes but not exceeding 7.5 tonnes mass (incl drawing trailer not exceeding 7.5 tonnes).	B, B+E, B1, C1+E, D1+E, F, K, L, N, P
D1	Passenger vehicle (not used for hire or reward) with between 8 and 16 seats (excl driver's) (incl drawing trailer not exceeding 750kg mass).	B, B+E, B1, C1, C1+E, D1+E, F, K, L, N, P
B+E	A motor vehicle in category B drawing a trailer exceeding 750kg mass.	

C1+E	A motor vehicle in category C1 drawing a trailer exceeding 750kg mass.	
D1+E	A motor vehicle in category D1 drawing a trailer exceeding 750kg mass.	
F	Agricultural tractor excluding category.	H
G	Road roller.	
H	Track laying vehicle steered by its tracks.	
K	Mowing machine or pedestrian-controlled vehicle.	
L	Electric vehicle	K
N	Vehicle exempted from duty under VEA* 1977s7.	
P	Moped	

Vehicles (Excise) Act 1977

NB: *In the above table the term 'mass' means the permissible maximum weight (pmw) for the vehicle/trailer.*
Full licence categories C and D respectively covering goods vehicles exceeding 3.5 tonnes pmw and passenger vehicles seating more than 8 persons in addition to the driver will be introduced by further legislation at a later date.

New driving licences issued to come into effect since 1 June 1990 show entitlements to drive under the new vehicle categories listed above.

All existing entitlements to drive will be maintained so that no existing licence holder will be deprived of his/her rights to drive particular vehicles either now or in the future, with one exception. This concerns those who currently drive large passenger vehicles (ie with more than 16 seats in addition to the driver's seat) on an ordinary group A driving licence. This particular entitlement is to be removed (currently anticipated by the end of 1990) and persons wishing to drive such vehicles may need to obtain the psv vocational driving qualification.

Euro Licences

The European Driving Licence, the 'pink' licence, has been issued in Britain since 1 January 1987 but only since 1 June 1990 has it become the unified licence carrying details of all of an individual's entitlements to drive (ie motorcycle, car, hgv and psv). It carries the words 'European Community Driving Licence' in eight languages including Greek and Gaelic. The holder's photograph can be added to the licence but this is not compulsory and, in any case, at present the Swansea computer cannot handle photographs. Northern Ireland issued driving licences do carry a photograph of the holder. The licences will also contain where appropriate a provisional driving entitlement document and an endorsement document, both of which are coloured green.

Existing green licences will continue to be valid in Britain and in other countries which recognise British licences.

Since 1 January 1983 national driving licences issued in EC member states have been recognised throughout the Community and when the 'Euro' licence is fully in use national licences will be obsolete.

Exchange of Driving Licences

Since February 1985 holders of valid licences in the following countries

6: ORDINARY DRIVING LICENCES

have been able to exchange these for full British driving licences: Barbados, British Virgin Islands, Cyprus, Finland, Malta and Zimbabwe. More recently the following countries have been added to the list: Austria, Japan. Previously this provision was extended to holders of licences in: Australia, Hong Kong, Kenya, New Zealand, Norway, Singapore, Sweden and Switzerland. Also, holders of British Forces Germany driving licences and holders of Gibraltar driving licences may exchange these for a British ordinary driving licence. The fee for exchange licences is £5.00.

Exchange Vocational Licences

European Community driving licence holders who require heavy goods or public service vehicle licences in addition to an ordinary British driving licence (which they can obtain under the Euro licence scheme mentioned above) should note this requirement when completing the ordinary licence exchange form and they will be sent appropriate application forms from their local Traffic Area office. In addition to holding an appropriate Community licence covering these vehicles, such applicants must provide proof of recent driving experience. Minimum periods of experience for vocational (ie hgv or psv) licence applicants are either six months in the 18 months preceding the date of becoming resident or one year in the previous three years. Holders of Northern Ireland public service vehicle driving licences are entitled to exchange them for a British public service vehicle driving licence.

Visitors Driving in the UK

Visitors to the United Kingdom may drive vehicles in this country provided they hold a domestic driving licence issued in their own country (ie outside the UK and the EC) or a Convention Driving Permit (issued under the Geneva Convention on Road Traffic by a country outside the UK). Holders of such permits are entitled to drive vehicles of a class which their own national or international licence covers for a period of 12 months from the date of their entry into the UK.

International Driving Permits

Certain foreign countries will not accept British ordinary driving licences (eg Bulgaria, East Germany including West Berlin, Hungary) in which case an International Driving Permit will be required by British licence holders wishing to drive in those countries.

These permits are obtainable from the RAC, AA or the National Breakdown Recovery Club (NBRC). The fee is £3.00 and a passport-type photograph is required for attachment to the permit.

7: HGV Drivers' Licences

As with the changes to the UK ordinary driving licence scheme described at the beginning of Chapter 6, so from 1 June 1990 changes are taking place with regard to vocational (ie hgv/psv) licensing. From this date vehicle classes will be categorised in accordance with EC requirements and applicants for new or renewed hgv/psv licences will receive a single 'unified' licence showing all of their driving entitlements in one document. Not all of the necessary legislative changes have been made in the UK as yet to bring us fully into line with the full requirements of the EC directive but these will be forthcoming in the near future.

In the meantime it should be emphasised that no existing hgv/psv drivers will lose their present entitlements to drive – with one exception (see p 123). Some drivers, however, may gain entitlement to drive vehicles in additional classes as described later in this chapter. Licence holders will encounter the new system of licences when they first apply to renew their existing hgv/psv driving licences after 1 January 1991 and new vocational licence applicants will also start to receive the new-type unified licences.

Besides the changes in vehicle categories, full introduction of the changes will involve a transfer of hgv/psv driving licence administration from the Licensing Authorities (Traffic Commissioners when dealing with psv matters) to the DVLA at Swansea with the LAs retaining only a disciplinary role in regard to vocational licensing. Other changes in licensing are expected to follow including medical examinations at five-yearly intervals after age 45 years (currently at three-yearly intervals after 60 years). Full details should be available for inclusion in the 1992 edition of this *Handbook*.

No person may drive a vehicle defined in law as a heavy goods vehicle of any class on a road unless they are at least 21 years old and hold a heavy goods vehicle (ie hgv) driving licence of the appropriate class permitting them to do so. They must not be employed by another person to do so either. *(A special exemption applies to members of the armed forces who may drive heavy goods vehicles in connection with the civilian community and registered drivers under the Young HGV Driver Training Scheme – see p 129).* It is an offence to cause or permit any person to drive any vehicle unless they hold an appropriate current and valid licence for driving that type and class of vehicle. Driving of a vehicle when not correctly licensed can invalidate the insurance and result in accident and damage claims being refused by the insurers.

The Issuing Authority

The hgv driving licence scheme is currently administered by the Licensing Authorities from the Traffic Area offices (Appendix I) and the decision on whether or not a licence will be granted to any applicant rests entirely with the LA. In due course this responsibility will be transferred to the Driver and

Vehicle Licensing Agency (DVLA – previously the DVLC) at Swansea.

Heavy Goods Vehicles

An hgv driving licence is required, in addition to an ordinary current Group A (or B for driving only vehicles with automatic transmission) driving licence (see Chapter 6 for changes to the ordinary driving licence scheme and licence categories), by drivers (including part-time or occasional drivers such as motor fitters and testers) of most goods vehicles which have a permissible maximum weight (pmw) exceeding 7.5 tonnes (ie heavy goods vehicles) as follows:
1. For driving rigid vehicles constructed or adapted to carry or haul goods and which exceed 7.5 tonnes pmw.
2. For driving articulated vehicle combinations with an pmw which exceed 7.5 tonnes (unless the tractive unit does not exceed 2 tons unladen weight in which case an hgv driving licence is not needed).
3. For driving rigid goods vehicle and trailer combinations (not articulated combinations) when the rigid goods vehicle has an pmw exceeding 3.5 tonnes and the total pmw of the combination is more than 7.5 tonnes (see exemption 19, p 115).

Drivers of vehicles below these weights and of other vehicles which are on the list of exemptions from the requirements (see pp 114–15) do not require hgv driving licences.

Unplated Trailers

For the purpose of the hgv driving licence regulations, where the permissible maximum weight of a trailer is not known (ie because it does not have a plate) a system of notional weights has been devised. These can be used as the basis for establishing a legal weight for calculating whether an hgv driving licence is needed when driving a combination of a vehicle and that trailer (see p 120).

Towed Vehicles

It has been held by the courts that a person who steers a disabled heavy goods vehicle on tow is 'driving' the vehicle and thus needs to hold current and valid ordinary and hgv driving licences of the appropriate class for that vehicle.

Types of Driving Licence

1. Standard Licences

Full	For those drivers who have qualified to drive vehicles of the Class for which the licence is issued.
Restricted	For those drivers who have qualified only to drive vehicles of Class 3 or 3A with an pmw not exceeding 10 tonnes.
Provisional	For those drivers who have not qualified to drive vehicles of the Class for which the licence is issued.

7: HGV DRIVERS' LICENCES

2. Trainee Licences

For drivers who comply with the requirements of the young driver training scheme detailed in Chapter 8.

HGV Driving Licence Classes

For the purpose of the pre-existing UK hgv driving licence scheme, vehicles are divided into six classes: three of these cover the range of vehicle sizes and types, depending on whether articulated or rigid construction and the number of axles, fitted with manually-operated gearboxes. The other three classes are those covering the same types of vehicle but fitted with automatic transmission instead of manual gearboxes.

The following is a list of the six classes with an indication of the other classes covered:

Class	Definition	Additional classes
Class 1	An articulated vehicle not with automatic transmission	1A, 2, 2A, 3 and 3A
Class 1A	An articulated vehicle with automatic transmission	2A, and 3A
Class 2	A heavy goods vehicle not with automatic transmission, other than an articulated vehicle, designed and constructed to have more than four wheels in contact with the road surface	2A, 3 and 3A
Class 2A	A heavy goods vehicle with automatic transmission, other than an articulated vehicle, designed and constructed to have more than four wheels in contact with the road surface	3A
Class 3	A heavy goods vehicle not with automatic transmission, other than an articulated vehicle, designed and constructed to have not more than four wheels in contact with the road surface	3A
Class 3A	A heavy goods vehicle with automatic transmission, other than an articulated vehicle, designed and constructed to have not more than four wheels in contact with the road surface.	

Licences for Draw-bar Combinations
When draw-bar (ie rigid vehicle and draw-bar trailer combinations) outfits are driven, an hgv licence for Class 2 or 3 only is required depending on whether the towing vehicle has more than two axles (ie Class 2) or only two axles (ie Class 3).

Licences for Articulated Tractive Units
Drivers of articulated tractive units (ie travelling on the road without semi-trailers) need only hold Class 2 (multi-axle) or Class 3 (two-axle) hgv driving licences as appropriate.

NB: See end of chapter for list of new EC vehicle categories corresponding to the above heavy goods vehicle classes.

Restricted HGV Driving Licences

Under transitional arrangements made in 1976 at the time of changing the weight threshold for hgv driving licences, certain drivers were granted 'Restricted' Class 3 hgv driving licences without taking the hgv driving test. Drivers holding these 'Restricted' licences are permitted to drive only goods vehicles with a permissible maximum weight not exceeding 10 tonnes. If they wish to drive other Class 3 vehicles (ie two-axle vehicles with pmw up to 16 tonnes) it is necessary for them to take the full hgv driving test on a Class 3 vehicle.

The Restricted licence can be used as a provisional licence for driving other Class 3 vehicles (ie over 10 tonnes pmw) but it does not qualify the holder to accompany a provisional licence holder learning on a Class 3 type vehicle.

Drivers of vehicles over 3 tons unladen weight but with an pmw not exceeding 7.5 tonnes do not require hgv driving licences for driving such vehicles.

At the time of renewing Restricted Class 3 licences applicants are only permitted to obtain a further Class 3 licence (restricted to vehicles of 10 tonnes pmw) unless in the meantime they have passed the hgv driving test for that or any other class of vehicle.

Exemptions

Exemptions from the need to hold an hgv driving licence when driving certain vehicles are contained in the Heavy Goods Vehicle (Drivers' Licences) Regulations 1977 as amended. The list of exemptions is as follows:

1. Track laying vehicles
2. Steam-propelled vehicles
3. Road rollers
4. Road construction vehicles used or kept on the road solely for the conveyance of built-in construction machinery
5. Engineering plant (which includes certain types of mobile crane)
6. Works trucks
7. Industrial tractors, that is tractors which are not land tractors, have unladen weights of not more than 3.5 tonnes, and which are designed and used primarily for work off roads, or for work on roads in connection with road construction or maintenance and which are constructed so as to be incapable of a speed of more than 20 miles per hour on the level under their own power
8. Land locomotives and land tractors (ie agricultural vehicles)
9. Digging machines
10. Vehicles used less than six miles per week on public roads (ie exempted from duty under the Vehicles (Excise) Act 1971)
11. Articulated tractive units weighing not more than 3050 kgs unladen which have no trailer attached
12. Vehicles used as public service vehicles
13. Vehicles used for no purpose other than the haulage of lifeboats and the conveyance of the necessary gear of the lifeboats which are being hauled

7: HGV DRIVERS' LICENCES

14. Vehicles manufactured before 1 January 1960 used unladen and not drawing a laden trailer
15. Vehicles in the service of a visiting military force or headquarters
16. Wheeled armoured vehicles, the property of, or under the control of, the Secretary of State for Defence
17. A heavy goods vehicle when driven by a police constable for the purpose of removing it to avoid obstruction to other road users or danger to other road users or members of the public, for the purpose of safeguarding property, including the vehicle and its load, or for other similar purposes
18. Any articulated vehicle which has a permissible maximum weight of not more than 7.5 tonnes, or the tractive unit of which does not exceed 2 tons (not tonnes) unladen weight
19. Any rigid vehicle which has a permissible maximum weight of not more than 3.5 tonnes which is towing a trailer (ie not an articulated vehicle)
20. Any vehicle other than an articulated vehicle with an unladen weight of not more than 10 tons which belongs to the holder of a psv licence when such a vehicle is going to or returning from a place where it is to give assistance to a disabled vehicle operating under a psv licence or when moving such a vehicle to prevent it causing an obstruction or to a place where it is to be repaired, stored or broken up
21. Breakdown vehicles which weigh less than 3 tons unladen, provided they are fitted with apparatus for raising a disabled vehicle partly from the ground and for drawing a vehicle when so raised, are used solely for the purpose of dealing with disabled vehicles, and carry no load other than a disabled vehicle and articles used in connection with dealing with disabled vehicles
22. Play buses
23. Fire fighting or salvage vehicles driven by a member of the armed forces
24. Vehicles driven by members of the armed forces on urgent work of national importance as ordered by the Defence Council.

Licence Application

The hgv driving licence application form DLG1, obtainable from the Licensing Authority at Traffic Area offices, has to be completed by the applicant – it is quite straightforward – and returned to the LA in whose area he resides (see Appendix I for list of addresses and areas covered). *See note above about proposed changes to the administration of the hgv licensing scheme.* Questions on the form are concerned with details of the applicant and any current ordinary driving licence which he holds, whether he has ever been refused a driving licence or been disqualified from driving and details of any convictions against him. Also the applicant is asked to declare whether or not he has 'ever suffered from sudden attacks of disabling giddiness or fainting, or from any disease, mental or physical, or disability likely to interfere with the efficient discharge of (his) duties as a driver or to cause driving (by him) of a heavy goods vehicle to be a source of danger to the public'.

The application for an hgv driving licence should be made not more than two months before the date from which the licence is required to run.

A warning is clearly stated on the form that any false statement given for the purpose of obtaining a licence could result in a fine or a term of imprisonment or both.

Medical Requirements

In order to make an application for an hgv driving licence, the applicant must be medically examined and must obtain a medical certificate (form DTP 20003) which must be completed by a registered medical practitioner (ie usually his family doctor). The medical examination cannot be carried out under the National Health Service and therefore must be paid for, on a private basis, by the applicant himself or it could be paid for by his employer.

Medical certificates are required on the first application for an hgv driving licence and on each renewal application after the age of 60. *This is to be reduced to 45 years with five-yearly examinations thereafter to age 65 years after which annual examinations will be required.* Further medical examinations may be called for if there is any doubt as to a driver's fitness to drive. The certificate must be signed by the doctor not more than three months before the date of commencement of the licence.

Doctors are given guidance on various aspects of the medical examination by the British Medical Association – these notes of advice from the BMA are, however, confidential to doctors. Among medical disabilities which may cause failure of the examination are sudden attacks of vertigo ('dizziness'), heart disease which causes disabling weakness or pain, a history of coronary thrombosis, or the use of hypertensive drugs for blood pressure treatment and diabetes requiring insulin injection or oral agents. Drivers who have suffered an epileptic attack since the age of five (previously age three) are ineligible for the grant of an hgv driving licence. Where the wearing of contact lenses was not acceptable for hgv drivers at one time, drivers may be permitted to drive if their vision with contact lenses meets the required standard (see also below).

A licence will be refused to a driver who is liable to sudden attacks of disabling giddiness or fainting. A driver who has had a cardiac pacemaker fitted is advised to discontinue hgv driving, although driving below the hgv threshold is permitted if a person who has disabling attacks which are controlled by a pacemaker has made arrangements for regular review from a cardiologist and will not be likely to endanger the public.

The vision requirement is that new drivers with spectacles must meet a standard of 6/9 in the better eye and 6/12 in the other; also 6/60 in both eyes separately without glasses. Existing drivers must meet a standard of 6/12 in the better eye, 6/36 in the other and 6/60 uncorrected. If they meet these requirements, new or existing drivers may drive with contact lenses or following a cataract operation.

The medical questionnaire to be completed by the doctor is extensive. Information is required about any previous electrocardiogram (ECG) and any chest X-ray examination which the applicant may have undergone, in order to screen out those patients who have had abnormal cardiographs, or X-ray results, as a result of investigations in relation to their previous medical history. The applicant has to sign his consent to allow the Licensing Authority to make direct approaches to his doctor and any specialists he has consulted with regard to his medical condition.

Licence Renewal

Heavy goods vehicle driving licences are renewable on application on form DLG 1(R) at three-yearly intervals. Normally the Traffic Area office sends out reminders six weeks in advance of the renewal date. A licence will be renewed even if the holder has not driven a heavy goods or any other kind of vehicle of the class for which the licence is applicable during the currency of the licence or within five years of its expiry date. The holder of an hgv driving test pass certificate who does not apply immediately for a licence can do so at any time within five years from the date on which the certificate was issued.

New Style HGV Driving Licences

A new style hgv driving licence was introduced in 1988 replacing the earlier hard-backed version. According to the DTp the new style licences will make forgery more difficult and help enforcement agencies detect offenders. The new licences contain a number of improvements including security printing and colouring and there is better provision for driver details and more legible guidance notes. Existing licences remain valid until renewal when the new version will be issued.

Late Renewal

The Licensing Authorities are concerned about drivers making late application to renew their hgv driving licences. Renewal can take up to four weeks from the date of application, consequently, once the expiry date has passed the driver is not entitled in law to drive heavy goods vehicles but in practice the licence will remain in force until the renewal application is granted.

Licence Fees

A full hgv driving licence is valid for three years. To be increased to five years. The fee is £10.00. A provisional hgv driving licence is valid for six months and the fee is £5.00. Replacement for lost, defaced or exchanged licences cost £5.00. A driver who holds a full hgv driving licence for any class of vehicle and subsequently passes the test for additional classes of vehicle can obtain an exchange licence (valid for the unexpired life of the surrendered licence) to show the new information by submitting a fresh application, his current ordinary driving licence and the hgv driving test 'pass' certificate.

Tax Relief

The cost of renewing an hgv driving licence, and the cost of medical examinations after the age of 60 years (see previous note about possible changes to this age limit), qualify for income tax relief. This does not, however, apply to the cost of obtaining the first licence, the first medical examination or the cost of taking the hgv driving test.

The LA's Considerations

The decision whether or not an applicant will be granted an hgv driving licence rests entirely with the LA and in making his decision he will take into account any driving convictions for motoring offences, drivers' hours and record offences and offences relating to the roadworthiness or loading of vehicles, against the applicant in the four years prior to the application and any offence connected with driving under the influence of drink or drugs during the 11 years prior to the application. The applicant has to declare such convictions on the application form but the LA has means of checking to ensure that applicants have declared any such convictions against them.

Suspension, Revocation and Disqualification

The holder of an hgv driving licence can have his licence revoked or suspended by the LA at any time on the grounds of misconduct or physical disability. In a recent tightening up of law enforcement LAs have taken to suspending the hgv driving licences of drivers for persistent speeding as indicated by examination of their tachograph charts. There is no endorsement procedure for hgv driving licences in the same way that ordinary driving licences can be endorsed but a person can be refused an hgv driving licence after having his existing licence revoked. This refusal to grant a licence can apply either indefinitely or for some other period of time which the LA specifies.

Appeals

If the LA refuses to grant an application for an hgv driving licence or revokes, suspends or limits a licence, the applicant or the holder may appeal against the decision under the Road Traffic Act 1972. He should first ask the LA, in writing, to reconsider the decision (and a personal hearing can be requested and the applicant can be represented if desired) and, if this is refused, then make an appeal to a Magistrates' Court acting for the petty sessions in England or Wales, or in Scotland to the local Sheriff.

Removal of HGV Driving Licence Disqualification

If a driver is disqualified from holding an hgv driving licence, as described above, he may apply to have the disqualification removed after two years if it was for less than four years, or after half the period if the disqualification was for more than four years but less than ten years. In any other case including disqualification for an indefinite period an application for its removal cannot be made until five years have elapsed. If an application for the removal of a disqualification fails another application cannot be made for three months.

Ordinary Licence Disqualification

In the event of a driver incurring a disqualification on his ordinary driving licence for an offence or offences committed, even if it is with a vehicle which does not come within the hgv driving licence system (for example, a private car), he must notify the LA 'forthwith' and immediately send his hgv driving licence to the Traffic Area office from where it was issued. The LA will hold the hgv licence until the holder can drive again and produces a valid ordinary driving licence. In the meantime, the driving of a heavy

7: HGV DRIVERS' LICENCES

goods vehicle would be illegal and could result in severe penalties.

Return of HGV Driving Licences

Experience has shown that the LAs will not readily restore hgv driving licences on application following disqualification of an ordinary driving licence. Such applicants can be called before a public inquiry at which the LA will inquire into the events which led to the disqualification and at which he may also decide that the applicant must wait a further period before applying again or must take an hgv driving test in order to regain his licence.

Licence Examination

A police officer or a Department of Transport examiner can demand to see a driver's hgv driving licence or the licence of a person accompanying a provisional hgv licence holder and request details of the name and address of the owner of the vehicle. If production is demanded by an examiner the licence holder must acknowledge the information which the examiner records on his sheet in connection with his name and address and his hgv driving licence by signing the examiner's sheet.

If the licence holder is not able to produce his licence at the time of the request for examination by a police officer he must produce it in person at a nominated police station within *seven* days. If he is unable to produce the licence when requested to do so by an examiner it must be produced within *ten* days at the office of the examiner or at any office of an LA nominated by the driver at the time of being requested to show his licence. In either case, if the licence cannot be produced within the seven or ten days it can be produced as soon as reasonably practicable thereafter. Failure to produce a licence on request is an offence.

An LA can also require the holder of an hgv driving licence to produce that licence and his ordinary licence at the Traffic Area office for examination within ten days.

Provisional HGV Driving Licences

Drivers learning to drive heavy goods vehicles must hold a provisional hgv driving licence and a full or provisional ordinary driving licence. A full hgv driving licence for any of the lower classes of vehicle can be used as a provisional licence while learning to drive a vehicle of a higher class (unless the licence holder specifically applies for his licence to be used as a full licence only, in which case his physical fitness to drive will only be considered in relation to the vehicle for which he has a full licence).

When a full licence is used as a provisional licence for a higher class vehicle the conditions applying to the holder of a provisional licence will have to be observed when driving a vehicle of a class for which a full licence is not held.

Applications for provisional hgv drivers' licences are made on the same forms as already mentioned for a full licence and the same medical examination is also required.

A provisional licence holder, when learning to drive on a heavy goods vehicle, must be accompanied by a person in the cab who holds a full driving licence for that class of vehicle. An 'L' plate of the approved type must be displayed on the front and on the rear of the vehicle where it is clearly visible to other road users from within a reasonable distance from the front and back of the vehicle. If the provisional hgv licence holder is also a provisional ordinary driving licence holder an ordinary 'L' plate must also be displayed on the front and rear of the vehicle. Vehicles used for the tuition of provisional hgv licence holders can be loaded with either test loads or normal loads for delivery (but not the latter if the reduced rate of VED is being paid – see p 318) but for taking the driving test the vehicle *must be unladen.*

Provisional Drivers on Motorways

Holders of provisional hgv driving licences who hold a full ordinary driving licence may drive heavy vehicles on motorways while under tuition. Those who hold only provisional ordinary and provisional hgv driving licences are not permitted to drive on motorways.

Notional Gross Weights

In cases where a goods vehicle or trailer does not have a manufacturer's specified or Department of Transport specified gross weight or gross train weight (ie for vehicle and trailer combinations) marked on it, a system of 'multipliers' is used to calculate the notional maximum gross weight for the purposes of determining driving licence requirements. The unladen weight of the vehicle (or trailer) is multiplied by the number given in the tables below for that class of vehicle, and the resulting figure is taken to be the gross or gross train weight, but only for the purposes of deciding what driving licence is required and not for any other purpose.

The relevant classes of vehicle and trailer and the multiplier (ie multiply unladen weight by the multiplier) are shown in the accompanying tables:

Motor Vehicles

Class of Vehicle	Number
1. Dual-purpose vehicles not constructed or adapted to form part of an articulated goods vehicle combination	1.5
2. Breakdown vehicles	2
3. Works trucks and straddle carriers used solely as works trucks	2
4. Electrically-propelled motor vehicles	2
5. Vehicles constructed or adapted for, and used solely for, spreading material on roads to deal with frost, ice or snow	2
6. Motor vehicles used for no other purpose than the haulage of lifeboats and the conveyance of the necessary gear of the lifeboats which are being hauled	2
7. Living vans	1.5
8. Vehicles constructed or adapted for, and used primarily for the purpose of, carrying equipment permanently fixed to the vehicle, in a case where the equipment is used for medical, dental, veterinary, health, educational, display or clerical purposes and such use does not directly involve the sale, hire or loan of goods from the vehicle	1.5

9. Three-wheeled motor vehicles designed for the purpose of street cleansing, the collection or disposal of refuse or the collection or disposal of the contents of gullies — 2
10. Steam-propelled vehicles — 2
11. Vehicles designed and used for the purpose of servicing, controlling, loading or unloading aircraft on an aerodrome — 2
12. Motor vehicles of a class not mentioned above where equipment, apparatus or other burden is permanently attached to and forms part of the vehicle and where the vehicle is only used on a road for carrying, or in connection with the use of, such equipment, apparatus or other burden — 1
13. Motor vehicles of a class not mentioned above which are either
    (a) heavy motor cars or motor cars first used before 1 January 1968, or
    (b) locomotives or motor tractors first used before 1 April 1973 — 2
14. Any motor vehicles not mentioned above. — 4

Trailers

Class of Vehicle — *Number*
1. Engineering plant — 1
2. Trailers which consist of drying or mixing plant designed for the production of asphalt or of bituminous or tar macadam — 1
3. Agricultural trailers — 1
4. Works trailers — 1
5. Living vans — 1.5
6. Any trailers not mentioned above. — 3

Articulated Vehicles

Class of Combination — *Number*
1. Articulated goods vehicle combinations where the semi-trailer is a trailer of a kind mentioned in paragraph 1, 2, 3, 4 or 5 of 'Trailers' above — 1.5
2. Any other articulated goods vehicle combination. — 3

New Unified Driving Licence Scheme

Under the new EC unified driver licensing scheme referred to above, which is being progressively introduced in the UK, hgv/psv drivers will be issued with a single vocational driving licence showing all of their entitlements to drive under the EC list of vehicle categories – see below.

Listed below are the new EC vehicle categories followed by a list of correspondences so that hgv drivers and their employers can determine what categories of vehicle they are covered to drive. It should be stressed that no current licence holder will lose any of his existing entitlements to drive in the licence changeover – some drivers will gain an additional entitlement (see note below).

EC Vehicle Categories

The new vehicle categories are as follows:

Category	Vehicle type	Other categories covered
A	Motorcycle (with or without sidecar) – excluding vehicles in categories K, P.	B1, P
B	Motor vehicle not exceeding 3.5 tonnes and not more than 8 seats (excl driver's), not included in any other category (incl drawing trailer not exceeding 750kg mass)	B+E, B1, C1, C1+E, D1, D1+E, F, K, L, N, P
B1	Motor tricycle not exceeding 500kg mass and engine over 50cc – excluding vehicles in categories K, L, P.	
C	Goods vehicles exceeding 3.5 tonnes mass.	B, B+E, B1, C1, C1+E, D1+E, F, K, L, N, P
C1	Goods vehicles exceeding 3.5 tonnes but not exceeding 7.5 tonnes mass (incl drawing trailer not exceeding 7.5 tonnes).	B, B+E, B1, C1+E, D1+E, F, K, L, N, P
D	Passenger vehicles with more than 8 seats (excl driver's).	B, B+E, B1, C1, C1+E, D1+E F, K, L, N, P
D1	Passenger vehicle (not used for hire or reward) with between 8 and 16 seats (excl driver's) (incl drawing trailer not exceeding 750kg mass).	B, B+E, B1, C1, C1+E, D1+E, F, K, L, N, P
B+E	A motor vehicle in category B drawing a trailer exceeding 750kg mass.	
C1+E	A motor vehicle in category C1 drawing a trailer exceeding 750kg mass.	
D1+E	A motor vehicle in category D1 drawing a trailer exceeding 750kg mass.	
E	Vehicles drawing trailers exceeding 750kg mass.	
F	Agricultural tractor excluding category.	H
G	Road roller.	
H	Track laying vehicle steered by its tracks.	
K	Mowing machine or pedestrian-controlled vehicle.	
L	Electric vehicle.	K
N	Vehicle exempted from duty under VEA* 1977s7.	
P	Moped.	

*Vehicles (Excise) Act 1977

NB: In the above table the term 'mass' means the permissible maximum weight (pmw) for the vehicle/trailer.
Full licence categories C and D respectively covering goods vehicles exceeding 3.5 tonnes pmw and passenger vehicles seating more than 8 persons in addition to the driver will be introduced by further legislation at a later date.

7: HGV DRIVERS' LICENCES

So that existing hgv drivers licence classes can be compared with the new EC vehicle categories the following table is provided:

Existing hgv licence classes	EC vehicle categories covered
1	B+E, C, C+E, D1, D1+E.
1A	As for 1 above but restricted to vehicles with automatic transmission.
2	B+E, C, C+E (limited to drawbar combinations only), D1, D1+E.
2A	As in 2 above but restricted to vehicles with automatic transmission.
3	As in 2 above.
3A	As in 2A above.

NB: It will be seen from this table that existing Class 3 hgv driving licence holders currently permitted to drive only rigid vehicles with two axles (ie 4 wheels) will gain a licence to drive multi-axle rigid vehicles (ie 6 and 8 wheeler rigids) when they first come to renew their hgv driving licences under the new scheme. Similarly, holders of existing Restricted Class 3 hgv driving licences (under which they can drive vehicles only up to 10 tonnes pmw) will gain a licence to drive all categories of rigid vehicle covered by category 2.

8: Driving Tests (Ordinary – HGV – Advanced)

With the progressive harmonisation of UK driver licensing with requirements applicable throughout the European Community certain aspects of the long-standing British hgv test are to be amended. However, the main principle of the test will remain valid which is to ensure that goods vehicle drivers are competent to drive heavy vehicles on the roads in safety. It also provides a measure of professionalism among commercial vehicle drivers. The test is more comprehensive and more complex than the ordinary driving test and, consequently, it demands greater skill and knowledge from the driver who wishes to pass.

For many years the advanced driving test organised by the Institute of Advanced Motorists has been looked upon as a severe test of driving skills requiring a high degree of knowledge of the 'rules of the road' for private car drivers. Commercial vehicle drivers who want to show that they too have attained an exceptional level of proficiency can take the advanced driving test designed specially for commercial vehicles and on passing they may display the coveted IAM badge.

This chapter contains details of the ordinary driving test, the hgv driving test (and the proposed EC changes) which must be passed to gain a licence to drive heavy goods vehicles, and the advanced driving test which drivers may take voluntarily. The chapter also covers heavy goods vehicle driver training provisions and the Young HGV Driver Training Scheme.

New rules require candidates for ordinary, hgv and psv driving tests to produce satisfactory evidence of identity otherwise the test will be cancelled and the test fee forfeited. Acceptable identity documents for this purpose would include existing driving licences (ordinary, hgv or psv or an overseas driving licence) or a passport. At the examiner's discretion valid bank cheque cards or credit cards could be accepted. If a test candidate cannot produce satisfactory means of identification the test will not be conducted and the fee will be forfeited.

Ordinary Driving Test

Before a person can be granted a licence to drive a motor vehicle on the road they must pass a driving test on the class of vehicle for which they require the licence.

The test is carried out by an examiner from the Driving Standards Agency (DSA – one of the Government's new executive agencies) and the test candidate has to meet the following requirements:

1. They must show that they are fully conversant with the contents of the Highway Code.
2. They must prove that they are able to read in good daylight (with the aid of spectacles, if worn) a motor vehicle's registration number in accordance with the vision requirements (see p 100).

3. They must show that they are competent to drive without danger to and with due consideration of other users of the road, including being able to:
   (a) start the engine of the vehicle;
   (b) move away straight ahead or at an angle;
   (c) overtake, meet or cross the path of other vehicles and take an appropriate course;
   (d) turn right-hand and left-hand corners correctly;
   (e) stop the vehicle in an emergency and in a normal situation, and in the latter case bring it to rest at an appropriate part of the road;
   (f) drive the vehicle backwards and while doing so enter a limited opening either to the left or to the right;
   (g) cause the vehicle to face the opposite direction by the use of forward and reverse gears;
   (h) indicate their intended actions at appropriate times by giving appropriate signals in a clear and unmistakable manner (in the case of a left-hand drive vehicle or a disabled driver for whom it is impracticable or undesirable to give hand signals there is no requirement to provide any signals other than mechanical ones);
   (i) act correctly and promptly on all signals given by traffic signs and traffic controllers and take appropriate action on signs given by other road users.

Since the introduction of the DSA in May 1990, candidates who fail the driving test are given an oral explanation of the reasons for their failure.

Driving Test Fee

The fee for an ordinary driving test is £19.50.

Driving Instruction

Only DTp-approved instructors (ADIs – now approved by the Driving Standards Agency) are permitted to give driving instruction for payment on the following classes of vehicle:
1. Private cars.
2. Light goods vehicles of less than 7.5 tonnes gross weight.
3. Articulated tractive units weighing less than 15 cwt unladen.

More stringent standards have been introduced for driving instructors, in particular extended training periods are necessary before instructors can become qualified.

Tuition given for payment on heavy goods vehicles does not come within the scope of this legislation despite the opinion of a certain number within the transport industry that it should do so. Consequently, registration of instructors with the DSA for this purpose is not necessary.

The HGV Driving Test

The heavy goods vehicle driving test is also conducted by DSA examiners (see above) and booking has to be made through the applicant's local Traffic Area office (see Appendix I for list of addresses and areas covered).

Application and Fees

Applications for the test have to be made on form DLG 26 obtainable from the Traffic Area office. The current test fee of £45.00 must be sent with the application. Applicants are warned to apply for a test in good time. This is important if an hgv driving licence is required – subject to passing the test – from a particular date; and applicants must also ensure that their driving is of a sufficiently high standard to be able to pass the test. Test candidates must be able to produce satisfactory identification on arrival at the test centre otherwise the examiner may refuse to conduct the test and the fee will be forfeited.

Certain test centres now offer Saturday morning hgv and psv driver testing.

Block Bookings

Block bookings may be made for hgv driving tests and in these cases trainees may be named up to one week (instead of the normal 28 days) before the test date. Training organisations can make provisional bookings with the local Traffic Area office but the appointment must be confirmed more than one month ahead on forms DLG 26X, Y and Z together with the fee.

Vehicles for the HGV Driving Test

The candidate has to provide the vehicle (or arrange for the loan of a suitable vehicle) on which he wishes to be tested and it must comply with the following requirements:
1. it must be unladen and of the class for which a licence is required;
2. it must display approved hgv 'L' plates (and ordinary 'L' plates if the candidate is to be tested for an ordinary licence at the same time) at the front and rear;
3. it must be in a thoroughly roadworthy condition;
4. seating accommodation in the cab must be provided for the examiner;
5. it must have sufficient fuel for a test lasting up to two hours.

The Test

The hgv driving test can be used as a combined test for both licences where the candidate holds both a provisional ordinary driving licence and a provisional hgv driving licence.

The test is in three parts consisting of:
1. The test of a driver's ability to manoeuvre a vehicle in a confined space. This test will take place off the highway at a DTp driving test centre.
2. A test drive over a route of about 25 miles of various types of road including fast open roads and urban roads and in varying traffic densities.
3. An oral test of the candidate's knowledge of the Highway Code and his knowledge of the function of those components of the vehicle affecting its safe operation and other functions.

Since 1 July 1986 the duration of the test has been reduced from two hours to one and a half hours but 'without any relaxation of standards'.

The specific operations that will be expected of a driver undergoing the test are on the same lines as the ordinary driving test and are as follows:
1. Start the engine of the vehicle.

2. Move off straight ahead or at an angle.
3. Maintain a proper position in relation to a vehicle immediately in front.
4. Overtake and take an appropriate course in relation to other vehicles.
5. Turn right and left.
6. Bring the vehicle to rest at a predetermined position while travelling forwards and backwards and make an emergency stop.
7. Manoeuvre the vehicle both forwards and backwards, including steering the vehicle along a predetermined course and make it enter a narrow opening.
8. Give by mechanical means appropriate signals in clear and unmistakable manner at appropriate times to indicate intended actions. Although the previous specific requirement to give arm signals has been removed, test candidates will still be expected to give arm signals to indicate their intention to slow down or stop when approaching pedestrian crossings and at times when it is necessary to emphasise the signal given by a direction indicator that the driver intends to turn right. The omission of arm signals when they should have been used or wrong arm signals would count as driving faults.
9. Act correctly and promptly in response to all signals given by traffic signs and persons regulating road traffic and take appropriate action on signs given by other road users.

Preparing for the HGV Driving Test

The detailed questions asked by the examiner in addition to random questions on the Highway Code will be to test the candidate's knowledge of the correct action to take in the event of a fault developing in a component affecting the safe operation of the vehicle. 'Workshop-type' answers will not be expected but only sufficient information to satisfy the examiner that the driver knows when a heavy goods vehicle is in a safe condition to be driven. The candidate will also be expected to have a knowledge of safe loading and correct load distribution on his vehicle and the reasons why this is important. In addition he may be expected to give details of the checks that should be carried out before starting on a journey. Drivers of articulated vehicles will be questioned to test their knowledge of the correct procedures for uncoupling and re-coupling a semi-trailer.

Before undertaking the hgv driving test a driver should study carefully the Highway Code, the Department of Transport free booklet (DL 68) *Your Driving Test and How to Pass* (which applies to both ordinary and hgv driving tests) and put the advice given in these booklets into practice when driving on the road before taking the hgv test to eliminate any bad habits acquired since passing the ordinary test. The manoeuvring exercises should also be practised as much as possible before taking the test, if facilities are available, to ensure a good chance of passing.

HGV Test Passes

A driver who passes the hgv driving test will be issued with a certificate to that effect. If he was the holder of both a provisional ordinary driving licence and a provisional hgv driving licence, passing the hgv driving test will also qualify him to apply for a full ordinary licence of Groups A or B. The hgv driving test pass certificate will remain valid for a period of five

8: DRIVING TESTS (ORDINARY – HGV – ADVANCED)

years during which time the holder can apply for an hgv driving licence of the appropriate class.

HGV Test Failures

A driver who fails the hgv driving test will be given an oral explanation of the reasons for his failure. He may apply for an immediate re-test unless the test was for both an ordinary driving licence and an hgv driving licence in which case the applicant must wait at least one month before being eligible to take another test.

New Test Procedures

With the progressive introduction of new driver licensing arrangements as described in Chapters 6 and 7, there are proposals to amend the current hgv driving test with regard to the vehicles which candidates must supply for the test. For category C tests (ie goods vehicles exceeding 3.5 tonnes pmw) the vehicle must be of at least 11000kg pmw and be capable of a speed of at least 80kph. For a category C+E test (ie articulated vehicles) the vehicle must have a permissible maximum weight of at least 21000kg and be capable of at least 80kph. Drawbar vehicle combinations provided for a C+E test must have a total combination weight of at least 21000kg and the wheelbase must be at least 4 metres. The 80kph minimum speed capability will apply.

Driver Training

Since the introduction of the hgv driving licence system there has been a great deal of activity in the field of driver training. Some of this training has been carried out by private training schools, some by operators training their own drivers and new recruits and some by transport operators who, unable to finance their own full-scale training activity, collaborated with others in the same situation to form Group Training Associations (GTAs).

These groups are formed with the help and guidance of the Road Transport Industry Training Board (RTITB) which in some cases also employs the group training officer and provides the vehicles which are used exclusively for training purposes.

The RTITB has its own training centres (MOTECs – multi-occupational training and education centres) at which it trains driving instructors as well as other classes of road transport employee.

Young Driver Training Scheme

Following measures introduced in the 1974 Road Traffic Act, a scheme has been established for the training of hgv drivers from the age of 18 years. A National Joint Training Committee has been set up through the RTITB and it has evolved a scheme for youngsters of 16 and upwards to be given progressive training for a Class 3 hgv driving licence which they will be able to hold at 18, working up to a Class 1 licence at 21. The course includes periods of further education on a day-release basis at colleges.

A trainee driver who has passed the appropriate test may drive heavy goods vehicles of the following classes without supervision while under the age of 21 years: 2, 2A, 3, 3A. However, when driving such vehicles a trailer must not be towed unless the trainee driver is accompanied by a full hgv driving licence holder. A trainee driver who has passed the test to drive vehicles of Classes 1 and 1A must be accompanied by a full hgv driving licence holder for that class of vehicle until he reaches the age of 21.

A recent amendment to regulations removed the anomaly which prevented an LA from renewing a young trainee hgv driver's licence when he has penalty points endorsed on his ordinary driving licence. A trainee will, however, still need to have a clean licence before he can obtain his first trainee hgv driving licence and more than three penalty points on his ordinary licence will still result in the revocation of his trainee hgv driver's licence.

Explanatory Notes for Employers from National Joint Committee

Introduction
This scheme, open to both men and women, has been designed to provide training leading to a career as a heavy goods vehicle driver. It will be administered by a Committee on which are represented the Road Haulage Association, the Freight Transport Association, the trade unions TGWU, URTU and NUR, the Road Transport Industry Training Board, the Department of Employment and the Royal Society of Arts. The National Joint Training Committee is the only authority legally empowered to administer training of this nature under Section 15 of the 1974 Road Traffic Act.

Condition for Licence Issue
For a trainee hgv driving licence to be issued the applicant's ordinary driving licence must be free from penalty points. Further, if during the validity of a trainee hgv driving licence the trainee obtains more than three penalty points on his ordinary driving licence the Licensing Authority is obliged to revoke the trainee licence.

Registration
An employer must apply to be registered before any training can take place. A representative of the Committee will make an inspection visit to ensure that an organisation maintains its own training facilities to the required standard, or proposes to use approved facilities for both the non-driving and driving training parts of the programme. The opportunity will be taken during this visit to discuss in detail the proposed training programme and any modifications needed to meet an employer's particular business requirements.

A company registration fee is required to cover general administration and inspection costs (a reduced fee is payable by companies with less than 25 hgv drivers). A fee in respect of trainees undergoing Class 3 vehicle training, and a further fee for each subsequent class, is payable to cover monitoring by the RTITB which will act as agent of the Committee in this matter.

The Training Programme
The training covers three main aspects:

8: DRIVING TESTS (ORDINARY – HGV – ADVANCED)

1. Initial job training and Group A (below hgv class) vehicle training.
2. The minimum age for applying for an ordinary Class A driving licence is 17. The minimum ages for applying for a provisional trainee heavy goods vehicle driver's licence in each of the classes of hgv are:
   Class 3 18 years
   Class 2 One year after passing Class 3 test
   Class 2A One year after passing Class 3 or 3A test
   Class 1 One year after passing Class 2 test
   Class 1A One year after passing Class 2 or 2A test.
   At each of the above stages, conversion of a provisional licence into a full licence must follow completion of the course of practical driver training on vehicles of the class in question and on the passing of the appropriate hgv driving test.
3. A one-year programme (it can be spread over a longer period if required) of further education is included in the scheme and is designed to teach the trainee the basic information a driver must know to carry out his duties legally and safely. The opportunity will be taken to reinforce the elements of reading and writing in a job-related manner. Included also are the elements of transport engineering, ie basic servicing, maintenance and fault-finding, and a short course on first aid. There will be an examination and a certificate awarded to successful candidates, but passing the examination is not mandatory and failure will not disqualify the trainee from obtaining an hgv licence.

Conditions of Employment

Employers are required to sign an agreement with the trainee. This should be completed in triplicate, one copy being held by the employer, one by the trainee and the third to be retained by the National Joint Training Committee. This agreement does not exempt the employer from his legal obligation to make a formal offer of contract as required by the Contracts of Employment Act 1972.

Rates of Pay

The trade unions in particular have approved the following recommendations on minimum rates of pay:
1. That the pay rate to which a trainee's pay should be related should be the lowest applicable basic rate payable to an adult hgv driver in the establishment where the training is being undertaken.
2. That while undergoing training, a trainee should be paid an agreed percentage of such basic rate. Suitable percentages might be:
   At age 16 – not less than 65 per cent
   At age 17 – not less than 75 per cent
   At age 18 – not less than 85 per cent
3. That after the Class 3 licence has been obtained, the trainee should be paid not less than the rate laid down above:
   (a) whenever he is employed without supervision on a revenue-earning vehicle; or
   (b) while undergoing training for the Class 2 test.
4. That a trainee entering the scheme at the age of 19 should be paid during his initial training not less than 85 per cent of the rate laid down above.

5. That no trainee should lose pay as a result of his attendance at any course of further education which he is required by the scheme to undertake.
6. That it should be made clear to a registered employer that, in pursuance of his undertaking in the agreement, he will be required to meet any appropriate further education fees and will also be expected to assist the trainee with the cost of any associated travel, books, etc.

Medical Examination
This is not mandatory on entry to the scheme but since an examination is required to obtain a licence, it is seen as a reasonable precaution for the intending trainee to be medically examined. This will virtually eliminate the possibility, and the inevitable distress and dissatisfaction, of young people embarking on a career for which they may later find they are medically unfit.

Legal Obligations
Clearly a scheme of this nature involving the training of young people to drive vehicles will require very close control if it is not to be subject to public criticism. It is important for potential employers to note that:
1. They are legally required to register with the National Joint Training Committee before employing a young driver.
2. A young driver must also be registered before he can undertake driver training.
3. A young driver's licence, for which he must apply to the Licensing Authority, will indicate the employer for whom he is allowed to drive. Should the employer named be unable to continue the programme of training – in the event of the company going out of business or the training standards not being maintained – a trainee may change his registration to another company with the approval of the National Joint Training Committee.
4. Under no circumstances may a young driver be employed by a company other than that named on his licence. Both the offending employer and trainee will incur legal penalties for infringement of this condition. Furthermore, driving for an employer other than that named on the licence means, effectively, that a young driver is unlicensed and therefore uninsured.
5. Disqualification as a private motorist will also result in the immediate loss of a young driver's hgv licence, and removal from the training programme: a fact which should be emphasised strongly at initial interview.

Insurance
One of the reasons for the strict control of the scheme is to satisfy the insurance companies that the scheme will not result in a preponderance of claims involving drivers from this age group. Discussions have taken place which indicate that insurance brokers are generally satisfied with the conditions of the scheme and will not normally require additions of

8: DRIVING TESTS (ORDINARY – HGV – ADVANCED)

premiums. They may well require an employer to accept responsibility for the first part of any damage claim – the amount depending on the experience of the driver concerned.

In any discussion with your insurance broker, you should emphasise that this is a professional training programme, and that there is no basis for the comparison with the notoriously accident-prone section of the younger age group who drive high performance cars – having had the minimum of instruction and training. Any employer experiencing difficulty regarding insurance premiums should contact the National Joint Training Committee immediately.

ITB Training Grants
The RTITB has agreed to pay grants to eligible companies for driver training and off-the-job training. Full details are given in the *Employers' Guide.* Other Training Boards may make similar grants and details may be obtained direct from the Board concerned.

Employers within the scope of the RTITB will be visited by Board staff acting as the official representatives of the National Joint Training Committee, to carry out periodic inspections of training facilities and to obtain reports on trainees' progress. Two documents have been prepared for this purpose – the *Training Record Book* and *Record of Progress.*

Procedure
Registration of Employers, Group Training Association, Trainees' Application for Licences.

Complete Form 1 – individual employer, or Form 2 – in the case of a GTA, returning it to the RTITB as indicated complete with a cheque for the fee in the case of employers. This sum is non-returnable, and covers the cost of initial registration administration, but is deductible from the full fee for full registration. You will then receive a visit from a National Joint Training Committee representative. If he is satisfied that your training arrangements are adequate, he will recommend approval. He will also discuss any problems you may have regarding the training programme.

Following the formal approval of your organisation's application to be registered, you will receive further documents.
Form 3 – to confirm acceptance of this application, the bottom half of this form should be returned with the balance of the registration fee.
Form 5 – one copy for each trainee should be returned to the National Joint Training Committee as soon as possible, together with the fee for each trainee.

Agreement forms in triplicate: one for your records, one for the trainee, and one to be forwarded to the National Joint Training Committee. A training record book and a supply of six-monthly report forms (Form 6).
Form 4 – a copy of this form will be sent to GTAs confirming acceptance of training facilities.

Licence application forms are obtainable from the National Joint Training Committee. When they have been completed by the applicant they should be sent back to the NJTC for endorsement. The licence application form and other appropriate documents should then be sent by the trainee to the Licensing Authority.

The minimum age for licence applications is as follows:
- Group A   17 years
- Class 3   18 years
- Class 2   19 years
- Class 1   20 years

NB: any change which will affect the licence holder must be notified to the National Joint Training Committee immediately. This can range from the simple matter of a change of address to withdrawal from the scheme by the trainee or employer. The general conditions of the scheme include this responsibility as a legal requirement.

The trainee should be registered as early as possible with the local College of Further Education running the course associated with this programme.

This document reproduced with acknowledgement to the National Joint Training Committee.

Young Driver Training Programme

A draft training programme has been established for young heavy goods vehicle drivers and this has been approved by both the DTp and the Department of Employment. This programme is outlined here:

Company Induction
General yard work. Assisting under supervision with: load preparation, loading, load security, use of mechanical handling equipment, warehouse work (if part of the company activity), etc.

Maintenance bay. Assisting under supervision with: routine maintenance and inspection, maintenance and inspection records, preparation of vehicles for annual test, etc.

Traffic office. Assisting traffic clerk with: vehicle and load documentation, driver documentation, routeing and scheduling, etc.

Driver's mate: route familiarisation, collection and delivery routine and procedure, driver maintained documentation.

Industrial Training
Driving instruction on light van or truck. DTp Group A test.

Controlled Experience
Normal driver duties under supervision. Supervision to include driving assessment by qualified instructor at intervals of 100 hours of driving or one month, whichever occurs first, with immediate remedial tuition. Trainee to be accompanied during first night drive. (This may be regarded as an assessment.)

Industrial Training
Driving instruction on hgv Class 3. DTp hgv Class 3 test.

8: DRIVING TESTS (ORDINARY – HGV – ADVANCED)

Controlled Experience
Normal driver duties on Class 3 vehicle under supervision. Supervision to include driving assessment by qualified instructor at intervals of 100 hours of driving or one month, whichever occurs first, with immediate remedial tuition. Trainee to be accompanied by qualified driver during first night drive. (This may be regarded as an assessment.)

Industrial Training
Driving instruction on hgv Class 2. DTp hgv Class 2 test.

Controlled Experience
Normal driver duties on Class 3 or 2 vehicle under supervision. Supervision to include driving assessment by qualified instructor at intervals of 200 hours of driving or one month, whichever occurs first, with immediate remedial tuition. Trainee to be accompanied by qualified driver during first night drive. (This may be regarded as an assessment.)

Industrial Training
Driving instruction on hgv Class 1. DTp hgv Class 1 test.

Controlled Experience
Normal driver duties under supervision (accompanied by qualified driver if in Class 1). Supervision to include driving assessment by qualified instructor at intervals of 200 hours of driving or one month, whichever occurs first, with immediate remedial tuition. Full Class 1 licence. Training completed.

Though the trainee may have passed an hgv test, he will not be entitled to accompany holders of provisional hgv licences as a supervising driver until he reaches the age of 21.

Advanced Commercial Vehicle Driving Test

The advanced commercial vehicle driving test is run by the Institute of Advanced Motorists (Empire House, Chiswick High Road, London W4 5TJ, telephone 081-994 4403) and is open to any heavy goods vehicle driver, subject to certain conditions as follows:
1. Loads, if carried, must be properly secured.
2. A safe seat at the front of the vehicle must be available for the examiner.
3. The driver must not, by taking the test, contravene the drivers' hours and records regulations.

On passing the test, the applicant becomes eligible for admission to membership of the Institute of Advanced Motorists.

Fees

The fee for the advanced commercial vehicle test is currently £20.00, and annual subscription to the Institute is £7.50. Applicants for the test must send £27.50 to include the first year's subscription of £7.50 and this amount is refunded if the applicant is unsuccessful in the test.

Exemption from the Test

Certain specially qualified drivers may apply to become Members of the Institute without taking the advanced driving test:
1. Royal Navy, Army and Royal Air Force hgv instructors and qualified testing officers who have passed an hgv instructor's course and whose application is supported by the recommendation of the applicant's Commanding Officer.
2. Holders of the Road Transport Industry Training Board Instructor's Certificate.
3. Fire Service hgv instructors who have completed an hgv instructor's course, and whose application is supported by the senior instructor.
4. Hgv driving examiners.

The Advanced Test

To pass the test the driver should show 'skill with responsibility' and any driver of reasonable experience and skill should be able to pass without difficulty. The Institute examiners are all ex-police drivers holding a Class 1 Police Driving Certificate, and they test candidates on routes located all over Britain.

The test lasts about 90 minutes, during which the test route of some 35-40 miles is covered. The route incorporates road conditions of all kinds including congested urban areas, main roads, narrow country lanes and residential streets. Candidates are not expected to display elaborate driving techniques. Examiners prefer to see the vehicle handled in a steady workmanlike manner without exaggeratedly slow speeds or excessive signalling. Speed limits must be observed (driving in excess of any limit results in test failure) and the driving manner must take into consideration road, traffic and weather conditions. However, the examiners expect candidates to drive briskly within the limits and to cruise at the legal limit (on the road or the vehicle, whichever is lower) whenever circumstances permit.

Drivers will be asked to reverse around a corner and to make a hill start. There will be spot checks on the driver's power of observation (ie the examiner will ask questions about road signs or markings recently passed or about other significant landmarks).

Examiners ask a number of questions of candidates but these are not trick questions. The requirement that once existed for the driver to give a running commentary during a portion of the route no longer exists – although the test regulations do state that candidates are free to give a commentary if they wish to make extra clear their ability to 'read the road'.

Test Requirements

The examiner will consider the following aspects of driving:

Acceleration: must be smooth and progressive, not excessive or insufficient and must be used at the right time and place.

8: DRIVING TESTS (ORDINARY – HGV – ADVANCED)

Braking: must be smooth and progressive, not fierce. Brakes should be used in conjunction with the driving mirror and signals. Road, traffic and weather conditions must be taken into account.

Clutch control: engine and road speeds should be properly co-ordinated when changing gear. The clutch should not be 'ridden' or slipped and the vehicle should not be coasted with the clutch disengaged.

Gear changing: should be smooth and carried out without jerking.

Use of gears: the gears should be correctly selected and used and the right gear engaged before reaching a hazard.

Steering: the wheel should be correctly held with the hands and the 'crossed arm' technique should not be used except when manoeuvring in confined spaces.

Driving position: the driver should be alert and should not slump at the wheel. Resting an arm on the door while driving should be avoided.

Observation: the driver should 'read' the road ahead and show a good sense of anticipation and the ability to judge speed and distance.

Concentration: the driver should keep his attention on the road and should not be easily distracted.

Maintaining progress: taking account of the road, traffic and weather conditions, the driver must keep up a reasonable pace and maintain good progress.

Obstruction: the candidate must be careful not to obstruct other vehicles by driving too slowly, taking up the wrong position on the road or failing to anticipate and react correctly to the traffic situation ahead.

Positioning: the driver must keep to the correct part of the road especially when approaching and negotiating hazards.

Lane discipline: the driver must keep to the appropriate lane and be careful not to straddle white lines.

Observations of road surfaces: the driver must keep an eye on the road surface especially in bad weather and should watch out for slippery conditions.

Traffic signals: signals, signs and road markings must be observed, obeyed and approached correctly and the driver should show courtesy at pedestrian crossings.

Speed limits and other legal requirements: these should be observed. The examiner cannot condone breaches of the law.

Overtaking: must be carried out safely and decisively maintaining the right distance from other vehicles and using the mirror, signals and gears correctly.

Hazard procedure and cornering: road and traffic hazards must be coped with properly, and bends and corners taken in the right manner.

Mirror: the mirror must be used frequently especially in conjunction with signals and before changing speed or course.

Signals: direction indicator, and hand signals when needed, must be given at the right place and in good time. The horn and headlamp flasher should be used in accordance with the Highway Code.

Restraint: the driver should show reasonable restraint, but not indecision, at the wheel.

Consideration: sufficient consideration and courtesy should be shown to other road users.

Vehicle sympathy: the driver should treat the vehicle with care, without overstressing it by needless revving of the engine and by fierce braking.

Manoeuvring: manoeuvres such as reversing should be performed smoothly and competently.

9: Vehicle Weights and Dimensions

EC and British law relating to the weights and dimensions of goods vehicles and trailers is extremely complex. Much of it is difficult for the operator to comprehend and apply and even worse for his driver who may, when loading, be the one having to make on-the-spot decisions which could later prove to be wrong, thereby breaching the law and bringing possible prosecution for himself and his employer. In May 1983 the maximum permissible weight for certain articulated vehicles was increased from 32.5 tonnes to 38 tonnes and other dimensional changes were introduced. In March 1990, the maximum length for certain articulated vehicles was increased to 16.5 metres with corresponding increases in semi-trailer length under the provisions of the Road Vehicles (Construction and Use) (Amendment) Regulations 1990. But these changes were combined with a more technically complex method of measurement and with very restrictive turning circle limitations which have caused many headaches in their interpretation and application. Other such vehicles not complying with the specification set out in regulations remain restricted to 15.5 metres. In due course there is the prospect of further weight increases to 35 tonnes for certain four-axle articulated vehicles and drawbar combinations, 40 tonnes for top weight articulated vehicles (and 44 tonnes for those carrying ISO containers) and further dimensional and weight increases as Britain aligns with European Directives aimed at ensuring Community-wide harmonisation by 1992 (see end of chapter).

The UK regulations in which these vehicle weights and dimension provisions are to be found are the Road Vehicles (Construction and Use) Regulations 1986 (as amended) as well as in specific EC Directives. These UK regulations also cover many other aspects of vehicle construction and use, but for ease of understanding the subject has been split into two separate chapters in this *Handbook*. This chapter deals with vehicle weights and dimensions and Chapter 10 deals with the other important topics under the Construction and Use regulations.

Length

Rigid and Articulated Vehicles

The maximum overall length permitted for rigid vehicles is 12 metres.

For certain articulated vehicles the maximum permitted length is 16.5 metres (see also below), provided the combination can turn within minimum and maximum swept inner and outer concentric circles of 5.3 metres radius and 12.5 metres radius respectively (see Figure 9.1), otherwise the maximum permitted length remains at the old limit of 15.5 metres. The swept circle requirements do not apply to low loader or step-frame low-loader combinations, car transporters, articulated vehicles constructed to carry indivisible loads of exceptional length, articulated vehicles with semi-trailers built or converted to increase their length prior to 1 April 1990 or to articulated vehicles not exceeding 15.5 metres overall length.

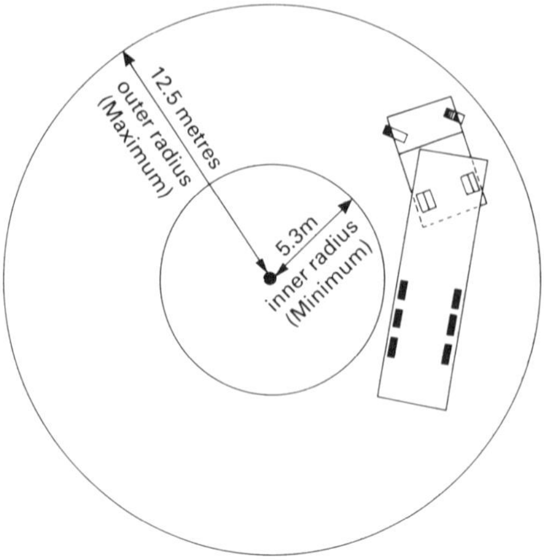

Figure 9.1 *The maximum and minimum outer and inner swept circles within which a new 16.5 metre long articulated vehicle must be able to turn*

For the purposes of enforcement of the turning circle requirements, the DTp has notified vehicle manufacturers that it will take a notional measurement from the king-pin to the centre line of the semi-trailer bogie. Where such a dimension does not exceed 7.8 metres the combination will be assumed to comply. Where this dimension exceeds 7.8 metres the DTp reserves the right to demand a turning circle demonstration on a steering pad.

The maximum overall length for an articulated vehicle incorporating a low-loader semi-trailer (but not a step-frame semi-trailer) is increased to 18 metres. Such vehicles do not have to meet the turning circle requirements described above.

Where an articulated vehicle is designed to carry indivisible loads of exceptional length there is no length restriction (an indivisible load means 'a load which cannot without undue expense or risk of damage be divided into two or more loads for the purpose of conveyance on a road').

Trailers

The maximum length for any drawbar trailer which has four or more wheels and is drawn by a vehicle which has a maximum gross weight exceeding 3500kg, is 12 metres. The same 12-metre maximum length limit also applies to agricultural trailers. The maximum permitted length for all other drawbar trailers is 7 metres.

Vehicle and Trailer Combinations (Drawbars)

When a rigid motor vehicle is drawing a trailer the maximum overall length for the combination is 18 metres. *NB: Although the maximum individual*

9: VEHICLE WEIGHTS AND DIMENSIONS

lengths for both drawing vehicle and trailer are 12 metres as stated, two such maximum length units obviously cannot be combined within the 18-metre limit.

The EC is proposing (in a draft Directive) to permit an increase in maximum length for drawbar combinations to 18.35 metres but combined with a maximum loadspace length of only 15.35 metres between the two bodies (current close-coupled drawbars operating within the present 18-metre length limit can achieve up to 16.2 metres loadspace). Also included in the proposal is a minimum cab length of 2.35 metres and a coupling length of 0.7 metres. This new limit is expected to apply to combinations used in international journeys from 1991, but has not yet been been legislated for in the UK.

When a trailer is designed for carrying indivisible loads of exceptional length the length of the drawing vehicle must not exceed 9.2 metres and the whole combination must not exceed 25.9 metres. When two or more trailers are drawn the overall length of the combination must not exceed 25.9 metres unless an attendant is carried and two days' notice is given to the police. When two trailers are drawn within the 25.9 metre limit mentioned here (ie only legally permissible with a vehicle classed as a motor tractor or locomotive), only one of the trailers may exceed an overall length of 7 metres. When three trailers are drawn (ie only legally possible with a vehicle classed as a locomotive) none of the trailers may exceed a length of 7 metres.

The limits do not apply when a broken-down vehicle (which is then legally classed as a trailer) is being towed.

Articulated Semi-trailers

The maximum permitted length for certain articulated vehicles was increased in March 1990 to 16.5 metres as stated above. This applies where such vehicles include a semi-trailer with a distance from the centre-line of the king-pin to the rear of the trailer which does not exceed 12 metres and where the distance from the king-pin (or rearmost king-pin if more than one) to the furthest point on the front corner of the trailer does not exceed 2.04 metres (4.19 metres for car transporters) – see Figure 9.2.

In practical terms this provides a loadspace length of up to 13.61 metres (including front and rear wall thicknesses/headboards, etc) with flat platform or dry-freight trailers (at 2.5 metres wide) or a maximum of only 13.57 metres in the case of refrigerated semi-trailers (at 2.6 metres wide) – see Figures 9.2 and 9.3. Dry freight semi-trailers built to the new lengths can accommodate 26 metric pallets (ie 1000 x 1200mm) or 33 Europallets (ie 800 x 1200mm).

Articulated semi-trailers built post-1 May 1983 are limited to a maximum length of 12.2 metres. There is no specified length limit for pre-May 1983 built semi-trailers. In measuring the 12.2-metre dimension no account need be taken of the thickness of front or rear walls or any parts in front of the front wall or behind the rear wall or closing device (ie door, shutter, etc). The thickness of any internal partitions must be included in the length measurement. This means effectively that the dimension relates only to load space between the front and rear walls (Figure 9.4).

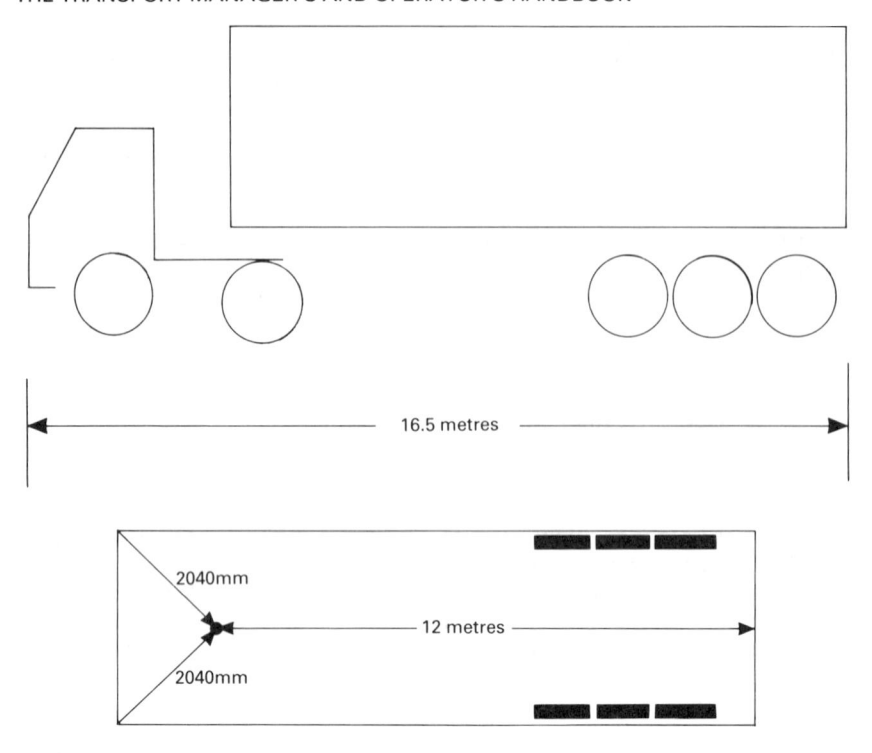

THE TRANSPORT MANAGER'S AND OPERATOR'S HANDBOOK

Figure 9.2 *The maximum dimensions for new articulated vehicles and semi-trailers*

Calculation of maximum front overhang (A) with 2.5 metre-wide semi-trailer

ie $2.04^2 - 1.3^2 = \sqrt{2.47} = A = 1.57$ metres

Total length 12 metres + 1.61 metres = 13.61m

Calculation of maximum front overhang (A) with 2.6 metre-wide (refrigerated) semi-trailer

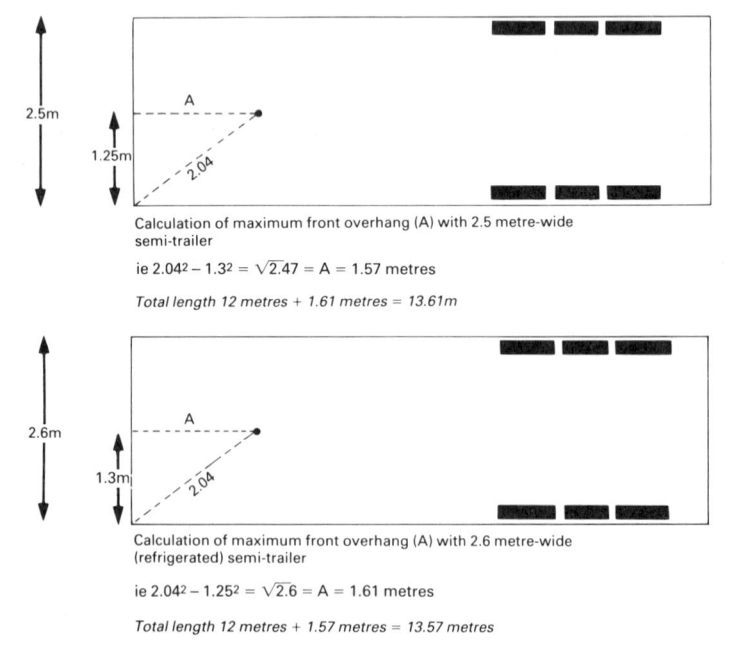

ie $2.04^2 - 1.25^2 = \sqrt{2.6} = A = 1.61$ metres

Total length 12 metres + 1.57 metres = 13.57 metres

Figure 9.3 *The calculation of semi-trailer lengths for operation under the new (1990) regulation amendments*

9: VEHICLE WEIGHTS AND DIMENSIONS

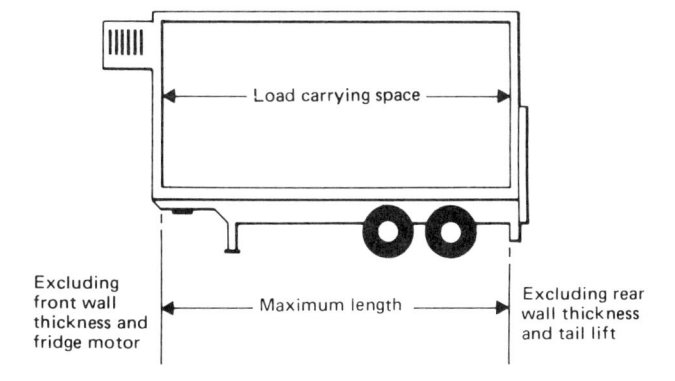

Figure 9.4 *Measurement of the maximum length dimension for pre-1990 and other semi-trailers not conforming to the new regulations*

The 12.2-metre length limit for semi-trailers as described does not apply to a trailer which is normally used on international journeys part of which are outside the UK. Similarly, articulated vehicles operating within the 15.5 metre on international journeys do not have to meet the turning circle requirements described above for 16.5 metre long vehicles.

Minimum Length

In the case of articulated combinations with maximum permissible weights above 32.5 tonnes, minimum overall length dimensions have to be observed. These range from 10 metres minimum length for 33 tonnes maximum weight to 12 metres minimum length for 38 tonnes maximum weight (see table on p 146). There is no minimum length requirement for articulated vehicles up to and including 32.5 tonnes maximum gross weight.

Measurement of Length

In measuring vehicle or trailer length account must be taken of any load-carrying receptacle (eg demountable body or container) used with the vehicle. In the case of drawbar combinations the length of the drawbar is excluded from overall length calculations. With dropside-bodied vehicles the length of the tailboard in the lowered (ie horizontal) position is excluded unless it is supporting part of the load in which case it must be included in the overall length measurement and for the purposes of establishing overhang limits (see below).

Overhang

Overhang is the distance by which the body and other parts of a vehicle extend beyond the rear axle. The maximum overhang permitted for rigid goods vehicles (ie motor cars and heavy motor cars) is 60 per cent of the distance between the centre of the front axle and the point from which the overhang is to be measured. The point from which overhang is measured is, in the case of two-axled vehicles, the centre line through the rear axle, and in the case of vehicles with three or more axles two of which are rear axles, 110mm to the rear of the centre line between the two rear axles (Figure 9.5).

This regulation does not apply to vehicles used solely in connection with street cleansing; the collection or disposal of refuse; the collection or disposal of the contents of gullies or cesspools; works trucks; or tipping vehicles, provided the total overhang does not exceed 1.15 metres (3ft 9in approx). There is no specified overhang limit on trailers.

Two-axled vehicles: Overhang 'x' must not exceed 60 per cent of length 'y'

110mm behind centre line of two axles

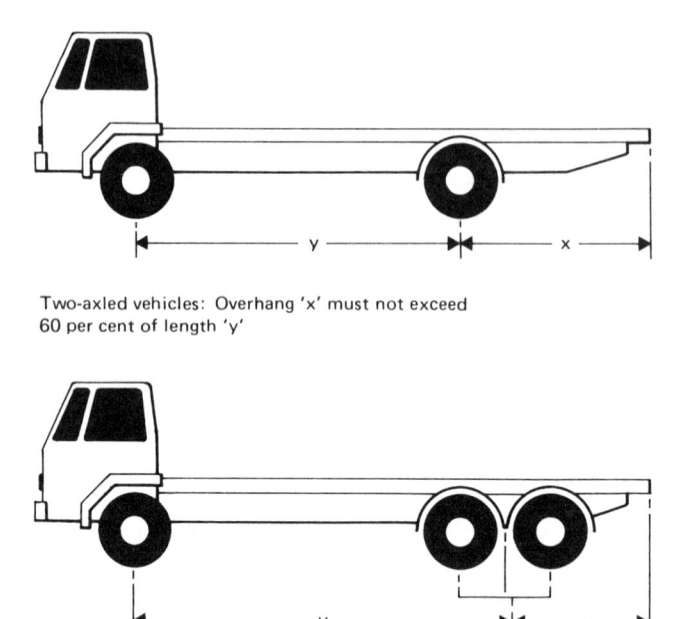

Figure 9.5 *How to measure overhang on vehicles with two axles, three axles and more. This measurement applies equally to two- and three-axled tractive units.*

Width

Motor Vehicles

The overall width of motor tractors, motor cars and heavy motor cars (most goods vehicles are included in these classifications) must not be more than 2.5 metres and the maximum width of locomotives must not be more than 2.75 metres.

Trailers

The maximum permissible width for trailers is 2.5 metres provided the drawing vehicle has a maximum permissible weight exceeding 3500kg. If the towing vehicle is below this weight, the width of the trailer must not exceed 2.3 metres.

Refrigerated Vehicles

The maximum permitted width for refrigerated (ie reefer) vehicles, semi-trailers and draw-bar trailers, is 2.60 metres provided the thickness of the side walls (inclusive of insulation) is at least 45mm. For the purposes of this regulation 'refrigerated vehicle' means a vehicle (or trailer) specially designed to carry goods at low temperature.

Height

Apart from the particular case mentioned below, there are currently no legal maximum height limits for other goods vehicles or for loads in Britain but these are, obviously, governed by the height of bridges on the routes on which the vehicles are operated. For general information, the minimum height of bridges on motorways, for example, is 16ft 6in and the maximum heights for buses is 4.57 metres.

The operator must bear in mind, however, that if he loads vehicles to a height which could cause danger he would be liable to prosecution under the Construction and Use Regulations. Also, if a vehicle were to be loaded to a height whereby the load hit a bridge on the route being used, the operator could be accused under these regulations of using a vehicle on a road for a purpose for which it was so unsuitable as to cause, or to be likely to cause, danger.

Regulations in some EC countries specify a height limit of 4 metres.

Height Limit on Vehicles over 32.5 tonnes

A maximum height limit of 4.2 metres is imposed on articulated vehicles operating at (ie laden to) weights in excess of 32.5 tonnes if the semi-trailer has a maximum permitted weight exceeding 26 tonnes. This height limit does not apply to any other articulated combination (or to any other vehicles or trailers – see above).

Measurement of the height is taken when the vehicle is standing on level ground and it extends to the top of any part of the structure of the vehicle, including the top of any detachable structure attached to the vehicle for containing a load (eg, demountable bodies and containers). The height limit does not include loads themselves or sheets, ropes, webbing straps, nets, chains or any other flexible securing device. It does not apply at the time when vehicles are being loaded or unloaded nor does it apply when their laden weight is reduced to 32.5 tonnes or less.

Height Marking

When vehicles or trailers are used to carry containers, engineering equipment or skip loaders, the height of the vehicle and its load must be indicated to the driver in the vehicle cab if the height exceeds 12 feet (3.66 metres). The height marking, in letters and figures at least 40mm tall, must show the 'travelling height' to within one inch. For the purpose of this regulation 'containers' means containers of a type which are not in themselves a vehicle or trailer (ie it excludes box vans and box van trailers) and which have a volume of at least 8 cubic metres. This clearly means that demountable bodies are included. Travelling height is the maximum height of the vehicle or its load measured from a level road surface.

Weight

Maximum permitted weights (the total weight of the vehicle and load, including the weight of fuel, and the driver and passenger if carried) for goods vehicles and trailers depend on their wheelbase, the number of axles, the outer axle spread (the distance between the centre of the wheels on the front and rearmost axles) or the relevant axle spacing in the case of articulated vehicles (see p 149).

All goods vehicles over 1525kg unladen weight (and trailers over 1020kg unladen weight) should be fitted with a DTp plate (see p 215) on which is shown, for that vehicle, the maximum permissible axle weights and gross weight (or in the case of articulated vehicles, the combined weight of the tractive unit and trailer) for that vehicle in Great Britain.

The maximum permissible weights for different types of vehicle are shown in the following tables:

Rigid Vehicle and Trailer Weights

	kg
Two-axled vehicles:	
• where the distance between the axles is less than 2.65 metres	14,230
• in the case of a trailer other than an articulated trailer, which has a wheelbase of less than 2.65 metres but the former axle of which is at least 4.2 metres from the rear axle of the drawing vehicle	16,260
• where the distance between the axles is at least 2.65 metres	16,260
• where the distance between the axles is at least 3.0 metres	17,000
• in the case of *trailers only* where the distance between the axles is at least 3.0 metres	18,000
Three-axled vehicles:	
• Must not exceed 16,260kg except as shown below:	
• where the distance between the foremost and rearmost axle is at least 3 metres	18,290
• where the distance between the foremost and rearmost axle is at least 3.2 metres and the maximum axle weight is not more than 8,130kg	20,330
• where the distance between the foremost and rearmost axle is at least 3.9 metres and the maximum axle weight is more than 10,170kg	20,330
• where the distance between the foremost and rearmost axle is at least 3.9 metres and the maximum axle weight is not more than 8,640kg	22,360
• where the distance between the foremost and rearmost axle is at least 4.6 metres and the maximum axle weight is more than 10,170kg	22,360

9: VEHICLE WEIGHTS AND DIMENSIONS

- where the distance between the foremost and rearmost axle is at least 4.9 metres and the maximum axle weight is not more than 9,400kg   24,390
- where the distance between the foremost and rearmost axle is at least 5.1 metres and the maximum axle weight is more than 10,170kg   24,390

Vehicles with four or more axles:
- Shall not exceed 18,290kg except as shown below:
- where the distance between the foremost and rearmost axle is at least 3.7 metres and the maximum axle weight is not more than 8,640kg   20,330
- where the distance between the foremost and rearmost axle is at least 4.6 metres and the maximum axle weight is not more than 8,640kg   22,360
- where the distance between the foremost and rearmost axle is at least 4.7 metres and the maximum axle weight is not more than 8,640kg   24,390
- where the distance between the foremost and rearmost axle is at least 5 metres and the maximum axle weight is not more than 9,150kg   24,390
- where the distance between the foremost and rearmost axle is at least 5.6 metres and the maximum axle weight is not more than 9,150kg   26,420
- where the distance between the foremost and rearmost axle is at least 6 metres and the maximum axle weight is not more than 9,660kg   26,420
- where the distance between the foremost and rearmost axle is at least 5.9 metres and the maximum axle weight is not more than 9,150kg   28,450
- where the distance between the foremost and rearmost axle is at least 6.3 metres and the maximum axle weight is not more than 9,660kg   28,450
- where the distance between the foremost and rearmost axle is at least 6.3 metres and the maximum axle weight is not more than 9,400kg   30,490
- where the distance between the foremost and rearmost axle is at least 6.5 metres and the maximum axle weight is not more than 9,660kg   30,490

Articulated Vehicle Weights

The maximum weights for different classes of articulated vehicles based on the number of axles (subject to plated weights and axle spacings) are as shown in the table below:

Type of articulated vehicle	Maximum weight (kg)
1. Motor vehicle and semi-trailer having a total of three axles	24,390
2. Motor vehicle and semi-trailer having a total of four axles or motor vehicle first used before 1 April 1973 and semi-trailer having a total of five or more axles	32,520

3. Motor vehicle first used on or after 1 April 1973 and semi-trailer having a total of five or more axles   38,000

Maximum permitted Laden Weights for Articulated Tractive Units
The maximum permitted laden weights for articulated *tractive* units based on the number of axles and the axle spacing (ie distance between foremost and rearmost axles – see Figure 9.6) is as follows:

Number of axles of motor vehicle	Spacings between foremost axle and rearmost axle (m)	Intermediate axle weight (kg)	Max weight transmitted to road by all wheels of vehicle (kg)
2	at least 2.0	–	14,230
2	at least 2.4	–	16,260
2	at least 2.7	–	17,000 (provided vehicle has a relevant train weight of more than 32,520 kg)
3 or more	at least 3.0	not over 8,390	20,330
3 or more	at least 3.8	not over 8,640	22,360
3 or more	at least 4.0	not over 10,500	22,500
3 or more	at least 4.3	not over 9,150	24,390
3 or more	at least 4.9	not over 10,500	24,390

Maximum permitted Laden Weights for Articulated Vehicles
The maximum permitted laden weight for *complete articulated vehicles* (ie tractive unit and semi-trailer) depending on the number of axles of the tractive unit, the relevant axle spacing (ie rearmost axle of tractive unit to rearmost axle of semi-trailer – see Figure 9.5) and the minimum overall length (in some cases only) is as follows:

Relevant axle spacing (m)		Maximum weight (kg)	Minimum overall length (m)
Where motor vehicle has 2 axles	Where motor vehicle has at least 3 axles		
less than 2.2	less than 2.2	20,330	–
at least 2.2	at least 2.2	22,360	–
at least 2.6	at least 2.6	23,370	–
at least 2.9	at least 2.9	24,390	–
at least 3.2	at least 3.2	25,410	–
at least 3.5	at least 3.5	26,420	–
at least 3.8	at least 3.8	27,440	–
at least 4.1	at least 4.1	28,450	–
at least 4.4	at least 4.4	29,470	–
at least 4.7	at least 4.7	30,490	–
at least 5.0	at least 5.0	31,500	–
at least 5.3	at least 5.3	32,520	–
at least 5.5	at least 5.4	33,000	10.0
at least 5.8	at least 5.6	34,000	10.3

9: VEHICLE WEIGHTS AND DIMENSIONS

at least 6.2	at least 5.8	35,000	10.5
at least 6.5	at least 6.0	36,000	11.0
at least 6.7	at least 6.2	37,000	11.5
at least 6.9	at least 6.3	38,000	12.0

Axle Spacing for Articulated Vehicles

For the purposes of determining articulated vehicle weights a dimension referred to as the 'relevant axle spacing' is used. This is defined as 'the distance between the rearmost axle of the drawing vehicle (ie the tractive unit) and the rearmost axle of the semi-trailer' (Figure 9.6).

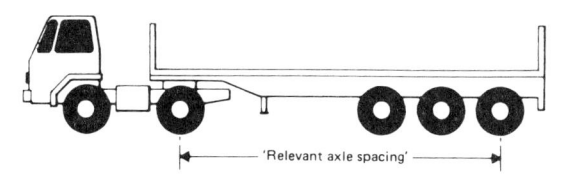

Figure 9.6 *Measurement of axle spacing for articulated vehicles*

Lorry and Trailer Combination Weights

Lorry and trailer (ie drawbar) combinations must not exceed 24390kg gross combination weight (gcw). If, however, the trailer is fitted with power assisted brakes which remain operative even when the drawing vehicle's engine is not running and a brake pressure warning device is provided in the driver's cab the combination may operate (if it is so plated) at up to 32520kg gross combination weight.

Trailer Weights

The maximum laden weight permitted for unbraked trailers is not more than half the unladen weight of the towing vehicle.

Trailers with overrun brakes are limited to a maximum laden weight of 3500kg unless they were first manufactured before 27 February 1977 in which case their maximum laden weight is 3560kg (these limits do not apply to agricultural trailers).

The maximum permissible weight for trailers used in draw-bar combinations is 18 tonnes provided the trailer has an axle spacing of at least 3 metres and is plated for 18 tonnes.

Axle and Wheel Weights

Maximum permitted axle and wheel weights (ie the total weight which may be imposed by an axle or a wheel on the road surface when the vehicle is fully loaded) for vehicles is as follows:

Axle/wheel type	Maximum permitted weight transmitted to road (kg)
1. Two wheels in line transversely each of which is fitted with a wide tyre or with two pneumatic tyres having the centres of their areas of contact with the road, not less than 300mm apart, measured at right angles to the longitudinal axis of the vehicle	
(a) if the wheels are on the sole driving axle of a motor vehicle and the relevant train weight shown on the plate of that vehicle exceeds 32,520kg	10,500
(b) if the vehicle is a bus which has 2 axles and of which the weight transmitted to the road surface by its wheels is calculated in accordance with C & U regulations	10,500
(c) in any other case	10,170
2. Two wheels in line transversely otherwise than as mentioned in item 1	9,200
3. More than two wheels in line transversely	
(a) in the case of a vehicle manufactured before 1 May 1983 if the wheels are on one axle of a group of two closely spaced axles or on one of three adjacent axles as mentioned in the C & U regulations	10,170
(b) in the case of a vehicle manufactured on or after 1 May 1983	10,170
(c) in any other case	11,180
4. One wheel not transversely in line with any other wheel	
(a) if the wheel is fitted as described in item 1	5,090
(b) in any other case	4,600
5. More than two wheels transmitting weight on to a strip of the road surface on which the vehicle rests contained between two parallel lines at right angles to the longitudinal axis of the vehicle	
(a) less than 1.02m apart	11,180
(b) 1.02m or more apart but less than 1.22m apart	16,260
(c) 1.22m or more apart but less than 2.13m apart	18,300
6. Two wheels in line transversely	9,200
7. One wheel, where no other wheel is in the same line transversely	4,600

Maximum permitted weights for two closely spaced axles

Distance between axles (m)	Max weight when plated weight of neither axle exceeds half of the specified weight in kg	Max weight in cases not within column 3 when plated weight of neither axle exceeds 10,170	Max weight in cases not within columns 3 or 4 (kg)
1. at least 1.02	16,260	12,200	10,500
2. at least 1.05	17,280	15,260	10,500
3. at least 1.20	18,300	16,270	15,260
4. at least 1.35	18,800	17,280	16,500
5. at least 1.50	19,320	18,300	18,000
6. at least 1.80	20,000	19,000	19,000
7. at least 1.85	20,340	19,320	19,320

9: VEHICLE WEIGHTS AND DIMENSIONS

Maximum permitted weights for three closely spaced axles

Smallest distance between any adjoining axles of three closely spaced axles	Maximum weight for any one of three closely spaced axles (m)
1. at least 0.70	6,000
2. at least 0.80	6,200
3. at least 0.90	6,400
4. at least 1.00	6,600
5. at least 1.10	6,900
6. at least 1.20	7,100
7. at least 1.30	7,500*

*NB See item below about tri-axle bogies with air suspensions.

Maximum permitted weights for three adjacent axles

Distance between foremost and rearmost axles (m)	Maximum intermediate axle weight (kg)	Maximum permitted total weight (kg)
1. Less than 3.0	10,170	18,290
2. At least 3.0	8,390	20,330
3. At least 3.8	8,640	22,360
4. At least 4.6	9,150	24,390

Maximum Weight for Air-sprung Tri-axle Bogies

Tri-axle bogies with air suspension are permitted a maximum laden weight of 8 tonnes per axle instead of the 7.5 tonnes allowed on individual axles in tri-axle bogies with other types of suspension. In order to qualify for this increase there must not be more than 500kg weight difference between the axles under any condition of load.

Overall Weight Limits

The total weight of the load on a vehicle, together with the weight of the vehicle itself, must not exceed the maximum permitted weight for each individual axle or for the vehicle.

Notional Weights (Multipliers)

Regulations enable a notional gross weight to be determined for unplated vehicles and trailers from an unladen weight for driver licensing purposes. The regulations specify a wide variety of vehicle types but the most important are:
1. Heavy motor cars or motor cars first used before 1 January 1968 or locomotives or motor tractors first used before 1 April 1973 – *multiply unladen weight by factor of 2.*
2. Articulated vehicles – *multiply the combined unladen weights of the tractive unit and the semi-trailer by a factor of 2.5.*

See p 120 for full list of multipliers.

Weight Offences

It is an offence on the part of both the driver and the vehicle operator (ie the driver's employer) to operate a goods vehicle on a road laden to a weight above that at which it has been plated by the DTp (ie above the maximum permitted gross and individual axle weights) and both are liable to prosecution. Such offences are 'absolute' in that once the actual overweight has been established – and there are *NO* tolerances allowed – the fact that it was a deliberate action to gain extra revenue or purely accidental, unintentional, outside the driver or vehicle operator's control or loading was in a place where no weighing facilities existed, is of no consequence in defending against the charge.

Defence
There is no defence of 'due diligence' against charges of overloading, something for which the Road Haulage Association has been campaigning, but it is a defence under the Road Traffic Act 1988 (section 42) to prove that at the time the contravention was detected the vehicle was proceeding to the nearest available weighbridge or was returning from such weighbridge to the nearest point at which it was reasonably practicable to remove the excess load. However, there have been instances reported where successful defences have been made against conviction where the operator was able to show that he had no way of knowing or controlling the weight placed on a vehicle.

It is a further defence, where the weight exceeds maximum limits by not more than 5 per cent, to prove that the weight was within legal limits at the time of loading the vehicle and that no person had since added anything to the load.

Penalties
Overloading offences are looked upon very seriously by the enforcement authorities and by the courts and very heavy penalties are imposed on offenders. In addition to punitive fines (currently a maximum of £2000 per offence – an overloaded vehicle could result in a number of individual offences related to gross and axle weights), the operator risks losing his 'O' licence and the driver could put his hgv driving licence in jeopardy.

Prohibition of Overweight Vehicles
Any vehicle on a road found by a vehicle examiner to be overloaded to the extent that it could endanger public safety will be ordered off the road immediately. The necessary powers to enable this step to be taken are included in Section 70 (2) and (3) of the 1988 Road Traffic Act and they empower an authorised officer to prohibit the driving of a goods vehicle on a road if after having it weighed it appears to him that the vehicle exceeds the relevant weight limits imposed by the Construction and Use Regulations, and as a result would be an immediate risk to public safety if it were used on a road. The officer may be one of the DTp's examiners or a specially authorised weights and measures inspector or a police constable.

A prohibition notice, form GV160, will be issued to the driver of a vehicle found to be overweight and it is the driver's responsibility to remove the excess weight to his own satisfaction and clear the GV160 before proceeding on his journey. The penalty for ignoring a prohibition notice is a fine of up to £1000.

Official Weighing of Vehicles
Under the Road Traffic Act 1988 an authorised officer can request the

9: VEHICLE WEIGHTS AND DIMENSIONS

person in charge of a vehicle to drive to a weighbridge to be weighed. If the journey is more than five miles and on arrival the vehicle is found to be within the legal limit then the vehicle owner can claim for the loss involved in making the journey. It is an offence to refuse to go to a weighbridge if requested (maximum fine currently £1000). Once a vehicle has been weighed it will be exempt from further requests for weighing while carrying the same load on that journey.

Dynamic Weighers
Provisions regarding the weighing of vehicles are contained in the 1974 and 1988 Road Traffic Acts which give the Secretary of State for Transport powers to make regulations regarding the method of weighing vehicles and to specify the limits within which a weight determined by a weighbridge is presumed to be accurate. Regulations are in force to permit the dynamic weighing of vehicles at the roadside (see also p 367).

Portable Weighers
There have been reports of Trading Standards officers in some areas using portable axle weigh-pads as a means of checking vehicle/axle weights and have brought overloading prosecutions against operators based on such weighings. There is considerable doubt about the accuracy of such machines and the Road Haulage Association has expressed its concern about their use.

Weight and Dimension Increases

There is constant discussion and press reportage of proposals to increase vehicle weights and dimensions. With the prospect of 1992 and all that this entails in regard to the harmonisation of vehicle weights and dimensions throughout Europe, there has been renewed pressure on the government to increase the limit for top weight articulated vehicles to the EC standard of 40 tonnes and the maximum weight for drawbar combinations – currently restricted to 32.52 tonnes – to 36 tonnes. For two, three and four axle rigid vehicles the EC requirements are for increases to 18, 25 and 32 tonnes respectively replacing the current limits of 17, 24.39 and 30.49 tonnes. We also need to see the introduction of EC-standard 11.5-tonne drive axles in Britain to enable these higher limits to be achieved.

Note: It should be stressed that at present all of these weights and dimensions are contained only in EC Directives; definite dates for their implementation in the UK have not yet been determined. The existing limits as shown in this chapter should be strictly observed until such changes are confirmed.

10: Construction and Use of Vehicles

In constructing goods vehicles and trailers, manufacturers and bodybuilders must observe requirements regarding the specification and standards of construction of components and the equipment used in the manufacture. While some of these items are covered by the Type Approval scheme (see Chapter 11), the majority are included in the Road Vehicles (Construction and Use) Regulations 1986 (Statutory Instrument 1078/1986 HMSO) and subsequent amendments to these regulations.

Once a goods vehicle or trailer has been built and put into service, it is the operator as the vehicle user (see p 18) who must then ensure that it complies fully with the law regarding its construction and use when on the road. It is worth pointing out that where a vehicle on the road is found to contravene the constructional aspects of the regulations, it is the operator who will be prosecuted and if convicted he will be liable to meet the penalty and may find that it jeopardises his 'O' licence. It is no defence or excuse to say that the fault with the vehicle rests with the manufacturer, bodybuilder or even the supplying dealer.

Only the main items from the regulations and amendments which concern the goods vehicle operator and transport manager are included in this chapter. Those aspects of the regulations dealing with the limitations on vehicle weights and dimensions are covered in Chapter 9. The provisions of the C & U regulations dealing with safe operation and safety of vehicles and loads are explained in Chapter 17. Many other points relating to a wide variety of other types of vehicle (motor bicycles and invalid carriages, for example) are not included because they are not generally thought to be relevant to the reader of this *Handbook*.

Definitions of Vehicles

For the purpose of these regulations the following definitions, as given in the Road Traffic Act 1988, apply:
- A **goods vehicle** is a vehicle or a trailer adapted or constructed to carry a load.
- A **motor car** is a vehicle which, if adapted for the carriage of goods, has an unladen weight not exceeding 3050kg but otherwise has an unladen weight not exceeding 2540kg.
- A **heavy motor car** is a vehicle constructed to carry goods or passengers with an unladen weight exceeding 3050kg.
- A **motor tractor** is a vehicle which is not constructed to carry a load and has an unladen weight not exceeding 7370kg.
- A **light locomotive** is a vehicle which is not constructed to carry a load and which has an unladen weight of more than 7370kg but not exceeding 11690kg.
- A **heavy locomotive** is a vehicle which is not constructed to carry a load and which has an unladen weight exceeding 11690kg.
- An **articulated vehicle** as defined in the Construction and Use Regulations is a motor car or heavy motor car with a trailer so attached

that when the trailer is uniformly loaded, at least 20 per cent of the weight of the load is imposed on the drawing vehicle.
- A **composite trailer** is a combination of a converter dolly and a semi-trailer, and is treated as one trailer only when considering the number of trailers which may be drawn.
- **Engineering plant** means movable plant or equipment in the form of a motor vehicle or trailer which is specially designed and constructed for the purposes of engineering operations and which cannot, for this reason, comply with the C & U Regulations. Also it is constructed to carry only materials which it had excavated from the ground and which is specially designed to treat while being carried. It also means mobile cranes which do not conform in all respects with the C & U Regulations.
- A **land tractor** means a tractor with an unladen weight not exceeding 7370kg which is designed and primarily used for work on the land in connection with agriculture, grass cutting, forestry, land levelling, dredging or similar operations. To comply with this definition the tractor must be owned by a person engaged in agriculture or forestry or a contractor engaged in this business; it must not be constructed or adapted to carry any load other than its own loose equipment, or a load consisting of agricultural or woodland produce within 15 miles of a farm or forestry estate owned by the person who owns the tractor, or implements fitted to the tractor, for work on land or for forestry.
- A **pedestrian controlled vehicle** means a motor vehicle which is controlled by a pedestrian and which is not constructed or adapted to carry a driver or passenger.
- A **works truck** means a motor vehicle (other than a straddle carrier) designed for use in private premises and used on a road only in delivering goods from or to such premises, or from a vehicle on a road in the immediate neighbourhood, or in passing from one part of the premises to another or to other private premises in the immediate neighbourhood, or in connection with road works or in the immediate vicinity of the site of such works.
- A **works trailer** means a trailer used for the same purposes as a works truck.

Constructional Requirements

Brakes

All goods vehicles must meet specified braking efficiencies. The regulations state minimum efficiencies for the service brake, for the secondary brake, and for the parking brake or handbrake. On pre-1968 vehicles the secondary brake can be the handbrake and on post-1968 vehicles it can be a split or dual system operated by the footbrake. If it is the latter it must be capable of meeting the secondary requirement if part of the dual system fails. The parking brake must achieve the required efficiency by direct mechanical action or by the energy of a spring without the assistance of stored energy.

Every vehicle must have a parking brake system to prevent at least two wheels from turning when it is not being driven. All vehicles first used after 1 January 1968 must have an independent parking brake.

10: CONSTRUCTION AND USE OF VEHICLES

Anti-lock (ie anti-skid) braking systems will be required on certain new articulated vehicles and drawbar trailer combinations under EC legislation and under British regulations currently in draft form. The vehicles affected are rigid goods vehicles over 16 tonnes equipped to draw trailers first used from 1 April 1992 and trailers over 10 tonnes built on or after 1 October 1991.

Specified Braking Efficiencies
Vehicles used before 1 January 1968:

Two-axle rigid vehicles	Service brake	45 per cent
	Secondary brake	20 per cent
Multi-axled rigid vehicles, trailer combinations and articulated vehicles	Service brake	40 per cent
	Secondary brake	15 per cent

Vehicles first used on or after 1 January 1968:

All vehicles	Service brake	50 per cent
	Secondary brake	25 per cent
	Parking brake – must be capable of holding the vehicle on a gradient of at least 1 in 6.25 without the assistance of stored energy (1 in 8.33 with a trailer attached).	

Maintenance of Brakes

The braking system on a vehicle, including all of its components and means of operation must be maintained in good and efficient working order and must be properly adjusted at all times.

Braking Standards

The regulations reflect the requirements for braking standards laid down in EC Directives 320/1973, 524/1975 and 489/1979 (as amended). These call for the fitting of load sensing valves or anti-lock braking on drive axles – most modern tractive units already comply with these requirements – and the overall emphasis is on stability, eliminating jack-knifing and trailer swing. EC rules permit the use of two-line air braking systems instead of the traditional British three-line systems. Most older tractive units in the UK have three-line braking systems fitted with yellow, blue and red couplings.

Vehicles built to the European standard have only two lines (red and yellow or two black). Coupling three-line tractive units to three-line trailers, two-line tractive units to two-line trailers and two-line tractive units to three-line trailers presents no difficulties. Problems arise when coupling three-line tractive units to two-line trailers. Such combinations must not be used unless they are specially designed or modified by fitting a fourth coupling or internal valves and connecting pipework.

On tractive units first registered before 1 April 1983 a notice should be displayed stating that the system is suitable for coupling. If no such notice is displayed the driver should check the system to see if it is suitable for coupling.

The Department of Transport has issued a free drivers' advice leaflet *'3 into 2 can Go'* which can be obtained from hgv goods vehicle testing stations. A poster with a similar message is also available for display in premises. For fleet operators a free booklet *Braking Connections for Goods Vehicles and Trailers* is available from: DOE/DTp Publicity Stores, Building No 3, Victoria Road, South Ruislip, Middlesex HA4 0NZ.

Brakes on Trailers
Trailers constructed before 1 January 1968 must have an efficient braking system on half the number of wheels. Trailers constructed after this date must be fitted with brakes operating on all wheels which are capable of being applied by the driver of the drawing vehicle and having maximum efficiencies matching the braking requirement for the drawing vehicle, emergency brakes operating on at least two wheels and a parking brake capable of holding the trailer on a gradient of at least 1 in 6.25.

Overrun Brakes
Overrun brakes may be fitted to trailers not exceeding 3500kg gross weight (or 3560kg if made before 27 February 1977). Overrun brake couplings must be damped and matched with the brake linkage. Normally, to ensure that these standards are met, the coupling design needs to be type approved. Trailer braking efficiency must be at least 45 per cent and the parking brake must be capable of holding the laden trailer on a gradient of 1 in 6.25 (ie 16 per cent). Modern braked trailers must also be fitted with an emergency device which automatically applies the brakes if the trailer becomes uncoupled from the towing vehicle. This does not apply to single axle trailers up to 1500kg gross weight provided they are fitted with a safety chain or cable to stop the coupling head touching the road if the trailer becomes detached.

Light Trailer Brakes
Light trailers must be fitted with brakes if:
1. Their maximum gross weight exceeds 750kg and their unladen weight exceeds 102kg; or
2. Their maximum gross weight exceeds 750kg and they were built on or after 1 October 1982; or
3. Their laden weight on the road exceeds half the towing vehicle's kerbside weight (this does not apply to agricultural trailers or to trailers whose unladen weight does not exceed 102kg and which were built before 1 October 1982).

Unbraked trailers must have their maximum gross weight marked in kilograms in a conspicuous position on the nearside.

Parked Trailers
When trailers are detached from the towing vehicle they must be prevented from rolling by means of a brake, chain or chock applied to at least one of their wheels.

Lifting Axles

Draft amendments to the Construction and Use regulations currently in

10: CONSTRUCTION AND USE OF VEHICLES

circulation (and planned for introduction on 1 January 1991) are intended to introduce controls on the use of manually and automatically-retractable axles. The object of the regulations is to ensure that the use, or incorrect use, of such axles does not result in the other axles of the vehicle becoming overloaded. The regulations will ban in-cab control of lift-axles except for a facility to provide additional traction for brief periods only (60 seconds or 90 seconds with trailer lift-axles). When one axle of a tandem bogie is retracted, it is proposed that the remaining axle will be limited to 50 per cent of the permitted bogie weight and with tri-axle bogies the remaining axles should bear not more than 60 per cent of the maximum permitted bogie weight. The current definition of overhang is to be amended to disregard rear-fitted retractable axles (measurement of the wheelbase with a tandem-axle bogie will then be to the drive axle, not from a point behind the midway point between the axles – see Figure 9.5) and the regulations will classify self-tracking axles as steering axles for the purposes of definitions.

Tyres

It is an offence to use, or cause or permit to be used on a road, a vehicle or a trailer with a pneumatic tyre which is unsuitable for the use to which the vehicle is being put. It is also an offence to have different types of tyres fitted to opposite wheels of the vehicle or trailer; for example, radial-ply tyres must not be fitted to a wheel on the same axle as wheels already fitted with cross-ply tyres and vice versa. Tyres must be inflated to the vehicle or tyre manufacturers' recommended pressures so as to be fit for the use to which the vehicle is being put (for example, motorway work or cross-country work). No tyre must have a break in its fabric or a cut deep enough to reach the body cords, more than 25mm or 10 per cent of its section width in length, whichever is the greater; also there must be no lump, bulge or tear caused by separation or partial fracture of its structure, neither must there be any portion of the ply or cord structure exposed.

Approval Marks on Tyres
It is an offence to sell motor car tyres unless they carry an 'E' mark to show compliance with EC load and speed requirements. It is also an offence to sell retreaded car or lorry tyres unless they are manufactured and marked in accordance with British Standard BS AU 144b 1977.

From 1 October 1990 it has been a requirement for tyres on heavy goods vehicles to show load and speed markings in accordance with UN ECE Regulation 30 or 54. It is a legal requirement that these limits of both loading and speed performance are strictly observed. Failure to do so can result in prosecution and could invalidate insurance claims in the event of an accident to a vehicle loaded above the weight limit of the tyres or travelling at a speed in excess of the tyre limit.

Tread Depth
All tyres must have a tread depth of at least 1mm across three-quarters of the breadth of the tread and around the entire circumference of the tyre. This 1mm tread depth must be in a continuous band around the entire circumference of the tyre. Further, on the remaining one quarter of the

width of the tyre where there is no requirement for the tread to be 1mm deep, the base of the original grooves must be clearly visible.

From 1 January 1992 the minimum tread depth for cars, light vans and light trailers will be increased to 1.6mm and this will apply across the central three-quarters of the width of the tyre and in a continuous band around the entire circumference. The 1mm limit stated above will remain in force for heavy goods vehicles.

Recut Tyres
Recut tyres may be fitted to goods vehicles of over 2540kg unladen weight which have wheels of at least 405mm rim diameter and to trailers weighing more than 1020kg unladen weight and electric vehicles. They must not be used on private cars, dual-purpose vehicles, goods vehicles or trailers of less than the weight or wheel size specified.

Run-Flat and Temporary Use Spare Tyres
The regulations permit the legal use of 'run-flat' tyres in a partially inflated or flat condition and what are described as temporary use spare tyres. This is of more consequence to motor car users because the only tyres of the former (ie run-flat) type currently available are designed for a limited range of private cars (eg Dunlop Denovo tyres). Where a temporary use spare tyre is being used the vehicle speed must not exceed 50mph otherwise the legal provision which permits their use ceases to apply. The temporary use spare tyre or the wheel to which it is fitted must be of a different colour to the other wheels on the vehicle and a label must be attached to the wheel giving clear information about the precautions to be observed when using the wheel.

Lightweight Trailer Tyres
Tyres fitted to lightweight trailers since 1 April 1987 must be designed and maintained to support the maximum axle weight at its maximum permitted speed (ie 60mph).

Guidance on Tyres
An explanatory leaflet called *Tyres and the Law* is available free of charge from: Usercare, SP Tyres UK Limited, Fort Dunlop, Birmingham B24 9QT.

Windscreen Wipers and Washers

All vehicles must be fitted with one or more efficient automatic windscreen wipers capable of clearing the windscreen to provide the driver with an adequate view to the front and sides of the vehicle. They must be maintained in good and efficient working order and must be adjusted properly. This provision does not apply if the driver can get an adequate view of the road without looking through the windscreen.

Washers
Vehicles required to be fitted with windscreen wipers must be fitted with a

10: CONSTRUCTION AND USE OF VEHICLES

windscreen washer which is capable, in conjunction with the wipers, of clearing the area of the windscreen swept by the wipers of mud or dirt. Washers are not required on land tractors, track-laying vehicles and vehicles which cannot travel at more than 20mph.

Mirrors

Goods vehicles and dual-purpose vehicles must be fitted with at least two mirrors. One of these must be fitted externally on the offside and the other must, in the case of vehicles first used since 1 June 1978, be fitted in the driver's cab or driving compartment. When an interior mirror does not provide an adequate view to the rear, a mirror must be fitted externally on the near side. The mirrors must show traffic to the rear or on both sides rearwards. Mirrors fitted to vehicles over 3500kg must conform to Class II and those fitted to other vehicles with Class II or III as described in EC Directive 127/71.

Fitment of Mirrors
External mirrors with a bottom edge less than 2 metres from the ground (when the vehicle is loaded) must not project more than 20cm beyond the overall width of the vehicle or vehicle and trailer. Mirrors fitted on the offside must be adjustable from the driving seat unless they are of the spring-back type. Internal mirrors fitted to vehicles first registered on or after 1 April 1969 must be framed with some material (usually plastic beading) which will reduce the risk of cuts to passengers who may be thrown against the mirror.

Type Approval for Mirrors
Since 1 June 1978 vehicles must be fitted with rear view mirrors bearing the EC type approval 'E' mark. The relevant date for the implementation of this requirement to Ford Transit vehicles was 10 July 1978 instead of 1 June 1978 which was the date for all other vehicles.

Wide Angle Mirrors
Goods vehicles over 12 tonnes maximum permissible weight first used since 1 October 1988 must be fitted with additional mirrors which provide close proximity and wide angle vision for the driver in accordance with EC Directive 205/85.

Horn

All vehicles with a maximum speed exceeding 20mph, except works trucks and passenger-controlled vehicles, must be equipped with an audible warning instrument. The sound emitted by a horn must be continuous and uniform and not strident. Gongs, bells, sirens and two-tone horns are only permitted on emergency vehicles but a concession allows similar instruments, except two-tone horns, to be used on vehicles from which goods are sold to announce the presence of the vehicle to the public. Any vehicle first used since 1 August 1973 must not be fitted with multi-toned or musical horns.

Restriction on Sounding Horns
Audible warning instruments must not be sounded at any time while the

vehicle is stationary or in built-up areas (ie where 30mph speed restriction is in force) between 11.30 pm and 7 am (see also item about reversing alarms on p 187). The use of the horn on a stationary vehicle in an emergency situation (ie 'at times of danger due to another moving vehicle on or near the road') is allowed.

Horns Used as Anti-Theft Devices

Audible warning instruments which are gongs, bells or sirens may be used to prevent theft or attempted theft of a vehicle provided a device is fitted which will stop the warning sounding continuously for more than five minutes.

Speedometer

Speedometers (and/or tachographs, as appropriate – see Chapter 5) must be fitted to all vehicles registered since 1 October 1937 except those which cannot or are not permitted to travel at more than 25mph, agricultural vehicles which are not driven at more than 20mph and works trucks first used before 1 April 1984. In the case of vehicles first used since 1 April 1984 the speedometer must indicate speed in both miles per hour and kilometres per hour. The instrument must be maintained in good working order at all material times and kept free from any obstruction which might prevent it being easily read.

Defence

It is a defence to be able to show that a defect to a speedometer or a tachograph occurred during the journey the vehicle was on when the offence was detected or that at that time steps had been taken to get the defect repaired as soon as reasonably practicable.

Seat Belts

Seat belts for the driver and one front-seat passenger must be fitted to goods vehicles not exceeding 1525kg unladen registered since 1 April 1967 and goods vehicles not exceeding 3500kg gross weight first used since 1 April 1980. From 1 October 1988 goods vehicles over 3500kg must be fitted with seat belt anchorage points for each forward facing seat to which lap-strap type seat belts can be fixed.

Vehicles to which this regulation applies, first used since 1 April 1973, must be fitted with belts which can be secured and released with one hand only and also with a device to enable the belts to be stowed in a position where they do not touch the floor. Vehicles to which this requirement applies will fail the annual test if seat belts are not fitted, are permanently obstructed or are not in good condition.

The legal requirement for drivers and passengers to wear seat belts came into effect in January 1983 with certain exemptions (see p 368).

10: CONSTRUCTION AND USE OF VEHICLES

Silencer

An adequate means of silencing exhaust noise and of preventing exhaust gases escaping into the atmosphere without first passing through a silencer must be fitted to all vehicles. Silencers must be maintained in good and efficient working order and must not be altered so as to increase the noise made by the escape of exhaust gases.

Safety Glass

Goods vehicles must be fitted with safety glass (ie toughened or laminated) for windscreens and windows in front of and on either side of the driver's seat. The windscreen and all windows of dual-purpose vehicles must be fitted with safety glass. The glass must be maintained so as not to obscure the vision of the driver while the vehicle is being driven on the road. This means that a driver could be prosecuted for having a severely misted up, iced up or otherwise dirty windscreen.

Wings

Goods vehicles and trailers must be fitted with wings to catch, as far as practicable, mud and water thrown up by the wheels unless adequate protection is provided by the bodywork.

Articulated vehicles and trailers used for carrying round timber are exempt from these requirements in respect of all except the front wheels of the tractive unit. Vehicles and trailers in an unfinished condition which are proceeding to a body builder for work to be completed and works trucks are also exempt from the need to have wings.

Fuel Tanks

Vehicles first used since 1 July 1973 and manufactured since 1 February 1973 which are propelled by petrol engines must have metal fuel tanks fitted in a position to avoid damage and prevent leakage. This provision does not apply where the vehicle complies with relevant Community regulations (EC 221/70 and is marked accordingly.

Power-to-Weight Ratio

All goods vehicles powered by diesel engines first used on or since 1 April 1973 must comply with a power-to-weight ratio of 4.4kW per 1000kg. The specific requirement in the regulations is that the power of the engine shown on the manufacturer's plate must be at least 4.4 times the gross weight shown on the plate (in kg).

When a vehicle is fitted with engine-driven ancillary equipment designed for use when the vehicle is in motion at a speed in excess of 5mph, the power from the vehicle's engine must be sufficient to provide power to drive such equipment and leave at least 4.4kW/1000kg available to drive the vehicle.

Exemptions to this requirement apply to vehicles first manufactured before 1 April 1973 and those first manufactured before 1 April 1973 propelled by a Perkins 6.354 engine.

Underrun Bumpers

Rear underrun bumpers (referred to in legislation as rear underrun protection) must be fitted to most rigid goods vehicles over 3.5 tonnes gross weight manufactured since 1 October 1983 and first used since 1 April 1984. Trailers, including semi-trailers, over 1020kg unladen weight manufactured since 1 May 1983 must also be fitted with bumpers. Certain vehicles and trailers are exempt (see below) from the fitting requirements and there were no retrospective fitting requirements for existing vehicles.

Strength of Bumpers
Rear underrun bumpers must be constructed so they are capable of withstanding a force equivalent to half the gross weight of the vehicle or trailer or a maximum of 10 tonnes, whichever is the *lesser,* without deflecting more than 400mm measured from the rearmost point of the vehicle or trailer — not from the original vertical position of the bumper.

Fitment of Bumpers
Bumpers must be fitted as near as possible to the rear of the vehicle and the lower edge must not be more than 550mm from the ground (see Figure 10.1). Normally, only one bumper would be fitted but where a tail-lift is fitted or the bodywork or other parts of the vehicle make this impracticable, two or more bumpers may be fitted. When a single full-width bumper is fitted it must extend on each side of the centre to within at least 100mm from the outermost width of the rear axle, but must not in any case extend beyond the width of the rear axle measured across the outermost face of the tyres. When two or more bumpers are fitted, for the reasons mentioned above, the space between each part of the bumper must not exceed 500mm and the outermost edge of the bumpers must extend to within at least 350mm from the outermost width of the rear axle (see Figure 10.2). Bumpers must not protrude beyond the width of the vehicle or trailer and the outside ends of the bumper must not be bent backwards.

Maintenance of Bumpers
Rear bumpers must be maintained free from any obvious defect which would adversely affect their performance in giving resistance to impact from the rear. It is also important to ensure that the dimensional requirements are met — particularly if the bumper is damaged (for example by fork-lift truck impact or reversing on to loading bays).

Exemptions
Rear underrun bumpers do not have to be fitted to vehicles and trailers in the following list:
1. Vehicles incapable of a speed exceeding 15mph on the level under their own power.
2. Tractive units of articulated vehicles.
3. Agricultural trailers, trailed appliances and agricultural motor vehicles.
4. Engineering plant.
5. Fire engines.
6. Road spreading vehicles (ie for salt and grit).

10: CONSTRUCTION AND USE OF VEHICLES

7. Rear tipping vehicles.
8. Naval, military or airforce vehicles.
9. Vehicles being taken to have bodywork fitted, or being taken for quality or safety checks by the manufacturer, distributor or dealer in such vehicles.
10. Vehicles being driven or towed to a place to have a rear underrun bumper fitted by prior arrangement.
11. Vehicles designed to carry other vehicles which are loaded from the rear (eg car transporters).
12. Trailers designed and constructed (not just adapted) to carry round timber, beams or girders of exceptional length.
13. Vehicles fitted with tail-lifts where the tail-lift forms part of the floor of the vehicle and extends to a length of at least one metre.
14. Temporarily imported foreign vehicles and semi-trailers.
15. Vehicles specially designed (not just adapted) for carrying and mixing liquid concrete.
16. Vehicles designed and used solely for the delivery of coal by means of a conveyor fixed to the vehicle so as to make the fitment of a rear underrun bumper impracticable.

Sideguards

Most heavy vehicles and trailers must be fitted with sideguards to comply with legal requirements except certain vehicles and trailers which are exempt from the fitting requirement as listed at the end of this section.

Sideguards must be fitted to the following vehicles and trailers:
1. Goods vehicles exceeding 3.5 tonnes maximum gross weight manufactured since 1 October 1983 and first used since 1 April 1984.
2. Trailers exceeding 1020kg unladen weight manufactured since 1 May 1983 and which, in the case of semi-trailers, have a distance between the foremost axle and the centre line of the kingpin (or rearmost kingpin if there is more than one) exceeding 4.5 metres (Figure 10.3).
3. Semi-trailers made before 1 May 1983 with a gross weight exceeding 26000kg and used in an articulated combination with a gross train weight exceeding 32520kg.

Sideguards are not required on vehicles and trailers, other than semi-trailers, where the distance between any two consecutive (ie front and rear) axles is less than 3 metres (Figure 10.4).

Strength of Sideguards
Sideguards must be constructed so they are capable of withstanding a force of 200kg (2 kilo newtons) over their length, apart from the rear 250mm, without deflecting more than 150mm. Over the last 250mm the deflection must not be more than 30mm under such force (Figure 10.5). These force resistance requirements *do not* apply where sideguards were fitted to existing semi-trailers (ie those built before 1 May 1985, and which were used at weights above 32520kg).

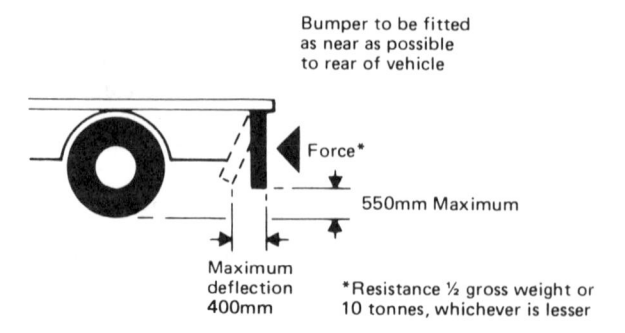

THE TRANSPORT MANAGER'S AND OPERATOR'S HANDBOOK

Bumper to be fitted as near as possible to rear of vehicle

Force*

550mm Maximum

Maximum deflection 400mm

*Resistance ½ gross weight or 10 tonnes, whichever is lesser

Figure 10.1 *Illustration of the rear underrun bumper force resistance requirements and ground clearance dimension*

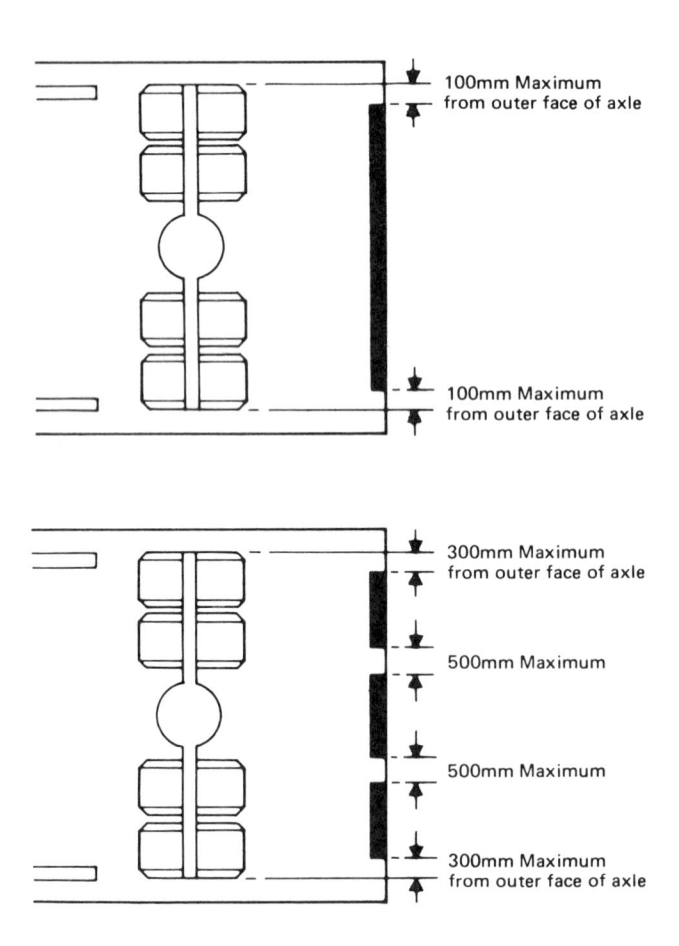

100mm Maximum from outer face of axle

100mm Maximum from outer face of axle

300mm Maximum from outer face of axle

500mm Maximum

500mm Maximum

300mm Maximum from outer face of axle

Figure 10.2 *Illustrations of the fitting dimensions for single and multiple rear underrun bumpers*

10: CONSTRUCTION AND USE OF VEHICLES

Fitment of Sideguards

The fitting position for sideguards depends on the type of vehicle or trailer as follows:
1. Rigid vehicles: at front – not more than 300mm behind the edge of the nearest tyre and the foremost edge of the sideguard; at rear – not more than 300mm behind the rearmost edge of the sideguard and the edge of the nearest tyre (Figure 10.6).
2. Trailers: at front – not more than 500mm behind the edge of the nearest tyre and the foremost edge of the sideguard; at rear – not more than 300mm behind the rearmost edge of the sideguard and the edge of the nearest tyre (Figure 10.7).
3. Semi-trailers with landing legs: at front – not more than 250mm behind the centre line of the landing legs and the foremost edge of the sideguard; at rear – not more than 300mm behind the rearmost edge of the sideguard and the edge of the nearest tyre (Figure 10.8).
4. Semi-trailers without landing legs: at front – not more than 3 metres behind the centre line of the rearmost kingpin and the foremost edge of the sideguard; at rear – not more than 300mm behind the rearmost edge of the sideguard and the edge of the nearest tyre (Figure 10.9).

In all cases sideguards must be fitted so they are not inset more than 30mm from the external face of the tyre excluding any distortion due to the weight of the vehicle (Figure 10.10).

The upper edge of sideguards must be positioned as follows:
1. In the case of vehicles or trailers with a body or structure which is wider than the tyres, no more than 350mm from the lower edge of the body or structure (Figure 10.11).
2. In the case of vehicles or trailers with a body or structure which is narrower than the tyres or which does not extend outwards immediately above the wheels, a vertical plane taken from the outer face of the tyre must be measured upwards for 1.85 metres above the ground. If this plane is dissected by the vehicle structure within 1.85 metres from the ground the sideguard must extend up to within 350mm of the structure where it is cut by the vertical plane (Figure 10.12); if the vertical plane is not dissected by the vehicle structure the upper edge of the sideguard must extend to be level with the top of the vehicle structure to a minimum height of 1.5 metres from the ground (Figure 10.13).

The lower edge of sideguards must not be more than 550mm from the ground. This dimension is to be measured on level ground and, in the case of a semi-trailer, when its load platform is horizontal.

When sideguards are to be fitted to extendible trailers and to vehicles and trailers designed to carry demountable bodies or containers, the following fitting provisions apply:
1. Sideguards must be fitted to extendible trailers in compliance with the original fitting specifications in regard to spacings from the nearest wheel, kingpin or landing leg when the trailer is at its shortest length. When the trailer is extended beyond its minimum length the spacings between the front edge of the sideguard and the semi-trailer landing legs or kingpin (if it has no landing legs) and the rear edge of the sideguard and the foremost edge of the tyre nearest to it are no longer applicable.

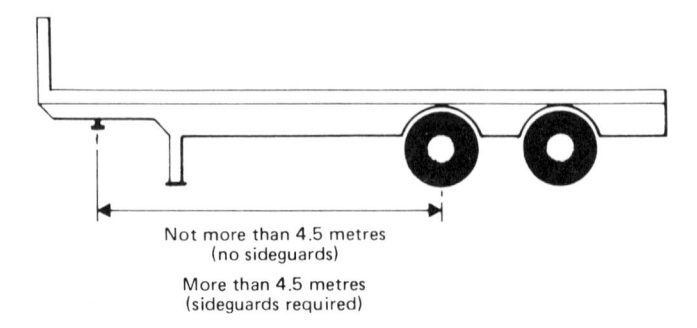

Figure 10.3 *Measurements of relevant distance between foremost axle and centre of kingpin for semi-trailers to determine if sideguards must be fitted*

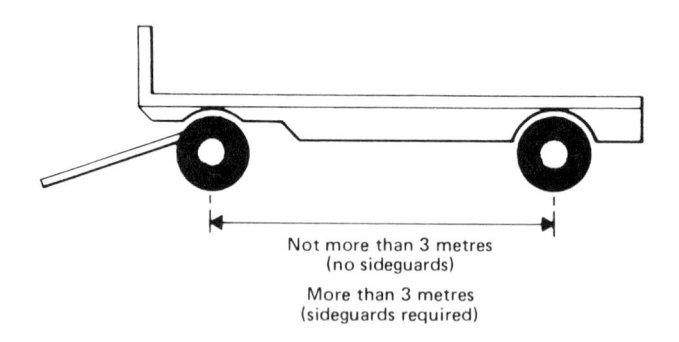

Figure 10.4 *Measurement of two consecutive axles on draw-bar trailers – the same dimension applies to rigid vehicles – to determine if sideguards must be fitted*

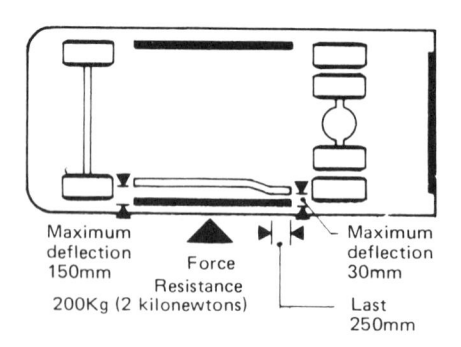

Figure 10.5 *How force resistance applies to sideguard on new vehicles and trailers (It does not apply to sideguard fitted to existing semi-trailers)*

10: CONSTRUCTION AND USE OF VEHICLES

2. Sideguards must be fitted to vehicles and trailers which are designed and constructed (not merely adapted) to carry demountable bodies or containers so that when the body or container is removed the sideguards remain in place. This means that if the vehicle runs without a body or container it must still comply with the sideguard requirements.

Construction of Sideguards

All parts of the sideguard which face outwards must be 'smooth, essentially rigid and either flat or horizontally corrugated'. Each face of the guard must be a minimum of 100mm wide (including the inward face at the forward edge) and the vertical gaps between the bars must not be more than 300mm wide.

Maintenance of Sideguards

Sideguards must be maintained free of any obvious defect which would impair their effectiveness. It is important to ensure that the fitting dimensions are observed particularly when the sideguards are damaged (eg by fork-lift truck impact).

Exemption to Fitting Dimensions

The specific requirements relating to the fitting positions for sideguards as previously described only apply so far as is practicable in the case of the following vehicles and trailers:
1. Those designed solely for the carriage of a fluid substance in closed tanks permanently fitted to the vehicle and provided with valves and hose or pipe connections for loading and unloading.
2. Those vehicles which require additional stability during loading and unloading or while working and which are fitted with extendible stabilisers on either side (eg lorry mounted cranes, tower wagons, inspection platforms).

Exemptions

Sideguards do not have to be fitted to vehicles and trailers in the following list:
1. Vehicles incapable of a speed of more than 15mph on the level under their own power.
2. Agricultural trailers.
3. Engineering plant.
4. Fire engines.
5. Land tractors.
6. Side and end tipping vehicles and trailers.
7. Vehicles with no bodywork fitted and being driven or towed for the purposes of a quality or safety check by the manufacturer, distributor or dealer in such vehicles, or being driven by prior arrangement to have bodywork fitted.
8. Vehicles being driven or towed to a place by prior arrangement to have sideguards fitted.
9. Vehicles designed solely for use in connection with street cleansing, the collection or disposal of refuse or the collection or disposal of the contents of gullies or cesspools.

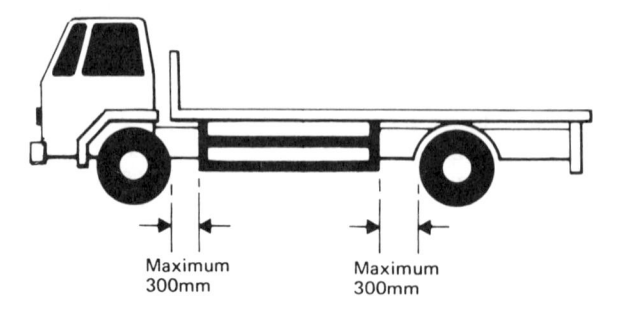

Figure 10.6 *Fitting position for sideguard on rigid vehicles*

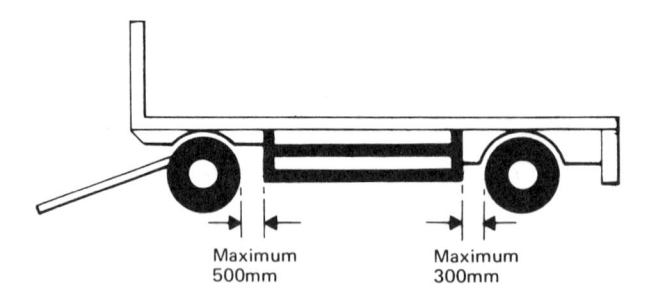

Figure 10.7 *Fitting position for sideguard on trailers*

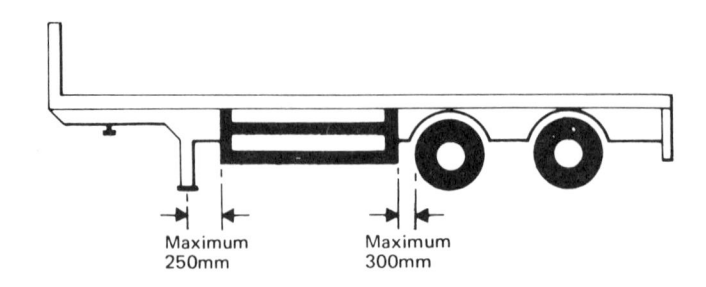

Figure 10.8 *Fitting position for sideguards on semi-trailer with landing legs*

10: CONSTRUCTION AND USE OF VEHICLES

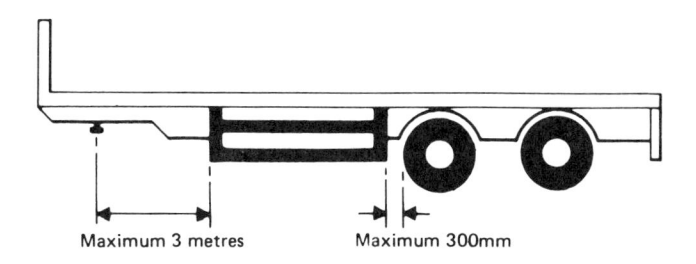

Figure 10.9 *Fitting position for sideguards on semi-trailer without landing legs*

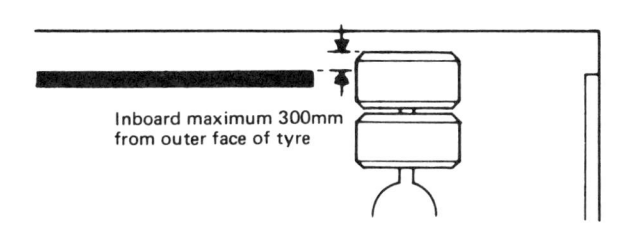

Figure 10.10 *Inboard mounting position for sideguards – all vehicles and trailers*

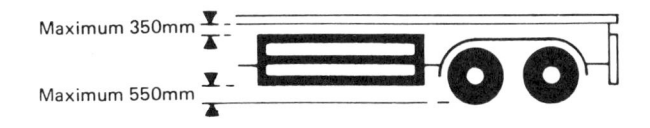

Figure 10.11 *Fitting position for sideguards where body or structure is wider than the tyres*

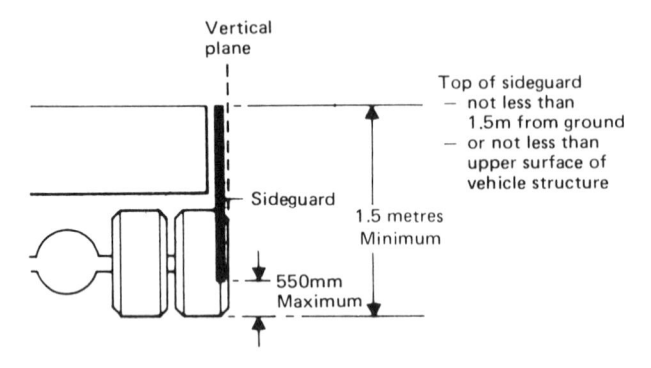

THE TRANSPORT MANAGER'S AND OPERATOR'S HANDBOOK

Figure 10.12 *Fitting position for sideguards where body or structure is narrower than the tyres up to a height of 1.85 metres*

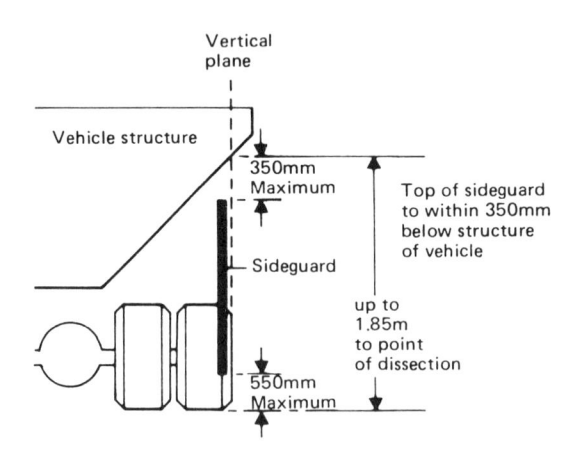

Figure 10.13 *Fitting position for sideguards where body or structure is narrower than the tyres*

10: CONSTRUCTION AND USE OF VEHICLES

10. Trailers specially designed and constructed to carry round timber, beams or girders of exceptional length.
11. Articulated tractive units.
12. Naval, military or airforce vehicles.
13. Trailers specially designed and constructed (not merely adapted) to carry other vehicles loaded from the front or rear (eg car transporters).
14. Temporarily imported foreign semi-trailers.
15. Low-loader trailers where:
    (a) the upper surface of the load platform is not more than 750mm from the ground, and
    (b) no part of the edge of the load platform is more than 60mm inboard from the external face of the tyre (discounting the distortion caused by the weight of the vehicle).

Ground Clearance for Trailers

Minimum ground clearances are specified for goods carrying trailers manufactured since 1 April 1984. Such trailers must have a minimum ground clearance of 160mm if they have an axle interspace of more than 6 metres and not more than 11.5 metres. If the interspace is more than 11.5 metres the minimum clearance is 190mm (Figures 10.14 and 10.15).

Measurement of the axle interspace is taken from the point of support on the tractive unit in the case of semi-trailers or the centre line of the front axle in other cases to the centre line of the rear axle or the centre point between rear axles if there is more than one (Figure 10.15).

In determining the minimum ground clearance no account should be taken of any part of the suspension, steering or braking system attached to any axle, any wheel and any air skirt. Measurement of the ground clearance is taken in the area formed by the width of the trailer and the middle 70 per cent of the axle interspace (Figure 10.16).

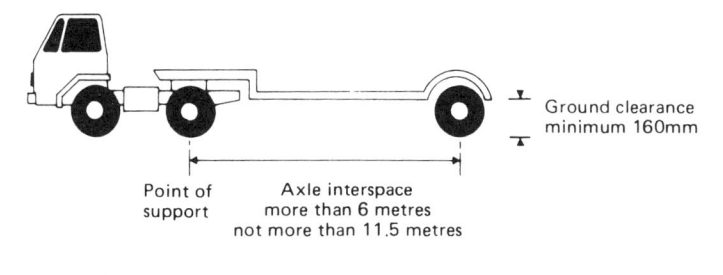

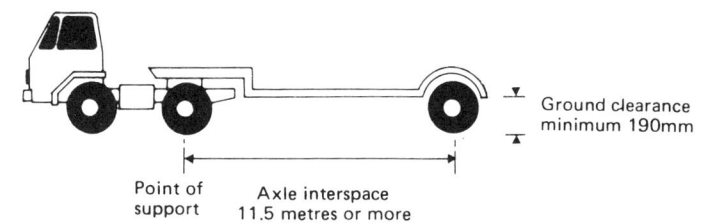

Figure 10.14 *Ground clearance for trailers – measure from the point of support to the centre line of the axle*

THE TRANSPORT MANAGER'S AND OPERATOR'S HANDBOOK

Midway between centres

Midway between centres

Midway between centres

Axle interspace
(see Figure 10.14
for dimensions)

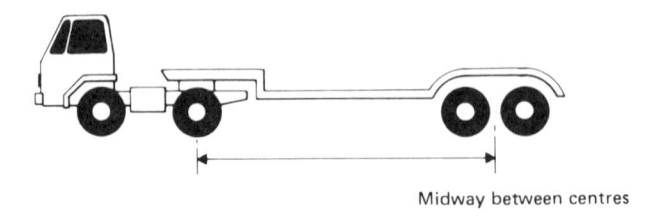

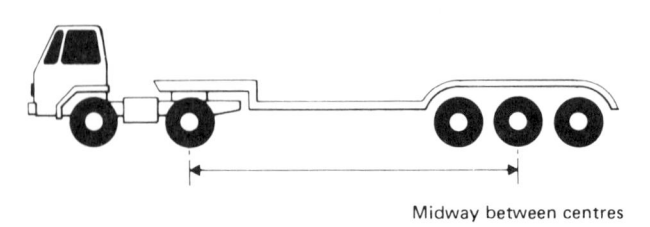

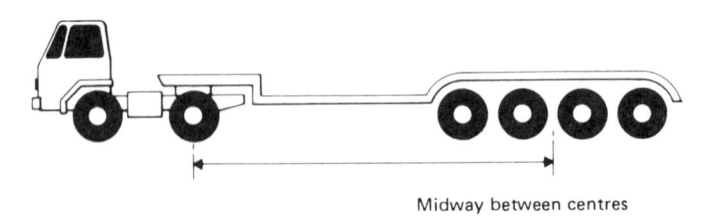

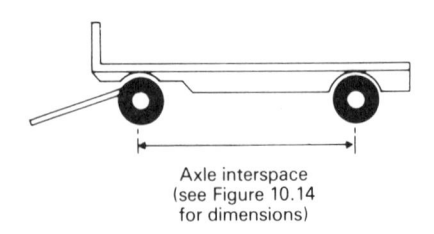

Figure 10.15 *The point for measuring axle interspace on multi-axle semi-trailers and on other trailers*

10: CONSTRUCTION AND USE OF VEHICLES

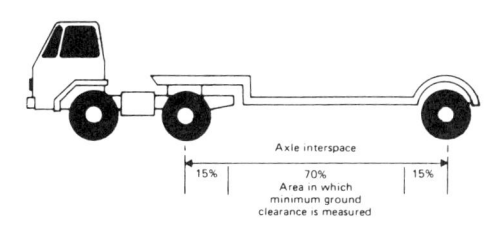

Figure 10.16 *The area in which minimum ground clearance is measured*

Anti-Spray

Regulations require certain vehicles and trailers to be equipped with anti-spray devices. The following vehicles and trailers must be fitted with approved equipment from the dates shown:
1. Motor vehicles over 12 tonnes gross weight made on or after 1 October 1985 and first used on or after 1 April 1986. Fitment required from date when vehicle first used on road from 1 April 1986.
2. Trailers over 3.5 tonnes gross weight made on or after 1 May 1985. Fitment required from date trailer first used on road from new.
3. Trailers over 16 tonnes gross weight with two or more axles
   (a) made before 1 January 1975. Fitment required from 1 October 1987;
   (b) made on or after 1 January 1975 but before 1 May 1985. Fitment required from 1 October 1986;
   (c) trailers made on or after 1 May 1985. Fitment required from 1 May 1985.

NB: The EC proposes reducing the weight threshold at which the fitment of anti-spray devices becomes mandatory from the present 12 tonnes to 3.5 tonnes.

Retrospective Fitting
When trailers which come within the scope of 3(a) and 3(b) above were in service before the end of 1984 and were fitted with anti-spray equipment or other spray suppression devices at that time, such equipment or devices will remain legally acceptable if they 'substantially conform' to the requirements of the regulations. Legal precedence has established that the word 'substantially' can mean as little as 60 per cent. The operator would also have to be in a position to prove fitment before the end of 1984.

Exemptions
Anti-spray requirements do not apply to those vehicles and trailers which are exempt under the C & U Regulations from the need for wings and to a further list of exemptions as follows:

  1. Four-wheel and multi-wheel drive vehicles.

2. Vehicles with a minimum of 400mm (approximately 16ins) ground clearance in the middle 80 per cent of the width and the overall length of the vehicle.
3. Works trucks.
4. Works trailers.
5. Broken down vehicles.
6. Vehicles which cannot due to their construction exceed 30mph on the level under their own power.
7. Vehicles specified in regulations as exempt from sideguards.
    (a) agricultural trailers and implements
    (b) engineering plant
    (c) fire engines
    (d) side and end tippers
    (e) military vehicles used for naval, military or airforce purposes
    (f) vehicles with no bodywork fitted being driven on road test or being driven by prior appointment to a place where bodywork is to be fitted or for delivery
    (g) vehicles used for street cleansing, the collection or disposal of the contents of gullies or cesspools
    (h) trailers designed and constructed to carry round timber, beams or girders of exceptional length
    (i) temporarily imported foreign semi-trailers
8. Concrete mixers.
9. Vehicles being driven to a place by prior arrangement to have anti-spray equipment fitted.
10. Land locomotives, land tractors and land implement conveyors.
11. Trailers forming part of an articulated vehicle or part of a combination of vehicles, having in either case, a total laden weight exceeding 46000kg.

British Standard

The British Standard on spray suppression was originally contained in two documents BS AU 200 (parts 1 and 2) 1984 which apply to vehicles fitted before 1 May 1987 but this has now been replaced by new Standards BS AU 200 Part 1a and 2a 1986 which apply to fitment since this date. The regulations require anti-spray devices to conform to the Standard set out in these documents. However, there is no requirement for existing equipment fitted to the requirements of the original BS AU standard to be changed to equipment which meets the new BS AU standard.

In order to comply with the law, relevant vehicles and trailers must be fitted with anti-spray systems which fall into one of two main categories:
1. A straight valance across the top of the wheel and a flap hanging vertically behind the wheel all made from approved spray suppressant material; or
2. A semi-circular valance following the curvature of the wheel with either:
    (a) air/water separator material round the edge; or
    (b) a flap of spray suppressant material hanging from the rear edge.

Spray Suppressant Material

Two types of material are referred to in the Standard. These are generally identifiable as follows:

10: CONSTRUCTION AND USE OF VEHICLES

1. Spray suppressant material – designed to absorb or dissipate the energy of water thrown from the tyre in order to reduce the degree to which water shatters into fine droplets on hitting a surface.
2. Air/water separator – 'a device forming part of the valance and/or wheel flap which permits air to flow through while reducing the emission of spray'.

Maintenance of Anti-Spray Equipment and Devices
The regulations stipulate that all devices fitted to comply with the legal requirement (and every part of such device) must be maintained, when the vehicle is on the road, so that they are free from 'any obvious defect which would be likely to affect adversely the effectiveness of the device'. It is also important that fitting dimensions are maintained especially if the flaps are damaged.

Fitment – Valances and Flaps
Where the choice is for spray suppression to be achieved by the use of valances and flaps (particularly on rear vehicle wheels and trailer wheels) the specific requirements for fitment are as follows:

NB: Capital letters in brackets in the following text refer to items on the adjacent diagrams illustrating fitment details.

- Valances of spray suppressant material must extend across the top of the tyre from a line vertical with the front edge of the tyre (A) to a line beyond the rear wheel which will allow the rear flap to be suspended no more than 300mm from the rear edge of the tyre (B). The valance must be at least 100mm deep (C).

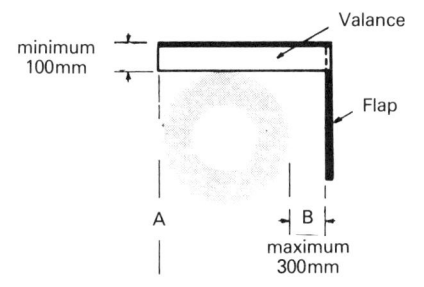

- The valance must extend downwards to be level with the top of the tyre (D) or it may overlap the top of the tyre (E).

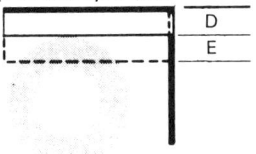

- In the case of multiple axle bogies the relevant dimensions are shown above with the additional requirement that where the gap between the rear edge of the front tyre and the front edge of the rear tyre is greater than 250mm (F) a flap must be fitted between the two. *Note:* no middle flap is required if the distance does not exceed 250mm.

177

This section
can be omitted

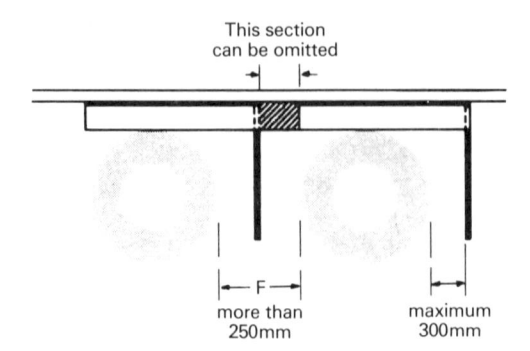

|← F →|
more than
250mm

maximum
300mm

Note: The top of the valance may be in two separate sections (see shaded part) so long as it otherwise conforms to the dimensions.

- Valances must extend the full width of the tyre and beyond to a maximum of 75mm (G) in the case of the rear wheels (non-steerable) and 100mm (H) in the case of steered wheels.

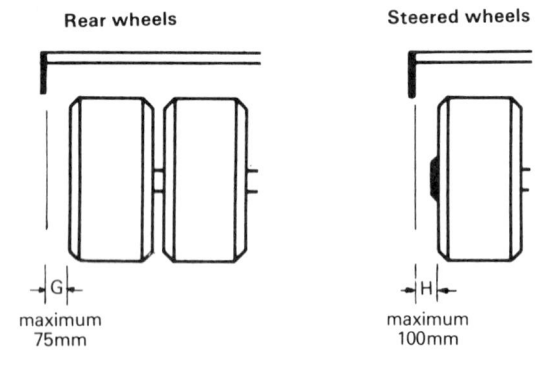

Rear wheels

maximum
75mm

Steered wheels

maximum
100mm

- If the valance extends below the level of the tyre on fixed wheels the gap between the tyre face and the valance can be extended to 100mm (J). There must be no gaps between the valance and the vehicle body.

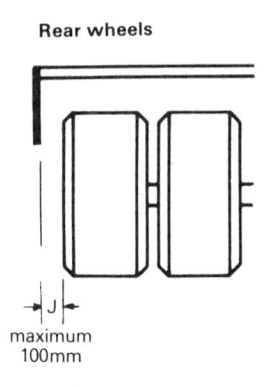

Rear wheels

maximum
100mm

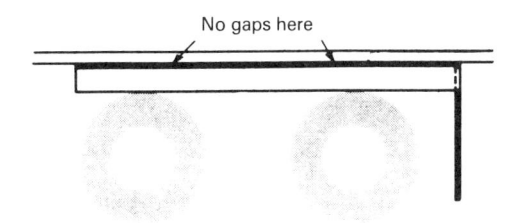

10: CONSTRUCTION AND USE OF VEHICLES

No gaps here

- Flaps used in conjunction with valances as described above must conform to the following dimensions:
1. They must extend the full width of the tyre/tyres (K).
2. They must reach down to within 200mm of the ground (L) when the vehicle is unladen (300mm on rearmost axles of trailers used on roll-on/roll-off ferries or on any axle where the radial distance of the lower edge of the valancing does not exceed the radius of the tyres fitted).

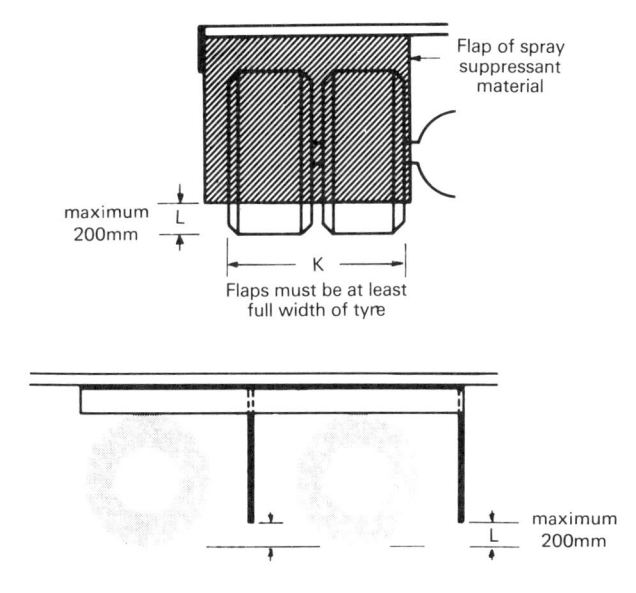

maximum 200mm — L
Flap of spray suppressant material
K
Flaps must be at least full width of tyre

maximum 200mm — L

3. When flaps are used in conjunction with mudguard valances the top of the flap must extend upwards at least to a point 100mm above the centre line of the wheel irrespective of the position of the lower edge of the mudguard.

Flap used in conjunction with mudguard valance

Guard or bodywork
Flap inside mudguard valance
minimum 100mm
maximum 200mm — L

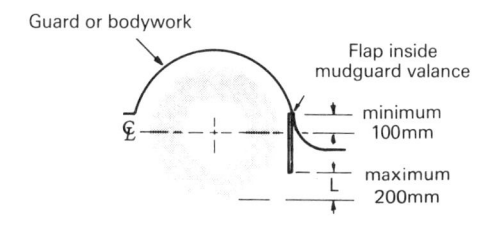

4. Where the flap extends inside the guard then it must be at least the width of the tyre tread pattern.

- If the flap used is of a type with an air/water separator device (ie bristles) fitted to the bottom edge the following dimensions apply:
  1. Rear edge of tyre to flap – maximum distance 200mm (M).
  2. The edge of the device must come to within 200mm of the ground (N).

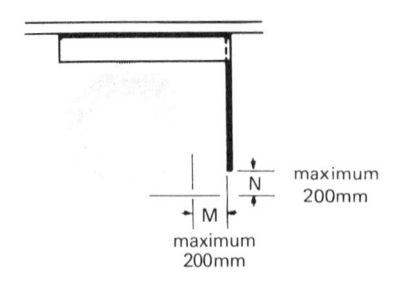

Deflection of Flaps
Wheels flaps must not be capable of being deflected rearwards more than 100m when subjected to a force of 3N (ie 4lbs) applied near the bottom of the flap.

Fitment – Mudguards and Air/Water Separator Devices
Where the choice for compliance with the regulations is by means of conventional mudguarding there are specific dimensions to be observed:
- If the mudguard is covering a steerable wheel (see later note about steerable axles on drawbar trailers) the radius of the edge of the valance must not be more than 1.5 times the radius of the tyre measured at three points (P) and in the case of non-steerable wheels, 1.25 times the same radius.

Three points of measurement of radial for mudguards (P)

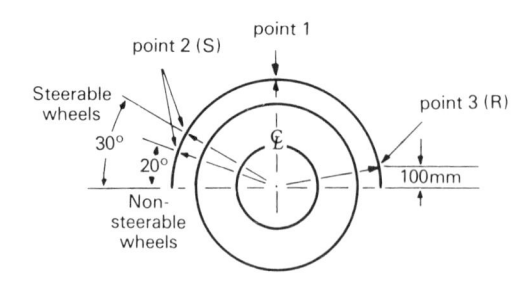

1. Vertically above the centre of the tyre.
2. A point at the front of the tyre 20 degrees above the horizontal centre line of the tyre (non-steerable wheels) or a point 30 degrees above the horizontal centre line of the tyre (steerable wheels).

10: CONSTRUCTION AND USE OF VEHICLES

3. A point at the rear of the tyre 100mm above the horizontal centre line of the tyre.

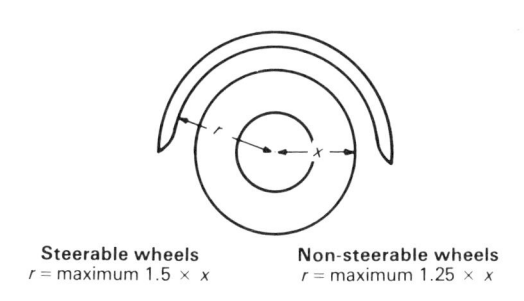

Steerable wheels
$r = $ maximum $1.5 \times x$

Non-steerable wheels
$r = $ maximum $1.25 \times x$

- Mudguard valances must be at least 45mm deep behind a point vertically above the wheel centre. They may reduce in depth forward of this point (Q).

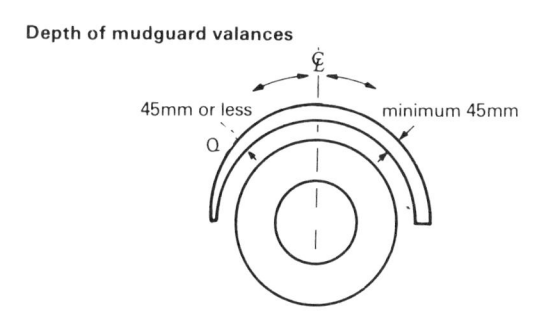

Depth of mudguard valances

45mm or less — Q

minimum 45mm

- In the case of drawbar trailers, the 1.5 times radius dimension applies as above for the front steerable axle unless the mudguards are fitted to the turntable and thus turn with the wheels in which case the maximum radius for the valance is 1.25 times the tyre radius.
- If the valancing on fixed wheel mudguards is provided by means of air/water separator material (ie bristles) the edge must follow the periphery of the tyre. On steerable wheels the edge must be not more than 1.05 times the tyre radius.

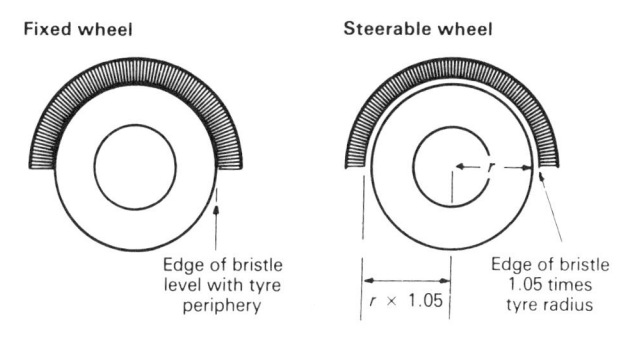

Fixed wheel

Edge of bristle level with tyre periphery

Steerable wheel

$r \times 1.05$

Edge of bristle 1.05 times tyre radius

The valances on mudguards must extend downwards at front and rear to at least the following dimensions:
1. at rear – to within 100mm above the centre line of the axle (point 3) (R).
2. at front – to within a line 20 degrees above the centre line of the axle. In the case of steerable wheels this dimension is raised to 30 degrees (point 2) (S).

- In the case of multi-mudguarding over tandem axles or bogies, the intersection of the guards between the wheels must conform to one of the two dimensions:
    1. The gap between the guards at the valance edges must not exceed 60mm (T); or
    2. The edges must come down to within 150mm of the horizontal centre line across the wheels (V).

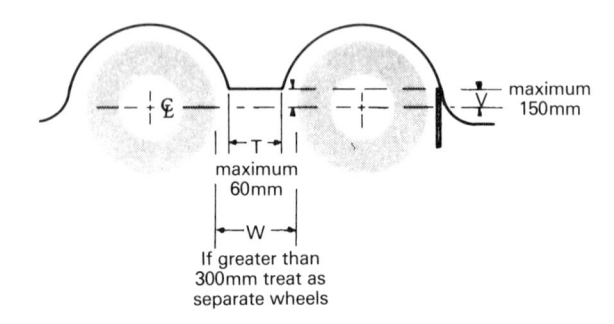

- If the gap between the tyre edges is greater than 250mm a flap must be provided between the wheels. If the gap is more than 300mm the wheels should be treated as though separate for mudguarding purposes (W).

Notes:
1. All dimensions in the regulations are to be taken when the vehicle is unladen, when steerable wheels are straight ahead and when the load platforms of articulated semi-trailers are level.
2. All suppression material or devices and air/water separator material or devices must be permanently and legibly marked with the following mark: BS AU 200/2, plus 'the name, trademark or other means of identification of the responsible manufacturer'.

Use of Vehicles

In addition to the foregoing constructional requirements which are mainly the responsibility of the vehicle manufacturer or the person building the bodywork, there are requirements regarding the use of vehicles which are the responsibility of the operator. However, as mentioned earlier, the vehicle user carries full legal responsibility for the mechanical condition of a vehicle on the road and its compliance with the constructional requirements even if the fault which led to an offence could be laid at the

10: CONSTRUCTION AND USE OF VEHICLES

> # Garphyttan
>
> ## Quality components for the majority of vehicles produced in Western Europe
>
> The Garphyttan Group comprises 14 companies operating in six countries, manufacturing components for buses, truck and trailers. In the UK, the Group is organised into three main divisions operating under the wing of Garphyttan Ltd.
>
> **HALDEX DIVISION**
> Formerly known as SAB Automotive Co., this division manufactures Haldex automatic brake adjusters (over 7 million in service throughout the world), single and twin air driers, automatic drain valves, and are also sole UK concessionaires for Knorr Dahl air brake systems, load sensing valves and compressors.
>
> **ELHYDRAULIC DIVISION**
> Their main products are Hesselman electro-hydraulic motors and powerpacks used for tailgate lifts and materials handling products; electric driving wheels for fork-lift trucks and mechanical handling equipment.
>
> **WIRE DIVISION**
> Manufactures the famous 'Oteva' spring wire used by leading producers of valve springs and piston rings throughout the world. Oteva spring wire currently account for approximately one-third of the world demand for valve spring material.
>
> ## Garphyttan
>
> **Garphyttan Ltd.** Hilton Road, Aycliffe Industrial Estate, Newton Aycliffe, Co. Durham DL5 6SX
> Tel: (0325) 310110. Telex: 587743. Fax: (0325) 311834

door of the chassis manufacturer, the bodybuilder, an ancillary equipment supplier or the dealer.

These requirements cover such items as vehicle weights (which were dealt with earlier), towing, fumes, the condition and maintenance of vehicles and their components, noise, smoke, and general safety in the use of vehicles. They also deal with the regulations regarding the number of trailers which a vehicle may draw.

Noise

It is an offence to use, or cause or permit to be used on a road a motor vehicle or trailer which causes an excessive noise because of a defect, lack of repair or faulty adjustment of components or load. Also no motor vehicle must be used on a road in such a manner as to cause any excessive noise which could have been reasonably avoided by the driver. Noise for these purposes is the combined noise emitted by the exhaust plus that from the tyres, engine, bodywork and equipment and the load. Noise levels for goods vehicles are measured by special meters either by the police or by DTp officers at hgv test stations and occasionally on roadside tests.

Noise Limits
The permissible noise levels specified in the regulations are based on a 'constructional' standard and an 'in use' standard. The 'in use' standards are as follows:

Motor vehicles first used from 1 April 1970
1. Plated goods vehicles with a maximum gross weight
   exceeding 3560kg   89 dB (A)
2. Other goods vehicles   85 dB (A)
3. Motor tractors, locomotives, land tractors, works trucks and
   engineering plant   89 dB (A)

Motor vehicles first used from 1 October 1983
1. Goods vehicles with a maximum gross weight not
   exceeding 3500kg   81 dB (A)
2. Plated goods vehicles with a maximum gross weight over
   3500kg   86 dB (A)
3. Goods vehicles over 12000kg maximum gross weight and
   with engine power of at least 200hp (DIN)   88 dB (A)

Exemption from Noise Limits
These limits do not apply in the case of a vehicle going by appointment to have the noise measured or for mechanical adjustments to reduce the noise level, or returning from such an appointment. It also does not apply to a stationary vehicle using a power take-off or a vehicle first used before 1 November 1970 if using an exhaust brake.

More stringent noise limits for goods vehicles were due to be introduced from 1 October 1990 in accordance with EC Directive 424/84. Broadly this means a reduction to 81dB(A) for vehicles over 3.5 tonnes with engine power less than 75kW per 1000kg, 83 dB(A) for those with power outputs between 75 and 150kW and 84 dB(A) for vehicles with engine power at or above this figure.

Smoke

Vehicles must not emit smoke, visible vapour, grit, sparks, ashes, cinders or oily substances which may cause damage to property or injury or danger to any person.

Excess Fuel Devices
Excess fuel devices must not be used on diesel vehicles while the vehicle is in motion. Such devices are incorporated in the vehicle fuel pump to enable extra fuel to be fed to the engine to aid cold starting. Their use when the engine is warm slightly increases the power of the engine, but in doing so black smoke is emitted from the exhaust. For this reason their use is forbidden while the vehicle is in motion.

Smoke Opacity Limits
Diesel engined vehicles first used after 1 April 1973 (but not manufactured before 1 October 1972) must comply with smoke opacity limits specified in BS AU 141a/1971. Engines fitted to such vehicles must be of a type for which a type test certificate in accordance with the British Standard Specification for *The Performance of Diesel Engines for Road Vehicles* has been issued by the Secretary of State for the Environment. The certificate

will indicate that engines of that type do not exceed the emission of smoke limits set out in the BS Specification.

Exemptions
Land tractors, industrial tractors, works trucks and engineering plant propelled by diesel engines with not more than two cylinders are exempt from this requirement; so too are vehicles fitted with the Perkins 6.354 engine manufactured before 1 April 1973.

Offences
It is an offence to use a vehicle to which this type test applies if the fuel injection equipment, the engine speed governor or others parts of the engine have been altered or adjusted in such a way that the smoke emission of the vehicle is increased. An offence is committed if a vehicle emits black smoke or other substances even without alteration or adjustment of the parts (eg as a result of lack of maintenance).

Control of Fumes
Petrol engined vehicles first used after 1 January 1972 must be fitted with a means of preventing crank-case gases escaping into the atmosphere except through the exhaust system.

Exhaust Emissions

Tighter standards for exhaust emissions from new vehicles are to be introduced by amendment to the Construction and Use Regulations in accordance with EC requirements (under EC Directives 89/458 – cars – and 88/77 – diesel-engined vehicles over 3.5 tonnes). These limits are already applied in Type Approval regulations to vehicles first used from 1 April 1991 (later for cars/vans with engines over 1400cc and those with diesel engines).

Even tougher (so-called Stage II) standards are to be applied to vehicles over 3.5 tonnes pmw from 1 January 1993 as a result of draft EC proposals currently under consideration with further, more stringent (Stage III), emission controls in prospect from 1996.

The vehicle user is required by law to keep the engine of his vehicle and any emission control equipment (ie catalytic converter) in good working order and in tune.

Gas Powered Vehicles

Regulations specify technical standards for fuel tanks or containers, the filling system and valves and general requirements for gas propulsion systems in motor vehicles. The regulations permit the use of LPG only in gas propelled vehicles, although this may be combined with petrol fuel systems, but the use of methane or hydrogen is prohibited. The DTp has published a free guide *Gas Installations in Motor Vehicles and Trailers* which is available from: Department of Transport, B3, Victoria Road, South Ruislip, Middlesex HA4 0NZ.

Towing

Goods vehicles may draw (ie tow) only one trailer. An exception to this is when a rigid goods vehicle tows a broken-down vehicle on a towing ambulance or dolly in which case although this is counted as towing two trailers it is allowed. In a case where an articulated vehicle has broken down, this may be towed by a rigid goods vehicle so long as the articulated vehicle is not loaded. In these circumstances the outfit is treated as one trailer only, but if it is loaded an articulated outfit being towed is considered to be two trailers and it is illegal for a normal goods vehicle (ie a heavy motor car) to tow it. Only a locomotive can tow a broken-down articulated vehicle which is laden (see below).

Motor tractors may draw one laden or two unladen trailers and locomotives may draw three trailers (see p 155 for definitions).

Composite Trailers
The C & U Regulations make it permissible for rigid goods vehicles (apart from locomotives and motor tractors) to draw two trailers instead of only one, when one of the trailers is a towing implement (ie a dolly) and the other is an articulated-type semi-trailer secured to and resting on, or suspended from, the dolly. This combination of dolly and semi-trailer is known as a composite trailer (Figure 10.17).

To comply with the regulations, the dolly needs to have two or more wheels and be specifically designed to support a superimposed semi-trailer. Dollies must display a manufacturer's plate and they are subject to the annual heavy goods vehicle test.

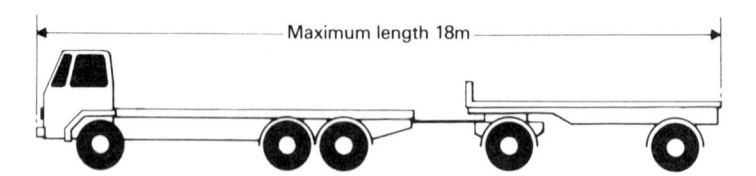

Figure 10.17 *A conventional six-wheeled rigid vehicle drawing a dolly mounted semi-trailer*

Towing Distance
The distance between the nearest points of two vehicles joined by a tow rope or chain must not exceed 4.5 metres. When the distance between the two vehicles exceeds 1.5 metres the rope, chain or bar must be made clearly visible from both sides of the vehicles. There is no specified maximum distance limit if a solid tow-bar is used for towing.

Televisions in Vehicles

It is illegal for a vehicle to be fitted with television receiving apparatus where the driver can see the screen either directly or by reflection except where such equipment displays nothing other than information:
1. About the state of the vehicle or its equipment.
2. About the location of the vehicle and the road on which it is located.
3. To assist the driver to see the road adjacent to the vehicle (eg to the rear when reversing).

10: CONSTRUCTION AND USE OF VEHICLES

4. To assist the driver to reach his destination.

Reversing Alarms

It is legally permissible to fit reversing alarms to certain goods and passenger vehicles if desired – *the regulations do not make it mandatory to do so.* Such alarms may be fitted and used on the following vehicles:
1. Commercial vehicles over 2 tonnes gross weight
2. Passenger vehicles with nine or more seats
3. Engineering plant
4. Works trucks.

Time Restriction on Use of Reversing Alarms
The alarms are subject to the same night-time restrictions that apply to the sounding of horns in built-up areas (ie not after 11.30 pm and before 7 am – 23.30 to 07.00) and the sound emitted must not be capable of being confused with the Pelican crossing 'safe to cross' signal.

Restriction on Fitment of Reversing Alarms
Such alarms *must not* be fitted to light goods vehicles below 2 tonnes gross weight or to motor cars.

Advice on Use of Alarms
A number of cases have arisen following reversing accidents resulting in death or injury where the Health and Safety Executive have prosecuted the vehicle operators concerned for not voluntarily fitting reversing alarms. In other words the HSE line is that the offender had not taken sufficient steps to ensure safety when his vehicles were reversing by fitting equipment which the law permits, but not mandatorily requires, him to do.

11: Type Approval

Type Approval is a scheme which requires vehicle manufacturers to submit new vehicles (ie new designs, new models and changes of specifications for existing approved models) for approval before they are put on the market. The Department of Transport examines the vehicle submitted to ensure that it meets all legal requirements and also meets minimum standards of construction and performance. When a vehicle has been approved the manufacturer is then required by law to build all vehicles of a similar type to exactly those standards and certify this fact to the customer by the issue of a Certificate of Conformity.

An EC directive lays down the basic procedures for the Type Approval scheme for vehicles and components. Subsidiary directives have also been issued setting out agreed standards on some aspects of vehicle safety or pollution. They cover the same ground as existing national regulations. The directives do not yet cover all vehicle features which need to be regulated so until the programme is complete both EC directives and national regulations apply to relevant items. The UK established a non-compulsory scheme to enable exporting vehicle manufacturers to gain the necessary Type Approval in order to sell their products in EC countries.

Eventually EC Type Approval requirements will supersede UK Construction and Use Regulations but initially vehicles which have a Type Approval Certificate will be exempt from certain Construction and Use requirements.

Vehicles Covered

Type Approval requirements apply to all passenger cars first licensed for use in the United Kingdom from 1 April 1978. The Motor Vehicles (Type Approval for Goods Vehicles) (Great Britain) Regulations 1982 (as amended) make the application of the Type Approval scheme compulsory for goods vehicles, motor caravans, motor ambulances and bi-purpose vehicles constructed for the carriage of both goods and passengers (but not more than eight passengers) which are not included in the car Type Approval scheme and which have been manufactured since 1 October 1982 and first used since 1 April 1983. Applications for Type Approval could be made from 1 October 1981 onwards.

While there is currently no Type Approval scheme for trailers or semi-trailers the EC is proposing that they should be included in Type Approval requirements and is currently endeavouring to harmonise national legislation to provide for the introduction of an EC-wide package covering marking, brakes, lighting, under-run protection and sideguards, spray suppression and bulkhead load strength by 1993.

Exemptions from Type Approval

Type Approval does not apply to the following vehicles:

1. Vehicles manufactured before 1 October 1982 whenever they are first registered.
2. Vehicles manufactured on or after 1 October 1982, providing they are first licensed before 1 April 1983.
3. Temporary imports of vehicles.
4. Vehicles proceeding for export from the UK.
5. Vehicles in the service of visiting forces or headquarters.
6. Certain vehicles which are, or were formerly, in use in the public service of the Crown.
7. Prototypes which are not intended for general use on the roads.
8. Motor tractors, light locomotives and heavy locomotives.
9. Engineering plant, pedestrian-controlled vehicles, straddle carriers, works trucks and track-laying vehicles.
10. Vehicles specially designed and constructed for use in private premises for moving excavated materials, vehicles fitted with movable platforms and vehicles designed and constructed for the carriage of abnormal indivisible loads.
11. Tower wagons.
12. Fire engines.
13. Road rollers.
14. Steam-propelled vehicles.
15. Vehicles constructed for the purpose of preventing or reducing the effect of snow or ice on roads.
16. Two-wheeled motorcycles with or without sidecars.
17. Electrically-propelled vehicles.
18. Breakdown vehicles.
19. Any vehicle not exceeding 1525kg unladen weight which is constructed or assembled by a person not ordinarily engaged in the manufacture of goods vehicles of that description.
20. Vehicles not exceeding 1525kg unladen weight providing that:
    (a) the vehicle has been purchased outside the UK for the personal use of the individual importing it or his dependants
    (b) the vehicle has been so used by that individual or his dependants on roads outside the UK before it is imported;
    (c) the vehicle is intended solely for such personal use in the UK; and
    (d) the individual importing the vehicle intends, at the time when the vehicle is imported, to remain in the UK for not less than 12 months from that date.

Responsibility for Compliance

Responsibility for complying with complex construction standards will rest with the manufacturer although users will still be responsible for maintaining vehicles in roadworthy condition. The construction standards applied by the scheme are limited to those which can be approved during the primary stage of manufacture. The standards are identical to those already required under the Construction and Use Regulations but under this scheme vehicles have to be approved before they can be used on the road.

Effects on Plating and Testing

The scheme requires plated weights for heavy goods vehicles to be set

11: TYPE APPROVAL

during the Type Approval process instead of waiting until the first annual plating and testing examination. This means that heavy vehicle operators need a Type Approval Certificate in order to get a Ministry plate for display in the vehicle cab (see Chapter 13). However, annual testing is retained so as to check the condition of vehicles and to ensure that plated weights are accurate.

Responsibility for Type Approval

All aspects of Type Approval are the responsibility of the Department of Transport, Standards Division, Tollgate House, Houlton Street, Bristol BS2 9DT.

The Standards Checked

To obtain goods vehicle national Type Approval it is first necessary to obtain individual systems approvals for the following items:
1. Power-to-weight ratio (not applicable to petrol-engined vehicles or dual-purpose vehicles).
2. Gaseous exhaust emissions (petrol-engined vehicles only).
3. Particle emission (ie exhaust smoke) (diesel-engined vehicles only).
4. External noise level.
5. Radio-interference suppression (petrol-engined vehicles only).
6. Brakes.

Arrangements for First Licensing of Vehicles

For vehicles which are over 1525kg unladen weight or which form part of an articulated vehicle, application for first licensing on Form V55 must be accompanied by two copies of the Type Approval Certificate, which should have been supplied with the vehicle. On one of these the applicant must complete a declaration saying whether or not the vehicle is exempt from the Plating and Testing Regulations (see Chapter 13 for full details) and whether it has been altered in any way that has to be notified to the DTp under the Type Approval Regulations and, if so, whether any action arising from the notification has been satisfactorily completed.

Issue of Plates

When application is made for first licensing a vehicle which is subject to plating and testing, the local Vehicle Registration Office (VRO) will send a copy of the Type Approval Certificate with the applicant's declaration to the Goods Vehicle Centre (GVC) at Swansea. The second copy will be stamped and returned to the applicant to serve as a temporary Ministry plate. When the GVC receives the copy of the certificate, and if the details compare satisfactorily with those on the copy sent direct by the vehicle manufacturers, the GVC will issue a Ministry plate and laminated plating certificate. These will be sent direct to the person or company in whose name the vehicle is registered. Thus, operators buying new vehicles receive their first plate and plating certificate for the vehicle from the GVC at the time of licensing rather than from the hgv testing station when the vehicle is presented for its first annual test as under previous arrangements. When application is made for licensing a vehicle which is exempt from plating and testing, a copy of the certificate and the declaration will be sent to the GVC so that they are aware that it is exempt.

Refusal to Licence

Since 1 April 1983 no vehicle subject to the Type Approval regulations will be first licensed unless the DTp registration Form V55 has a valid Type Approval number on it or it is an exempt vehicle.

Alteration to Vehicles

If a vehicle, which has been issued with an Approval Certificate and supplied to a dealer or direct to an operator, is modified by them, prior to first licensing, they must notify the VCA at Bristol and send the certificate for the vehicle together with full technical details, drawings of the alterations and details of the weights on the certificate which need, or may need, changing.

The VCA will judge whether the alterations affect the vehicle's compliance with the regulations; if they do not affect compliance the certificate will be returned so the vehicle can be licensed. If they do contravene compliance, the certificate will be cancelled and fresh approval will need to be obtained before the vehicle can be licensed. This is a complex and costly procedure that most operators will want to avoid; they can do so by registering and licensing the vehicle before any alterations are carried out.

12: Vehicle Lighting and Marking

The legal requirements for vehicles to be fitted with and to display lights at night and other times, and for the fitment of reflectors and other markings on vehicles are contained in the Road Vehicles Lighting Regulations 1989 (as amended). These regulations specify in considerable detail all the requirements for the position of lamps and reflectors and the angles from which they must be visible. This chapter can only include a summary of the relevant requirements and dimensions as they apply to goods vehicles which, for most normal purposes, is satisfactory because vehicles and trailers are generally ready-fitted with lamps and reflectors conforming to legal requirements when supplied from new.

However, for a variety of reasons, operators may find it necessary to replace and re-locate lamps from time to time when carrying out repairs and conversions, and at this time they are advised to check the regulations carefully to ensure strict compliance with the law. Not only can prosecution follow for incorrectly positioned or non-functioning lights and reflectors, but vehicles could fail their annual test on this account which adds to operating costs and wastes time. There are also the safety considerations with the lives of both vehicle drivers and other road users at risk if vehicles are not showing correct or adequate lights.

The Regulations require that lights and reflectors which are fitted to vehicles must be maintained so as to enable them to be driven on a road between sunset and sunrise, or in seriously reduced visibility between sunrise and sunset, or to be parked on a road between sunset and sunrise, or between the hours or darkness, without contravening the regulations. All lights must be kept clean and in good working order. It is an offence to have defective or obscured lighting on a vehicle at any time, but there is a defence against conviction under certain circumstances (see overleaf).

Obligatory Lights

Between sunset and sunrise vehicles used on a public road must display the following obligatory lights, other lights and reflectors:
1. Two front position lamps (ie sidelamps) showing white lights to the front.
2. Two rear position lamps (ie rear lamps) showing red lights to the rear.
3. Two headlamps showing white lights to the front (alternatively, the light may be a yellow light).
4. Illumination for the rear number (ie registration) plate when the other vehicle lights are on.
5. Certain goods vehicles and trailers additionally require side marker lamps plus side-facing reflectors and rear reflective markings – see below.
6. One or two red rear fog lamps on post-1 April 1980 vehicles.
7. Two red reflex retro reflectors at the rear.
8. End-outline marker lamps.

9. Direction indicators on either side showing to the front and rear and capable of giving hazard warning on post-1 April 1986 vehicles.
10. And any other lights or lighting devices with which the vehicle is fitted (eg stop lamps, hazard warning signals, running lamps, dim-dip devices and headlamp levelling devices).

It is illegal except in certain specified cases for a goods vehicle to show a white light to the rear (showing such a light when reversing and indirect illumination of the rear registration plate are permitted for example) or a red light to the front.

Defence

A defence is provided to a charge of having defective lights on a vehicle if it can be proved that the defect occurred during the journey on which the contravention had been detected or that when the contravention had been detected steps had been taken to have the defect remedied 'with all reasonable expedition'. This defence does not apply in the case of a vehicle used with defective lights during the period when the law requires the lights to be in use (ie between sunset and sunrise).

Headlamps

Motor vehicles must be fitted with two headlamps capable of showing a white or yellow light to the front – both lamps must emit the same colour light. Headlamps must be either permanently dipped or fitted with dipping equipment. Vehicles first used since 1 April 1987 must have dim-dip lighting devices unless their lighting equipment complies with EC requirements (see below).

Headlamps must be mounted so that they are not lower than 500mm from the ground and not higher than 1200mm. They must be placed on either side of the vehicle with their illuminated areas not more than 400mm from the side of the vehicle. They must be equipped with bulbs or sealed-beam units of not less than 30 watts in the case of vehicles first used before 1 April 1986. For vehicles used since this date no minimum wattage requirement is specified.

Headlamp Exemptions

Certain vehicles are exempt from the headlamp requirements. These include vehicles with less than four wheels, pedestrian-controlled vehicles, agricultural implements, land tractors, works trucks, vehicles not capable of travelling at a speed of more than 6mph and military vehicles.

Headlamps on Electric Vehicles

Electrically-propelled goods vehicles with four or more wheels registered before October 1969 and electric vehicles with two or three wheels first used before 1 January 1972 and capable of a speed of more than 15mph are required to comply with the headlamp requirements. Those electrically-propelled vehicles which are incapable of speeds of more than 15mph are exempt from the headlamp requirements.

Use of Headlamps

Headlamps must be adjusted so that they do not cause dazzle. When

12: VEHICLE LIGHTING AND MARKING

vehicles which require headlamps are being driven on unlit roads during the hours of darkness and in seriously reduced daytime visibility the headlamps must be illuminated. They must be switched off when the vehicle is stationary except at traffic stops.

Unlit roads are roads on which there are no street lamps or on which the street lamps are more than 200yds apart.

Headlamps in Daylight
It is a legal requirement for vehicles to use side position lights (ie sidelights) and headlights when travelling in seriously reduced daytime visibility conditions such as in fog, smoke, heavy rain, spray or snow. If matching fog or fog and spot lights are fitted in pairs these may be used instead of headlights, but sidelights must still be used and the other vehicle lights must be on (eg side marker lights).

There is no specific definition of 'seriously reduced visibility' in the regulations. It is left to the driver to judge whether it is advisable and sensible to use his lights to enable his vehicle to be seen by others.

Dim-Dip Lighting

Since 1 April 1987 newly registered vehicles must be fitted with dim-dip lighting devices which operate automatically when the obligatory lights of the vehicle are switched on and ensure that either 10 per cent (with halogen) or 15 per cent (with grading filament lamps) of the normal dipped beam intensity shows when the vehicle ignition key is switched on or the engine is running. The European Court of Justice has ruled that it is unfair for the British government to legislate for the fitment of dim-dip lighting devices for vehicles which already comply with the EC lighting directive (EC 756/1976).

Front Position Lamps (Sidelamps)

Two front position lamps (ie sidelamps) emitting a white light through a diffused lens must be fitted to all motor vehicles and trailers. If such lamps are incorporated within a headlamp showing a yellow light then the side position lamps may be yellow. No minimum wattage is specified for these lights. The lights must be equal in height from the ground and mounted not more than 1500mm from the ground (in exceptional circumstances this height can be increased to 2100mm) in the case of vehicles first used on or after 1 April 1986 and 2300mm in other cases, and not more than 400mm from the outer edge of the vehicle for vehicles first used since 1 April 1986 and 510mm in other cases. No minimum height above the ground is specified.

Exemptions

Exemptions apply to trailers not more than 1600mm wide and those no longer than 2300mm (excluding the drawbar), built before 1 October 1985.

Optional Lamps

Fog and spot lamps (ie optional lamps) if required should be fitted and used in symmetrical pairs. They must emit either a white or yellow light, must be adjusted so that they do not cause dazzle to other road users, must not be lit when the vehicle is parked and must not be used at any time other than in conditions of seriously reduced visibility. If they are fitted and used singly, the headlamps must also be illuminated. Spot lamps may be used singly and without headlamps if at the time, use of headlamps was not legally required (eg when driving through built-up areas at night when sidelights only are required).

These lamps should be positioned not more than 1200mm from the ground and not more than 400mm from the sides of the vehicle. They should be aligned so that the upper edge of the beam is, as near as practicable, 3 per cent below the horizontal when the vehicle is at its kerbside weight and has a weight of 75kg on the driver's seat.

Reversing Lamps

White reversing lamps (not more than two) may be fitted to vehicles provided they are only used while the vehicle is reversing and operate automatically only when reverse gear is selected. Alternatively, they may be operated manually by a switch (which serves no other purpose) in the driver's cab provided that a warning device indicates to the driver that the lights are illuminated. The lights must be adjusted so as not to cause dazzle to other road users. Such lamps when bearing an 'e' approval mark do not have to meet minimum wattage requirements but those without approval marks must not exceed 24 watts.

Number Plate Lamp

Rear number plates (ie registration plates) on vehicles must be indirectly illuminated when the other obligatory lamps on the vehicles are lit. The light must be white and must be shielded so that it only illuminates the number plate and does not show to the rear.

Rear Position Lamps (Rear Lamps)

Two red rear position lamps (ie rear lamps) must be fitted to all motor vehicles and trailers. There is no specified wattage for these lights. They must be mounted not less than 350mm and not more than 1500mm (2100mm in exceptional circumstances) from the ground. They must be at least 500mm apart (no specified distance on pre-1 April 1986 registered vehicles) and not more than 400mm (800mm on pre-1 April 1986 registered vehicles) from the outside edge of the vehicle.

Stop Lamps

All goods vehicles (except those not capable of more than 25mph) must be fitted with red stop lamps which are maintained in a clean condition and in good and efficient working order. Vehicles registered before 1 January 1971 need only one such lamp which must be fitted at the centre or to the offside of the vehicle, although a second matching lamp may be fitted on the near side. Vehicles registered since that date need two such lamps (specified wattage 15 to 36 watts except with pre-1 January 1971 registered vehicles) mounted not less than 350mm from the ground and not more than 1500mm (in exceptional circumstances this may be increased to 2100mm) and they must be at least 400mm apart. Such lamps must be visible horizontally from 45 degrees on either side and normally from 15 degrees above and below vertically (from only 5 degrees below where fitted less than 750mm from the ground and only 10 degrees below when fitted not more than 1500mm from the ground).

Direction Indicators

All goods vehicles must be fitted with amber-coloured direction indicators (on pre-September 1965 registered vehicles indicators can be white facing to the front and red facing to the rear) at the front and rear which must be fixed to the vehicle not more than 1500mm (2300mm in exceptional cases) and not less than 350mm above the ground, at least 500mm apart and not more than 400mm from the outer edges of the vehicle. Side repeater indicators are required on vehicles first used since 1 April 1986 and these must be fitted within 2600mm of the front of the vehicle. Normally vehicles should have one indicator on each side at the front and rear but may have two on each side at the rear. They must not have more than one on each side at the front.

Indicators bearing approval marks do not have to meet minimum wattage requirements but those without such marks must be between 15 and 36 watts. They must flash at a rate of between 60 and 120 times a minute and a visible or audible warning must indicate to the driver when they are operating. The indicators must be maintained in a clean condition and in good and efficient working order.

Semaphore Arm Indicators

Vehicles first registered before 1 September 1965 are allowed to have either semaphore arm or flashing indicators. The semaphore arm type must be amber in colour but the flashing indicators may show a white light to the front and a red light to the rear.

Hazard Warning

Direction indicators operating on both sides of the vehicle simultaneously as a hazard warning to other road users are required by law on all vehicles first used since 1 April 1986. They must be actuated by a switch solely controlling that device and a warning light must indicate to the driver that the device is being operated. The hazard indicators may be used when the vehicle is stationary on a road, or any part of the road (ie not just the carriageway), because of a breakdown of it or another vehicle, an accident or other emergency situation, or when the vehicle is causing a temporary obstruction on a road when loading or unloading.

Emergency Warning Triangles
As an additional warning of a hazard, drivers *may* (ie it is not compulsory to do so) place a red warning triangle on the road to the rear of a vehicle

causing a temporary obstruction (eg through breakdown). The triangle must be made and marked to British Standard Specification BS AU47: 1965. It must be placed upright on the road, 45 metres to the rear of the obstruction and on the same side.

Other safety devices may be used to warn of vehicles broken down on the roadside. These include traffic cones, warning lamps and traffic pyramids, as well as conventional warning triangles mentioned above.

Rear Fog Lamps

Rear fog lamps (at least one, but two may be fitted) must be fitted to new vehicles and trailers manufactured on or after 1 October 1979 and first used since 1 April 1980. There is no legal requirement to fit such lamps on pre-1 October 1979 registered vehicles but if they are fitted voluntarily they must comply with the regulations in regard to mounting position, method of wiring and use.

Rear Fog Lamps on Articulated and Towing Vehicles

In the case of articulated combinations, the relevant date in this connection is the date of the older of the tractive unit or semi-trailer. Thus if a post-April 1980 registered tractive unit is coupled to a pre-October 1979 built trailer there appears to be no legal requirement for the vehicle to carry rear fog lamps. This means there is no retrospective fitting requirement for such lamps on older trailers. A broken-down vehicle being towed does not need rear fog lamps. However, it is important to remember the dangers which arise if such a combination is used when the tractive unit or towing vehicle itself has rear fog lamps which would, in some instances, be visible to following motorists who, in bad visibility, might not be aware of some 40 feet of trailer or another vehicle on tow behind the lights.

Mounting of Rear Fog Lamps

Rear fog lamps must be mounted either singly on the offside of the vehicle or in a matched pair not less than 250mm and not more than 1000mm from the ground (in the case of agricultural vehicles this height limit is increased to 1900mm or in cases where, because of the shape of the vehicle, 1000mm is not practical it may be increased to 2100mm). The lamps must be at least 100mm from existing stop lamps.

Restriction on Wiring of Rear Fog Lamps

The lights must be wired so that they only operate when the other statutory lights on the vehicle are switched on; they must not be wired into the brake/stop light circuit and the driver must be provided with an indicator to show him when the lights are in use.

Use of Rear Fog Lamps

The lights should only be used in conditions affecting the visibility of the driver (ie in fog, smoke, heavy rain or spray, snow, dense cloud, etc), when the vehicle is in motion or during an enforced stoppage (a motorway hold-up, for example). They must not cause dazzle. The Highway Code recommends these lights should not be used unless visibility is below 100 metres.

Side Marker Lamps

Side marker lamps must be fitted on long vehicles and trailers as follows:
1. Vehicles (including a combination of vehicles) over 18.3 metres long (including the length of the load):
    (a) one lamp within 9.15 metres of the front
    (b) one lamp within 3.05 metres of the rear
    (c) additional lamps at 3.05-metre intervals between front and rear side marker lamps
2. Vehicles in combination between 12.2 metres and 18.3 metres long (but not articulated vehicles) carrying a supported load:
    (a) one lamp within 1530mm of the rear of the rearmost vehicle in the combination
    (b) one lamp within 1530mm of the centre of the load, if the load extends further than 9.15 metres to the rear of the drawing vehicle.
3. Trailers more than 9.15 metres long (6 metres for post-1 October 1990 trailers):
    (a) one lamp within 1530mm of the centre of the trailer length.

Side marker lamps fitted to pre-1 October 1990 built trailers may show white side marker lights to the front and red lights to the rear, in all other cases such lights must be amber. They must be positioned not more than 2300mm from the ground.

End-Outline Marker Lamps

Vehicles (except those less than 2100mm wide and those first used before 1 April 1991) and trailers (except those less than 2100mm wide and those built before 1 October 1990) must be fitted with two end-outline marker lamps visible from the front and two visible from the rear. They must be positioned no more than 400mm in from the outer edges of the vehicle/trailer and mounted at the front at least level with the top of the windscreen. They must show white lights to the front and red lights to the rear.

Warning Beacons

Amber warning beacons must be fitted to vehicles with four or more wheels and having a maximum speed no greater than 25mph when using unrestricted dual-carriageway roads except where such use is merely 'for crossing the carriageway in the quickest manner practicable in the circumstances'.

Amber warning beacons may also be fitted to vehicles used at the scene of an emergency, when it is necessary or desirable to warn of the presence of a vehicle on the road (eg Special Types vehicles carrying abnormal loads) and to breakdown vehicles used at the scene of accidents and breakdowns and when towing broken-down vehicles.

Green warning beacons may be used on vehicles by medical practitioners registered with the General Medical Council when travelling to or dealing with an emergency.

Blue warning beacons and other special warning lamps may only be used on emergency vehicles (ie ambulance, fire brigade or police service vehicles; Forestry Commission fire fighting vehicles; military bomb disposal vehicles; RAF Mountain Rescue vehicles; Blood Transfusion Service vehicles; British Coal mines rescue vehicles; HM Coastguard and Coast Life Saving Corps vehicles; RNLI vehicles and those used primarily for transporting human tissue for transplanting).

In all cases such beacons should be fitted with their centres no less than 1 200mm from the ground and visible from from any point at a reasonable distance from the vehicle. The light itself must show not less than 60 and not more than 240 times per minute.

Swivelling Spotlights

White swivelling spotlights for illumination purposes may be used at the scene of an accident or breakdown provided that the vehicle carrying the lamp also has an amber warning beacon and that this beacon is in use.

Rear Retro Reflectors

Motor vehicles must be fitted with two red reflex retro reflectors facing squarely to the rear. Reflectors must be fitted not more than 900mm and not less than 350mm from the ground. For normal goods vehicles and trailers they must be within 400mm of the outer edge of the vehicle or trailer and not less than 600mm apart. Reflectors must be capable of being seen from an angle of 30 degrees on either side.

Triangular Rear Reflectors
Triangular rear reflectors if used on a voluntary basis may only be fitted to trailers or broken-down vehicles being towed. There is no longer any specific legal requirement for such reflectors to be fitted. They must not, in any event, be used on other vehicles.

Side Retro Reflectors

Vehicles more than 6 metres long first used since 1 April 1986 (more than 8 metres long if first used before 1 April 1986) and trailers more than 5 metres long must be fitted with two (or more as necessary) amber side retro reflectors on each side. One reflector on each side must be fitted not more than 1 metre from the extreme rear end of the vehicle and another no more than 4 metres from the front of the vehicle with further reflectors at minimum 3-metre intervals (or can be 4 metre intervals) along its length. They must be mounted not more than 1500mm and not less than 350mm from the ground. On pre-April 1986 vehicles one reflector must be positioned in the middle third of the vehicle length and the other within one metre of the rear. Where such reflectors are mounted within one metre of the rear of the vehicle/trailer they may be coloured red instead of amber.

Front Retro Reflectors

Trailers built since 1 October 1990 must be fitted with two obligatory front retro reflectors, white in colour and mounted facing forwards, at least 350mm but not more than 900mm from the ground and no more than 150mm in from the outer edges of the trailer and at least 600mm apart.

Vehicle Markings

Number (Registration) Plates

All vehicles first registered since 1 January 1973 must be fitted with number plates made of reflecting material complying with BS AU 145a. This requirement does not apply to goods vehicles over 7.5 tonnes gross weight which are required to display rear reflective markers (see overleaf) or works trucks, agricultural machines and trailers or pedestrian-controlled vehicles. If a vehicle over 3050kg unladen is exempt from the requirement to fit rear reflective markers then it must be fitted with reflective number plates.

Unladen Weight

Goods vehicles of more than 3050kg unladen weight (ie heavy motor cars), motor tractors and locomotives must have their unladen weight shown in a conspicuous place on the outside of the vehicle where it can easily be seen. This does not apply where the unladen weight is shown on the DTp (ie Ministry) plate attached to the vehicle.

Plates

Goods vehicles over 1525kg and trailers over 1020kg unladen weight must display a DTp plate and/or a manufacturer's plate showing the maximum permissible gross vehicle weight and individual axle weights (see Chapter 13).

Special Types Plates

Since 1 October 1989 it has been a legal requirement for vehicles carrying abnormal loads to display a manufacturer's plate showing the maximum weights at which the vehicle can operate and the relevant speeds for travel at those weights. The weights shown must be those approved by the vehicle or trailer manufacturer and the vehicle must not exceed specified Special Types speed limits when travelling loaded to the weight shown on the plate (see details of speeds for different classes of Special Types vehicles p 284).

Food Vehicles

Vehicles which are used in connection with a food business or from which food is sold must display in a clearly visible place the name and address of the person carrying on the business and the address at which the vehicle is kept or garaged. If the vehicle bears a fleet number and is kept or garaged on that person's premises the garage address is not required but the local authority must be notified.

Height Marking

The travelling height of vehicles and trailers carrying engineering equipment, containers and skips, where the height of the vehicle and load exceeds 12ft, must be marked in the cab where the driver can see it (see p 145 for further details).

Hazard Marking

Vehicles which carry hazardous, radioactive or explosive loads must display appropriate hazard warning symbols on the vehicle whether a bulk tanker, a tank container or a normal delivery vehicle used for carrying hazardous consignments and on the individual packages too in the latter case. Further details are given in Chapter 20.

Rear Reflective Markings

All vehicles with a maximum permissible weight exceeding 7500kg and trailers with a maximum permissible weight exceeding 3500kg (see also p 287) must be fitted with rear reflective markers which make them more conspicuous at night and in poor visibility (Figures 12.1 and 12.2). The markers may also be displayed on loads such as builders' skips (see below).

Which Markers to be Fitted

Vehicles not exceeding 13 metres in length and trailers in combinations not exceeding 11 metres must be fitted with the markers shown in diagrams 1 and 2 in Figure 12.1 or if this is not practical the markers shown in diagram 3 may be fitted. Trailers in combinations of more than 11 metres but not more than 13 metres may fit the markers shown in diagrams 1, 2, 3, 4 or 5. Vehicles more than 13 metres long and trailers in combinations more than 13 metres long must be fitted with the markers shown in diagram 4 or 5.

Types of Markers

There are two types of markings, each in two sizes:

1. Alternating red fluorescent and yellow reflective diagonal strips. Diagrams 1, 2, 3.
2. A central yellow reflective panel overprinted with the words LONG VEHICLE and having a red fluorescent surround. Diagrams 4 and 5.

Specification for Markers

Markers fitted to vehicles and trailers must comply with the regulations regarding size and colour and they must be in the form of durable plates stamped with the mark 'BS AU 152'. They must not be simulated by being painted on the vehicle and the plates must not be defaced, cut or modified to aid fitting to the vehicle.

Fitting Position

The height from the ground to the lower edge of the marker when fitted

12: VEHICLE LIGHTING AND MARKING

Diagram 1

140mm (5½ in)
1400mm (55 in)

Diagram 2

140mm (5½ in)
700mm (27½ in)   700mm (27½ in)

Diagram 3

700mm (27½ in)

Diagram 4

LONG VEHICLE
225mm (8¾ in)
1265mm (50 in)

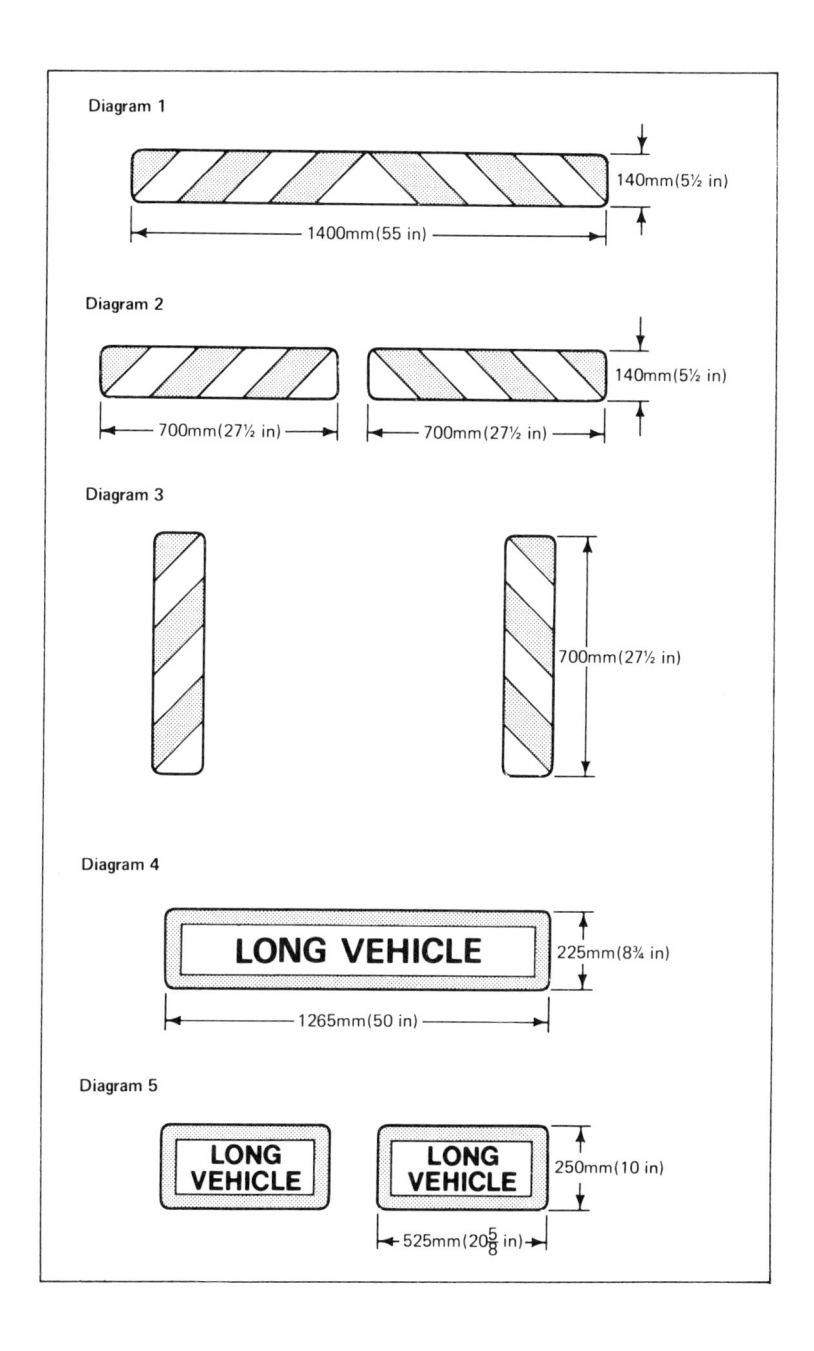

Diagram 5

LONG VEHICLE   LONG VEHICLE
250mm (10 in)
525mm (20⅝ in)

Figure 12.1 *Rear reflective markers required on certain goods vehicles. The plates comprise red fluorescent material background. The lettering is in black on yellow reflex reflecting.*

203

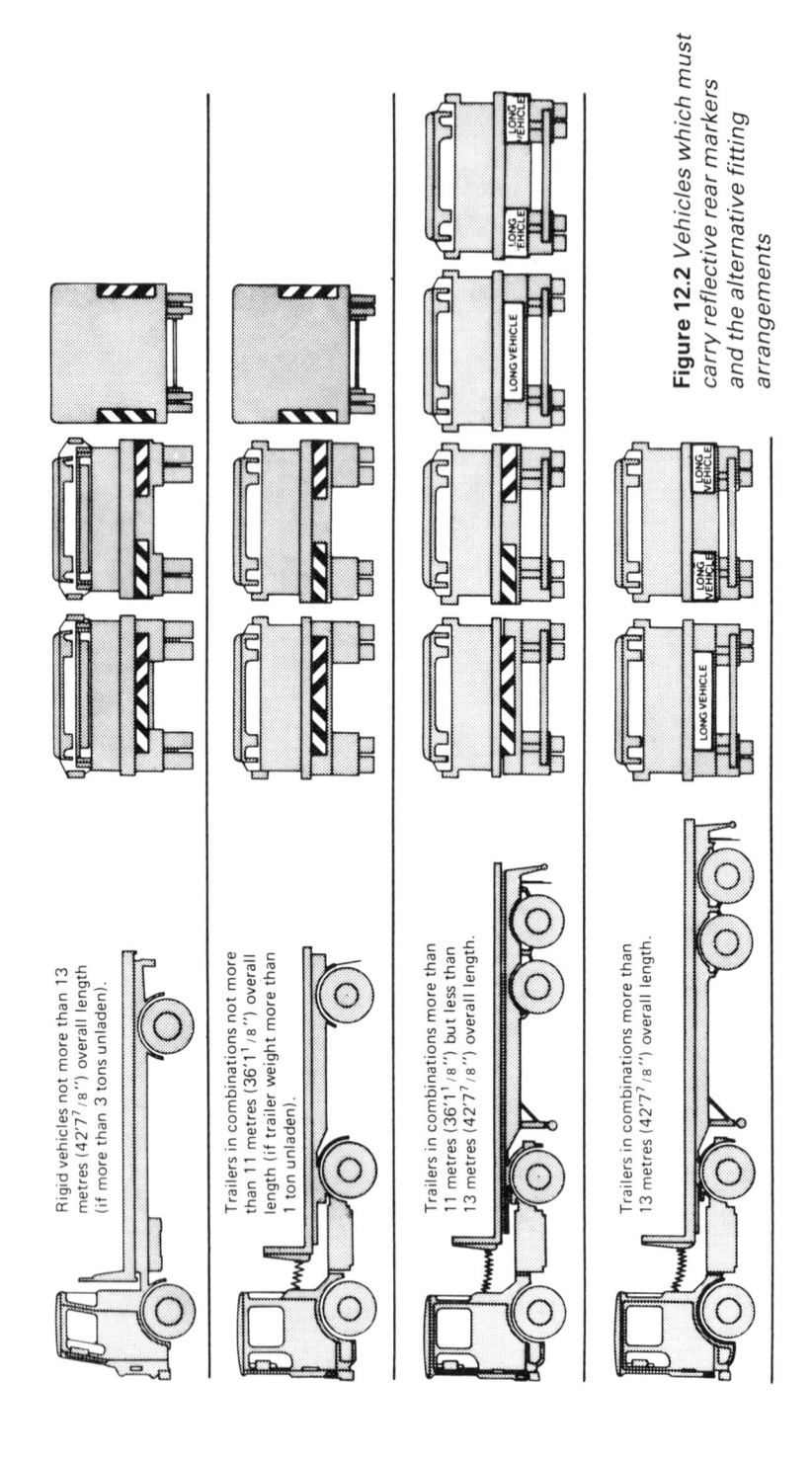

Figure 12.2 *Vehicles which must carry reflective rear markers and the alternative fitting arrangements*

12: VEHICLE LIGHTING AND MARKING

must not exceed 1700mm but must be at least 400mm. It must be fitted parallel to the ground and be facing square to the rear.

Alternative Fitting Position

When a vehicle, which by law requires rear reflective markers to be displayed, is carrying a load which obscures partly or wholly the markers so that they are not clearly visible from the rear, the reflective markers may be fitted to the rear of the load.

Exemptions

Certain vehicles as indicated in the following list are exempt from the requirement to fit these markers. Previously it was illegal to fit the markers to these vehicles, but a change in the regulations permits the fitting of such markers to exempt vehicles on a voluntary basis, provided the vehicles exceed the specified weight limit. It is illegal to display these markers on vehicles which do not require them by law except as mentioned below.

Exempt Vehicles
1. Vehicles with a maximum gross weight not exceeding 7500kg
2. Passenger vehicles other than articulated buses
3. Land tractors, land locomotives, land implements, land implement conveyors, agricultural tractors or industrial tractors
4. Works trucks or works trailers
5. Vehicles in an unfinished condition proceeding to a works for completion or to a place where they are to be sorted or displayed for sale
6. Motor vehicles constructed or adapted for the purpose of forming part of articulated vehicles
7. Broken-down vehicles while being drawn in consequence of the breakdown
8. Engineering plant
9. Trailers, not being part of an articulated bus, drawn by public service vehicles
10. Vehicles designed for fire fighting or fire salvage purposes
11. Vehicles designed and used for the purpose of servicing or controlling aircraft
12. Vehicles designed and used for the transportation of two or more motor vehicles carried thereon, or of vehicle bodies or two or more boats
13. Vehicles proceeding to a place for export
14. Vehicles brought temporarily into Great Britain by persons residing abroad
15. Vehicles in the service of a visiting force or of a headquarters
16. Motor vehicles first used before 1 January 1940
17. Vehicles owned or in the service of the Army, Navy or Air Force
18. Vehicles designed for heating or dispensing tar or similar material for road construction or maintenance
19. Trailers being drying or mixing plant designed for the production of asphalt, bitumen or for macadam

20. Trailers made before 1 August 1982 with an unladen weight not exceeding 1020kg
21 Trailers with a gross weight not exceeding 3500kg.

Builders' Skips

Rear reflective markings of the type described above (as shown in diagram 3, Figure 12.1) must be fitted to the ends of builders' skips which are placed on the highway. They must be fitted as a matched pair as near to the outer edge as possible, mounted vertically and no more than 1.5 metres from the ground to the top edge. They must be kept clean, in good order and be visible from a reasonable distance. Such skips are required to be illuminated when standing on roads at night.

13: HGV Plating, Annual Testing and Vehicle Inspections

Most goods vehicles are required to be tested annually to ensure they are safe to operate on the road and meet the legal requirements relating to mechanical condition. In particular, this annual inspection is intended to determine whether vehicles and trailers meet the standards specified in the Road Vehicles (Construction and Use) Regulations 1986 (as amended). Additionally, it is necessary for goods vehicles and trailers to be 'Ministry plated' to show the maximum permissible gross weight and maximum axle weights at which they may be operated on roads in the United Kingdom. The requirement for annual plating and testing of goods vehicles is contained in the Road Traffic Act 1988 and is detailed in the Goods Vehicles (Plating and Testing) Regulations 1982 as amended.

The Department of Transport Vehicle Inspectorate is responsible for goods vehicle testing stations, as well as the Transport and Road Research Laboratory (TRRL). References in this chapter to the DTp in regard to goods vehicle plating and testing and to DTp vehicle examiners should be taken to be for the purposes of absolute accuracy, references to the DTp Vehicle Inspectorate.

Annual Testing

Articulated tractive units, rigid goods vehicles over 1525kg unladen weight (this changes to over 3.5 tonnes pmw from 1 April 1991), goods carrying semi-trailers and drawbar trailers over 1020kg unladen weight and converter dollies must be tested annually at a DTp heavy goods vehicle testing station. Certain specialised vehicles are exempt from the test, as shown on p 221, and the regulations do not apply to vehicles used under a trade licence. Hgv test stations also carry out the Group V test, which is the light vehicle MOT-type test, on large passenger vehicles which cannot get into normal MOT test garages (see also Chapter 14).

Types of Test

There are various types of test as follows:
1. *First test:* the first annual test of the vehicle or trailer (carried out no later than the end of the anniversary month in which it was first registered) at which it is provided with its DTp plate.
2. *Part 2 re-test:* examines the vehicle which has failed its first test.
3. *Periodical test:* the annual test which applies to all relevant vehicles after the first test.
4. *Part 3 re-test:* re-tests a vehicle which has failed its annual or periodical test.
5. *Part 4 test:* a test provided for in the regulations which may be required if a notifiable alteration has been made to the vehicle or if the operator wants the plating certificate amended to show different weights as a result of changes to the vehicle or, for example, if different tyre equipment has been fitted.

6. *Re-test following appeal:* to area mechanical engineer or the Secretary of State for Transport.

Test Dates

Vehicles may be submitted for test at any one of the full-time or part-time goods vehicle test stations selected by the vehicle operator. Vehicles are due for test each year no later than the end of the anniversary month in which they were first registered (eg a vehicle registered on 1 January 1989 would be due for its first test no later than 31 January 1990 and for subsequent tests by 31 January in each following year). A scheme has been introduced for Saturday testing at certain selected test stations at an additional fee. Operators wishing to take advantage of this facility must mark their applications very clearly 'SATURDAY TEST' and show the appropriate date.

Trailer Test Dates
Articulated semi-trailers and other goods carrying trailers which come within the scheme are due for test during the month indicated by the last two figures of the serial number which the DTp allocates to all trailers when making application for their first test (eg if the last two figures of the serial number are 01 the trailer has to be tested in January each year; 07 means testing in July; 12 means testing in December etc). The first test for trailers is due by the end of the first anniversary month from *when they were sold.* At this test the serial number mentioned above is given.

Year of Manufacture/Registration
There is an anomaly with due test dates when a vehicle or trailer is manufactured in one year and is not registered (or sold in the case of a trailer) before 1 July of the following year. In this case they must be tested by the end of December in the year in which they were first registered or sold.

Phased Programmes and Missed Test Dates
The DTp allows vehicle operators the facility of having vehicles voluntarily tested before their due date to accommodate phased programmes of test preparation rather than having a large number of vehicles due for preparation and test in any particular month of the year. This concession is only permitted once during a vehicle's life and when the particular date has been chosen the vehicle will become due for test in the same month in subsequent years, and not in the month of its first registration.

When a vehicle misses its due test date (possibly because it has been off the road for a period) then provided it is tested more than ten months but less than one year after the date it was originally due for its test, a test certificate issued will be valid for up to 14 months from the date of issue. This will save vehicles being tested twice within a short period of time.

Test Applications

Initial application for a first test and for subsequent tests of vehicles and

13: HGV PLATING, ANNUAL TESTING AND VEHICLE INSPECTIONS

trailers has to be made direct to the DTp, Goods Vehicle Centre, Welcombe House, 91/92 The Strand, Swansea (not to be confused with the DVLC at Swansea). The following forms, which may be obtained from goods vehicle test stations or Traffic Area offices, are used for making the application:

VTG1L   First test of a vehicle
VTG2L   First test of a trailer
VTG40L   For subsequent tests of both vehicles and trailers

Time for Application
Applications for test should be made during the two months prior to the month in which the test is required to take place (ie the last day on which the vehicle may legally operate without a test certificate). Applications should ideally be made at least one month before the date on which the test is preferred by the operator (see note above about the new Saturday test facility).

Test Fees
The appropriate test fee, as follows, should be sent to the Goods Vehicle Centre with the application form:

	Vehicles	Semi-trailers and trailers
First and subsequent tests	£28.00	£15.25
Re-tests	£14.25	£ 8.25
Notifiable alterations	£11.75	£11.00
Saturday supplement	£ 7.50	£ 7.50

Block Bookings
Large fleet operators may make block bookings for vehicles or trailers of similar type to be tested at a test station so that any available vehicle or trailer of the block may be submitted for test at the appointed time. The test station must, however, be advised two or three days before the appointed date as to which particular vehicle or trailer will be submitted for test.

Trailer Testing
Many operators have more semi-trailers and trailers than tractive units or drawing vehicles and in order to have these additional trailers tested it may be necessary for them to be submitted for test with a vehicle which has already been tested and has a current valid test certificate. In these cases only the trailer will be examined and the fee payable will be the trailer fee only.

Test Appointments
Following application to the Goods Vehicle Centre for a first or subsequent

test (see note above about new Saturday testing facility), the test station selected by the operator will confirm the test booking in due course with an appointment card, and all further communications regarding the test must be made with the test station, not with Swansea. If, owing to excessive workload or staff shortage, the chosen test station cannot accommodate the test an appointment will be made at the nearest alternative test station and a card will be sent from that station. The appointment card and the vehicle registration document must be produced on arrival at the test station.

It is essential that vehicles arrive at the test station at the appointed time. Late or non-arrival of a vehicle can mean cancellation of the test and the fee will be forfeited unless an acceptable reason citing 'exceptional circumstances' is put forward. Exceptional circumstances include accident, fire, epidemic, severe weather; failure in the supply of essential services or other unexpected happenings. Breakdown, mechanical defect or non-availability of the vehicle because of shortages in spare parts supply or for operational reasons for example are not looked upon as exceptional circumstances.

Cancellations

If it is necessary to cancel a test booking after making application, provided seven days' notice is given to the test station either a new test date will be arranged or the fee will be refunded after deduction of a £1.50 charge. In exceptional circumstances, such as an accident to the vehicle on the way to the test station, if notification is given to the station within three days of the accident the fee will be carried forward or refunded less £1.50. If other exceptional circumstances arise within seven days of the due date for the test, providing satisfactory evidence is given to the test station, the fee will be similarly carried forward or refunded less £1.50.

Refusal to Test

Test station officials have the right to refuse to test a vehicle or trailer for the following reasons, in these circumstances form VTG12 will be issued:
1. Arrival after the appointed time.
2. Appointment card or vehicle registration document not produced.
3. If it is found that the vehicle brought to the test station does not conform to the details given on the application form.
4. If the vehicle was booked for the test with a trailer but the trailer is not taken to the test station.
5. If the chassis number cannot be found by the examiner or if the serial number given for the trailer by the DTp is not stamped on it.
6. If the vehicle is in a dirty or dangerous condition.
7. If the vehicle does not have sufficient fuel or oil to enable the test to be carried out.
8. If the test appointment card specified that the vehicle should be loaded for the test and it is taken to the test station without a load. Under normal circumstances the decision whether the vehicle is to be tested in a laden or unladen condition is left to the owner to suit his convenience but in some circumstances the test station may request that the vehicle is fully or partially loaded to enable the brakes to be accurately tested on the roller brake tester.
9. In the case of a trailer if the vehicle submitted with it is not suitable to draw it.

13: HGV PLATING, ANNUAL TESTING AND VEHICLE INSPECTIONS

10. If the vehicle breaks down during the test.
11. If the vehicle is submitted for its annual test (ie not for the first test) or a re-test and the previous test and plating certificates are not produced.

Test Procedure

Goods vehicle test stations vary in size and in the number of examination staff. Testing normally takes approximately 45 minutes during which the driver must be available to assist and move the vehicle as required. Examination of vehicles is carried out by DTp examiners based at the station in accordance with *The Goods Vehicle Tester's Manual* published by HMSO. All items which have to be inspected are listed in the *Manual* together with, where necessary, details of how the inspection of each item should be carried out and the reasons for failing the item. Under the 'reasons for rejection' column in the *Manual* where the item inspected is one that is subject to wear, the maximum tolerance will be indicated (see example, Figure 13.1).

The examination is conducted in four stages: items 1 to 40 in the *Tester's Manual* are inspected on the hard standing outside the test building. Items 41 to 61 are inspected at the second stage of the examination over the test pit inside the building. The third section of the test, items 62 to 69, are inspected at the next point where a beam setter is used for checking headlamp alignment. The braking tests, under items 70 to 73, which comprise the fourth section of the examination are the last to be carried out at the end of the test line. A roller brake tester is used for these purposes; the machine indicates on dials on a console the braking force of all the wheels on an axle and each individual wheel (or a pair of twin wheels) when the vehicle's footbrake, handbrake and emergency brake are applied by the driver when directed to do so.

Inspection Sheet
During the test the examiner has an inspection sheet on which all items in the *Tester's Manual* are listed and in the case of failure of any item the sheet is marked accordingly. Four inspection sheets are used as follows:

1. Form VTG4A   For tests of rigid vehicles
2. Form VTG4B   For re-tests of rigid vehicles
3. Form VTG4C   For tests of trailers
4. Form VTG4D   For re-tests of trailers

Items to be Inspected
The list of items shown in *The Goods Vehicle Tester's Manual* to be inspected is as follows:
1. Ministry plate position
2. Ministry plate details
3. Seat belts *
4. –
5. Smoke emission *
6. Road wheels and hubs
7. Size and type of tyres
8. Condition of tyres

9. Sideguards, rear underrun device and bumper bars
10. Spare wheel carrier
11. Trailer couplings *
12. Coupling on trailer
13. Trailer landing legs
14. Condition of wings
15. Cab mountings *
16. Cab doors *
17. Cab floor and steps *
18. Driving seat *
19. Security of body
20. Condition of body
21. –
22. Mirrors *
23. View to front *
24. Condition of glass or other transparent material *
25. Windscreen wipers and windscreen washers
26. Speedometer *
27. Audible warning *
28. Driving controls *
29. Tachograph *
30. Play at steering wheel *
31. Steering wheel *
32. Steering column *
33. –
34. Pressure/vacuum warning *
35. Build-up of pressure/vacuum *
36. Hand lever operating mechanical braking systems (except trailers)
37. Service brake pedal *
38. Service brake operation *
39. Hand-operated brake control valves *
40. –
41. Condition of chassis
42. Electrical wiring and equipment
43. Engine and transmission mountings *
44. Oil leaks *
45. Fuel tank and system *
46. Exhaust system *
47. –
48. Suspension pins and bushes
49. Suspension spring units and linkages
50. Attachment of spring units, linkages and sub-frames
51. Shock absorbers (dampers)
52. –
53. Stub axles/wheel bearings
54. Steering linkage
55. Steering gear *
56. Power steering *
57. Transmission *
58. –
59. Mechanical brake components
60. Brake actuators
61. Braking systems and components
62. Rear markings

13: HGV PLATING, ANNUAL TESTING AND VEHICLE INSPECTIONS

63. Front positional lamps
64. Rear positional lamps and rear fog lamps
65. Reflectors
66. Direction indicators
67. Aim of headlights *
68. Headlamps
69. Stop lamps
70. Trailer parking brake
71. Service brake performance
72. Secondary brake performance
73. Parking brake performance
74. –
75. –

* These items do not apply when trailers are being inspected and the blank spaces are left to enable the DTp to add any further items at a later time.

Examination of spray suppression equipment fitted to heavy vehicles and trailers has been included as part of the test since January 1989.

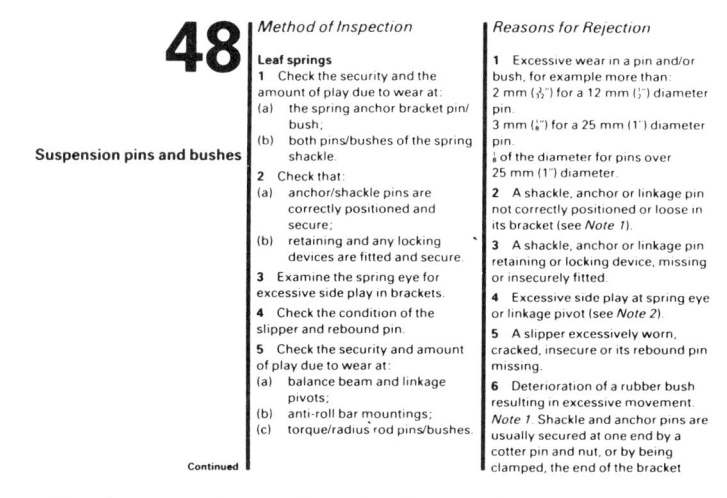

	Method of Inspection	Reasons for Rejection

48
 	
Suspension pins and bushes
	Leaf springs
	1 Check the security and the amount of play due to wear at:
	  (a) the spring anchor bracket pin/bush;
	  (b) both pins/bushes of the spring shackle.
	2 Check that:
	  (a) anchor/shackle pins are correctly positioned and secure;
	  (b) retaining and any locking devices are fitted and secure.
	3 Examine the spring eye for excessive side play in brackets.
	4 Check the condition of the slipper and rebound pin.
	5 Check the security and amount of play due to wear at:
	  (a) balance beam and linkage pivots;
	  (b) anti-roll bar mountings;
	  (c) torque/radius rod pins/bushes.
	Continued
		1 Excessive wear in a pin and/or bush, for example more than:
		  2 mm ($\frac{3}{32}$") for a 12 mm ($\frac{1}{2}$") diameter pin.
		  3 mm ($\frac{1}{8}$") for a 25 mm (1") diameter pin.
		  $\frac{1}{8}$ of the diameter for pins over 25 mm (1") diameter.
		2 A shackle, anchor or linkage pin not correctly positioned or loose in its bracket (see *Note 1*).
		3 A shackle, anchor or linkage pin retaining or locking device, missing or insecurely fitted.
		4 Excessive side play at spring eye or linkage pivot (see *Note 2*).
		5 A slipper excessively worn, cracked, insecure or its rebound pin missing.
		6 Deterioration of a rubber bush resulting in excessive movement.
		Note 1. Shackle and anchor pins are usually secured at one end by a cotter pin and nut, or by being clamped, the end of the bracket

Figure 13.1 *An example page from the Goods Vehicle Tester's Manual*

Test Pass

When a goods vehicle is found to be in satisfactory order a test certificate is issued by the test station. For goods vehicles the certificate is form VTG5 and for goods-carrying trailers it is VTG5A which is issued together with a trailer test disc (VTG5B). The trailer test disc is included with the certificate and this must be removed and fixed on to the trailer in a protective holder in a position where it is conspicuous, readily accessible and clearly visible from the nearside.

The heavy goods vehicle test certificate must be produced when applying for an excise licence for a vehicle which comes within the scope of these regulations and otherwise at the request of a competent authority (see also p 000).

Replacement Documents
Replacement test certificates and trailer test date discs and replacement

plates and plating certificates (see later in chapter) may be obtained from the Goods Vehicle Centre at Swansea at a cost of £8.25 each. Application in both cases should be made on form VTG59 obtainable from goods vehicle test stations or Traffic Area offices. Automatic replacement of lost or defaced documents is not guaranteed. The Secretary of State has powers to order a re-test before issuing such replacements, in which case full test fees become payable.

Test Failure and Re-tests

When the vehicle is sent for test, it is recommended that a mechanic with a tool-kit and minor spares items (light bulbs, for example) accompanies it so that any minor defects can be rectified on the premises and the test can be completed. The examiner may allow certain minor defects to be repaired during the test if they do not take up too much time and delay the test schedule. In some instances the vehicle may be allowed to be taken out of the test line for minor repairs to be carried out but this again is at the discretion of the examiner.

If it is necessary to take the vehicle away to get the defects rectified and it is submitted again later that day or during the next working day, no additional charge is made. These free re-tests are restricted to those cases where the vehicle failed because of certain prescribed defects in items as follows:
- Legal plate position
- Legal plate details
- Bumper bars
- Spare wheel carrier
- Cab doors
- Mirrors
- View to front
- Speedometer
- Audible warning
- Oil leaks
- Fuel tanks, pipes and system
- Obligatory side lamps
- Obligatory rear lamps
- Reflectors
- Direction indicators
- Headlamps – vertical aim
- Obligatory headlamps
- Obligatory stop lamps.

If the vehicle which fails the test is submitted to the same test station again within 14 days, a reduced re-test fee is charged and only the items on which the test was failed are re-examined. The re-test fee is £14.25 for vehicles and £8.25 for trailers. Arrangements for re-tests have to be made with the manager of the test station concerned.

Appeals against Test Failure
If a vehicle or trailer undergoing test or re-test failed for a reason which the operator believes is not justified he has a right of appeal to the DTp Area Mechanical Engineer, who is based at the Traffic Area office, provided it is made within ten days of the test. If the operator is not satisfied with the Area Mechanical Engineer's decision, a further appeal may be made to the Secretary of State for Transport within 14 days of this decision.

13: HGV PLATING, ANNUAL TESTING AND VEHICLE INSPECTIONS

Appeals must be made on form VTG8 and the fees are £15 in the case of appeals to the Area Mechanical Engineer and £25 for appeals to the Minister. Appeal fees are refunded if the appeal is upheld.

Plating of Goods Vehicles and Trailers

Manufacturer's Plating

All new goods vehicles and new trailers over 1020kg unladen weight must be fitted with a plate (see Figure 13.2) by the manufacturer which shows specified information as follows:
- The manufacturer's name
- The date of manufacture
- Vehicle type
- Engine type and power rating
- Chassis or serial number
- Number of axles
- Maximum weight allowed on each axle
- Maximum gross weight for the vehicle (including the weight imposed on the tractive unit by a semi-trailer in the case of articulated vehicles)
- Maximum train weight.

The plate containing this information is normally fitted inside the driver's cab on the nearside.

For trailers, the information shown on the plate is:
- The manufacturer's name
- Date of manufacture
- Chassis or serial number
- Number of axles
- Maximum weight allowed on each axle
- Maximum weight imposed on the drawing vehicle in the case of semi-trailers
- Maximum gross weight for the trailer.

The plate for trailers is usually riveted to the chassis frame on the nearside.

Design Weights
The weights stated are those at which the manufacturer has designed the vehicle to operate. Where these weights exceed those permitted by law (ie in the Construction and Use Regulations) for the type of vehicle in question then, until such time as the vehicle is plated by the Department of Transport, the lower statutory weight limits apply. Conversely, if the manufacturer's design weight is lower than that permitted by law for the type of vehicle then it is the lower limit which applies.

DTp (ie 'Ministry') Plating

When Type Approved goods vehicles are first registered an official plate is issued showing the maximum permissible gross vehicle weight and individual axle weights at which the vehicle or trailer is allowed to operate within Great Britain.

A plating certificate (Figure 13.3) and a plate (Figure 13.4), giving similar details to those on the manufacturer's plate, is issued by the Goods

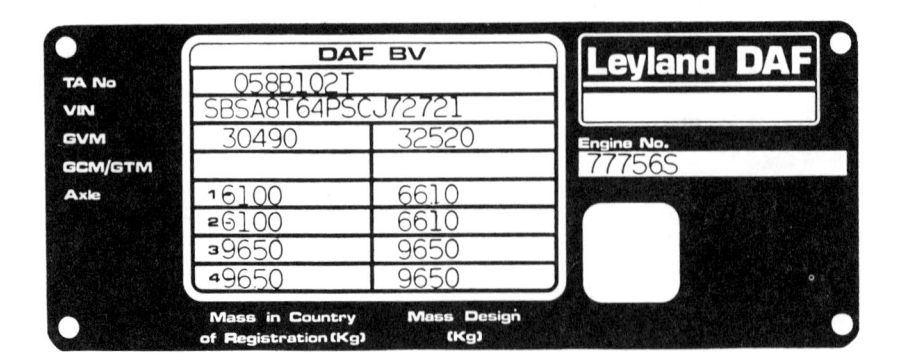

Figure 13.2 *An example of a manufacturer's plate for a rigid 8-wheel chassis*

Vehicle Centre at Swansea after receipt of the necessary documents (including the Type Approval Certificate) when a new vehicle is first registered. The plating certificate must be retained by the vehicle operator but the plate (made of laminated paper, not metal as is the manufacturer's plate) which is also issued must be fixed to the vehicle in an easily accessible position. Generally it should be fitted inside the cab of vehicles on the nearside (but not affixed to the door) and in a suitable position on the nearside of trailers (it is usually fitted to the chassis frame). In all cases the plates should be protected against the weather, kept clean and legible and secure against accidental loss.

Tractive units and semi-trailers in articulated outfit combinations are plated separately and the individual plates must be fixed separately to the tractive unit and the trailer.

Articulated Vehicle Matching

When planning loads for or when loading articulated outfits, the plated weights of both the tractive unit and the trailer must be taken into consideration. If the outfit normally operates as a matched pair at all times there is little difficulty, but if various trailers covering a range of plated weights are used with the tractive unit, care must be taken by the people concerned (drivers, loaders, weighbridge staff, etc) to ensure that the correct weights are observed so that no offence is committed. For example, if a two-axle tractive unit plated for operation at 38 tonnes gross weight is normally used at this weight with a tri-axle semi-trailer but on a particular occasion a tandem-axle semi-trailer is used, a lower weight, limited by the semi-trailer's gross plated weight (say 32.5 tonnes), must be observed and an offence would be committed if the outfit was still loaded to 38 tonnes gross weight. With 38 tonnes operation permitted for certain articulated vehicles, it is important in this context to ensure that the minimum overall length requirements are also observed (see p 143).

Standard Lists

Vehicles are plated by the DTp in accordance with 'standard lists'. These

13: HGV PLATING, ANNUAL TESTING AND VEHICLE INSPECTIONS

Figure 13.3 *DTp plating certificate VTG 7*

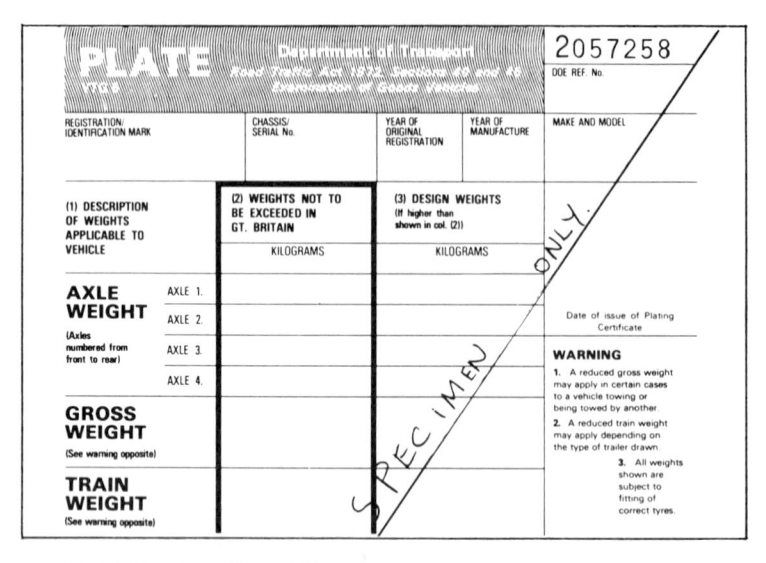

Figure 13.4 *DTp plate (form VTG 6)*

lists, one for each make of vehicle and trailer, are published by HMSO and they are based on information provided by the manufacturer relating to all the models and types of vehicle or trailer, with their respective serial/chassis numbers, manufactured in recent years.

The designed axle weights and gross vehicle weights are shown in the lists together with differences in design weights which apply when alternative options in suspension systems (such as a differing number of leaves in the springs), wheels and tyres are selected on any particular model. For example, the use of leaf springs with one or more additional leaves or the use of tyres of a different size or ply rating could possibly mean an increase of a few kilos on the axle or gross vehicle weights. Conversely, by selecting an alternative lower specification, reduced axle or gross vehicle weights may apply (eg to come below the levels at which 'O' licensing or hgv drivers' licensing apply).

Provided vehicles submitted for test comply with the details set out in the standard lists, they will be plated by the DTp at the standard list weights. Plating at lower than standard list weights will only be done if the tyres fitted to the vehicle at the time of the test are not of the ply rating shown in the standard list for that vehicle. In such circumstances the vehicle will be plated at axle and gross weights suitable for the tyres fitted. The weights will be decided by reference to a tyre data sheet, also obtainable from HMSO, which indicates the loadings on tyres of various size and ply ratings.

In *no* circumstances will a vehicle which has an inefficient braking performance or is not maintained to the required standard be plated at lower than standard list weights to compensate for these defects. In such cases the examiners will refuse to plate the vehicle.

Non-Standard Vehicles
Vehicles which are non-standard and therefore do not appear in the standard lists are plated at gross and axle weights decided by the test

station staff on the basis of the following:
1. Information supplied by the operator concerning the specification of the vehicle.
2. Information contained in the particular manufacturer's standard list relating to the vehicle of the nearest standard type.
3. The vehicle's braking efficiency as indicated on the roller-brake tester.
4. The load rating of the tyres fitted and the general chassis, axle and suspension.

Applicable Weights
If the maximum axle and gross vehicle weights shown on the manufacturers' plates for particular vehicles are higher than the current Construction and Use limit for that type of vehicle, then the Construction and Use weights prevail. For example, many of the heaviest tractive units and semi-trailers are designed and plated for operation at up to 44 tonnes or even more in anticipation of future increases in permitted vehicle weights or for carrying abnormal loads, but for the present such vehicles, while operating in the UK on normal operations (ie not Special Types applications), are limited to the Construction and Use maximum gross weight of 38 tonnes which applies in this country.

International Plates

International Proof of Compliance plates are available to and may be voluntarily fitted to vehicles by international hauliers. These plates show compliance with the weights and dimension requirements of EC Directives 85/3 and 86/364. They have been introduced to speed up clearance times through customs for vehicles on international journeys, showing that the vehicles to which they are fitted do meet the regulations on weights, widths and lengths. Operators wishing to fit these plates should apply to the Goods Vehicle Centre at Swansea using application forms obtainable from Swansea direct or from heavy goods vehicle testing stations. Eventually the new style plate will replace the present style of 'Ministry' plates.

Notifiable Alterations

Operators who make any alteration to the structure of their vehicle must notify the DTp before the vehicle is used on the road. Details of the alterations which require notification on form VTG10 are as follows:

(a) *Alterations to the structure or fixed equipment of a vehicle which vary its carrying capacity*
These include alterations to any of the following items:
(i) *Chassis frame or structure*
Any alteration which increases or decreases the front or rear overhang by more than 1 foot. Any structural alteration (other than normal adjustment of an extensible structure) which reduces or extends the wheelbase (or in the case of a semi-trailer the equivalent distance). Any other extension, deletion or alteration including cutting, welding, riveting, etc which materially weakens the chassis frame or structure or changes its torsional stiffness.

(ii) *Steering suspension, wheels and axles (including stub axles and wheel hubs)*
The fitting of steering gear, axles, hubs or road springs of a different design or load bearing capacity. The fitting of additional wheels and axles, or the removal of such items. Any addition, deletion or alteration which reduces the inherent strength of the above components.

(iii) *The fitting of an alternative body of different design, construction or type*
Any alteration which reduces materially the strength of the body structure or the means by which it is attached to the chassis. Any alteration which causes the body to extend beyond the rear of the chassis frame.

(b) *Alterations to braking system*
These comprise alterations which adversely affect either the braking system or the braking performance of the vehicle. They include the addition or deletion of components such as reservoirs, servo motors, brake actuators, exhausters and compressors. They would also include the addition of any equipment which it is necessary to connect to any part of the braking system, and the fitting of different brake drums or shoes or liners of a smaller contact area.

(c) *Other alterations to the structure or fixed equipment*
Any other alteration made in the load bearing structure or fixed equipment of the vehicle, eg the coupling gear, which could make the vehicle unsafe to travel on roads at any weight shown on the plate and plating certificate. In the case of a motor vehicle this could include such alterations as changing the type of engine or re-positioning the engine or its mountings (eg petrol to diesel, normal control to forward control, etc).

Exemptions from Plating and Testing

Vehicles which are subject to the Goods Vehicle (Plating and Testing) Regulations 1982 (as amended) are exempt from the need to hold current plating and testing certificates while being taken to a test station, when used on a road during the test, returning to base from the test station after a test and being taken (unladen) to a working or repair centre for work to be carried out on them in connection with the test.

Temporary Exemption
Temporary exemption from the need to hold a test certificate for not more than three months can be granted by the test station manager if for some special reason it is not possible for a vehicle or trailer to be submitted for test by the last day of the month in which it was due to be tested.

Temporary exemption may be granted in the event of severe weather, fire, epidemic, a failure in the supply of essential services, an industrial dispute, or other unexpected happenings to either a vehicle or the test station. A normal mechanical breakdown of the vehicle will not be considered a circumstance for temporary exemption. A certificate (form VTG33) confirming the exemption will be issued and this can be produced either to

13: HGV PLATING, ANNUAL TESTING AND VEHICLE INSPECTIONS

the police if they ask for the test certificate, or when applying for an excise licence for the vehicle.

Exempt Vehicles
Vehicles to which the regulations do not apply are as follows:
1. Dual-purpose vehicles not constructed or adapted to form part of an articulated vehicle.
2. Mobile cranes as defined in Schedule 3 of the Vehicles (Excise) Act 1971.
3. Breakdown vehicles.
4. Engineering plant and movable plant and equipment specially designed and constructed for the special purposes of engineering plant.
5. Trailers being drying or mixing plant designed for the production of asphalt or of bituminous or tar macadam.
6. Tower wagons as defined in Schedule 4 of the Vehicles (Excise) Act 1971.
7. Road construction vehicles as defined in Section 4(2) of the Vehicles (Excise) Act 1971 and road rollers.
8. Vehicles designed for fire fighting or fire salvage purposes.
9. Works trucks, straddle carriers used solely as works trucks, and works trailers.
10. Electrically-propelled motor vehicles.
11. Motor vehicles used solely for clearing frost, ice or snow from roads by means of a snow plough or similar contrivance, whether forming part of the vehicle or not.
12. Vehicles constructed or adapted for, and used solely for, spreading material on roads to deal with frost, ice or snow.
13. Motor vehicles used for no other purpose than the haulage of lifeboats and the conveyance of the necessary gear of the lifeboats which are being hauled.
14. Living vans not exceeding 1525kg unladen weight.
15. Vehicles constructed or adapted for, and used primarily for the purpose of, carrying equipment permanently fixed to the vehicle which equipment is used for medical, dental, veterinary, health, educational, display or clerical purposes, such use not directly involving the sale, hire or loading of goods from the vehicle.
16. Trailers which have no other brakes than a parking brake and brakes which automatically come into operation on the overrun of the trailer.
17. Vehicles exempted from duty because they do not travel on public roads for more than six miles in any week and trailers drawn by such vehicles (Vehicles (Excise) Act 1971 Section 7[1]).
18. Agricultural motor vehicles.
19. Agricultural trailers and trailed appliances drawn on roads only by a land tractor.
20. Passenger-carrying vehicles and hackney carriages.
21. Vehicles used solely for the purpose of funerals.
22. Goods vehicles proceeding to a port for export and vehicles in the service of a visiting force.
23. Vehicles equipped with new or improved equipment or types of equipment and used solely by a manufacturer of vehicles or their equipment or by an importer of vehicles, for or in connection with the test or trial of any such equipment.

24. Motor vehicles temporarily in Great Britain.
25. Motor vehicles for the time being licensed in Northern Ireland.
26. Vehicles having a base or centre in any of the following islands, namely Arran, Bute, Great Cumbrae, Islay, Mull or North Uist, from which the use of the vehicle on a journey is normally commenced.
27. Trailers temporarily in Great Britain, a period of 12 months not having elapsed since the vehicle in question was last brought into Great Britain.
28. Track-laying vehicles.
29. Steam-propelled vehicles.
30. Motor vehicles manufactured before 1 January 1960 used unladen and not drawing a laden trailer, and trailers manufactured before 1 January 1960 and used unladen.
31. Three-wheeled vehicles used for street cleansing, the collection or disposal of refuse, and the collection or disposal of the contents of gullies.
32. Vehicles designed and used for the purpose of servicing or controlling aircraft, while so used on an aerodrome within the meaning of the Airports Authority Act 1965 or on roads to such extent as is essential for the purpose of proceeding directly from one part of such an aerodrome to another part thereof or, subject as aforesaid, outside such an aerodrome unladen and not drawing a laden trailer.
33. Vehicles designed for use, and used on an aerodrome mentioned in the last preceding paragraph solely for the purpose of road cleansing, the collection or disposal of refuse or the collection or disposal of the contents of gullies or cesspools.
34. Vehicles provided for police purposes and maintained in workshops approved by the Minister as suitable for such maintenance, being vehicles provided in England and Wales by a police authority or the receiver for the metropolitan police or, in Scotland, by a police authority or a joint police committee.
35. Heavy motor cars or motor cars constructed or adapted for the purpose of forming part of an articulated vehicle which are used for drawing only a trailer falling within a class of vehicle specified in paragraphs 14, 15 or 16 above or a trailer being used for or in connection with any purpose for which it is authorised to be used on roads under the Special Types general order.
36. Play buses.

NB: The following definitions apply in the above exemptions:
'Break-down vehicle' means a motor vehicle on which is permanently mounted apparatus designed to lift, wholly or partly, one disabled vehicle and tow the vehicle when so lifted and which is not equipped to carry any load other than articles required for the operation of or in connection with that apparatus, or for repairing disabled vehicles.

'Engineering plant' means movable plant or equipment being a motor vehicle or trailer (not constructed primarily to carry a load) specially designed and constructed for the purposes of engineering operations.

'Works truck' means a motor vehicle designed for use in private premises and used on a road only in delivering goods from or to such premises to or from a vehicle on a road in the immediate neighbourhood, or in passing from one part of any such premises to another or to other private premises in the immediate neighbourhood or in connection with road works while at or in the immediate neighbourhood of the site of such works.

Taxing Exempt Vehicles
When applying for a vehicle excise licence for a vehicle exempt from plating and testing, it is necessary to complete declaration form V112G (available from VROs) in order to obtain the licence without a valid test certificate.

Tachograph Testing
Inspection of tachographs is now included in the annual test, but only in respect of the following items:
1. That a tachograph is fitted (ie where the vehicle requires to have it fitted by law).
2. That it can easily be seen from the driving seat.
3. The condition of the instrument.
4. That the instrument can be illuminated.
5. That all seals are present and intact.

Operators submitting vehicles for test, which are exempt from the requirement for tachograph fitment, must declare the exemption on an appropriate form which lists the exempt categories (see p 89 for list of tachograph exemptions).

Production of Documents

The police can request production of both test and plating certificates for goods vehicles when such vehicles have been involved in an accident or if they believe an offence has been committed. If these documents cannot be produced at the time they may be produced within seven days at a police station convenient to the person to whom the request was made, or as soon as reasonably practicable thereafter.

DTp Checks on Vehicles

Roadside Checks

In addition to carrying out annual vehicle tests at the goods vehicle testing stations, the DTp operates roadside checks on commercial vehicles. These roadside checks are carried out at intervals on main roads by examiners who usually take over a lay-by which will accommodate several large vehicles. The DTp has stepped up its normal system of roadside checks in recent times and occasionally carries out checks during the night and during weekends. A police officer, in uniform, standing on the road directs vehicles *(NB: only a police officer in uniform can stop a moving vehicle)* which are required for examination into the lay-by where they are inspected mainly for visible wear and defects of the brakes, steering gear, silencers, tyres, lights and reflectors and for the emission of black smoke when the engine is revved up. The examiners only have a limited amount of equipment on these checks so the extent of their examination is likewise limited but nevertheless the inspection is undertaken by skilled and observant people and very little escapes their attention.

Vehicle Inspections on Premises

Besides roadside checks, DTp examiners and police officers in uniform are, at any reasonable time, free to enter any premises on which goods vehicles are kept and examine the vehicles. The owner's consent has to be obtained to carry out the examination or he must be given at least 48 hours' notice of such a proposal to carry out an examination *(if the notice is sent by recorded delivery post the period is increased to 72 hours)*. If on these inspections defects are found on the vehicles examined, the same procedure applies regarding the prohibition of their use as explained for roadside checks.

A police officer in uniform or a DTp vehicle examiner on production of suitable identification can instruct a driver in charge of a stationary goods vehicle on a road (by the issue of form GV3) to take the vehicle to a suitable place to be examined but this must not be for a distance of more than five miles.

Prohibition notices can be issued by examiners at a goods vehicle test station if defects of a serious enough nature are found. Also the police may be notified if prosecution is warranted, although it is not usual for vehicles in such a precarious state to be submitted for test.

Defect Notices and Prohibitions

Defect Notice

When vehicles are checked by DTp examiners various forms may be issued if defects are found. Form GVDN is used when defects are not of a serious nature but are such that it is in the operator's and other road users' interest to have them quickly rectified.

Prohibition Notices

The driver of any vehicles found by DTp examiners to have serious defects is given a form PG9 (Figure 13.5) on which these are listed. The form PG9 (previously designated form GV9 – see below) is the examiner's authority to stop the use of the vehicle on the road for carrying goods. Depending on how serious the defects are, the prohibition will either take effect immediately, in which case the vehicle, if loaded, has to remain where it is until either it is repaired or has been unloaded and then taken away for repair for which the examiner will give authority by issuing form PG9B (Figure 13.6), or it may be delayed for 12 to 24 hours or more depending on the seriousness of the fault. In this case the vehicle may continue to operate until the limit of the period of exemption of the prohibition by which time, if it is not repaired and cleared, it must be taken off the road. If defects recorded as requiring immediate attention are repaired quickly on the roadside (either by the driver or by a mechanic or repair garage staff who come out to the vehicle) the examiner may issue a variation to the PG 9 notice with form PG9A (Figure 13.7) which then allows the vehicle to be removed and used until the new time specified on the variation notice.

C & U Offences
If defects are found at a roadside check which make the vehicle unsafe to be on the road (usually brakes, steering or suspension defects) or if the defects are such that an offence under the Construction and Use

13: HGV PLATING, ANNUAL TESTING AND VEHICLE INSPECTIONS

Figure 13.5 *Prohibition on driving a vehicle on a road GV9*

Exemption from a Prohibition on the Driving of a Vehicle on a Road

Road Traffic Act 1972

West Midland Traffic Area
Cumberland House
200 Broad Street
Birmingham B15 1TD

Identification No. of Vehicle................................ Make................................

Licence No. (if any)..

By virtue of the powers vested in me by the above Act, and subject to the conditions specified below at Nos..I hereby exempt the vehicle specified above from the terms of the prohibition issued with respect to it

at..hrs............................

the..day of.. 19............

CONDITIONS

That:—1. The vehicle is unladen
    2. The vehicle proceeds at a speed not exceeding..................miles per hour
    3. The vehicle does not tow a trailer
    4. The vehicle is towed by a rigid tow bar
    5. The vehicle is towed by a suspended tow
    6. The vehicle is not used after lighting up time
    7. The vehicle proceeds only between..
        ....and..

This notice of exemption expires at....................hrs the..

day of..19..............

Signed..Goods Vehicle Examiner

At....................................hrs the........................day of....................19............

Copy to..Traffic Area

GV9B

IMPORTANT—Please see Note overleaf.

CP 56-00

Figure 13.6 *Exemption from a prohibition on the driving of a vehicle on a road GV9B*

Road Traffic Act 1972

Variation in the Terms of a Prohibition on Driving a Vehicle on a Road

West Midland Traffic Area
Cumberland House
200 Broad Street
Birmingham B15 1TD

A	B	C	D
E	F	G	H
J	K	L	M

Identification No. of Vehicle............................ Make............................
Licence No. (if any)............................

By the powers vested in me by the above Act I hereby vary the terms of the prohibition notice, issued at............................hrs the............................day of
............................19............................in respect of the vehicle specified above and

1. suspend it until............................hrs the............................day of............................
   19............................or
2. alter the time at which the prohibition shall come into force to............................hrs
   the............................day of............................19............................and/or
3. alter the list of defects occasioning the prohibition.

Defects Occasioning Prohibition

No's............................as specified on the above-mentioned prohibition notice.

Signed............................ Goods Vehicle Examiner

The prohibition will continue in force until it is removed by a Goods Vehicle Examiner appointed by the Secretary of State for the Environment.

At............................hrs the............................day of............................19............................

Signature of person to whom the notice was given at the time of inspection

....

Copy to............................Traffic Area

IMPORTANT—Please see Notes overleaf.

WM 56-ST

GV9A

Figure 13.7 *Variation in the terms of prohibition on driving a vehicle on a road GV9A*

Figure 13.8 *Removal of a prohibition on driving a vehicle on a road GV10*

REFUSAL TO REMOVE A PROHIBITION ON DRIVING A VEHICLE ON A ROAD

Road Traffic Act 1972

West Midland Traffic Area
Cumberland House
200 Broad Street
Birmingham B15 1TD

Identification No. of Vehicle .... Make ....

Licence No. (if any) ....

By virtue of the powers vested in me by the above Act, I hereby refuse to remove the prohibition on driving the vehicle specified above on a road, which was issued at ....hrs.................... day of.................... 19........on the grounds that the vehicle is not fit for service because of defects Nos.......................... listed on the prohibition.

Signed...(Goods Vehicle Examiner)/(Certifying Officer)

at..............................hrs. the...................................day of.................................19..........

Copy to...Traffic Area
IMPORTANT:–See notes overleaf

CP 56-ST

GV9C

Figure 13.9 *Refusal to remove a prohibition on driving a vehicle on a road GV9C*

Regulations is committed (particularly in respect of lights, reflectors, smoke emission or the horn), the DTp examiners will report these items to the police in attendance for consideration for prosecution.

Clearance of prohibition

An operator having a vehicle placed under an immediate or a delayed prohibition notice has to get the defects repaired and then submit the vehicle to his local DTp heavy goods vehicle testing station to be re-examined and obtain a clearance certificate, PG10 (Figure 13.8) if the examiner is satisfied with the repair. If the examiner is not satisfied with the repair he will issue a form PG9C (Figure 13.9) 'Refusal to Remove a Prohibition' or form PG9A if some of the defects are cleared and others are not. If because of the better inspection facilities at the test station he finds further defects another form PG9 may be issued.

Effects of prohibition

A vehicle must not, under any circumstances, be used to carry goods while it is the subject of a PG9 prohibition notice, but despite the prohibition notice a vehicle may be driven unladen to a goods vehicle test station or to a place agreed with a goods vehicle examiner (both by previous appointment only) in order to have the vehicle inspected. The vehicle may also be driven on the road for test purposes, provided it is unladen, within three miles of where it has been repaired.

Forms PG9 and PG9A have a panel of boxes identified by letters of the alphabet A to M (see Figures 13.5 and 13.7). These boxes are used by enforcement staff to codify certain aspects of the vehicle check as follows:

A	Whether vehicle laden or unladen
B	Whether examination took place on a road or off the road
C	To indicate if defects appeared to be from neglect in which case a letter 'N' is entered*
D	To indicate whether a prosecution will follow (the letter 'P' in this box indicates prosecution by the police and 'PE' by the enforcement authorities)
E	If vehicle is issuing smoke ('S' equals smoking in service; 'S/A' equals smoking under free acceleration when vehicle is stationary)
L	Indicates number of pages of prohibition notice served at the time (ie page 1 of 1 – page 1 of 2). This indicates to the examiner, who is asked to clear the prohibition, that there was another sheet(s) to the prohibition notice issued at the time
F,G, H, K and M	Not currently used.

* If a letter 'N' appears in box C of a PG9 the vehicle examiners, to quote their own words, 'will be after the operator's hide!'.

New Forms

In taking steps to combine prohibition notices for both goods and passenger vehicles, the DTp has re-numbered documents with a PG prefix. Thus, GV9 has become PG9, GV9A has become PG9A, GV9B has become

13: HGV PLATING, ANNUAL TESTING AND VEHICLE INSPECTIONS

PG9B, GV9C has become PG9C and GV10 has become PG10. The way in which the prohibition system works as described in this chapter is not changed in any way as a result of the re-numbering of the relevant documents.

Light Vehicle Testing

Light goods vehicles under 1525kg unladen weight (3.5 tonnes pmw from 1 April 1991) and dual-purpose vehicles (see p 318 for definition) under 2040kg unladen weight are required to be tested on the third anniversary of the date of their original registration and annually thereafter (commonly known and referred to as the MOT test). The tests are carried out at private garages approved by the Department of Transport and displaying the blue and white triple-triangle sign. For full details of the light vehicle testing scheme, see Chapter 14 which deals with light vehicle testing.

All in all: it's a winner

The Voith Retarder - available in two sizes:

VHBK 130 for vehicles over 15ft
VHBK 120 for vehicles of 7.5t/20t

The advantages:
- less wear due to fully hydraulic operation, 90% of all braking done by retarder
- higher average speeds while reducing driver fatigue
- greater comfort with smooth jolt-free braking
- safer, particularly for long descents.

Voith Engineering Ltd.
6 Beddington Farm Road
Croydon
Surrey CRO 4XB

Phone 01-667 03 33
Telex: 946 129
Fax No. 01-667 04 03

14: Light Vehicle Testing

Private cars, motor caravans (irrespective of weight), dual-purpose vehicles (see p 318 for definition) under 2040kg unladen weight and light goods vehicles not exceeding 1525kg unladen weight (to change to 3.5 tonnes permissible maximum weight from 1 April 1991) are subject to annual testing (commonly referred to as the MOT test) at DTp approved commercial garages, starting on the third anniversary of the date of their first registration and each year thereafter.

Testing is carried out at garages displaying the blue and white MOT triple-triangle symbol, and application is made direct to the garage for a suitable appointment. Some centres claim to provide MOT testing 'while you wait'. There is no application form to be completed.

The fee for the light vehicle test is £14.26 per vehicle, payable at the garage at the time of the test. Duplicate test certificates cost £7.13 each.

Vehicle Classes

Vehicles subject to the MOT test are classified as follows:

Class I — Light motor bicycles not exceeding 200cc cylinder capacity with or without sidecars.
Class II — All motor bicycles (including Class I) with or without sidecars.
Class III — Light motor vehicles with three or more wheels (excluding Classes I and II) not exceeding 450kg unladen weight.
Class IV — Heavy motor cars and motor cars (excluding Classes III and V); ie any vehicle with an unladen weight of more than 450kg which is:
  (a) a passenger vehicle (ie private car, taxi, vehicle licensed as private, with 12 passenger seats or less, or small public service vehicle with less than eight passenger seats)
  (b) a dual-purpose vehicle not exceeding 2040kg unladen weight
  (c) a goods vehicle not exceeding 1525kg unladen weight (3.5 tonnes pmw from April 1991)
  (d) a motor caravan irrespective of weight.
Class V — Large passenger carrying vehicles; ie motor vehicles which are constructed or adapted to carry more than 12 seated passengers in addition to the driver, and which are not licensed as public service vehicles.
Class VI — Public service vehicles other than those in Class V above.

Exemptions
Public service vehicles with seats for eight or more passengers excluding the driver, track-laying vehicles, vehicles constructed or adapted to form part of an articulated vehicle, works trucks and all trailers are excluded

from the above classes and the following vehicles are also exempted from the test:
1. Heavy locomotives.
2. Light locomotives.
3. Goods vehicles over 1525kg unladen weight (3.5 tonnes pmw from 1 April 1991).
4. Articulated vehicles other than articulated buses.
5. Vehicles exempt from duty under section 7(1) of the Vehicles (Excise) Act 1971.
6. Works trucks.
7. Pedestrian-controlled vehicles.
8. Vehicles kept and used by invalids.
9. Vehicles temporarily in Great Britain.
10. Vehicles proceeding to a port for export.
11. Vehicles provided for use by the police force.
12. Imported vehicles owned or in the service of HM navy, army or airforce.
13. Vehicles which have Northern Ireland test certificates.
14. Electrically-propelled goods vehicles not exceeding 1525kg unladen weight.
15. Certain hackney carriages.

Many of these vehicles are subject to the heavy goods vehicle testing and plating scheme (see Chapter 13 for details).

There is also an exemption which applies to vehicles which come within the MOT test scheme while they are being driven to a place by previous arrangement for a test or bringing it away, if it fails, to a place to have work done on it. This means that such vehicles can be driven on the road without a valid test certificate being in force, but only in the circumstances mentioned and no other.

The Test

Testing is carried out in accordance with *The MOT Tester's Manual* (copies available from HMSO). *Note: This publication should not be confused with The Goods Vehicle Tester's Manual which relates solely to the goods vehicle annual test and which is also available from HMSO.*

When presenting a vehicle for test the following conditions must be observed:
1. The vehicle registration document must be produced.
2. The vehicle must be sufficiently clean so as not to make the test unreasonably difficult.
3. The vehicle must have sufficient petrol and oil to enable the test to be completed.
4. If the vehicle is presented for the test in a loaded condition (ie in the case of light goods vehicles) the load must be secured or else removed.

Refusal and Discontinuance of Test

Failure to observe any of the above conditions can lead to a refusal to test the vehicle, and the test fee will be refunded. Furthermore, if the tester finds a defect of a serious nature which, in his opinion, makes it essential to discontinue the inspection on the grounds of risk to his own safety, risk to the test equipment or to the vehicle itself, he may do so and issue form VT 30 showing the defects which caused the test to be discontinued.

Items Tested

The following items are tested and must meet the conditions specified in *The MOT Tester's Manual:*

Section I	Function of obligatory front and rear lamps
	Function of obligatory headlamps
	Function of stop lamps
	Obligatory rear reflectors
	Function of direction indicators
	Aim of headlamps
Section II	Steering wheel and column
	Steering mechanism
	Power steering
	Front wheel bearings
	Suspension
	All suspension types
	Suspension assemblies (springs, torsion bars, etc)
	Shock absorbers
Section III	Parking brake and operating lever
	Parking brake mechanism (under vehicle)
	Service brake operating pedal
	Service brake mechanism under vehicle
	Brake performance test
Section IV	Tyres
	Roadwheels
Section V	Seat belts
Section VI	Function of windscreen washers
	Function of windscreen wipers
	Exhaust system
	Function of audible warning device
	Condition of the vehicle structure.

Test Failure

If the vehicle fails to reach the required standard of mechanical condition a 'notification of refusal of a test certificate' (Form VT 30) is issued. This indicates the grounds on which the vehicle failed the test (ie it names the faulty components or component area and the actual fault).

Re-tests

If a vehicle fails the test, no further test fee is payable if it is left at the garage for the necessary repairs to be carried out. If the vehicle is taken away after the test failure but is returned to the original garage or another test garage within 14 days of the original test date for repairs and re-test, only 50 per cent of the test fee is payable. Re-tests carried out more than 14 days after the original test are charged at the full rate (ie £14.26). The full rate is also charged if a vehicle is repaired other than at the original test garage or any other approved testing station and is returned for test even if it is within 14 days of the original test.

Issue of Test Certificate

On completion of the test, if the vehicle is found to be in satisfactory condition and in compliance with the law, a test certificate (form VT 20) is issued. Additionally, a copy of form VT 29 is issued to indicate to the vehicle owner the general state of the vehicle and to point out components which may need attention in the future to keep it in good, safe working order. Comments on form VT 29 are made against the following headings:
    I. Lighting equipment
   II. Steering and suspension
  III. Braking system
  IV. Tyres and wheels
   V. Seat belts
  VI. General items.

Appeals

A vehicle owner can appeal if he is not satisfied with the result of the test. He must complete form VT 17 and send it to the local Traffic Area office within 14 days of taking the test.

Production of Test Certificates

It is necessary to produce a current, valid test certificate when taxing a vehicle to which the regulations apply, otherwise an excise licence will not be issued. A police officer can ask to see a vehicle test certificate. If the driver does not have it with him he can be asked to produce the certificate at a police station nominated by him within seven days.

Vehicle Defect Rectification Scheme

Operators of light vehicles (up to 1525kg unladen) found on the road with non-endorsable minor vehicle defects (ie lights, wipers, speedometer, silencer etc) in certain areas may be offered the VDRS procedure by the police whereby no prosecution will result if:
1. Immediate arrangements are made for the repair of the defect.
2. The repaired vehicle and VDRS notice are presented to an MOT garage for examination and certification that the defects have been rectified.
3. The certificate is sent to a local Central Ticket Office.

Failure to follow the procedure will result in prosecution.

15: Vehicle Maintenance

The requirements of the Road Traffic Act 1988 for the annual testing of goods vehicles and trailers, the requirements of the current Construction and Use Regulations, and the parts of the Transport Act 1968 setting out the conditions relating to vehicle maintenance under which an 'O' licence will be granted create a situation where operators must ensure that their vehicles and trailers are always safe, are in a fit and roadworthy condition and that their maintenance, vehicle inspection and maintenance record systems meet the requirements laid down in the legislation.

In order for the operator to meet these requirements he must maintain his vehicles and trailers (no matter how old they are) to a sufficiently high standard to enable them to pass the stringent annual goods vehicle test which they should be able to do on the test day *and on every other day when they are on the road.* To be able to do this, it is not sufficient merely to take the vehicle off the road for a short period once a year just before test day and work frantically to get it up to scratch, and for the rest of the year allow it to run on the road in a condition which is something below the required standard.

The risk of the vehicle encountering a roadside check, or being on the operator's premises when DTp vehicle examiners or the police decide to make an inspection, as they are empowered to do, is too great to take when the penalties for failure to maintain vehicles are so high. Besides the risk of heavy fines, there is the possibility that the operator may lose his 'O' licence since a satisfactory state of maintenance is one of the factors taken into account by the Licensing Authority in considering applications and renewals for such licences.

DTp Maintenance Advice

A DTp team along with operator associations is currently in the process of producing a Code of Practice on vehicle maintenance for transport operators and this is expected to be published shortly after this edition of the *Handbook* goes to press. In the meantime the DTp's free guide *A Guide to Goods Vehicle Operators' Licensing* (reference GV 74), contains some specific advice on vehicle maintenance arrangements for licence applicants. The following notes are included as an appendix to the *Guide*.

There are two separate vehicle checks and inspections which should be carried out:
- daily running checks
- vehicle safety inspections and routine maintenance at set intervals on items which affect vehicle safety, followed by repair of any faults.

Daily running checks are normally carried out by drivers before a vehicle starts its daily journey. They are checks on such basic items as engine oil, brakes, tyre pressures, warning instruments, lights, windscreen wipers and washers and trailer coupling.

Vehicle safety inspections and routine maintenance should be carried out at set intervals of either time and/or mileage whichever occurs first.
Note: the West Midland Licensing Authority insists on inspections being carried out on a time basis only.

How often these inspections are done should be decided by the nature of the operator's business. A vehicle used on long-distance work will need inspecting at different intervals from one employed in heavy traffic on local work with frequent stops and starts. The items inspected should include wheels, tyres, brakes, steering, suspension, lighting, and so on. More detailed information can be found in the Department of Transport's publication *The Goods Vehicle Tester's Manual* (available from HMSO). Vehicle checks and inspections are extra to a routine maintenance schedule. It is vital to the vehicle's safety that both types of checks and inspections are done.

Staff doing inspection checks must be able to recognise faults they find, such as excessive wear of components. They should also be aware of the acceptable standard of performance and wear of parts. Trade associations offer regular inspections for their members' vehicles.

Records

Records must be kept of all safety inspections to show the history of each vehicle. These records must be kept for at least 15 months. If vehicles from several operating centres are inspected and repaired at a central depot, the records may be kept at that depot, although DTp examiners are entitled to request inspection of records at the operating centres where vehicles are based.

If an outside garage does the inspections and repairs, you must still keep maintenance records. You are responsible for the condition of any vehicle or trailer on your licence.

Facilities

These will depend on the number, size and types of vehicles to be inspected. It must be possible to inspect the underside of a vehicle with sufficient light and space to examine individual parts closely. Ramps, hoists or pits will usually be necessary, but may not be needed if the vehicles have enough ground clearance for a proper underside inspection to be made on hard-standing. Creeper boards, jacks, axle stands and small tools should be available.

As well as providing facilities for checking the underside of vehicles, operators should whenever possible use equipment for measuring braking efficiency and setting headlights. If many vehicles have to be inspected, it may be worthwhile providing a roller brake tester. If this cannot be justified, a decelerometer (Tapley-meter) to measure braking efficiency might be worthwhile.

Drivers' Reports

Drivers must report vehicle faults to whoever is responsible for having them put right. The maintenance system should allow for these reports, which must be recorded in writing either by the driver himself or by the person responsible for maintaining the vehicle. Owner-drivers must note faults as they arise and keep these notes as part of their maintenance record.

Hired Vehicles and Trailers

In the case of hired, rented or borrowed vehicles or those belonging to other operators used in inter-working arrangements, it is the user who is responsible for their mechanical condition on the road. If disciplinary action is taken as a result of a mechanical fault, it is against the user's licence, not the company from whom the vehicle is hired, or the owner.

The Choice: To Repair or Contract Out

The first decision an operator has to make when planning his vehicle maintenance is to determine whether it is to be carried out in his own workshops, by his own staff, or whether it is to be contracted out to a repair garage. The size of the fleet and what existing facilities and premises he already has will usually determine the method to be used. It is unlikely to be an economic proposition for a very small operator with a fleet of less than five or six vehicles to establish his own workshop unless he actually does the work himself. On the other hand it is unlikely to be an economic proposition for a large operator to contract out the work. There are, however, many examples in industry where the opposites apply, and very successfully too; so it remains very much a matter for the operator to assess his own requirements, balance out the costs of the alternatives and make arrangements accordingly.

Choice of Repairer

When choosing a repairer to do the work preference should be given to a garage which is a main distributor for the make of vehicle operated or an agent for that make of vehicle. The reason for this is that such a firm, as part of its arrangement with the manufacturer it represents, will have had to send some of its mechanics to the factory for training in the repair and servicing of that particular make of vehicle. This ensures that skilled staff are working on the vehicle. Moreover, the distributors are also usually required by the manufacturer to hold considerable stocks of spare parts, with a predominance of fast moving items. By using such a garage the risk of a vehicle being kept off the road waiting for spare parts is therefore considerably reduced, and since vehicle downtime is a heavy cost burden these days this is an important consideration. If a garage of this type is not available locally and a second choice has to be made, this should be a firm which is experienced in heavy vehicle repair work and which has suitably trained staff and the necessary equipment. A garage which normally only handles motor car repair work should not be used.

Repair Arrangements

Any arrangements made with a repairer should be in writing. The 'O' licence application form requests that copies of any maintenance contract should be sent with the application but in any event the LA will want to know what arrangements have been made with a repairer. Verbal arrangements or the practice of sending vehicles in for repair as necessary on an ad hoc basis are not acceptable to the LAs, some of whom have said that a verbal agreement for these purposes is no agreement at all.

Maintenance Agreements
The agreement should include provisions for the repairer to be responsible for supplying the operator with suitable records of the inspections and repair work carried out. The operator should ensure that he can escape reasonably quickly and easily from any agreement in the event of the standard of work deteriorating and thereby placing his 'O' licence at risk.

Care should be taken when discussing or making an agreement that the repairer is aware of the consequences of any negligent action on his part on the livelihood of the operator, remembering that it is the vehicle 'user' who remains responsible at all times for the safe and satisfactory mechanical condition of the vehicle, and it is he who is responsible for keeping and producing records of vehicle inspections and other maintenance work.

There is no standard or recommended form of maintenance agreement in universal use; it is left to the parties concerned to agree on terms. *NB: a suitable format for agreements is suggested by the DTp in its guide to 'O' licensing. A copy of this is reproduced here for reference.* The agreement should clearly set out in detail the work to be done, the intervals at which it is to be done, the responsibilities of the operator and the garage, the form which records should take and the action to be taken if defects are discovered or repairs over a certain value are found to be necessary.

Maintenance Contracts

Some of the prominent commercial vehicle repair specialists offer contract maintenance schemes. There are usually a number of options in such schemes which, for instance, give the operator a choice of having his vehicles inspected only at set intervals; inspected and serviced according to the manufacturer's recommendations; or inspected, serviced and all repair work carried out (excluding damage caused by the vehicle having been involved in an accident) including the supply of materials except for such things as tyres and batteries.

The charges (both labour and materials) for the various options are usually incorporated in the contracts and these remain fixed for the period of the contract with a clause which enables the garage to make additional charges if the vehicle exceeds, by a large margin, the mileage estimated by the operator at the time of negotiating the contract. The additional charges are usually based on the excess mileage at an agreed figure per mile.

In offering a fixed charge agreement to include all normal repair work, the garage is dependent to quite an extent on the good faith of the operator in using his vehicles in a manner which is not likely to involve the garage in excessive costs above what may be normally estimated in advance. Again, a clause may be included in the contract stating that additional charges will be raised for the repair of damage or defects because of misuse by the owner.

If a full maintenance contract under one of these schemes is negotiated, the garage usually accepts the responsibility for ensuring that the vehicle is always in a fully roadworthy condition, able to pass through DTp roadside checks and pass its annual test without difficulty. In the event of a vehicle getting a PG 9 prohibition for defects, the operator has some grounds for a claim against the garage but, unfortunately, he has no defence to present to the LA if he is called to explain why the vehicle was not maintained to the required standard because of the condition of 'O' licensing which makes the vehicle user totally responsible for the condition of his vehicles on the road (see below).

The garage offering a full fixed price contract maintenance scheme will prefer, wherever possible, to negotiate a contract for a vehicle from the day it is new because it is much easier to plan and cost the amount of work likely to be necessary for an estimated annual mileage and the spare parts required.

The effective working of a contract agreement needs the co-operation of both parties if it is to be successful. The operator may feel that in return for paying the garage a fixed price for full maintenance he is left with little responsibility. But he must make it his business to ensure that whatever other considerations may be pressing, the vehicle is sent to the garage when it is required if the contract is one in which the garage calls the vehicle in at specified intervals for the work to be done.

Although armed with what appears to be a fair agreement with a reputable repairer, the operator should not become complacent. It is strongly recommended that wherever possible he should arrange for a physical check of the work that the repairer claims to have carried out. While not suggesting that a repairer is likely to claim to have done work that he knows has not been done, it must be remembered what is at stake and an operator should therefore doubly check the quality of the work.

Contract Maintenance Schemes

A number of package contract maintenance schemes are available to the operator. Which he chooses, if indeed he chooses any, will depend on a number of considerations: the make of the vehicles he owns, the trade association to which he belongs, the availability of a suitable repairer, etc.

FTA Maintenance Services
Under the FTA quality control maintenance inspection service a member operator contracts to have his vehicles inspected one or more times a year by Association inspectors (only skilled and highly experienced people are appointed) to see that they meet the requirements of the law. The inspections can be used by the operator either as a second check on his own inspection and maintenance system, or as the sole means of inspection of his vehicles to comply with the law in this respect, the actual maintenance work being carried out by his own staff. Alternatively, the scheme can be used as a means of checking the maintenance work carried out by a repair garage or agent.

The FTA vehicle check system is not purely a maintenance scheme as such. It is an inspection and maintenance advisory service available to Association members as a do-it-yourself scheme using the documents, checklists and advice provided. It can include contract inspections of vehicles by a qualified inspector.

A model agreement between the operator and a garage or agent for safety inspections and/or repair of vehicles and trailers subject to operators' licensing

This Agreement is made the .... day of .... 19 .... between

(a) .... whose address [registered office] is

.... ("the operator") of the one part, and

(b) .... whose address [registered office] is

.... ("the contractor") of the other part.

1. The Contractor agrees that he [it] will, in relation to every vehicle mentioned in the Schedule below, on every occasion when that vehicle is submitted by the operator as mentioned in Article 2 below on or after the date of this Agreement —

   (a) inspect all the items specified in the maintenance record in the form for the time being approved by the Department of Transport which relate to the vehicle;

   (b) if the operator so consents, carry out such renewals and repairs as may be necessary to ensure that the vehicle and every part of it specified in that maintenance record is in good working order and complies with every statutory requirement applying to it; and

   (c) complete that maintenance record to show —

      (i) which items were in good working order and complied with the relevant statutory requirements when the vehicle was submitted and which remain in that condition;

      (ii) which (if any) items were not in good working order or failed to comply with those requirements when the vehicle was submitted but have been replaced or repaired so that those requirements are satisfied; and

      (iii) which (if any) items were not in good working order or failed to comply with those requirements when the vehicle was submitted and which has not been so replaced or repaired.

2. The operator agrees that he [it] will —

   (a) submit to the contractor each vehicle mentioned in the Schedule below in order that the contractor may, as regards that vehicle, comply with the provisions of Article 1 above —

      (i) within .... weeks of the date of this Agreement, and, thereafter;

      (ii) within .... weeks of the last submission or, in the case of a motor vehicle, when the mileage shown on the odometer has increased by .... miles, whichever is the sooner;

   (b) pay to the contractor such reasonable charges as the contractor may make pursuant to his [its] obligations under Article 1 above; and

   (c) retain, and make available for inspection by an officer mentioned in section 82(1) of the Transport Act 1968, every maintenance record mentioned in Article 1 above for a period of at least 15 months commencing with the date of its issue.

3. This Agreement shall be determinable by either party giving to the other .... months written notice of his [its] intention to determine it.

Schedule

(Motor Vehicles and trailers which [are authorised vehicles] [it is intended shall become authorised vehicles] under an operator's licence [held] [applied for] by the operator under Part V of the Transport Act 1968).

1. Motor Vehicles (give registration numbers and brief descriptions).

2. Trailers (give brief descriptions).

As witness etc.

(Signature(s), or seal operator)

(Signature(s), or seal, or contractor)

With acknowledgement to the Department of Transport (reproduced from GV 74)

After carrying out a vehicle check, the inspector completes a checklist indicating whether items are satisfactory within reasonable tolerances, or whether attention is needed. When the inspector returns to carry out the next check on the vehicle he will expect to see that his previous recommendations have been followed. If they have not, the operator is told that there is little point in paying for a service which he is not using to its fullest advantage.

Following the experience of many operators who have received PG9s on brand new vehicles, the FTA offers a service whereby it will conduct a full inspection of a brand new vehicle before it goes into service. One of the obvious advantages of this independent check is that it provides the operator with evidence to support claims to the vehicle supplier and manufacturer for new vehicles delivered in faulty condition.

Responsibility for Maintenance

The major point to remember when making any arrangements with a garage is that it is the operator (ie the vehicle 'user' – see p 18 for definition), not the repairer, who remains responsible for the mechanical condition of the vehicle, even where defects are due to negligence by the repairer. In *A Guide to Operators' Licensing* available from local Traffic Area offices the following warning is given:

> 'Operators who contract out their inspections and maintenance work are still the legal 'users' of their vehicles and as such will be held fully responsible by the LA for the arrangements they make and the condition of their vehicles. If either are unsatisfactory it is the operator's licence which will be placed in jeopardy.'

The same responsibility applies in the case of vehicles hired without drivers and trailers even if the hire company, as part of the agreement, carries out the inspection and repair work.

Responsibility for Records
Operators are also responsible for ensuring that proper records of maintenance work are kept. Even if the repairer makes the records and holds them on file it is up to the operator to ensure, first, that they are properly kept with all the necessary information recorded and, second, that they are retained on file, available for inspection, for a minimum period of 15 months. In completing the 'O' licence application 'declaration of intent' (see p 249) the vehicle operator promises to 'keep records'. This can be interpreted as meaning that the operator keeps the record rather than the repair garage keeping it on his behalf (see also p 252 and Chapter 16).

Negligence by Repairers

Unfortunately, however satisfactory the arrangements made with a garage may be in other ways, there is very little that the operator can do contractually to protect himself completely from negligence on the part of the repairer or the repairer's employees. It is unlikely that the repairer would agree to be party to a contract in which he has fully to indemnify the operator against failure of his employees to carry out work to a required standard, even though he may agree that morally he should be held responsible (moral responsibility, incidentally, has no standing in law). Moreover, most small operators are not likely to be in a position to have sufficiently persuasive powers to get the repairer to agree to such terms.

The operator has no protection against poor workmanship other than relying on the reputation of the garage. However, if he is a member of one of the trade associations (the Freight Transport Association for own-account operators and the Road Haulage Association for haulage contractors) he could try to enlist their help in pressing a claim.

In-House Repairs

The advantages of the operator having his own workshop and being able to do his own safety inspections and repairs are many, provided that sufficient vehicles are operated to justify the overheads involved. Principal among them is that by employing the staff he has direct control over the work carried out, the standard of the work and the record keeping which is so important.

If the operator provides his own maintenance facilities they must be of a suitable standard, although once again no specific details are given in the regulations. The main requirement is for a covered area with hard-standing and facilities including adequate lighting for conveniently inspecting the underside of vehicles. Ideally this means that either a pit in the ground or an hydraulic lift should be provided. The former is the most commonly used and it is very much the cheaper of the two alternatives. Suitable lighting, either fixed in the pit shining upwards to the underside of the vehicles or by means of portable inspection lamps, is necessary.

The remainder of the tools and machines with which a workshop should be equipped are left entirely to the operator's choice, but such items as a beam-setter and a portable Tapley brake-efficiency recorder are useful to check that vehicles comply with the test requirements. Servicing equipment such as jacks, high-pressure greasing equipment, high-pressure washing or steam cleaning equipment make maintenance work much less of a chore. Hand tools are, of course, essential and in general the better the equipment available (including the availability of the special tools often needed to carry out work on today's sophisticated vehicles) the more likelihood there is of the work meeting the required standard.

Vehicle Inspections

Vehicle inspections are an essential part of the maintenance programme, and legislation covers this aspect. Section 59 of the Road Traffic Act 1972 requires operators of goods vehicles to have them regularly inspected by a 'suitably qualified person' to ensure that they comply with Construction and Use Regulations (Chapter 10) and, of course, it is in the operator's best interests to have vehicles regularly inspected to ensure that they are kept in a fully safe and roadworthy mechanical condition.

Frequency of Inspection

Legislation does not specify the intervals at which vehicles should be inspected, what form the inspection should take or what is meant by a 'suitably qualified person'. In the case of the first-mentioned, it is very much a question of the type of operation on which the vehicle is used. A tipping vehicle, for example, which spends much of its time on rough sites, with perhaps a fairly high mileage on the road as well, certainly should be inspected at least weekly. The same applies to a vehicle which, although it remains on normal roads, does perhaps 800 to 1200 miles a week. On the other hand, a monthly inspection may be quite sufficient for a local delivery vehicle doing low weekly mileages on good roads and spending a great deal of its time standing while deliveries are being made. The operator's own experience of his type of operation should indicate the intervals between which wear and tear takes place and defects become apparent. It has even been suggested that vehicles standing out of use in depots should be checked at least monthly. Although there is some suggestion that inspection intervals can be based on either a time or miles/kilometres alternative it is becoming clear that some LAs at least will not accept anything other than a time based frequency from 'O' licence applicants. The new DTp Code of Practice on vehicle maintenance referred to on page 237 recommends that the maximum time interval between safety inspections should be six weeks with no mileage alternatives. It also recommends operators to have flow charts covering at least 12-monthly periods to indicate when vehicle safety inspections are due.

Items for Inspection

A full list of the items to be inspected at regular intervals is not laid down in regulations but it is obviously necessary that the inspection at the very least covers all the items set out in *The Goods Vehicle Tester's Manual* (see p 211), with particular emphasis on those items (eg brakes, steering, wheels, tyres, suspension systems and lights) that have special relevance to the safe operation of the vehicle. Tyres on vehicles used on site work or on local delivery work should receive particularly careful examination for damage.

The Inspector

There are no specified qualifications for a vehicle inspector. Clearly, the most obvious one is wide experience in the repair of heavy commercial vehicles. A person with such experience would know where and how to look for wear and for defects and would recognise the symptoms of hidden faults, such as uneven tyre wear indicating that the steering is out of alignment or that kingpins or wheel bearings are worn.

It is possible, however, to train a person specifically as a vehicle inspector, and this is being done in the industry. The emphasis in training in such cases must be on following a predetermined list, such as *The Goods Vehicle Tester's Manual,* examining every individual item carefully and methodically, testing the wear in components and measuring the tolerances of moving parts accurately.

It is desirable, although not a legal requirement, that the person carrying out the vehicle inspection should not be expected to carry out repairs, however small, at the time of making the inspection. To have to do this would cause a lack of concentration and could lead to other items being missed if repairs took up too much of the inspector's time. In the case of an owner-driver carrying out his own inspections and repairs this can be a difficult situation and in such instances it is useful to have the work verified and an audit-type check carried out by an outside agency, such as the FTA, to ensure that the vehicle is kept up to a high standard.

Authority to Stop Use of Vehicles

The inspector, besides being suitably qualified and experienced to spot defects, should have the authority to prevent a vehicle being taken on the road in the event of a serious or potentially dangerous defect being found.

Vehicle Servicing

Regular servicing as opposed to specific inspections and repairs is an important part of vehicle maintenance and as such it should be carried out with unfailing regularity at predetermined intervals of time or mileage. The importance of servicing cannot be too highly emphasised for two reasons. First, because the vehicle must meet the requirements of the law and second, because the operator will benefit by always having his vehicles ready for work and able to carry out a job without breakdowns and delays. It also increases the life of the working parts and consequently of the whole vehicle as well as reducing down-time costs and disrupted delivery schedules.

The intervals at which servicing should be carried out are left to the owner's discretion depending on the work on which the vehicle is employed, in much the same way as the intervals for inspection are decided. To give the owner some guidance, however, vehicle manufacturers usually provide a service schedule which the owner can use in his own workshop or which his agent will use when vehicles are sent in for servicing.

A useful guide to service intervals is 5000/6000 mile services carried out at least monthly with more extensive services at 15000/20000 mile/three-monthly intervals and 30000/40000 mile/six-monthly intervals. Progressively, service intervals are being extended with the use of longer life components and particularly improved filters and lubricating oils which can go for very much longer periods these days without detriment to their lubricating properties.

Cleaning of Vehicles

Particular reference is made in the instructions to operators submitting vehicles for DTp heavy goods vehicle tests, that those which are not sufficiently clean will be refused the test. Again, it is difficult to specify a standard of cleanliness for the underside of a vehicle, but the main point is that all the components listed for the examination must be easily visible so that inspectors can see without difficulty if wear or damage exists. To achieve and keep a suitable standard of cleanliness it is desirable for vehicles to be washed with either a steam cleaner or a high-pressure water washer at regular intervals and certainly immediately before they are taken to the test station.

If the maintenance of the vehicles is contracted out to a garage on a maintenance scheme, the operator should arrange either for the garage to clean the vehicle before inspection or for one of the many specialist vehicle cleaners to do it.

Enforcement of Maintenance Standards

There has been increasing concern in recent times about the standards of vehicle maintenance. As a result of this concern, the DTp, following on from recommendations in the Foster Committee Report on 'O' licensing, has stepped up the levels of checking on vehicles by enforcement staff particularly at night and at weekends. The purpose of these additional checks is to catch vehicles operating outside normal working hours – many legitimately but some possibly deliberately running the gauntlet.

Recovery Services

There has been a proliferation of heavy vehicle recovery services and roadside aid services to help the driver with a broken-down truck. Many such services have a freefone contact arrangement. These services are operated by independent firms and by the vehicle manufacturers. Examples of the former are BRS Rescue (British Road Services Ltd) and National Breakdown Recovery Service and of the latter include DAF Aid and Action Volvo.

16: Maintenance Records

There is a legal requirement under the Road Traffic Act 1988 for goods vehicle operators to keep records of maintenance work carried out on their vehicles. When completing form GV 79, 'O' licence application, operators have to make the statutory 'declaration of intent' in which they promise to fulfil undertakings made at that time throughout the duration of the 'O' licence. A number of items in the declaration of intent relate to maintenance records. From this can be determined what records are needed by law.

In the declaration of intent the operator promises to ensure that the following records will be kept:
1. Safety inspections.
2. Routine maintenance.
3. Repairs to vehicles.

A promise is also made that drivers will report 'safety faults' in their vehicles and the Licensing Authorities insist that these reports should be in writing and therefore they become part of the vehicle record-keeping system. The operator promises to keep all these records for a minimum period of 15 months and to make them available on request (ie by DTp enforcement staff or the Licensing Authority).

Additionally, operators are frequently asked by DTp vehicle examiners and the LAs to keep a wall chart showing vehicles in the fleet and when they are due for inspection, service and annual DTp test. The new DTp Code of Practice on vehicle maintenance (see p 237) recommends annual flow-charts showing vehicle inspection-due dates).

Driver Reports of Vehicle Faults

It is a specific requirement (and part of the declaration of intent on an 'O' licence application form) that arrangements must be made for drivers to have a proper means of reporting 'safety faults' (ie defects) in the vehicle they are driving as soon as possible. As already mentioned, the LAs expect these defect reports to be made in writing, not verbally. Ideally, the report should be made either on an individual form which is completed and handed in by the driver, or in a defect book reserved for recording defects found on a vehicle which is kept in a convenient place where all drivers have easy access to it, and where whoever is responsible for ensuring that repair work is carried out can also easily reach it. To reiterate, it has been made abundantly clear that verbal reporting of defects is not in itself a system acceptable to the Licensing Authorities.

Whichever method is used it is important that the repair of the defects is recorded on the form or in the book by a note of the work done and the signature of the person who has done it (see also under repair records). It is also important for the operator to ensure that whatever system of defect reporting is used, he makes regular checks on drivers and repair staff to see that the procedure is being followed correctly. This requirement has been pointed out by the LAs on a number of occasions. Using separate pads of defect sheets (see Figure 16.1) is the best alternative and where these can be made out in duplicate they provide the driver with his own copy of the report for future reference.

Systems of defect reporting which rely on a centrally located defect book or on verbal reports by drivers are open to the risk of drivers forgetting to report defects when they return to base. If a driver's attention is distracted by his manager who wants to talk to him, for example, just as he is about to report a defect, the defect is not reported and another driver may take the vehicle out next day with a defect which could result in a prohibition notice being issued in a roadside check. A driver may also forget to report a defect when he returns late from a journey and is in a rush to get home or if he cannot find the defect book.

It is the operator's responsibility to make sure that the system used is infallible in all these circumstances firstly because it is an offence to fail to cause the defect to be reported and secondly because the vehicle could be found on the road subsequently with a safety fault not reported and not repaired.

Inspection Reports

The 1972 Road Traffic Act requires that records of regular safety inspections to vehicles must be made. For this purpose the vehicle inspector (see p 246) should have a sheet on which are listed all the items to be inspected (preferably in accordance with the contents of *The Goods Vehicle Tester's Manual* – see p 211).

The inspection sheet should identify the necessary items for inspection with a cross-check reference number to the *Tester's Manual* to enable, if necessary, full details of the method of inspection of that item – and the reason for its rejection as not being within acceptable limits – to be determined. The sheet should have provision for the inspector to mark against each item whether it is 'serviceable' or 'needs attention' and space to comment on defects for immediate rectification and other items for attention at a future date or on which a watch should be kept if attention is not required immediately. The form should contain space for the inspector to sign his name and add the date.

Defect Repair Sheets

Besides ensuring that proper records are kept of vehicle safety fault reports made by drivers and of regular safety inspections, the operator must also keep a record showing that any defects reported or found on inspection are rectified in order to keep the vehicle in a fit, serviceable and safe condition. Records of such repairs may be added to the driver defect report or the inspection report to provide combined records or a separate repair or job sheet may be used.

The important points about repair records are, first, that they should show comprehensive details of the actual repair work carried out, identifying components which were repaired or replaced and new parts added, and,

16: MAINTENANCE RECORDS

DRIVER'S DAILY VEHICLE DEFECT REPORT	
Date:	Driver's name:
Vehicle No:	Trailer Fleet/Serial No:

Note: Drivers are responsible for the safe condition of their vehicle and load. You are required by law to report defects to your employer.

Tick items on this check list that are in order; put cross against defective items.

DAILY CHECK	Tick or cross
Fuel:	Lights:
Oil:	Reflectors:
Water:	Indicators:
Battery:	Wipers:
Tyres:	Washers:
Brakes:	Horn:
Steering:	Mirrors:
Security of body:	Markers:
Security of load:	Sheets/ropes/chains:
Artics/Lorry & trailer combinations	
Brake hoses:	Electrical connections:
Coupling secure:	Trailer No. plate:

REPORT DEFECTS HERE

WRITE NONE HERE IF NO DEFECTS

Driver's signature:

Action Taken By:

Signature:

A model agreement between the operator and a garage or agent for safety inspections and/or repair of vehicles and trailers subject to operators licensing

With acknowledgement to the Department of Transport (reproduced from GV 74)

Figure 16.1 *A typical example of a driver's vehicle defect report available in pad form.*

251

second, that there should be a matching repair sheet for every defect reported or found on inspection so that the Licensing Authority's vehicle examiners, when they visit to examine records, can see the report of the defect and then subsequently a report of the repair work carried out to rectify it. Reports of defects which do not have a corresponding repair record can arouse suspicion in the examiner's mind that perhaps the necessary repair has not been carried out and that the defect still exists. This is a good reason for him then to consider examining that vehicle, or perhaps the whole fleet.

Service Records

In addition to the records of defects and vehicle inspections which have to be kept, a record should also be kept of all other work carried out on the vehicle, whether it is repair or replacement of working parts or normal servicing (oil changes and greasing, etc).

Retention of Records

It is a legal requirement that records of maintenance must be retained by operators. The original inspection report, or a photocopy of it, with the inspector's comments, the date and the mileage at which the inspection was carried out, must be retained and kept available for inspection if required by the LA's examiners for 15 months from the date of the inspection. Work sheets showing the repair work carried out following the inspection and all other work done on the vehicle, including repairs following defect reports by drivers, as well as defect reports themselves, must be kept for 15 months, available for inspection by DTp enforcement staff or the Licensing Authority, if requested.

Repair Records from Garages

When vehicle safety inspections, servicing and repair work are carried out for the operator by repair garages, the operator should obtain from the garage comprehensive documentation to enable him to meet the legal requirements detailed above. In many cases the LA's vehicle examiners are quite happy if the garage retains the records of inspection and repair, so long as they can be made available for examination when required. The operator must be certain, in these instances, that the garage is keeping proper records (for a period of 15 months) which satisfy the legal requirements and that they are being kept available for inspection, not bundled away out of easy reach in a store with thousands of others.

In the event of failure of the garage to keep records as required, the operator's licence would be at risk but there would be no penalty imposed on the garage. On the GV 79 declaration of intent (see p 249) the operator promised that he would '...make proper arrangements so that records are kept for (15 months) of all safety inspections, routine maintenance and repairs to vehicles and make them available on request'.

It is important to note that in this respect, invoices, or copies of invoices from garages, for repair work are not in themselves sufficient to satisfy the record-keeping requirement. It is the actual inspection sheet and repair sheets, or photocopies of them, which are needed because of the greater

16: MAINTENANCE RECORDS

and more precise detail which they contain. Similarly, maintenance records in computer print-out form are unlikely to satisfy the requirement of enforcement staff to examine actual records – they will still want to see the original inspection sheets. This is an important point to consider with the increasing application of computers to transport operations and vehicle maintenance functions.

Location of Records

Where companies hold operators' licences in a number of separate Traffic Areas the maintenance records for the vehicles under each licence should be kept in the area covered by the individual licence (preferably at the vehicle operating centre). With the sanction of the local LA, records may be kept centrally at a head office or central vehicle workshop, although the vehicle examiners may ask for them to be produced for inspection at the operating centre of the vehicles in the Traffic Area – probably giving three days' to a week's notice to enable the records to be obtained from the central files.

Wall Planning Charts

While it is not strictly a legal requirement, many DTp vehicle examiners (and the current West Midland LA) like to see operators using wall planning charts (see note above about use of flow charts in accordance with new DTp Code of Practice on vehicle maintenance) to provide a visual reminder of important dates such as:
1. Vehicle/trailer due for inspection
2. Vehicle/trailer due for service
3. Vehicle/trailer due for DTp annual test
4. Excise duty due.

Such charts usually provide facilities for a whole year's recording of these items for the fleet (either shown by vehicle registration number or by fleet number).

Vehicle History Files

For efficiency in record keeping, a system of vehicle history files – one for each vehicle and trailer in the fleet – is most useful. This provides the facility for keeping all relevant records relating to individual vehicles and trailers together and in one place. Individual files can have all the important details of the vehicle/trailer on the front cover for easy reference, as follows:
1. Registration number/fleet number
2. Make/type
3. Date of original registration
4. Price new plus extras/options
5. Annual test date
6. Taxation (ie VED) date
7. Base/location
8. Model designation
9. Wheelbase (in/mm)
10. Body type

11. Special equipment
12. Chassis number
13. Engine number
14. Gearbox type/number
15. Rear axle type
16. Electrical system – 12v/24v
17. Plated weights – gross/axle
18. Supplier's name and address.

17: Safety – Vehicles, Loads and at Work

Transport operators, along with all other sectors of business and industry, are under increasing pressure to becoming ever more conscious of the need for safety in their operations and in the way their employees work and conduct themselves on work premises. Predominantly, this is influenced by the demands of the Health and Safety at Work Act and the stringent requirements which it imposes on employers and employees alike. But in transport, the requirements of the Construction and Use Regulations, regarding the safety of vehicles and loads, place additional legal burdens on operators and drivers alike. The problems of safe loading and avoidance of vehicle overloading are not new but increased enforcement activity has accelerated concern in these areas. There is concern also on the wider front of safety in load handling and in the use of loading aids (fork-lift trucks for example) and with regard to vehicle manoeuvring in depots and works premises.

C & U Requirements

The Road Vehicles (Construction and Use) Regulations 1986 require that all vehicles and trailers, and all their parts and accessories, and the weight, distribution, packing and adjustment of their loads, shall be such that no danger is caused or likely to be caused to any person in or on the vehicle or trailer or on the road. Additionally, no motor vehicle or trailer must be used for any purpose for which it is so unsuited as to cause or be likely to cause danger or nuisance to any person in or on the vehicle or trailer or on the road.

Under the regulations, provisions relating particularly to bulk and loose loads make it an offence if a load causes a nuisance as well as a danger to other road users and such loads must be secured, if necessary by physical restraint, to stop them falling or being blown from a vehicle.

These regulations include two notable terms relating to the term load safety: one is the use of the term 'nuisance' in addition to 'danger'; so that to commit an offence the operator does not have to go so far as causing danger, merely causing nuisance is sufficient to land him in trouble. The other term is 'physical restraint' which clearly implies the need for sheeting and roping any load, such as sand or grain, hay and straw and even builder's skips carrying rubble, which may be blown from the vehicle.

The Safety of Loads on Vehicles

A Code of Practice – The Safety of Loads on Vehicles published by the DTp (available from HMSO) sets out general requirements in regard to the legal aspects of safe loading, information on the forces involved in restraining loads, the strength requirements of restraining systems and load securing equipment, and then details specialised requirements for containers, pallets, engineering plant, general freight, timber, metal and loose bulk loads. It provides a list of do's and don'ts for drivers and others concerned with the loading of vehicles as shown below.

For particular note is the basic principle on which the Code is based which is that:

'the combined strength of the load restraint system must be sufficient to withstand a force not less than the total weight of the load forward and half the weight of the load backwards and sideways'.

SAFE LOADING

Your own life and the lives of others may depend upon the security of your load

DO'S

1. Do make sure your vehicle's load space and the condition of its load platform are suitable for the type and size of your load.

2. Do make use of load anchorage points.

3. Do make sure you have enough lashings and that they are in good condition and strong enough to secure your load.

4. Do tighten up the lashings or other restraining devices.

5. Do make sure that the front of the load is abutted against the headboard, or other fixed restraint.

6. Do use wedges, scotches etc., so that your load cannot move.

7. Do make sure that loose bulk loads cannot fall or be blown off your vehicle.

DON'TS

1. Don't overload your vehicle or its individual axles.

2. Don't load your vehicle too high.

3. Don't use rope hooks to restrain heavy loads.

4. Don't forget that the size, nature and position of your load will affect the handling of your vehicle.

5. Don't forget to check your load.

   a. Before moving off.

   b. After you have travelled a few miles

   c. If you remove or add items to your load during your journey.

6. Don't take risks.

Taken from DTp Code of Practice on the Safety of Loads on Vehicles

Safety Report

The Health and Safety Executive has produced a report entitled *Transport Kills* (HMSO 1982) based on a study of fatal accidents in industry in which it indicates that motor vehicles are one of the biggest causes of industrial deaths. These motor vehicle related deaths occur during vehicle loading, unloading, maintenance and, of course, movement and are mainly caused by poor management, failure to provide safe working systems and inadequate training. *NB: Although now dated, nevertheless the contents of this report and the advice it gives are still valid and extremely valuable today.*

Included in the report is a checklist which is intended to help transport operators and others to reduce unnecessary risks and dangers. Companies should use it to help examine their current practices and to institute new and safer procedures. The checklist (reproduced below with acknowledgement to the HSE) is only a general guide, and it is emphasised that safety requirements vary with different types of operation. *However, it is important to note that firms could face prosecution if they do not meet the minimum safety standards outlined in the list.*

This checklist is intended as a general guide only. It will not necessarily be comprehensive for every operation and all points will not be relevant for all work.

Organisation, Systems and Training

- Have all health and safety aspects of the transport operation been assessed?
- Has an organisation (and arrangements) for securing such safety been detailed in the safety policy?
- Has a person been appointed to be responsible for the transport safety?
- Have safe systems of work been set up?
- What monitoring is carried out to ensure that the systems are followed?
- Have all drivers been adequately trained and tested?
- Is there a satisfactory formal licensing or authorisation system for drivers?
- Have all personnel been trained, informed and instructed about safe working practices where transport is involved?
- Is there sufficient supervision?

External Roadways and Manoeuvring Areas

- Are they of adequate dimensions?
- Are they of good construction?
- Are they well maintained?
- Are they well drained?
- Are they scarified when smooth?
- Are they gritted, sanded, etc, when slippery?
- Are they kept free of debris and obstructions?
- Are they well illuminated?
- Are there sufficient and suitable road markings?
- Are there sufficient and suitable warning signs?
- Are there speed limits?
- Is there a one-way system (as far as possible)?
- Is there provision for vehicles to reverse where necessary?
- Are there pedestrian walkways and crossings?

- Are there barriers by exit doors leading on to roadways?
- Is there a separate vehicle parking area?
- Is there any storage positioned close to vehicle ways?
- Is the yard suitable for internal works transport, eg smooth surface, hard ground, no slopes?

Internal Transport

- Are internal roadways demarcated and separated where possible from pedestrian routes with crossings and priority signs?
- Are there separate internal doors for trucks and pedestrians? Have these vision panels?
- Are blind corners catered for by mirrors, etc?
- Are trucks kept apart from personnel where possible?
- Do the trucks use a satisfactory warning system?

Vehicles

- Is there a maintenance programme for vehicles and mobile plant?
- Is there a fault reporting system?
- Are there regular checks to ensure that the vehicles are up to an acceptable standard?
- Are keys kept secure when vehicles and mobile plant are not in use?
- Are vehicles and mobile plant adequate and suitable for the work in hand?
- Is suitable access provided to elevated working places or vehicles?
- Are tractors and lift trucks equipped with protection to prevent the driver being hit by falling objects and from being thrown from his cab in the event of overturning?
- Are there any unfenced mechanical parts on vehicles, eg power take-offs?
- Are there fittings for earthing vehicles with highly flammable cargoes?
- Are loads correctly labelled (especially hazardous substances)?
- Are the vehicles suitable for use in all the areas they enter? Do they need to be to Division I or II standards, etc?
- If passengers ride on vehicles, do they have a safe riding position?

Loading and Unloading

- Do loading positions obstruct other traffic? Do pedestrian ways need diverting?
- Are there special hazards, eg flammable liquid discharge? Do pedestrians need to be kept clear?
- Is there a yard manager to supervise the traffic operation, to control vehicular movement and to act as a banksman during reversing?
- Has he received satisfactory training? Does he use recognised signals, and has he cover during his absences?
- Are there loading docks? Will the layout prevent trucks falling off or colliding with objects or each other?
- Are there any mechanical hazards caused by dock levellers, etc?

17: SAFETY – VEHICLES, LOADS AND AT WORK

- Are methods of loading and unloading assessed? Are loads stable and secured?
- Are safe arrangements made for sheeting?
- Is there a pallet inspection scheme?

Motor Vehicle Repair

- Are appropriate arrangements made for tyre repair and inflation?
- Are arrangements made for draining and repair of fuel tanks?
- Is access available to elevated working positions?
- Are arrangements made to ensure brakes are applied and wheels checked?
- Is portable electrical equipment low voltage and properly earthed?
- Are moving vehicles in the workshop carefully controlled?
- Are vehicles supported on both jacks and axle stands where appropriate?
- Are engines only run with the brakes on and in neutral gear?
- Are raised bodies always propped?

Health and Safety at Work

Since the introduction of the Health and Safety at Work etc Act 1974 employers have had to take positive steps to draw up policy statements regarding health and safety at work, appoint safety representatives and establish safety committees in addition to ensuring that work places meet all the necessary safety requirements of the law. These responsibilities apply equally to employers in transport, and it should be remembered that here the requirements of the law apply to the transport operator's premises (ie offices, workshops, warehouses and yard) and to his vehicles which constitute the work place of drivers.

The Act replaces certain parts of the Factories Act and the Offices, Shops and Railway Premises Act, and adds other provisions. There are four parts to the Act:
- Part I relates to health, safety and welfare at work
- Part II relates to the Employment Medical Advisory Service
- Part III amends the law regarding building regulations
- Part IV covers a range of general and miscellaneous provisions.

The main effects of the Act are:
1. To maintain and improve standards of health and safety for people at work.
2. To protect people other than those at work against risks to their health or safety arising from the work activities of others.
3. To control the storage and use of explosives, high flammable or dangerous substances, and to prevent their unlawful acquisition, possession and use.
4. To control the emission into the atmosphere of noxious or offensive fumes or substances from work premises.
5. To set up the Health and Safety Commission and the Health and Safety Executive.

Duties of Employers

The Act prescribes the general duties of all employers towards their employees by obliging them to ensure their health, safety and welfare while at work. This duty requires that all plant (including vehicles) and methods of work provided are reasonably safe and without risks to health. A similar injunction relates to the use, handling, storage and transport of any articles or substances used in connection with the employer's work.

Provision of Necessary Information
In order that employees are fully conversant with all health and safety matters, it is the duty of the employer to provide all necessary information and instruction by means of proper training and adequate supervision.

Condition of Premises
Work places generally, if under the employer's control, must be maintained in such a condition that they are safe and without risks to health, have adequate means of entrance and exit (again this applies equally to vehicles as it does to 'premises') and must provide a working environment that has satisfactory facilities and arrangements for the welfare of everybody employed in the premises.

Statements of Safety Policy
It is necessary for an employer of five or more employees to draw up and bring to the notice of all his work force *a written statement of company policy* regarding their health and safety at work with all current arrangements detailed for the implementation of such a policy. Stress is laid on the necessity of updating the 'statement' as the occasion arises and of communicating all alterations to the personnel employed.

Appointment of Safety Representatives
Involvement of all employees in health and safety activities is envisaged by the appointment (by a recognised trade union) or election of safety representatives from among the work force. A safety representative should be a person who has been employed in the firm for at least *two years* or who has had two years' similar employment 'so far as is reasonably practicable'. The broad duties of safety representatives are concerned with the inspection of work places, investigating possible hazards and examining the cause of accidents, investigating employees' complaints regarding health and safety matters and making representations to their employer on health and safety at work matters.

Safety Committees
At the written request of at least two safety representatives employers must establish a safety committee to review health and safety at work matters. The establishment of a safety committee creates a joint responsibility with the employer for concern with all health and safety measures at the work place, together with any other duties arising from regulations or codes of practice.

Duty to Public
Employers and self-employed persons are required also to ensure that

their activities do not create any hazard to members of the general public. In certain circumstances, information must be made publicly available regarding the existence of possible hazards to health and safety.

Summary of Duties of Employers to their Employees
1. It shall be the duty of every employer to ensure so far as is reasonably practicable the health, safety and welfare at work of all his employees. That duty includes in particular:
    (a) The provision and maintenance of plant and systems of work that are so far as is reasonably practicable safe and without risks to health.
    (b) Arrangements for ensuring so far as is reasonably practicable safety and absence of risks to health in connection with the use, handling, storage and transport of articles and substances.
    (c) The provision of such information, instruction, training and supervision as is necessary to ensure so far as is reasonably practicable the health and safety at work of his employees.
    (d) So far as is reasonably practicable the maintenance of any place of work that is under the employer's control in a condition that is safe and without risks to health, and the provision and maintenance of means of access to and egress from it that are safe and without such risks.
    (e) The provision and maintenance of a working environment for his employees that is so far as is reasonably practicable safe and without risk to health and adequate as regards facilities and arrangements for their welfare at work.
2. Except in such cases as may be prescribed it shall be the duty of every employer to prepare and as often as may be appropriate revise a written statement of his general policy with respect to the health and safety at work of his employees and the organisation and arrangements for the time being in force for carrying out that policy, and to bring the statement and any revision of it to the notice of all his employees.
3. It shall be the duty of any person who erects or installs any article for use at work in any premises where the article is to be used by persons at work to ensure, so far as is reasonably practicable, that nothing about the way in which it is erected or installed makes it unsafe or a risk to health when properly used.
4. No employer shall levy or permit to be levied on any employee of his any charge in respect of anything done or provided in pursuance of any specific requirement of the relevant statutory provisions.

Duties of Employees

The Act states in general terms the duty of an employee to take reasonable care for the safety of himself and others and to co-operate with others in order to ensure that there is a compliance with statutory duties relating to health and safety at work.

In this connection no person shall interfere with or misuse anything provided in the interests of health, safety or welfare either intentionally or recklessly.

Summary of Duties of Employees at Work
1. It shall be the duty of every employee while at work:

(a) to take reasonable care for the health and safety of himself and of other persons who may be affected by his acts or omissions at work, and
(b) as regards any duty or requirement imposed on his employer or any other person, to co-operate with him so far as is necessary to enable that duty or requirement to be performed or complied with.
2. No person shall intentionally or recklessly interfere with or misuse anything provided in the interests of health, safety or welfare.

General Duties of Employers and Self-employed to Persons other than their Employees

1. It shall be the duty of every employer and of every self-employed person to conduct his undertaking in such a way as to ensure so far as is reasonably practicable that persons not in their employment are not thereby exposed to risks to their health and safety.
2. It shall be the duty of every employer and of every self-employed person to give to persons not in their employment who may be affected the prescribed information about such aspects of the way in which he conducts his undertaking as might affect their health and safety.

Improvement and Prohibition Notices

Improvement Notice
An improvement notice may be served on a person by a health and safety inspector in cases where he believes (ie is of the opinion) that the person is contravening or has contravened, and is likely to continue so doing or will do so again, any of the relevant statutory provisions. Such a notice must give details of the inspector's reason for his belief and requires the person concerned to remedy the contravention within a stated period.

Prohibition Notice
A prohibition notice with immediate effect may be served on a person under whose control activities to which the relevant statutory provisions apply are being carried on, or are about to be carried on, by an inspector if he believes that such activities involve or could involve *a risk of serious personal injury*. A prohibition notice must specify those matters giving rise to such a risk, the reason why the inspector believes the statutory provisions are, or are likely to be, contravened, if indeed he believes that such is the case. The notice must direct that the activities in question shall not be carried on unless those matters giving rise to the risk of serious personal injury, and any contravention of the regulations, are rectified.

Remedial Measures
Both improvement and prohibition notices may include directions as to necessary remedial measures and these may be framed by reference to an approved code of practice and may offer a choice of the actions to be taken. Reference must be made by the inspector to the Fire Authority before

serving a notice requiring, or likely to lead to, measures affecting means of escape in case of fire.

Withdrawal of Notices and Appeals
A notice, other than a prohibition notice with immediate effect, may be withdrawn before the end of the period specified in the notice, or an appeal against it made. Alternatively, the period specified for remedial action may be extended at any time provided an appeal against the notice is not pending.

Control of Substances Hazardous to Health (COSHH)

New regulations under this heading (commonly referred to as the COSHH regulations) which came into force on 1 October 1989 under the auspices of the Health and Safety Commission are designed to further protect the health and safety of people at work and place additional responsibilities on employers to assess the risks to employees' health of working with hazardous substances. Employers must undertake an assessment of their work environment (which should have been completed by 1 January 1990) to determine the potential hazards and to take steps to minimise any such hazards. They must inform employees of any risks which exist and train them in safety procedures such as the handling of hazardous materials and the monitoring of the work environment. Failure to comply with the regulations will result in prosecution under these regulations and under the Health and Safety at Work Act.

Notification of Accidents

The Reporting of Injuries, Diseases and Dangerous Occurrences Regulations 1985 (commonly referred to as RIDDOR) which came into effect in April 1986 require employers to notify fatal accidents, major accidents and those causing more than three days' incapacity for work, work related diseases, gas incidents and any dangerous occurrence whether or not anybody is injured.

The report of any notifiable accident or occurrence must be made to the appropriate authority (see below) by a 'responsible person'. Usually this is the employer himself in the case of his employees, but if the accident or occurrence involves a member of the general public, the responsible person is the person who controls the premises.

In cases where an accident occurs to an employee when he is away from base (as may be the case with lorry drivers and sales representatives, for example), although it remains the responsibility of his employer to report the accident or occurrence, the Health and Safety Executive suggests that it would be helpful if the owner or occupier of the premises where the event occurred were to advise the person's employer as soon as possible (although there is no legal obligation for him to do so). Where a dangerous occurrence involves the carriage of dangerous goods by road the person responsible is the 'O' licence holder.

Reporting Authorities

Reports of fatal and injury accidents and notifiable dangerous occurrences must be made to the 'enforcing authority' (ie the authority responsible for enforcing the Health and Safety at Work Act). Principally, the authority is the Health and Safety Executive but reports should be made to its individual Inspectorates as listed below, depending on the type of premises activity:

Premises by main activity | *To whom to report*
1. Factories and factory offices — HM Factory Inspector
2. Mines and quarries — HM Mines and Quarries Inspector
3. Farms (and associated activities), horticultural premises, and forestries — HM Agricultural Inspector
4. Civil engineering and construction sites — HM Factory Inspector
5. Statutory and non-statutory railways — Inspecting Officer of Railways
6. Shops, offices, separate catering services, launderettes — District Council (or equivalent)
7. Hospitals, research and development water supply, postal services and telecommunications, entertainment and recreational services, local government services, educational services and road conveyance. — HM Factory Inspector services

Reporting an Accident

Report should be made to the local office of the enforcing authority as soon as possible, preferably by telephone:
1. any accident causing death or major injury to an employee
2. any accident which occurs on premises which are under a person's control causing death or major injury to a self-employed person or to a member of the public
3. any notifiable dangerous occurrence; incidents of these types affecting the work or equipment either of a firm or self-employed persons working on premises which are under a member of the firm's control should be reported even if nobody is injured.

'Major injury' is defined as follows:
   (a) fracture of the skull, spine or pelvis;
   (b) fracture of any bone:
      (i) in the arm other than a bone in the wrist or hand;
      (ii) in the leg other than a bone in the ankle or foot;
   (c) amputation of a hand or foot;
   (d) the loss of sight of an eye; or
   (e) any other injury which results in the person injured being admitted into hospital as an inpatient for more than 24 hours, unless that person is detained only for observation.

If the person responsible does not know whom to report to, he should tell the nearest office of the Health and Safety Executive who will pass on the report.

Details of the accident/dangerous occurrence should be entered in the record book (or other record system). Form F2509 may be used for this purpose.

Within seven days a written report must be sent, on form F2508 (available from Health and Safety Executive offices), to the enforcing authority. This form should be used to report on all accidents causing fatal or major injury and notifiable dangerous occurrences. In the case of a reportable disease form F2580A is used.

Other injuries to employees are also notifiable if they result in more than three days' absence from normal work, but all that is needed is to:
(a) enter details of the accident in the accident record book (or other record system). Form F2509 may be used for this purpose.
(b) complete form B176 (relating to a claim for Industrial Injury Benefit) when requested to do so by the local DHSS office.

Dangerous Occurrences

The list of dangerous occurrences in the regulations is selective, the aim being to obtain information about incidents with a high potential for injury but with a low frequency of occurrence.

It is important to note that dangerous occurrences must be reported even though no injury was actually caused to any person.

Examples of incidents which constitute dangerous occurrences are as follows:
1. Failure, collapse or overturning of lifts, hoists, cranes, excavators, tail-lifts, etc
2. Explosion of boiler or boiler tube
3. Electrical short circuits followed by fire or explosion
4. Explosion or fire which results in stoppage of work for more than 24 hours
5. Release of flammable liquid or gas (ie over one tonne)
6. Collapse of scaffolding
7. Collapse or partial collapse of any building
8. Failure of a freight container while being lifted
9. A road tanker to which the Hazchem regulations apply either overturning or suffering serious damage to the tank while a hazardous substance is being carried.

Note 1: This list is abbreviated. Where appropriate the regulations themselves should be consulted.

Note 2: A useful leaflet on the subject is available free from local offices of the Health and Safety Executive.

First Aid

Regulations require employers to train members of their staff in first aid techniques and to provide first aid equipment and facilities under The Health and Safety (First Aid) Regulations 1981. An approved code of practice has been established by the Health and Safety Commission providing both employers and the self-employed with practical guidance on how they may meet the requirements of the regulations. Further, HMSO has published a booklet in their health and safety series entitled *First Aid at Work* (HS(R) 11 Price: £2.50) from which these guidelines are extracted.

The regulations state that 'an employer shall provide, or ensure that there are provided, such equipment and facilities as are adequate and appropriate in the circumstances for enabling first aid to be rendered to his employees if they are injured or become ill at work.'

Trained First-Aiders

The employer must provide suitable persons to administer first aid and these persons must have had proper training or hold appropriate qualifications. The requirement is for one trained first-aider for every 150 persons employed in low hazard operations (ie shops and offices) and one first-aider for 50-150 employees and one for every other 150 employees in high hazard operations (ie factories, sites, dockyards etc). Where the numbers of employees fall between these levels at least one person should be appointed to take responsibility for dealing with accidents (ie for looking after first aid kits and telephoning for medical assistance).

First Aid Boxes

First aid boxes must be provided. These should be properly identified as first aid containers, preferably with a white cross on a green background, and contain only first aid supplies. The list of recommended contents and quantities is as follows:

Item	Number of employees				
	1-5	6-10	11-50	51-100	101-150
Guidance card	1	1	1	1	1
Individually wrapped sterile adhesive dressings	10	20	40	40	40
Sterile eye pads, with attachment	1	2	4	6	8
Triangular bandages	1	2	4	6	8
Sterile coverings for serious wounds (where applicable)	1	2	4	6	8
Safety pins	6	6	12	12	12
Medium sized sterile unmedicated dressings	3	6	8	10	12
Large sterile unmedicated dressings	1	2	4	6	10
Extra large sterile unmedicated dressings	1	2	4	6	8

17: SAFETY – VEHICLES, LOADS AND AT WORK

Soap and water and disposable drying materials, or suitable equivalents, should also be available. Where tap water is not available, sterile water or sterile normal saline, in disposable containers each holding at least 300ml, should be kept easily accessible, and near to the first aid box, for eye irrigation.

Where sterile water or sterile normal saline in disposable containers needs to be kept near the first aid box because tap water is not available, at least the following quantities should be kept:

Item	Number of employees			
	1-10	11-50	51-100	101-150
Sterile water or saline in disposable containers (where tap water is not available) (minimum capacity 300ml)	1	3	6	6

The contents of first aid boxes should be replenished as soon as possible after use and items which deteriorate will need to be replaced from time to time. For this reason boxes and kits should be examined frequently to make sure they are fully equipped.

Travelling First Aid Kits
An employer does not need to make first aid provisions for employees working away from his establishment. However, where the work involves travelling for long distances in remote areas, from which access to NHS accident and emergency facilities may be difficult, or where employees are using potentially dangerous tools or machinery, small travelling first aid kits should be provided.

The contents of such kits may need to vary according to the circumstances in which they are to be used. The regulations suggest that in general the following items should be sufficient:
1. Six individually wrapped sterile adhesive dressings.
2. One medium-sized sterile unmedicated dressing (approx 10cm x 8cm. Examples of suitable dressings currently available are the Standard Dressings No 8 and No 13 BPC).
3. One triangular bandage (this should, if possible, be sterile; if not, a sterile covering appropriate for serious wounds should also be included).
4. Six safety pins.

First Aid Rooms

When the siting of a new first aid room is under consideration it should be borne in mind that there should, where possible, be toilets nearby. Any corridors and lifts which lead to the first aid room may need to allow access for a stretcher, wheelchair, carrying chair or wheeled carriage. Consideration should also be given to the possibility of providing some form of emergency lighting.

The following facilities and equipment should be provided in first aid rooms:
1. Sink with running hot and cold water always available.

2. Drinking water when not available on tap.
3. Paper towels.
4. Smooth topped working surfaces.
5. An adequate supply of sterile dressings and other materials for wound treatment. These should be at least equivalent in range and standard to those listed above, and kept in the quantities set out on p 266.
6. Clinical thermometer.
7. A couch with pillow and blankets frequently cleaned.
8. A suitable store for first aid materials.
9. Soap and nail brush.
10. Clean garments for use by first-aiders and occupation first-aiders.
11. Suitable refuse container.

Safety Signs

A safety sign is defined as one which combines geometrical shape, colour, and a pictorial symbol to provide specific health or safety information or an instruction whether or not any text is included on the sign. Regulations concerning the specification of safety signs in work premises has applied to all such signs since 1 January 1986. Specifications for various types of safety sign are given in BS 5378 (Part I). They are briefly described as follows:

Prohibition Sign: round in shape with a white background and a circular band and cross bar in red. The symbol must be black and placed in the centre of the sign without obliterating the cross bar. Typical examples of such signs are those prohibiting smoking, pedestrians or the use of water for drinking purposes.

Warning Sign: triangular in shape with a yellow background and black triangular band. The symbol or words must be black and placed in the centre of the sign. Typical examples of such signs are those warning of the danger of fire, explosion, toxic substances, corrosive substances, radiation, overhead loads, industrial trucks, electric shocks, proximity of laser beams, etc.

Mandatory Sign: round in shape with a blue background with the symbol or words placed centrally and in white. Typical examples of such signs are those advising that certain pieces of protective clothing must be worn (eg goggles, hard hats, breathing masks, gloves, etc).

Safety Sign: square in shape with a green background and white symbol or words centrally placed. Typical examples of such signs are those for fire exits, first aid posts and rescue points.

Vehicle Reversing

Among the statistics of industrial accidents and road accidents, those resulting from vehicles reversing feature significantly. It is in consequence of this that legislation was changed to permit the voluntary fitment of reversing bleepers on certain goods and passenger vehicles (see p 187 for full details).

With the introduction of these voluntary provisions there is the risk that any operator deciding not to fit such equipment on a voluntary basis who then has one of his vehicles involved in a reversing accident could face proceedings under the Health and Safety at Work Act for not taking sufficient care in safeguarding the health of others. A number of successful prosecutions on this account have been reported and in some cases very heavy fines were imposed.

Fork-Lift Truck Safety

There has been much concern in recent years about the high level of industrial accidents which are caused or which result from fork-lift truck misuse. In consequence of this a system of fork-lift truck driver licensing is to be established in order to ensure a safe standard of operation.

The scheme is voluntary but a Code of Practice will be established which employers will be bound to follow if they wish to avoid conflict with the Factory Inspectorate who have powers to order an employer to have drivers trained, to order that the use of fork-lift trucks be stopped immediately if they believe that danger is being caused, and to take an employer to court if an untrained driver causes an accident with a fork-lift truck.

Manual Handling

Legislation is proposed by the Health and Safety Commission to limit the weight of loads which may be lifted manually. In a consultative document the Commission shows its intention of placing on employers responsibility for identifying the capabilities of their staff in relation to their lifting abilities and the risks which would be encountered by them lifting weights at certain levels.

The draft regulations divide weights into four categories. Below 16kg (ie 35lb) no special action is required provided the few individuals who are likely to face serious risks when handling weights of this order have been identified. In the weight range 16kg to 34kg (ie 35lb to 75lb) employers would be required to establish 'procedures to identify those individuals unable to handle such weights regularly without unacceptable risk unless mechanical assistance is provided'.

Unless the regular handling of weights between 34kg and 55kg (ie 75lb to 120lbs) is limited to 'effectively supervised, selected and trained individuals' mechanical handling systems should be employed. Above this level, the draft says that mechanical handling or 'team' systems should always be considered. Where this is not reasonably practicable, selective recruitment and special training is essential, the draft suggests. The reason it gives for this is that even with effective supervision, very few people can regularly handle weights of this order with safety.

The regulations themselves contain nothing onerous. They merely require the employer not to employ a person to handle any load likely to injure him because of its weight, shape, size or lack of rigidity; to the frequency with which he handles loads; or the conditions under which the load is to be handled. Further, the employer must ensure that systems of work involving manual handling of loads must be, as far as reasonably practicable, safe and without risk to health. Employees are given responsibility to co-operate with their employer in implementing systems of work involving manual handling.

The HSE notes, *Manual Handling Framework Guidance,* are in two parts. The first identifies the sources of the risks and hazards involved in manual handling and the second contains guidance on what positive steps can be taken to minimise those risks. A checklist is also provided.

These notes will provide useful guidance to employers on many aspects of manual handling. But they will not help to overcome the undoubted difficulties which will arise when employers actually get down to trying to assess the health or capabilities of their employees. If the firm employs a medical officer the problem may be easily overcome but not otherwise.

For a start, it is questionable as to whether the majority do, or would be prepared to, disclose to their employer the true state of their health in regard to its effect on their lifting capacity. Furthermore, employees may not want to appear inferior in strength to their workmates by having limitations placed on their lifting capacity by the employer, no matter how beneficial this may be in health terms.

Another major problem area is the fact that only in a proportion of instances can the employee, or indeed even the employer, know the precise weight of objects to be lifted. Even if the weights of objects are known, the scheduling problems likely to be encountered by employers trying to ensure that employees with the right lifting capabilities are on hand to lift appropriate loads may be almost insurmountable.

Freight Container Safety Regulations

Owners and lessees and others in control of freight containers must ensure that they comply with the International Convention for Safe Containers – Geneva 1972. The Freight Containers (Safety Convention) Regulations 1984 apply to containers designed to facilitate the transport of goods by one or more modes of transport without intermediate reloading, designed to be secured or readily handled or both, having corner fittings for these purposes and which have top corner fittings and a bottom area of at least 7 square metres or, if they do not have top corner fittings, a bottom area of at least 14 square metres.

Containers must have a valid approval issued by the Health and Safety Executive or a body appointed by the HSE (or under the authority of a foreign government which has acceded to the Convention) for the purpose confirming that they meet specified standards of design and construction and should be fitted with a safety approval plate to this effect. If they are marked with their gross weight such marking must be consistent with the maximum operating gross weight shown on the safety approval plate. Containers must be maintained in an efficient state, in efficient working order and in good repair. Details of the arrangements for the approval of containers in Great Britain are set out in a document *Arrangements in GB for the Approval of Containers* available from the Health and Safety Executive.

17: SAFETY – VEHICLES, LOADS AND AT WORK

The safety approval plate (issued by the HSE) as described in the regulations must be permanently fitted to the container where it is clearly visible and not capable of being easily damaged and it must show the following information:

CSC SAFETY APPROVAL
1. Date Manufactured
2. Identification Number
3. Maximum Gross Weight ...kg ...lb
4. Allowable Stacking Weight for 1.8g ...kg ...lb
5. Racking Test Load Value.

Operation of Lorry Loaders

The use of hydraulically operated lorry loaders or lorry mounted cranes as they are more commonly called (in fact the name Hiab is becoming a generic term for this equipment) 'has reduced the risk of accident from the arduous and potentially injurious manhandling of loads and they reserve the strength of the driver for safe conduct of the vehicle', according to the Association of Lorry Loader Manufacturers and Importers of Great Britain (ALLMI). But, the Association says, despite the inherent safety of a properly designed and installed lorry loader, accidents still occur through lack of knowledge and understanding. For this reason ALLMI has published an excellent booklet called *Code of Practice for the Safe Application and Operation of Lorry Loaders*. Copies are available from the Association C/o Tindal Oatts & Roger, 113 St Vincent Street, Glasgow G2 5HS.

Safety in Dock Premises

Under the Docks Regulations 1988 (SI 1655/88) made under the Health and Safety at Work etc Act 1974, when goods vehicle drivers work in or visit docks premises including roll-on/roll-off ferry ports they must be provided with high visibility clothing to be worn when they leave the vehicle cab. The clothing may take the form of fluorescent jackets, waistcoats, belts or sashes and must be worn at all times when out of the cab on such premises including when on the vehicle decks of the ferry. Protective headgear (hard hats) must be supplied and worn in such areas where there is likely to be danger of falling objects from above (eg where cranes are working).

Drivers must leave the vehicle cab when parked on a straddle-carrier grid or where containers are being lifted on to or off the vehicle.

The HSC has published an approved code of practice *Safety in Docks* which is available from HMSO.

18: Loads – General

In addition to the regulations referred to in Chapter 10 regarding the way in which vehicles are constructed and used, the operator will find many more regulations imposed on him which depend on the types of load he carries. Some of these provisions are included in the Road Vehicles (Construction and Use) Regulations 1986, and its many amendments, but others are to be found elsewhere. This chapter deals with normal loads and also covers some of the special points applicable to carrying food, animals, sand and ballast, solid fuel and containers.

Distribution of Loads

When loading a vehicle, care must be taken to ensure that the load is evenly distributed to ensure stability of the vehicle and to conform to the vehicle's individual axle weights as well as the overall gross weight. It is important on multi-delivery work to make sure that when part of the load has been removed in the course of a delivery, none of the axles has become overloaded because of the transfer of weight. This can happen even though the gross vehicle weight is still within permissible maximum limits and in such cases it is necessary for the driver to attempt to correct the situation by shifting the load, or part of it.

All loads should be securely and safely fixed and roped and sheeted, chained or lashed if necessary. It is an offence to have an insecure load or a load which causes danger to other road users. Furthermore, it is a legal requirement (C and U Regulations 1986 s100) that loads must not cause or be likely to cause a danger or nuisance to other road users and that they should be physically restrained (ie roped and sheeted) if necessary to avoid parts of the load falling or being blown from the vehicle. It is an offence also for the securing ropes or other devices and sheets to flap and cause nuisance or danger to other road users. Heavy penalties, with maximum fines of up to £2000, can be imposed on conviction for offences relating to these matters.

Axle Load Calculations

Imposed axle loads can be calculated to determine whether a vehicle is operating legally in particular circumstances by using the following formula:
1. Determine the vehicle wheelbase.
2. Determine the weight of the load (ie payload).
3. Calculate the front loadbase (ie centre line of front axle to centre of gravity of load).
4. Apply the formula as follows.

Length and Width of Loads

Loads on normal goods vehicles (ie which come within the C and U Regulations) in excess of the actual vehicle dimensions of length and width

Example of axle weight calculation:

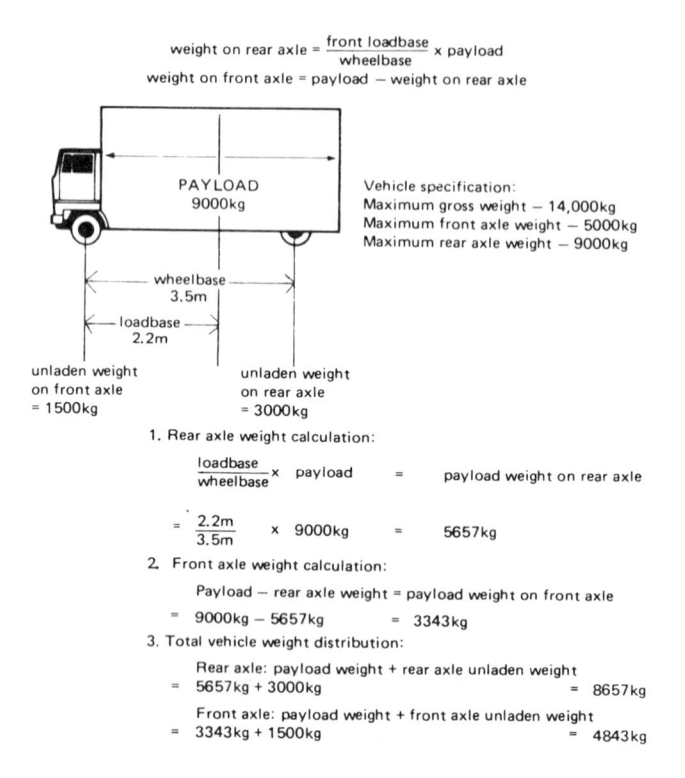

$$\text{weight on rear axle} = \frac{\text{front loadbase}}{\text{wheelbase}} \times \text{payload}$$

weight on front axle = payload − weight on rear axle

PAYLOAD 9000kg

wheelbase 3.5m
loadbase 2.2m

unladen weight on front axle = 1500kg

unladen weight on rear axle = 3000kg

Vehicle specification:
Maximum gross weight — 14,000kg
Maximum front axle weight — 5000kg
Maximum rear axle weight — 9000kg

1. Rear axle weight calculation:

$$\frac{\text{loadbase}}{\text{wheelbase}} \times \text{payload} = \text{payload weight on rear axle}$$

$$= \frac{2.2m}{3.5m} \times 9000kg = 5657kg$$

2. Front axle weight calculation:

Payload − rear axle weight = payload weight on front axle
= 9000kg − 5657kg = 3343kg

3. Total vehicle weight distribution:

Rear axle: payload weight + rear axle unladen weight
= 5657kg + 3000kg = 8657kg

Front axle: payload weight + front axle unladen weight
= 3343kg + 1500kg = 4843kg

may be carried provided that certain special conditions are met, as indicated here. Details of the requirements relating to abnormal and projecting loads is given in Chapter 19.

Length

When moving a vehicle which complies with C and U Regulations and its load is more than 18.3 metres long, the police must be notified two clear days in advance and a statutory attendant must also be carried. If a long load is carried on an articulated vehicle which is specially designed to carry long loads but in all other respects complies with the C and U Regulations the 18.3 metre dimension is measured excluding the length of the tractive unit. Notice must also be given to the police and an attendant carried if the combination of a number of vehicles carrying one load is more than 25.9 metres long.

An overall limit of 27.4 metres is set for the length of a trailer and its load (the length of the towing vehicle is excluded from this dimension) above which movement can only be allowed by special order from the Secretary

18: LOADS – GENERAL

of State for Transport. *Further details of the requirements for markers, police notification and attendants on long loads is given in Chapter 19.*

Width

The overall width of a normal load (ie not an indivisible load – see p 281 for definition) carried on a vehicle complying with the Construction and Use Regulations must not be more than 2.9 metres. The load itself must not project more than 305 millimetres on either side of the vehicle. There is an exception to this requirement when loose agricultural produce is carried.

If an indivisible load is carried on a normal vehicle which complies in all respects with the C and U Regulations and the load is more than 2.9 metres wide, two days' notice must be given to the police of every district through which it is to pass. If such a load exceeds 3.5 metres width then the police must be notified as stated and an attendant must be carried.

If the load on a vehicle is more than 5 metres wide, two days' notice must be given to the police, a statutory attendant must be carried and a Special Order must be obtained from the Secretary of State for Transport on form VR1.

Loads in London

Before moving loads in central London which are more than 2.6 metres wide or 10.98 metres long or one and a quarter times the length of the vehicle, between the hours of 10 am and 7 pm on weekdays, police permission must be obtained.

Animals

There are regulations to ensure that animals do not suffer distress or discomfort during transport by road and that the risk of the spread of disease is minimised. In the event of an outbreak of foot and mouth disease there are severe restrictions on the movement of cloven-hoofed animals. Pigs are not allowed to be moved away from sale premises without a local authority inspector licensing the movement. Separate regulations cover the carrying of horses and calves.

In general, vehicles used for carrying animals should have non-slip floors with footholds, and the interior should not have any projections such as bolt-heads. Adequate ventilation is a necessity, proper loading ramps must be used and a roof must be provided to protect animals from the weather. Vehicles must not be overcrowded and animals must not be mixed. Even horses of different breeds must be separated. There are minimum heights laid down for the decks of two-tier vehicles used for carrying sheep and pigs. Where journeys of more than 12 hours' duration are involved, arrangements must be made to provide the animals with a supply of food and water.

Vehicles must be cleaned and disinfected after animals have been carried and before the next lot are loaded unless more than one load of the same class of animals is carried on the same day between the same points. It is an offence under the Movement and Sale of Pigs Order 1975 to use any vehicle whether owned by a farmer or hired which has been carrying pigs, unless the vehicle is cleansed and disinfected immediately after the pigs have been unloaded and before it is used again for carrying pigs or any other animal or thing. The disinfectant to be used for this purpose must be one approved officially for swine vesicular disease.

Different categories of pigs must not be carried together in the same vehicle. It is important to ensure that all pigs being picked up from one or more farms have the same kind of licence, or are slaughter pigs clearly marked with a red cross being moved to a slaughter market or slaughterhouse.

Records must be kept of the movement of horses giving details of the vehicle owner, the vehicle, the animals, the sender and the person taking delivery, the journey and the date and place where the vehicle is disinfected. The record must be made within 18 hours of the journey and kept for three months. In the case of journeys taking more than three hours a record must be kept on the vehicle showing loading, feeding and watering times and the unloading time.

Food

Special regulations (The Food Hygiene [Markets, Stalls and Delivery Vehicles] Regulations 1966) apply to vehicles used for the carriage of food, excluding milk and drugs. All mobile shops and food delivery vehicles and the equipment carried by such vehicles must be constructed and maintained so that the food carried can be kept clean and fresh.

The driver of a food vehicle should wear clean overalls and if meat or bacon sides are carried, which the driver has to carry over his shoulder, he should wear a hat to prevent the meat touching his hair. He must not smoke while loading or unloading or serving the food (but he may do so in the cab of the vehicle if this is separate from the part of the vehicle in which the food is carried), and any cuts or abrasions on his hands must be covered with waterproof dressings.

If a driver or any other person concerned in the loading and unloading of food develops any infectious disease, his employer must notify the local authority health department immediately.

Food vehicles must have the name and address of the person carrying on the business shown on the nearside and the address at which the vehicle is garaged if this is a different address. If, however, a vehicle based in England or Wales has a fleet number clearly shown and is garaged at night on company premises, then the garage address is not required.

A wash hand basin and a supply of clean water must be provided on vehicles which carry uncovered food (except bread) unless the driver can wash his hands at both ends of his journey before he has to handle the food. When meat is carried, soap, clean towels and a nailbrush must be provided on the vehicle. In Scotland all food-carrying vehicles must be provided with these items.

Mobile shops and food delivery vehicles must not be garaged with food still inside unless it can be kept clean.

An authorised officer of a council may enter and detain (but not stop while it is in motion) any food-carrying vehicle except those owned by British Rail or vehicles operated by haulage contractors.

18: LOADS – GENERAL

Perishable Food

A whole range of legislation covers the carriage of food and particularly perishable food both in the UK and in Europe. When perishable foodstuffs are carried on international journeys to and through Austria, Belgium, Bulgaria, Czechoslovakia, Denmark, Finland, France, Germany, Italy, Luxembourg, Morocco, the Netherlands, Norway, Poland, Spain, Sweden, USSR and Yugoslavia the conditions of the Agreement on the International Carriage of Perishable Foodstuffs (known as the ATP agreement) must be observed.

The ATP agreement also applies in Britain (vis the International Carriage of Perishable Foodstuffs Act 1976) and under its provisions vehicles used to carry perishable food must be constructed and tested (at six-yearly intervals) to certain specified standards and must display an ATP approval plate to this effect. The principal requirement is that vehicles carrying certain specified perishable foodstuffs must comply with the body and temperature control equipment test standards and must be certified to this effect. The ATP agreement applies broadly to quick frozen, deep frozen, frozen and non-frozen foodstuffs but not fresh vegetables and soft fruit (see Chapter 26 for more detail).

Information relating to food transport may be obtained from the Department of Health which has published a number of Codes of Practice, and from the Ministry of Agriculture, Fisheries and Food and the Royal Society of Health.

Chilled Food Controls

Following a series of food poisoning (salmonella and listeria) outbreaks in 1989 the government is planning to change existing legislation (the Food Hygiene Regulations 1970) to control the maximum temperature at which chilled food can be transported. The current proposal is to set maximum limits of plus 5° C and plus 8° C for the two main categories of chilled food. At the present time, a government consultation paper is circulating in the food manufacturing, retailing and controlled temperature distribution industries. Transfrigoroute (UK), the trade association representing the major chilled food carriers has its own code of conduct and is energetically promoting the idea of self-regulation for the industry starting with the production of a new cold-chain training video.

Waste Food

Vehicles used to collect unprocessed waste food, intended for feeding to livestock and poultry, must be drip-proof, covered and enclosed with material capable of being cleansed and disinfected.

Vehicles must be thoroughly cleansed and disinfected on the completion of unloading. No livestock or poultry or foodstuff or anything intended for use for any livestock or poultry may be carried in any vehicle which is carrying unprocessed waste food intended for feeding to livestock or poultry. Furthermore, processed and unprocessed waste food may not be carried in the same vehicle at the same time.

Sand and Ballast Loads

The movement of sand and ballast comes to the attention of the

Department of Trade and Industry and Trading Standards Inspectors principally because under the Weights and Measures Act 1985 these materials must be sold in weighed quantities (normally by volume in metric measures – in multiples of 0.2 cubic metres) and carried in calibrated vehicles which display a stamp placed on the body by the Trading Standards department of the local authority.

When sand and ballast (including shingle, ashes, clinker, etc) loads are carried, the driver must have a signed note (ie conveyance note) from the supplier indicating the following facts:
1. The name and address of the sellers.
2. The name of the buyer and the address for delivery of the load.
3. A description of the type of ballast.
4. The quantity by net weight or by volume.
5. Details of the vehicle.
6. The date, time and place of loading the vehicle.

The document containing these details must be handed over to the buyer before unloading, or if he is not there it must be left at the delivery premises. Where a delivery is to be made to two or more buyers each must be given a separate document containing the details shown above. Similar requirements apply to the carriage of ready-mixed cement.

Solid Fuel Loads

When solid fuel is carried a document giving similar details to those mentioned above for sand and ballast carrying must be held by the driver of the vehicle. When solid fuel is carried for sale in open sacks a notice on the vehicle in letters at least 60mm high must contain the following words: 'All open sacks on this vehicle contain 25kg or 50kg'.

Container Carrying

Container carrying has come to the fore in recent years, and while there are no specific regulations on this subject apart from the general safety provisions of the C and U Regulations and the vehicle weight limitations, the authorities are concerned about the dangers arising from inadequate securing of containers. Containers, ideally, should be carried only on vehicles fitted with proper twistlocks or, failing this, should be secured by chains of sufficient strength with tensioners for adjustment and taking account of the recommended strength of restraint systems given in the DTp code of practice *Safety of Loads on Vehicles* (see pages 255–6).

The use of ropes for securing containers should be avoided because the corner castings through which they are passed are rough and will cut through the rope. Containers where possible should be loaded against the headboard and directly on the platform of the vehicle, not on timber packing which is liable to move.

Under the Freight Containers (Safety Convention) Regulations 1984 owners and lessees and others in control of freight containers used or supplied must ensure that they comply with the conditions of use as stated in the International Convention for Safe Containers 1972 (see also Chapter 17).

Fly Tipping

The Environmental Protection Bill currently before parliament is intended to tighten up existing measures to prevent the illegal tipping (fly-tipping) of waste, demolition rubble and such materials in unauthorised places. Among the specific proposals included are plans to introduce the registration of waste transporters and tipper operators, the licensing of authorised operators, restriction of tipping to authorised sites and further powers to impound (and possibly sell) vehicles belonging to operators who dump loads illegally (such powers already exist through the Criminal Justice Act 1988 – see also Chapter 20).

19: Loads – Abnormal and Projecting

The Construction and Use Regulations, as previously described in Chapter 9, relating to the lengths, widths and weights of vehicles do not apply to heavy vehicles specially designed, constructed and used solely for the carriage of abnormal indivisible loads (commonly known as 'Special Types' vehicles). Certain conditions apply to these Special Types vehicles when abnormal indivisible loads are carried under the provisions of the Motor Vehicles (Authorisation of Special Types) General Orders of 1979 and 1981 and the Amendment Order 1987 which raised the threshold above which this legislation applies to 38 tonnes from 1 October 1989, divide such vehicles into three weight categories and set speed limits for such operations. This chapter details the legal requirements that apply when abnormal loads are carried and for the carriage of projecting loads.

Abnormal Indivisible Loads

For the purpose of regulations, abnormal indivisible loads (sometimes abbreviated to AILs) are loads which cannot, without undue expense or risk of damage, be divided into two or more loads for the purpose of carriage on the road and which cannot be carried on a vehicle operating within the limitations of the C and U Regulations as described in Chapter 9.

Number of Abnormal Loads

While normally the carriage of only one abnormal load is permitted, two such abnormal loads may be carried on one vehicle within Category 1 or Category 2 (see below) provided the loads are from the same place and are destined for the same delivery address.

Engineering Plant
In the case of engineering plant, such plant and parts dismantled from it may be carried on the same vehicle (ie to constitute more than one or two loads) provided that the carriage of the parts does not cause the overall dimensions of the vehicle and the main load to be exceeded and that the parts are loaded and discharged at the same place as the main load.

Special Types Vehicles

Dimensions

Width
Special Types vehicles, locomotives and trailers and their loads are normally permitted to be up to 2.9 metres wide but, if necessary to ensure

the safe carriage of large loads, they may be up to a maximum of 6.1 metres wide.

Length
The overall length of a Special Types vehicle and its load must not exceed 27.4 metres which applies normally but where the abnormal load is carried on a combination of vehicles and trailers or on a long articulated vehicle the dimension of 27.4 metres is measured excluding the drawing vehicle.

Weight
The permissible maximum weight of a Special Types vehicle must not exceed 150000kg. There is a limit on the maximum weight which may be imposed on the road by any one wheel of the vehicle, of 8250kg and the maximum weight imposed by any one axle must not exceed 16500kg. These limits may be exceeded only if authorisation by Special Order is obtained from the Secretary of State for Transport (see p 286).

Vehicle Categories
The Special Types Order specified three separate weight categories for abnormal load vehicles as follows:
Category 1 – up to 45 tonnes gcw
Category 2 – up to 80 tonnes gcw
Category 3 – up to 150 tonnes gcw

Category 1 Vehicles
Vehicles within this category will normally fall within the Construction and Use Regulations in regard to permissible maximum weight, axle spacings and axle weights but where it is a five-axle articulated vehicle the weight may exceed 38 tonnes up to a maximum of 46000kg (ie 46 tonnes) provided the following minimum relevant axle spacings are observed:

Relevant axle spacing	*Maximum Weight*
At least 6.5 metres	40000kg
At least 7.0 metres	42000kg
At least 7.5 metres	44000kg
At least 8.0 metres	46000kg

Category 2 Vehicles
Vehicles within this category may operate up to a maximum weight of 80000kg (ie 80 tonnes) but they must have a minimum of five axles with a maximum weight of 50000kg on any group of axles and they must meet the minimum axle spacing requirements specified below.

Individual wheel and axle weight weight limits are as follows:

19: LOADS – ABNORMAL AND PROJECTING

Distance between adjacent axles	Maximum axle weight	Maximum wheel weight
At least 1.1 metres	12000kg	6000kg
At least 1.35 metres	12500kg	6250kg

Minimum axle spacings and applicable maximum weights are as follows:

Distance between foremost and rearmost axles	Maximum weight
5.07 metres	38000kg
5.33 metres	40000kg
6.0 metres	45000kg
6.67 metres	50000kg
7.33 metres	55000kg
8.0 metres	60000kg
8.67 metres	65000kg
9.33 metres	70000kg
10.0 metres	75000kg
10.67 metres	80000kg

Category 3 Vehicles

A minimum of six axles is needed on Category 3 vehicles operating up to a permissible maximum weight of 150000kg (ie 150 tonnes) with a limit of 100000kg on any group of axles or 90000kg on any group of axles where the distance between adjacent axles is less than 1.35 metres. Vehicles in this category must meet the minimum axle spacing requirements specified below.

Individual wheel and axle weight limits are as follows:

Distance between adjacent axles	Maximum axle weight	Maximum wheel weight
At least 1.1 metres	15000kg	7500kg
At least 1.35 metres	16500 kg	8250kg

Minimum axle spacings and applicable maximum weights are as follows:

Distance between foremost and rearmost axles	Maximum weight
5.77 metres	80000kg
6.23 metres	85000kg
6.68 metres	90000kg
7.14 metres	95000kg
7.59 metres	100000kg
8.05 metres	105000kg
8.50 metres	110000kg
8.95 metres	115000kg
9.41 metres	120000kg
9.86 metres	125000kg
10.32 metres	130000kg
10.77 metres	135000kg
11.23 metres	140000kg
11.68 metres	145000kg
12.14 metres	150000kg

VED for Special Types Vehicles

A separate VED taxation class applies to Special Types vehicles – see Chapter 21 for details.

Braking Standards

Vehicles operating within Category 1 must meet the C and U Regulation braking standards requirements and those operating within Categories 2 and 3 from 1 October 1989 must meet the EC braking standards (ie EC 230/71, 132/74, 524/75, 489/79).

Identification Sign

Vehicles operating under the Special Types Order must display an identification sign at the front. This sign on a plate at least 250mm x 400mm will have white letters on a black background as follows:

STGO	letters 105mm high
CAT...	letters and figures 70mm high

NB: A figure 1, 2 or 3 must follow the word 'CAT' as appropriate depending on the category of vehicle.

Special Types Plates

Vehicles falling within Category 2 and 3 which have been manufactured since 1 October 1988 must display Special Types plates (in a conspicuous and easily accessible position) showing the maximum operational weights recommended by the manufacturer when travelling on a road at varying speeds as follows: 12, 20, 25, 30, 35, 40mph. The weights to be shown are the permissible maximum gross and train weights and the maximum weights for each individual axle. Plates on trailers (including semi-trailers) must show the permissible maximum weight for the trailer and the maximum-weights for each individual axle. The plates must be marked with the words 'Special Types Use'.

Speed Limits

Maximum permitted speeds* are specified for for Special Types vehicles as follows:

Vehicle category	Motorways	Dual-carriageways	Other Roads
1. Up to 46 tonnes	60mph	50mph	40mph
2. Up to 80 tonnes	40mph	35mph	30mph
3. Up to 150 tonnes	30mph	25mph	20mph

Speeds for Wide Loads
Vehicles carrying loads over 4.3 metres but not over 6.1 metres wide are restricted to 30mph on motorways, 25mph on dual-carriageways and 20mph on other roads.

*NB: It is important to note that tyre equipment on vehicles and trailers must be compatible with both the gross weight of the vehicle and the authorised maximum speed of operation.

19: LOADS – ABNORMAL AND PROJECTING

Attendants

An attendant must be carried on Special Types vehicles:
1. when the vehicle or its load is more than 3.5 metres wide;
2. if the overall length of the vehicle is more than 18.3 metres (not including the length of the tractive unit in the case of articulated vehicles);
3. if the length of a vehicle and trailer exceeds 25.9 metres;
4. if the load projects more than 1.83 metres beyond the front of the vehicle;
5. if the load projects more than 3.05 metres beyond the rear of the vehicle.

If three or more vehicles carrying abnormal loads or other loads of dimensions that require statutory attendants to be carried travel in convoy, attendants need only be carried on the first and last vehicles in the convoy.

Police Notification

The police of every district through which a Special Types combination is to be moved must be given two clear days' notice (excluding Saturdays, Sundays and bank holidays in the case of notification under the STGO and excluding Sundays and bank holidays for notificaiton under the C and U Regulations) if:
1. the vehicle and its load is more than 2.9 metres wide;
2. the vehicle and its load (or trailer and load) is more than 18.3 metres long;
3. a combination of vehicles and trailers carrying the load is more than 25.9 metres long;
4. if the load projects more than 3.05 metres to the front or rear of the vehicle;
5. the gross weight of the vehicle and the load is more than 80000kg.

The notice given must include details of the vehicle and the weight and dimensions of the load, the dates and times of the movement through the police district and the proposed route to be followed through that district.

In the case where notice has been given to the police of the movement of an abnormal load, they have the power to delay the vehicle during its journey if it is holding up other traffic or in the interests of road safety.

Notification of Highway and Bridge Authorities

If a Special Types vehicle and its load weighs more than 80000kg, or the weight imposed on the road by the wheels of such a vehicle exceeds the maximum limit laid down in the C and U Regulations (see pp 150–51), five clear days' notice must be given to the Highway and Bridge Authorities for the areas through which the vehicle is to pass. Two days' notice is required when only the C and U axle weight limit is exceeded. The operator of such a vehicle is also required to indemnify the Authority against damage to any road or bridge over which it passes. These requirements also apply to vehicles which exceed the C and U gross weight limits and those which exceed their plated axle weight limits, plus mobile cranes and engineering plant which exceed the limits specified.

Stopping on Bridges
The driver of a vehicle carrying an abnormal load must ensure that no

other such vehicle and load are on a bridge before he drives on to the bridge and once on the bridge he must not stop unless forced to do so.

Where a vehicle weighing more than 38000kg gross has to stop on a bridge for any reason it must be moved off the bridge as soon as possible. If it has broken down, the advice of the bridge authority (usually the Highways Department of the local authority) must be sought before the vehicle is jacked up on the bridge. In the event of damage being caused to a road or bridge by the movement of a heavy or large load over it the highway authority can take steps to recover from the vehicle operator the costs of repairing the damage.

Special Orders

Written notice has to be given to the Secretary of State for Transport where movement may only be by Special Order (ie where vehicle and load exceed 5 metres in width, exceed the length limit of 27.4 metres or the weight limit of 150 tonnes). Application is made on form VR 1 (ie the movement order) and a copy of this completed form must be carried on the vehicle.

Dump Trucks

When dump trucks (ie vehicles designed for moving excavated material) are used on the road the maximum permissible gross weight is limited to 50800kg and the maximum axle weight allowed for such vehicles is 22860kg. They must not exceed a speed of 12mph on normal roads and an attendant must be carried if the width exceeds 3.5 metres. If a dump truck is more than 4.3 metres wide, permission in the form of a Special Order from the Secretary of State for Transport is required before it is moved. Where three or more such vehicles over 3.5 metres wide travel in convoy only the first and last vehicles need carry attendants.

Other Plant

The Special Types General Order also makes special provision for other items of plant such as grass cutting machines and hedge trimmers, track-laying vehicles, pedestrian-controlled road maintenance vehicles, vehicles used for experimental trials, straddle carriers, land tractors used for harvesting, mechanically propelled hay and straw balers, vehicles fitted with moveable platforms and engineering plant. Any person proposing to move such items on public roads is advised to check that the appropriate legal requirements are met.

High Loads

While there are no specific legal height restrictions on vehicles or loads (except those mentioned on p 202), clearly vehicles must be loaded so that they can pass under bridges on the routes to be used. In particular it should be noted that motorway bridges are built to give a clearance of 16ft 6ins and overhead power cables crossing roads are set at a minimum height of 19ft (5.8 metres) where the voltage carried does not exceed 33000 volts and at 6 metres where this voltage is exceeded. When planning to move loads above 19ft it is a legal requirement to make contact with the National Grid Company (ie previously the CEGB) or the appropriate regional electricity

19: LOADS – ABNORMAL AND PROJECTING

distribution company (ie previously the regional electricity boards) beforehand. It is also recommended that contact should be made with British Telecom regarding the presence of its overhead lines on the routes to be used. Some police forces now report that they will not action notification of abnormal load movements until both National Power and British Telecom have been notified.

Projecting Loads

Projecting loads may be carried on normal C and U regulation vehicles as well as on Special Types vehicles as described above. A projecting load is one that projects beyond the foremost or rearmost points or the side of the vehicle and, depending on the length or width of the projection, certain conditions apply when such loads are carried on normal vehicles including requirements for lighting and marking.

Forward Projections

A load projecting more than 2.0 metres beyond the foremost part of the vehicle (on both C and U and Special Types vehicles) must be indicated by an approved side and end marker board (Figure 19.1) and an attendant must be carried. On Special Types vehicles only, where the load projects more than 1.83 metres to the front, an end marker must be displayed and an attendant carried.

If a load projects more than 3.05 metres beyond the front (on both C and U and Special Types vehicles), the police must be given two days' notice of its movement, both side and end approved marker boards must be displayed and an attendant must be carried.

If a load projects more than 4.5 metres beyond the front of the vehicle the provisions mentioned above must be observed and additional side marker boards must be carried within 2.5 metres of the first set of side markers.

Rearward Projections

Where a load projects more than 1.0 metre beyond the rear of a C and U vehicle (1.07 metres on Special Types vehicles) it must clearly be marked (the form which this must take is not specified, but a piece of rag tied to the end is usually sufficient).

If the projection is more than 2.0 metres on C and U vehicles (1.83 metres on Special Types vehicles) an end marker board must be displayed.

If the rearward projection is more than 3.05 metres the police must be notified, an attendant carried and approved side and end marker boards displayed. An end marker is not required if the projecting load is fitted with a rear reflective marker.

If the rearward projection exceeds 5.0 metres additional side marker boards must be carried within 3.5 metres of the first set of side markers.

Marker Boards

Marker boards carried in accordance with the requirements described above must conform to the dimensions and colours shown in Figure 19.1 and they must be indirectly illuminated at night.

Lighting on Projecting and Long Loads

Rearward Projections

When carrying a load projecting more than 1.0 metre beyond the rear end of the vehicle an additional red rear position light must be carried within 1.0 metre of the end of the load or if the projecting load covers the rear lights and reflectors of the vehicle, additional lights and reflectors must be fixed to the load. This is usually best accomplished by having a complete lighting set and reflectors fitted to a board which can be fixed to the load.

Side Projections

When a load projects sideways more than 400mm beyond the front and rear position lights of a vehicle, side position lights must be carried within 400mm of the outer edges of the load and additional rear lights must also be carried within 400mm of the outer edges of the load.

Long Vehicles

A vehicle or combination of vehicles which, together with their load, are more than 18.3 metres long must, when on the road during the hours of darkness, carry side marker lights on each side positioned within 9.15 metres of the front of the vehicle or load and within 3.05 metres of the rear of the vehicle or load and other lights positioned between these at not more than 3.05 metre intervals. These requirements do not apply if approved illuminated marker boards are carried or if the combination is formed of a towing vehicle and a broken-down vehicle.

In the case of a combination of vehicles carrying a supported load (a load not resting on a vehicle except at each end) when the total length of the combination exceeds 12.2 metres but not 18.3 metres, side marker lights must be carried when on the road during the hours of darkness, positioned not more than 1.53 metres behind the rear of the drawing vehicle and if the load extends more than 9.15 metres beyond the drawing vehicle an additional side marker light must be carried not more than 1.53 metres behind the centre line of the load.

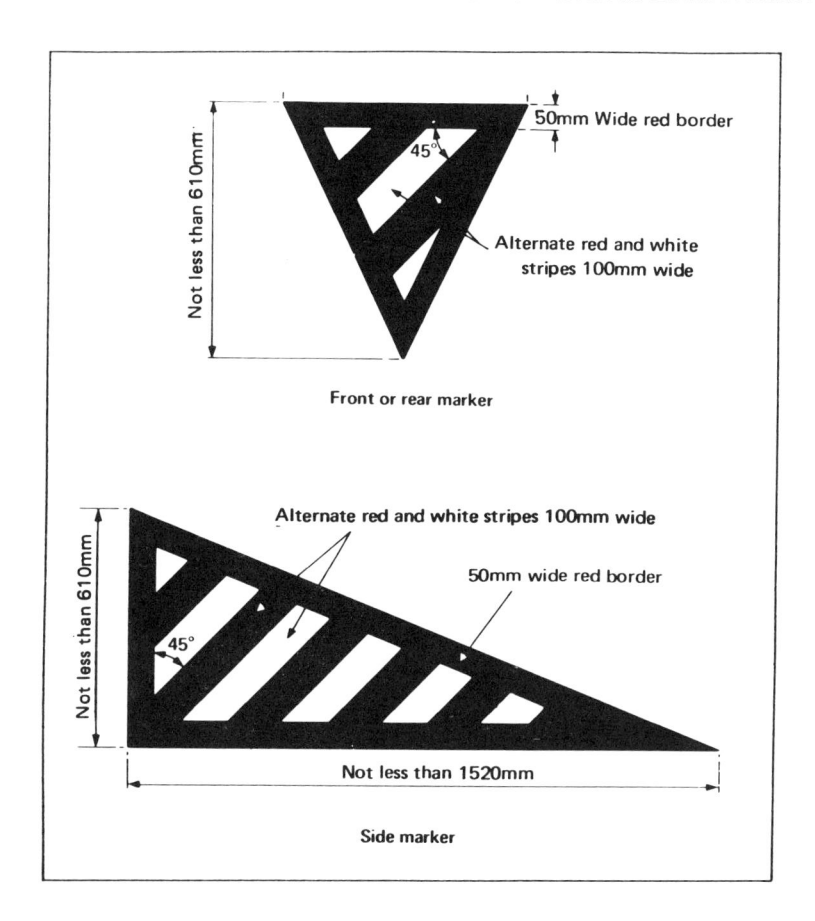

Figure 19.1 *The approved type marker boards which must be displayed when projecting loads are carried*

20: Loads – Dangerous and Explosive

Four sets of regulations cover most of the legal requirements relating to the packaging, labelling and carriage by road of dangerous and explosive substances whether in bulk loads or small consignments. The relevant legal requirements are to be found in the following regulations (in abbreviated form):
1. The packaging and labelling regulations
2. The bulk tanker regulations
3. The carriage of dangerous substances in packages regulations
4. The explosives regulations.

Under proposals put forward by the United Nations Economic Commission for Europe, transport operators who carry dangerous substances could be held liable to pay compensation for any damage or pollution resulting from spillages or vehicle accidents. Specifically, any carrier who, in transporting dangerous substances causes loss of life, personal injury, loss or damage to property or damage to the environment by contamination will be liable to meet compensation claims from victims who, because the principle of *strict* liability will apply, will not have to prove that the carrier is liable.

Packaging and Labelling

The Classification, Packaging and Labelling of Dangerous Substances Regulations 1984 (SI 1244/84) (commonly referred to as the CPL regulations) which came into effect on 1 January 1986 impose requirements regarding the packaging of dangerous substances supplied or conveyed by road, the methods by which packages should be marked or labelled and the particulars to be shown on labels. For the purposes of these regulations substances are dangerous for supply and conveyance if they are specified in the Health and Safety Executive (HSE) 'Approved List' (ie *Information Approved for the Classification, Packaging and Labelling of Dangerous Substances* – copies available from HMSO) and any substances not in the list which have characteristic properties equally dangerous to those in the list.

Packaging

The regulations place responsibilities on the supplier of relevant substances to use only receptacles which are designed, constructed and maintained to prevent leakage when being handled and moved; to use receptacles of suitable material which will not be adversely affected by the chemical properties of the substances put into them; and to use only receptacles with replaceable closing devices where these devices are capable of being repeatedly re-closed with leakage of the contents.

Labelling

Packages and receptacles containing substances must be properly labelled

(on the container or receptacle and on any outer packaging in which they are enclosed) to show the following information:
1. Name and address of manufacturer, importer, wholesaler or supplier
2. The official designation of the substance
3. Indications of the nature of risk associated with the substance
4. The risk and safety phrases associated with the substance
5. Additional information relating to pesticides.

The regulations specify details concerning the size and nature of the labels to be used, that labels must be securely fixed and capable of being clearly seen against the background of that package, even if the package is not in its usual position (ie if it is turned on its side or upside down).

Codes of Practice

The Health and Safety Commission (HSC) has published Codes of Practice in connection with these regulations as follows:
1. *Packaging of Dangerous Substances for Conveyance by Road*
2. *Classification and Labelling of Substances Dangerous for Supply and/or Conveyance by Road.*

It has also published *A Guide to the Classification, Packaging and Labelling of Dangerous Substances Regulations 1984*. All of these documents are available from Her Majesty's Stationery Office.

NB: In the main these regulations concern the manufacturer and consignor of dangerous materials rather more than the transport operator and driver but nevertheless it is useful that they should understand the main requirements of the regulations as described above.

Dangerous Loads in Bulk Tankers/Tank Containers

The Dangerous Substances (Conveyance by Road in Road Tankers and Tank Containers) Regulations 1981 (SI 1059/81) are concerned with the carriage by road of dangerous substances in bulk either in conventional road tanker vehicles or in tank containers which can be lifted on and off road vehicles and conveyed by other transport modes (eg rail and ship). The main body of the legislation came into effect on 1 January 1982, but certain measures were scheduled for commencement on later dates.

The regulations are obviously important in their own right but there are four very important pieces of supporting literature. The first is the *Approved Substance Identification Numbers, Emergency Action Codes and Classifications for Dangerous Substances Conveyed in Road Tankers and Tank Containers* published by the Health and Safety Executive and commonly referred to as the 'Approved List' (not to be confused with the Approved List referred to on p 291). The second document is the *Operational Code of Practice* which explains to transport operators what the regulations are really all about and, more particularly, it indicates to them in very clear language precisely what they must and must not do to comply with the law.

The third document is the *Code of Practice on Road Tanker Testing* and the fourth is the *Guide to the Regulations*. Additionally, there is a Health and Safety Executive explanatory booklet called *Transport of Dangerous*

Substances in Tank Containers and another Code of Practice dealing with the construction of road tankers. All of these documents can be obtained from Her Majesty's Stationery Office.

Definitions

An understanding of the definitions of the main terms used is important to appreciate how the law applies.

Conveyance by Road
The term 'conveyance' which is used in the title of the regulation is precisely defined and it means rather more than would be generally expected in that it applies 'from the commencement of loading ... until the (tank) has been cleaned or purged ... whether or not the vehicle is on a road at the material time'. During the whole of this time the full weight of the legislation applies so that, for example, if a trained driver delivered a load of chemicals but another driver, untrained in the handling of that substance, drives the vehicle before the empty tank has been cleaned, then clearly an offence has been committed.

Tanker Operator
Operators of road tankers and other vehicles are defined in the regulations along with operators of tank containers. The 'operator' of a road tanker is the person who holds or who is required to hold an Operator's Licence under the provisions of section 60 of the Transport Act 1968. Where there is no requirement to hold an 'O' licence the operator is the keeper of the vehicle. The 'operator' of a tank container is defined as the tank owner or his agent or, in the absence of either of these, the operator of the vehicle on which the container is conveyed. In the case of leased or hired tanks the operator is the person to whom the tank is leased or hired. The significance of the definition of the term 'operator' is that it is he who is fully responsible for ensuring that the regulations are met.

Approved List
'Approved List' means the list previously referred to (see p 292) in its up-to-date form (see below). The List shows for each substance the exact chemical name, the substance identification number, the emergency action code and the classification (eg flammable liquid, corrosive substance, toxic gas). The relevance of the identification numbers, emergency action codes and classification will be seen by reference to the text on the Hazchem marking scheme – see p 297.

Dangerous Substance
'Dangerous substance' means a substance specified in the Approved List plus any substance which 'by reason of its characteristic properties creates a risk ...which is comparable with the risk created by substances specified in the approved list'.

Road Tanker/Tank Container
For the purposes of the regulations, a road tanker is a goods vehicle with a

tank structurally attached to or which is an integral part of the frame of the vehicle. A tank container is defined as being one (whether or not divided into separate compartments) which has a capacity greater than 3 cubic metres.

Restriction on Substances to be Carried

Strict limits are placed on the carriage of certain substances in that the regulations prohibit the carriage in a tanker or tank container of any organic peroxide unless the substance is named in the approved list or, if it is not named in the list, if its characteristic properties create no greater risk than other substances of similar characteristic properties which are specified in the list. The regulations also stipulate that if a substance is greater in concentration than that specified as the maximum concentration in the list it must not be carried.

Where a substance is not included in the Approved List it must not be carried. The omission may be due to the fact that the substance is too dangerous to travel in a road tanker or tank container or it may be because the substance is new and has not yet been classified. Advice in these circumstances can be obtained from the Health and Safety Executive.

Exemptions

The regulations do not apply to vehicles carrying non-dangerous bulk powder, granule or liquid goods (eg certain food products such as sugar and glucose, cement and sand, gas oil, derv and so on). They also do not apply to vehicles which are carrying dangerous goods in the following circumstances:
1. When engaged in international transport under the International Convention for the Conveyance of Goods by Rail (CIM).
2. When engaged in international transport under the European Agreement concerning the International Carriage of Dangerous Goods by Road (ADR).
3. When under the control of the armed forces of the Crown or of visiting forces.
4. When exempted from excise duty (VED) under the Vehicles Excise Act 1971, section 7(1).
5. When a road construction vehicle (other than a road tanker) is used for conveying liquid tar (ie substance identification number 1999 in approved list).

The regulations also do not apply when the substance being carried is a radioactive substance within the meaning of The Ionising Radiations (Unsealed Radioactive Substances) Regulations 1968 (SI 780/ 1958).

Condition of Tanker Vehicle/Tank Container

A road tanker vehicle or tank container must not be used for the conveyance of dangerous goods unless it is properly designed; is of adequate strength and good construction from sound and suitable material which would not be adversely affected by contact with the substance being carried. It must be designed, constructed and maintained so that the contents cannot escape and be suitable for the purpose for which it is being used. It must have adequate and correct ancillary fittings (eg flanges, fittings and hoses).

20: LOADS – DANGEROUS AND EXPLOSIVE

In accordance with the *Road Tanker Testing Code of Practice* the tank should be periodically tested and a tank certificate should have been issued indicating the substances that may be carried. Furthermore, following accident damage, repair or modification, the effects on the tank should be assessed and it should be re-tested and certified.

Information in Writing

Operators must not convey dangerous substances by road in a road tanker or tank container, unless they have first obtained from the consignor information which enables them to comply with the regulations and to be aware of the risks created by the substance to the health and safety of any person. It is the responsibility of the person supplying such information to ensure that it is accurate and sufficiently detailed.

Transport operators in turn must give to their vehicle drivers information *in writing* to enable them to know the identity of the substance, the nature of the dangers which may arise with that substance and the emergency action to be taken in the event of spillage, accident or other dangerous incident. The regulations place a duty on drivers to ensure that the written information they are given is kept in the cab of the vehicle and is readily available at all times while the substance in question is being carried.

While the legal requirement to supply information in writing can be satisfied by typing the details on a piece of the company's letter-headed paper, normally the most convenient method of providing drivers with written information on the products carried and which conforms with legal requirements is by means of commercially produced, re-usable, laminated 'Tremcards'. These transport emergency cards cover either a single product or a group of products and detail the nature of the hazard and describe what protective devices should be used or worn to deal with any spillage of the substance. The emergency action to be taken is detailed and first aid advice is also given on the card along with a reference telephone number. Standard Tremcards are prepared by the Conseil Europeen des Federations de l'Industrie Chimique (ie European Council of Chemical Manufacturers Federations, commonly known and referred to as CEFIC).

It is an important requirement that written information about substances which are not being carried at the time are removed from the vehicle, destroyed or placed in a 'securely closed container clearly marked to show that the information does not relate to a substance then being conveyed'. This is to avoid any confusion of the emergency services should they have to attend an incident involving spillage, leakage or a vehicle accident as to what substance is and is not currently being carried on the vehicle.

Safety Measures

The regulations specify precautions for preventing fire and ensuring that tanks are not overfilled. In particular, the operator should notify his drivers the maximum quantity of the dangerous substance to be loaded. There must be no smoking in the vicinity of the vehicle especially during loading and discharging and smoking materials and other sources of ignition such as torches and radios should also be kept well away at such times. The vehicle should be equipped with suitable serviceable fire extinguishers and with master switches and earthing leads which must be used at all times.

The driver should be aware of all the potential dangers and should take all possible precautions to ensure the safety of the load, the vehicle, premises and, most importantly, all persons in the vicinity of the vehicle especially when on the public highway.

Parking of Dangerous Goods Vehicles

Dangerous goods vehicles must be parked in a safe place or they must be supervised at all times by the driver or another competent (ie trained) person over 18 years of age. This applies to tankers displaying hazard warning panels on which the emergency action code ends with the letter E. However, it does not apply if the driver can show that the tank is empty or that, if the identification code number 1270 is displayed, no petrol is being conveyed and the tank is empty; or if the number 1268 is displayed that no toluene or petroleum distillate (flash point less than 21° C) is being conveyed and the tank is empty.

Labelling of Road Tankers/Tank Containers

The regulations impose requirements for notices to be displayed on road tankers and tank containers which are being used to carry prescribed dangerous substances. References in the regulations (and this text) to hazard warning notices refer in fact to what are commonly known as Hazchem labels or markers.

The relevant substances to which the regulations refer and which are the subject of tanker labelling are specified in the Health and Safety Commission *Approved Substance Identification Numbers, Emergency Codes and Classifications for Dangerous Substances conveyed in Road Tankers and Tank Containers* referred to earlier together with a substance identification number and appropriate emergency action code.

Emergency Action Codes

The emergency action codes are as follows:
1. By numbers 1 to 4 indicating the equipment suitable for fire fighting and for dispersing spillages (ie 1 = water jets, 2 = water fog, 3 = foam, 4 = dry agent)
2. By letters indicating the appropriate precautions to take as follows:

Letter	Danger of violent reaction	Protective clothing and breathing apparatus	Measures to be taken
P	Yes	Full protective clothing	Dilute
R	No	Full protective clothing	Dilute
S	Yes	Breathing apparatus	Dilute
S*	Yes	Breathing apparatus for fire	Dilute
T	No	Breathing apparatus	Dilute
T*	No	Breathing apparatus for fire	Dilute
W	Yes	Full protective clothing	Contain
X	No	Full protective clothing	Contain
Y	Yes	Breathing apparatus	Contain
Y*	Yes	Breathing apparatus for fire	Contain
Z	No	Breathing apparatus	Contain
Z*	No	Breathing apparatus for fire	Contain

*These symbols are shown as white letters on a black background.

20: LOADS – DANGEROUS AND EXPLOSIVE

Where a letter 'E' is shown at the end of an emergency action code this means that consideration should be given to evacuating people from the neighbourhood of an incident.

The Hazchem Label

The Hazchem label must be orange with black borders, figures and letters except for the space where the individual hazard warning sign is placed which is white (see Figure 20.1). Hazard warning panels and Hazchem labels must be displayed at all times in accordance with the regulations, they must be kept clean and free from obstruction (except that a rear mounted panel may be fitted behind a ladder 'of light construction which does not prevent the panel from being easily read') and when the tank is emptied of the substance indicated the label must be covered or removed. For cross reference a pocket card (Figure 20.2) is provided for firemen and other emergency service personnel which indicates the nature of the hazard and advises whether protective clothing and/or breathing apparatus should be used (see above for details of emergency action codes).
Hazchem labels are divided into a number of individual panels as follows:
1. Top left – a combined code which identifies the equipment to be used for fire fighting and dispersal of spillage (see codes above)
2. Second down on left – the substance identification number from the Approved List (also the name of the substance can be added)
3. On right – appropriate hazard warning symbol on white background
   (a) flammable liquid
   (b) corrosive substance
   (c) toxic substance
   (d) harmful substance
   (d) non-flammable compressed gas
   (f) toxic gas
   (g) flammable gas
   (h) oxidising substance
   (i) organic peroxide
   (j) other hazardous substance (including explosive substances (see Figure 20.1)).
4. Across bottom – telephone number for specialist advice and, if desired, the manufacturer's/supplier's name.

Single/Multi-load Labelling

All relevant vehicles must be labelled in accordance with the regulations, depending on whether a single or multi-load is carried, as follows:

For Single loads: An orange/black Hazchem warning label containing the following details:
1. Emergency action code for the substance
2. Substance identification number
3. Appropriate hazard warning sign
4. Telephone number where specialist advice can be obtained plus, if required:
5. The name of the substance
6. If required, the name of the manufacturer.

For Multi-loads: An orange/black Hazchem warning label containing the following details:
1. Appropriate multi-load emergency action code
2. The word 'multi-load'
3. The appropriate hazard warning sign
4. Telephone number where specialist advice can be obtained
5. If required, the name of the manufacturer.

Additionally, for multi-loads, on each tank or each compartment there should be a label showing:
1. The appropriate substance identification number (and the name if desired)
2. The hazard warning sign applicable to the contents of that tank or compartment where this is different from the hazards of any other substance on the vehicle.

Hazard Warning Signs/Symbols

Individual hazard warning signs or symbols (sometimes also called diamonds) are coloured as follows (see Figure 20.3):

Description of signs	Symbol	Lettering	Background
Flammable liquids	Black or white	Black or White	Red
Flammable solids	Black	Black	White with vertical red stripes
Flammable gases	Black or white	Black or white	Red
Toxic gases	Black	Black	White
Non-flammable compressed gases	Black or white	Black or white	Green
Toxic substances	Black	Black	White
Harmful substances	Black	–	White
Corrosive substances	Black	White	White upper half, black lower half
Organic peroxides	Black	Black	Yellow
Oxidising substances	Black	Black	Yellow
Substances which in contact with water emit flammable gases	Black or white	Black or white	Blue
Spontaneously combustible substances	Black	Black or white	White upper half, red lower half
Other hazardous substances and multi-loads of different hazards	Black	–	White

NB: It is useful to note that the Hazchem labels and the individual hazard warning signs are shown, in colour, in the latest edition of the Highway Code.

20: LOADS – DANGEROUS AND EXPLOSIVE

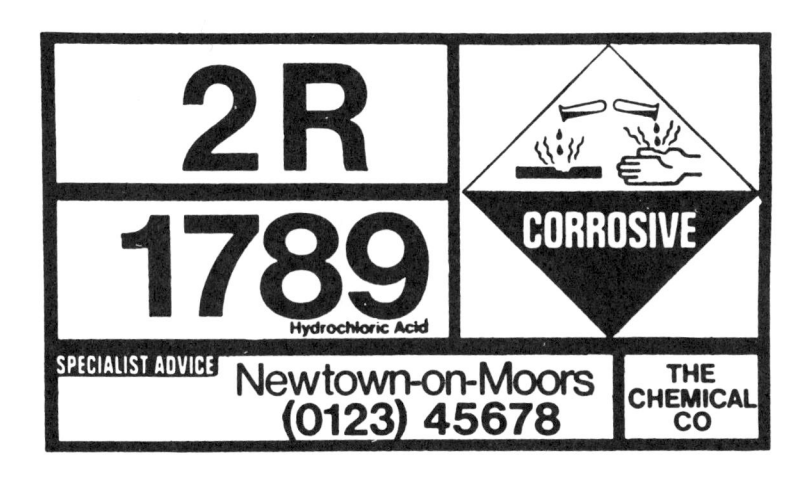

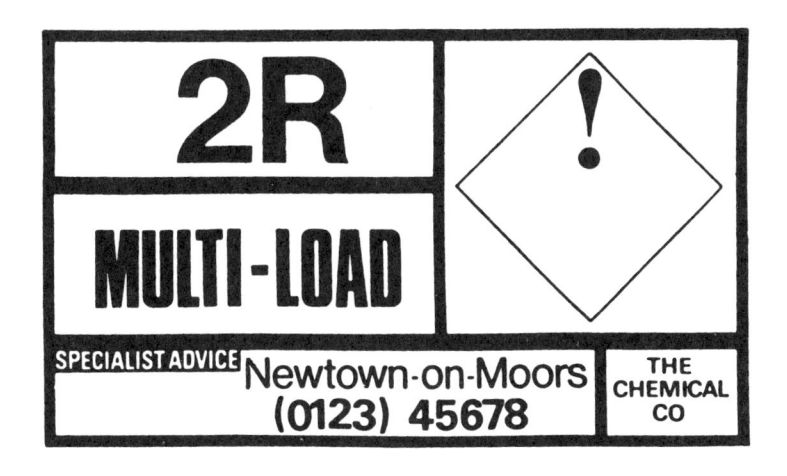

Figure 20.1 *Illustrations showing hazard warning labels for:
top: full/single loads, bottom: multi-loads*

Hazchem pocket reference card

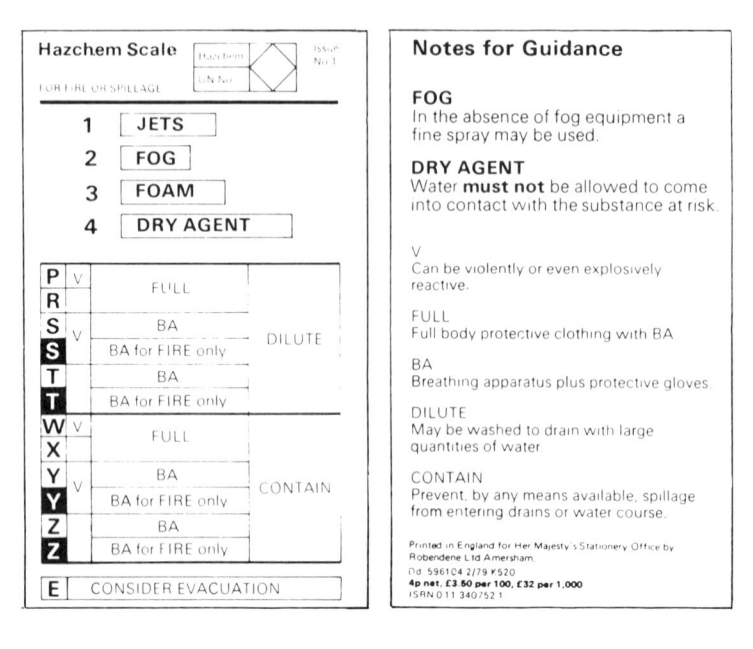

Hazchem Scale			Notes for Guidance
FOR FIRE OR SPILLAGE			
1	JETS		**FOG** In the absence of fog equipment a fine spray may be used.
2	FOG		
3	FOAM		**DRY AGENT** Water **must not** be allowed to come into contact with the substance at risk.
4	DRY AGENT		

P	V	FULL		V — Can be violently or even explosively reactive.
R				
S	V	BA	DILUTE	FULL — Full body protective clothing with BA
S		BA for FIRE only		
T		BA		BA — Breathing apparatus plus protective gloves.
T		BA for FIRE only		
W	V	FULL		DILUTE — May be washed to drain with large quantities of water
X				
Y	V	BA	CONTAIN	CONTAIN — Prevent, by any means available, spillage from entering drains or water course.
Y		BA for FIRE only		
Z		BA		
Z		BA for FIRE only		
E	CONSIDER EVACUATION			

Printed in England for Her Majesty's Stationery Office by Robendene Ltd Amersham.
Dd. 596104 2/79 K520
4p net, £3.50 per 100, £32 per 1,000
ISBN 0 11 340752 1

Figure 20.2 *Hazchem pocket reference card*

Exemptions to Marking

There are certain exemptions that apply regarding the marking of vehicles. These are as follows:

1. If a vehicle is carrying dangerous substances transferred from another tanker or tank container which has broken down or has been damaged in an accident provided the vehicle is escorted by the police or fire brigade or alternatively if it displays the hazard warning signs shown to the regulations.
2. If the road tanker or tank container is travelling to a port for carriage by sea or from a port having been carried by sea and it is marked in accordance with the provisions of the International Maritime Dangerous Goods Code (IMDG Code) of the International Maritime Organisation (IMO).
3. If the road tanker or tank container is in the service of armed forces of the Crown or visiting forces engaged in manoeuvres or training subject to proper authority.

There is an exemption to the requirement for multi-load marking where such loads comprise only substances specifically listed in the approved list as being suitable for treatment as a single bulk load, in which case the bulk load labelling requirements will apply.

When a tanker or tank container has been emptied and cleaned, the hazard warning panels must be completely removed or completely covered except for the telephone number which may be left exposed. When two or more substances have been carried and one or more have been discharged and the respective tank compartments cleaned, the hazard warning labels referring to those substances must be removed or completely covered and the panels changed to those appropriate to the remaining load.

20: LOADS – DANGEROUS AND EXPLOSIVE

Flammable liquids

Flammable solids

Flammable gases

Toxic gases

Non-flammable compressed gases

Toxic substances

Harmful substances — keep away from food

Corrosive substances

Organic peroxides

Oxidizing substances

Substances which in contact with water emit flammable gases

Spontaneously combustible substances

Other hazardous substances and multi-loads of substances of different hazards

Figure 20.3 *Illustrations showing signs for hazard warning*

301

Driver Training

The vehicle operator must ensure that drivers who are likely to encounter dangerous substance loads in their work receive adequate training (and re-training and refresher training as necessary) to enable them to understand 'the nature of the dangers to which the substances being carried may give rise and the emergency action (he) should take'. The training must cover the hazards of dangerous substances that the driver will need to deal with, safe loading and unloading procedures, the use of safety equipment and the emergency procedures to be followed in the event of spillage or accident, the checks to be carried out before a journey, the vehicle marking requirements and the general requirements of the legislation. Drivers must also be given specific instruction regarding the particular loads they are to handle in their work. Employers must keep a record of the training given to drivers and must give a copy of the record to a driver if he requests it.

Certification of Training

There is no legal requirement under these regulations, applicable to UK operations, for the training to be provided by the DTp or by any other official or approved body, and there is no legal requirement for a driver to be given, to carry or to produce any document or certificate confirming such instruction and training. Therefore fleet operators are free to provide training for drivers themselves in whatever manner they think is appropriate and sufficient to satisfy the regulations.

This has been a point of confusion because the ADR requirements, applicable to international operations, are for training under an approved scheme and for the driver to carry some evidence of such training. In Britain the Hazfreight/Hazpak* training schemes sponsored jointly by the Road Transport Industry Training Board, the Road Haulage Association and the Chemical Industries Association and conducted by a number of training establishments approved under The National (Dangerous Substances) Driver Training Scheme (NDSDTS) satisfies the training requirements of ADR and the Hazfreight/Hazpak Driver Identity Card satisfies the certification requirement of ADR.

Although, as stated, formal training is not essential under British regulations, the use of this facility is an organised and comprehensive way of providing the training needed under the UK tanker regulations.

Hazpak is a registered service mark which should only be used to describe the two-day course run by approved training centres within The National (Dangerous Substances) Driver Training Scheme.

Vocational training certificates will be required by drivers of dangerous goods tankers (ie over 3000 litres) and explosives vehicles from 1 January 1992 and by drivers of other dangerous goods vehicles from 1 January 1995. Such certificates will be issued after drivers have completed a suitable training course and will be renewable five-yearly following refresher training but those drivers who have had at least five years' dangerous load driving experience prior to these dates will be exempt from the training requirement.

Exemption Certificates

The regulations provide scope for Exemption Certificates to be issued by the Health and Safety Executive in special cases where there is a need because the regulations cannot be practically applied provided there is no risk to health or safety. A number of such certificates have been issued.

Enforcement

This legislation is enforced by two agencies, namely officers of the Health and Safety Executive and by the police in the course of their normal enforcement procedures against vehicles on roads.

Defence

Provision is made for any person to claim in his defence in any proceedings against him under the regulations that 'he took all reasonable precautions and exercised all due diligence to avoid...' committing the offence.

Conveyance of Dangerous Substances by Road in Packages

Regulations broadly similar to those described previously for the bulk carriage of dangerous substances by road, control the carriage of dangerous goods by road in packages, drums and other individual containers (referred to in the regulations as 'receptacles'). The Road Traffic (Carriage of Dangerous Substances in Packages etc) Regulations 1985 (SI 1951/86)(commonly referred to as the 'PGR') apply:

1. When self-reactive organic peroxides, flammable solids and other substances of similar risk (ie toxic gases, flammable gases, organic peroxides, asbestos or asbestos waste) are carried in any quantity and when dangerous substances are carried in bulk other than in tankers and tank containers (eg tippers).
2. When United Nations Packing Group 1 substances are carried in receptacles with a capacity of 5 litres or more.
3. When UN medium risk substances (ie packing group II) are carried in receptacles with a capacity of 200 litres (ie 44 gallons) or more. They also apply when notionally empty receptacles (having previously carried specified substances) are carried.

Currently, there is no statutory control over the carriage by road of substances listed as packing group III which comprise those presenting the lowest level of hazard. However, the Health and Safety Commission (HSC) is proposing to extend the regulations to bring substances in this group (and those in group II) into line with the requirements of group I (ie those presenting the most serious hazards).

Code of Practice

In addition to the regulations mentioned above, there is an Approved List (see below) an *Operational Code of Practice* and a guide to the regulations. All these documents are available from Her Majesty's Stationery Office.

The Operator

For the purposes of these regulations, as with the tanker regulations, the term 'operator' is defined as the person who holds the Operator's Licence where such a licence is needed but otherwise the keeper of the vehicle.

Substances Covered

The substances covered by the regulations are those included in the 'Approved List' referred to in the text on Packaging and Labelling of dangerous substances (see p 291) namely *Information Approved for the Classification, Packaging and Labelling of Dangerous Substances* (not to be confused with the Approved List referred to in the text on the tanker regulations – p 292) which are toxic or flammable gases, organic peroxides, substances listed in UN Packing Group 1 and 2, asbestos in any form, other hazardous wastes plus any other substances which are not specified in the list but which have similar chemical properties and present similar hazards to those in the list, and mixtures of both types of substance (ie listed and non-listed similar substances).

The regulations also cover LPG carried in cylinders with a capacity (ie water capacity) of 5 litres or more except where such a cylinder is carried to provide fuel for a piece of equipment.

Limitations on Carriage

There are strict limitations on the carriage of certain dangerous substances. Particularly, operators must not carry substances in greater concentrations than those specified in the Approved List or in contravention of any conditions specified in the list about inerting or stabilising substances.

When carrying organic peroxides and flammable solids (specified as having a 'self-accelerating decomposition temperature' of 50° C or below) which can only be safely conveyed under controlled temperature conditions the driver must have adequate means to ensure that the temperature is maintained at a safe level. The regulations apply to these particular substances irrespective of the quantity being carried. Further advice on the carriage of these substances is to be found in the HSC Code of Practice.

Construction of Vehicles

Vehicles used for carrying dangerous goods in packages must be properly designed, constructed and maintained and be suitable for the purpose for which they are used. Specialised vehicles are *not* required and no special provisions relating to the construction of vehicles apart from that just mentioned are included in the regulations.

Information

Vehicle operators have responsibility under the regulations for ensuring that they receive from consignors of dangerous substances adequate information about the substances to be carried to enable them to comply with the regulations in giving the driver instruction, in marking vehicles correctly, and in being aware of the risks created by the substances to the health or safety of any person. They should not commence the carriage of any substance until such time as they have received the necessary information described here – it is illegal to do so.

20: LOADS – DANGEROUS AND EXPLOSIVE

Drivers must be given appropriate information *in writing* on the substances in their charge (ie identification of the substances, the dangers inherent in carrying and handling the substances and the action to be taken in the event of emergency) by their employer and must at all times carry in the vehicle cab these written details of the substances on board. They have a duty to ensure that written notices for substances no longer on the vehicle are removed, destroyed or locked away securely. The provision of Tremcards (although not obligatory – the information in writing can be in any form) satisfies this requirement (see p 295)*. Alternatively, the requirement for written information can be met by the labels on the packages (and the accompanying written statements which are required in any case where single receptacles of 250 litres or more are carried) so long as they comply with legal requirements. Information carried on vehicles must be given to the police and traffic examiners on request.

NB: The Health and Safety Executive has said that Multi-Load Tremcards can be illegal and should not be used unless the entire load is carried for the whole of the journey. Such cards can conflict with the legal requirement to remove or lock away information in writing relating to dangerous goods no longer on the vehicle.

Driver Training

Drivers of vehicles carrying dangerous substances in packages (ie those included in the Approved List and in appropriate quantities) must have received proper training (and refresher training where necessary) in the hazards of handling and conveying dangerous substances, in loading and unloading procedures, in the checks they should make before commencing a journey, in the use of safety equipment, in the emergency procedures to be followed in the event of accident or dangerous occurrence, about vehicle marking and generally about the requirements of the regulations. They should also be given instruction regarding their duties under the regulations and about the particular load they are to carry. Failure to comply with this requirement is an offence and the HSC has warned that operators can face fines of up to £2000 on conviction.

While training by official or approved sources is not implied, nevertheless driver employers must either establish some form of adequate in-house training scheme or make the necessary arrangements with suitable training establishments (eg those approved under the National (Dangerous Substances) Driver Training Scheme) for Hazpak* training to ensure that their drivers are competent to handle all the products likely to be encountered and to deal with emergency situations.

Hazpak is a registered service mark which should only be used to describe the two-day course run by approved training centres within the National (Dangerous Substances) Driver Training Scheme.

Vocational training certificates will be required by drivers of dangerous goods vehicles (ie except tankers over 3000 litres and explosives vehicles – see p 302) from 1 January 1995. See also note on p 302 about qualifying for such certificates.

Supervision of Vehicles

Similar requirements apply for the supervision of vehicles loaded with dangerous substances to those already mentioned for tanker vehicles. In particular, if the products carried amount to 3 tonnes or more, the vehicle must be parked in a safe place or must be supervised by the driver at all times or by some other competent (ie trained) person over the age of 18 years.

Labelling of Vehicles

Vehicles used for carrying 500kg or more of dangerous goods in packages must be correctly marked with reflectorised orange-colour plates at both the front and rear. These plates are rectangular and plain orange in colour surrounded by a broad black border. They must be kept clean and free from obstruction and may remain in place when an amount less than 500kg of dangerous substance is being carried. *However, they must be removed or covered when no such substances are being carried.* Additionally, hazard warning symbols (see p 298) *may* be displayed – they are not legally required.

Loading, Stowage and Unloading

Everybody involved in the loading, stowage and unloading of dangerous goods on vehicles must ensure that the requirements relating to health and safety are observed at all times and that goods are secured in the vehicle safely with minimum risk of damage to the packages. In general, the requirements for safe loading contained in the C and U regulations should be carefully observed (see pp 255–6).

Safety Precautions

The driver has a duty to observe precautions against fire or explosion, to ensure that loading, stowage and unloading is carried out safely and generally to be aware of the need for care particularly when on the highway and when near to members of the public.

Petroleum

The carriage of petroleum spirit in bulk tankers comes within the tanker regulations previously described. Petroleum spirit vehicles, when loaded, must not be left unattended except in a place approved by a local authority. The person in attendance must be either the driver or a competent person who is not less than 18 years old. A similar person must be in attendance during discharge to ensure there is no spillage, to ensure that all connections have been properly made and in particular to confirm that there is sufficient capacity in the storage tank to accept the delivery. At the time of petroleum spirit delivery a Certificate of Delivery must be completed. One copy is retained by the driver and returned to his employer, the other is retained by the owner of the storage tank.

Petroleum spirit carrying tanker vehicles must be constructed to conform with the regulation specification which includes such items as the provision of a fire screen between the vehicle power unit and the tank, location of the exhaust, the wiring specification and a master power cut-off switch.

Schedule 4 to the Dangerous Substances (Conveyance by Road in Road Tankers and Tank Containers) Regulations 1981 specifies details regarding the transfer of petroleum spirit into storage tanks at filling stations or other premises licensed for keeping 100000 litres or less in storage.

CIA Voluntary Code

The Chemical Industries Association has a voluntary code of practice for road transport operators who carry dangerous substances. This code is the *Road Transport of Hazardous Chemicals – A Manual of Principal Safety Requirements.*

The manual is concerned with setting guidelines for good operating practice and covers the following items:
1. Responsibilities of the manufacturer, the transporter and the receiver.
2. Factors to be considered before chemicals are consigned.
3. Driver selection and training.
4. Operational standards, including vehicle construction and maintenance, loading and discharge procedures, vehicle routeing, safety equipment, the issue of instructions in writing and the marking of vehicles.
5. Dealing with emergencies.

A suggested general safety checklist for the road transport of chemicals is included in the manual as follows:
1. Is the vehicle roadworthy and suitable for the load to be carried?
2. Is the load secure and correctly stowed on the vehicle?
3. Are the containers of hazardous chemicals suitably labelled?
4. Does the vehicle display the appropriate statutory and other information relating to the chemical(s) being carried?
5. Has the driver been informed of the name, nature and hazardous properties of the chemical(s) being carried and the procedure to be followed in the case of emergency such as the spillage or escape of chemicals?
6. Have instructions in writing been placed in the cab of the vehicle or on the packages by way of a suitable label?
7. Is the vehicle properly equipped with first aid requirements, fire extinguishers and protective clothing and equipment?
8. Has consideration been given to routeing the vehicle to avoid traffic hazards and areas of high population density and areas especially vulnerable to contamination?
9. Has the driver been informed of any particular procedures which apply to the loading and discharge of the product involved?
10. Where haulage contractors are employed, has the contractor been checked for competency and informed of:
    (i) The nature and hazards of the load to be carried?
    (ii) Whether the conveyance of the chemical in question is controlled by legislation?
    (iii) The action to be taken in the event of emergency?
11. Has the driver been given specific instructions as to the procedure to be followed in bad weather, eg fog, ice, heavy rain, etc?

Hazardous Poisonous Waste

Many transport operators are concerned with the disposal of waste materials and, as such, they are affected by the Disposal of Poisonous Waste Act 1972 which makes it an offence to dispose of poisonous waste in an irresponsible way, by the Control of Pollution (Special Waste) Regulations 1980, the Criminal Justice Act 1988 (which provides powers for the authorities to impound vehicles engaged in illegal fly-tipping) and eventually by the Environmental Protection Bill when this becomes law and requires operators to be licensed by the Waste Regulation Authority.

Broadly the law requires that waste which is poisonous, noxious or polluting is not deposited on land where its presence is liable to give rise to an environmental hazard. And it is necessary for anyone removing or depositing poisonous material to notify both the local authority and the river authority before doing so.

An environmental hazard is defined as waste that is deposited in a manner or in such quantity that it would subject persons or animals to material risk or death, injury or impairment of health or threaten the pollution or contamination of any water supply. A booklet *Guidelines on the Responsible Disposal of Wastes* is available from the Confederation of British Industry. The European Commission has also produced a booklet on this subject for local authorities in Community countries.

Hazardous Waste Disposal

The site licensing provisions of the Control of Pollution Act 1974 require all commercial, industrial or domestic wastes to be disposed of at a site licensed for that purpose and nowhere else. The licences are issued by the Waste Disposal Authorities (these are the County Councils in England and the District Councils in Wales and Scotland). These licences, which are a matter of public record, set conditions for the operation of each site including the types of waste which can be disposed of at that site, the manner of disposal, site supervision, boundary fences, notice boards etc. Waste Disposal Authorities must inspect sites regularly and make sure the operators are following the conditions of the licence. Failure to comply with licence conditions is a criminal offence. In addition to prosecution, the Authority can amend or even revoke the licence.

In addition to this, there are additional controls over the carriage and disposal of particularly hazardous waste. The Control of Pollution (Special Waste) Regulations 1980 were introduced in order to comply with EC directives:

The main requirements of these regulations are outlined below:
1. Certain types of waste are to be regarded as special waste and subject to the additional controls. These are wastes that are regarded as dangerous to life as set out in the regulations.
2. Waste producers have to give not less than three days' and not more than one month's prior notice to Waste Disposal Authorities of their intention to dispose of a consignment of special waste.
3. A set of consignment notes must be completed when special wastes are transported. This means that a consignment of special waste can be transported from the producer to the disposal site only if each person has signed for it and taken on responsibility for it. This is to ensure that Waste Disposal Authorities know who is carrying the waste and they have to be informed within 24 hours of when it reaches the disposal site. Waste producers should take particular note of the requirement that all

notices must be made on the statutory forms. Each form contains a unique reference number to assist the Authority in making sure that waste is safely disposed of.
4. A record of the location of the point of disposal on site of all special wastes must be kept in perpetuity. This is to ensure that proper arrangements can be made to bring the site back into use after the waste disposal operation has ceased.
5. Proper registers of consignments must be kept by the producers, carriers and disposers.
6. There will be a 'Season Ticket' arrangement for regular consignments of special wastes of similar composition disposed of at the same site. The Waste Disposal Authorities will decide which producers and disposers in their areas qualify.
7. The Secretary of State will have emergency powers to direct receipt of special wastes at a particular site. This is likely to be rarely used.
8. Radioactive waste which also has the characteristics of special waste will be subject to the new controls.

Failure to comply with any of the requirements of the Regulations is an offence.

Two documents have been prepared which explain the procedures in much more detail and provide technical guidance on applying them to special wastes.
These are:
1. DoE Circular No 4/81
   Welsh Office Circular No 8/81 (available from HMSO)
   The Control of Pollution (Special Waste) Regulations 1980 and
2. Waste Management Paper No 23 *Special Wastes: A Technical Memorandum.*
   (Available from the Department of the Environment and from HMSO.)

Advice on particular problems can be obtained from Waste Disposal Authorities and further guidance can be obtained from the Department of the Environment, Land Wastes Division, Becket House, 1 Lambeth Palace Road, London SE1 7ER (for England) and the Welsh Office, Local Government Division, New Crown Building, Cathays Park, Cardiff CF1 3NQ (for Wales).

Hazardous Waste Tankers

A draft Code of Practice on the design and construction of vacuum-operated road tankers used to carry hazardous waste has been published by the Health and Safety Commission for consultation.

Carriage of Explosives

New regulations which mainly came into force on 3 July 1989 control the movement of explosives by road. The Road Traffic (Carriage of Explosives) Regulations 1989 (SI 615/1989) were made under the Health and Safety at Work etc Act 1974 and replace the requirements of the Explosives Act 1875.

For the purposes of the regulations the term 'explosives' means explosive articles or substances which have been classified under the Classification and

Labelling of Explosives Regulations 1983 (SI 1140/1983) as being in Class 1 or those which are unclassified. An 'explosive article' is an article which contains one or more explosive substances and an 'explosive substance' is a solid or liquid substance or a mixture of solid or liquid substances, or both,

> which is capable by chemical reaction in itself of producing gas at such a temperature and pressure and at such speed as could cause damage to surroundings or which is designed to produce an effect by heat, light, sound, gas or smoke or a combination of these as a result of non-detonative self-sustaining exothermic chemical reactions.

The term 'Compatibility Group' also has a meaning assigned to it by the 1983 regulations referred to above. The term 'carriage' means from the commencement of loading explosives into a vehicle or trailer until they have all been unloaded, whether or not the vehicle is on a road at the time. However, the term carriage is not applied where explosives are loaded on an unattached trailer or semi-trailer; carriage begins and ends when the trailer is attached to and later is detached from the towing vehicle or when the explosives have been unloaded whichever is the sooner.

The new regulations prohibit the carriage of any explosive in Compatibility Group K (see 1983 regs) in a vehicle and any unclassified explosive except where it is being carried in connection with an application for their classification and in accordance with conditions approved in writing by the Health and Safety Executive (or, in the case of military explosives, by the Secretary of State for Defence).

Explosives must not be carried in any vehicle being used to carry passengers for hire or reward except that a passenger in such a vehicle may carry explosives under the following conditions:

- the substance carried is an explosive listed in Schedule 1 to the regulations (eg certain cartridges, fireworks distress-type and other signals, certain flares, fuses, igniters, primers and other pyrotechnic articles), gunpowder, smokeless powder or any mixture of them

- the total quantity of such explosive carried does not exceed 2kg

- the explosives are kept by that person and are kept properly packed

- all reasonable precautions are taken by the person to prevent accidents arising from the explosives.

The person carrying the explosives on the vehicle remains totally responsible for them and no responsibility for them is legally attached to the driver or the vehicle operator.

Suitability of Vehicles and Containers

It is the vehicle operator's duty under the regulations to ensure that any vehicle or any freight container used for the carriage of explosives is 'suitable' to ensure the safety and security of the explosives carried bearing in mind their type and quantity. The operator is also responsible for ensuring that the specified maximum quantities of any particular class of explosive carried on a vehicle or in a freight container are not exceeded and that a greater quantity of explosive is carried than that for which the vehicle or container is 'suitable'.

20: LOADS – DANGEROUS AND EXPLOSIVE

The limits on quantities of explosives permitted to be carried are shown in the following table:

Type of explosives		Maximum quantity
Division	Compatibility Group	
1.1	A	500kg
1.1	B, F, G or I	5 tonnes
1.1	C, D, E or J	16 tonnes
1.2	Any	16 tonnes
1.3	Any	16 tonnes
Unclassified explosives carried solely in connection with an application for their classification		500kg

The operator must ensure that explosives in different Compatibility Groups are not carried unless permitted as shown in Schedule 3 to the regulations.

Marking of Vehicles

Vehicles used for the carriage of explosives must be marked at the front and rear with a 400mm x 300mm rectangular reflectorised orange plate with black border (max 15mm wide). Additionally a square placard set at an angle of 45° must be displayed on each side of the vehicle container or trailer containing the explosives (see Fig 20.4). The placard must conform to minimum dimensions as shown in the illustration below and have an orange-coloured background with a black border and with a 'bomb blast' pictograph and any figures or letters denoting classification and Compatibility Group shown in black.

Certain exemptions apply to the display of markings as described above where the quantities of explosives of particular categories carried are below limits set out in Schedule 4 to the regulations.

Markings on vehicles and containers must be clearly visible, be kept clean and free from obstruction and must be completely covered or completely removed when all explosives have been removed from the vehicle or container. Both the vehicle driver and operator are responsible for ensuring these marking provisions are complied with.

Duty to Obtain Information

Operators must obtain information in writing from consignors of explosives which enable them to comply with the regulations. The consignor's duty is to ensure the information given is both accurate and sufficient to allow the operator to comply.

Information to be given to Drivers

The operator must give the driver or the vehicle attendant the following information in writing:
1. The division and Compatibility Group for classified explosives
2. The net mass (in tonnes or kg) of each type of explosive carried (or the gross mass if the nett mass figure is not available)
3. Whether the explosives carried are explosive articles or explosive substances (in the case of Group C, D or G explosives)

Fig. 20.4 *Placard to be displayed on either side of vehicle or freight container carrying explosives*

4. The name and address of the consignor, the operator of the vehicle and the consignee
5. Such other information as necessary to enable the driver to know the dangers which may arise and the emergency action to be taken.

This information must be carried on the vehicle at all times during the carriage from the start of the journey and must be shown on request to a police officer or goods vehicle traffic examiner. It must also be shown to a fire brigade officer or inspector if required. Information must not be carried on a vehicle when the explosives it refers to are no longer on that vehicle. It must be removed, destroyed or placed in a securely closed container marked to show that that the contents do not relate to explosives then being carried. If the necessary information is not available to the driver or vehicle attendant the explosives must not be carried.

Safe and Secure Carriage

The vehicle operator and the driver and any other person involved in the carriage of explosives must take all reasonable steps to prevent accidents and minimise the harmful effects of any accident. They must also prevent unauthorised access to, or removal of, all or part of the load. The operator and driver must ensure that a competent person is constantly in attendance with the vehicle whenever the driver is not present except during stops in a safe and secure place (as defined in the regulations – namely within a factory or magazine licensed under the Explosives Act 1875 or at a place with an exemption certificate granted under the Explosives Act 1875 (Exemptions) Regulations 1979 (SI 1885/1974) and when the vehicle is on a site where adequate security precautions are taken.

The operator and driver of a vehicle used to carry more than 5 tonnes of explosives in Division 1.1 must follow a route agreed with the chief officers of police for each area through which it is to pass.

Procedure in the Event of Accident

The driver or vehicle attendant must contact the police, fire brigade and vehicle operator as quickly as possible in the event of the following circumstances:
1. Spillage of explosives such as to constitute a safety risk
2. Damage to the explosives or their packaging such as to constitute a safety risk
3. If the vehicle overturns
4. If a fire or explosion takes place on the vehicle.

When such circumstances arise the driver, vehicle attendant and the operator must take all proper precautions to ensure the security of the explosives and the safety of persons likely to be affected and the vehicle operator must immediately notify the Health and Safety Executive.

Duration of Carriage and Delivery

Both the vehicle operator and the driver are responsible for ensuring that the carriage of explosives is completed within a reasonable period of time having regard to the distance involved, that explosives are unloaded as soon as reasonably practicable on arrival, that the explosives are delivered to the consignee or his agent or to another person who accepts them in custody for onward despatch provided they are delivered to a safe and secure place or a designated parking area in an airport , a railway transhipment depot or siding, a harbour or harbour area. If they cannot be delivered as required they must be returned to the consignor or his agent. If loaded in a trailer the trailer must not be detached except in a safe place or in an emergency.

Training of Drivers and Attendants

Vehicle operators must ensure that drivers and vehicle attendants have received adequate training and instruction to enable them to understand the nature of the dangers which may arise from the carriage of the explosives, the action to be taken in an emergency and their duties under these regulations and under the Health and Safety at Work etc Act 1974.

Currently the only body able to approve explosives training courses is the Confederation of British Industry (CBI) and the only approved course available is that run by Chemfreight Training of Runcorn. However, the regulations do not specifically state that training must be provided by such an organisation, the employer can quite legally establish his own in-house training courses if he so wishes.

Vocational training certificates will be required by drivers of explosives vehicles from 1 January 1992.

The operator must keep a record of his own training and instruction if he is a driver or attendant and that given to drivers and attendants in his employment. A copy of the training record must be made available to the employees concerned.

Minimum Ages

The regulations specify a minimum age of 18 years for those engaged in the carriage of explosives as a driver or vehicle attendant, for being made responsible for the security of explosives or for travelling in a vehicle carrying explosives unless in the presence of and supervised by a competent person over 18 years of age.

21: Vehicle Excise Duty

Vehicle Excise Licences

All mechanically-propelled vehicles, whether used for private or business purposes, which are used or parked on public roads in Great Britain must have, and display, excise licences (often called road fund licences or road tax) indicating that the appropriate amount of vehicle excise duty (ie VED) has been paid unless they are being driven, by previous appointment, to a place where they are to have their annual test. It is an offence under the Vehicles (Excise) Act 1971 to use or keep an unlicensed vehicle on the road for any period, however short. In the event of a conviction for such an offence heavy fines may be imposed and back duty may be claimed. Operators' licence holders also jeopardise their licences when committing excise duty offences.

The present system of excise licences for most goods vehicles is based on gross weights and axle configurations while goods vehicles not exceeding 3500kg gross weight (1525kg unladen until 30 September 1990) are in the same class as private vehicles which is called private/light goods (PLG) (see p 371 for full details).

Exemptions

Exemption from vehicle excise duty applies to:
1. Vehicles owned or operated by the Crown
2. Vehicles used for fire brigade or ambulance services
3. Road rollers
4. Vehicles used for the haulage of lifeboats and lifeboat gear
5. Vehicles travelling to or from a place where they are to have an annual roadworthiness test by prior appointment
6. Vehicles carrying built-in road construction machinery
7. Vehicles designed and built specially for spreading grit on snow and ice-covered roads
8. Tower vehicles used for street lighting maintenance
9. Local authority road watering and gulley cleaning vehicles
10. Electric vehicles.
11. Pedestrian-controlled vehicles

Six-mile Exemption
In addition to the exemptions mentioned above there is one other important exemption from vehicle excise duty. This applies to vehicles intended to be used on a public road *only* when travelling from one place to another, both of which places must be occupied by the registered owner of the vehicle, and provided the distance travelled on the road is not more than six miles in a week.

In order to take advantage of this exemption, application has to be made to a local Vehicle Registration Office on form V325/1 (see local telephone directory for address). Details must be given of the roads used, the location of the two points at either end of the journey, the actual distance and the number of trips per week. A special windscreen disc is issued showing the vehicle is exempt from VED.

Payment of Duty

Excise duty is payable once annually, or every six months. To assist the private motorist in saving towards vehicle excise duty licence stamps valued at 5.00 each can be purchased at certain post offices.

Application for initial registration or renewal of duty is made on the appropriate form as follows:

First registration	– Form VE 55/1 for new vehicles
	– Form VE 55/5 for re-imported vehicles
Renewal of duty (12 or 6 months)	– Form V10 for all vehicles

A circular licence disc is issued by the DVLC when the duty is paid and this must be displayed in the vehicle windscreen where it can be clearly seen from the near side. It is an offence to fail to display a current and valid excise licence disc.

Reduced, Extended Periods and Refunds
A vehicle may be licensed for only six months at a time if this is preferred but this method of licensing means that a higher amount of duty is paid annually. All licences are valid only from the first day of the month in which they come into force. Alternatively, new vehicles may be licensed part way through a month (but only at local Vehicle Registration Offices) with the duty period commencing on the tenth, seventeenth or twenty-fourth day of the month and continuing through to the end of the 12-month period from the first day of the following month.

In cases where a vehicle is only to be used for a shorter period than either 6 or 12 months or is taken out of service during the currency of the licence, a licence has to be taken out for one or other of these periods and then surrendered to the VRO (see local telephone directory for addresses of local Vehicle Registration Offices) when it is no longer required; the VRO will refund the duty for each complete month remaining on the licence. To gain a full month refund the licence must be surrendered at least by the last day of the previous month. Application for a refund should be made on form V14.

Rates of Duty
The rate of duty payable varies depending on the way in which the vehicle is constructed, the way that it is used and, in the case of light vehicles, its unladen weight, and for heavy goods vehicles, their gross weight and the number of axles.

Duty is categorised in tables as follows:
  1. Private/light goods vehicles (ie not exceeding 3500kg gross weight)

- rates for ordinary vehicles plus those registered by farmers and showmen.
2. Plateable rigid and articulated vehicles (not exceeding 12000kg gross weight)
   - rates for ordinary vehicles plus those registered by farmers and showmen
   - up to 7500 and 7500 to 12000kg.
3. Plateable rigid goods vehicles (exceeding 12000kg gross weight)
   - rates for ordinary vehicles plus those registered by farmers and showmen
   - rates for vehicles with 2 axles, 12000kg to 17000kg
   - rates for vehicles with 3 axles, 12000kg to 24390kg
   - rates for vehicles with 4 or more axles, 12000kg to 30490kg.
4. Trailers
   - rates for ordinary trailers plus those towed by vehicles registered by farmers and showmen
   - rates for trailers 4000kg to 12000kg gross weight (ie towed by vehicles over 12 tonnes gvw).
   - rates for trailers over 12000kg gross weight (ie towed by vehicles over 12 tonnes gvw).
5. Plateable articulated goods vehicles (exceeding 12000kg gross train weight)
   - Table A, 2-axled tractive unit used with any semi-trailer
   - Table B, 2-axled tractive unit used with 2- or more axled semi-trailers only
   - Table C, 2-axled tractive unit used with 3- or more axled semi-trailers only
   - Table D, 3-axled (or more) tractive unit used with any semi-trailer
   - Table E, 3-axled (or more) tractive unit used with 2- or more axled semi-trailers only
   - Table F, 3-axled (or more) tractive unit used with 3- or more axled semi-trailers only.

(All tables contain rates for goods vehicles and those registered by farmers and showmen.)

6. Non-plateable vehicles (ie vehicles over 1525kg ulw – over 3500kg gross weight from 1 October 1990 – exempt from plating and testing)
   - rates for ordinary vehicles and those registered by farmers and showmen
   - single rate only for 'restricted' vehicles falling in this category.
7. Special Types vehicles – for movement of indivisible loads
8. General haulage tractors
   - rates based on unladen weights in imperial tons – no special farmers' or showmen's rates.
9. Hackney carriages
   - rates based on number of seats – minimum rate 20 seats.
10. Showmen's haulage vehicles
    - rates based on unladen weights in imperial tons.
11. Agricultural machines, works trucks, etc
    - single rate to cover all machines in this category.
12. Trade licences
    - covering trade licences for vehicles and those for motor bicycles.
13. Recovery vehicles.

Articulated Combinations

In the case of articulated tractive units which are used with a variety of trailers, the determining factor for taxation purposes is the number of axles on the trailer likely to be used with it. This is so that the maximum amount of duty is paid to prevent a vehicle operating on the road at a rate less than that which is applicable. In general terms, the system operates so that the fewer the axles the greater the duty payable and vice versa. This is because the duty relates to the road damage caused and greater damage arises with fewer axles. In consequence of this it is illegal to operate a vehicle on a road for which the incorrect (ie insufficient) excise duty has been paid.

Trailers

Where drawbar trailers are drawn, if the gross weight of the trailer exceeds 4 tonnes and the gross weight of the towing vehicle exceeds 12 tonnes, additional duty is payable in accordance with published duty tables but not otherwise. So, if the towing vehicle or the trailer falls below these weights no trailer duty is payable.

Goods Carrying Vehicles

The goods vehicle rate of duty is payable if the vehicle is built or has been converted to carry goods, and is actually used to carry goods in connection with a trade or business. In general this rate of duty applies to all types of lorries, vans, trucks, estate cars, dual-purpose vehicles and also passenger vehicles if they are converted for carrying goods. If, however, dual-purpose vehicles (see below) and goods vehicles are never used for carrying goods in connection with a trade or business they may be licensed at the private/light goods (PLG) rate of duty which is currently £100.00 per year.

Driver Training and Non-Goods Carrying Vehicles

Heavy goods vehicles which are used exclusively for driver training purposes may be licensed at the private rate of duty even if they carry ballast (eg concrete blocks) to simulate driving under loaded conditions – *but not other loads*. Similarly, other goods vehicles used for private purposes (ie carriage of goods but not in connection with a trade or business – for example, privately used horse boxes) may also be licensed at the private rate of duty – currently £100.00.

Dual-Purpose Vehicles

For the purposes of the regulations a dual-purpose vehicle (as referred to above) is defined as a vehicle, built or converted to carry both passengers and goods of any description, which has an unladen weight of not more than 2040kg and has either four-wheel drive or:

(a) has a permanently fitted roof
(b) is permanently fitted with one row of transverse seats (fitted across the vehicle) behind the driver's seat (the seats must be cushioned or sprung and have upholstered back-rests)
(c) has a window on either side to the rear of the driver's seat and one at the rear.

The majority of so-called estate cars, shooting-brakes, station wagons, certain Land Rovers and Range Rovers are dual-purpose vehicles under this definition. It should be noted, however, that vehicles used for *dual operations* are not dual-purpose vehicles in terms of the legal requirements.

21: VEHICLE EXCISE DUTY

Special and Reduced Rates of Duty

Farmers' Vehicles
Goods vehicles registered in the name of a person engaged in agriculture and used on public roads only for carrying the produce of, or materials for, the agricultural land he occupies and for no other purpose, can be licensed at a reduced rate of duty.
These reduced rate licences, known as 'Farmers' or 'F' licences, are issued conditional on the vehicle being used for no purposes other than those stated, except that there is a concession that allows the holder of an 'F' licence to carry the produce of, or articles for, another farmer provided that this is only done occasionally, that the goods carried represent only a small proportion of the total goods carried on the vehicle, and that no payment is asked and no reward is given.

Travelling Showmen
Goods vehicles registered in the name of a travelling showman, and used only for his business, and vehicles fitted with a living van type of body or some special type of body or superstructure, are subject to a special rate of duty.

Works Trucks and Mobile Cranes
Works trucks and trailers, agricultural machines, small dumpers, mobile plant, fork-lift trucks and mobile cranes are all subject to special rates of duty. If a works truck or fork-lift truck is used on a public road only when travelling from one set of premises to another set of premises occupied by the same person or company and it does not travel on the road more than six miles in a week, then no licence duty has to be paid. If, however, such vehicles are used on public roads for more than six miles in a week or if they are used on a road for loading or unloading, the rate of duty payable is currently £16.00 per year. Mobile cranes may be licensed at the £16.00 rate provided they do not carry any load on the road except equipment used in connection with the crane assembly. The heavier types of dumper can be licensed at the £100.00 private rate only if they are used on roads when travelling empty between sites.

Mobile Engineering Plant
Other types of mobile engineering plant such as mowing and digging machines, excavators, agricultural machines and mobile compressors may be licensed at the £16.00 annual rate.

Electric Vehicles
Electric vehicles have been exempted from vehicle excise duty altogether since the 1980 Budget.

Registration and Renewal of Duty

A new vehicle has to be registered with local Vehicle Registration Offices or the Driver and Vehicle Licensing Centre at Swansea and a registration number has to be obtained for the vehicle. The number has to be displayed on a plate at both the front and rear of the vehicle.
Form VE 55, which is used for motor vehicle registrations, consists of a single sheet which will be used for first licensing and registration purposes. Attached to it is a two-sheet section with carbon paper inserts, so that the official details of the vehicle and the dealer's name and town (but nothing more) will copy through on to those sheets. These will be sent to an agency acting for the motor industry which will also act for the DTp in the assembly of official vehicle registration statistics.

A feature on these additional sheets is a voluntary statistical section, in which applicants are invited to supply, if they wish to do so, information which will be of value for government and motor industry statistical purposes. It includes questions about the purchaser's occupation and previous vehicle and about the main use to which he intends to put the new vehicle. The information given will help the industry to obtain a better knowledge of the market and therefore to give the best possible service to its customers. Also, if the purchaser chooses to give his name and address, this will enable the manufacturer to get in touch with him direct over any safety matters which may arise. Any information given in this section will be treated as confidential.

Most of the main vehicle manufacturers and importers will have entered the details of each vehicle on the form before it reaches the dealer. This will have two advantages, both for motor dealers and for the purchaser himself. In the first place, they will no longer have to fill in the details themselves, and, in the second place, the association of one form with one vehicle right from the start is intended to make it more difficult to register a stolen vehicle as new. If the manufacturer or importer has not completed the form in advance, copies are available on demand at licensing offices.

Documents

Besides the completed form V55, a certificate of insurance and a copy of the supplier's invoice, a Type Approval Certificate (TAC) is required for goods vehicles which are subject to the type approval regulations, or alternatively a Minister's Approval Certificate (MAC); these documents must be produced when first registering a goods vehicle with form V55 and with form V205 if the vehicle is exempt from plating and testing, if a concessionary rate of duty is applicable or if it is to be used with a trailer when the additional trailer duty is payable (ie over 12 tonnes and 4 tonnes gross weight respectively).

Issue of Registration Document/Licence Disc

The DVLC, on receipt of the above mentioned items, will issue a licence disc and a registration document, form V5, for the vehicle showing its registration number and details of the vehicle such as make, type, type of body (van or tipper, for example), engine number, chassis number, colour, method of propulsion (petrol, heavy oil or battery) and the gross weight. Police officers and certain officers of the DTp may request production of the registration document for inspection at any reasonable time.

Renewal of Licence

When the licence expires after six months or 12 months it has to be renewed by completing renewal form V10. Renewal reminders are sent out from the DVLC on form V11 and this may be used as an alternative to form V10 to renew the licence at certain post offices (provided the vehicle is not over 3500kg gross weight (1525kg unladen weight until 30 September 1990) where form V10 is used, there is no change in ownership or address which has not been recorded and no change to the vehicle or its use) or at local Vehicle Registration Offices. The vehicle registration document, the appropriate fee, a valid certificate of insurance and, if the vehicle is subject to annual testing, a current test certificate, must accompany the application.

21: VEHICLE EXCISE DUTY

Where to Apply
When registering a vehicle for the first time, application must be made to the local Vehicle Registration Office (VRO) or to the Driver and Vehicle Licensing Centre (DVLC) at Swansea SA99 1AR.
Applications for renewal of duty may be made as follows:

1. If you have the official licence renewal reminder, form V1 (providing there is no change in the details on the form) — In person to main post offices or VROs, or by post to VROs
2. If you have form V11 but there are changes in the details — In person or by post to VROs
3. In the London area (providing there is no change in details) — In person to the London VROs or main post offices or by post to these post offices
4. In the London area if you have not received form V11 or if the details on form V11 are not correct (eg changed address or changed particulars of the vehicle). — In person or by post to VROs.

Replacement Licences and Discs
Duplicates or replacements for lost or defaced vehicle registration documents or windscreen discs are available on application. They cost £3.50 each (except in certain exceptional cases – eg if stolen with the vehicle, if for a VED exempt vehicle, if lost in the post). As a security measure, when future application is made for a replacement registration document, the DTp may contact the previous vehicle owner to ensure that the applicant is entitled to have possession of the vehicle and the registration document.

Alteration of Vehicles

If a vehicle is altered during its life by adding or removing equipment, by changing the type of body or even the colour of the vehicle, by changing the plated weight or increasing the unladen weight by fitting a heavier body or heavier components, the DVLC must be advised of the changes at once. If the changes mean that the vehicle goes into a higher weight range, then the additional licence duty becomes payable from the date of the changes.

If a van is converted to carry passengers or has side windows fitted to the body behind the driver's seat the owner becomes liable to pay car tax to HM Customs and Excise. The amount of tax payable is based on the current wholesale value of the vehicle. Any person making such a conversion must report the fact to the Customs and Excise authorities immediately.

Sale of Vehicles

When a vehicle is sold, the seller must notify the DVLC by completing the bottom tear-off portion of the registration document (Form V5), which is perforated for this purpose, with the name and address of the new owner of the vehicle. It is an offence to fail to notify a change of vehicle ownership (maximum fine £400.00) and it can lead to the original owner being prosecuted for offences committed with the vehicle by the new owner and leaving the previous owner to pay any fixed penalty fines incurred. The new owner has to fill in his name and address in the changes section of the registration document and send the document to the DVLC for registration in his name. If a vehicle is sold for scrap or is broken up, the registration document has to be sent to the DVLC with a note advising them of this.

Production of Test Certificates

A valid goods vehicle test certificate has to be produced at the time of re-licensing any goods vehicle over one year old (ie vehicles over 3500kg gross weight and articulated vehicles which are subject to the goods vehicle annual test), and a light vehicle or private car type (ie MOT) test certificate when re-licensing any vehicle not over 3500kg gross weight which is over three years old and is subject to the light vehicle annual test scheme.

Vehicles Exempt from Plating and Testing

When applying to license or re-license goods vehicles which are exempt from plating and testing, a declaration has to be made on form V112G (available from VROs) to cover the non-production of a valid test certificate.

Data Protection

In accordance with the provisions of the Data Protection Act the DVLC at Swansea is registered as a Data User and as such must make available, on request, details held on file concerning individual persons. Such information is normally shown on driving licences and vehicle registration documents but an enquiry to establish details held on file can be made (on payment of a fee) to the: Vehicle Enquiry Unit (Data Protection Queries), DVLC, Swansea SA99 1AN.

Trade Licences

Trade licences (trade plates) are available for use by motor traders and vehicle testers to save them the inconvenience of having to license individually every vehicle which passes through their hands.

Fees and Validity

A trade licence can be obtained from the local Vehicle Registration Office (VRO) in whose area the applicant has his business; it is valid either for one year or for six months (licences are issued on 1 January and 1 July) and the licence fee is £100.00 for one year and £55.00 for six months. Replacements for lost or defaced trade licences cost £11.00 per set or £6.50 for the plate containing the licence and £4.50 for other plates.

Display of Trade Licences

The VRO will, when they have approved the application, issue a pair of special number plates with the registration number in red letters on a white background. One of the plates has a licence holder attached to it and the licence affixed (it does not have to be displayed on the windscreen); this plate must always be carried at the front of the vehicle on which the plates are being used. The other plate is carried at the rear.

Issue of Licences

There are considerable restrictions on the issue and use of trade licences; as already mentioned they are issued only to:
(a) motor traders, defined as 'manufacturers or repairers of, or dealers in mechanically-propelled vehicles' (this also includes dealers who are in business consisting mainly of collecting and delivering mechanically-propelled vehicles), plus those who modify vehicles (eg by fitting accessories) and those who provide valet services for vehicles who may use the licence for all vehicles which are from time to time temporarily in their possession in the course of their business as motor traders;
(b) vehicle testers for all vehicles which are from time to time submitted to them for testing in the course of their business as vehicle testers.

Vehicles such as service vans or general run-about vehicles owned by motor traders cannot be used under trade licences; the full rate of duty has to be paid for such vehicles.

Use of Trade Licences

The following are the purposes for which vehicles operated under a trade licence may be used by a motor trader or vehicle tester:
 1. For test or trial in the course of construction or repair of the vehicle or its accessories or equipment and after completing construction or repair.
 2. Travelling to or from a weighbridge to check the unladen weight or travelling to a place for registration or inspection by the Council.
 3. For demonstration to a prospective customer and for travelling to or from a place of demonstration.
 4. For test or trial of the vehicle for the benefit of a person interested in promoting publicity for the vehicle.
 5. For delivering the vehicle to a purchaser.
 6. For demonstrating the accessories or equipment to a prospective purchaser.
 7. For delivering a vehicle to, or collecting it from, other premises belonging to the trade licence holder or another trader's premises.
 8. For going to or coming from a workshop in which a body or equipment or accessories are to be, or have been fitted or where the vehicle is to be or has been valeted, painted or repaired.
 9. For delivering the vehicle from the premises of a manufacturer or repairer to a place where it is to be transported by train, ship or aircraft or for returning it from a place to which it has been transported by these means.
 10. Travelling to or returning from any garage, auction room or other place where vehicles are stored or offered for sale and where the vehicle has been stored or offered for sale.
 11. Travelling to a place to be tested (and return), dismantled or broken up.

It should be noted that the use of a vehicle on trade plates does not exempt the driver or operator from the need to ensure that it is in sound mechanical condition when on the road, even if being driven for the purposes of road testing or fault finding prior to repair or after repair. The police will prosecute if they find trade licensed vehicles on the road in an unsafe or otherwise illegal condition.

Carriage of Goods on a Trade Licence
Goods may only be carried on a vehicle operating under a trade licence:
1. When a load is necessary to demonstrate or test the vehicle, its accessories or its equipment – the load must be returned to the place of loading after the demonstration or test unless it comprised water, fertiliser or refuse.
2. When a load consists of parts or equipment designed to be fitted to the vehicle being taken to the place where they are to be fitted.
3. When a load is built in or permanently attached to the vehicle.
4. When a trailer is being carried for delivery or being taken to a place for work to be done on it.
5. If the goods are another fully licensed vehicle being carried for the purpose of travel from or to the place of collection or delivery (ie the driver's own transport to get him out or back home).

Carriage of Passengers on a Trade Licence
The only passengers who are permitted to travel on a trade licensed vehicle are:
1. The driver of the vehicle, who must be the licence holder or his employee
    – other persons may drive the vehicle with the permission of the licence holder but they must be accompanied by the licence holder or his employee (this latter proviso does not apply if the vehicle is only constructed to carry one person).
2. Persons required to be on the vehicle by law, a statutory attendant for example.
3. Any person carried for the purpose of carrying out his statutory duties of inspecting the vehicle or trailer.
4. Any person in a disabled vehicle being towed including persons from the disabled vehicle being carried provided this is not for hire or reward.
5. A prospective purchaser or his servant or agent.
6. A person interested in promoting publicity for the vehicle.

NB: It is illegal for transport fleet operators to road test their own vehicles on trade plates. This has been established on the grounds that the vehicles are not 'temporarily' in their possession and are therefore outside the permitted terms of a trade licence use.

Recovery Vehicles

Since 1 January 1988 a recovery vehicle is no longer permitted to undertake recovery operations on trade plates. A separate class of VED at an annual rate of duty of £50.00 and £27.50 for six months (currently) applies to these vehicles. Any vehicle used for recovery work which does

21: VEHICLE EXCISE DUTY

not conform to the definition given below must be licensed at the normal goods vehicle rate according to its class and gross weight.

Definition of Recovery Vehicle

For the purpose of this new taxation class, a recovery vehicle is one which is 'either constructed or permanently adapted primarily for the purpose of lifting, towing and transporting a disabled vehicle or for any one or more of those purposes'.

A vehicle will no longer be a recovery vehicle under the regulations (ie Vehicles (Excise) Act 1971 Schedule 3 as amended by the Finance Act 1987) if at any time it is used for a purpose other than:

(a) the recovery of a disabled vehicle (this has been extended to two vehicles)
(b) the removal of a disabled vehicle from the place where it became disabled to premises at which it is to be repaired or scrapped
(c) the removal of a disabled vehicle from premises to which it was taken for repair to other premises at which it is to be repaired or scrapped
(d) carrying any load other than fuel and any liquids required for its propulsion and tools and other articles required for the operation of, or in connection with, apparatus designed to lift, tow or transport a disabled vehicle.

Plating and Testing

Recovery vehicles licensed under the recovery vehicle taxation class are not exempt from goods vehicle plating and testing unless they satisfy the definition of a 'breakdown vehicle'.

Operation of Recovery vehicles

Licensed recovery vehicles are exempt from 'O' licensing, the EC drivers' hours rules and the tachograph requirements but those persons who drive them must comply with the British Domestic driving hours rules (see p 67 for details).

Rebated Heavy Oil

Commercial vehicles powered by diesel (heavy oil) engines must use diesel fuel on which the full rate of duty has been paid. A lower rate of duty is payable on fuel used for purposes other than driving road vehicles, such as driving auxiliary equipment, for contractors' plant which does not use public roads, bench testing of engines and space heating. Fuel on which the lower rate of duty has been paid is known as rebated heavy oil but is more commonly called gas oil or red diesel.

Rebated heavy oil must be marked, when delivered from bonded oil warehouses, with a red dye so that its use can easily be detected, and the supplier must deliver to the recipient a delivery note bearing a statement that the oil is 'not to be used as road fuel'. If both rebated and unrebated oils are stored in the same place a notice bearing the same wording must be placed at the outlet of the rebated oil supply.

Road fuel testing units staffed by officers of Customs and Excise operate throughout the UK to test fuel in vehicles and in storage tanks. Under the Hydrocarbon Oil Regulations 1973 Customs and Excise officers are empowered to examine any vehicle and any oil carried in it or on it and may also enter and inspect any premises and inspect, test or sample any oil on the premises whether the oil is in a vehicle or not. Vehicle owners and drivers must give the officers facilities for inspecting oils in vehicles or on premises.

The following vehicles may use rebated heavy oil as fuel. All other vehicles must use unrebated (full-duty paid) oil at all times:
- Vehicles not used on public roads and not licensed for road use
- Road rollers
- Road construction machinery (vehicles used or kept on a road solely for carrying built-in road construction machinery)
- Vehicles exempted from excise licence duty which use public roads for not more than six miles in a week
- Agricultural machines
- Trench digging and excavating machines
- Mobile cranes
- Mowing machines
- Works trucks.

Heavy penalties, including fines and repayment of duty, are imposed on offenders convicted of using illegal diesel fuel.

22: Insurance – Vehicle, Premises and Business

Owners and operators of motor vehicles using the public highway must insure against third-party* injury and passenger claims. Further, an essential part of any investment in property (buildings, vehicles, plant, etc) is to obtain protection by insurance against loss or damage by theft, fire or any other eventuality. It is also wise to be protected against claims made by third parties for compensation following injury to themselves or damage to their property as a result of some occurrence involving you, your employees, your property, or taking place on your premises.

The insurance company is the first party; the insured person(s) is the second party, and anybody else involved (particularly if they make a claim for compensation) is termed the third party.

Motor Vehicle Insurance

Third-Party Cover

The Road Traffic Acts require that all motor vehicles, except invalid carriages and vehicles owned by local authorities or the police, used on a road must be covered against third-party risks. This can be achieved by means of an insurance policy or, alternatively, by a deposit of £15000 in cash or securities to the Accountant-General of the Supreme Court but this is only applicable if authorisation is granted by the Secretary of State for Transport. Normally, such authorisation is only granted to public bodies and authorities and to major organisations with access to the substantial funds which may be needed to meet major accident claims.

Where the cover is obtained by conventional insurance means the Road Traffic Act 1988 stipulates that cover is only valid if taken out with insurers who are members of the Motor Insurers' Bureau (MIB) which is a body established to meet claims for compensation (in respect of death or personal injuries only) by third parties involved in accidents with motor vehicles which subsequently prove to be uninsured against third-party risks.

Section 145 (3a) and (3c) of the Road Traffic Act 1988 states that the insurance policy:

> ...must insure such person, persons or classes of persons as may be specified in the policy in respect of any liability which may be incurred by him or them, in respect of the death or bodily injury to any person caused by, or arising out of, the use of the vehicle on a road...(and)... must also insure him or them in respect of any liability which may be incurred by him or them...relating to payment for emergency treatment.

The emergency treatment referred to is that provided at the scene of an accident by a doctor or hospital authority and that provided by and charged for by a hospital for in-patient or out-patient care.

Passenger Liability

Passenger liability insurance cover for motor vehicles is compulsory. This requirement applies to all vehicles which are required by the Road Traffic Act to have third-party insurance and the cover must extend to authorised passengers (other than employees of the insured who are covered separately by the compulsory employers' liability insurance), other non-fare paying passengers and also to what may be termed 'unauthorised passengers' such as hitch-hikers and other people who are given lifts.

Unauthorised Passengers
The display in a vehicle of a sign which says 'No passengers...' or 'No liability...' does not indemnify a vehicle operator or driver from claims by so-called 'unauthorised' passengers who may claim for injury or damage received when travelling in or otherwise in connection with the vehicle resulting from the driver's or vehicle operator's negligence. The law ensures that such liabilities are covered within the vehicle's policy on insurance.

Property Cover

In accordance with an EC Directive (EC 5/84), from 1 January 1989 all UK motor insurance policies have been required to cover liability for damage to property (up to a maximum liability of £250000 arising from one accident or a series of accidents from one cause). Damage to property in this context includes that caused by the weight of the vehicle (eg to road surfaces, paving slabs etc) and by vibration which may damage services (eg gas and water mains, gullies and sewers, telephone cables etc) below the road surface and third parties whose property is damaged in a vehicle accident have the right to request details of the vehicle insurance.

Certificate of Insurance

A policy of insurance does not provide the cover required by the Act until the insured person or organisation has in their possession a Certificate of Insurance. Possession meaning, in this context, exactly what it says: 'promised' or 'in the post' is not sufficient to satisfy the law. The policy itself is not *proof* of insurance cover it only sets out the terms and conditions for the cover and the exclusion and invalidation clauses.

The Certificate (or a temporary cover note proving cover until the Certificate is issued) which is *proof* (or evidence) of cover must show the dates between which the cover is valid, give particulars of any conditions subject to which the policy is issued (eg the permitted purposes for which the vehicle may be used and those which are not permitted) and must relate to the vehicles covered, either individually by registration number or by specification and to the persons who are authorised to drive them.

Production of Insurance Certificate
It is necessary to produce a current Certificate of Insurance when making application for a excise licence (road tax) for a vehicle. Alternatively, a temporary cover note may be produced and this will be accepted, but the insurance policy itself is not acceptable.

The owner (ie registered keeper) of a motor vehicle must produce a Certificate of Insurance relating to the vehicle if required to do so by a police officer. If he is not able to produce the Certificate on the spot, or if an employed driver is required to produce a Certificate of Insurance for the vehicle he is driving, it may be produced for inspection, no later than *seven* days from the date of the request by the police officer, at any police station which the owner or driver, chooses. The person to whom the request is made does not have to produce the Certificate personally, but may have somebody else take it to the nominated police station for him. A valid temporary cover note would suffice instead of the Certificate if this has not yet been issued.

Duty to Give Information

If requested to do so, the owner of a vehicle must give the police any information they ask for to help determine whether on any particular occasion a vehicle was driven without third-party insurance cover in force. The owner must also give information about the identity of a driver who may at any time have been driving a vehicle which is registered in his name, or information which may lead to the identification of a driver if he is asked to do so by the police.

When the vehicle or vehicles concerned in such a request are the subject of a hiring agreement, the term 'owner' for the purposes of these insurance provisions includes each and every party to the hiring agreement.

Invalidation of Cover

Insurance cover may be invalidated and claims refused if policy conditions are not strictly adhered to. In particular these circumstances may arise if the vehicle is operated illegally (for example, in excess of its permissible weight, without a valid test certificate, in an unsound mechanical condition, outside the terms of an 'O' licence, with an incorrectly or unlicensed driver or one who is disqualified, or if replacement components fitted to the vehicle are not to manufacturer's specification).

By way of example, a case was reported where liability was rejected by an insurance company when a fast sports saloon motor car was fitted with tyres not approved for the top speed of which the car was capable (well in excess of 100mph), although the claim arose out of an accident at less than 30mph.

It is important to stress the need to examine carefully all the clauses contained in a motor insurance policy and to take steps to avoid any action which may invalidate the policy. The employment of unlicensed or incorrectly licensed drivers or the use of unroadworthy vehicles (ie vehicles which do not comply with legal requirements or are found to be on the road in a dangerous condition) are two examples of the most likely ways of invalidating a motor insurance policy. Similarly, the policy should cover *all persons* who may be required (or may need in an emergency) to drive vehicles, not just employees.

Use of Unfit Drivers
It is important not to use drivers who are, or who are believed to be, medically unfit to drive. Insurance companies have a duty to notify the Secretary of State for Transport of the names and addresses of people

refused insurance cover on medical grounds so their driving licences can be withdrawn.

Payment to Travel
Previously, motor insurance cover could be invalidated if passengers paid towards the cost of car-running expenses. As a result of provisions in the Transport Act 1980, the receipt of travel expenses contributions from passengers in private cars does not invalidate insurance policies provided no profit is made.

Cancellation of Insurance

When an insurance policy is cancelled, the Certificate of Insurance – there may be one or more depending on the number of vehicles covered by the policy – relating to that policy must be surrendered to the insurer within seven days of the cancellation date.

Cover in EC Countries

It is a requirement that every motor insurance policy issued in an EC country, including Britain, must include cover against those liabilities which are compulsorily insurable under the laws of every other EC member state *(Article 7 (2) of the EEC Directive on Insurance of Civil Liabilities arising from the use of Motor Vehicles (No 72/166/CEE))* and some non-EC states. Motor policies issued in the UK contain provisions for such cover but this only provides very limited legal minimum cover and, while an international motor insurance 'green card' is no longer essential to enable EC member state boundaries to be crossed by vehicles (private or commercial), it is wise to obtain a green card when travelling or sending goods vehicles abroad, in order to obtain the much wider cover provided by the policy. Possession of a green card provides adequate evidence of insurance when abroad and it also eliminates problems of language and different procedures in foreign countries.

Cover in non-EC Countries

The EC insurance arrangements described above have been extended to five non-EC countries in Europe – Austria, Finland, Norway, Sweden and Switzerland. Vehicles from these countries are exempt from checks on their insurance documents at UK ports of entry and drivers of British vehicles will enjoy reciprocal arrangements in these five countries as well as in the other 11 EC member countries (ie France, Belgium, Holland, Germany, Luxembourg, Italy, Denmark, Eire, Greece, Spain, Portugal).

British motor policies have been extended to cover vehicles in all 16 countries so that they meet the national law of each country on motor insurance. In their own interests, drivers should continue to carry either a green card or their British Insurance Certificate when travelling abroad because, although they will not be subjected to routine border crossing checks for insurance, they may be required to produce evidence of insurance in the event of an accident.

International Accident Report Form

A special accident report form has been devised by the European Insurance

Committee (CPA) for use as an agreed statement and accident report to be completed by drivers at the time of an accident when travelling in a foreign country (ie a country other than that in which the vehicle is insured). The use of such a form (available from insurers), particularly when dealing with persons from other countries who cannot speak your language, can help to resolve matters later.

Fleet Insurance

Most large fleet operators obtain insurance cover on a 'blanket' basis. Under this arrangement vehicles are not specified on the Certificate of Insurance by registration number but there is a statement on the Certificate to the effect that cover is provided for any vehicle owned, hired or temporarily in the possession of the insured person or company. With blanket insurance it is normal to advise the insurance company by means of a quarterly return of the registration numbers of all vehicles added to or deleted from the fleet strength during that period.

The basic insurance premium is calculated on the total fleet at the beginning of the policy year and adjustments are made by the insurance company issuing debit or credit notes as necessary following receipt of the quarterly returns. This system saves the insurance companies having continually to issue and cancel cover notes and Certificates for vehicles in fleets where there may be many changes during a year because of staggered replacement programmes. The insured company also benefits by not having to get in touch with their insurers every time a vehicle is obtained or disposed of and, further, by being able to obtain an excise licence for a new vehicle without having to wait to receive a cover note from the insurance company.

Additional Vehicle Insurance Cover

Extended Cover

The minimum cover against third-party risks mentioned above is not sufficient protection for the owner of a vehicle in the event of it being involved in an accident, damaged in any way (eg by vandals or by another vehicle when the driver was not present) or stolen. To obtain extra protection against such contingencies it is necessary to extend the insurance cover beyond the third-party legal minimum. This can be done in varying stages depending on what the vehicle owner considers necessary for his purpose. The basic policy can be extended to cover loss of the vehicle or damage to it as a result of fire or theft. The insurance can be further extended to give comprehensive cover which provides protection against third-party claims, fire and theft risks and accidental damage to the vehicle itself.

Loading and Unloading Risks

Goods vehicle insurance policies should include clauses which give protection against claims arising from the loading or unloading of vehicles or the activities of employees engaged on such work.

Loss of Use

Most motor vehicle policies do not include cover for the loss of use of a vehicle or for the hire of a replacement vehicle following an accident. If the accident proves to be the fault of the third party, a claim has to be made against him for the loss of use or the hiring charges incurred but such claims are often difficult to substantiate (particularly the value of loss of use of the vehicle) and may result in only meagre awards. An extension to the policy covering such eventualities is the most satisfactory means of protection against this type of loss.

Mechanical Failure

Mechanical failure is another item which is not normally included in motor insurance policies and generally it is not possible to obtain this type of cover for motor vehicles (although it is for some items of heavy engineering plant). Damage to engines caused by frost is covered in the majority of commercial vehicle insurance policies although there are certain qualifications. It is necessary, for example, if a claim is to be met, for the vehicle to have been sheltered in a properly constructed garage between specified hours of the night. It is a condition of all policies that all reasonable steps should be taken to safeguard the vehicle from such loss or damage, and this clause particularly is one which the insurance company can use to escape a claim if it feels the policy conditions have not been complied with.

Windscreen Breakage

Insurance companies normally provide cover for windscreen breakage within the standard motor insurance policy. Claims made for broken windscreens are generally limited to a fixed amount but are paid to the policy holder without detriment to any existing no-claims bonus and irrespective of whether or not an 'excess' clause is in force on the policy. Similar cover applies on most goods vehicle policies providing for the cost of replacement of the broken windscreen and for repairs to paintwork damaged by the broken glass.

Towing

Insurance cover for towing a vehicle which has broken down is normally provided under a goods vehicle policy, but the cover does not extend to damage caused to the vehicle while it is being towed, or to loss or damage of any goods being carried by the broken-down vehicle.

Damage by Weight

A goods vehicle insurance policy should provide cover against claims for damage caused to roads, bridges, manhole covers and such like by the weight of the vehicle passing over them. Some policies have a limit on the maximum liability acceptable for damage to property and this amount should be checked to ensure that it is adequate to meet likely claims in this respect.

Defence Costs

A motor insurance policy can be extended to cover legal costs incurred in

22: INSURANCE – VEHICLE, PREMISES AND BUSINESS

defending a driver faced with manslaughter or causing death by reckless driving charges.

Goods in Transit Insurance

A motor vehicle insurance policy does not provide cover for claims made for damage or loss to goods carried on or in the vehicle. Goods in Transit (GIT) insurance cover is needed to provide protection for this eventuality.

Most GIT insurance policies provide cover in accordance with the limits included in the Road Haulage Association Conditions of Carriage which is normally a maximum liability of £800 per tonne for goods carried within the UK. If goods are of relatively low value (bulk traffics, such as coal, gravel and other excavated materials, for example) a lower limit of liability and consequently a lower premium can be considered. However, in many cases the £800 per tonne limit can be totally inadequate. Many loads these days are valued at tens of thousands of pounds with an equivalent value per tonne way in excess of the RHA level and it is necessary to ensure that the amount of insurance cover is adequate to cover the value of such loads.

When goods of this level of value are carried regularly the insurance company will provide suitable annual cover but in some instances goods vehicle operators may find that a lower level of cover is suitable for most of their activities since they only occasionally carry high-value loads. It is important when this happens that the haulier makes himself aware of the load value and that the insurance company is advised of such loads and the appropriate cover obtained. Failure to do so could leave a haulier facing expensive loss or damage claims from his own pocket.

Some GIT policies specifically exclude certain high-risk loads such as cigarettes, tobacco, spirits, livestock, computers, etc, so the operator faced with a request to carry such a load should check that his policy covers the value and consult his insurers before accepting an order to move the goods.

The GIT policy can be on an 'All-Risks' basis but it is usual for the policy to meet the particular requirements of the operator to give him protection against the liabilities he assumes when he accepts goods for carriage. Such liabilities may be accepted under Conditions of Carriage (see later in this chapter) or under a contract or agreement or, in the abbsence of any specific contract or conditions, at common law. If the operator is carrying his own goods in addition to other people's he should make sure that these are also covered under the policy.

Liability for Goods

Most transport managers are aware that it is essential that they should effect a Goods in Transit insurance policy in respect of the goods carried, but it is most important to consider very carefully the liabilities which are assumed for the goods handled on behalf of customers and that there is full understanding of the Goods in Transit insurance contract which has been arranged.

If transport contractors for commercial reasons assume total responsibility for very high-value loads and do not in any way limit their liability by contract or by the application of conditions of carriage (see p 335), they will soon realise that the claims which are being handled by their Goods in Transit insurers become so expensive that the premium subsequently demanded will be far too high to bear.

It is for this reason that the majority of transport contractors find it sensible to limit their liability in accordance with Conditions of Carriage such as those published by the RHA (it has drawn up Conditions, dated 1982, which are the copyright of the RHA and may not be used by non-members – see Figure 22.1) where the liability is based on a value of £800 per tonne on the actual weight of the goods carried or on the computed weight if the volume of the goods exceeds 80 cubic feet per tonne. This limit can be varied on the insurance policy to suit individual demands but otherwise retaining for the operator the legal liability limitations.

High-Value Loads

There may be a temptation for haulage contractors to accept high-value loads because the freight rate being offered by the consignor is generous in comparison to normal haulage rates. Such loads, however, are notoriously attractive to thieves so it is important before accepting them to examine the Goods in Transit insurance policy to make sure that such high-value goods are not specifically excluded and that any special requirements which the insurance company may have imposed regarding overnight parking and general vehicle security and protection are complied with.

Night Risk and Immobiliser Clauses
Insurance policies frequently contain clauses requiring vehicles carrying high-value goods to be securely parked in locked or guarded premises overnight (known as the 'Night Risk' clause) or to be fitted with approved vehicle protection devices such as steering column locks, engine immobilisers and alarm systems (known as the 'Immobiliser' clause). It is a condition of the insurance that such devices must be maintained in good working order and must be put into effect when the vehicle is left unattended. Failure to comply with such conditions can render the cover invalid.

Sub-Contracting
Before valuable loads are sub-contracted to other hauliers, operators should take considerable pains to satisfy themselves as to the genuineness of any driver calling at their premises for a load (telephoning the driver's employer is one suggested method of checking). Experience shows that drivers with criminal intent will state that they are employed by a certain firm and that they require a return load; documents are frequently handed to the driver in such cases; he picks up the load and disappears. A few days later, when investigations are made, it is only then discovered that the driver obtained the load by false pretences. Goods in transit insurers may not accept responsibility for such losses, or indeed any losses involving sub-contracted loads unless they have had prior notification of the loads and the circumstances.

GIT on Hired Vehicles

The increasing use of vehicles on contract hire raises an important issue regarding liabilities for goods carried. Normally under the terms of the hire contract it is made quite clear by the hire company supplying the vehicle that it assumes no responsibility for loss or damage to the goods which are carried on the vehicle.

Vehicles Hired with Drivers
If, however, under the terms of the contract the hire company offers to provide a driver, the driver acts under its instructions. Should he act in a way which would be considered contrary to normal reasonable action (for example, leaving a fully laden vehicle overnight in the open when he had been specifically instructed to empty the vehicle or to place it in a locked garage), the hire company may find itself held liable at law for a 'fundamental breach of contract' and be faced with having to pay the full amount of any loss incurred. A method of overcoming this difficulty is for the hire company to arrange with the owner of the goods for a Goods in Transit insurance policy to be effected in their joint names and for the owners of the goods to pay the premium in the contract hire agreement.

Conditions of Carriage

An operator carrying goods for hire or reward is advised to set out conditions of carriage under which he contracts to carry goods. In these conditions the carrier can define his liabilities by stipulating limits on the value of goods for which he will normally accept responsibility, with goods of higher value being carried only on special terms, and stating circumstances and provisions under which no compensation is payable. For example, an operator could make it a condition that he accepts no liability under the following circumstances:
- Act of God.
- Act of war or civil war.
- Seizure under legal process.
- Act or omission of the trader, his employees or agents.
- Inherent liability to wastage in bulk, or weight, latent defect inherent defect vice or natural deterioration of the merchandise.
- Insufficient or improper packing.
- Insufficient labelling or addressing.
- Riots, civil commotions, strikes, lock-outs, stoppage or restraint of labour from whatever cause.
- Consignee not taking or accepting delivery within a reasonable time.
- Loss of a particular market whether held daily or at intervals.
- Indirect or consequential damages.
- Fraud on the part of the trader. In this context trader means either consignor or consignee.
- If non-delivery of a consignment, whether in part or whole, is not notified in writing within a specified number of days of despatch and a claim made in writing within a further specified number of days of despatch.
- If pilferage or damage is not notified in writing within a specified number of days of delivery, and a claim made in writing within a further specified number of days of delivery.

A note to the effect that goods are carried only under the Conditions of Carriage should be made on all relevant business documents, particularly consignment and delivery notes, invoices and quotations. Conditions of Carriage should always be drawn to the customer's attention and copies made available for customers to examine before they give orders for movements to commence.

RHA Conditions of Carriage

The Conditions of Carriage used by members of the Road Haulage Association are an excellent example of the sort of conditions which could be used by a haulage contractor to define his responsibilities. The conditions referring to general traffics are shown in full in Figure 22.1. Further sets of conditions for livestock carrying and sub-contracting are also prepared for members.

NB: The RHA conditions of carriage are the copyright of the Association and their use by a non-member would be a breach of copyright and therefore illegal – the RHA has taken legal action in cases of unauthorised use of its conditions.

Cover for International Haulage Journeys

The Goods in Transit cover described above is not sufficient or even legally acceptable where vehicles are engaged on international haulage work. In most cases, such operations are governed by the provisions of the *Convention on the Contract for the International Carriage of Goods by Road,* commonly known and referred to as the CMR convention. This Convention automatically applies where an international haulage journey takes place between different countries at least one of which is party to the Convention (with the exception of UK – Eire and UK mainland – Channel Islands journeys which are ruled not to be international journeys for this purpose).

Road hauliers who carry goods on any part of an international journey, whether they know it or whether they choose to or not, fall within the legal confines of the CMR Convention under which compensation levels for loss or damage to goods are much higher than the standard Conditions of Carriage GIT cover applicable in National transport operations. CMR levels of cover vary according to a set standard which is published daily in the financial press. For this reason it is important to obtain adequate cover when involved in international transport. See also Chapter 26.

Unfair Contract Terms

The Unfair Contract Terms Act 1977 affects such contracts as Conditions of Carriage. The effect of this legislation is to increase the liability of transport operators, particularly in respect of instances where liability for negligence is disclaimed by contract or by notice. Further, it prevents a business from excluding its liabilities for breach of contract when dealing with the general public. Consequently, any term in a contract purporting to exclude liability for personal injury by negligence is void. Any term excluding liability for damage to property by negligence is also void unless the term used is reasonable as between the parties to the contract.

22: INSURANCE – VEHICLE, PREMISES AND BUSINESS

Road Haulage Association Limited

CONDITIONS OF CARRIAGE 1982

(hereinafter referred to as "the Carrier") is not a common carrier and accepts goods for carriage only upon that condition and the Conditions set out below. No servant or agent of the Carrier is permitted to alter or vary these Conditions in any way unless expressly authorised to do so.

1. Definitions

In these Conditions:

"*Trader*" means the customer who contracts for the services of the Carrier.

"*Contract*" means the contract of carriage between the Trader and the Carrier.

"*Consignment*" means goods in bulk or contained in one parcel, package or container, as the case may be, or any number of separate parcels, packages or containers sent at one time in one load by or for the Trader from one address to one address.

"*Dangerous Goods*" means:

(a) goods which are specified in the special classification of dangerous goods issued by the British Railways Board or which, although not specified therein, are not acceptable to the British Railways Board for conveyance on the ground of their dangerous or hazardous nature, or

(b) goods which, although not included in (a) above, are of a similar kind.

2. Parties and Sub-Contracting

(1) The Trader warrants that he is either the owner of the goods in any Consignment or is authorised by such owner to accept these Conditions on such owner's behalf.

(2) The Carrier and any other carrier employed by the Carrier may employ the services of any other carrier for the purpose of fulfilling the Contract in whole or in part and the name of every such other carrier shall be provided to the Trader on request.

(3) The Carrier contracts for itself and as agent of and trustee for its servants and agents and all other carriers referred to in (2) above and such other carrier's servants and agents and every reference in Conditions 3-17 inclusive hereof to "The Carrier" shall be deemed to include every such other carrier, servant and agent with the intention that they shall have the benefit of the Contract and collectively and together with the Carrier be under no greater liability to the Trader or any other party than is the Carrier hereunder.

3. Dangerous Goods

If the Carrier agrees to accept Dangerous Goods for carriage such goods must be accompanied by a full declaration of their nature and contents and be properly and safely packed and labelled in accordance with any statutory regulations for the time being in force for carriage by road.

4. Loading and Unloading

(1) When collection or delivery takes place at the Trader's premises the Carrier shall not be under any obligation to provide any plant, power, or labour in addition to the Carrier's carmen, required for loading or unloading at such premises.

(2) The Carrier shall not be required to provide service beyond the usual place of collection or delivery but if any such service is given by the Carrier it shall be at the sole risk of the Trader who shall indemnify the Carrier against all claims and demands whatever which could not have been made if such service had not been given.

(3) (a) Goods requiring special appliances for unloading from the vehicle by which they are carried are accepted for carriage only on condition that such appliances are made available by the Trader at destination.

(b) When the Carrier is, without prior arrangement in writing with the Trader, called upon to load or unload goods requiring special appliances for loading or unloading, the Carrier shall be under no liability whatever to the Trader for any damage whatever, however caused, arising out of such loading or unloading and the Trader shall indemnify the Carrier against all claims and demands whatever which could not have been made if such assistance had not been given.

5. Consignment Notes

The Carrier shall, if so required, sign a document prepared by the sender acknowledging the receipt of the Consignment but no such document shall be evidence of the condition or of the correctness of the declared nature, quantity, or weight of the Consignment at the time it is received by the Carrier.

6. Transit

(1) Transit shall commence when the Carrier takes possession of the Consignment whether at the point of collection or at the Carrier's premises.

(2) Transit shall (unless otherwise previously determined) end when the Consignment is tendered at the usual place of delivery at the consignee's address within the customary cartage hours of the district. Provided that:

(a) if no safe and adequate access or no adequate unloading facilities there exist then transit shall be deemed to end at the expiry of one clear day after notice in writing (or by telephone if so previously agreed in writing) of the arrival of the Consignment at the Carrier's premises has been sent to the consignee; and

(b) when for any other reason whatever a Consignment cannot be delivered or when a Consignment is held by the Carrier 'to await order' or 'to be kept till called for' or upon any like instructions and such instructions are not given or of the Consignment is not called for and removed, within a reasonable time, then transit shall be deemed to end.

7. Undelivered or Unclaimed Goods

Where the Carrier is unable for any reason to deliver a Consignment to the consignee or as he may order, or where by virtue of the proviso to Condition 6(2) hereof transit is deemed to be at an end, the Carrier may sell the goods and payment or tender of the proceeds after deduction of all proper charges and expenses in relation thereto and of all outstanding charges in relation to the carriage and storage of the goods shall (without prejudice to any claim or right which the Trader may have against the Carrier otherwise arising under these Conditions) discharge the Carrier from all liability in respect of such goods, their carriage and storage.

Provided that:

(a) the Carrier shall do what is reasonable to obtain the value of the Consignment and

(b) the power of sale shall not be exercised where the name and address of the sender or of the consignee is known unless the Carrier shall have done what is reasonable in the circumstances to give notice to the sender or, if the name and address of the sender is not known, to the consignee that the goods will be sold unless within the time specified in such notice, being a reasonable time in the circumstances from the giving of such notice, the goods are taken away or instructions are given for their disposal.

8. Carrier's Charges

(1) The Carrier's charges shall be payable by the Trader without prejudice to the Carrier's rights against the consignee or any other person. Provided that when goods are consigned 'carriage forward' the Trader shall not be required to pay such charges unless the consignee fails to pay after a reasonable demand has been made by the Carrier for payment thereof.

(2) Except where a quotation states otherwise all quotations based on a tonnage rate shall apply to the gross weight unless:

(a) the goods exceed 2.25 cubic metres in measurement per tonne, in which case the tonnage rate shall be computed upon and apply to each measurement of 2.25 cubic metres or any part thereof, or

(b) the size or shape of a Consignment necessitates the use of a vehicle of greater carrying capacity than the weight of the consignment would otherwise require, in which case the tonnage rate shall be computed upon and apply to the carrying capacity of such vehicle as is reasonably required.

(3) Charges shall be payable on the expiry of any time limit previously stipulated and the Carrier shall be entitled to interest at the average of the overdraft interest rates being charged at Lloyds Bank Limited and Barclays Bank Limited current at this time, calculated on a daily basis on all amounts overdue to the Carrier.

9. Liability for Loss and Damage

(1) The Trader shall be deemed to have elected to accept the terms set out in (2) of this Condition unless, before the transit commences, the Trader has agreed in writing that the Carrier shall not be liable for any loss or misdelivery of or damage to goods however or whenever caused and whether or not caused or contributed to directly or indirectly by any act, omission, neglect, default or other wrongdoing on the part of the Carrier.

Figure 22.1 *RHA Conditions of Carriage*

337

(2) Subject to these Conditons the Carrier shall be liable for:
  (i) loss or misdelivery of or damage to livestock, bullion, money, securities, stamps, precious metals or precious stones only if
    (a) the Carrier has specifically agreed in writing to carry any such items and
    (b) the Trader has agreed in writing to reimburse the Carrier in respect of all additional costs which result from the carrying of the said items and
    (c) the loss, misdelivery or damage is occasioned during transit and results from negligent act or omission by the Carrier;
  (ii) any loss or misdelivery or damage to any other goods occasioned during transit unless the same has arisen from, and the Carrier has used reasonable care to minimise the effects of,
    (a) act of God;
    (b) any consequences of war, invasion, act of foreign enemy, hostilities (whether war or not), civil war, rebellion, insurrection, military or usurped power or confiscation, requisition, or destruction of or damage to property by or under the order of any government or public or local authority;
    (c) seizure or forfeiture under legal process;
    (d) error, act, omission, mis-statement or mis-representation by the Trader or other owner of the goods or by servants or agents of either of them;
    (e) inherent liability to wastage in bulk or weight, latent defect or inherent defect, vice or natural deterioration of the goods;
    (f) insufficient or improper packing;
    (g) insufficient or improper labelling or addressing;
    (h) riot, civil commotion, strike, lockout, general or partial stoppage or restraint of labour from whatever cause;
    (i) consignee not taking or accepting delivery within a reasonable time after the Consignment has been tendered.
(3) The Carrier shall not in any circumstances be liable for loss of or damage to goods after transit of such goods is deemed to have ended within the meaning of Condition 6(2) hereof, whether or not caused or contributed to directly or indirectly by any act, omission, neglect, default or other wrongdoing on the part of the Carrier.

10. Fraud

The Carrier shall not in any circumstances be liable in respect of a Consignment where there has been fraud on the part of the Trader or the owner of the goods or the servants or agents of either in respect of that Consignment, unless the fraud has been contributed by the complicity of the Carrier or of any servant of the Carrier acting in the course of his employment.

11. Limitation of Liability

(1) Except as otherwise provided in these Conditions the liability of the Carrier in respect of loss or mis-delivery of or damage to goods shall in all circumstances be limited as follows:
  (a) where loss, misdelivery or damage, however sustained, is in respect of the whole of the Consignment, to a sum calculated at the rate of £800 per tonne on either the gross weight of the Consignment or, where applicable, the tonnage computed in accordance with Condition 8(2)(a) or (b) hereof;
  (b) where loss, misdelivery or damage, however sustained, is in respect of part of the Consignment, to the proportion of the sum ascertained in accordance with (1)(a) of this Condition which the actual value of that part of the Consignment bears to the actual value of the whole of the Consignment.

Provided that:
  (i) nothing in this Condition shall limit the liability of the Carrier to less than the sum of £10;
  (ii) the Carrier shall be entitled to require proof of the value of the whole of the Consignment and of any part thereof lost, misdelivered or damaged;
  (iii) the Trader shall be entitled at any time prior to commencement of transit to give seven days' written notice to the Carrier requiring that the afore mentioned £800 per tonne limit be increased but not so as to exceed the value of the Consignment and in the event of such notice being given the Trader shall within the said seven days agree with the Carrier an increase in the carriage charges in consideration of the said increased limit.

(2) Notwithstanding condition 11(1), the liability of the Carrier in respect of the indirect or consequential loss or damage, however arising and including loss of market, shall not exceed the amount of the carriage charges in respect of the Consignment or the amount of the claimant's proved loss, whichever is the smaller, unless;
  (a) at the time of entering into the Contract with the Carrier the Trader declares to the Carrier a special interest in delivery in the case of loss or damage or of an agreed time limit being exceeded and agrees to pay a surcharge calculated on the amount of that interest, and
  (b) prior to the commencement of transit the Trader has delivered to the Carrier written confirmation of the special interest, agreed time limit and amount of the interest.

12. Indemnity to the Carrier

The Trader shall indemnify the Carrier against:
(1) all consequences suffered by the Carrier (including but not limited to claims, demands, proceedings, fines, penalties, damages, costs, expenses, and loss of or damage to the carrying vehicle and to other goods carried) of any error, omission, misstatement or misrepresentation by the Trader or other owner of the goods or by any servant or agent of either of them, insufficient or improper packing, labelling or addressing of the goods or fraud as in Condition 10;
(2) all claims and demands whatever by whoever made in excess of the liability of the Carrier under these Conditions;
(3) all losses suffered by and claims made against the Carrier in consequence of loss of or damage to property caused by or arising out of the carriage by the Carrier of Dangerous Goods whether or not declared by the Trader as such;
(4) all claims made upon the Carrier by H.M. Customs and Excise in respect of dutiable goods consigned in bond whether or not transit has ended or been suspended.

13. Time Limits for Claims

The Carrier shall not be liable for:
(1) loss from a parcel, package or container or from an unpacked Consignment or for damage to a Consignment or any part of a Consignment unless he is advised thereof in writing otherwise than upon a consignment note or delivery document within three days, and the claim is made in writing within seven days, after the termination of transit;
(2) loss, misdelivery or non-delivery of the whole of a Consignment or of any separate parcel, package or container forming part of a Consignment unless he is advised of the loss, misdelivery or non-delivery in writing otherwise than upon a consignment note or delivery document within twenty-eight days, and the claim is made in writing within forty-two days, after the commencement of transit.

Provided that if the Trader proves that:
  (a) it was not reasonably possible for the Trader to advise the Carrier or make a claim in writing within the time limit applicable and
  (b) such advice or claim was given or made within a reasonable time,
the Carrier shall not have the benefit of the exclusion of liability afforded by this Condition.

14. General Lien

The Carrier shall have a general lien against the owner of the goods for any monies whatever due from the Trader or such other owner to the Carrier. If any such lien is not satisfied within a reasonable time the Carrier may at his absolute discretion sell the goods, or part thereof, as agent for the owner and apply the proceeds towards the monies due and the expenses of the retention, insurance and sale of the goods and shall, upon accounting to the Trader for any balance remaining, be discharged from all liability whatever in respect of the goods.

15. Unreasonable Detention

The Trader shall be liable for the cost of unreasonable detention of any vehicle, trailer, container or sheet but the rights of the Carrier against any other person in respect thereof shall remain unaffected.

16. Computation of Time

In the computation of time where any period provided by these Conditions is seven days or less, Saturdays, Sundays and all statutory public holidays shall be excluded.

17. Impossibility of Performance

The Carrier shall be relieved of its obligation to perform the Contract to the extent that the performance thereof is prevented by failure of the Trader, fire, weather conditions, industrial dispute, labour disturbance or cause beyond the reasonable control of the Carrier.

Road Haulage Association Limited 1982
Registered with Office of Fair Trading, Ref. No. S/91

Figure 22.1 *(continued)*

RHA 1982 Conditions of Carriage

Explanatory Notes
The revised conditions have been produced to meet the requirements of the Restrictive Trade Practices Act 1976 and the Unfair Contract Terms Act 1977 and the opportunity has been taken also to attempt to meet the changing needs of the industry and to achieve greater clarity.

The conditions have been submitted to the office of Fair Trading and have been placed on the public register. Members are now free to operate in accordance with the conditions and they are recommended to do so. The conditions are not compulsory but if any member intends to modify the conditions, he should take the greatest care to ensure that the conditions meet the requirement of 'reasonableness' in the Unfair Contract Terms Act 1977.

The conditions are the copyright of the RHA and may not be used by non-members.

To use the Conditions
A member who intends to trade under the conditions should take the following action:
1. Refer the conditions to his insurers or brokers and secure any necessary adjustments to existing insurance covers.
2. Inform existing customers, in writing, preferably by Recorded Delivery, of the intention to trade subject to the new conditions saying, for example, 'Please note that as from (date) goods will be accepted for carriage only subject to the RHA Conditions of Carriage 1982, copies of which are available free on application' (or 'a copy of which is attached').
3. Inform existing sub-contractors in writing, preferably by Recorded Delivery, that as from (date), goods will be accepted for carriage and sub-contracted only subject to the RHA Conditions of Carriage 1982.
4. Retain Recorded Delivery receipts or, if the above letters are not sent by Recorded Delivery, maintain a permanent record of customers and sub-contractors and the dates on which the letters were dispatched.
5. Print (or overprint) at the foot of the letter headings, quotation forms, confirmation notes, consignment notes, and invoices, etc 'Goods are accepted for carriage and sub-contracted only subject to the RHA Conditions of Carriage 1982 , copies of which are available free on application'.
(NB '1982' should be included to stress that the new conditions and not any previous editions are to apply. However, if existing letter headings etc refer to the current RHA Conditions of Carriage this reference will probably suffice until reprinting of documents becomes necessary.)
6. Maintain a stock of the conditions for issue to customers or sub-contractors as and when required.

Effects of the Conditions
The conditions have been set out in the logical sequence of a haulage operation, starting with definitions and proceeding through the parties to the contract, loading, unloading, transit, etc.

Condition 1. Defines 'Trader', 'Contract', etc. As and when new statutory regulations relevant to the packaging etc of dangerous goods are published, it may be necessary to amend the definition of 'Dangerous Goods'.

Condition 2. Sets out the parties to the contract and authorises the employment by the carrier of other contractors. However, at the behest of the OFT, the names of other contractors (ie sub-contractors) must be advised to the trader on request. Normally such advice will be required to be given before transit commences. The carrier remains responsible as if he had himself performed the whole of the contract but he is entitled to recover from the sub-contractor provided the carrier makes quite clear to the sub-contractor before the sub-contract is entered into that the carriage of goods is sub-contracted subject to the 1982 RHA Conditions of Carriage.

Condition 3. Requires the customer to identify dangerous goods and to package and label them in accordance with the appropriate regulations.

Condition 4. Makes clear that the carrier is not normally required to provide service beyond the usual place of collection and delivery and any additional facilities beyond the assistance of the driver, such as mechanical loading and unloading devices, must be provided for in advance and be the customer's responsibility.

Condition 5. Does not mean that the consignment note is of no value as a receipt. However, because of the difficulty or impossibility of a driver being able to establish the true facts, particularly when goods are in containers or are palletised, the consignment note is not intended to be indisputable evidence of the nature, condition or quantity of the goods.

Condition 6. Defines when transit begins and ends.

Condition 7. Gives the carrier the right to sell undelivered or unclaimed goods, after giving notice to the sender or consignee when transit is at an end.

Condition 8 (1) requires the carrier's charges to be paid by the customer without prejudice to the carrier's rights against the consignee or any other person, but when goods are consigned 'carriage forward' the carrier must do his best to recover 'carriage forward' charges from the consignee before he makes any claim against the trader.

Condition 8 (2) provides for charging for bulk as an alternative to weight and condition 8 (2)(b) provides a new facility for charging for the use of a vehicle of greater carrying capacity than the weight of the consignment.

Condition 8 (3) is new and provides for the charging of interest on overdue accounts.

Condition 9 (1) has been introduced at the behest of the OFT to allow traders to elect to have the goods carried at their own risk.

Condition 9 (2) deals with the carrier's liability for loss or misdelivery of or damage to the goods. Condition 9 (2) (i) is new and deals with goods normally excluded from Goods in Transit insurances. These goods will only be carried if the costs, including insurance, are met by the trader. Condition 9 (2) (ii) acknowledges the carrier's liability relevant to the goods, save for acts of God, war, etc and now additionally in (d) 'error, act, omission', which could provide a carrier with a defence in a case of overloading, for example.

Condition 9 (3) relieves the carrier of liability after the transit is at an end.

Condition 10. Corresponds to the proviso to the 1967 Condition II but, at the behest of the OFT, the carrier no longer avoids liability if the carrier or his agents or servants, acting in the course of their employment, have contributed to the fraud by complicity.

Condition 11. Retains the previous limit of 800 but this now applies per tonne, instead of per ton. The amount remains adequate for all but a few consignments and the proviso (iii) to condition 11 (1) requires this limit to be increased if the trader gives seven days' written notice of such a requirement and agrees an increase in the carriage charges to take into account the increased limit of liability. However, in no case will the carrier's liability in respect of goods exceed the value of those goods.

Condition 11 (2) varies proviso (b) to the 1967 condition 12 and the carrier now has a liability for indirect or consequential loss or damage, including loss of market, to the amount of the carriage charges or the amount of the proved loss, whichever is the smaller, unless the trader has previously declared a special interest in delivery or an agreed time limit and has also agreed special terms. The carrier's Goods in Transit insurance should be extended to cover this risk.

Condition 12. Brings together in one condition the circumstances in which the trader must indemnify the carrier. In previous conditions these matters were dealt with in a number of different conditions.

Condition 12 (2) relates only to the liability of the carrier under these Conditions of Carriage and not to claims in respect of injury to or damage to the property (not being the Goods Carrier) of third parties.

Condition 13. Lays down the time limits for claims but the proviso does permit claims beyond the time limit in specified circumstances.

Condition 14. Gives a general lien for all unpaid monies due from the trader to the carrier. This lien and, in particular, the right of sale should not normally be exercised without legal advice and, even then, care must be taken to ensure that the goods remain in the ownership of the trader or such other party on whose behalf the trader is authorised to contract. In the event of sale of the goods there is an obligation on the carrier to obtain the best possible price under the circumstances of the sale. Further, notwithstanding the words 'be discharged from all liability in respect of the goods', the carrier will be responsible in accordance with the conditions in respect of any damage to the goods before the sale takes place.

Condition 15. Enables the carrier to charge if his vehicles, containers, sheets, etc are unreasonably detained by the trader.

Condition 16. Indicates which days are to be excluded in applying the time limits provided by the conditions.

Condition 17. States the circumstances under which the carrier is relieved of his obligation to perform the contract.

Security

Insurance claims relating to vehicle thefts have increased in recent years and this is a serious problem of concern to insurance companies as well as to vehicle operators and the police. It is important that when away from base drivers should be encouraged to park their vehicles, especially if they are loaded with valuable goods, in guarded security parks. While the number of suitable security parks is limited and they are not conveniently located, it is nevertheless in everybody's interest that vehicles should not be left parked overnight on the roadside or on pieces of wasteland.

Over a number of years the RHA, in addition to the other help which it gives to its members, has taken considerable steps to fight crime involving goods vehicles and their loads. To combat the menace of lorry thefts the Association formed a voluntary organisation called the Vehicle Observer Corps (VOC) which helps the police in tracing stolen vehicles and loads. RHA member firms provide thousands of volunteers to search for reported stolen vehicles and for finding a vehicle with its load intact the Association will pay a VOC member a reward. This payment does not prevent the finder from receiving other awards which might be on offer.

Security Warning

The RHA issues a security warning to members as follows:
1. Make every effort to ensure you are employing honest staff. Take up references over at least the previous five years and be suspicious of unexplained gaps. When checking references by telephone be sure to look in the telephone directory yourself for the number. A number supplied by a dishonest applicant could connect you to his accomplices. A staff enrolment form is available on application to RHA Area Offices and this form or a similar one should be completed.
2. Until you have seen his driving licence and have in your possession his P45 tax form and photograph, do not allow a newly-engaged driver to take out a vehicle.
3. Fit a vehicle immobiliser and/or alarm in as inaccessible a position as possible. Choose one which provides protection without the driver

having to perform any operation which he normally would not have to do to stop his vehicle. Inspect the device frequently.
4. Drivers of vehicles carrying valuable loads should not get out of their cab if stopped. Even if a policeman requests them to do so, they should offer to go to the nearest police station. Bolts on the inside of the cab doors give added protection against hijackers.
5. A trouble-free cash bonus, from which a driver can be fined if he does not observe your security drill, is helpful.
6. Vehicles should not be left unattended for long periods, especially at night. At no time should keys be left in an unattended vehicle. Remember, a stationary vehicle with its windscreen wipers or indicators operating gives a clear signal to any watching criminal that it is his for the taking.
7. Discourage drivers from using the same cafes at the same time each day, particularly where their vehicles are not parked within sight.
8. Starter or ignition switches, security lock keys: remove numbers and keep the keys for each vehicle on a ring which is welded so that they cannot be separated.
9. If a vehicle's keys are lost, change switches and locks. It is much cheaper than losing a load.
10. Invite drivers to report to the police any suspicious circumstances, such as transfer of goods from one vehicle to another without apparent reason, which they might see on their travels, or the registration number of any vehicle which is persistently following them.
11. When disposing of a vehicle, remove the name of your firm so that a thief cannot use it to secure a load by false pretences.

Other Insurance – Business and Premises

While vehicle operators may be particularly concerned about obtaining appropriate insurance cover for their vehicles and the loads carried, they also need adequate insurance protection for other business contingencies in exactly the same way as any other employer or firm. Some of these insurances are listed and briefly described below.

Employers Liability

It is a legal requirement for employers to cover their liabilities for any bodily injury incurred or disease contracted by their employees during or arising from their employment in the employer's business activities. In the case of a haulage contractor the business activities for which cover is required would be both as a haulage contractor and as an owner or occupier of property (ie the business premises).

The minimum cover required by law is £2 million, but usually policies are issued with unlimited liability. Premiums are based on the total payroll of the firm divided into categories (eg clerical staff, drivers, maintenance staff). Extensions to the basic policy can provide cover for employees engaged on private work for directors or senior management, against liability incurred in work/employment related sporting, social, first aid or welfare activities and against liabilities arising through sub-contracting work. Legal costs are recoverable in addition to any compensation awards.

Public Liability

Public liability policies provide cover against legal liability to third parties for bodily injury or illness or loss of or damage to their property arising out of the insured's business activities because of the insured's negligence. The policy can be extended to cover contractual liability which is essential for hauliers operating under printed Conditions of Carriage.

The policy conditions should be such that they cover contingencies not covered by the motor vehicle policies for damage caused by the vehicle or driver. It should also provide cover for liability arising from goods or vehicles being sold, supplied, altered, serviced or repaired.

Indemnity is usually set at a fixed figure per occurrence. A minimum of £500000 is recommended as court awards have reached this figure for injuries to just one person.

Money Cover

Insurance cover can be obtained for the loss of cash, bank notes, currency notes, cheques, postal orders, postage or revenue stamps, national insurance stamps (now available only for limited use by self-employed people), 'holiday with pay' stamps, luncheon vouchers, trading tokens, credit vouchers, travellers' cheques, VAT vouchers and other negotiable instruments.

Extensions to the policy should include assault benefits to employees and other persons lawfully carrying these items and provide cover in respect of damage to and loss from slot machines, franking machines and safes. Premiums are usually based on estimated carryings of money to and from banks in a year.

Credit Insurance

Cover is available for financial loss because of customers defaulting on payment or their insolvency.

Indirect or Consequential Loss

When operating under RHA Conditions of Carriage which exclude liability for indirect or consequential loss and delay, the owner of the goods is not covered under a Goods in Transit policy. Cover is available under indirect or consequential loss insurance at a premium amounting to approximately 20 per cent of the Goods in Transit insurance premium.

Theft

Theft cover provides protection in the event of loss or damage resulting from entry to or exit from property by violent or forceable means. Usually, no cover is provided in such policies against larceny if there is no damage or visible sign of entry.

Petrol Installations and Oil Storage Tanks

Cover for accidental damage to fuel pumps, surface tanks and piping (but not for the loss of the contents, which is covered under the normal theft or fire insurance) is provided by such insurance. It also covers collapse, rupture or weld failure of these items.

Storm Damage

These policies compensate for losses resulting from the entry of water into petrol and diesel tanks as a result of heavy rain storms.

Fire and Special Perils

Cover can be obtained under this form of insurance for damage caused by fire, aircraft falling on the premises, explosion, riot and civil commotion, lightning, impact (including by own vehicles which is important because you cannot claim for this under your own vehicle insurance), and burst pipes.

Particular attention has been drawn to the need for adequate cover in respect of riot and civil commotion following well-publicised disturbances in some of Britain's inner city areas. Unless a fire insurance policy is extended to provide such cover, fire damage by rioters is not covered. It is possible to claim on the local authority under the Riot Damages Act 1886 but this would hardly provide adequate compensation for full reinstatement of premises.

Glass

This cover provides compensation for broken windows and for the cost of temporary boarding up.

Pressure Vessels and Boilers

This type of policy includes provision for the regular and statutory inspection of compressors and air receivers, together with compensation in the event of their explosion or collapse.

Lifting Equipment

The law requires such equipment to be regularly inspected and certificated. Insurance cover can be obtained which provides the inspection and protection against claims arising from the use of hoists, lifts, cranes, fork-lift trucks, pulley blocks, chains, and so on.

Personal Accident

A firm can cover its principals, directors, staff, drivers and maintenance staff against personal accident while driving or while away from the premises (not on the premises). This will provide set levels of regular income for various contingencies or lump-sum damages for loss of limbs. Where the firm is large enough there are special schemes available which have significant tax advantages to the employer.

Medical Expenses

When drivers are required to travel abroad they should be covered for medical expenses incurred in foreign countries, for compensation for taking relatives out to visit them if they are detained in hospital and for bringing the patient back to the UK for further treatment if necessary. Compensation for the loss of drivers' personal effects and baggage can usually be included in this type of policy.

Legal Expenses

Cover may be obtained to protect against the legal costs incurred in contesting unfair dismissal claims and other breach of employment contract issues such as pension rights and matters arising from legislation on equal pay, sex discrimination and race relations. Such policies also usually provide cover for legal expenses incurred in other disputes over liability or responsibility for the action of individuals or firms and for legal expenses following criminal prosecution under any statute. Other schemes are available to cover actual compensation awards.

Loss of Profit

This type of insurance would apply if a transport operator lost his vehicles and warehouse as a result of, for example, a fire. While the fire insurance would cover the cost of damage incurred, a loss of profit policy would compensate the operator for his business losses to competitors during the period of disruption until he got his business back on its feet again.

Usually the policy would provide this cover for at least 12 months and possibly even longer in view of the delays experienced in obtaining new vehicles and in getting premises replanned and rebuilt.

Book Debts

This insurance provides cover for debts caused by loss of records as a result of fire or other physical causes which leave no trace of amounts owed.

Fidelity Guarantee

Fidelity guarantee insurance provides cover against fraud or dishonesty by employees in connection with their employment during or within 18 months of the period of the fraud occurring or termination of the employment, whichever comes first.

Hired-In Plant

This type of policy covers all the liabilities imposed by hiring agreements including damage to the plant (vehicles, fork-lift trucks, cranes, etc), losses in hiring revenue incurred by the owner and claims made by third parties. 'The Contractor's Plant Association Conditions of Hire' also impose such liabilities while hired plant is on the highway. A motor insurance certificate is also required in these instances.

Motor Contingencies

Operators will find that their existing motor policies and other insurances exclude such things as liabilities incurred when hiring-in vehicles and drivers. A motor contingency policy would protect the insured by covering the liabilities of the person or firm owning the vehicle or employing the driver if its insurance was not current or was invalidated for some reason (eg premiums not paid). Similarly, a motor contingency policy would cover employees' use of their own cars on company business. The cover would be for any liability of the employer resulting from the use of the car on his business (eg if the employee had not paid his premium or, for example, if the vehicle was not taxed or not in roadworthy condition thus causing his cover to be invalid), but it would not provide any cover for the liability of the employee himself.

All Risks

This is a policy which could be used to cover any eventuality which is not specifically covered in any other policy held by a business. For example, it would provide compensation for loss or damage to any valuable paintings or antiques on company premises or in directors' offices, the firm's sporting trophies, awards of merit, and so on.

Computers

Policies are available to provide cover for material damage to computer systems resulting from accidental causes, electrical or mechanical breakdown. Such policies also cover consequential loss. Further policies cover software against loss or damage – even coffee spillage – and accidental or malicious erasure of data and provide for the costs of re-establishing information.

Obtaining the Best Cover

When negotiating with an insurance company for cover the premiums and policy conditions should be carefully considered and it is usually advisable to compare the terms offered with those available from other insurers. The services of an insurance broker can be helpful in finding the most satisfactory terms and competitive premium rates. Brokers retained for this purpose will give advice on the terms and conditions, handle claims and generally ensure that you are getting the best possible cover at economic rates. No payment is made to insurance brokers; they obtain their payment by way of commissions or discounts on premiums paid to the insurance company.

Insurance Claims

When making claims on insurance policies there are a number of points which deserve particular attention if a broker has not been engaged to handle these problems. The first and most important point in regard to claims following motor vehicle accidents is that insurance companies must be given immediate notice of an accident to any vehicle for which they supply cover, followed by a properly and fully completed accident report and claim form. A time limit is specified for this, normally seven days.

Completion of Claim Form

If the claim is being made as a result of a vehicle accident the driver, if possible, should complete a claim form giving as much detail of the accident as he can: time, place, conditions of the weather and road, his position on the road and his speed, his direction of travel and the location of identifying objects, and the names and addresses of other parties involved and of any witnesses. A description of events leading up to the occurrence and a sketch of the position of the vehicles involved, both before and after the collision, should also be made on the report form, together with an indication of the damage to vehicles and property. The driver should not make any statement at the scene of the accident admitting or indicating liability (eg by apologising for his mistake).

Processing Claims

Once the insurance company has received the claim form they will get on with the business of deciding where the responsibility for the accident lies and how it should be apportioned. They will arrange for their motor vehicle assessor to examine the damaged vehicle and give permission for the repairs to be carried out if the estimate which the repairer has submitted is acceptable and, of course, if the vehicle is repairable. If the vehicle is beyond economical repair the assessor will authorise a 'write-off'.

Recovery of Uninsured Loss

In the event of the third party being at fault in an accident and the insured having an excess on the policy (by which the insured person volunteers to pay part of the cost of the repairs to their own vehicle, usually the first £25.00 to £250.00, for which there is usually a reduction in premium), he will need to make a claim against the third party for recovery of the excess (usually termed the 'uninsured loss'). The insurance company (or brokers) will deal with this matter if the damage is more than the excess and they are meeting the difference, but if the damage is slight and it is not intended to make a claim on the insurance company, a claim must be made direct to the third party for the 'uninsured loss'.

23: Road Traffic Regulations

Road traffic regulations are very complex and are to be found in a number of Acts and statutory instruments relating to all aspects of road use by pedestrians, cyclists and motorcyclists, motorists and, of course, heavy goods and passenger vehicle drivers and operators. Following a recent major review of road traffic law (published as the *Road Traffic Law Review Report* – commonly referred to as the North Report – available from HMSO) the DTp produced a White Paper *The Road User and the Law* in which it proposed a new 'dangerous driving' offence, tougher measures to deal with drink drivers (with 5 years' imprisonment for drink drivers who cause a death), a new 'endangerment' offence to deal with vandals who place road users' lives at risk by placing dangerous objects on a road or interference with traffic signs or signals (with up to 7 years' imprisonment for convicted offenders), a new tougher driving test to be taken by bad drivers before their licences are restored following disqualification, the introduction of new technology to improve the detection of speeding and traffic light offences.

Many of the particular legal requirements relating to the use of vehicles on the road are identified in the Highway Code along with much useful advice on driving and road usage although it should be remembered that the Code is intended for guidance and is not, in itself, a book of traffic law. Among more recent provisions included in the Code are such topics as child safety in cars, alcohol and the road user and the use of in-car telephones.

In this chapter some of the more important aspects of traffic regulations affecting goods vehicle operators are covered.

Speed Limits

Three levels of speed limit are imposed on road users:
1. Limits applying to particular roads.
2. Limits applying to particular classes of vehicle.
3. Temporary speed limits introduced for special reasons such as in potentially hazardous situations and in times of fuel shortages.

Speed Limits on Roads

On roads where street lights are positioned at intervals of not more than 200 yards (defined as a 'restricted' road), an overall speed limit of 30mph applies to all classes of vehicle unless alternatively lower speeds are indicated by signs or unless the vehicle itself is subject to a lower limit by reason of its construction or its use. In some instances, speeds in excess of 30mph are permitted on such roads and this is indicated by appropriate signs showing the higher maximum limits.

The present maximum speed limits on roads outside built-up areas are 60mph on single-carriageway roads and 70mph on dual-carriageway roads and motorways, except where specified temporary or permanent lower limits are in force.

Advisory speed limits on motorways should be observed. These are shown by illuminated signs and indicate hazardous situations and road works ahead and by temporary speed limits signs at road works. The amber flashing warning lights positioned on the nearside of motorways (two lights, one above the other) indicate an advisory maximum speed of 30mph until the danger is passed. Mandatory speed limits may also been seen at roadworks sites on motorways (indicated by white signs with black letters and a red border). Failure to comply with these mandatory motorway speed warning signs can result in prosecution.

Speed Limits on Vehicles

Vehicles are restricted to certain maximum speeds according to their construction, weight or use but when travelling on roads which themselves are subject to speed restrictions it is the lowest permitted speed (ie of the vehicle or of the section of road) which must be observed.

Private cars
Motor cars and dual-purpose vehicles must observe the 70mph limit on motorways and dual-carriageway roads and 60mph on single-carriageways and the appropriate lower limits on all other occasions.

Car-Derived Vans
Light vans derived from private-type motor cars (ie car-derived vans which also includes car-derived open-back, pick-up-trucks) may travel at the same speeds as private cars on these roads (ie 70mph on motorways and dual-carriageways and 60mph on other roads unless lower limits are in force).

Private cars and car-derived vans towing trailers
The speed limit for motor cars (including dual-purpose vehicles), car-derived vans and motor caravans towing trailers and caravans is 50mph on single-carriageway roads and 60mph on dual-carriageways and motorways. There is no longer any legal requirement for such vehicles towing trailers and caravans to display a '50' mph plate at the rear.

Light Goods Vehicles
Light goods vehicles (apart from car-derived vans mentioned above) for the purposes of speed limits are vehicles up to and including 7.5 tonnes maximum laden weight (mlw). Speed limits for rigid vehicles in this category are 50mph on single-carriageway roads, 60mph on dual-carriageway roads and 70mph on motorways.

The maximum speed for rigid vehicles up to 7.5 tonnes maximum laden weight drawing trailers and articulated vehicles up to 7.5 tonnes maximum laden weight on single-carriageway roads is 50mph and on dual-carriageways and motorways the limit is 60mph.

Heavy Goods Vehicles
There is no distinction in terms of maximum speed between rigid and

articulated heavy goods vehicles and those with drawbar trailers. Heavy goods vehicles are those over 7.5 tonnes maximum laden weight (mlw) which, under other regulations, are required to display rear reflective markers so making them readily identifiable for speed limit enforcement purposes. Speed limits for all vehicles in this category are 40mph on single-carriageway roads, 50mph on dual-carriageway roads and 60mph on motorways.

Passenger Vehicles
The maximum speed limit for buses and coaches over 3.05 tonnes unladen weight and with more than eight passenger seats is dependent upon the overall length. For those not exceeding 12 metres in length the limits are 50mph on single-carriageway roads, 60mph on dual-carriageway roads and 70mph on motorways. For those over 12 metres in length the limits are 50mph on single-carriageway roads and 60mph on dual-carriageways and motorways.

NB: In all cases mentioned above, it must be stressed that these limits only apply where no lower limit is in force.

Special Types Vehicles
Vehicles operating outside the C and U regulations for the purposes of carrying abnormal indivisible loads come within scope of the Special Types General Order (STGO) as described in Chapter 19 and must conform to specified speed limits depending on their category. These speed limits are stated on p 284 but are repeated here with other speed limits for ease of reference:

Vehicle category	*Motorways*	*Dual-carriageways*	*Single-carriageways*
Category 1	60mph	50mph	40mph
Category 2	40mph	35mph	30mph
Category 3	30mph	25mph	20mph

NB: The category 3 speed limits also apply when wide loads between 4.3 metres and 6.1 metres are being carried on Category 1 and 2 Special Types vehicles.

Works Trucks and Industrial Tractors
The maximum speed limit for works trucks and industrial tractors is 18mph but the latter are not permitted on motorways.

Agricultural Vehicles
Agricultural vehicles are limited to 40mph. They are not permitted on motorways.

Motor Tractors/Locomotives
Where such vehicles (including their trailers) are fitted with springs and

wings their maximum permitted speeds are 40mph on motorways and 30mph on other roads. When they do not have springs and wings the maximum speed limit is 20mph on all roads.

Track-Laying Vehicles
These vehicles are limited to maximum speeds of 20mph or 5mph depending on their construction (ie whether they have springs and wheels fitted with pneumatic or resilient tyres – see below).

Vehicles with Non-Pneumatic Tyres
Vehicles with resilient, non-pneumatic (ie solid) tyres are restricted to a maximum speed of 20mph on all roads. Those with non-resilient tyres (eg traction engines) are restricted to 5mph – see also above: track-laying vehicles.

Emergency Vehicles
Fire, police and ambulance service vehicles are exempt from all speed limits if, by observing the speed limit, they would be hampered in carrying out their duties. However, drivers of such vehicles have a duty to take particular care when exceeding statutory limits and could face proceedings if an accident results while exceeding the limits.

Table of Vehicle Speed Limits

	Motorway mph	Dual carriageway mph	Other roads mph
Private cars			
– solo	70	70	60
– towing caravan or trailer	60	60	50
Buses and coaches			
– not over 12 metres length	70	60	50
– over 12 metres length	60	60	50
Goods vehicles			
Car-derived vans			
– solo	70	70	60
– towing caravan/trailer	60	60	50
Not Exceeding 7.5 tonnes mlw			
– solo	70	60	50
– articulated	60	60*	50
– draw-bar	60	60*	50
Over 7.5 tonnes mlw			
– solo	60	50	40
– articulated	60	50	40
– draw-bar	60	50	40

Note : mlw means maximum laden weight (ie maximum gross weight for a vehicle as specified in Construction and Use Regulations).

* In Northern Ireland the speed limit for vehicles in these two categories is only 50mph.

NB: See above for speed limits for Special Types and other vehicles.

Lighting-Up Time

All mechanically-propelled vehicles must display front and rear position lights between sunset and sunrise and headlamps (where required by regulations) during the hours of darkness, which is from half-an-hour *after* sunset to half-an-hour *before* sunrise (see Chapter 12 for lighting details) and during daytime hours when visibility is seriously reduced.

Night Parking

Goods vehicles not exceeding 1525kg unladen do not require lights at night when standing on restricted roads (ie on which a 30mph speed limit – or lower limit – is in force), if they are parked either in a recognised parking place (ie outlined by lamps or traffic signs) or on the nearside, close to and parallel to the kerb, facing the direction of travel and with no part of the vehicle within 10 metres of a junction (ie on the same side as the vehicle or on the other side of the road). On any road where these conditions are not met lights must be shown (ie front and rear position lights).

All goods vehicles exceeding 1525kg unladen weight must display lights at all times when parked on roads between sunset and sunrise. Trailers and vehicles with projecting loads must not be left standing on roads at night without lights.

Vehicles should be parked on the nearside of the road when left standing overnight except when parked in a one-way street or in a recognised parking place and they must not cause obstruction.

Increasing attention is being given by the police and local authorities to drivers sleeping overnight in heavy vehicles with sleeper cabs while parked in lay-bys. Drivers should be warned against this practice which is usually considered illegal on the grounds that the vehicle is causing an obstruction. A similar situation applies when draw-bar trailers and semi-trailers are left in lay-bys.

Stopping, Loading and Unloading

Leaving Engine Running

Whenever a driver leaves his vehicle on a road, the engine must be stopped (except in the case of fire, police or ambulance service vehicles or when the engine is used to drive auxiliary equipment or for providing power for batteries to drive such equipment).

Obstruction

A vehicle must not be left in a position where it is likely to cause obstruction or danger to other road users, eg near an entrance to premises, near a school, a zebra crossing or a road junction (see pp 357–8 for full list).

Trailers must not be left on a road when detached from the towing vehicle.

Loading and Unloading Restrictions

Vehicles must not stop or park on clearways to load or unload. In some areas loading and unloading restrictions are indicated by yellow lines

painted on the kerb at right angles to it (Figure 23.1) as follows:
1. A single yellow line at intervals indicates restrictions during certain hours, for example, peak hours.
2. Double yellow lines at intervals indicate a complete ban on loading and unloading during the whole of the working day, for example, 8 am to 6.30 pm.
3. Three yellow lines at intervals indicate a ban at all times.

The times quoted vary from place to place but where this type of road marking is used there is always a sign stating the hours during which loading and unloading must not take place.

Parking Meter Zones
Loading and unloading in parking meter zones during the working day (the times are indicated on signs) is not allowed unless a gap between meter areas or a vacant meter space can be found. A vehicle using a meter space for loading or unloading can stop for up to 20 minutes without having to pay the meter fee (this does not apply when parking for any purpose other than loading or unloading the vehicle).

Waiting and Parking Restrictions
Single, double or broken yellow lines painted on the road parallel to the kerb apply to waiting and parking at various times, but they do not indicate a ban on loading or unloading and the same applies to 'no waiting' prohibitions indicated by 'no waiting' signs (see Highway Code for full details of waiting and parking restrictions).

Motorway Driving

Use of Lanes

Goods vehicles with operating weights in excess of 7.5 tonnes and vehicles drawing trailers (and certain other heavy motor cars not included in the categories mentioned) must not use the outer or offside lane of three- and four-lane motorways. Following a High Court appeal ruling goods vehicles which are over 3050kg unladen weight but which do not exceed 7.5 tonnes gross weight must not use the third lane of motorways.

On some steep slopes of two-lane motorway sections heavy goods vehicles (ie over 7.5 tonnes) are banned from using the outside lane; these bans are clearly signposted on the approaches to the appropriate section indicating the extent of the banned section and the vehicles prohibited from using the outer lane.

It is intended in the next edition of the Highway Code to emphasise that the middle and third lanes of motorways are to be used for overtaking only and are not for normal cruising.

Temporary Speed Limits

Where carriageway repairs take place on motorways or where contraflow traffic systems are used an *advisory* 50mph speed limit is usually imposed. This is considered by the police to be a maximum speed, and they may prosecute drivers found speeding in these sections for a 'driving without

23: ROAD TRAFFIC REGULATIONS

due consideration...' type of offence. However, it is becoming more common for a *mandatory* temporary speed limit to be imposed in such cases and where drivers are detected speeding in these sections they will be prosecuted for this offence.

Speed Limits for Recovery Vehicles on Motorways

For the purposes of motorway speed limits recovery vehicles may travel at up to 60mph. This follows a High Court ruling (on an appeal by the Director of Public Prosecutions) that such vehicles are constructed to carry a load and therefore may travel at the same maximum speed as other heavy goods vehicles. Previously such vehicles were required to observe the 40mph maximum limit applicable to vehicles classified as motor tractors, light and heavy locomotives.

Other Vehicles on Motorways

Light and heavy locomotives which do not comply with C and U Regulations, dump trucks, engineering plant and vehicles for export which do not comply with the C and U Regulations may be driven on motorways provided they are capable of attaining a speed of 25mph on the flat when unladen and so long as they are not drawing a trailer.

Learner Drivers on Motorways

Learner drivers are not allowed to drive on motorways, but holders of provisional hgv driving licences may drive heavy goods vehicles on motorways provided they hold a full ordinary licence and are accompanied by a qualified driver.

Lights on Motorways

Hazard Warning
Motorways are equipped with amber hazard warning lights located on the nearside verge and placed at one-mile intervals. When these lights flash, vehicles must slow down to an advisory 30mph until the danger which the lights are indicating has passed.

Rural Motorways
Rural motorways have amber lights, placed at not more than two-mile intervals and usually located in the central reservation, which flash and indicate either a maximum speed limit or, by means of red flashing lights, that one or more lanes ahead are closed. The speed limit indicated applies to *all* lanes of the motorway and should not be exceeded.

Urban Motorways
Urban motorways have overhead warning lights placed at 1000-yard intervals. Amber lights flash in the event of danger ahead and indicate a maximum speed limit or an arrow indicating that drivers should change to another lane. If red lights flash above any or all of the lanes, vehicles in those lanes must stop at the signal. It is as much of an offence to fail to stop at these red lights as it is to ignore automatic traffic signals.

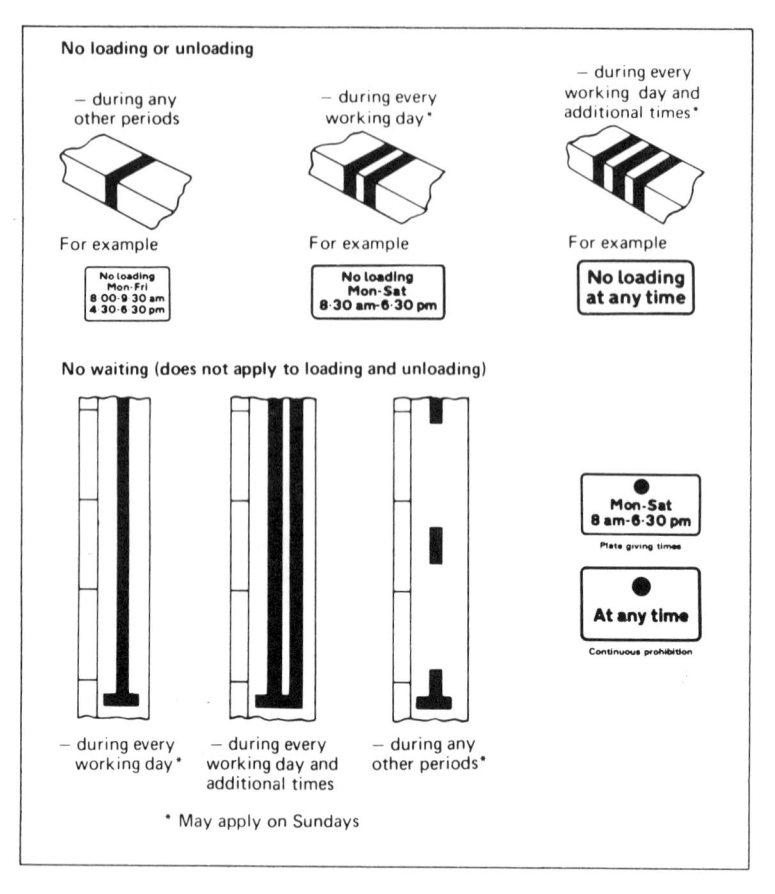

THE TRANSPORT MANAGER'S AND OPERATOR'S HANDBOOK

Figure 23.1 *Waiting and loading restriction road markings and plates giving times*

Motorway Fog Code

To help drivers avoid the grave hazards of fog on motorways and to meet the special dangers of mixed traffic, an eight-point drivers' Code applies as follows:

Fog Code
1. Slow down; keep a safe distance. You should always be able to pull up within your range of vision.
2. Don't hang on to someone else's tail lights; it gives you a false sense of security.
3. Watch your speed; you may be going much faster than you think.
4. Remember that if you are in a heavy vehicle you need a good deal longer to pull up.
5. Warning signals are there to help and protect. Do observe them.
6. See and be seen – use headlights or fog lamps.
7. Check and clean windscreen, lights, reflectors and windows whenever you can.

23: ROAD TRAFFIC REGULATIONS

8. If you must drive in fog, allow more time for your journey.

Segregation
1. Drivers of cars, light goods vehicles and coaches should move out of the left-hand lane when it is safe to do so but not if they will soon be turning off the motorway. When they want to leave the motorway, they should start their move to the left well before the exit. They should be prepared to miss the exit if they cannot reach it safely.
2. Drivers of heavy lorries should keep to the left-hand lane; but be ready to let other drivers into the lane at entry points and well before exit points.

The Code and the Segregation advice, which can be found in the Highway Code, apply on motorways throughout Great Britain whenever there is fog.

Hazard Warning

Four-way direction-indicator flasher systems fitted to vehicles may be legally used to indicate that a vehicle is temporarily obstructing the road or any part of the carriageway either while loading or unloading, when broken down or for emergency reasons (previously their use was only permitted in emergencies). Further details of vehicle lighting requirements are to be found in Chapter 12.

Lights During Daytime

If visibility during the daytime is poor, because of adverse weather conditions, drivers of all moving vehicles must switch on both front position lights and headlamps or front position lights and matched fog and spot lights. This applies in the case of heavy rain, mist, spray, fog or snow or similar conditions. When vehicles are equipped with rear fog lights (see p 198) these should be used when the other vehicle lights are switched on in poor daytime visibility conditions. Further details of vehicle lighting requirements are to be found in Chapter 12.

Parking

Drivers who park their vehicles in a position which causes danger or obstruction to other road users can be prosecuted. The Highway Code lists the following as being areas where danger or obstruction may be caused by a parked vehicle:
(a) in a 'no-parking' area
(b) on a clearway
(c) alongside yellow lines
(d) where there are double white lines
(e) near a road junction
(f) near a bend
(g) near the brow of a hill
(h) near a humpback bridge
(i) near a level crossing
(j) near a bus stop

(k) near a school entrance
(l) near a pedestrian crossing
(m) on the right-hand side of the road at night
(n) where the vehicle would obscure a traffic sign
(o) on a narrow road
(p) on fast main roads and motorways
(q) near entrances and exits used by emergency service vehicles
(r) near road works
(s) alongside or opposite another parked vehicle.

This list does not leave many alternative places for parking for the goods vehicle driver who has collections or deliveries to make particularly in town, and for this reason drivers should be instructed to take reasonable care when parking in congested areas to avoid causing obvious obstruction or danger. For example, drivers should not double park, block entrances and exits of business or private premises, park near dangerous junctions or near pedestrian crossings, as well as avoiding the areas mentioned above.

Bus-only Lanes

Traffic lanes on urban roads reserved solely for use by buses are a common feature in many towns and cities. Uniform traffic signs and road markings indicate bus lanes. A single wide solid white line is used to mark the edge of the reserved lanes. Upright signs incorporating international symbols combined with arrows will show to other traffic the number of lanes available for their use. When the signs and restrictions are in operation on a road, all other vehicles, except for pedal cycles (and taxis if signed to this effect), are prohibited from using the bus lane.

Level Crossings

Most level crossings are now fitted with automatic half-barrier crossing gates and appropriate warning signs are given in advance. When a train is approaching such crossings, red lights flash and a bell rings to warn drivers and pedestrians. Once these warnings start the barrier comes down immediately, and drivers should not zig-zag around the barriers. When the train has passed, the barriers will rise unless another train is following, in which case the warnings will continue.

Drivers of vehicles which are large or slow (ie with their loads that are more than 9ft 6in [2.9 metres] wide or more than 55ft [16.8 metres] long or weighing more than 38 tonnes gross or incapable of a speed of more than 5mph) wishing to cross one of these crossings must, before attempting to cross, obtain permission to do so from the signalman by using the special telephone which is provided at the crossing. Failure to do this is an offence. In the event of a vehicle becoming stuck on the crossing the driver should advise the signalman immediately by using the telephone.

Weight-Restricted Roads and Bridges

Where signs indicate that a particular section of road or a bridge is restricted to vehicles not exceeding a specified weight limit or axle weight limit, unless otherwise expressly stated, the weight limit shown relates to the actual weight of the vehicle or to an individual axle of the vehicle not the relevant plated weights. Where doubt exists about any particular sign it

23: ROAD TRAFFIC REGULATIONS

is advisable to consult the local authority responsible for its erection and to determine the precise wording of the Traffic Management Order under which authority the sign would have been erected.

Owner Liability

Under the Road Traffic Act responsibility for payment of fixed penalty fines or excess parking charges rests with the registered vehicle owner (ie the keeper of the vehicle, not necessarily the legal owner), if the driver who committed the offence cannot be identified or found. The registered owner of the vehicle is sent details of the alleged offence and is obliged to pay the fine or submit a Statutory Statement of Ownership in which he states whether he was the vehicle owner at the time of the alleged offence (in which case he should name the driver), had ceased to be the owner at that time or had not yet become the owner at that time. Where the person was not the owner he must give the name of the previous owner or the new owner to whom he transferred the vehicle if he knows it.

When a vehicle is hired out for less than six months, and such an incident arises, the hiring company can declare that the vehicle was on hire and send a copy of the hiring agreement together with a signed statement of liability from the hirer accepting responsibility for the fine or excess parking charge. Such a clause is normally included in the hiring agreements which the hirer signs. Failure to pay a fixed penalty or excess charge, or to give information as required by the police in such matters, can result in a fine of up to £400 on conviction.

Fixed Penalties

In order to reduce the pressure on the courts, a system of fixed penalties exists by which both traffic wardens and the police can issue fixed penalty notices requiring the vehicle driver or owner to pay the fixed penalty or to elect to have the case dealt with in court in the normal way. The fixed penalty system operates on two levels of non-endorsable offences (mainly dealt with by traffic wardens) and driving licence endorsable offences which only the police can deal with since traffic wardens have no general authority to request the production of driving licences (see below).

Non-endorsable Offences

For non-endorsable offences a white ticket/notice (penalty £16.00) is issued either to the driver if present or is fixed to the vehicle windscreen. Since no driving licence penalty points are involved for such offences there is no requirement to examine the licence. Traffic wardens have authority to issue fixed penalty tickets for the following non–endorsable offences:
1. leaving a vehicle parked at night without lights or reflectors
2. waiting, loading, unloading or parking in prohibited areas
3. unauthorised parking in controlled parking zone areas
4. contravention of the Vehicles (Excise) Act 1971 by not displaying a current licence disc
5. making 'U' turns in unauthorised places
6. lighting offences with moving vehicles
7. driving the wrong way in a one-way street
8. overstaying on parking meters, returning to parking places before the expiry of the statutory period, or feeding meters to obtain longer parking facilities than those permitted in a meter zone

9. parking on pavements or verges by commercial vehicles exceeding 3050kg unladen weight (see p 364).

Endorsable Offences

The extended fixed penalty system covering driving licence endorsable offences which can be dealt with only by the police (ie not traffic wardens who have no general authority to examine driving licences) came into force from 1 October 1986. The extended scheme includes some 250 driving and vehicle use offences divided between those which are driving licence endorsable offences and those which are non-endorsable offences as described above. For endorsable offences a yellow ticket/notice with a different level of penalty applies as described below.

For driving licence endorsable offences the police issue a yellow ticket/notice for which a penalty of £32.00 is payable. These tickets are only issued after the police officer has seen the offender's driving licence and has established that the addition of penalty points appropriate to the current offence, when added to any points already on the licence, will not result in automatic disqualification under the 12-point totting-up procedure. If this is the case, the ticket will be issued and the driving licence will be confiscated (an official receipt will be given) being returned to the holder with the appropriate penalty points added when the penalty has been paid.

If the offender does not have his driving licence with him at the time, the penalty notice will not be issued on the spot but will be issued at the police station when the driving licence is produced there within seven days – subject again to the number of penalty points already on the licence.

Where the addition of further points in respect of the current offence would take the total of penalty points on the licence to 12 or more thus leading to automatic disqualification, the ticket will not be issued and the offence will be dealt with by the offender being summoned to appear in court in the normal manner.

Payment or Election to Court

Fixed penalty notices must be paid in accordance with the instructions on the notice and within the specified time limit of 28 days. Alternatively, the offender can elect to have the charge dealt with by a court so he has the opportunity of defending himself against the charge or, even if he accepts that he is guilty of the offence, of putting forward mitigating circumstances which he feels may lessen any penalty which may be imposed.

The address of the fixed penalty office to which the penalty payment should be sent is given in the notice together with instructions for making application for a court hearing if this course of action is chosen.

Failure to Pay

With both the white and yellow ticket systems, failure to pay the statutory penalty within the requisite period of 28 days will result in the offender being automatically considered guilty and the penalties being increased by 50 per cent (ie to £24.00 and £48.00 respectively). These increased amounts become fines and continued non-payment will lead to the arrest of the

23: ROAD TRAFFIC REGULATIONS

offender and appearance before a court in the district where the alleged offence was committed. This could be many miles from where the offender lives and may necessitate him being transported there under arrest and possibly held overnight.

Summary of Offences

Among the offences covered by the extended scheme are the following:

White Ticket (non-endorsable)
1. Not wearing seat belt.
2. Driving and stopping offences (reversing, parking, towing, etc).
3. Contravention of traffic signs, box junctions, bus lanes, etc.
4. Contravening driving prohibitions.
5. Vehicle defects (speedometer, wipers, horn etc).
6. Contravening exhaust and noise regulations.
7. Exceeding weight limits (overloading, etc).
8. Contravention of vehicle lighting requirements.
9. Contravention of vehicle excise requirements.

Yellow Ticket (endorsable)
1. Speeding.
2. Contravention of motorway regulations.
3. Defective vehicle components (brakes, steering, tyres, etc) and vehicle in dangerous condition.
4. Contravention of traffic signs.
5. Insecure and dangerous loads.
6. Leaving vehicles in dangerous positions.
7. Contravention of pedestrian rights.

This is only a summary of a very extensive list of offences included within the scheme.

Traffic Wardens

In addition to the powers of traffic wardens to issue fixed penalty tickets as described in the previous section, they also have powers to act as parking attendants at street parking places, to carry out special traffic control duties, to inquire into the identity of drivers of vehicles, to act in connection with the custody of vehicles at car pounds and to act as school crossing patrols.

It is *only* when on duty at 'car pounds' that traffic wardens have the power to request production of a driving licence.

Drink-Driving and Breath Tests

It is an offence to drive or attempt to drive a motor vehicle when the level of alcohol in the breath is more than 35 microgrammes per 100 millilitres of breath, where this can be monitored by means of an initial breath test (conducted on the spot when the driver is stopped) and later substantiated by a test on a breath-testing machine (ie Lion Intoximeter) at a police station (see also text in Chapter 6 on this subject). The breath/alcohol limit mentioned above equates to the blood/alcohol limit of 80 milligrammes of alcohol in 100 millilitres of blood or the urine/alcohol limit of 107 milligrammes of alcohol in 100 millilitres of urine.

If the person suspected of an alcohol-related offence cannot, due to health reasons, produce a breath sample or if a breath test shows a reading of not more than 50 microgrammes of alcohol per 100 millilitres of breath they may request a blood test.

Prosecution will follow a failure to pass the test which will result in a fine or imprisonment and automatic disqualification from driving. Failure to submit to a breath test and to a blood or urine test are serious offences and drivers will find themselves liable to heavy penalties on conviction and potentially long-term disqualification or driving licence endorsement (endorsements for such offences remain on a driving licence for 11 years – see page 106).

The police *do not* have powers to carry out breath tests at random but they *do have* powers to enter premises to require a breath test from a person suspected of driving while impaired through drink or drugs or who has been driving or been in charge of a vehicle which has been involved in an accident in which another person has been injured.

Pedestrian Crossings

There are two types of pedestrian crossing. Zebra crossings are bounded on either side by areas indicated by zig-zag road markings in which overtaking, parking and waiting are prohibited. The marked areas extend to about 60ft on either side of the crossing. A 'give-way' line 3ft from the crossing is the point at which vehicles must stop to allow pedestrians to cross. Pelican crossings are controlled by traffic lights which vehicle drivers must observe and pedestrians should cross only when the green light signal indicates that they should do so (at some Pelican crossings an audible bleeper is provided to assist blind people to cross with safety). With either type of crossing, if there is a central refuge for pedestrians each side of the refuge is considered to be a separate crossing.

Builder's Skips

Provisions are contained in the Highways Act 1971 to control the placing of builders' skips on the road. Before such a skip is placed on the road, permission must be obtained from the local authority. This will be given subject to conditions relating to the size of the skip, its siting, the manner in which it is made visible to oncoming traffic, the care and disposal of its contents, the manner in which it is lit or guarded and its removal when the period of permission ends.

Owners must ensure that skips carry proper reflective markers (see p 202), are properly lit at night, are clearly marked with their name and telephone number or address, and that they are moved as soon as is practical after they have been filled.

The police and highway authorities have powers to re-position or remove a skip from the road and recover the cost of doing so from the owner, and a fine may be imposed.

For the purposes of the Act the definition of a builder's skip is 'a container designed to be carried on a road vehicle and to be placed on a highway or other land for the storage of builders' materials, or for the removal and disposal of builders' rubble, waste, household and other rubbish or earth'.

Abandoned Motor Vehicles

It is an offence under the Refuse Disposal (Amenity) Act 1978 to abandon a motor vehicle or any part of, or part removed from, a motor vehicle in the open air or on any other open land forming part of a highway. Such offences, on conviction, can lead to fines of up to £200 for a first offence and up to £400 and a term of imprisonment for a subsequent offence.

Vehicles which are illegally or obstructively parked can be removed and statutory charges imposed as follows:
1. Removal from a motorway – £80.00.
2. Removal from other roads and loading areas in London – £80.00.
3. Removal from other roads and loading areas elsewhere – £75.00.

The additional charge for storage of a removed vehicle is £10.00 per day and £50.00 is charged for its disposal. Removed and impounded vehicles are not released until all relevant charges have been paid.

Wheel Clamps

Vehicles which are illegally parked or which cause obstruction, in a wide area of central London, will be immobilised by the Metropolitan Police or by contractors on their behalf. A wheel clamp, known as the 'Denver Boot', will be fixed to one wheel of the vehicle thereby preventing it being driven away. A notice will be stuck to the vehicle giving the driver notice of the offence committed and instructions for securing release from the clamp.

It is an offence to try to remove a wheel clamp or to attempt to drive off with one fitted. Vehicle drivers finding a clamp fixed to their vehicle must go to the Metropolitan Police pound in Hyde Park underground car park and request removal of the clamp. Both a removal charge (currently £30.00) and a fixed penalty (currently £16.00) have to be paid before the clamp is removed.

Lorry Routes and Bans

Local authorities identify preferred routes for heavy vehicles passing through their areas and display on them appropriate signs. The type of sign shown in Figure 23.2 is used to:
1. Mark the most suitable route between dock areas and the nearest convenient connection with the primary route/motorway network.
2. Mark a suitable alternative route at any place on the primary route network where drivers of goods vehicles might be advised to avoid a particular part of that route, but where it is not appropriate to direct all traffic on to the alternative route, or to the primary route itself.
3. Mark routes from the primary/motorway route system to local inland centres which generate a high level of goods vehicle traffic (industrial estates, for example).

Certain areas and especially London impose bans on the movement of goods vehicles and the parking of goods vehicles. These bans and restrictions are always marked with appropriate signs and operators are advised to ensure that their drivers observe them.

London Bans

Vehicles more than 12.2 metres long are banned from Central London unless they are delivering to or collecting from specific addresses within the Central London area.

Vehicles over 16.5 tonnes pmw are prohibited from travelling along many routes through Greater London at certain times unless the operator holds an exemption permit (issued under the London Boroughs Transport Scheme) which must be carried on the vehicle and the vehicle must display exemption plates at the front and rear in a conspicuous position. The routes on which the ban applies are well signposted and the times at which it applies are also given on the signs.

It is an offence for a driver of a goods vehicle over 16.5 tonnes pmw to travel on the banned routes at the relevant times unless a valid exemption permit has been issued and is carried on the vehicle. Application for exemption permits and vehicle plates should be made to the London Boroughs Transport Committee, Rooms 301–305, Hampton House, 20 Albert Embankment, London SE1 7TJ. Tel: 071-582 6220.

The London ban applies at the following times:
Sunday   at all times
Monday to Friday   midnight to 7am and 9pm to midnight
Saturday   midnight to 7am and 1pm to midnight

Parking on Verges

The Road Traffic Act 1988 (sections 19 and 20) make it an offence to park a heavy commercial vehicle (ie a vehicle over 7.5 tonnes maximum laden weight including the weight of any trailer) on the verge of a road, on any land between two carriageways or on a footway whether the vehicle is totally parked on those areas or only partially so.

There are exemptions to this: when a vehicle is parked on such areas with the permission of a police officer in uniform, or in the event of an emergency, such as for the purposes of saving life or extinguishing fire, or for loading and unloading, provided that the loading or unloading could not have been properly performed if the vehicle had not been so parked and that the vehicle was not left unattended while it was parked.

Operators should, however, remember that it was made an offence under the Road Traffic Act 1972 to drive a heavy commercial vehicle on a pavement or cause obstruction of the pavement in urban areas with such a vehicle. This provision has since been supplemented by the Road Traffic Act 1974 which extends the restriction to vehicles other than heavy commercial vehicles – in other words, light goods vehicles and private cars.

It remains an offence (under the Road Traffic Act 1988 s34) for any person to drive a motor vehicle on to common land, moorland or other land which does not form part of a road or on any footpath or bridleway, beyond a distance of 15 yards except where legal permission exists to do so but then only for the purpose of parking or to meet an emergency such as saving life or extinguishing fire.

Overloaded Vehicles

It is an offence to drive an overloaded vehicle on a road. Under the Road

23: ROAD TRAFFIC REGULATIONS

Traffic Act 1988 (sections 70 and 71) an authorised examiner or police officer may prohibit the use of an overloaded vehicle on the road until the weight is reduced to within legal limits and may direct, in writing, the person in charge of an overloaded vehicle to remove the vehicle to a specified place. See also page 152.

The government is currently committed to increasing enforcement of vehicle weight regulations and proposes to weigh at least 100000 heavy vehicles annually. It intends that penalties for serious or persistent offenders should be such as to deter others from overloading their vehicles.

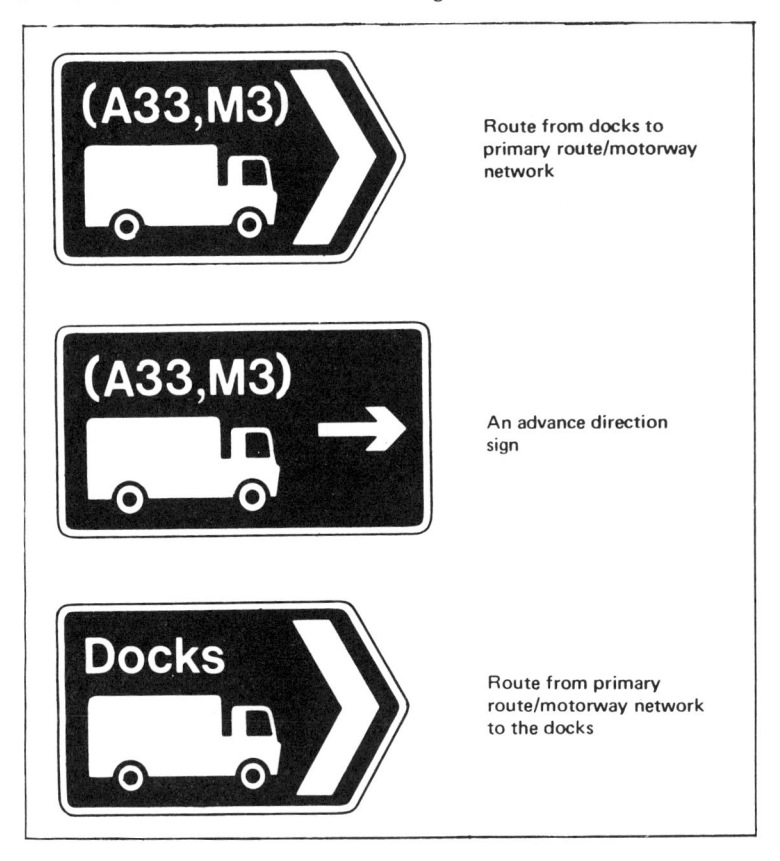

Figure 23.2 *Signs to be used in connection with the routeing of goods vehicles to avoid congested and unsuitable areas*

A driver may be instructed to drive for a distance of up to five miles to a weighbridge for the weight of his vehicle and load to be checked. If he is directed to drive more than five miles to the weighbridge and his vehicle is found to be within the maximum permitted weights then a claim may be made against the appropriate highway authority for the costs incurred.

The maximum fine for an overloading offence is £2000 but any one instance of an overloaded vehicle could result in conviction for more than one offence, each of which carries this maximum penalty. Subsequent convictions for such offences could lead to higher fines. Convictions for overloading offences also jeopardise the operator's licence (see also Chapter 9 on vehicle weights and overloading).

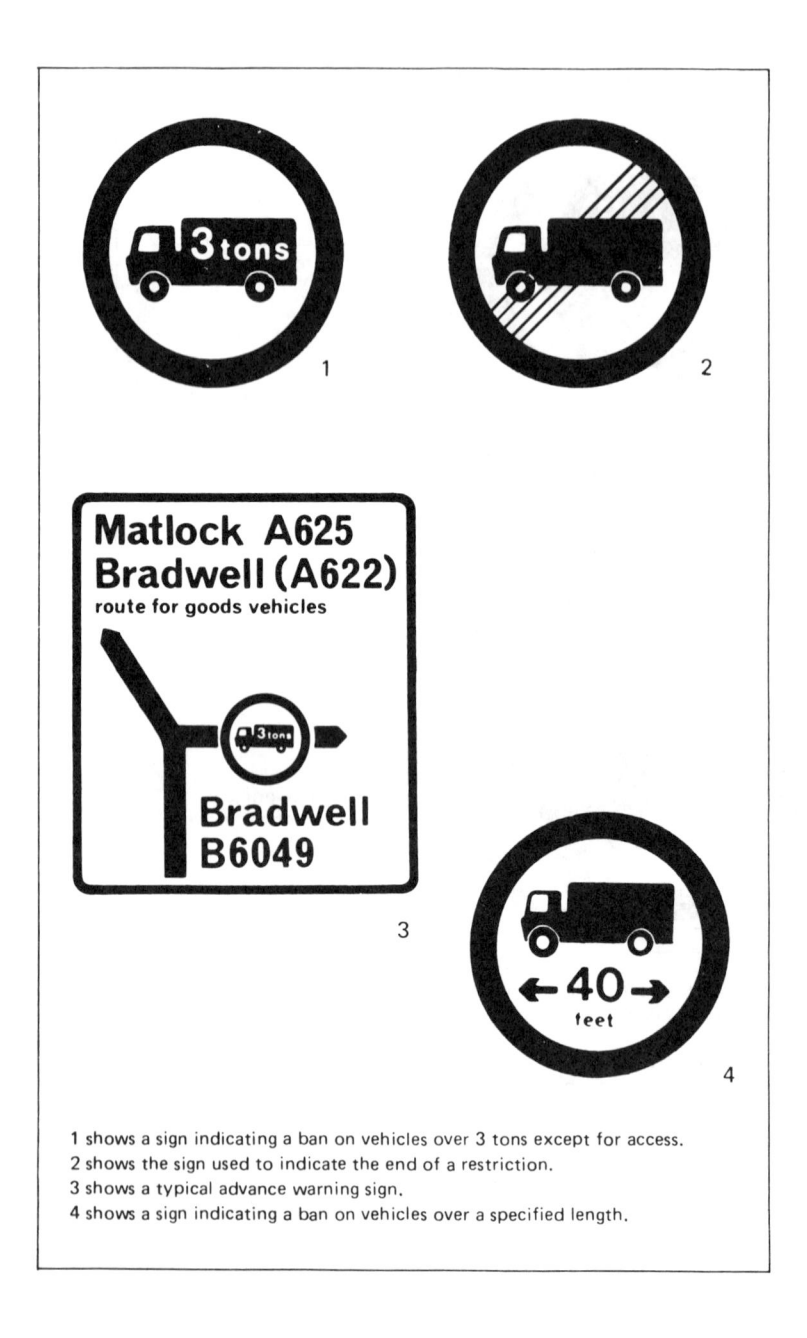

1 shows a sign indicating a ban on vehicles over 3 tons except for access.
2 shows the sign used to indicate the end of a restriction.
3 shows a typical advance warning sign.
4 shows a sign indicating a ban on vehicles over a specified length.

Figure 23.3 *Signs indicating route bans on heavy goods vehicles*

23: ROAD TRAFFIC REGULATIONS

Dynamic Weighing

The use of dynamic axle weighing machines has increased for weight enforcement purposes. These are permitted under regulations (the Weighing of Motor Vehicles (Use of Dynamic Axle Weighing Machines) Regulations 1978) which specify that an enforcement officer can require a vehicle to be driven across the weighing platform of a machine for this purpose. The permitted weights for the vehicle are measured to within plus or minus 150kg for each axle and within plus or minus 150kg multiplied by the total number of axles to determine the tolerance on the total vehicle weights.

The Government is stepping up its enforcement activities on vehicle overloading and warns operators that they must allow a margin for safety if they cannot keep within the limits.

Accident Reporting

Any driver involved in a road accident in which a personal injury is caused to any person other than himself, or damage is caused to any vehicle other than his own vehicle, or damage is caused to any animal* other than animals carried on his own vehicle or to any roadside property (see below for definition) MUST STOP. Failure to stop after an accident is an offence and fines of up to £2000 can be imposed on conviction.

The driver of a vehicle involved in an accident must give to anybody having reasonable grounds for requiring it his own name and address, the name and address of the vehicle owner and the registration number of the vehicle.

If the accident results in injury or damage to any person other than the driver himself or to any other vehicle or to any reportable animal,* or to roadside property, then the details of the accident must be reported to the police *as soon as reasonably practicable afterwards, but in any case no later than 24 hours after the event*. This obviously does not apply if police at the scene of the accident take all the necessary details. Failure to report an accident is an offence which also carries a maximum fine of £2000.

* NB: For these purposes an animal means any horse, ass, mule, cattle, sheep, pig, goat, dog (in Northern Ireland only, a 'hinnie' is added to this list).

Under the Road Traffic Act 1988 the need to stop following accidents extends to cover any damage caused to any property 'constructed on, fixed to, growing on, or otherwise forming part of the land in which the road is situated or land adjacent there to'. This means that if a vehicle runs off the road and no other vehicles or persons are involved the driver still has to report damage to fences, hedges, gate-posts, street bollards, lamp-posts, and so on.

Third parties injured in accidents who find when making claims for damages that the vehicle was uninsured at the time can make a claim for personal injuries only to the Motor Insurers' Bureau (MIB) (see also Chapter 22). More recently the MIB compensation scheme has been extended to cover claims for damage to property by uninsured vehicles. Such claims for property damage will only be accepted if the vehicle driver is traced – not otherwise – and provided no claim for the damage can be made elsewhere. There is a limit of £250000 on claims and they are subject to a £175 excess clause.

Road Humps

Regulations permit the construction of road humps on sections of the highway where a 30mph speed limit is in force. The road hump will be treated as part of the highway provided it complies with the regulations. A DTp review was taking place in 1988 'to make a greater diversity of road humps and locations available to local highway authorities...so that maximum benefits can be gained from the use of these cost effective accident reduction measures'. New regulations were introduced in 1989 to enable local authorities to reduce pedestrian casualties by the introduction of more road humps.

Sale of Unroadworthy Vehicles

It is an offence to sell, supply, offer to sell or expose for sale or supply a vehicle which is in such a condition that it does not comply with the Construction and Use Regulations, and is therefore legally unroadworthy.

This means that to display a vehicle for sale which needs attention to bring it up to the required standard is an offence, even though the intention would have been to remedy any defects before a purchaser paid for or took the vehicle away. However, it would not be an offence if the buyer was made aware of the defects and he intended to remedy them or have them remedied before using the vehicle on the road.

It is also an offence to fit any part to a vehicle which, by its fitting, makes the vehicle unsafe and causes it to contravene the regulations. For example, fitting a tyre which is below the limits regulating tread depth would be to commit such an offence.

Seat Belts

The compulsory wearing of seat belts came into effect on 31 January 1983. The seat belt regulations specify that compulsory wearing applies to drivers and front-seat passengers of motor cars, light vehicles not exceeding 1525kg unladen weight registered on or after 1 April 1967 and vehicles not exceeding 3500kg gross weight registered since 1 April 1980.

Children between the age of one year and 14 years must wear the seat belt provided when travellin in the front seat of a vehicle which is required to have seat belts fitted. Children under ony year old must be in an approved child seat if they travel in the front of a vehicle. Where such a seat is not available, they must travel in the back seat of the vehicle, as must older children if the existing seat belts are not suitable.

From 1 September 1989 if seat belts or child restraints are fitted in the rear of a motor car, it is the *driver's** legal responsibility to ensure that any child under 14 years old is secured by the belt or restraint.

*It must be emphasised that irrespective of whether the child's parents, guardians, or other responsible person in whose charge they are, are in the car it remains the driver's responsibility to ensure that any children are secured.

Where a light goods vehicle is fitted with bench-type or double front passenger seats, the requirement for seat belt wearing applies only to the person riding in the outer part of the seat (ie furthest from the driver) and not to a person in the middle part of the seat provided the nominated

23: ROAD TRAFFIC REGULATIONS

passenger seat is occupied. It is illegal to occupy the centre part of the seat (ie next to the driver) where no belt may be provided if the outer part of the seat with the belt provided is unoccupied.

Responsibility for wearing seat belts in a vehicle rests with the person sitting in the seat for which the belt is provided. The driver is not responsible for the failure of a front seat passenger to wear a belt as required by law except if the passenger is a child under 14 years old travelling in the front or back seats of the vehicle – see also above.

A court has ruled that if, as a result of an accident, injuries were sustained which may have been prevented or lessened had the injured person been weargin a seat belt, then the damage awarded to that person in any claim should be reduced by an appropriate amount. Subsequently, other cases involving motor accident claims have followed the same lines.

Exemption from seat belt wearing applies to:
1. Drivers holding a medical exemption certificate.
2. Collection and delivery drivers (including mail collections and deliveries).
3. Drivers in the process of reversing.
4. Taxi and private hire car drivers.
5. A driving examiner.
6. A qualified driver accompanying a learner driver but only when the learner is reversing.
7. A driver or passenger in a vehicle being driven on trade plates for the purpose of investigating or repairing a mechanical fault in the vehicle.
8. Drivers or passengers sitting in a seat for which a seat belt is required if the belts are defective.

Use of Radios and Telephones in Vehicles

The Highway Code contains advice against using a hand-held microphone or telephone handset while the vehicle is moving except in an emergency. Drivers should not stop on the hard shoulder of a motorway to answer or make a call no matter how urgent. The Code recommends that a driver should only speak into a fixed, neckslung, or clipped-on microphone when it would not distract his attention from the road.

Autoguide in London

The government is proceeding with its proposals to introduce a pilot Autoguide scheme in London. Licences were to be issued from 1 June 1990 for the operation of a pilot scheme commencing in 1992 with approximately 1000 vehicles involved in the trials. The initial plan is for the scheme to cover a 400 square mile area within the M25 London Orbital motorway ring controlled by 200 roadside beacons. It is anticipated that motorists will be able to have the Autoguide equipment in their cars within the 1990s.

Autoguide is a system that gives drivers recommended routes to their destination using a display fitted to the dashboard of their vehicle. Roadside beacons transmit the advice data to vehicles and also keep the central Autoguide computer abreast of current traffic conditions. The system is self-adjusting so it will not shift traffic congestion from one location to another.

24: Fleet Car and Light Vehicle Operations

Transport managers and other staff responsible for the operation of heavy goods vehicles within companies frequently have additional responsibilities for the operation of company-owned motor cars used by management, sales and service personnel, and light commercial vehicles which are outside the general scope of much of the legislation explained in this book. It is equally important that such vehicles should be operated strictly within the law. Most of the offences and penalties described in earlier chapters apply when operating such vehicles and the consequences of operating illegally can be serious. As already mentioned, for example, Licensing Authorities will take account of failure to operate light vehicles safely and within the law when deciding whether an applicant is a fit person or is of sufficient good repute to hold an 'O' licence for heavier vehicles.

For the purposes of this chapter, light goods vehicles are vehicles with an unladen weight not exceeding 1525kg or a gross plated weight not exceeding 3.5 tonnes (ie below the 'O' licensing, hgv plating and testing and the EC drivers' hours and tachograph requirement thresholds).

Much of the legislation applicable to the use of private motor cars and light goods vehicles has already been dealt with under such headings as excise duty, insurance and traffic regulations. The same system as described previously in Chapter 21 applies to the registration and excise licensing of such vehicles and the legal requirements for insurance cover have been outlined in Chapter 22. Most of the traffic restrictions, particularly with regard to parking and waiting, road signs, motorway lights, breath tests and zebra crossings which apply equally to the private car and light vehicle driver and to the heavy goods vehicle driver, have been dealt with in Chapter 23. Nevertheless, some of these items of legislation are worth emphasising here for the benefit of the light vehicle fleet manager along with other matters applicable to such operations within firms.

Excise Duty

Private-type motor cars owned by firms and used for business purposes can be licensed at the private/light goods (PLG) rate of duty – currently £100 per year. Similarly, estate cars can be taxed at the £100 duty rate. If on the other hand a private car is adapted for carrying goods, or an estate car is used for carrying goods, tools or samples, the appropriate goods rate of duty must be paid if the permissible maximum weight exceeds 3500kg.

In determining whether an estate car or dual-purpose vehicle (see p 318 for definition) is subject to the goods vehicle rate of duty, if its permissible maximum weight exceeds 3500kg consideration has to be given to the nature of the goods or burden carried. No specific guidelines are laid down but local Vehicle Registration Offices take the view that if any goods or samples, service equipment or spare parts are carried in connection with a business from which profit may result, then the vehicle should be taxed as a goods vehicle. Samples which can be accommodated in a normal briefcase would not generally constitute goods for this purpose.

The tax (ie VED) disc must be displayed on the windscreen of the vehicle on the near side where it can be easily seen. See Chapter 21 for details of vehicle excise duty requirements.

Insurance

Private-type motor cars and light goods vehicles, like all other vehicles, are required by law to be covered for third-party insurance risks as a minimum, but clearly in the case of fleet cars additional cover would be taken out, and in most instances comprehensive cover is advisable. Most insurance policies contain a variety of option clauses, some of which are included in the basic premium and others are available at extra cost.

Correct Cover

Of importance to the fleet manager is the need to ensure that company cars are fully insured for business use by employees of the company. The difference in insurance classification for business cars used for commercial travelling and for those which are not used for this purpose is an important point for the fleet manager to consider. Most policies differentiate between such use, and in a car fleet where vehicles are used by both salesmen and other staff and management it is essential to ensure that either the policy covers the whole of the car fleet for commercial travelling or, if it does not do so, the sales force should be restricted to driving only those cars which have this cover. If a salesman, or indeed any other staff member, uses a car for a purpose which can in any way be described as soliciting an order, then in insurance terms this use is classed as commercial travelling and the cover on the car must include this clause.

Dual-purpose vehicles registered and licensed as goods vehicles must be insured with cover permitting goods to be carried for business purposes.

Cover for Special Cars

There can be problems in a fleet with certain individual cars on insurance cover which may not be driven by certain employees. For example, if the managing director has a high powered sports-type car it is likely that the insurers would impose severe restrictions on the driving of that car, for whatever purpose (chauffeuring, ferrying back and forth for service or repairs, for example), by relatively inexperienced drivers or by, say, young drivers under 25 years of age. Alternatively, such cars may be restricted to named drivers only.

Private Use of Company Cars

A further point which needs consideration is cover for the employee's use of a company car for private purposes. It is general practice for firms to allow their employees this concession both for commuting to work and for family motoring at the weekends and for holidays. The cover taken out for fleet cars should specifically include this provision if such use is permitted, otherwise the vehicle owner (the firm) may be guilty of permitting the use of an uninsured car. In these circumstances, if an accident and claim were to result, the consequences for the employee could be very serious in terms of meeting damage claims and in prosecution for using an uninsured car. The same provisions should be applied if the firm permits the employee's wife (or husband) or even his children (if they are qualified drivers) to drive the car at any time.

Employees' Use of Own Cars

If employees are ever required, or likely to be required, to use their own private car for business purposes, even for only the occasional errand, the fleet manager should ensure that the employee has adequate insurance cover on his own vehicle for such purpose. This usually means that the employee's own policy must include provision for his car to be used in connection with the business of his employer.

The fleet manager, confronted with this type of situation, should ask to see evidence of the cover (ie a valid Certificate of Insurance or a temporary cover note showing the conditions for use covered by the policy) and not just rely on the word of the employee. Similarly, he would be wise to inform all other persons in the firm, management and staff alike, that employees should not use, or be requested to use, their own cars on company business without first having the insurance cover verified.

To avoid the dangers which could arise from an employee using his own private car for business purposes when it was not covered for such use, when the policy was not in force at all because the premium had not been paid, or because the policy was invalid as a result of the employee giving incorrect information at the time of completing the policy application, the company can take out a motor contingency policy which will indemnify it against any claims arising from an accident involving an employee undertaking company business in his own uninsured car. This type of policy is very cheap to obtain and well worth the cost when considered against the risks. For example, if the employee had an accident causing serious injury to one or more third parties and his own insurance proved to be void, the third parties would look to the employer on whose business the employee was engaged at the time of the accident to meet their claims.

Dual Car Use

When an employee who is provided with a company car also owns a car which his wife uses, an anomalous situation on insurance cover can arise if his own car is insured in his, and not his wife's name. This problem occurs because the cover provided on his own car automatically provides him with third-party cover while driving any other car not belonging to him. Consequently, when driving the firm's car for pleasure purposes he has the double cover provided by both the firm's policy and his own policy. If he should then be involved in an accident resulting in a third-party claim, his own insurers could be held partially liable for the damages arising out of the claim.

In order to overcome this particular problem the major insurance companies have made an undertaking indicating that it is not their intention to take advantage of the cover provided by the driver's own personal insurance policy in such circumstances. However, not all insurance companies are party to this undertaking.

Payment by Passengers

Payment by passengers towards the cost of petrol consumed on a journey no longer infringes the 'hiring' exclusion clause on insurance cover. However, payment towards other motoring expenses such as parking fees or depreciation could still fall within the 'prohibition of hiring' clause in most insurance policies. In cases where this situation arises a check should be made with insurers to ascertain the current position.

Company Cars and Income Tax

Directors and higher paid employees are assessed for schedule E income tax on the 'personal benefit' which they derive from the provision of a car by their employer for their business and private use.

Higher paid employment for the purposes of company car tax assessment is employment where total remuneration including all expense payments and benefits in kind or cash amounts to £8500 for 1990-91.

If the business use of the car is 'insubstantial' (the annual business mileage must be over 2500 to avoid a car being treated as substantially for private use) compared with private use, the benefit of having the car will be assessed for tax purposes at one-and-a-half times the scale figure shown in the table. The same one-and-a-half times increase in assumed benefit will apply to a second car provided to a person by a company.

If business use of the car is 'substantial' tax is based on the benefit derived according to a scale which covers both the capital value and the running costs of the car. If the business use of the car exceeds 18000 miles per year the assumed taxable benefit will be reduced by half.

Car Benefits 1990-91

	Age of car	
	Under 4 years annual benefit	4 years or more annual benefit
Cars having a market value not exceeding £19250 when first registered		
Cars having a cylinder capacity:		
1400cc or under	£1700	£1150
1401cc to 2000cc	£2200	£1500
2001cc or more	£3550	£2350
Cars having a market value exceeding £19250 when first registered:		
Original market value		
£19251 to £29000	£4600	£3100
More than £29000	£7400	£4900

Car Fuel Benefits for 1990-91

Cylinder capacity of car in cubic centimetres	Original market value	Annual benefit
1400cc or under	or less than £6000	£480
1401cc to 2000cc	or £6000 to 8499	£600
2001cc or more	or £8500 or more	£900

Construction and Use Regulations

Apart from the sections of the C and U Regulations which apply to private cars concerning their construction, lighting, noise, silencing and all the provisions which require the motor car to be maintained in accordance with the regulations, they are not involved in the special requirements relating to goods vehicles, unless the car has in any way been adapted to carry goods, for example, by removing seats or fitting racks on which goods can be carried. In this case the goods vehicle rate of excise duty applies and the vehicles become subject to certain aspects of the C and U Regulations regarding goods vehicles (see Chapter 10).

It should be remembered that the overriding requirement of the C and U Regulations for all vehicles to be maintained at all times in such a condition that they shall not cause danger to people carried on the vehicle and other road users applies equally to private cars and to goods vehicles irrespective of their size or weight.

New cars manufactured for sale in Britain have to meet the braking system requirements of EC Directive 71/320 unless the system is of the dual-line type. This directive specifies maximum stopping distances equivalent to a braking efficiency of 27 per cent.

Also as a result of EC directives, reversing lamps and four-way hazard warning flashers will eventually become compulsory on all cars made in Britain. Regulations require rear fog lights to be fitted to new vehicles manufactured since 1 October 1979 and first used since 1 April 1980 (see p 279 for more details).

Drivers' Hours and Records

Light Goods Vehicles

Light goods vehicles coming within the scope of this chapter are exempt from the EC regulations (ie because they do not exceed 3.5 tonnes gross weight) and in consequence of this only the relevant British provisions will apply.

The applicable limits to goods vehicles not exceeding 3.5 tonnes gvw are as follows:

Maximum daily driving time	10 hours
Maximum daily duty time	11 hours

There are no specified break or daily or weekly rest period requirements, no limits on continuous duty or weekly limits on duty or driving.

Drivers of light goods vehicles of not more than 3.5 tonnes gross plated weight and dual-purpose vehicles (see p 318 for definition) of any weight

used for certain specialised duties are required to observe only a daily maximum driving time of 10 hours. This applies to light goods vehicles used:
1. By doctors, dentists, nurses, midwives or vets.
2. For any service of inspection, cleaning, maintenance, repair, installation or fitting.
3. By a commercial traveller and carrying only goods used for soliciting orders.
4. By an employee of the AA, the RAC or the RSAC.
5. For business of cinematography or of radio or television broadcasting.

Record Keeping
Light goods vehicle drivers (ie vehicles under 3.5 tonnes gross weight) and drivers of dual-purpose vehicles are exempt from the requirements to keep records of their driving, duty and rest periods.

Private Cars

Employees driving company owned private-type motor cars are exempt from the requirements of the goods vehicle drivers' hours and record requirements, but only so long as they do not drive vehicles to which these requirements do apply. If at any time an employee who normally drives only motor cars also as part of his work needs to drive a goods vehicle to which the drivers' hours regulations do apply then any time spent driving a private car (his own or the company's) for his firm's business must be counted within his total daily working time (ie duty time). If the goods vehicle exceeds 3.5 tonnes gross weight the driving of the car should be shown on his record sheet (ie tachograph chart) for the day on which he drives a goods vehicle as 'other work'.

Full details of the goods vehicle drivers' hours and records are given in Chapters 3 and 4.

Tachographs

Light goods vehicles of not more than 3.5 tonnes gross plated weight are exempt from the EC tachograph regulations requiring tachograph fitment and use, but if such a vehicle is coupled to a goods carrying trailer so that the total of the combined gross weights exceeds 3.5 tonnes then the vehicle will come within the scope of the EC tachograph regulations, unless it is otherwise exempt due to special use. This means that a DTp calibrated tachograph must be fitted and must be used by the driver when the trailer is drawn (see Chapter 5 for full details of the tachograph regulations) and the EC drivers' hours rules must be followed (see Chapter 3 for details).

Speed Limits

Private cars and dual-purpose vehicles not drawing trailers are restricted to maximum permitted speeds on certain roads in accordance with the restriction sign-posted on the section of road and to overall maximum speeds of 60mph on single-carriageway roads and 70mph on dual-carriageways and motorways.

24: FLEET CAR AND LIGHT VEHICLE OPERATIONS

Speed limits for cars and light goods vehicles are as follows:

	Motorways	Dual-Carriageways	Other Roads
1. Cars and car-derived vans	70	70	60
2. Cars and car-derived vans towing trailer	60	60	50
3. Rigid goods vehicles not exceeding 7.5 tonnes	70	60	50
4. Articulated vehicles and rigid goods vehicles not exceeding 7.5 tonnes drawing trailer	60	60*	50

*In Northern Ireland the limit for this category of vehicle is 50mph.
NB: In all cases of speed restrictions mentioned above, if specific lower limits are in force on any section of road, then it is the lower limit which must be observed.

Seat Belts

Compulsory fitment of seat belts applies in the case of the following light vehicles (see also p 368):
1. Goods vehicles not exceeding 1525kg unladen (first registered since April 1967).
2. Dual-purpose vehicles registered since 1 January 1965.
3. Private cars registered since 1 January 1965.

Vehicles to which the regulations apply first used since 1 April 1973 must be fitted with belts which can be secured and released with one hand only and must also be fitted with a device to enable the belts to be stowed in a position where they do not touch the floor. The belts must be maintained in a fit and serviceable condition and kept free from permanent or temporary obstruction which would prevent their being used by a person sitting in the seat for which the belt is provided. Failure to comply with these requirements is an offence and can lead to failure of the MOT test.

In cases where the regulations apply, as above, belts must be provided for the driver and one front seat passenger.

Wearing of Seat Belts

The wearing of seat belts in vehicles fitted with them by law has been compulsory since 1 January 1983. Certain exemptions to the wearing of belts have been included in the regulations (see p 369 for list of exemptions). From 1 September 1989 children up to 14 years of age riding in the back seats of motor cars fitted with rear seat belts must wear those belts or restraints. A maximum fine of £100 may be imposed on conviction for failing to wear a seat belt as required by law. The responsibility for seat belt wearing rests with the person sitting in the seat for which the belt is provided except that responsibility for ensuring that children wear seat belts as required by law rests with the driver of the vehicle (ie not the parent or guardian who may be accompanying the child).

Fuel Consumption Tests

Concern about energy conservation led to the Energy Act 1976 and the

Passenger Car Fuel Consumption Order 1977 being enacted. Because of interest among readers of the *Handbook* in this subject, details of the legal requirements and the scheme are outlined here.

Since 1 April 1978 new cars on display in showrooms and on forecourts must carry a label showing official fuel consumption figures for that model of car. Every dealer must have details of officially approved fuel consumption tests for all cars listed in this booklet available in his showroom for buyers to consult on request. In addition, where reference is made in promotional literature, such as advertisements, technical specifications and sales brochures, to the petrol consumption of a new car the test results must be included. In all such cases the results of all tests carried out must be quoted (urban cycle, 90km/h – and 120km/h where appropriate) in both miles per gallon and litres per 100km. These requirements do not apply in the Channel Islands or the Isle of Man.

Official Tests

The official tests are carried out in approved laboratories or on test tracks. They have been designed to be representative of real-life driving situations and the results achieved provide a guide to the models which are likely to be more economical in their fuel use.

The test results do not guarantee the fuel consumption of any particular car. Each new car has not itself been tested and there will inevitably be differences between cars of the same model. The driver's style, the loading of the car, road, weather and traffic conditions, the overall mileage of the car and its standard of maintenance will all affect its fuel consumption. For all these reasons the fuel consumption achieved on the road will not necessarily accord with the tests results.

The Standard Test
The tests follow an internationally agreed procedure and consist of two compulsory parts:
1. A cycle simulating urban driving
2. A constant speed test at 55mph (90km/h).

Models Included in the Tests
Almost all types of new passenger cars are covered by the tests. However, certain types are excluded as follows:
1. Cars manufactured before 1 January 1978
2. Second-hand cars
3. Cars adapted to carry more than eight passengers (excluding the driver)
4. Three-wheelers
5. Invalid carriages
6. Van-derived passenger cars
7. Cars built specially for export
8. Cars operating on four-wheel drive only
9. Cars whose engines run on diesel, liquefied petroleum gas or other such fuels.

These vehicles will not, therefore, be labelled in the showrooms. Heavy goods vehicles, vans and motorcycles are also excluded from these tests.

Also, a small number of manufacturers and importers have been granted exemption from testing because of the low volume of production involved. Consequently, these particular makes and models are not likely to be of significant interest or concern to the fleet user.

Urban Test Cycle
The urban test cycle is carried out in a laboratory where equipment simulates the loads experienced under normal driving conditions and the standard patterns of urban driving. The car is driven from a fully warmed-up start and is taken through a cycle of acceleration, deceleration and idling with a maximum speed not exceeding 31mph (50km/h).

Constant Speed Test
The constant speed test at 56mph (90km/h) is intended to be representative of open road driving. It may be carried out in the laboratory or on a test track (under strictly controlled road and weather conditions).

Optional Constant Speed Test
This test is carried out at 75mph (120km/h) in a laboratory or on a test track. Although it is recognised that this test exceeds the UK maximum speed limit, it is included to illustrate to car drivers the worsening fuel consumption at higher speeds. It may also be useful to manufacturers exporting to some parts of Europe where speed limits are higher.

Only one production car is tested as a representative of each model. It must have been run in and have been driven for at least 1800 miles (3000km) before testing. In some cases several models, which do not differ significantly in certain technical characteristics thought to be important in determining fuel consumption, may be grouped together into a 'class'. Only one car in the class needs to be tested.

The Testing

The responsibility for testing lies with the manufacturers and importers themselves. They must either carry out the tests themselves or arrange for them to be carried out on their behalf. Department of Energy officials have the right to inspect the test laboratories and to witness tests in progress to ensure that they are being carried out correctly.

Manufacturers must submit their fuel consumption test results to the Department of Energy who record the results in an official fuel economy certificate.

25: Northern Ireland Operations

Vehicles based and registered in England, Wales and Scotland must comply with all the normal legal requirements (eg vehicle condition, excise duty, insurance and observance of traffic rules) set out in this *Handbook* when operating in Northern Ireland, but particularly so in regard to 'O' licensing (Chapter 1), professional competence (Chapter 2), drivers' hours and record-keeping regulations (Chapters 3 and 4), tachographs (Chapter 5), drivers' licensing (Chapters 6 and 7) and plating and testing (Chapter 13). It should be noted that in regard to road traffic and road traffic offences there are differences between the Northern Ireland requirements and those on the British mainland. A separate edition of the Highway Code is published for Northern Ireland.

Vehicles based and operated in Northern Ireland must comply with the law as it applies in the Province which, although substantially similar to that applicable in the rest of the United Kingdom, does vary in some respects as shown in this chapter.

Road Freight Operator Licensing

In order to carry goods by road for reward (but not for purely own-account operations) with vehicles over 3.5 tonnes permissible maximum weight in Northern Ireland it is necessary to hold a Road Freight Operator's Licence (RFO) issued under the provisions of the Transport Act (Northern Ireland) 1967.

Since 1 January 1978 regulations have been in effect to ensure that road freight operators are better qualified. These regulations, The Road Transport (Qualification of Operators) Regulations (Northern Ireland) 1977, implement EC Directive 561/74 *On admission to the occupation of road haulage operator*. Thus the requirements for obtaining a road freight operator's licence in Northern Ireland take account of this requirement and depending on the qualifications of the operator the licence may or may not be restricted to operations within the United Kingdom. The type and scope of the licence will be indicated clearly in the licence – covering either national operations or both national and international operations.

Conditions for Grant of 'O' Licence

Under the statutory requirements for the grant of a road freight operator's licence, an operator has to satisfy the issuing authority that he is:
1. Of good repute
2. Of appropriate financial standing
3. Professionally competent or that he employs a full-time manager who is professionally competent and of good repute.

The requirements of good repute and appropriate financial standing are as stated in detail in Chapter 1 of the *Handbook*. While the professional

THE TRANSPORT MANAGER'S AND OPERATOR'S HANDBOOK

competence requirement in Northern Ireland is largely as explained in Chapter 2 there are some differences as shown below.

Professional Competence by Examination
A separate syllabus for the Royal Society of Arts examination is applicable to Northern Ireland. It differs mainly in section C, *Access to the Northern Ireland Market*, which covers vehicle and operators' licences and professional competence requirements. Copies of the syllabus *Examinations for the Certificates of Professional Competence in Road Transport (Northern Ireland)* may be obtained from: Royal Society of Arts Examinations Board, Westwood Way, Westwood Business Park, Coventry CV4 8HS. The current examination syllabus applicable to Northern Ireland national goods and national passenger operations was published in 1988 and both NI national examinations have taken the modular form, with a core examination common to both passenger and goods sectors.

Issuing Authority
For operations in Northern Ireland, the issuing authority for operators' and vehicle licences is: Department of the Environment for Northern Ireland, Road Transport Licensing Branch, Upper Galwally, Belfast BT8 4FY.

Objections to Road Freight 'O' Licences
Objections to the grant of a Road Freight 'O' Licence may be made to the DOE by the Road Haulage Association (RHA) and the Freight Transport Association (FTA) on the grounds that the statutory conditions for the grant of such a licence are not or will not be met.

Appeals
Appeals against refusal by the DOE to grant a road freight operator's licence or where such a licence has been suspended or revoked may be made within 28 days to the County Court.

Application for Road Freight Operator's Licence
Application for a road freight operator's licence must be made to: Department of the Environment (NI), Road Transport Licensing Branch, Upper Galwally, Belfast BT8 4FY.

Form RFL 1 is used for the application. This requires details to be supplied as follows:
1. Name and place of business.
2. Type of licence required (ie national or national and international operations).
3. Address of operating centre (ie where vehicles are to be parked when not in use). Where premises are not owned the 'original' rental agreement must be sent with a first application.
4. Number of vehicles to be operated (original receipts or hire purchase agreements for vehicles and trailers to be operated must be sent with the application).
5. Whether professional competence requirements are met
6. If applicant is not professionally competent, the name and address of the full-time transport manager who is qualified must be given.

25: NORTHERN IRELAND OPERATIONS

7. Evidence of professional competence (the original certificate must be sent).
8. Whether the applicant or his named transport manager has any convictions offences in the past five years which are not spent.
9. Details of convictions.
10. Names and addresses (and past addresses) of the applicant, the named transport manager, and all directors and/or partners.
11. Name and address of bank from which a reference can be obtained.
12. Declaration (signature, status and date).

Licences are usually valid for three years.

Further information may be required in support of a road freight operator's licence regarding the applicant's financial status and a statement of estimated operating costs for vehicles specified in the application. The former requires the applicant to send the following items:
1. Bank status report
2. Details of any credit facilities from bank or any other financial resources available (eg deposit accounts)
3. Copy of latest bank statement
4. Rental agreement for operating premises
5. Receipts or hire purchase agreements in respect of vehicles
6. Original certificate of competence
7. A statement showing a breakdown of estimated annual costs and receipts of running the proposed road transport business.

The requirement to supply statements of estimated operating costs for vehicles involves the need to complete a form designed for this purpose. The following information must be provided:
1. Details of vehicles
   (a) type and model
   (b) registration number and date of first registration
   (c) type of trailer
   (d) gross weight
   (e) unladen weight
   (f) carrying capacity
   (g) number of tyres fitted and size (including trailer)
   (h) estimated fuel consumption (miles per gallon)
   (i) estimated annual mileage
   (j) vehicle length (in feet).
2. Estimated running costs and standing costs for one year (one vehicle only):
   (a) wages (including National Insurance)
   (b) motor tax
   (c) insurance for vehicle
   (d) insurance for goods in transit
   (e) fuel
   (f) maintenance
   (g) tyres
   (h) shipping charges if applicable
   (i) hire purchase payments on vehicle and trailer (if applicable)
   (j) rent and rates for business premises
   (k) depreciation on vehicle
   (l) miscellaneous expenses (eg telephone, stationery, etc)

Total costs
3. Estimated income from one year's operation (one vehicle only).

It is generally believed (although never officially stated) that the DOE is looking for 'O' licence applicants to have at least 25 per cent of first year operating costs in the bank at the start of the operation or assets equivalent to £7500 for each rigid vehicle and £15000 for each articulated vehicle either in the form of bank credits or agreed overdraft facilities.

Penalties for Improper Use

Anyone operating internationally on a Road Freight 'O' licence that is restricted to national operations only will be liable, on conviction, to a fine and his 'O' licence and vehicle licences may be revoked or suspended. There are also penalties laid down for using unlicensed vehicles on national operations.

Changing Licences

The holder of a Road Freight 'O' licence which is restricted to national transport operations may have the restriction removed to enable him to engage in both national and international operations if he can meet the additional requirements (namely professional competence in both national and international transport operations) for engaging in international operations.

Vehicle Licences

Northern Ireland motor vehicles over 3.5 tonnes gross weight may not be used to carry goods for hire or reward except under a Road Freight Vehicle Licence granted under Section 17 of the Transport Act (NI) 1967 (as amended). Vehicle licences may only be granted to a person who holds a Road Freight Operator's Licence and will cover either:
1. National transport operations only (ie covering Northern Ireland and the remainder of the UK) – Blue disc
2. National and international transport operations – Green disc.

Vehicle licences are valid for one year and are issued in the form of a disc for display in the vehicle windscreen. They are serial numbered and show the vehicle registration number, the name of the owner and the date of expiry. Application is made on form RFL 3 to the DOE Northern Ireland (see address below) enclosing both the vehicle excise licence disc and the goods vehicle certificate as evidence that the vehicle is taxed and tested, if applicable (see p 387), on the date of issue of the vehicle licence.

Application for Road Freight Vehicle Licences

Applications for road freight vehicle licences have to be made on form RFL3 to the DOE at the address given above. Details which must be provided by the person or firm using the vehicles are as follows:
1. Name, address and telephone number of applicant
2. Road Freight Operator's Licence number
3. Whether RFOL is valid for international operations

25: NORTHERN IRELAND OPERATIONS

4. (a) Registration numbers of vehicles which are owned or in possession under an agreement for hire, hire purchase, credit sale or loan for which road freight licences are required
   (b) Type of vehicle
   (c) Type of body
   (d) Gross weight of vehicle
5. Address where vehicles will be parked overnight
6. Declaration that statements given are true.

Penalties for Illegal Use

Making a false statement to obtain the grant of a road freight operator's licence or a road freight vehicle licence is an offence punishable on conviction by a fine or imprisonment for up to six months or both. The 'O' licence could also be suspended or revoked. Use of a motor vehicle on a road for the carriage of goods for reward without a road freight vehicle licence can result in a fine which increases for subsequent convictions.

Own-Account Transport Operations

Under Northern Ireland operations, own-account operators who do not engage in hire or reward haulage operations are exempt from the requirement to hold road freight operators' licences. However, if an own-account operator wishes to send vehicles across to Great Britain, they must carry an 'own-account document' indicating details of the user of the goods vehicle, his trade or business, the goods being carried, their loading and unloading points, the vehicle and the route.

This information may be set out on a firm's letter-headed notepaper but generally form GV 243 should be obtained from the Road Freight Licence Office to formalise presentation of the information. The purpose of this document is to cover vehicles travelling in Great Britain without displaying a British 'O' licence disc.

Period Permits for Northern Ireland Operators

Hauliers who wish to engage in cross-border haulage of goods for reward into Eire must obtain a Period Permit for the territory of the Republic of Ireland. In order to obtain a Period Permit an applicant must hold a current road freight operator's licence valid for international operations and current road freight vehicle licences. Permits do not permit the operator to engage in internal transport in the Republic of Ireland. It is reported that there is no longer any check on these permits when vehicles cross the border and that NI operators are no longer applying for them.

Validity and Duration of Permits

Period permits are valid for any number of cross-border journeys within the period stipulated on the Permit but may only be used in respect of one vehicle at any one time. Permits are normally issued for 12 months but they may be issued for shorter periods in certain circumstances.

A Period Permit is not transferable to any other person and must be returned to the issuing office within 15 days of the expiry date.

Statistical Returns

Within ten days of the end of each month, the holder of a Period Permit has to make a statistical return to the issuing office giving detailed information of all loads carried across the border in each direction. If no cross-border haulage has been undertaken during a month a 'nil' return must be made.

Application and Fee

Application has to be made on form RFL 58 to: Department of the Environment (NI), Road Transport Licensing Branch, Upper Galwally, Belfast BT8 4FY.

Exemptions from Period Permits

The following transport activities are exempt from the need for Period Permits for cross-border haulage into the Republic of Ireland:
1. Types of carriage listed in Annex 1 of the First Directive of the Council of the EC of 23 July 1952 as amended, that is:
   (a) Frontier traffic in an area extending for a distance of 25 kilometres as the crow flies, on each side of the frontier, provided that the total distance covered does not exceed 100 kilometres as the crow flies
   (b) Occasional carriage of goods to or from airports, in the event of air services being diverted
   (c) Carriage of luggage in trailers coupled to passenger-carrying vehicles and the carriage of luggage in all types of vehicle to and from airports
   (d) Carriage of mails
   (e) Carriage of vehicles which have suffered damage or breakdown
   (f) Carriage of refuse and sewage
   (g) Carriage of animal carcasses for disposal
   (h) Carriage of bees and fish fry
   (i) Funeral transport
   (j) Carriage of goods in motor vehicles the permissible laden weight of which, including that of trailers, does not exceed 6 tonnes or the permissible payload of which, including that of trailers, does not exceed 3.5 metric tons
   (k) Own-account transport as provided for in EC Council Directive 80/49/EC of 20 December 1979
   (l) Carriage of articles required for medical care in emergency relief, in particular for natural disasters
   (m) Carriage of valuable goods (eg, precious metals) effected by special vehicles accompanied by the police or other security guards.
2. The carriage of goods under an authorisation granted pursuant to Council for the carriage of goods by road between member states as amended, or by virtue of a licence issued pursuant to the scheme adopted by Resolution of the Council of Ministers of the European Conference of Ministers of Transport (ECMT) on 14 June 1973.
3. Transport on own account, provided that an appropriate own-account document is carried on the vehicle.
4. Transport of spare parts and provisions for ocean-going ships.
5. Transport of works and objects of art for fairs and exhibitions or for commercial purposes.

25: NORTHERN IRELAND OPERATIONS

6. Transport of articles and equipment intended exclusively for advertising and information purposes.
7. Unladen runs by goods vehicles, but if the vehicle is entering to collect goods, the permit applying to the transport operation which is to follow should be carried on the vehicle on entry.
8. Transport of properties, accessories and animals to or from theatrical, musical, film, sports or circus performances, fairs or fetes and those intended for radio, recording, or for film or television production.

Cabotage

Northern Ireland licensed operators must not collect and deliver goods within the British mainland. Similarly, British 'O' licensed operators must not collect and deliver goods within the province of Northern Ireland. These prohibited activities are known as cabotage.

Now that cabotage is legalised throughout the European Community, Northern Ireland operators can take advantage of the opportunity to undertake such work within European states provided that they hold the necessary cabotage permit issued by the IRFO at Newcastle upon Tyne. Only a very limited number of such permits have been made available initially to NI road hauliers.

Drivers' Hours and Records

The EC requirements regarding drivers' hours and record keeping as described in Chapters 3 and 4 of the *Handbook* apply in Northern Ireland on substantially the same basis.

Tachographs

Legal requirements for the fitment and use of tachographs in Northern Ireland operations are the same as those described for the United Kingdom in Chapter 5.

Hgv Drivers' Licensing

Drivers of heavy goods vehicles in Northern Ireland must comply with the regulations for hgv driving licences and the requirements for hgv driving tests as set out in Chapters 7 and 8.

Plating & Testing of Vehicles (Northern Ireland Certification)

The United Kingdom system of heavy goods vehicle plating and annual testing does not apply in Northern Ireland. The Province has its own Goods Vehicle Certification scheme (commonly known and referred to in the Province as the PSV test) which requires heavy goods vehicles to be submitted to the Department of the Environment (NI) for an annual mechanical examination. Under The Goods Vehicles (Certification) Regulations (Northern Ireland) 1982 , owners of goods vehicles (other than those specifically exempted – see p 390) must obtain a test certificate for each vehicle no later than one year from the date of first registration and annually thereafter (see exemption 10 on p 391).

Application for a certificate must be made to the following address at least one month before the date on which the certificate is to take effect: Department of the Environment, Vehicle and Driving Test Centre, Balmoral Road, Belfast BT12 6QL.

Re-test fees apply where application is made within 21 days from the date of service of the notice and the vehicle is presented for re-examination within 28 days.

Applications by Non-NI Based Bodies

Where an application is made by a corporate body with its principal or registered office outside Northern Ireland or by a person residing outside Northern Ireland the following conditions must be observed:
1. During the currency of the certificate a place of business must be retained in NI.
2. They must be prepared to accept, at such a place of business, any summons or other document relating to any matter or offence arising in NI in connection with the vehicle for which the certificate is applied for.
3. They must undertake to appear at any court as required by such a summons or by any other document.
4. They must admit and submit to the jurisdiction of the court relative to the subject matter of such summons or other document.

Failure to comply with any of the above-mentioned requirements will involve immediate revocation of the certificate.

Examination of Vehicle

When notified by the Department the applicant must present the vehicle for examination, in a reasonably clean condition, together with the registration book and previous certificate, if any, at the time and at the centre specified in the notice.

Issue of Certificate
If, after examining the vehicle, the Department is satisfied that it complies in all respects with the regulations in respect of the construction, use, lighting and rear marking of vehicles, a certificate will be issued.

Refusal of Certificate
If the vehicle does not meet the requirements of the regulations a certificate will be refused and the applicant will be notified of the reasons why.

Re-Examination of Vehicles
When a certificate has been refused and the defects specified in the notice have been put right, an application may be made for a further examination of the vehicle. A reduced re-test fee will be payable if the re-test is conducted within 21 days of the original test.

Refund of Fees

Prepaid test fees may be refunded in the following circumstances:

1. If an appointment for an examination of a vehicle is cancelled by the Department;
2. If the applicant cancels the appointment by giving the Department (at the centre where the appointment is made) three clear working days' notice;
3. If the vehicle is presented to meet the appointment but the examination does not take place for reasons not attributable to the applicant or the vehicle;
4. If the applicant satisfies the Department that the vehicle could not be presented for examination on the day of the appointment because of exceptional circumstances which occurred no more than seven days before the day of the appointment, and providing notice is given to the centre where the examination was to take place within three days of the occurrence.

Duplicate Certificates

Duplicate certificates may be issued in replacement of those which have been accidentally lost, defaced or destroyed. A fee is payable for replacement certificates. If subsequently the original certificate is found, it must be returned to the nearest examining centre or to any police station.

Display of Certificates

The certificate issued on satisfying the examiners must be attached to the vehicle in a secure, weather-proof holder and must be displayed on the nearside windscreen or on the nearside of the vehicle not less than 610mm and not more than 1830mm above the road surface so that the particulars of the certificate are clearly visible (ie at eye level) to a person standing at the nearside of the vehicle.

Conditions of Certificate

It is a condition of the certificate that the vehicle owner:
1. Must not permit the vehicle to be used for any illegal purpose;
2. Must not deface or mutilate the certificate or permit anybody else to do so;
3. Must, at all reasonable times, for the purpose of inspection, examination or testing of the vehicle to which the certificate relates:
   (a) produce the vehicle at such a time and place as may be specified by any Inspector of Vehicles;
   (b) afford to any Inspector of Vehicles full facilities for such inspection, examination or testing including access to his premises for that purpose;
   (c) must ensure that the vehicle and all its fittings are maintained and kept in good order and repair and must take all practical steps to ensure that all parts of the mechanism, including the brakes, are free from defects and are in efficient working order;
   (d) must immediately notify the nearest examination centre of any alteration in design or construction of the vehicle since a certificate was issued.

Transfer of Certificates

If a vehicle owner sells or changes the ownership of a vehicle, he must return the certificate for the vehicle to the nearest examination centre and notify the Department of the name and address of the transferee. The Department may then transfer the certificate on request by the new owner.

If a vehicle owner dies or becomes infirm of mind or body, on application of any person the Department may transfer the certificate to such a person.

Change of Address

If a certificate holder changes his address during the currency of a certificate, he must notify details of such changes to the nearest examination centre.

Markings on Vehicles

When certificates have been issued for vehicles, those vehicles must be marked with:
1. The name and address of the owner in legible writing and in a conspicuous position on the nearside of the vehicle; and
2. Where the unladen weight of the vehicle exceeds 1020kg, the unladen weight should be painted, or otherwise clearly marked, in a conspicuous position on the offside of the vehicle. In the case of articulated vehicles the unladen weight of the tractive unit and the trailer must be marked on the respective unit and trailer.

For security reasons in the Province this provision is not strictly enforced.

Offences

It is an offence to operate when a certificate has expired, to alter, deface, mutilate or fail to display a certificate. Failure to observe such rules will result in the certificate being declared invalid. It is also an offence to assign or to transfer a certificate to another person with the same resultant penalty. Fines or six months' imprisonment may be imposed on summary conviction for such offences or up to two years' imprisonment upon any further conviction or indictment.

Renewal of Certificates

At least one month before the expiry date of a certificate the holder should apply for a new one using an application form obtainable from any examination centre or Local Vehicle Licensing Office of the Department.

Exemptions from Certification

The following vehicles are exempt from the requirements of NI certification:
1. Vehicles constructed or adapted for the sole purpose of spreading material on roads or used to deal with frost, ice or snow;
2. A land tractor, land locomotive or land implement;
3. An agricultural trailer drawn on a road only by a land tractor;
4. A vehicle exempted from duty under section 7(i) of the Vehicles (Excise) Act (Northern Ireland) 1972 and any trailer drawn by such a vehicle;
5. A motor vehicle for the time being licensed under the Vehicles (Excise) Act 1971, paragraph (a);

6. A trailer brought into NI from a base outside NI if a period of 12 months has elapsed since it was last brought into NI;
7. A pedestrian-controlled vehicle;
8. A track-laying vehicle;
9. A steam-propelled vehicle;
10. A vehicle used within a period of 12 months prior to the date of it being registered for the first time in NI or the UK; or, where a vehicle has been used on roads in NI or elsewhere before being registered, the exemption applies for the period of 12 months from the date of manufacture rather than from the date of registration. For this purpose any use before the vehicle is sold or supplied retail is disregarded.

Builders' Skips

Under regulations applicable in Northern Ireland builders' or rubbish skips must not be left on any footpath, cycle track, central reservation or verge on roads where a vehicle is prohibited from waiting or which are subject to a 30mph speed limit without the written consent of the Northern Ireland Department of the Environment.

Skips must be clearly visible, both ends must be painted yellow and a red and yellow reflective chevron strip must be shown along the top. The skip owner's name and address or telephone number must be displayed. Traffic cones must be placed on the approaches to a skip and yellow lights must be attached to each corner at night. No danger must be caused through the siting of the skip.

SALLY
FERRIES

RAMSGATE - DUNKERQUE

7 days a week the Sally route gives you fast access to the French motorway system as well as permit free transit to Benelux, Germany and Austria.

The Port of Ramsgate offers effective DTI customs clearance.

Sally's rates are competitive for both accompanied and unaccompanied vehicles.

Sally Freight

Please contact us for further information
(0843) 585496 TX 96352

26: International Transport Operations

Europe, Scandinavia, Eastern Bloc countries, the Middle East and Asia are destinations covered regularly by British hauliers and own-account delivery fleets. The trend has been towards a substantial increase in this traffic over the years and this may be expected to increase with the advent of the European single market in 1992.

Easy though international travel by road now is, the inexperienced operator will find that he is taking on a great deal of additional responsibility in setting out to offer a delivery service to Europe and beyond. There are still many legal and commercial requirements to be observed, documents to be carried and other points needing attention if the own-account operator or professional haulier is not to fall foul of foreign customs, frontier officials or the local gendarmerie, all of whom are well known for the extensive delays and severe penalties which they can impose on defaulters.

Heavy on-the-spot fines are a frequent hazard on the other side of the channel and, in a serious case, vehicles can, and will, be impounded and drivers imprisoned and no amount of persuasion will effect their release until the legal requirements have been satisfied.

For the professional haulier, the decision to extend his operations to Europe or beyond will, most likely, emanate from a desire to become part of what is for some a very profitable sphere of operations. Alternatively, it may result from pressure by existing customers to carry their exports as well as their domestic traffic. Whatever the cause, the effect will be that operations will have to be re-scaled, the administrative system revised to cope with the documentation, drivers trained and suitable vehicles acquired.

With the haulier, once the decision to 'go international' has been made, he can set up the appropriate organisation measuring the cost against the potential profits. But for the own-account operator the situation is less clear. Since he already owns vehicles for the distribution of his products within the UK he will, naturally, want to consider whether he should use these vehicles to deliver his exports to European markets.

There are advantages in making direct deliveries by road in one's own vehicles; reduced handling costs, minimum despatch to delivery times, direct control over the goods throughout their movement, the advertising value, and so on. On the other hand, the value of these cost and service advantages should be compared with costs and the administrative and operational burdens which will be incurred in setting up a continental delivery operation.

In making this comparison, the following factors will need serious consideration:
1. Are the existing vehicles suitable for operation in Europe?
2. Will additional vehicles have to be purchased if these are not suitable or if, by using them, the home delivery fleet will be depleted?

3. What are the merits, if any, either in terms of prestige or financial value, in providing the customer with a personal door-to-door service?
4. Are there worthwhile advantages – such as security or safety factors – in having one's own driver accompany loads to their final destination?
5. Are there savings in the cost of packing and insurance and is there less risk of theft or damage to offset the total delivery costs if these prove to be higher than those which would be incurred in using other transport modes or services?
6. Is the existing transport administration system adequate to complete the necessary documentation and make the necessary, and often quite involved and complicated, arrangements or would this be better left to professional forwarders?
7. Is the whole scheme financially justified when compared with the other services and transport modes available?

While these example considerations are directed primarily to the own-account operator some of them are equally applicable to the professional haulier. In addition to these commercial considerations there are the legal requirements to be met. These are outlined in the following pages.

In order to assist operators taking goods vehicles abroad the International Road Freight Office (see below for address) publishes a free guide called *Your Lorry Abroad*. Similarly, for those operators venturing further afield to Middle Eastern countries, the Freight Transport Association has published an excellent detailed guide covering journeys to such countries.

An outline of the major items of legislation affecting those who take goods vehicles abroad follows in this chapter. However, because of regularly and rapidly changing circumstances operators should check carefully details of current documentation requirements and fiscal charges with the relevant authorities when planning journeys.

Permits

Bilateral Permits

Although the system of road haulage permits between EC member states is to be abolished with the advent of 1992 and the Single European market, for the time being anyone operating goods vehicles on a road haulage (ie hire or reward) basis to or through a country with which the British government has concluded a bilateral agreement must, in most cases, obtain a bilateral journey or period permit to do so from the International Road Freight Office, Westgate House, Westgate Road, Newcastle upon Tyne N61 1TW, telephone ~~091-261-0031~~. 091 261 40000

Application should be made well in advance of the journey although with the current plentiful supply of permits to most countries as a result of the relaxation of the quota system, there is no longer a queuing delay.

The cases when permits may not be required are when own-account vehicles travel to some European countries which allow such vehicles entry without permits, but usually a document giving facts about the ownership of the vehicle and the load is required.

The non-EC countries with which Britain has concluded or is negotiating bilateral arrangements are:
Austria   Norway

Bulgaria
Cyprus
Czechoslovakia
Finland
East Germany (as was)
Hungary
Jordan
Poland
Romania
Sweden
Switzerland
Turkey
USSR
Yugoslavia

Multilateral (EC) Permits

Operators regularly running European services for hire and reward – professional road hauliers – can use the system of multilateral (ie EC) permit quotas for transit of EC member states. Under this system EC member countries each have a share of permits which they may issue to such hauliers (see note above about effects of the Single European Market measures coming into effect in 1992). The permits are issued to specific operators who may use the permits to cover any of their vehicles making any number of journeys in any one year – the validity of the permit – but the permit must only cover one vehicle at a time. There are a number of other conditions attached to the use of such permits:

1. The permits are intended for multilateral use rather than bilateral use. In other words, they enable the haulier to carry goods between EC countries rather than between the UK and one named country (which is all that bilateral agreements permit).
2. The permits cannot be used to cross EC countries to collect or deliver goods in non-EC countries.
3. Full details of all journeys under such permits must be recorded for statistical purposes.
4. These permits apply only to hire and reward operations. Own-account operators travelling to countries which require permits cannot obtain multilateral permits to do so but must apply for a bilateral permit.
5. Cabotage (collection and delivery within one country) is prohibited in all countries where multilateral permits are valid.
6. The permits cannot be used for unaccompanied trailer or semi-trailer operations.

Application for multilateral permits for road hauliers has to be made to the International Road Freight Office and these (because they are in short supply) are issued on the basis of previous usage of permits to ensure that they only go to operators who can be certain to use them fully.

ECMT Permits

These permits cover haulage operations between the 12 EC member states and seven other countries (ie Austria, Finland, Norway, Sweden, Switzerland, Turkey and Yugoslavia).

Cabotage Permits

Cabotage operations within EC member states have been legalised on a limited basis subject to road hauliers holding a valid cabotage authorisation permit issued by the IRFO in the UK or the relevant authority in other member states. Each authorisation is valid for one vehicle for one month only but any number of cabotage movements may be undertaken by that vehicle within the one-month period. The authorisation permit must accompany the vehicle at all times (in the case of articulated vehicles it relates to the tractive unit) and a special record sheet must be completed for each consignment of goods carried on a cabotage basis.

Operators are warned by the IRFO that when undertaking cabotage operations that they must comply with the internal laws of the countries in which such movements take place and should beware of special conditions and restrictions relating to the carriage of particular traffics and of the application of special rates and tariffs. Normal EC standards apply to vehicle construction, use and weights and dimensions and to driver's hours rules and the use of tachographs.

Operators should ensure that they comply with national VAT/IVA requirements and may need to register in the member states in which they are operating or appoint a suitable VAT/IVA agent to handle these matters.

Permit Fees

Bilateral permits cost £2.00 each (for one return journey) and £40.00 for a period permit. The cost for multilateral permits, authorising an unlimited number of journeys during their validity is £80. An ECMT permit costs £80 and an EC Removals permit (applicable for domestic furniture removal movements) costs £25.00. Road-rail certificates (for operators using the French SNCF and German rail DB system to transit France and Germany) cost £2 per outward and return journey. Community Cabotage authorisations cost £5 each and are valid for one month only.

Exemption from Permit Requirements

Countries which do not require own-account operators to hold permits are:

Austria	Luxembourg
Belgium	Netherlands
Bulgaria	Norway
Denmark	Poland
East Germany (as was)	Romania
Finland	Sweden
Greece	Switzerland
Hungary	Germany

Road hauliers do not need permits to operate in:

Belgium	Luxembourg
Bulgaria	Netherlands
Denmark	Norway
Finland	Poland
East Germany (as was)	Romania
Greece	Sweden
Jordan	Switzerland

If vehicles are to go to these countries without permits they must not land in, or pass through, neighbouring countries where permits are required.

Exemption by Weight

No permit at all is required for either haulage or own-account vehicles travelling to or through any European or Scandinavian country provided the maximum permissible gross weight of the vehicle does not exceed 6000kg (6 tonnes).

Non-Agreement Countries

If vehicles are to travel to or through a country with which Britain has no agreement, permission to operate in that country has to be sought direct from its transport authority (apply to FTA or RHA for addresses). Application should be made well before the journey is due and full details of the vehicle, the load and the route should be given.

Permit Checks

As a result of the exposure of a number of cases of permit frauds, more stringent regulations have been made to prevent vehicles leaving Britain on international journeys without valid permits and inspectors check vehicles leaving Britain to ensure that these regulations are complied with. A vehicle will be prevented from leaving the country if it does not carry a valid permit.

The International Road Haulage Permits Act 1975 makes it an offence to forge or alter permits, to make a false statement to obtain a permit or to allow one to be used by another person.

Customs Procedures

Two Customs transit procedures, which are described in the following pages, are currently in operation: the TIR Convention and the Community Transit system. The former has been in existence for some years and applies, if the transport operator elects to conform to the Convention's requirements, to journeys to all countries which are party to the Convention; this includes all EC and many other European countries. The Community Transit system was introduced with Britain's entry to membership of the EC (1 January 1973). All inter-EC journeys operate only under the Community Transit – or T-form – system but TIR still exists for journeys to non-EC countries. Since January 1988 the new Single Administrative Document (SAD) system has applied for export, import and transit movements.

The TIR Convention System

Under the Customs Convention on the International Transport of Goods by Road (TIR Carnets) 1959, to which the UK is party, goods in Customs sealed vehicles or containers may transit intermediate countries with the minimum of Customs formalities provided a TIR carnet has been issued in respect of the journey. The system cannot be used for purely inter-EC journeys.

The carnet is a recognised international Customs document intended purely to simplify Customs procedures; it is not a substitute for other documents; it is not mandatory for any operator to use it; and it does not give any operator the right to run vehicles in any European country. Use of a carnet frees the operator from the need to place a deposit of duty in respect of the load he is carrying in each country through which the vehicle is to pass. The issuing authorities for the carnets, in this country the FTA and the RHA, act as guarantors on behalf of the IRU which is the international guarantor, and for this reason carnets are only issued to bona fide members of these two associations.

Vehicle Approval

Goods may only be carried under a TIR carnet provided the vehicle in which they are carried complies with special requirements and has been approved by the DTP as meeting these requirements.

Approval for vehicles will only be given if they are constructed so that the load-carrying space can be sealed by Customs, after which it must not be possible for any goods to be removed from or added to the load without the seals being broken and there must be no concealed spaces where goods may be hidden.

TIR Plates

When a vehicle has been approved it must display at the front and the rear a plate showing the letters TIR in white on a blue background. Such plates are obtainable from the FTA and RHA.

TIR Carnets

Carnets (printed in French) are in four parts and contain 6, 14 or 20 pages (ie volets in French). A six-page carnet is valid only for a journey between the UK and one other country. One pair of pages, or in some cases three pages, are required for each Customs' entry so this means one pair for use at the point of exit from a country, three pages for use at the point of entry of the country of destination and the remainder for Customs' use at intermediate border crossings. Thus a 14-page carnet will cover a journey with four intermediate border crossings. Journeys to more than one other country require 14- or 20-page carnets which are valid for two months and three months respectively.

A carnet covers only one load and if a return load is to be collected a separate carnet is needed and the driver should take this with him on the outward journey. Careful attention to the completion of the carnet is vital if delays and difficulties are to be avoided on the Continent. The four parts of the carnet comprise the following:
1. Details of the issuing authority, the carnet holder, the country of departure, the country of destination, the vehicle, the weight and value of the goods as shown in the manifest (part 3).
2. A declaration that the goods specified have been loaded for the country stated, that they will be carried to their destination with the Customs seals intact and that the Customs' regulations of the countries through which the goods are to be carried will be observed.
3. A goods manifest giving precise details of the goods, the way in which they are packed (so many parcels or cartons) and their value.
4. Vouchers which Customs officials at frontier posts will remove, stamping the counterfoil section which remains in the carnet.

26: INTERNATIONAL TRANSPORT OPERATIONS

Before obtaining a carnet, the operator (ie Association member) must sign a form of contract with the Association agreeing to abide by all the necessary legal and administrative requirements. A financial guarantee will be required as a means of ensuring that the member meets any claims which may be made against him.

Carnets are valid until completion of the journey for which they are issued and if not used they must be returned to the issuing authority for cancellation. Those which are used and which bear all the official stampings acquired *en route* must also be returned within ten days of the return of the vehicle.

Strict instructions regarding the use of carnets are issued by the Associations both for the operator and for the driver. For example, the driver should never leave the carnet with any Customs authority without first obtaining a signed, stamped and dated declaration quoting the carnet number and certifying that the goods on the vehicle conform with the details contained on the carnet. Drivers should also ensure that the Customs at each departure office, transit office and arrival office take out a voucher from the carnet and stamp and sign the counterfoil accordingly.

Seal Breakage

If a Customs seal on a TIR vehicle is broken during transit as a result of an accident or for any other reason, Customs or the police must be contacted immediately to endorse the carnet to this effect.

Parties to the TIR Convention

Besides EC member states the following non-EC member countries are party to the TIR Convention:

Afghanistan	Kuwait
Albania	Luxembourg
Austria	Malta
Bulgaria	Morocco
Canada	Norway
Cyprus	Poland
Czechoslovakia	Romania
Finland	Sweden
East Germany (as was)	Switzerland
Hungary	Tunisia
Iran	Turkey
Israel	USA
Japan	USSR
Jordan	Yugoslavia

Non-TIR Journeys

Goods may be sent abroad in vehicles without TIR cover and no carnet is required. In this case, however, it will be necessary to comply with the individual Customs' requirements of each country through which the vehicle passes. A guarantee in lieu of import duty, or a deposit against such duty, will have to be paid before the vehicle is allowed to enter the country to which it is travelling, or any country through which it needs to pass, and the vehicle will be subject to stringent Customs' scrutiny not only at the port of exit from the UK and the port of entry to the Continent, but at all further frontier crossings during the journey.

The Community Transit System

The Community Transit system was introduced on 1 January 1973 in connection with the reduction in Customs duties between EC member countries which came into effect from 1 April 1973. Between this date and July 1977 such duties reduced to nil and tariff barriers between the member states are being removed. Normal rates of duty still apply to trade with non-EC member countries.

To take advantage of duty concessions, special documents comprising the Community Transit system are required. These documents confirm that the goods being carried originated in, and are travelling to, EC countries and are, therefore, eligible for the reduced duty. Full details of the system may be found in *Customs Notices 750, 750A, 750B and 755* available free from offices of HM Customs and Excise.

Two different procedures apply in this system. First is the use of a movement certificate – form T2L – which solely establishes the origin of the goods and has no authority as a transit document.

The second procedure is the full transit procedure when the T-form is used as a transit document, replacing the TIR system. In this case one of two coded forms will be used as follows:
1. Code T1 – For goods not eligible for free entry or reduced rates of duty since they are not in free circulation in the EC.
2. Code T2 – For goods eligible for free entry to any of the original six EC member countries and reduced rates of duty entry to the new EC member countries. Plus forms T2ES and T2PT.

The operator has to complete the appropriate form which can be obtained from local Customs and Excise offices (see local telephone directory for addresses), and have it certified when it has been completed by a Customs officer. The certified document must travel with the vehicle and be shown on request to Customs officials *en route*.

On arrival at the destination one copy of the document must be given to local Customs officials, the other two copies must be brought back, one to be given to Customs at the point of origin of the journey to match a copy which they retained when it was certified, the other to be retained for statistical purposes.

A deposit or guarantee against Customs claims will have to be made when using the Community Transit system, as with TIR operation. This guarantee can be arranged through banks or other approved sources either on an individual trip basis or it can be a comprehensive guarantee. Community transit guarantee vouchers can be used to relieve the necessity for making individual guarantees or deposits of duty. They can be obtained from the FTA, the RHA and the Prudential Assurance Company Ltd. The price of the vouchers varies according to the source and value of goods.

The acceptance of any guarantee will be subject to the approval of the guarantor by the Customs. In order to protect the interests of guarantors it is important for operators to ensure that documentation relating to loads is properly completed and that the T-form is returned to the office of departure on completion of the journey in order to release the guarantor from his obligations, provided, of course, that there was no irregularity while the goods were in transit.

This system is intended to ease the passage of loads between EC member countries to comply with the concept of a Customs-free Community with no tariff barriers – finally destined to be achieved in 1992 (ie the European Single Market). It replaces the need for TIR carnets and the involved procedures for the technical approval of TIR vehicles for all inter-EC journeys, although loads will still need to be 'satisfactorily sealed', a term which is not officially defined. Existing approved TIR vehicles will obviously comply but there may be difficulties with other vehicles not up to this standard of load area security.

Customs Entry Procedure

When goods are exported an 'entry' or declaration must be made to Customs and Excise (with certain exceptions). There are four procedures used for export clearance. They are as follows:
1. Pre-entry
2. Low Value Procedure
3. Local Export Control
4. Simplified Clearance Procedure (SCP).

Pre-entry is the standard scheme for making export declarations prior to clearance of goods using the appropriate forms (available from HM Customs and Excise). For certain low value goods (not exceeding £475 FOB and with a net weight not exceeding 1000kg) the Low Value Procedure can be used where the goods are non-dutiable and not destined for the Channel Islands. Local Export Control (LEC) procedure is for clearance of export goods at the consignor's premises with Customs and Excise approval (pre-authenticated form C44B is used together with C273 declaration). An alternative to Pre-entry is the use of the Simplified Clearance Procedure (SCP) but only where prior Customs approval has been obtained and a CRN (Customs Registered Number) has been issued.

Customs Documentation – SAD Scheme

The new 8-page Single Administrative Document (SAD) (Form C88) was introduced on 1 January 1988 to replace a large number of existing export, import and transit documents. This scheme applies throughout the whole of the European Community and is referred to as the 'Customs 88 Project'. Also part of the scheme is the introduction of a new Customs tariff based on the world-wide harmonised commodity description and coding system (HS) which is currently being adopted by all the world's major trading nations. The new tariff is referred to as TARIC. Full details are available from local offices of HM Customs and Excise and free explanatory publications are also available.

Carnets de Passage

Most European countries permit the temporary importation of foreign vehicles and containers (not to be confused with the loads they carry) free

of duty or deposit and without guaranteed Customs documents. However, a *carnet de passage en douane* is required for the following:
1. Vehicles and trailers entering Gibraltar, Iran, Iraq, Jordan, Kuwait, Lebanon, Saudi Arabia, Syria, Turkey and other Middle East countries.
2. Unaccompanied trailers entering France.
3. Vehicles remaining in Italy for more than three months and those remaining in Portugal for more than one month.

A deposit of duty in lieu of a *carnet de passage* is required for unaccompanied trailers entering Norway and Denmark.

Vehicles entering the Benelux countries (the Netherlands, Belgium and Luxembourg) do not require carnets provided they show signs of use (ie are not new imports). *Carnets de passage* are issued by the Automobile Association, the Royal Automobile Club and the Royal Scottish Automobile Club.

ATA Carnets

Goods which are only being temporarily imported into Europe, such as samples and items for display at exhibitions and fairs which will be returned to the UK can be moved under an ATA carnet (an international Customs clearance document), issued by Chambers of Commerce [or by the RHA] to members without the need for payments of, or deposits against, duty. Holding an ATA carnet does not relieve the operator from observing Customs' requirements in each individual country.

Carnets cost £40.00 to Chamber of Commerce members and £67.00 to non-members. They are valid for 12 months from the date of issue.

Dangerous Goods (ADR)

The European Agreement concerning the International Carriage of Dangerous Goods by Road (ADR) applies when vehicles travelling in certain European countries are carrying dangerous goods. Its purpose is to ensure that such goods being conveyed by road will be able to cross international frontiers without hindrance, provided they are packed and labelled in accordance with the Agreement and that the vehicles carrying the goods also comply with the special conditions laid down in the Agreement.

Operators taking vehicles containing dangerous goods by sea to European ports should also be aware of the stringent regulations applying to the delivery of such goods to ports (in the UK notice must be given to the harbour master at least 24 hours in advance) and to the carriage of such goods in ships. Advice on the suitability of vehicles and loads to be carried in ships can be obtained from the Marine Division, Department of Transport, Dangerous Goods Branch, 2 Marsham Street, London SW1P 3EB.

Tank vehicles and certain other vehicles carrying explosives under ADR are subject to technical inspection and a certification procedure in their country of registration to ensure that they conform to ADR requirements and with the normal safety regulations in force in the country of origin governing such things as brakes, steering and lights. Applications for test should be made to the Goods Vehicle Centre, The Strand, Swansea.

UK road transporters intending to carry dangerous goods to or through the countries which are party to the Agreement (Austria, Belgium, Finland, France, Germany, Hungary, Italy, Luxembourg, the Netherlands, Norway, Poland, Portugal, Spain, Sweden, Switzerland, Yugoslavia and the United Kingdom) will require an ADR certificate which must accompany the vehicle. Inspection of vehicles for this certificate will be carried out at certain DTp goods vehicle testing stations by DTp vehicle examiners and application forms for this inspection may be obtained from Traffic Area offices. The inspection fee is £95.00 for rigid vehicles and £95.00 each for the tractive unit and semi-trailer of articulated combinations, which is additional to the normal plating and testing fee (see p 209) if this is carried out at the same time.

Before the inspection is carried out the tanks of tank vehicles must be examined and tested by an inspecting authority approved by the Health and Safety Executive (see below for list). Tank testing will include examination for corrosion, cracking and faults at attachment points and at seams and valve connections. They are also pressure tested.

Tank Vehicle-Approved Inspecting Authorities

Associated Offices Technical Committee
St Mary's Parsonage,
Manchester M60 4DT
Tel 061-834 8124

Bureau Veritas
Ocean House,
Great Tower Street,
London EC3
Tel 071-623 1665

Cornhill Insurance Co Ltd
Engineering Dept, PO Box 10,
57 Ladymead, Guildford, Surrey
Tel 0483 68161

Eagle Star Insurance Co Ltd
Hagley House, 83 Hagley Road,
Edgbaston,
Birmingham B16 8QP

British Inspecting Engineers Ltd
66 Wilton Road, Victoria,
London SW1
Tel 071-834 1137

Guardian Royal Exchange
Assurance
Civic Drive,
Ipswich IP1 2AN

Imperial Chemical Industries
Central Inspection Services,
Sunley Building, Piccadilly Plaza,
Manchester M60 7JT

Lloyd's Register of Shipping
Non-Marine Dept,
Norfolk House, Wellesey Road,
Croydon CR9 2DT
Tel 081-686 2455

Vehicle Equipment

In order to meet the ADR requirements vehicles must have protected wiring circuits and electrical equipment and specifically positioned exhaust systems and fuel tanks. Tool kits for use in an emergency must be carried on the vehicle, together with at least two fire extinguishers and vehicles must be specially marked with orange reflex reflecting markers (see Chapter 17). In some cases a second man must be carried on the vehicle. Two amber flashing lights are required which operate independently of the vehicle and which must be used on the Continent. If the vehicle stops at night without lights the amber flashing lamps must be placed on the road, one 10 metres in front of the vehicle, the other 10 metres behind the vehicle. A suitable wheel chock must also be carried which is capable of holding the vehicle.

Driver Training and Certification

Vehicle crews should be properly trained and briefed on parking, loading and unloading procedures and what to do in case of an emergency and should also have details of authorities to contact in the event of a dangerous situation arising. They should carry certificates confirming their dangerous goods training – see also p 302.

Copies of the ADR agreement and its technical annexes which give all this information in detail may be obtained from HMSO. Details of how UK transport operators wishing to carry dangerous goods to and from the Continent are affected are contained in a free leaflet (ADR 2) obtainable from the Dangerous Goods Branch, Department of Transport, 2 Marsham Street, London SW1P 3EB.

Perishable Foodstuffs (ATP)

Operators sending vehicles carrying perishable foodstuffs for delivery to, or passing through, Austria, Belgium, Bulgaria, Denmark, Finland, France, Germany, Italy, Luxembourg, Morocco, the Netherlands, Norway, Portugal, the Soviet Union, Spain, Sweden, Switzerland and Yugoslavia must observe the strict regulations regarding the movement of food and produce under the *European Agreement on the International Carriage of Perishable Foodstuffs* (commonly known as the ATP agreement).

The UK introduced the International Carriage of Perishable Foodstuffs Act 1979 to enable requirements of the ATP agreement to be enforced in this country. Under these regulations specified temperature conditions and standards of thermal efficiency are set out for the carriage of prescribed frozen foodstuffs as follows:

Quick deep frozen and frozen (Annex 2 of ATP)
Ice cream and concentrated fruit juices	$-20°c$
Fish, all other quick (deep) frozen foodstuffs	$-18°c$
Butter and other frozen fats	$-14°c$
Frozen red offal, egg yolks, poultry and game	$-12°c$
Frozen meat; all other frozen foodstuffs	$-10°c$

A brief rise in temperature of $3°c$ maximum is allowed if caused by certain technical operations, eg defrosting of the mechanical refrigerated equipment.

Foodstuffs which are neither quick (deep) frozen nor frozen (Annex 3 of ATP)
Red offal	$+3°c$
Milk (raw or pasteurised) in tanks, for immediate consumption	$+4°c$
Industrial milk	$+6°c$
Yoghurt, kefir, cream, and fresh cheese	$+4°c$

Maximum transit time should not exceed 48 hours' duration for the above items.
Meat products (except those stabilised by salting, smoking, drying or sterilisation)	$+6°c$
Butter	$+6°c$
Game, poultry and rabbits	$+4°c$
Meat, other than red offal	$+7°c$

26: INTERNATIONAL TRANSPORT OPERATIONS

Fish, molluscs and crustaceans (other than smoked, salted, dried or live fish, live molluscs and live crustaceans) must always be carried in melting ice.

Insulated or controlled temperature vehicles must be used for frozen or chilled foods and the vehicle must carry an ATP certificate showing that it conforms to the requirements laid down for temperature control of the cargo. Vehicles and equipment used for carrying foodstuffs have to be individually tested or type approved (from 21 November 1980) and the Act gives powers to examiners to enter premises for inspection purposes.

Fiscal Charges

Operators sending vehicles to the Continent will find themselves, depending on which countries are visited, faced with a variety of taxes, duties and tolls which have to be paid. In all countries, except those listed below, goods vehicles are subject to the normal vehicle taxes of the country through which they pass. The amount of the taxation varies from time to time, and from place to place. Some countries, alternatively or additionally, levy a tax on ton-mileage or length of stay.

As a result of UK adherence to the relevant *International Taxation Convention* and taxation agreements with certain countries, goods vehicles registered in the United Kingdom will not be charged any vehicle taxes while in:

Belgium
Bulgaria
Czechoslovakia
Denmark
Eire
Finland (see below)
France
Germany
Greece
Yugoslavia
Hungary (see below)
Irish Republic
Luxembourg
Netherlands
Norway (see below)
Poland
Romania
Switzerland
Turkey

Motor fuel on the Continent is normally taxed and the tax included in the fuel price as it is in this country. The tax is not normally levied on fuel entering the country in the tanks of a vehicle, but the amount of fuel carried may be limited.

NB: Customs and Excise in Britain will charge duty on fuel brought back into Britain by British registered vehicles if the fuel is carried in supplementary or long-range tanks as opposed to the vehicle's normal fuel tank.

Among those countries with which the British government has made bilateral agreements concerning road transport operation the following examples show the type of fiscal charges payable:

Austria	Lorry tax payable by weight and distance.
Finland	UK vehicles are exempt from vehicle tax so long as certain Customs regulations for temporary admission are observed. This exemption does not apply to taxes on fuel consumption or on tolls.

405

Hungary	No taxes payable by British operators unless certain axle weight limits are exceeded (10 tonnes one axle, 16 tonnes two axles 2 metres or less apart).
Norway	No vehicle taxes payable by British operators but a kilometre tax is payable.
Sweden	Diesel powered vehicles are subject to a kilometre tax based on total vehicle weight, payable at the frontier.
Turkey	Vehicles in transit through Turkey are taxed on payload capacity, weights and dimensions.
Yugoslavia	Vehicles operating under permit within the country are exempt from payment of taxes. Those not covered by a permit and those travelling through are liable to a road tax based on the gross weight of the vehicle.

NB: *VAT may be payable on goods entering some European countries.*

Vehicle Insurance

In some countries insurance against third-party risks is compulsory, as it is in the UK, and in some cases liabilities for damage to the property of third parties must also be covered. An international motor insurance card (ie 'green card') issued by an insurance company will provide the necessary evidence of insurance against compulsory insurable liabilities in those countries in which the card is shown to be valid. While no longer required when transiting the EC and other near European countries, in certain other countries a sight of the card may be requested along with the other essential documents (see also below).

Most British insurance companies belong to the UK Bureau (the Motor Insurers' Bureau) and will arrange for 'green cards' to be issued to their policy holders on request and on payment of an additional premium.

Since 1 January 1974 a green card has not been a mandatory requirement for British vehicles when travelling to EC member countries and to Austria, Sweden, Norway, Finland and Switzerland. It will be required when travelling to any other European country. Insurers, however, advise that it should still be used since it provides more protection than the minimum EC requirement which British policies provide, namely indemnity for third-party personal injury but not indemnity for any property damage.

Under a new scheme launched in 1989 insurance company Eagle Star has introduced a European-wide fleet vehicle insurance scheme. Under this arrangement, holders of the new-style policy will not need a 'Green Card' when travelling to or through the following countries: all EC member states (except Italy – see below), Austria, Czechoslovakia, Finland, East Germany (as was), Hungary, Norway, Sweden and Switzerland. The company advises that in the case of Italy, it is still advisable to carry a Green Card because of Italian legal requirements governing civil liability.

Some countries insist on insurance of goods carried. Failing adequate proof of such insurance cover a premium will be payable on entry to a country. When a vehicle is to travel in Spain, an additional insurance requirement is a Spanish Bail Bond providing cover of at least £1000 which should be taken out to protect the driver in the event of his being involved in an accident or infringing local regulations. The cost of the premium for this is usually minimal. It is the practice of the Spanish police to hold all the

26: INTERNATIONAL TRANSPORT OPERATIONS

parties involved until blame for an accident or 'incident' has been firmly established. The Bond will probably secure the release of the driver and the vehicle pending an investigation.

Middle East Journeys

Special insurance cover is needed for journeys to the Middle East because once beyond Turkey the 'green card' system ceases to operate. In countries such as Syria, Jordan, Saudi Arabia and Qatar, third-party indemnity does not operate unless special arrangements for cover have been made before beginning the journey. Cover purchased at the border crossings will not provide sufficient protection in the event of a claim arising for third-party injury or death.

Even in countries which operate compulsory insurance purchase schemes, such as Iran, the level of cover obtained is absolutely minimal and, in the event of a bad accident involving injury or damage claims by third parties, the sum insured is unlikely to be anywhere near the amount required.

For these reasons, operators are advised to ensure that they have adequate cover for such journeys before setting out.

Medical Aid Schemes

A scheme to provide cover for medical aid for hauliers on international operations has been established by the Transporters Medical Service. Under the Transmed scheme, cover is provided for payment of medical expenses arising from illness or accident abroad and it includes the cost of repatriation where this is necessary by air ambulance or by regular air service with the provision of qualified medical attention.

International Carriage of Goods for Reward/CMR Convention

For loads other than furniture removals which are transported abroad, the carrier is controlled by the *Convention on the Contract for the International Carriage of Goods by Road* (CMR Convention) which is concerned with the international movement of goods by road for reward (ie by hauliers rather than own-account operators) between different countries of which at least one is a party to the CMR Convention. These countries are: Austria, Belgium, Denmark, France, Germany, Gibraltar, Hungary, Italy, Luxembourg, the Netherlands, Norway, Poland, Portugal, Sweden, Switzerland, UK and Yugoslavia. The CMR Convention does not apply to international movements by road between the UK and Eire and between the UK and Jersey (rules by the High Court to be not a different country from the UK).

The CMR Convention does not apply to international movements by road between the UK and Eire and between the UK and Jersey (ruled by the High Court to be not a different country from the UK). CMR is also not applicable to cabotage operations which are classed as domestic transport within the countries concerned. UK hauliers undertaking cabotage operations should ensure they are separately covered by insurance for these movements.

CMR regulations automatically apply to every contract for the international carriage of goods by road in vehicles for reward even when the vehicle containing the goods is carried over part of its journey by sea, rail or inland waterway and a CMR type consignment note must be completed. Even where a haulier is not aware that the load being moved is on an international journey or aware of the conditions and implications of CMR the provisions still apply.

Under the terms of the carriage contract the carrier taking over the goods must check the accuracy of the statements in the consignment note as to the number of packages, their marks and numbers, the apparent condition of the goods and their packaging. Under these regulations the carrier is responsible for loss, damage or delay from the time of taking over the goods until the time of their delivery.

CMR liability is set at a limit of approximately £6000 plus per tonne on the weight of the goods carried plus carriage charges. The actual valuation is based on Special Drawing Rights (SDR) per kilogramme at a current rate of 8.33 SDR per kilogramme (see daily financial press for conversion rate – on 30 August 1990 the rate was 0.721293 so the value for CMR insurance purposes was $8.33 \times 0.721293 \times 1000 = £6008.37$ per tonne). Customs duties and 5 per cent interest on the value of the goods have also to be included. It can be seen, therefore, that it is important for the operator to have goods in transit insurance cover sufficient to protect his liabilities to this extent.

If goods are handled by a number of carriers on an overseas journey, provisions are contained in CMR to apportion the liability for loss or damage between all the carriers because of the difficulties which may arise in pinpointing the exact time and place when the damage occurred.

It is not practical for own-account operators to undertake the carriage of return loads for hire or reward – despite their freedom to do so in the UK under their operators' licence – because such operations are not covered by CMR regulations and to do so can present problems which outweigh the reward obtained. This does not apply if the operator obtains return loads from associate companies on the Continent.

CMR Consignment Notes

Operators carrying goods for hire and reward on overseas journeys within the provisions of the *Convention on the Contract for the International Carriage of Goods by Road* (CMR) as described above must complete special CMR consignment notes to be carried on the vehicle. The details required on consignment notes, which must be made out in triplicate and signed by the sender and the carrier, are as follows:

Box 1. Sender (name, address, country).
Box 2. Customs reference/status.
Box 3. Sender's/agent's reference.
Box 4. Consignee (name, address, country).
Box 5. Carrier (name, address, country).
Box 6. Place and date of taking over the goods.
Box 7. Successive carriers.
Box 8. Place designated for delivery of goods.
Box 9. Marks and numbers; number and kind of packages; description of goods.*
Box 10. Gross weight (kg).
Box 11. Volume (m3).
Box 12. Carriage charges.

Box 13. Sender's instructions for Customs.
Box 14. Reservations.
Box 15. Documents attached.
Box 16. Special agreements.
Box 17. Goods received.
Box 18. Signature of carrier.
Box 19. Company completing the note.
Box 20. Place, date, signature.
Box 21. Copies to:
    (i) Sender
    (ii) Consignee
    (iii) Carrier.

*For dangerous goods indicate:
(i) Correct technical name (ie proper shipping name)
(ii) Hazchem class
(iii) UN number
(iv) Flashpoint (°C), if applicable.

Where applicable, the consignment notes must also contain the following particulars:
1. A statement that transhipment to another vehicle is not allowed.
2. The charges which the sender undertakes to pay.
3. The amount of 'cash on delivery' charges.
4. A declaration of the value of the goods and the amount representing special interest in delivery.
5. The sender's instructions to the carrier regarding insurance of the goods.
6. The agreed time limit within which the carriage is to be carried out.

The consignor or consignee can also add to the consignment note any other particulars which may be useful to the operator. One copy of the note is retained by the sender, the second by the carrier, and the third must accompany the goods. Own-account operators are not required to use this particular consignment note for continental journeys. For most countries a simple consignment note is all that is necessary to prove that the journey is on own-account (not for hire or reward). It should contain details of the following:
1. The vehicle operator.
2. His trade or business.
3. The goods being carried.
4. Their loading and delivery points.
5. The vehicle being used.
6. The route to be followed.

In the case of own-account traffic to Germany a more detailed document is required containing the following particulars:
1. The place at which the document was made out and the date it was made out.
2. The name and address of the own-account operator and an accurate description of the nature of his business.
3. If the goods are to be accepted from, or delivered to, any other person, the name and address of that person and an accurate description of the nature of his business.
4. Details of the loading point or points.
5. Details of the place or places at which the vehicle is to deliver.

6. Details of the nature of the load.
7. The gross weight or other indication of the quantity of the load.
8. The carrying capacity of the vehicle by weight.
9. The index mark and registration number of the vehicle or, if these do not exist, the chassis number.
10. The distance of the loaded journey in the German Federal Republic in kilometres.
11. The point or points at which the frontier is to be crossed.
12. A signature of the operator or his authorised representative.

Documents to be Carried

Vehicle Registration Document

The vehicle registration document (ie the original not a copy) should always be carried on the vehicle when it is travelling on international journeys. The driver should also have written authority from his employer on the company's letter-headed paper showing that he is the authorised driver of the vehicle.

If a hired or borrowed vehicle is taken abroad (or any vehicle not registered in the operator's name) the driver must carry written authority from the owner permitting his use of the vehicle together with the vehicle registration document. Alternatively, a special registration certificate can be obtained from the motoring organisations in which case there will be no need for the registration document to be carried.

On all journeys abroad British vehicles must display a valid vehicle excise disc.

Nationality Sign

All vehicles must display the British nationality sign – GB – when travelling outside the UK. The yellow and black reflective type occasionally seen on vehicles in this country is illegal in some European countries, so the official black lettering on a white background type should be used.

'O' Licences for International Operations

Road hauliers wishing to carry goods for hire and reward outside the UK need to hold a standard 'O' licence covering both national and international operations and will need to be professionally competent, or employ a person who is professionally competent, in national and international operations (see Chapter 1 for full details).

Own-account operators with restricted 'O' licences may operate internationally on these licences.

When under British transport regulations a vehicle is required to be specified on an operator's licence, the licence disc must be displayed on the vehicle during all international journeys.

Invoices

The manner in which invoices for goods should be made out is specified by the authorities of the country of destination. In addition to invoices, certificates of origin for the goods, certificates of health and consular certificates are sometimes required.

The requirements vary widely depending on the country of destination and the nature of the goods. The exporter should seek advice on these matters from the FTA, RHA, local Chambers of Commerce or the embassy of the country concerned.

Selling Documents

Many of the delays to export traffic occur as a result of incomplete, inaccurate or missing documentation. This is particularly so in the case of goods sold for export on an 'FOB' (the selling price including transport to the port of exit and loading to ship only) or 'CIF' (selling price comprising cost, insurance and freight) basis. The changeover of legal responsibility for the goods from the exporter to the importer either at the port of entry or on board ship at the port of departure is a major source of documentation problems. Such problems can be avoided by quoting a delivered price to the customer's door.

This method of selling is common in Europe and has additional advantages for the UK exporter by:
1. Saving his customer the need to convert 'FOB' or 'CIF' prices to a door-to-door price for comparison with the delivered price of products from other sources.
2. Easing transport planning by enabling him to arrange complete through movements through one source – either his own vehicles, a transport contractor or a forwarding agent.
3. Allowing him the opportunity to take advantage of any economies in transport costs resulting from his making all the arrangements for the through movement.
4. Enabling him to control the whole through movement and consequently taking advantage of savings in documentation costs, warehousing and possibly even in reduced packing costs.
5. Enabling him to reduce the time of goods in transit by efficient planning and therefore improving his cash flow.

Maximum Weight and Load Certificates

A certificate showing the maximum weight and load for the vehicle may be needed in certain European countries although generally the manufacturer's plate and the DTp plate fixed to the vehicle and/or trailer should suffice. The FTA or RHA will advise when a certificate is necessary in which case application for a certificate has to be made to the DTp area mechanical engineer at any Traffic Area office in the UK (see Appendix I).

Passports and Visas

Drivers and other crew members or passengers must carry a valid passport. This is required to satisfy immigration authorities on entry to a country and the British authorities on returning to the UK, to enable travellers' cheques to be cashed if money is carried in this form and to establish identity if apprehended by foreign police or authorities for any reason. Passports should be carried on the person at all times, when driving and when out in the evening or at any other time. They should not be left in the vehicle.

Certain countries require an entry or transit visa in addition to a passport. This does not apply in EC countries but such visas are required when travelling in:

Bulgaria
Czechoslovakia
Hungary
Poland
Romania
USSR

British citizens travelling in these countries are advised, in their own interests, to contact the nearest British consulate on arrival in the country and provide details of their passport and home address. If they are staying for more than a few days they should maintain contact with the consulate and advise it when they leave the country.

Passports are obtained from the Passport Office at Peterborough or from local passport offices, the addresses of which will be found in the telephone directory. Application for visas should be made to the consulate in the UK for the country concerned. Besides providing the visa it will also give information regarding any special regulations which must be observed in that country.

Driving Licences/International Driving Permits

Those European countries listed below accept a current British driving licence valid for the type of vehicle being driven. An international driving permit, issued by the AA, the RAC or the Royal Scottish Automobile Club (price £2.00) to applicants who produce a passport-type photograph and a valid British driving licence (not a provisional licence) covering the category of vehicle being driven, is also accepted.

Austria	Holland
Belgium	Luxembourg
Bulgaria	Norway
Czechoslovakia	Portugal
Denmark	Romania
Finland	Sweden
France	Switzerland
Germany	Turkey
Greece	USSR
Yugoslavia	

Countries not mentioned above require the international driving permit and do not recognise a British driving licence. Italy (not listed above) accepts a British driving licence provided it is accompanied by an Italian translation of the licence which the motoring organisations will provide. See p 108 for further details of the new 'Euro-Licence'.

Drivers' Hours and Work Records

Goods vehicles over 3.5 tonnes gross weight travelling in EC countries

26: INTERNATIONAL TRANSPORT OPERATIONS

must be equipped with a fully operational and officially calibrated tachograph (see Chapter 5) in order to enable drivers to keep a record of the hours worked in a day, the amount of this time spent driving, and the rest periods taken. Goods vehicle drivers within the EC, the rest of Europe and beyond are limited in the time they may spend driving and must take specified periods of rest and breaks between driving periods. When driving within the territories of EC member states drivers must observe the EC rules as contained in EC regulation 3820/85 and which are summarised below. Beyond the EC the requirements of the AETR rules on drivers' hours apply as shown on page 69 and these should be followed for the whole of the journey. Full details of the requirements for drivers' hours and records are given in Chapters 3 and 4.

Maximum Driving/Minimum Rest Period Times

Daily driving	9 hours
	10 hours on 2 days in week (all vehicles)
Weekly driving	6 daily driving periods
Fortnightly driving	90 hours
Driving before a break	4½ hours
Breaks after driving	45 minutes or other breaks of at least 15 minutes each totalling at least 45 minutes
Daily rest	11 hours
Reduced daily rest	9 hours on up to 3 days per week (must be made up by following week)
Split daily rest	11-hour daily rest period may be split into 2 or 3 periods – one at least 8 hours, the others at least one hour each – total 12 hours
Weekly rest	45 hours once each fixed week
Reduced weekly rest	36 hours at base
	24 hours elsewhere (reduced weekly rest must be made up *en bloc* by end of 3rd following week)
Rest on Ferries/Trains	May be split if:
	- part taken on land
	- not more than 1 hour between parts
	- drivers must have bunk/couchette
	- total rest must increase by 2 hours

Tachographs

European countries require goods vehicles arriving from Britain to be fitted with tachographs. Full details of the requirements for the fitment and use of tachographs are given in Chapter 5.

Construction and Size of Vehicles

Goods vehicles which comply fully with the UK Construction and Use Regulations will generally meet the requirements of the European countries in which they may have to operate. Regulations regarding vehicle weights and dimensions vary from country to country and are subject to occasional change. Operators should check with the transport associations before the departure of any vehicle constructed in such a way, or of such a size, that it may infringe regulations in countries to which it is travelling or through which it may pass.

Weighing of Vehicles for Ferry Crossings

Since 1 February 1989 goods vehicles over 7.5 tonnes have to be weighed before being loaded onto a roll-on/roll-off passenger ferry ship leaving a UK port. Additionally, this requirement applies to other 'qualifying cargo items' such as containers, demountable bodies, skips and other items of deck cargo. The regulations (the Merchant Shipping [Weighing of Goods Vehicles and Other Cargo] Regulations 1988) apply to UK registered vessels and other vessels registered under other national flags (eg French vessels such as those of SNCF and Brittany Ferries operating regularly from British ports).

Driving

Vehicles in Europe are driven on the right, but this normally presents little difficulty to British drivers with right-hand drive vehicles, although care and concentration are needed particularly when attempting it for the first time.

Special care is needed at road junctions and traffic islands where traffic approaching from the right has priority except in Germany and Sweden where traffic already on the roundabout has priority. Care is needed when overtaking, and because of the difficulty of pulling out 'blind' from behind other big vehicles it is good practice to leave extra space when following other vehicles to obtain better vision. Additional mirrors fitted on the nearside are very helpful.

When travelling on *autobahns* or *autostradas* the driver should remember that the speeds at which many continental drivers cruise is far higher than on British motorways. Cars travelling at 100 to 120mph are still common despite speed restrictions, so the goods vehicle driver must take great care when pulling out to overtake, especially on two-lane roads, to ensure that the road is clear for a long distance.

Traffic signs are to international standards and identical, in most cases, to those used in the UK. There are some signs which may be unfamiliar to the British driver so it is helpful to display on the vehicle windscreen or side window a small transfer showing all continental road signs. The motoring organisations will supply these.

In most European countries a red warning triangle must be displayed on the road behind a broken-down vehicle to warn approaching traffic of the hazard. Drivers should have these signs in case they are needed and they can also be obtained from the motoring organisations and from garages and motoring shops.

On-the-spot fines are common on the Continent. These fines, imposed by the police for even minor infringements of the law, can be heavy but the driver can decline to pay and have the case heard in court. This may involve making a special journey to Europe, so in the interests of reducing delays it is usually best and cheapest to pay the fine.

Driver's Accommodation

Drivers who travel regularly to the Continent invariably sleep in their vehicles these days with the proliferation of sleeper cabs otherwise they are usually able to find their own suitable accommodation at acceptable prices since there are a great number of cafes, hostels and roadhouses on all major routes and in towns. British drivers can join the French organisation *Les Routiers* , which vets eating and sleeping places for lorry drivers on the Continent. Approved establishments display a red, white and blue circular *'Les Routiers'* plaque and can be relied on to provide a welcoming atmosphere, food at reasonable prices for good helpings, and generally good value for money. Members receive a guide showing approved places across the Continent and a few in the UK, a badge to display on their vehicle and membership of the UICR *(Union International des Chauffeurs Routiers)*, a European lorry drivers' union.

Other benefits of membership include insurance protection in the event of accident abroad, benefits to next-of-kin in the event of death following an accident in France, an international membership which is recognised on the Continent as a valid identity document (it has a passport-type photograph of the holder attached), and an international notebook containing useful information for the trans- European driver.

It is common practice on the Continent (and a legal requirement in France) for restaurants and cafes to display a priced menu outside so the driver can check what is offered and what the charges are. If a menu is not displayed the place is best avoided.

Driver's Subsistence

Since the level of expenditure by drivers on subsistence while abroad is normally much greater than when operating in the UK it is important to obtain evidence of expenditure to back up expense claims. The Inland Revenue can ask to see evidence of payments to drivers for subsistence.

Bans on Goods Vehicles

Some countries do not allow goods vehicles to use the roads at weekends or on public holidays. Operators should make inquiries about this through their road transport association before planning journeys since public holidays vary from country to country and do not always coincide with those in Great Britain.

France, for instance, restricts the movement of goods vehicles on certain days – Bastille Day, for example – and over some routes. Germany prohibits the use of goods vehicles over 7.5 tons gross weight between 07.00 hours on Saturdays and 22.00 hours on Sundays and on public holidays. Goods vehicles may not be driven in Switzerland on Sundays, public holidays and during certain night hours. Restrictions apply in Italy to vehicles of 5 tonnes laden and over, on Sundays, public holidays, feast days and during certain night hours. On holiday weekends this restriction is extended to cover specified busy main roads. Italy also requires operators to obtain prior permission to take extra long or wide loads into the country.

Austria has introduced new bans on goods vehicles over 7.5 tonnes from crossing the Brenner Pass between Austria and Italy between 22.00 hours and 05.00 hours starting from 1 December 1989.

Middle East*

Journeys to the Middle East present special problems but the increasing volume of trade necessitates that some notes on the subject should be included here. It is not possible, however, to detail all the requirements likely to be encountered in countries forming the Middle Eastern bloc because of space limitations and rapidly changing situations resulting from economic and political manoeuvring.

Operators planning such journeys are strongly advised to spend considerable time checking up-to-the-minute requirements of all the countries they plan to visit or pass through to ensure that adequate precautions are taken for a safe journey, that the correct documentation is provided, and that drivers are fully briefed on what they might expect once they get beyond Turkey.

Turkey itself, which is on the main route to the Middle East and the last of the countries which really matches European standards and requirements, can present the operator or driver with difficulties. Anything can happen from delays of a few days to several weeks if paperwork is not in order, and imprisonment of drivers in the event of mishap is common. Beyond Turkey, the situation is worse so journeys should not be contemplated without a great deal of care and attention to detail.

Detailed guidance for operators is available from a number of sources as follows:
1. International Road Freight Office
   Northern Traffic Area Office, Westgate House, Westgate Road, Newcastle upon Tyne. Tel: 091-261 0031.
2. Freight Transport Association
   Hermes House, 157 St John's Road, Tunbridge Wells, Kent. Tel: 0892 26171.

The International Road Freight Office's notes, *Road Transport to the Middle East*, which are available free, provide information on travel to or through the following countries:

Afghanistan	Lebanon
Arab Republic of Egypt	Oman
Iran	Qatar
Iraq	Saudi Arabia
Israel	Syria
Jordan	Turkey
Kuwait	

The notes do not cover the Yemen Arab Republic since roads in that country are not suitable for goods vehicles.

*At the time of going to press, the situation in the Middle East was extremely uncertain, as a result of the Iraqi invasion of Kuwait. Any information provided here which relates to either Iraq or Kuwait should, therefore, be checked with outside sources.

26: INTERNATIONAL TRANSPORT OPERATIONS

The following includes extracts from these notes:
Drivers are strongly advised to prepare themselves properly before starting Middle Eastern journeys with particular emphasis on knowledge of operational conditions and climate, the possession of good road maps, sufficient money (a common and unfortunate failing among many drivers), and a good supply of vehicle spare components for roadside repairs. They should know what procedures to follow in the event of accidents and what is likely to happen to them in the hands of local police or authorities and the addresses of sources of help, especially the British Embassy in each country.

Timing of journeys can be seriously affected by long delays at Customs and frontier posts and by special holidays. It should be remembered that Saturday is the Jewish sabbath and that Friday is a holiday in Moslem countries, although they do not observe our Saturday/Sunday weekends. A frequent cause of delay is incomplete documentation and passport and visa problems. Drivers should check their personal documentation before departure to ensure that their visas are in order. Similarly, medical documents, such as a smallpox vaccination certificate, should be valid and drivers should check whether other innoculations are required or advised (TAB, cholera and yellow fever are required for those drivers on the Nigeria and other West African routes).

Road accidents are much more likely and generally are more serious in these countries and drivers are advised to be as prepared as possible for such eventualities and for sickness which can cause difficulties.

Insurance should receive special attention, as mentioned earlier, because normal coverage which would be adequate in Europe is not sufficient protection in the Middle East. Operators should consult brokers or insurers experienced in providing cover in this area.

experienced in providing cover in this area.

Middle Eastern countries, it should be remembered that vehicles still have to pass through Europe to get there. Regulations and permit and other documentation requirements applicable in Europe still have to be met.

Specific Requirements

Visas
Entry visas are necessary for drivers and crew members entering the following countries:

Bulgaria	Lebanon
Iran	Saudi Arabia
Iraq	Syria
Jordan	Turkey
Kuwait	

Passports
A full passport is required by drivers and crew members entering all European and Middle Eastern countries.

Driving Licences
British driving licences are acceptable in all countries except the following

417

which require an international driving permit (see p 109):

Iran
Iraq
Jordan
Kuwait
Lebanon
Saudi Arabia
Syria

Vehicle Permits
Hauliers and own-account operators require permits to enter or transit Saudi Arabia and Syria. Vehicles making deliveries in Jordan require permits but not if they are only passing through the country.

TIR Carnets
TIR carnets are generally acceptable outside Europe. See list of applicable countries on p 399. In countries where TIR carnets are not acceptable, vehicles will be expected to conform to TIR specifications (see p 399) in regard to Customs sealing and evidence of TIR certification may be requested.

ATA Carnets
These are not applicable in the Middle East.

Carnets de Passage
Carnets de passage en douane are required in all Middle Eastern countries. In their absence substantial deposits of duty or guarantees for the value of the vehicle and trailer (sometimes many times the actual value) will be demanded.

CMR
CMR is not recognised in the Middle East since none of these countries is party to the CMR Agreement but hauliers must still meet CMR requirements and use CMR consignment notes for transit through Europe.

Vehicle Documents
In all cases vehicles should display current excise licence and 'O' licence discs and for European countries the driver should carry the vehicle registration document or a copy of it. In the Middle East an international motor vehicle certificate will be required rather than the registration document. These are obtainable from the motoring organisations. Vehicles should display a black on white nationality sign (the reflective black on yellow type is not acceptable).

The driver should carry with him a letter from the vehicle owner authorising him to drive the vehicle which should be specified by its registration number and description and to act on behalf of the owner in respect of any incident in which the vehicle may be involved.

26: INTERNATIONAL TRANSPORT OPERATIONS

Taxes
Vehicle and fuel taxes are not generally imposed in Middle Eastern countries apart from Syria.

Drivers' Hours and Records
In the main, EC or AETR driving hours and records requirements apply to the whole of any international journey from the time of starting the journey in the UK depending upon the countries visited or passed through (see p 69).

Drivers' Ages
European requirements in regard to the age of drivers in relation to vehicle weights apply in all Middle Eastern countries namely:
For vehicles up to 7.5 tonnes gross weight – minimum age 18 years
For vehicles over 7.5 tonnes gross weight – minimum age 21 years

Traffic and Vehicle Construction Requirements
Each country has its own traffic regulations which should be observed especially in regard to speed limits, parking, and so on. Bans on driving at specified times should be checked and observed; so too should specific requirements relating to the construction, dimensions, loading and use of vehicles and trailers.

Money
Drivers should be provided with sufficient money for their journey and for unexpected contingencies. They should be briefed on exchange procedures and normal exchange rates (although these will fluctuate substantially depending on when and where exchanges are made) and they should be especially warned about the need for the security of their money.

General
In Turkey and beyond drivers must be prepared to encounter different conditions, attitudes, customs and formalities from those in Britain and the rest of Europe.

Many operators and drivers now have extensive experience of the Middle East, having learned the hard way. Advice from them is well worth seeking and observing if they are prepared to give it.

27: Rental, Hiring and Leasing of Vehicles

Rental, hiring and leasing of commercial vehicles is now seen as a major and very cost effective alternative to fleet ownership. Transport operating companies have shown increasing interest in the advantages of these means of vehicle acquisition. In many cases operators have reduced their owned fleets to the bare minimum required to service basic and predictable delivery requirements, topping up with short-term rental vehicles to meet peak trading demands, or using this source for the replacement of vehicles off the road for service, repair or annual test preparation. At the other extreme, firms have disposed completely of their owned fleets in favour of contract hire arrangements where vehicles are provided by a third-party contractor and maintenance is taken care of as part of the contractual arrangement. Between these extremes are the firms who use a combination of owned vehicles, long-term hired vehicles and short-term rental, to ensure the most economical and efficient overall transport operation whatever the seasonal fluctuations or other trading exigencies of their business.

These alternative means of adding vehicles to the fleet have both legal and operational implications; hence the reason for including this basic outline of the subject in the *Handbook*.

The Vehicle User

One of the most significant legal points in connection with the renting, hiring or leasing of vehicles concerns the status of the vehicle 'user'. If the person or company renting or hiring a vehicle provides the driver, then that person or company, as the employer of the driver and consequently as the user of the vehicle, carries the full weight of legal responsibility for both the safe mechanical condition and the safe operation of the vehicle when it is on the road.

It is the user's responsibility to ensure that the vehicle complies fully with the Construction and Use Regulations in all respects but especially with regard to safety items such as brakes, lights, steering, horn, tyres, speedometer/tachograph and vehicle markings. The fact that the rental or hiring company which owns the vehicle *should* ensure that all these items are in order (and indeed usually proclaims that it does ensure they are in order) makes no difference to where the blame lies and where the prosecution will be aimed if they are found not to be in order when the vehicle is being used on the road.

Furthermore, it is the user's responsibility to ensure that operator's licence provisions where applicable are fully complied with and that the drivers' hours and tachograph requirements are observed where these are applicable.

Rental

Rental of vehicles on a short-term basis of a few days or a few weeks, which is the usual arrangement, does not impose onerous contractual obligations on the hirer.

However, it does involve other legal obligations in respect of the vehicle itself and its use. For a start, much depends on the gross weight of the vehicle. If it is over 3.5 tonnes maximum permissible weight and has been rented for use in connection with a trade or business, then the person or firm renting it must hold an operator's licence and there must be a margin on that licence to cover the renting of one or more additional vehicles.

There is no need to advise the Licensing Authority of details of the vehicle unless it is to be retained on hire for more than 28 days, after which time the Licensing Authority must be notified so an 'O' licence windscreen disc can be issued for the vehicle. If the vehicle is rented for a shorter period and then returned to the rental company to be replaced by another vehicle, the LA does not have to be notified if the combined total of the two rental periods exceeds 28 days unless both are part of the same rental agreement.

If the over 3.5 tonnes vehicle is rented by a firm for use in another traffic area different from the one in which the 'O' licence is held, then an 'O' licence must be obtained in that other traffic area before a vehicle is permitted to operate from a base there.

Where the gross weight of the rented vehicle does not exceed 3.5 tonnes there are no legal obligations in respect of 'O' licensing unless it is used to tow a goods-carrying trailer with an unladen weight over 1020kg when the combined weights may take it over the 3.5 tonnes limit and into 'O' licensing.

Whether or not the rented vehicle comes within the scope of 'O' licensing, the person or firm renting it carries the user responsibility for its safe mechanical condition when it is on the road. Consequently, if vehicle faults result in prosecution the user will have to pay any fines imposed (not the rental company) and the user's 'O' licence will be put in jeopardy (even if the vehicle is not specified on his 'O' licence). Therefore careful selection of a reputable rental company with high maintenance standards is essential.

Charges for rented vehicles are usually on a time plus mileage basis in accordance with published scales so there is little scope for improvement in prices, although large users can sometimes negotiate discounts.

The particular advantage of rental is that payment for a vehicle is only made when the use of the vehicle is really required, and then the payment is out of revenue and not out of capital reserves. Further, because rental is normally for short periods only, it is easy to establish the total costs involved because there are no additional costs for the upkeep of the vehicle. Maintenance, tyre replacements, licences and most other costs apart from fuel and insurance are built into the rental price.

The disadvantage of rental is its high price if vehicles are taken for longer periods, because the rental companies try to recover their costs over a short time and the price covers the fact that only a certain number of hire days can be sold in a period.

Hiring

Hiring of vehicles, as opposed to rental, implies a longer-term arrangement

CONTRACT HIRE
(COMMERCIAL VEHICLES) LTD

WILL SUPPLY ANY MAKE OF NEW COMMERCIAL VEHICLE
OR PURCHASE YOUR EXISTING FLEET
FOR USE ON CONTRACT HIRE, WITH OR WITHOUT DRIVERS.
OUR SERVICE INCLUDES:

FULL MAINTENANCE COVER
•
24 HOUR RECOVERY
•
RELIEF VEHICLES

AND LOTS MORE TO EASE TRANSPORT OPERATIONS
AND SAVE YOU MONEY.
FOR FURTHER DETAILS OR A FREE QUOTATION
WITHOUT OBLIGATION.

CONTACT US NOW.

BRISTOL
(HEAD OFFICE)
SEVERNSIDE TRADING ESTATE AVONMOUTH BS11 8AG.
Tel: 0272 825571 Fax: 0272 235141

BOLTON
RAIKES LANE IND. ESTATE MANCHESTER ROAD BL3 2NS
Tel: 0204 32441 Fax: 0204 27574

TDG

A Transport Development Group Company

with a more rigid agreement as to the obligations of the parties involved. Hiring arrangements vary considerably since the vehicle provider and the customer draw up a contract to incorporate the services required. There are two principal forms of contract hire – vehicles supplied with drivers and vehicles supplied without drivers.

The important difference is that in the former case the contract hire company, as the employer of the driver, is the 'user' of the vehicles in law and therefore holds the 'O' licence and shoulders the legal responsibilities previously described, while the hirer merely operates the vehicles exclusively to suit his requirements. However, in the latter case the hirer is the 'user' and 'O' licence holder and, as with vehicles purchased and leased with his own employee drivers at the wheel, he carries the full legal responsibilities.

Between these two categories, a package is made up to suit individual company needs. A complete package normally includes full maintenance (ie safety inspections, service and repairs), fuel, licensing, insurance, parking areas, administration (ie checking of records, etc), replacement vehicles to cover downtime at no extra cost and free driver replacement to cover holidays and sickness.

Contract hire charges are normally made on a time and mileage basis (ie a fixed or standing charge and running charge). These charges are either increased annually to cover the hiring company's increased costs or linked to a published index. Sometimes such items as fuel surcharges are raised.

This method of vehicle acquisition offers a number of advantages. Principally, there is no investment of capital (generally not even an initial deposit to be found) and cash flow for transport services is predictable throughout the year, thus allowing easy budgeting. One regular monthly invoice covers all capital and operating costs. The hire charges are fully allowable against tax.

Overall, full contract hire with driver is advantageous to the operator, because it relieves him of the burdens of capital expenditure on an ancillary activity and of a welter of legal responsibilities and yet provides him with the right vehicles for his exclusive use to fulfil his delivery requirements as he wishes. He thus has the best of both worlds – all his transport needs met without the major burdens usually encountered by own fleet operators.

A further financial advantage can arise for a firm operating its own fleet but wishing to switch to contract hire to gain the benefits outlined. Contract hire companies will usually purchase a whole existing fleet and then contract-hire it back to the operator, thus still giving him resources to meet his transport needs and yet providing him with an immediate refund of the capital tied up in vehicles. This proposition can be used to advantage in relieving cash flow pressure.

Leasing

Leasing is a totally different concept from outright purchase or hire purchase in that the operator (ie the lessee) never actually owns the vehicle but he has the full use of it as though it was his own. It is also a different concept from rental and hiring arrangements in that it is purely a financial means of acquiring vehicles. In other words those putting up the money are not transport or vehicle operators, they are finance houses.

27: RENTAL, HIRING AND LEASING OF VEHICLES

Several different forms of leasing are available (basically divided by the assumption of risk with the lessee taking the risk with a pure finance lease and the lessor retaining the risk with an operating lease) and legislation governing leasing arrangements is subject to change. Also, the way in which the accountancy profession treats leasing is subject to variation, so it is important to discuss any proposed leasing arrangement with a professional accountant before commitment to an agreement.

The basic concept of leasing is that a finance house (ie the lessor) purchases a vehicle, for which the operator has specified his requirements and negotiated the price and any available discount from the supplier, and then it spreads the capital cost, interest charges, overhead costs and its profit margin over a period of time to determine the amount of the periodic repayments.

The three basic types of finance lease are as follows:
1. Full amortisation lease which runs for an agreed fixed period (the primary lease) followed by an optional secondary period (if the vehicle is still required) when the lease is extended for a nominal (ie 'peppercorn') rental.
2. Open-ended lease which allows the lessee to terminate the agreement on payment of a previously agreed settlement figure at any time after a fixed period (normally one year).
3. Balloon lease which has one large payment and a number of relatively low rental payments. The balloon can be at the beginning with a large payment to start the lease or at the end of the lease term with a large pre-calculated final payment reflecting a forecast residual value for the vehicle.

Usually this full range of choice only applies in the case of smaller vehicles. For heavy vehicles it is customary to apply 'full pay-out' types of lease, whereby the vehicle is fully paid for in the rentals with no residual value.

Because no capital outlay is involved in a leasing agreement, beyond the initial lease payment which is sometimes a number of monthly rentals lumped together, the lessee is able to obtain the vehicles he needs and yet still invest his own capital in more profitable business avenues.

Changes in accounting practice brought into effect (from the start of accounting years beginning after 30 June 1987) by the introduction of the accounting profession's Statement of Accounting Practice 21 (SSAP21) mean that no longer is it a case where leased vehicles do not appear as assets in the lessee's balance sheet. Consequently leased vehicles and plant appear on the balance sheet as assets matched by outstanding lease payments showing on the other side as liabilities.

Leasing is a complex financial area and, as already mentioned, it is important that proper professional advice is obtained before signing any agreement, otherwise the promised tax and other benefits may not materialise.

Where leasing is purely a financial arrangement, the advantages and disadvantages from an operational viewpoint are the same as for outright purchase. Because in principle the lessee operates the vehicle as though he owns it and he employs the driver, the full weight of legal responsibility, as already outlined, applies to him so he needs to have a full transport back-up of administration and operational staff, maintenance facilities and policies for selection of the correct vehicles and for replacement at the most economic intervals.

An excellent review of the merits of various alternative methods of vehicle acquisition is to be found in the National Freight Consortium's* publication Financing the *Acquisition of Commercial Vehicles* prepared independently by Andrew B. Jones C.A. , Partner in Charge, Tax Department, Ernst & Young, London.

NB: The NFC through its various operating companies is one of the UK's leading providers of vehicles on hire, contract hire, contract distribution and vehicle rental.

28: Vehicle Fuel Economy

Next to wage costs, fuel is the most expensive vehicle operating cost item. It is a high-cost commodity which is a major budget feature of all goods vehicle fleet operations. It is also subject to occasional and dramatic shortages as a result of political unrest in some of the major oil-producing countries, as we have seen with the Middle East. Scientists predict total extinction as world supplies of crude oil are consumed ever more rapidly by developed nations which have become increasingly dependent on transportation systems powered by oil-based fuels. Even the once much-heralded finds of oil in offshore waters of the British Isles and Eire are now known to have limited life expectancy.

While the search for and research into acceptable alternative fuels and power units goes on, it is important to take steps to minimise consumption of our present fuel supplies. As well as being a problem for nations, this is a problem which concerns all fleet operators, whatever their size. Besides any conscience they may have about energy conservation they will readily appreciate that fuel consumption must be reduced in the campaign to keep vehicle operating costs down.

Fuel and the Vehicle

Fuel consumption is substantially related to the type of vehicle, its power unit and drive line, its mechanical condition, the use to which it is put and how it is driven. In recent times manufacturers have offered fuel economy models within their ranges so the cost-conscious operator can choose between economy or outright performance.

The fuel-conscious operator who is in a position to buy new vehicles will undoubtedly choose fuel economy models where these are suited to his particular needs. However, for the most part, fleet operators have to stick with the vehicles they already have in their fleets and are faced with the need to consider how improved fuel economy can be achieved with existing vehicles.

Three principal areas exist for improvement in the vehicle itself. These are as follows:
1. Mechanical condition
2. Efficient use
3. Addition of fuel economy aids.

Mechanical Condition

A vehicle which is poorly maintained will inevitably consume more fuel. Particular attention should be paid to efficient maintenance of the following items:
1. *Fuel system* (fuel tank, pipe lines, filters, pump and injectors). There

should be no leaks and the vehicle should not emit black smoke. Both of these are causes or consequences of excessive consumption as well as matters which could result in test failure and prosecution. Fuel pumps and injectors should be properly serviced as recommended by the manufacturers.
2. *Wheels and brakes.* Wheels should turn freely and without any brake binding. Front wheels should be correctly aligned. Brake binding and misalignment cause unnecessary friction which is only overcome by the use of more fuel. Axles on bogies should be correctly aligned because tyres running at slip angles have a high rolling resistance and therefore are a source of increased fuel consumption.
3. *Driving controls.* Throttle cables, clutch and brake pedals should be correctly adjusted so the driver has efficient control over the vehicle. In particular, engine tickover should be accurately adjusted to save throttle 'blipping' to keep it running when the vehicle is stationary.

Efficient Use

Inefficient use of vehicles constitutes the greatest waste of fuel. The following activities should be avoided by careful route planning, scheduling and prior thought about the cost consequences:
1. Vehicles running long distances when only partially loaded.
2. Vehicles covering excessive distances to reach their destination.
3. Large vehicles being used for running errands or making small item deliveries which could be accomplished more efficiently, and certainly more economically, by other means.
4. Vehicles running empty.

It is frequently argued that traffic office staff have little control over these matters, since customer demands for orders and the need to give drivers freedom to choose routes are dictates which overrule efficient planning. Nevertheless, attempts should be made to persuade those concerned of the need for restraint in the quest of saving fuel and thereby reducing costs.

Fuel Economy Aids

The quest for fuel saving has led to a market for economy aids which can be added to existing vehicles. These aids fall into three general categories:
1. Streamlining devices such as cab-top air deflectors, under-bumper air dams, front corner deflectors for high trailers and box vans, in-fill pieces for lorry and trailer combinations and shaped cones for addition to the front of van bodies.
2. Road speed governors which restrict maximum speed – one of the greatest causes of excessive fuel consumption.
3. Engine fans and radiator shutters which are designed to ensure that diesel engines are always operating at the correct temperature to give the most efficient performance and fuel economy.

All these types of device can be economically justified to a varying degree, but it is important to note that fitting streamlining devices in isolation only reduces fuel consumption if vehicle speeds are kept down. If the driver is able to use the few extra miles per hour which these devices provide –

ZERO DEGREE

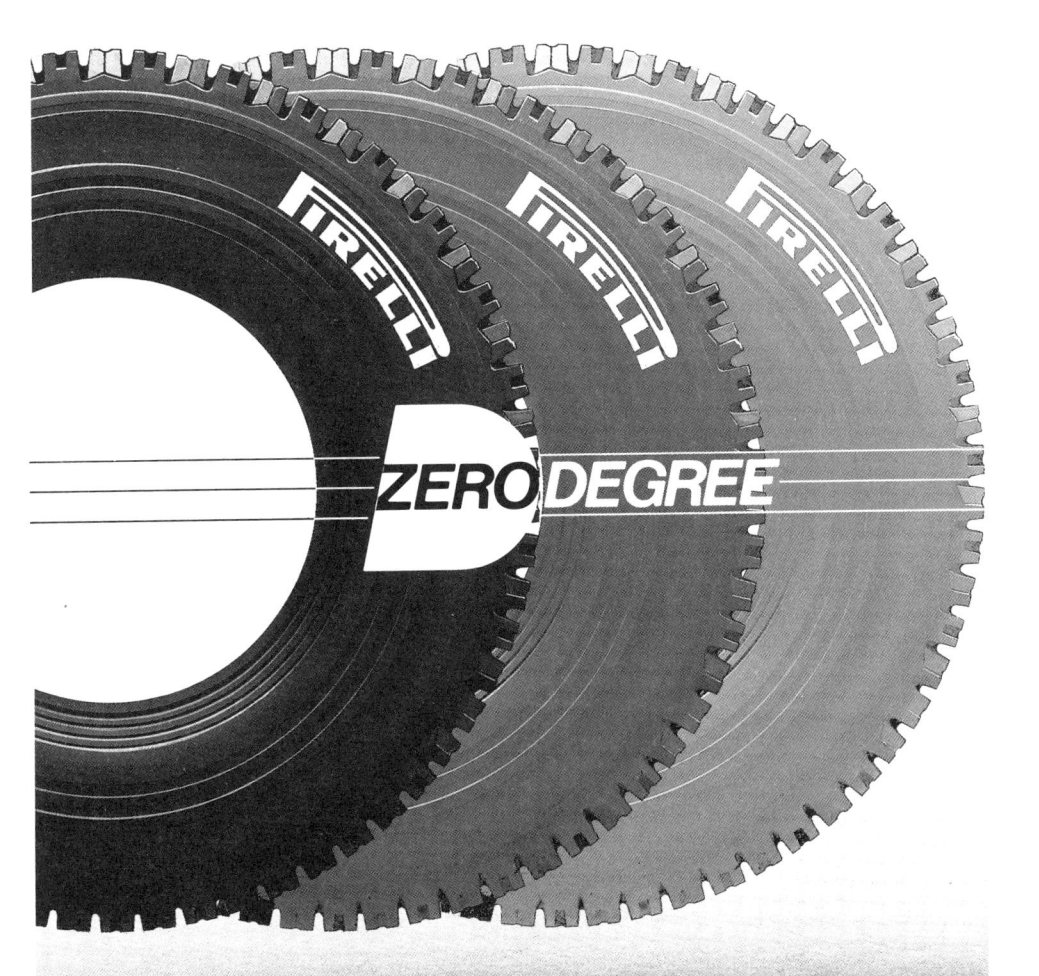

THE ULTIMATE
— from the forefront of the very latest tyre technology

PIRELLI
COMMERCIAL VEHICLE TYRES

Pirelli Limited, Derby Road, Burton-on-Trent DE13 0BH. England. Tel: 0283 66301 Telex: 34545 Fax: 0283 32042

which he will do unless otherwise restricted – then there will be little fuel saving and the cost of fitting would not be wholly justified.

Fuel and Tyres

The type and condition of tyres on a vehicle play a significant part in its fuel consumption. It is a proven fact that the lower rolling resistance inherent in radial ply tyres adds considerably to the fuel economy of the vehicle compared to the greater resistance of cross ply tyres.

Improvements in fuel consumption of 5 to 10 per cent can be expected from the use of radial ply tyres. Low profile tyres which offer a number of operational benefits over conventional radial tyres – such as reduced platform height and reduced overall height – also offer further possibilities for fuel saving.

The savings mentioned will only be achieved if the tyres are in good condition, are correctly inflated to the manufacturer's recommended pressures and are properly matched, especially when used in twin-wheel combinations. Neglect of tyre pressures is common in fleets and under-inflation is one of the major causes of tyre failure. It is also a major contributor to excessive fuel consumption.

Fuel and the Driver

Driving techniques, above all else, influence the overall fuel consumption of vehicles. A driver with a heavy right foot will negate all fuel-saving measures and devices and destroy any expectations of acceptable fuel consumption. Poor driving which has these consequences falls into two categories:
1. High speed driving
2. Erratic, stop-go driving.

Fast driving consumes excessive fuel: this fact is beyond question but the extent of the extra consumption is difficult to assess accurately. Tests carried out some time ago (but still make a valid point) by the National Freight Company with a 32-ton articulated vehicle on motorway operation indicated that fuel consumption increased quite dramatically when the vehicle was travelling at over 40mph. In the tests, at 40mph the fuel consumption was 10.5mpg, at 50mph this reduced by 2.6mpg to 7.9mpg and at 60mph a further reduction of 1.5mpg was experienced making a 3.75mpg difference between 40mph and 60mph travelling speeds. This represents a 35.7 per cent increase in fuel consumption. The real significance of these figures will be fully appreciated when annual motorway travel is calculated and this is multiplied by the increase in consumption, by the number of vehicles in the fleet and by the cost per gallon of diesel fuel.

In round figures the consequences of results of the calibre shown above may be as follows:*
    Vehicles travel 40000 miles per year on motorways;
        @ 10.5mpg = 3809.5 galls @ £1.75 per gall = £6666.62 pa
        @ 6.4mpg = 6250 galls @ £1.75 per gall = £10937.50 pa

Extra consumption = 2441 galls @ £1.75 per gall = £4272.00 pa
If five vehicles are involved the extra cost of fuel amounts to
£21360.00 pa.

*A pre-gulf crisis fuel price estimate has been used in this example.

The effects of erratic driving are more difficult to determine in quantitative terms, but it is sufficient to say that it results in abnormally high fuel consumption as well as causing excessive wear and tear on vehicle components. Impatience behind the wheel and an inability to assess in time what is happening on the road ahead leads the driver to see-saw between fierce acceleration to keep up with the traffic and violent braking to avoid running into the vehicle in front. Hence, the excessive use of fuel.

More economical driving is achieved by concentration on the road and traffic conditions ahead, anticipating well in advance how the traffic flow will move, and what is happening in front so that acceleration and braking can be more progressive and a smooth passage assured.

One other fuel-saving practice which the driver can adopt is to stop the engine while the vehicle is stationary rather than letting it tick over for unnecessarily long periods. If he feels this is necessary because his battery is in poor condition, then it is much cheaper to deal with the battery and charging problems than pay for the extra fuel to compensate.

Fuel and Fleet Management

Fleet operators can take a number of steps to reduce fuel consumption besides ensuring that the measures already mentioned are implemented.

Bulk Supplies/Buying

Control over the buying of bulk supplies and issues and over the buying of supplies outside from filling stations at the higher pump prices are important aspects for management attention. So too is accurate record keeping without which it is impossible to compare the fuel consumption of vehicles or to see which vehicles are consuming excessive amounts of fuel. Without records to identify these problems, there is no hope of remedying high fuel costs.

Recording Issues

Overfilling of vehicle tanks causing spillage is a common occurrence which wastes fuel and prevents accurate consumption records being obtained, as well as causing a mess and a health hazard. Accurate recording of issues against individual vehicles is another area which demands close attention. Modern electronic and computerised fuel-dispensing systems are available which ensure security of bulk supplies by preventing access except with a known key or card. This stops unauthorised drawing of fuel and it monitors issues to identified vehicles or key holders. The cost of such systems can be quickly recouped through savings in missing or unaccounted fuel and through better record keeping which enables high vehicle consumption to be quickly identified and investigated.

Buying Away from Base

Where bulk supplies are available at base, drivers should be discouraged from buying supplies from outside sources at higher prices except when absolutely necessary and even then they should buy only sufficient to get them home. Commonly, drivers fill tanks to the top which is enough to cover the trip home and to do further journeys as well on fuel which cost much more than that which they could have drawn once they got back to base. It is important to keep watch on the purchase of outside fuel supplies especially for cash because of the incentives which are offered to drivers to fill to the top. If outside fuel drawings are necessary then recognised bunkering card systems should be established.

Long Range Tanks

In the case of vehicles which operate regularly on long distances — on international work, for example — the fitting of long-range tanks is an economic proposition because of the savings achieved by using bulk-purchased supplies. A word of caution though, the extra fuel carried should not be at the expense of payload unless this can be justified and on international work there is the cost of fuel levies or taxes to be borne in mind. These are chargeable when entering some countries (see p 405) and are based on the amount of fuel in the tank. British hauliers returning to the UK may also find they have to pay an excess fuel tax on supplies bought outside the UK.

Route Planning/Scheduling

Better planning of vehicle schedules and routes offers the prospect of quite considerable fuel savings, besides other savings which may also result. A reduction in the miles travelled to fulfil particular delivery schedules will inevitably result in fuel savings. If the schedules can be planned so that fewer vehicles are needed to carry out the operation then, besides the broader savings in vehicle costs, the fleet as a whole will use less fuel. Therefore, the elimination of unnecessary trips or trips where vehicles are only partly loaded is a major priority in the search for fuel cost savings.

Tachographs in Fuel Saving

The use of tachographs in vehicles and detailed analysis of tachograph charts are steps which have provided many fleet operators with fuel savings if nothing else. The value of chart recordings in this connection should not be overlooked.

Agency Cards

There are a number of agency and fuel cards available to fleet operators. Generally they can be categorised between those from the major oil companies (eg Shell, Esso, BP) and those from other commercial organisations (eg All-Star, Overdrive, Dial Card, Petrocheck, BRS Transcard).

Principally these systems offer the opportunity to buy fuel at pump prices, paying only when fuel is actually purchased. The differences in the various schemes is in the levels of service which they offer.

Shell Scheme
Shell claims to lead the field with its Gold Card. This is intended mainly for

28: VEHICLE FUEL ECONOMY

the car and light vehicle operator with 20 plus vehicles but heavy trucks can be included, although the convenient Shell agency card is more appropriate for this purpose.

The Shell scheme offers a complete fleet management service enabling the authorised card holder to purchase all the legitimate items a vehicle user would need on the road (eg fuel, oil, tyres, batteries, windscreens, other parts, repair assistance). Prices charged are those which reflect maximum fleet discount no matter who or where the supplier. Thus the small fleet operator gets the same benefit as the large operator. Purchases are consolidated on to one VAT invoice and these invoices are submitted twice monthly. A 25-day credit period is given.

Where it is not possible to use the Gold Card (ie at a Shell garage) the driver can pay for his purchases with his own personal Access or Barclaycard and Shell will refund the amount back to him (on receipt of a completed voucher) within four days. In these circumstances the driver gains because he receives payment some 45 days before he has to meet his commitment.

Use of the Shell Gold Card automatically confers AA membership and this can be voluntarily extended to include AA's Relay and Home Start services. The balance of any existing AA membership at the time of joining the Shell scheme is refunded by the AA.

In addition to the invoice, Shell send the operator three computer 'reports' as follows:
1. Vehicle Transaction Report and Analysis
2. Cost Centre Summary
3. Fleet Report.

Automatic Bunkering

A number of automatic diesel fuel bunkering systems have been established recently to improve fuel supply services to heavy truck operators. Notable among these are Kuwait Petroleum (GB) Limited (selling under the Q8 brand name) which has introduced its International Diesel Service (IDS) in the UK in addition to its European-wide network. The Kuwait scheme features fully-automatic diesel sites, operating round the clock every day of the year, at which card-holding truck drivers can obtain fuel at an agreed price. The scheme is secure because the cards have a unique and secret 4-digit PIN code which prevent unauthorised use. The latest-technology pumps enable drivers to refuel rapidly in their own currency and their own language. The operator receives a comprehensive invoice at regular intervals with fuel drawn charged at a competitive price with VAT recorded and a facility to reclaim VAT where appropriate.

A basically similar scheme is operated by Mobil Oil with its Mobil Diesel Club (MDC). The company has about 100 outlets on key truck routes in 14 countries including the UK. A security-coded card is used as described above to obtain fuel from automatic high-speed pumps.

Fuel Economy Checklist

Check

- Fuel systems free from leaks.
- Fuel pump and injectors serviced and correctly adjusted.
- Exhaust not emitting black smoke.
- Air cleaners not blocked.
- Engine operating at correct temperature.
- Wheels turning freely.
- Controls properly adjusted and lubricated.

Tyres

- Condition and inflation pressures.
- Possibility of changing to radials on all vehicles.

Drivers

- Speed limits not being exceeded.
- Driving methods smooth and gentle.
- Engines stopped when vehicle standing.

Management

- Control over supplies and issues.
- Avoidance of spillage, loss and unauthorised use.
- Purchases from outside suppliers kept to a minimum.
- Record systems accurate and up to date.
- Possibility of installing fuel issue and monitoring systems.
- Possibility of fitting fuel economy aids (deflectors, engine fans, etc).
- Possibility of using long-range fuel tanks on vehicles.
- Routeing and scheduling practices to reduce wasted journeys and unnecessary mileage.
- Fuel economy programme to ensure all possible steps being implemented efficiently and recorded accurately.

29: Mobile Communications

There has been a significant increase in interest in all types of mobile communications in recent years. No longer is the in-vehicle radio or radio telephone an executive toy to be fitted only in the chairman's car. These days such equipment has proved and continues to prove itself to be a very cost-effective and efficient aid to a wide range of vehicle users from the company chairman down through all levels of executive vehicle users, to the sales representative, the service engineer and the delivery driver. In fact, wherever it can be established that there is a need and justification for the vehicle driver to be in contact with his base, with colleagues, with customers and with others here are the requirements for vehicle-based mobile communications.

Before looking at the systems of communication available it is useful to consider just what the benefits are to have vehicle drivers – whatever their status or purpose – in contact with others outside the vehicle. It is widely recognised that once a person gets into a vehicle and drives off he is totally cut off from his work place and the people with whom he normally deals in the way of business. And until he arrives at a known destination where a message can be relayed to him, or unless he manages to find a roadside telephone which operates (it is commonly felt that few of them do so when needed) he remains out of contact and out of touch with what is going on in his business or the business of his employer.

Clearly, in these days of high costs, competitive market places and a fast pace of business life, and taking account of technological developments, this is becoming an unacceptable penalty of having people travel by road especially during working hours. The inability to contact a top executive could, in the extreme, result in missed opportunities in business deals. The inability to contact a sales representative or a service engineer could mean a lost order or at least an irate customer; the same applies with a delivery driver. In addition, the inability to contact a driver could mean wasted journeys because of cancellations or changed plans which arise after they have set out on their journey. It could mean a driver getting back to base and having to go back to a customer visited earlier, simply because he could not be contacted *en route* to be warned of late or forgotten orders or items.

It is a common experience in transport operations for considerable cost to be wasted through late, changed, redirected, cancelled orders and instructions. Try as he might, the transport or fleet manager can rarely avoid his share of these annoying frustrations and there is nothing that he can do usually because he cannot contact the driver while he is travelling.

Vehicle-based mobile communications at today's level of sophistication can change all this and the wasted costs of the past can be turned into savings and even into profit quite simply by being able to contact the driver, relay details of the changed plans and generally divert vehicles to meet the current needs of the business. The savings in wasted time and miles, the avoidance of heavy vehicles returning home empty because they can be directed to pick up return loads, and the response to last minute customer demands are significant benefits which in themselves, or with other benefits, add up to offset the capital costs of buying and installing communications equipment and the on-going costs of rentals and call charges.

Choice of Communications

Mobile communications can be reviewed under four broad headings as follows:
1. CB radio.
2. Radio paging.
3. Private mobile radio (PMR).
4. Cellular telephone.

CB Radio

Citizens' Band (ie CB) radio was officially inaugurated in Britain in 1982 when the law made it permissible to operate such systems which had hitherto been illegal and had caused difficulty because their use interfered with the radio links of the emergency services and other official networks. Initially, CB was used by enthusiasts as a means of 'friendly' communication, to chat to other users and generally communicate non-business information. In time however, it proved capable of serving more important needs such as the reporting of accidents and other emergencies, breakdowns, road blockages, diversions and so on. Similarly, it proved to have some use in providing communication between vehicle drivers and their base – within limited range – for the purposes of passing information about loads, schedules and changed instructions for example.

Despite its obvious use for these purposes, CB has significant disadvantages: the frequencies are cluttered with undisciplined, long, sometimes foul and frequently frivolous conversation and chatter which can be heard by all users due to lack of privacy. This in itself is another disadvantage along with the general interference experienced and the congestion on channels. Furthermore, the equipment itself has its limitations in terms of power and range and in some areas there is less than satisfactory reception.

CB Licences
CB users (who must be over 14 years of age) must, by law, obtain an annual radio licence from a post office (using form CB 01) at a cost of £10.00 which covers the operation of a maximum of three sets. Further, licences costing £10.00 each per annum, are needed where more sets are to be operated but where licences are required for more than 15 sets postal application has to be made to the CB Licensing Unit, Chetwynd House, Chesterfield, Derbyshire S49 1PF (the same CB 01 application form is used). The application form in both cases requires only the name of the person applying (who becomes the licensee), and their address with post code.

The licence permits the licensee to operate only the specified number of CB 'sending and receiving stations for wireless telegraphy using only apparatus which conforms in all respects to the Department of Trade and Industry (DTI) specifications MPT 1320 and/or MPT 1321'. Suitable equipment may be recognised by the presence of one or other of the DTI approval marks.

Power Limits
Power limits must not be increased above that stated in the specification mentioned above and there are limits on the antenna which may be used. With 27 Mhz apparatus, the maximum length permitted is 1.65 metres and maximum diameter is 55 millimetres and with 934 MHz apparatus – with provision for connection to an external antenna – a maximum of four elements is permitted none of which must exceed 17 centimetres in length. Power amplifiers and antenna are not permitted.

Code of Practice
A Code of Practice (copies available free from post offices) has been established by the Radio Regulatory Division of the DTI along with representatives of CB groups and a Parliamentary Working Party on CB Radio. The following is extracted from this Code:

How to Operate
1. LISTEN BEFORE YOU TRANSMIT. Listen with the Squelch control turned fully down (and Tone Squelch turned off if you have Selective Call facilities) for several seconds, to ensure you will not be transmitting on top of an existing conversation.
2. KEEP CONVERSATIONS SHORT when the channels are busy, so that everyone has a fair share.
3. KEEP EACH TRANSMISSION SHORT and listen often for a reply – or you may find that the station you were talking to has moved out of range or that reception has changed for other reasons.
4. ALWAYS LEAVE A SHORT PAUSE BEFORE REPLYING so that other stations may join the conversation.
5. CB SLANG ISN'T NECESSARY – plain language is just as effective.
6. BE PATIENT WITH NEWCOMERS AND HELP THEM.

Emergencies and Assistance
7. AT ALL TIMES AND ON ALL CHANNELS GIVE PRIORITY TO CALLS FOR HELP.
8. LEAVE CHANNEL 9 CLEAR FOR EMERGENCIES. If you have to use it (for instance to contact a volunteer monitor service) get clear of it as soon as you can.
9. IF THERE IS NO ANSWER ON CHANNEL 9, then call for help on either channel 14 or 19 where you are likely to get an answer.
10. IF YOU HEAR A CALL FOR HELP – WAIT. If no regular volunteer monitor answers, then offer help if you can.
11. THERE IS NO OFFICIAL ORGANISATION FOR MONITORING CB AND NO GUARANTEE THAT YOU WILL ALWAYS BE IN REACH OF A VOLUNTEER MONITOR.

CB IS NOT A SUBSTITUTE FOR THE 999 SERVICE ASHORE OR FOR VHF RADIO (CHANNEL 16) AFLOAT.

Choice of Channel
12. RESPECT THE FOLLOWING CONVENTIONS:
    Channel 9:   Only for emergencies and assistance.

Channel 14: The calling channel. Once you have established a contact, move to another channel to hold your conversation.

Channel 19: For conversations among travellers on main roads. (Remember, if you are travelling in the same direction as the station you are talking to, not to hog this channel for a long conversation.) Give priority to the use of this channel by long distance drivers to whom it can be an important part of their way of life.

Other: You may find that particular groups in particular areas also have other preferred channels for particular purposes.

Interference

13. INTERFERENCE can be caused by any form of radio transmission. Avoid the risks. Put your antenna as far away as possible from others, and remember that you are not allowed to use power amplifiers. In the unlikely event that your CB causes interference, co-operate in seeking a cure using the suggestions from a good CB handbook. Moving the set or antenna a few feet may cure the problem.

Safety

14. NEVER ERECT OR USE AN ANTENNA UNDERNEATH OR NEAR AN OVERHEAD ELECTRIC LINE. Several CB enthusiasts have been killed because they did not appreciate the dangers involved. Keep antennas well clear of overhead lines at all times. If an antenna is already sited near a power line, do not attempt to remove it but get in touch with the local Electricity Board for advice.

15. WHEN MOUNTING ANTENNAS ON HIGH VEHICLES make sure that the top of the antenna is not so high that it is likely to foul overhead electrified lines at railway level crossings.

16. USE COMMON SENSE WHEN USING CB and do not transmit when it could be risky to do so. For example, don't transmit:
    a. when fuel or any other explosive substance is in the open – eg at petrol filling stations, when petrol or gas tankers are loading or unloading, on oil rigs or at quarries.
    b. when holding a microphone may interfere with your ability to drive safely.
    c. with the antenna less than 6 inches from your face.

Radio Pagers

Radio pagers (commonly called bleepers) are a portable means of contact but only on a one-way basis from the sender to the receiver. Pagers fall into two main categories, tone pagers and voice pagers. With either type a person can be alerted to the fact that he or she is required and with more sophisticated equipment can be advised by varying tones to follow specific predetermined instructions, for example, to ring one telephone number or another. Voice pagers or 'talking bleepers' convey a spoken message which is usually repeated twice, thereby, alerting the user to follow specific courses of action. Some pagers are capable of alerting the user by vibration (silent pagers) so that outsiders are not aware of the sound or so that the user is not interrupted in mid-conversation by an audible 'bleep'. Others have the ability to display messages on a liquid crystal screen from a text memory of up to some 800 characters.

While the cost of pagers is relatively low (usually only a few pence per day) and the unit itself is small and unobtrusive to carry around in the pocket

29: MOBILE COMMUNICATIONS

(some are no bigger than credit cards) there are disadvantages to their use. First, is the limited range (generally not more than about 15 miles) and second, is the need for the receiver to find a working telephone in order to make the call for which he has been alerted.

Private Mobile Radio (PMR)

Portable radios are used for private two-way communication usually between a base station and a number of mobiles (ie radio equipped vehicles) with the added facility in some cases of the mobile units being able to talk to each other. Generally, mobile radio operates over a limited range of some 10 to 20 miles depending on location and the height of the base station aerial. Much depends on the type of terrain between the base station and the mobile unit. In open country far greater range may be obtained than in a city with built-up areas and many tall buildings.

Many systems have the disadvantage that anybody in the vehicle or within earshot can hear the message being relayed and that all mobile units hear a message intended for one only. However, some equipment has a facility for selective calling so that only one unit need be contacted at a time.

In the main, mobile radio is restricted to a closed system but there are facilities whereby this can be extended by linking into one of the national relay networks which have many base stations throughout the country. The Securicor 'Relayfone' system is a good example. Developments are in hand to allow, in the future, interconnection of private mobile radio systems into the public switched telephone network (PSTN).

Typical of PMR systems are those used by local taxi services where the driver has a hand-held microphone with an 'ON/OFF' switch. This PTT (press to talk) switch must be depressed to enable the driver to talk to the base station and then released while he listens to the returning message. The disadvantage of this is the road safety risk created by a driver trying to control his vehicle and operate the microphone switch (the new Highway Code warns against such practices and the police are alert to this habit and will take action against offending drivers).

Mobile radio operates on a number of alternative radio frequencies as follows:

Low band VHF (25-50 Mhz) provides the greatest range but it suffers from high noise levels and heavy channel loadings (used by police and emergency services).

High band VHF (150-174 MHz) provides good coverage in built-up areas with less noise but there is still heavy usage of the channels.

UHF (450-512 MHz) has a much shorter range than VHF but there is much less congestion on the channels and it provides good penetration in urban areas where there are many buildings and tall structures.

Within these radio frequencies equipment may be obtained for AM or FM operation.

Band 3

Increased demand for mobile communication has led to the allocation by the Government of the VHF slot left vacant by the old 405-line black and white TV network for use in providing communications services. This is now called Band 3 PMR and is operated by the two official franchise holders GEC and Band Three Radio each with 200 channels.

This system will be of interest to those requiring only brief communication (ie not full conversation) between base station and vehicle (mobile unit), but with little need for communication outside and who wish to avoid the relatively high call costs of cell-phones and the rather higher capital costs of the cellular telephone units themselves.

Cellular Telephone

The advent of the cellular telephone system has revolutionised mobile communications. Today it is possible to have a telephone inter-connected to the national and international telephone networks from a vehicle-based (ie mobile) installation or from a set carried neatly in an executive briefcase or even in a jacket pocket. Such systems provide the user with the facility to dial direct to almost any telephone number in the UK or to reach such numbers via the British Telecom operator and to make international calls and calls to any other cellular telephone. Similarly, any telephone user can dial direct to a mobile cell-phone number.

The principle of the Total Access Communications System (TACS) cellular telephone system is that instead of a connection by wire as with the conventional telephone, the link is made by radio airwaves in the 900 MHz radio band frequency using only 50 MHz bandwidth. The UK is now divided into a number of individual cells like a honeycomb. Each cell is anything from 2 kilometres to 30 kilometres across with a transceiver which relays cellular calls to and from the normal public switched telephone network (PSTN) as well as from one cellular telephone to another.

A central computer (the brains of the system) monitors all traffic in the system and switches calls from one transceiver to another as the mobile cell-phone user travels from one cell into another. Calls go through both the cellular network and the British Telecom network hence the reason why call charges are higher than with the normal PSTN system and especially in the London area.

The Government has licensed two operators to provide the network, namely British Telecom (Cellnet) and Racal (Vodafone) and currently some 90 per cent of the UK population is covered by both systems.

Equipment for operation within the cellular telephone system can be divided into three groups:
1. Mobile units (eg installed in vehicles).
2. Transportable units (for use in vehicles or can be carried in a briefcase for example).
3. Portable units (small units which can be readily carried around and even fitted into a jacket pocket).

Voice Activation

A relatively new development in vehicle-based mobile units is voice activation to overcome the problems (and illegalities*) of answering the telephone and dialling numbers for outward calls while actually driving the vehicle. This equipment is programmed to recognise a voice signal (usually just a single word) spoken into the handset which sets off the dialling of a predetermined number (eg base, office, home). Other equipment is dashboard mounted so calls can be received and made 'hands off' to avoid the road safety risks and contravention of the advice given in the new Highway Code against using 'phones' while on the move.

*NB: While it is not strictly illegal to answer or dial-out when driving, a policeman may, however, prosecute for not exercising full control of the vehicle (but the same could apply when changing a cassette tape or unwrapping a toffee!).

Equipment and Charges

A wide range of equipment is currently available from many suppliers in the market, operating on either or both Cellnet and Vodafone systems. Equipment can be purchased outright, leased or rented for a short period. The costs and charges incurred fall under the following headings:
1. Purchase/lease of equipment.
2. Installation charges (ie fitting transceiver and aerial to vehicle).
3. Connection charges (once only).
4. Monthly subscription charge.
5. Call charges.

Call charges are invoiced to the user on a monthly or quarterly basis along with the subscription charge. These call charges are not governed by distance in the same way as normal BT call charges, thus a local call costs the same as a long distance call of the same duration. Outsiders making calls from a BT (ie PSTN) telephone to a cellular telephone number also incur higher costs at the 'M' rate (currently equivalent to a call from the UK to the Republic of Ireland).

Developments

Such is the rapid pace of development in this field that already a wide range of 'add on' facilities are, or soon will be, available to users. Links to data transmission equipment to allow communication between computers, the ability to send telexes and to interface with FAX machines are all current possibilities which substantially extend the use of a mobile or transportable cellular telephone.

Choosing Cell-Phone Suppliers

Potential cell-phone users should contact a number of suppliers for details and demonstrations of the variety of equipment available before selecting alternatives and making final decisions. The RHA has negotiated a special deal with Racal Vodac for its members. In particular, attention should be given to the strength of signal obtained on each system (Cellnet or Vodafone) in certain areas, the efficiency of installation and the back-up services provided as well as the equipment itself. There is a great deal of choice and competition in this field so keen prices should be obtained.

Warning
It is useful to caution users and potential users of cellular telephones about three particular matters as follows:
1. Proper installation of equipment in vehicles is essential for both efficient operation and for safety reasons. Special care is needed in the case of installation in heavy vehicles with 24 volt electrical systems to avoid wiring faults and other electrical problems.
2. Insurance of equipment in vehicles is important; it is highly attractive to thieves. If stolen or lost in a vehicle accident or fire an insurer may decline to accept a claim if the installation of the equipment had not been notified beforehand. In general, motor insurance does not cover a cellular phone. It is relatively easy for the subscriber to prevent fraudulent use of a stolen set by notifying the air-time retailer. The retailer can disconnect the stolen unit remotely thus preventing further use. Mobile cell phones are not easy to steal because the handset, transceiver and wiring loom have to be removed.
3. Users should be aware that foreign customs officials may impound mobile communications handsets when entering certain countries because use of the equipment is not compatible with overseas telecommunications networks and might interfere with emergency services.

Safety

The Highway Code now includes a special section on the use of microphones and car telephones. It advises against using a hand-held microphone or telephone handset while driving except in an emergency. It says the driver should only speak into a fixed, neckslung or clipped-on microphone when it would not distract attention from the road. Drivers should not stop on the hard shoulder of a motorway to answer or make a call, no matter how urgent.

Appendices

Appendix I   Licensing Authorities and Areas Covered
Appendix II FTA Regional Offices
Appendix III RHA Regional Offices
Appendix IV Organisations Connected with Transport
Appendix V   Approved Tachograph Centres

Appendix I

Licensing Authorities and Areas Covered

Traffic Area	Counties Covered
North-Eastern Westgate House, Westgate Road, Newcastle upon Tyne NE1 1TW Tel 091-261 0031/Fax 091-222 0824 and Hillcrest House, 386 Harehills Lane, Leeds LS9 6NF Tel 0532 499433	the Metropolitan Counties of South Yorkshire, Tyne and Wear and West Yorkshire, the Counties of Cleveland, Durham, Humberside, Northumberland and North Yorkshire.
North-Western Portcullis House, Seymour Grove, Manchester M16 0NE Tel 061-872 5077	the Metropolitan Counties of Greater Manchester and Merseyside, the Counties of Cheshire, Clwyd, Cumbria, Gwynedd and Lancashire, the Borough of High Peak, in the County of Derbyshire.
West Midland Cumberland House, 200 Broad Street, Birmingham B15 1TD Tel 021-631 3300	the Metropolitan County of West Midlands, the Counties of Hereford and Worcester, Shropshire, Staffordshire and Warwickshire.
Eastern Terrington House, 13-15 Hills Road, Cambridge CB2 1NP Tel 0223 358922 and Birkbeck House, 14-16 Trinity Square, Nottingham NG1 4BA Tel 0602 475511	the Counties of Bedfordshire, Cambridgeshire, Leicestershire, Lincolnshire, Norfolk, Northamptonshire, Nottinghamshire and Suffolk, the County of Derbyshire except the Borough of High Peak, the County of Essex except the Districts of Basildon, Brentwood, Epping Forest and Harlow and the Borough of Thurrock.
South Wales Caradog House, 1-6 St Andrews Place, Cardiff CE1 3PW Tel 0222 395426/Fax 0222 371675	the Counties of Dyfed, Gwent, Mid Glamorgan, Powys, South Glamorgan and West Glamorgan.
Western The Gaunts' House, Denmark Street, Bristol BS1 5DR Tel 0272 297221	the Counties of Avon, Cornwall, Devon, Dorset, Gloucestershire, Somerset and Wiltshire.
South-Eastern Ivy House, 3 Ivy Terrace, Eastbourne, East Sussex BN21 4QT Tel 0323 21471/Fax 0323 21057	the Counties of Berkshire, Buckinghamshire, East Sussex, Hampshire, Isle of Wight, Oxfordshire and West Sussex, the County of Kent except the Borough of Dartford and the District of Sevenoaks, the Borough of Surrey Heath and the District of Waverley in the County of Surrey.

THE TRANSPORT MANAGER'S AND OPERATOR'S HANDBOOK

Metropolitan
PO Box 643,
Charles House,
375 Kensington High Street,
London W14 8QU
Tel 071-605 0300/Fax 071-605 0499

the administrative area of Greater London, the County of Hertfordshire, the County of Surrey except the Borough of Surrey Heath and the district of Waverley, the districts of Basildon, Brentwood, Epping Forest and Harlow and the Borough of Thurrock in the County of Essex, the Borough of Dartford and the District of Sevenoaks in the County of Kent.

NB: The following special telephone numbers are now in operation to provide improved service when contacting the Metropolitan Traffic Area.
Hgv drivers querying licensing matters should dial 071-605 followed by;

A–E 0347   F–M 0346   N–Z 0344

(these initials relate to the first letter of the licence holder's surname).

'O' licence holders querying licensing matters should dial 071-605 followed by;

A–E 0328 0329 0330 0331 0332

F–Q 0327 0335 0336 0337 0338 0426

R–Z 0325 0326 0339 0340 0417

(these initial letters relate to the first letter of the name of the individual or company holding the licence, not the trading name of the business).

Scottish
Head Office,
83 Princes Street,
Edinburgh EH2 2ER
Tel 031-225 4677/Fax 031-225 5494

Whole of Scotland and Western Isles. Also the Orkneys and Shetlands.

International Road Freight Office
Northern Traffic Area Office,
Westgate House,
Westgate Road,
Newcastle upon Tyne NE1 1TW
Tel 091-261 0031/Fax 091-222 0824

Appendix II

FTA Regional Offices

Head Office:
Hermes House,
157 St John's Road,
Tunbridge Wells,
Kent TN4 9UZ
Tel 0892 26171

Midlands (East Midland, West Midland):
Hermes House,
Hall Street,
Dudley,
West Midlands DY2 7BQ
Tel 0384 237321

*Northern (Northern, North-Western,
Merseyside and North Wales, Yorkshire):*
Springwood House,
Low Lane,
Horsforth,
Leeds LS18 5NU
Tel 0532 589861

Scottish (including Northern Ireland):
Hermes House,
Melville Terrace,
Stirling FK8 2ND
Tel 0786 71910

South-Eastern (London and Home Counties):
Hermes House,
157 St John's Road,
Tunbridge Wells,
Kent TN4 9UZ
Tel 0892 26171

South-Western (South-Western and South Wales):
Hermes House,
Queen's Avenue.
Clifton,
Bristol BS8 1SE
Tel 0272 731187

Appendix III

RHA Regional Offices

Head Office:
Roadway House,
104 New King's Road,
London SW6 4LN
Tel 071-736 1183

Scotland:
Roadway House,
17 Royal Terrace,
Glasgow G3 7NY
Tel 041-332 9201

North-western:
124 Market Street,
Farnworth,
Bolton BL4 9EP
Tel 0204 71521

North-eastern:
Roadway House,
Beaumont Street West,
Darlington,
Co. Durham DL1 5SY
Tel 0325 281495

Eastern:
Roadway House,
Rightwell,
Bretton Centre,
Peterborough PE3 8DR
Tel 0733 261131

Western:
Roadway House
Cribbs Causeway
Bristol BS10 7TU
Tel 0272 503600

Midlands:
Roadway House,
50 Sedgley Road West,
Dudley,
West Midlands DY4 8AL
Tel 021-557 4911

Appendix IV

Organisations Connected with Transport

Association of District Councils
26 Chapter Street,
London SW1P 4ND
Tel 071-233 6940

Association of Vehicle Recovery
Operators (AVRO)
201 Great Portland Street,
London W1N 6AB
Tel 071-580 9122

Automobile Association (AA)
Fanum House,
Basing View,
Basingstoke,
Hants RG21 2EA
Tel 0256 20123

British Association of Removers (BAR)
3 Churchill Court,
58 Station Road,
North Harrow HA2 7SA
Tel 081-861 3331

British Road Federation (BRF)
Cowdray House,
6 Portugal Street,
London WC2A 2HG
Tel 071-242 1285

British Standards Institution (BSI)
2 Park Street,
London W1
Tel 071-629 9000

British Vehicle Rental and Leasing
Association (BVRLA)
13 St Johns Street,
Chichester,
West Sussex PO19 1UU
Tel 0243 786782

Chartered Institute of Transport (CIT)
80 Portland Place,
London W1N 4DP
Tel 071-636 9952

Department of Transport (DTp)
2 Marsham Street,
London SW1P 3EB
Tel 071-276 3000

Electric Vehicle Association (EVA)
Aberdeen House,
Headley Road,
Grayshott,
Hindhead,
Surrey GU26 6LA
Tel 0428 735536

British International Freight Association
(BIFA) previously the Institute of Freight
Forwarders
Redfern House,
Browells Lane,
Feltham,
Middx TW13 7EP
Tel 081-844 2266

Institute of Logistics and Distribution
Management (ILDM)
Douglas House,
Queens Square,
Corby,
Northants NN17 1PL
Tel 0536 205500

Institute of Materials Management (IMM)
Cranfield Institute of Technology
Cranfield,
Bedford MK43 0AL
Tel 0234 750662

Institute of the Motor Industry (IMI)
'Fanshaws',
Brickendon,
Hertford SG13 8PQ
Tel 099 286 521

Institute of Road Transport Engineers
(IRTE)
1 Cromwell Place,
Kensington,
London SW7
Tel 071-589 3744

Institute of Transport Administration
(IoTA)
32 Palmerston Road,
Southampton SO1 1LL
Tel 0703 631380

Institution of Mechanical Engineers (IME)
1 Birdcage Walk,
London SW1
Tel 071-222 7899

International Road Transport Union (IRU)
Centre International
1-3 rue de Varembe,
1202 Geneve,
Switzerland
Tel 34 13 30

Retail Motor Industry Federation (RMI)
previously the Motor Agents Association (MAA)
201 Great Portland Street,
London W1
Tel 071-580 9122

National Association of Warehouse Keepers (NAWK)
Walter House,
418-422 Strand,
London WC2R 0PT
Tel 071-836 5522

National Association of Waste Disposal Contractors (NAWDC)
Mountbarrow House,
6–20 Elizabeth Street,
London SW1W 9RB
Tel 071-824 8882

National Tyre Distributors Association (NTDA)
Broadway House,
The Broadway,
Wimbledon,
London SW19 1RL
Tel 081-540 3859

Road Transport Industry Training Board (RTITB)
Capitol House,
Empire Way,
Wembley,
Middx HA9 0NG
Tel 081-902 8880

Royal Automobile Club (RAC)
83-85 Pall Mall,
London SW1 5HW
Tel 071-930 4343

Royal Society of Arts (RSA)
(Examinations Dept),
Westwood Way,
Westwood Business Park
Coventry CV4 8HS
Tel 0203 470033

Royal Society for the Prevention of Accidents (RoSPA)
Cannon House,
Priory Queensway,
Birmingham B4 6BS
Tel 021-200 2461

Society of Motor Manufacturers and Traders (SMMT)
Forbes House,
Halkin Street,
London SW1
Tel 071-235 7000

Vehicle Builders and Repairers Association (VBRA)
Belmont House,
Finkle Lane,
Gildersome,
Leeds LS27 7TW
Tel 0532 538333

Vehicle Inspectorate – Executive Agency
Goods Vehicle Centre,
Welcombe House,
91–92 The Strand,
Swansea,
Glamorgan SA1 2DH
Tel 0792 458888

Transport Journals

Commercial Motor
Quadrant House,
The Quadrant,
Sutton,
Surrey SM2 5AS
Tel 081-661 3500

Distribution
Trinity House,
Hercies Road,
Hillingdon,
Middx UB10 9NA
Tel 0895 58431

Export and Freight
Carn Industrial Estate
Portadown BT63 5RH
Northern Ireland
Tel 0762 334272

Fleet News Truck Edition
Response Publishing Ltd,
Wentworth House,
Wentworth Street,
Peterborough PE1 1DS
Tel 0733 63100

Focus (Journal of Institute of Logistics and Distribution Management)
Douglas House,
Queens Square,
Corby,
Northants NN17 1PL
Tel 0536 205500

Freight Transport (Journal of FTA)
Hermes House,
St John's Road,
Tunbridge Wells TN4 9UZ
Tel 0892 26171

Freight Management
PO Box 96,
Coulsdon,
Surrey CR3 2TE
Tel 01-660 2811

Freight News Express
24 Chiswick High Road,
London W4 1TE
Tel 081-994 8582

Headlight
PO Box 96
Coulsdon,
Surrey CR5 2TE
Tel 081-660 2811

International Freighting Weekly (IFW)
Maclean Hunter House,
Chalk Lane,
Cockfosters Road,
Barnet,
Herts EN4 0BU
Tel 081-975 9759

Materials Handling News
Quadrant House,
The Quadrant,
Sutton,
Surrey SM2 5AS
Tel 081-661 3500

Motor Transport
Quadrant House,
The Quadrant,
Sutton,
Surrey SM2 5AS
Tel 081-661 3500

Removals and Storage (Journal of British Association of Removers)
3 Churchill Court,
58 Station Road,
North Harrow HA2 7SA
Tel 081-861 3331

Road Law
Barry Rose Law Periodicals
Little London,
Chichester,
Sussex PO19 1PG
Tel 0243 783637

Roadway (Journal of RHA)
Roadway House,
104 New King's Road,
London SW6 4LN
Tel 071-736 1183

Transport (Journal of Chartered Institute of Transport)
80 Portland Place,
London W1N 4DP
Tel 071-636 9952

Transport Management (Journal of Institute of Transport Administration)
32 Palmerston Road,
Southampton SO1 1LL
Tel 0703 31380

Transport Week
30 Calderwood Street,
London SE18 6QH
Tel 081-855 7777

Truck
97 Earl's Court Road,
London W8 6QH
Tel 071-370 0333

Trucking International
Central House,
154-162 Southgate Street,
Gloucester GL1 2EX
Tel 0452 307181

Appendix V

Approved Tachograph Centres

The following are Department of Transport approved Tachograph Centres (ie 'approved workshops' as referred to in EC legislation) in the UK, based on lists issued and updated from time to time by the DTp. This list is based on the DTp official listing dated March 1990.
*Remote area centres are shown with an asterisk

England

Avon

BRISTOL GB H 105
Swan National Motors (Bristol) Ltd,
Coventry & Jeffs,
Anchor Road,
Bristol BS1 5TT
Tel 0272 26031

BRISTOL GB H 117
Evans Halshaw SW Ltd,
Avonmouth Way,
Avonmouth,
Bristol BS11 8DB
Tel 0272 824611

BRISTOL GB H 118
A D Forsey (Transport) Ltd,
Weston Super Mare Motors,
Days Road,
Barton Hill,
Bristol BS5 0AI
Tel 0272 551571

BRISTOL GB H 222
Lex Tillotson Bristol,
Days Road,
St Phillips,
Bristol BS2 0OP
Tel 0272 557755

BRISTOL GB H 202
Bryan Bros Trucks Ltd,
Albert Crescent,
St Phillips,
Bristol BS2 0UD
Tel 0272 772671

BRISTOL GB H 216
S A Trucks (Bristol) Ltd,
Third Way,
Avonmouth,
Bristol BS11 9YL
Tel 0272 821241

BRISTOL GB H 303
Moreys Daf Trucks Ltd,
T/A ATAC,
Unit 3B,
Severnside Trading Estate,
St Andrews Road,
Avonmouth,
Bristol BS11 9YQ
Tel 0272 828583

BRISTOL GB H 314
Welch & Company Ltd,
Avon Street,
Bristol BS2 0PZ
Tel 0272 770411

CHIPPING SODBURY GB H 110
Dando's (Motor Services) Ltd,
Hatters Lane,
Bridge Road Works,
Chipping Sodbury BS17 6AS
Tel 0454 310136

WESTON-SUPER-MARE GB H 313
Weston-Super-Mare Motors,
Bridge Road Works,
Weston-Super-Mare BS23 3NF
Tel 0934 628127

Bedfordshire

BEDFORD GB F 105
Charles King (Motors) Ltd,
Hudson Road,
Elms Farm Industrial Estate,
Bedford MK41 0JQ
Tel 0234 40041

BEDFORD GB D 208
Arlington Motor Co Ltd,
The Embankment,
Barkers Lane,
Bedford MK41 9SD
Tel 0234 270000

BEDFORD GB F 317
Banks Truck Centre Ltd,
3 Brunel Road,
Barkers Lane Industrial Estate,
Bedford MK41 9TL
Tel 0234 211241

DUNSTABLE GB N 222
Trimoco Luton Ltd,
Skimpot Road,
Dunstable LU5 4JX
Tel 0582 597575

LEIGHTON BUZZARD GB E 100
Chassis Developments Ltd,
Grovebury Road,
Leighton Buzzard LU7 8SL
Tel 0525 374151

LEIGHTON BUZZARD GB E 315
Dawson Freight Commercials Ltd,
Stoneleigh Garage,
Billington Road,
Leighton Buzzard LU7 8TG
Tel 0525 851851

Berkshire

BRACKNELL GB K 307
John Lewis & Co Ltd,
Central Vehicle Workshop,
Doncastle Road,
Southern Industrial Area,
Bracknell RE12 4YB
Tel 0344 424680

READING GB K 104
Penta Truck & Van Centre,
Station Road,
Theale RG7 4AG
Tel 0734 323383

READING GB K 200
Zenith (Reading) Trucks Ltd,
20 Commercial Road,
Reading RG2 0RN
Tel 0734 312660

READING GB K 215
Lucas Service UK Ltd,
16-20 Long Barn Lane,
Reading RG2 7SZ
Tel 0734 861202

Buckinghamshire

AYLESBURY GB E 202
Perrys Ltd,
Griffen Lane,
Aylesbury HP19 3BY
Tel 0296 26162

COLNBROOK GB N 333
Scantruck West Limited,
Skyway 14,
Calderway (Off Horton Road),
Colnbrook SL3 0BQ
Tel 0753 686467

HIGH WYCOMBE GB N 306
Biffa Ltd,
Kingsmill,
London Road,
High Wycombe
Tel 0494 21221

MILTON KEYNES GB E 216
City Truck Sales Ltd,
10, Northfield Drive,
Milton Keynes MK15 0DE
Tel 0908 665152

MILTON KEYNES GBN 113
Leyland/DAF Distribution,
Chesney Wold,
Bleak Hall,
Milton Keynes MK6 1LH

MILTON KEYNES GB E 306
Perrys Ltd,
Clarke Road,
Mount Farm Estate,
Milton Keynes MK1 1NP
Tel 0908 74011

Cambridgeshire

CAMBRIDGE GB F 100
Marshall (Cambridge) Ltd,
Airport Garage,
Newmarket Road,
Cambridge CB5 8SQ
Tel 02205 3131

CAMBRIDGE GB F 212
Lucas Service UK Ltd,
442 Newmarket Road,
Cambridge CB5 8JU
Tel 0223 315931

CAMBRIDGE GB F 312
Gilbert Rice Ltd,
Commercial Vehicle Division,
375-381 Milton Road,
Cambridge CB4 1SR
Tel 0223 315959

HUNTINGDON GB F 307
Murkett Bros Ltd,
Ringroad,
Huntingdon PE18 6HX
Tel 0480 52697

HUNTINGDON GB F 108
Ouse Valley Motors,
Station Road,
St Ives,
Huntingdon PE17 4BL
Tel 0430 62641

453

PETERBOROUGH GB F 213
Sellers & Batty Ltd,
Unit A Morley Way,
Woodston,
Peterborough
Tel 0733 60591

PETERBOROUGH GB F 215
T C Harrison Group Ltd,
Truck Division,
Oxney Road,
Peterborough PE1 5YN
Tel 0733 558111

PETERBOROUGH GB F 315
BRS Midlands Ltd,
Fengate Commercials,
Nursery Lane,
Fengate,
Peterborough PE1 5BG
Tel 0733 65201

PETERBOROUGH GB F 111
Ford & Slater of Peterborough,
316 Padholme Road,
Peterborough PE1 1BA
Tel 0733 47100

Cheshire

ALTRINCHAM GB C 236
PDO Ferrymasters Ltd,
Engineering Division,
Station House,
Station New Road,
Altrincham

BRETTON GB C 108
H & J Quick Ltd,
Premier Garage,
Bretton,
Nr Chester CH4 0DS
Tel 0244 660681

CREWE GB C 116
Crewe Tachograph Centre,
Chamberlains Transport Ltd,
Brodley Road,
Haslington,
Crewe CW1 1PU
Tel 0270 581224

ELLESMERE PORT GB C 225
Tachograph Chester Ltd,
Rossfield Road,
Rossmore Trading Estate,
Ellesmere Port L65 3AN
Tel 051-355 2101

MIDDLEWICH GB C 232
ERF Service Centre,
Road Beta,
Brooks Lane,
Middlewich CW10 0JZ
Tel 060-684 4711

NORTHWICH GB C 302
North West Truck Engineering Ltd,
Griffiths Road,
Lostock Gralam,
Northwich CW9 7NU
Tel 0606 48611

SANDBACH GB C 227
Sandbach Truck Centre Ltd,
Station Road,
Elworth,
Sandbach CW11 9JG
Tel 0270 763291

STALYBRIDGE GB C 233
Tameside Tachograph Centre,
Bayfreight Garages,
Premier Mill,
Tame Street,
Stalybridge SK15 1ST
Tel 061-338 8700

STOCKPORT GB C 202
Gordon Ford Trucks,
Greyhound Industrial Estate,
Macclesfield Road,
Hazel Grove,
Stockport SK7 6DB
Tel 061-456 6333

SUTTON WEAVER GB C 125
Leyfield Commercial Services Ltd,
Ashville Way,
Sutton Weaver,
Nr Runcorn WA7 3EZ
Tel 0928 790098

WARRINGTON GB C 330
Ryland Vehicle Group North West Ltd,
Winwick Street Factory,
John Street,
Warrington WA2 7UD
Tel 0925 33271

WARRINGTON GB C 300
C D Bramall Ltd,
Winwick Road,
Dallam Lane,
Warrington WA2 7NY
Tel 0925 51111

WIDNES GB C 321
Sutton & Son (St Helens) Ltd,
6 Tanhouse Lane,
Widnes WA8 0RZ
Tel 051-424 3078

Cleveland

BILLINGHAM GB B 317
North East Leyland DAF Ltd,
Cowpen Bewley Road,
Haverton Hill,
Billingham TS23 4EX
Tel 0642 370555

STOCKTON ON TEES GB A 100
Hargreaves Vehicle (North East) Ltd,
Bowesfield Lane,
Stockton on Tees TS18 3HF
Tel 0642 614121

STOCKTON ON TEES GB A 202
Auto Electrics (Tees-side) Ltd,
Thornaby House,
Thornaby,
Stockton on Tees TS17 6BW
Tel 0642 607901

STOCKTON ON TEES GB A 208
Electro Diesel North East Ltd,
Portrack Grange Road,
Portrack Industrial Estate,
Stockton on Tees
Tel 0642 605050

Cornwall

HELSTON GB H 206
Wincanton Garages Ltd,
St Johns,
Helston TR13 8EX
Tel 03257 2561

LAUNCESTON GB H 214*
Pannell Commercials,
Pennygillam Industrial Estate,
Launceston PL15 7ED
Tel 0566 3896/4361

LAUNCESTON GB H 319*
T H Cawsey Commercials Ltd,
Newport Industrial Estate,
Launceston PL15 8EX
Tel 0566 2805

ST AUSTELL GB H 106
People 2000 Ltd,
Slades Road,
St Austell PL25 4HP
Tel 0724 672333

ST AUSTELL GB H 212
ECC International Ltd,
Westhaul Park,
Par Moor Road,
St Austell PL25 3RA
Tel 0726 812382/4/5

Cumbria

CARLISLE GB A 206
Thomas Armstrong
(Transport Services) Ltd,
Workington Road,
Flimby,
Maryport CA15 8RY
Tel 0900 68114

CARLISLE GB A 102
Duncan's Tachograph Centre,
Kingstown Industrial Estate,
Kingstown,
Carlisle CA3 0EP
Tel 0228 515284

CARLISLE GB A 303
Carlisle Commercials Ltd,
Kingstown Industrial Estate,
Kingstown,
Carlisle CA2 7NS
Tel 0228 29262

CARLISLE GB A 304
C G Truck,
Wakefield Road,
Kingstown Estate,
Carlisle CA3 0HE
Tel 0228 24234

CARLISLE GB C 235
Solway Leyland DAF Ltd,
Kingstown Broadway,
Kingstown Industrial Estate,
Carlisle CA3 0HD

DISTINGTON GB A 311*
Myers & Bowman Ltd,
Prospect Works,
Distington CA14 5XH
Tel 0946 830247/8/9

KENDAL GB A 201
Lakeland Commercials Ltd,
Mintsfeet Road North,
Mintsfeet Trading Estate,
Kendal LA9 6LZ
Tel 0539 23956

MILNTHORPE GB A 107
J Douthwaite & Sons (Milnthorpe) Ltd,
Bridge End Garage,
Milnthorpe LA7 7AB
Tel 05395 62291

Derbyshire

CASTLE DONINGTON GB E 500
BFI Trucks Ltd,
Trent Lane,
Castle Donington DE7 2NP
Tel 0332 811310

DERBY GB E 307
BRS Midlands Ltd,
Meadow Lane,
Alvaston DE2 8QR
Tel 0332 571931

DERBY GB E 201
T C Harrison Group Ltd ,
Chequers Road,
Derby DE2 6EN
Tel 0332 31188

THE TRANSPORT MANAGER'S AND OPERATOR'S HANDBOOK

DERBY GB E 223
F B Atkins & Son Ltd,
Burton Road,
Findern DE6 6BG
Tel 0332 516151

DERBY GB E 308
Kays Mackworth Ltd,
Ashbourne Road,
Mackworth DE3 4NB
Tel 0331 24371

DERBY GB E 226
Sherwood Leyland DAF Ltd,
Berristowe Lane,
Blackwell DE55 5HP
Tel 0773 863311

Devon

BARNSTAPLE GB H 100
P M Clarke (Commercials) Ltd,
Severn Brethren Trading Estate,
Barnstaple
Tel 0271 45151

BARNSTAPLE GB H 209
S & B Commercials,
Roundswell Industrial Estate,
Old Torrington Road,
Barnstaple EX31 3NL
Tel 0271 76658

EXETER GB H 204
Lucas Service UK Ltd,
Grace Road,
Marsh Barton,
Exeter EX2 8PE
Tel 0392 70235

EXETER GB H 213
Frank Tucker (Commercials) Ltd,
Peamore Garage,
Alphington,
Exeter EX2 9SL
Tel 0392 832662

EXETER GB H 300
Evans Halshaw SW Ltd,
Grace Road,
Marsh Barton,
Exeter
Tel 0392 76561

NEWTON ABBOT GB H 305
Newton Abbot Motors Ltd,
Bradley Lane,
Newton Abbot TQ12 1JT
Tel 0626 65081

PLYMOUTH GB H 116
Vospers Trucks Ltd,
Hobart Street,
Plymouth PL1 3LW
Tel 0752 668040

PLYMOUTH GB H 225
Lucas Service (UK) Ltd,
Plymouth City Bus,
Milehouse,
Plymouth

TOTNES GB H 224
Wincanton Distribution Services Ltd,
Dart Hills,
Babbage Road,
Totnes TQ 5JA
Tel 0803 867910

Dorset

BOURNEMOUTH GB K 114
Lucas Service UK Ltd,
Elliot Road,
West Howe Industrial Estate,
Bournemouth BH11 8LN
Tel 0202 570507

POOLE GB H 318
Morey Leyland DAF Trucks Ltd,
Unit 2,
Willis Way,
Fleets Industrial Estate,
Poole BH15 3SZ
Tel 0202 675131

POOLE GB K 216
New English Trucks,
Unit 2,
61-63 Willis Way,
Fleets Industrial Estate,
Poole BH15 3SX
Tel 0202 671122

DORCHESTER GB H 114
Executors of R W Toop (Dec'd)
T/A Bere Regis & District Motor Services,
Grove Trading Estate,
7 Bridport Road,
Dorchester DT1 1RW
Tel 0305 62992

WEYMOUTH GB H 308
Marsh Road Garages,
Marsh Road,
Weymouth
Tel 03057 76116

Durham

CHESTER-LE-STREET GB A 106
Millbay Truck & Van Centre,
Drum Road,
Chester-Le-Street DH3 2AF
Tel 091-410 4261

CHESTER-LE-STREET GB A 309
Transfleet Services Ltd,
Penshaw Way,
Portabello Trading Estate,
Birtley,
Chester-Le-Street DH3 2SA
Tel 091-410 4437

DARLINGTON GB A 104
Skipper of Darlington Ltd,
Allington Way,
Yarm Road Industrial Estate,
Darlington
Tel 0325 59242

DARLINGTON GB A 300
North Riding Garages Ltd,
Middleton St George,
Darlington DL2 1HR
Tel 0325 332941

DARLINGTON GB A 301
Darlington Commercials,
Lingfield Way,
Yarm Road Industrial Estate,
Darlington DL1 4PY
Tel 0325 55161

SPENNYMOOR GB A 105
Exel Logistics Regional Services,
Green Lane Industrial Estate,
Green Lane,
Spennymoor DL16 6DW
Tel 0388 815900

SHOTTON COLLIERY GB B 131
Geoffrey Division,
Victoria Fleet Services,
Victoria Garage,
Back Friar Street,
Shotton Colliery DH6 2NX

Essex

BASILDON GB N 232
Arlington Commercial Vehicle Sales &
Repairs
Cranes Close,
Basildon SS14 3JD
Tel 0268 20223

BENFLEET GB F 102
W Harold Perry Ltd,
Stadium Way,
Benfleet SS7 3NU
Tel 0268 775544

CHELMSFORD GB F 110
Lucas Service UK Ltd,
3 Montrose Road,
Dukes Park Industrial Estate,
Chelmsford CM2 6TE
Tel 0245 466166

CHELMSFORD GB F 205
Trimoco plc,
11 Montrose Road,
Dukes Park Industrial Estate,
Chelmsford CM2 6TF
Tel 0245 466619

CHELMSFORD
County Motor Works (Chelmsford) Ltd,
Eastern Approach,
Springfield,
Chelmsford CM2 6PT
Tel 0245 466333

COLCHESTER GB F 209
Colchester Fuel Injections Ltd,
Haven Road,
Colchester CO2 8HT
Tel 0206 862049

COLCHESTER GB F 500
Candor Motors Ltd,
114 Ipswich Road,
Colchester CO4 4AB
Tel 0206 571171

DAGENHAM GB N 229
Unigate Garage (Dairy Crest),
Selinas Lane,
Chadwell Heath,
Dagenham RH8 10H
Tel 081-517 5444

GRAYS GB N 329
Harris Commercial Repairs Ltd,
601 London Road,
West Thurrock,
Grays RM16 1AN
Tel 0708 864426

HARLOW GB N 205
Arlington Motor Co Ltd,
Potter Street,
Harlow CM17 9NP
Tel 0279 22391

PURFLEET GB N 206,
Scan Truck Ltd,
Arterial Road,
Purfleet RM16 1TR
Tel 0708 864915

Gloucestershire

GLOUCESTER GB H 217
Watts Truck Centre Ltd,
Mercia Road,
Gloucester
Tel 0452 25721

GLOUCESTER GB H 218
Target of Gloucester Ltd,
Bristol Road,
Hempsted,
Gloucester GL2 5YS
Tel 0452 21581

GLOUCESTER GB H 120
BRS Western Ltd,
St Oswald Road,
Gloucester GL1 2RP
Tel 0452 20387/500529

GLOUCESTER GB H 320
ATAC (Gloucester),
Unit 55a,
Gloucester Trading Estate,
Hucclecote,
Gloucester GL3 4AA
Tel 0452 371047

GLOUCESTER GB H 321
Richard Read (Transport) Ltd,
Longhope,
Gloucester GL17 0GQ
Tel 0452 830456/7

TEWKESBURY GB H 111
Mudie Bond Ltd,
New Town Trading Estate,
Tewkesbury GL20 8JD
Tel 0684 294896

Hampshire

ALDERSHOT GB K 220
P D E (Farnham) Ltd,
Pavilion Road,
Aldershot GU11 3NX
Tel 0252 316504

ALDERSHOT GB K 302
Baker Aldershot,
1 Lower Farnham Road,
Aldershot GU12 4DZ
Tel 0252 24401

ANDOVER GB K 109
Spartrucks Ltd,
Stephenson Close,
Portway Industrial Estate,
Andover SP10 3RY
Tel 0264 66224

BASINGSTOKE GB K 113
Jacksons (Baskingstoke) Ltd,
Roentgen Road,
Daneshill East Industrial Estate,
Basingstoke RG24 0NT
Tel 0256 461656

EASTLEIGH GB K 100
Hendy Lennox (Southampton) Ltd,
Bournemouth Road,
Chandlers Ford,
Eastleigh SO5 3ZG
Tel 0703 266388

FAREHAM GB K 119
Spartrucks Ltd,
Standard Way,
Fareham Industrial Estate,
Fareham PO16 8XL
Tel 0329 286224

PORTSMOUTH GB K 112
Wadham Stringer Commercials,
Burrfields Road,
Copnor,
Portsmouth PO3 5NN
Tel 0705 664900

PORTSMOUTH GB K 221
Lucas Service UK Ltd,
Airport Services Road,
Portsmouth PO19 5PY
Tel 0705 661504

PORTSMOUTH GB K 301
Arlington Motor Co (Portsmouth) Ltd,
Norway Road,
Hilsea,
Portsmouth PO2 9QZ
Tel 0705 661321

SOUTHAMPTON GB K 201
Morey Leyland DAF,
The Causeway,
Redbridge,
Southampton SO9 4YS
Tel 0703 663000

SOUTHAMPTON GB K 223
Taplin's Auto Electrical Ltd,
36/37 St Mary's Street,
Southampton SO9 5GE
Tel 0703 331331

SOUTHAMPTON GB K 304
Bristol Street Motors (Southampton) Ltd,
2nd Avenue,
Millbrook,
Southampton SO1 0LP
Tel 0703 701500

SOUTHAMPTON GB K 310
Princes Commercials (Southampton) Ltd,
Test Lane,
Nursling Industrial Estate,
Southampton SO1 9JX
Tel 0703 701900

SOUTHAMPTON GB K 121
Hendy Truck Cosham Ltd,
Southampton Road,
Cosham,
Portsmouth PO6 4RW

Hereford & Worcester

BROOMHALL GB D 300
Carmichael Trucks Ltd,
Bath Road,
Broomhall,
Worcester WR3 3HR
Tel 0905 820377

EVESHAM GB D 217
Coulters Garage (Evesham) Ltd,
Four Pools Lane,
Evesham WR11 5DW
Tel 0386 47111

HEREFORD GB D 211
Lucas Service UK Ltd,
Mortimer Road,
Hereford HR4 9JG
Tel 0432 265571/267678

HEREFORD GB D 302
The Praill Motor Group Ltd,
Holmer Road,
Hereford HR4 9SD
Tel 0432 268181

Hertfordshire

BOREHAMWOOD GB N 302
W H Perry Ltd,
Stirling Corner,
Stirling Way,
Borehamwood WD6 2AX
Tel 081-207 3100

HATFIELD GB N 217
S & B Commercials Ltd,
Huggins Lane,
Welham Green,
Hatfield AL9 7LA
Tel 0707 261111

HITCHIN GB N 309
Swan Garage (Hitchin) Ltd,
Grove Road,
Hitchin
Tel 0462 59744

HITCHIN GB N 341
Commercial Vehicle Recovery & Repair,
48 Bury Mead Road,
Hitchin SG5 1RT

KINGS LANGLEY GB N 331
E J Masters Ltd,
Railway Terrace,
Kings Langley WD4 8JA
Tel 09277 68921

ST ALBANS GB N 310
Godfrey Davis (St Albans) Ltd,
Bricknell Park Industrial Estate,
Ashley Road,
St Albans
Tel 0727 59155

SOUTH MIMMS GB N 340
Scan Truck Ltd,
Bignells Corner,
20 St Albans Road,
South Mimms EN6 3NG
Tel 0707 49955

WATFORD GB N 219
Vales Truck Centre Ltd,
Tolpits Lane,
Watford WD1 8QP
Tel 0923 776688

Humberside

BROUGH GB B 208
Humberside Motors Ltd,
Junction 38, M62,
Newport,
Brough HU15 2RD
Tel 04342 2297

GOOLE GB B 124
BRS Northern Ltd,
Mariner Street,
Goole DN14 5BW
Tel 0405 764251

GRIMSBY GB E 214
Hartford Motors (Grimsby) Ltd,
Corporation Road,
Grimsby DN31 1UH
Tel 0472 358941

GRIMSBY GB B 315
Scan Truck Ltd,
Estate Road One,
South Humberside Industrial Estate,
Grimsby DN31 2TA
Tel 0472 46913

HULL GB B 109
Thompson of Hull Ltd,
230-236 Anlaby Road,
Hull HU3 2RR
Tel 0482 23681

HULL GB B 110
Crossload Commercials Group,
Valletta Street,
Hedon Road,
Hull HU9 5NP
Tel 0482 781831

HULL GB B 213
Lex Tillotson (Hull) Ltd,
Hedon Road,
Hull HU9 5PJ
Tel 0482 795111

HULL GB B 216
Crystal of Hull Ltd,
Little Fair Road,
Hedon Road,
Hull HU9 5LA
Tel 0482 25732

HULL GB B 313
Torridan Commercial Vehicles Ltd,
Ann Watson Street,
Stoneferry,
Hull HU8 0BJ
Tel 0482 839677

SCUNTHORPE GB E 112
BRS Northern Ltd,
Grange Lane North,
Scunthorpe DN16 1BY
Tel 0724 865316

SCUNTHORPE GB B 218
H & L Garages Ltd,
Grange Lane North,
Scunthorpe DN16 1BT
Tel 0724 856655

SCUNTHORPE GB E 302
Lex Tillotson Scunthorpe,
Midland Industrial Estate,
Kettering Road,
Scunthorpe DN16 1VW
Tel 0724 282444

SOUTH KILLINGHOLME GB E 219
H & L Garages Ltd,
Humber Road,
South Killingholme DN40 3DL
Tel 0469 571666

Isle of Wight

NEWPORT GB K 120
Riverside Motors Ltd,
Riverside Works,
Little London,
Newport PO30 5BT
Tel 0983 522552

Kent

ASHFORD GB K 209
Crouch's Garage Ltd,
Station Road,
Ashford TN23 1PJ
Tel 0233 23451

ASHFORD GB K 306
Channel Commercials plc,
Brunswick Road,
Cobbs Wood Estate,
Ashford TN23 1EH
Tel 0233 29271

BROADSTAIRS GB K 116
Thanet Commercials PLC,
Unit 12, Hornet Close,
Pysons Road Industrial Estate,
Broadstairs CT10 2TD
Tel 0843 603480/602194

CANTERBURY GB K 102
Invicta Motors Ltd,
134 Sturry Road,
Canterbury CT1 1DR
Tel 0227 762783

CANTERBURY GB K 204
Lucas Service UK Ltd,
Maynard Road,
Wincheap Industrial Estate,
Canterbury CT1 3RH
Tel 0227 453510

CRAYFORD GB N 335
Acorn Truck Sales Ltd,
Acorn Industrial Park,
Crayford Road,
Crayford DA1 4AL
Tel 0322 56415

DARTFORD GB N 105
K T Trucks Ltd,
Datford Industrial Estate,
Hawley Road,
Dartford DA1 1NQ
Tel 0322 229331

ERITH GB N 226
South Eastern Auto
Electrical Services Ltd,
Unit 26,
Manford Industrial Estate,
Erith
Tel 0322 342277

MAIDSTONE GB K 105
Drake & Fletcher Ltd,
Parkwood Sutton Road,
Maidstone ME15 9NW
Tel 0622 55531

MAIDSTONE GB K 222
South Eastern Auto Electrical Service Ltd,
Wharf Road,
Tovil,
Maidstone ME15 6RT
Tel 0622 690010

MAIDSTONE GB K 303
Volvo (GB) Ltd,
T/A Maidstone Commercials Ltd,
Beddow Way,
Forstal Road,
Aylesford,
Maidstone ME20 7BT
Tel 0622 70811

ST MARY'S HOO GB K 118
Squires & Knight,
Fenn Corner,
St Mary's Hoo,
Nr Rochester ME3 8RF
Tel 0634 271987/270772

SITTINGBOURNE GB K 212
Sparshatts of Kent Ltd,
Unit 10,
Eurolink Industrial Estate,
Murston,
Sittingbourne ME10 3RN
Tel 0795 479571

TONBRIDGE GB N 101
Stormont Engineering Co Ltd,
Commercial Vehicle Div,
Hildenborough,
Tonbridge TN11 8NN
Tel 0732 833005

TUNBRIDGE WELLS GB K 107
J Rawson (Trucks) Ltd,
Longfield Road,
North Farm Industrial Estate,
Tunbridge Wells TN2 3EY
Tel 0892 515333

TUNBRIDGE WELLS GB K 224
Lucas Service UK Ltd,
North Farm Road,
High Brooms Industrial Estate,
Tunbridge Wells TN2 3EA
Tel 0892 510444

Lancashire

ACCRINGTON GB C 220
Gilbraith Commercials Ltd,
Market Street,
Church,
Accrington BB5 0DN
Tel 0254 31431

ACCRINGTON GB C 124
Lynch Truck Services Ltd,
Unit 3, Plot 8,
Newhouse Road,
Huncoat Industrial Estate,
Accrington BB5 6NT
Tel 0254 301331

BLACKBURN GB C 305
J D S Truck Centre,
Fox Commercial Vehicles Ltd,
Navigation Garage,
Forrest Street,
Blackburn
Tel 0254 675111/7

BURNLEY GB C 329
Burnley & Pendle Transport
Company Ltd,
Queensgate,
Colne Road,
Burnley BB10 1HH
Tel 0282 25244

CHORLEY GB C 114
Gilbraith Commercials Ltd,
Botany Bay,
Chorley PR6 8XA
Tel 02572 76421

CLITHEROE GB C 229
Steadplan Ltd,
Salthill Industrial Estate,
Clitheroe BB7 1QL
Tel 0200 27415

FORTON GB C 128
Cabus Garage,
A6 Lancaster Road,
Forton,
Lancashire
Tel 0524 791417

HAYDOCK GB C 325
Haydock Commercial Vehicles Ltd,
Yew Tree Trading Estate,
Kilbuck Lane,
Haydock WA11 9XW
Tel 0942 714103

LANCASTER GB C 317
Pye Motors Ltd,
Parliament Street,
Lancaster LA1 1DA
Tel 0524 63553

LEYLAND GB C 500
SVAP Leyland DAF Ltd,
Leyland Service Centre,
Croyston Road Gate No 1,
Starter Works,
Leyland PR5 1SN
Tel 0772 421400

LITTLE HOOLE GB C 109
BRS Northern Ltd,
Liverpool Road,
Little Hoole,
Nr Preston PR4 5JT
Tel 0772 617668

MORECAMBE C 133
Carlisle Commercials Ltd,
White Lund Industrial Estate,
Morecambe LA3 3BY
Tel 0228 29262

PRESTON GB C 230
Lucas Service Ltd,
160-164 Lancaster Road,
Preston PR1 1SR
Tel 0772 58326

PRESTON GB C 303
Ribblesdale Auto-Electrics Ltd,
Marsh Lane,
Preston PR1 8YN
Tel 0772 555011

PRESTON GB C 127
Leyland Auto Electrical & Diesel Ltd,
Unit 220,
Walton Summit Industrial Estate,
Bamber Bridge,
Preston PR5 8AL
Tel 0772 38583

PRESTON GB C 328
Ryland Vehicle Group Preston,
Unit 224,
Walton Summit Centre,
Bamber Bridge,
Preston PR5 8AL
Tel 0772 38111

ROCHDALE GB C 201
Rochdale Motor Garage,
T/A Tom Mellor Ford,
Durham Street,
Rochdale OL11 1LR
Tel 0706 355355

Leicestershire

BLABY GB E 120
BRS Midlands Ltd,
Lutterworth Road,
Blaby LE8 3DU
Tel 0533 773373

HINCKLEY GB E 210
Paynes Garages Ltd,
Watling Street,
Hinckley LE10 3ED
Tel 0455 38911

LEICESTER GB E 206
Cossington Commercial Vehicles Ltd,
System Road,
Cossington,
Leicester LE7 8UZ
Tel 0533 607111

LEICESTER GB E 217
A B Butt Ltd,
Frog Island,
Leicester LE3 5AZ
Tel 0533 513344

LEICESTER GB E 300
Batchelor Bowles & Co Ltd,
Freemens Common,
Aylstone Road,
Leicester LE2 7SL
Tel 0533 557667

LEICESTER GB E 305
Ford & Slater of Leicester,
Hazel Drive,
Narborough Road South,
Leicester LE3 2JG
Tel 0533 896561/630630

LOUGHBOROUGH GB E 106
Charnwood Trucks Ltd,
M1 Truck Centre,
Ashby Road,
Shepshed,
Loughborough LE12 5BR
Tel 0509 502121

Lincolnshire

BOSTON GB E 204
C F Parkinson Ltd,
Fydell Crescent Workshop,
Fydell Crescent,
George Street,
Boston PE21 8XQ
Tel 0205 63008

LINCOLN GB E 102
John Longden Ltd,
PO Box 19,
Crofton Road,
Lincoln LN3 4PJ
Tel 0522 538811

LINCOLN GB E 203
C F Parkinson Ltd,
Outer Circle Road,
Lincoln LN2 4HU
Tel 0522 530176

LINCOLN GB E 224
Ford & Slater of Lincoln,
Sleaford Road,
Bracebridge Heath,
Lincoln LN4 2NQ
Tel 0522 22231

SPALDING GB F 308
R C Edmondson (Spalding) Ltd,
St Johns Road,
Spalding PE11 1JA
Tel 0775 67651

Greater London

ALPERTON GB N 311
Godfrey Davis (London) Ltd,
374 Ealing Road,
Alperton,
Middlesex HA0 1HG
Tel 081-997 3388

BARKING GB N 216
Dagenham Motors (1981) Ltd,
51 River Road,
Barking IG11 0SW
Tel 081-592 6655

BARKING GB N 322
Gifford Tachograph Services &
Commercial Ltd,
Assured House,
Cheques Lane,
Dagenham
Tel 081-593 1550

CHARLTON GB N 332
Henleys London Ltd,
Units 5 & 9,
Maritime Industrial Estate,
Horizon Way,
Charlton SE7 7AY
Tel 081- 871 3021

CHINGFORD GB N 334
Rydale Truck & Coach Ltd,
47 Sewardstone Road,
Chingford E4 7PU
Tel 081-529 8686

CROYDON GB N 200
Dees of Croydon Ltd,
Dees Commercial Centre,
2 Imperial Way,
Croydon CR0 4RR
Tel 081-681 6711

CROYDON GB N 338
C Barber & Sons Ltd,
Barbers Tachograph Centre,
87 Beddington Lane,
Croydon CR0 4TD
Tel 081-689 4414

DAGENHAM GB N 111
Lancaster Trucks Ltd,
Lakeside Estate,
Heron Way,
West Thurrock RM16 1WJ
Tel 0708 861321

ENFIELD GB N 100
Hunter Vehicles Ltd,
Unit 7,
Trafalgar Trading Estate,
Jeffreys Road,
Enfield
Tel 081-805 5175

ENFIELD GB N 228
Arlington Motor Co Ltd,
Mollison Avenue,
Brimsdown,
Enfield EN3 7NE
Tel 081-804 1266

FELTHAM GB N 223
Heathrow Commercials Ltd,
Staines Road,
Bedfont,
Feltham TW14 8RP
Tel 0784 243571

GREENFORD GB N 225
Normand Commercial Vehicles Ltd,
Auriol Drive,
Oldfield Lane,
Greenford UB6 0AY
Tel 081-578 5688

HAYES GB N 213
Dagenham Motors (Hayes) Ltd,
Dawley Road,
Hayes UB3 1EH
Tel 081-573 2209

ISLEWORTH GB N 224
Currie Trucks Ltd,
207/209 Worton Road,
Isleworth TW7 6DS
Tel 081-568 4343

LONDON GB N 336
The Londoners Tacho Centre Ltd,
1A Brabourn Grove,
Peckham SE15 2BS
Tel 071-639 1212

LONDON GB N 201
Arlington Motor Co Ltd,
Brentfield Road,
Willesden NW10 8HH
Tel 081-956 5982

LONDON GB N 315
BRS Southern Ltd,
Victory Place,
Off Balfour Street,
SE17 1PH
Tel 071-703 5071

LONDON GB N 316
BRS Southern Ltd,
Leyton Repair Centre,
Ruckholt Lane,
Leyton E10 5PB
Tel 081-539 1298

LONDON GB N 327
Transfleet Services Ltd,
17 Western Road,
Western Trading Estate,
Park Royal NW10 7LT
Tel 081-961 5225

LONDON GB N 318
Hunts Trucks (Wandsworth) Ltd,
2 Airport Way,
Wandsworth SW18 1SH
Tel 081-871 3021

LONDON GB K 225
A23 Tacho Centre Ltd,
146/156 Brixton Hill,
London SW2 1SD
Tel 081-671 7781

LONDON GB N 231
East London Tachograph & Speed
Limiter Service,
London Buses (West Ham Garage),
Greengate Street,
London E13 0AS
Tel 081-471 7243

UXBRIDGE GB N 337
Hunt Engineering Co Ltd,
91 Cowley Road,
Uxbridge UB8 2AG
Tel 0895 57841

Greater Manchester

BOLTON GB C 118
Harris Road Services Ltd,
Raikes Lane Industrial Estate,
Manchester Road,
Bolton BL3 2NS
Tel 0204 32441

BOLTON GB C 308
BRS Northern Ltd,
Kay Street,
Bolton VL1 2HX
Tel 0204 26141

HYDE GB C 120
D Hulme Ltd,
Broadway Industrial Estate,
Dukinfield Road,
Hyde SK14 4QZ
Tel 061-366 9400

MANCHESTER GB C 130
ERF Manchester Ltd,
Trafford Park Road,
Trafford Park M17 1NJ
Tel 061-848 8331

MANCHESTER GB C 309
Manchester Garages (Trucks) Ltd,
Gorton Lane,
Gorton M18 8BT
Tel 061-223 7131

MANCHESTER GB C 123
Chatfield Martin Walter Ltd,
T/A CGL Truck Services,
Ashburton Road East,
Trafford Park M17 1GT
Tel 061-872 6855

MANCHESTER GB C 327
Quicks Trucks Ltd,
Moseley Road,
Trafford Park M17 1PG
Tel 061-872 7711

MANCHESTER GB C 204
Chatfields of Manchester,
40-46 Ashton Old Road,
Ardwick M12 6NA
Tel 061-273 7351

MIDDLETON GB C 324
West Pennine Trucks Ltd,
Stakehill Industrial Estate,
Middleton M24 2RL
Tel 061-653 9700

OLDHAM GB C 111
Main Line Trucks Manchester Ltd,
Fields New Road,
Chadderton,
Oldham OL9 8NH
Tel 061-652 4218

SALFORD GB C 234
Salford Leyland DAF Ltd,
West Egerton Street,
Salford M5 4DY
Tel 061-872 7241

STRETFORD GB C 223,
Lucas Service UK Ltd,
Severnside Trading Estate,
Textilose Road,
Trafford Park M17 1WB
Tel 061-872 5275

STRETFORD GB C 129
BRS Northern Engineering,
Barton Dock Industrial Estate,
Barton Dock Road,
Stretford M32 0XP
Tel 061-872 7551

WORSLEY GB C 119
Roy Braidwoods & Sons,
Worsley Trading Estate,
Lester Road,
Little Hulton,
Worsley M28 6PT
Tel 061-799 3801

Merseyside

LIVERPOOL GB C 105
Woodwards SVS,
Merton Street,
Bank Road,
St Helens WA9 1HU
Tel 07048 20266

LIVERPOOL GB C 501
J Blake & Co Ltd,
178 Lodge Lane,
Liverpool L8 0QW
Tel 051-727 4501

LIVERPOOL GB C 205
Lucas Service UK Ltd,
Vandries Road,
Liverpool L3 7BJ
Tel 051-236 7063

LIVERPOOL GB C 307
Peoples (Liverpool) Ltd,
Hawthorn Road,
Bootle,
Liverpool L20 9DA
Tel 051-922 8481

LIVERPOOL GB C 314
Thomas Hardie Commercials Ltd,
Newstet Road,
Knowsley Industrial Park (North),
Nr Liverpool L33 7TJ
Tel 051-546 5291

LIVERPOOL GB C 215
Perris & Kearon Ltd,
173-175 Crown Street,
Liverpool L7 3LZ
Tel 051-709 4262

LIVERPOOL GB C 331
North West Truck Engineering,
Unit 22,
Interchange Estate,
Wilson Road,
Huyton
Tel 051-480 0098

ST HELENS GB C 113
Roberts Motors Ltd,
St Helens Ford,
City Road,
St Helens WA10 6NZ
Tel 0744 26381

Norfolk

DISS GB F 219
Trumber Truck Care Ltd,
57 Victoria Road,
Diss IP22 3JD
Tel 0379 652161

FAKENHAM GB F 501
R C Edmondson (Fakenham),
Oak Street,
Fakenham NR21 9DU
Tel 0328 51122

GREAT YARMOUTH GB F 306
L G Perfect (Engineering) Ltd,
Jubilee Works,
Hafreys Road,
Great Yarmouth NR31 0JL
Tel 0493 675131

KING'S LYNN GB F 112
GDM Transport Engineering Ltd,
Leyland Truck Centre,
Maple Road,
Kings Lynn PE34 3AH
Tel 0553 761112

KING'S LYNN GB F 310
BRS Southern Ltd,
Oldmeadow Road,
Hardwich Trading Estate,
King's Lynn PE30 4TZ
Tel 0553 773671

NORWICH GB F 206
Lucas Service UK Ltd,
Weston Road North,
Norwich NR3 3TL
Tel 0603 410301

NORWICH GB F 305
Ford & Slater of Norwich,
Roundtree Way,
Mousehold Lane,
Norwich NR7 8SJ
Tel 0603 429451

NORWICH GB F 313
Busseys Ltd,
Whiffler Road,
Norwich NR3 2AW
Tel 0603 424022

NORWICH GB F 116
Carrow Commercials Ltd,
Unit 8 Industrial Estate,
Kerrison Road,
Norwich NR1 1JA
Tel 0603 621415

NORWICH GB F 220
Gales Commercial Vehicles Ltd,
Ayton Road,
Wymondham NR18 0QQ
Tel 0953 601222

THETFORD GB F 309
B & B Motor Repairs Ltd,
Caxton Way,
Thetford IP24 3RY
Tel 0842 752457

Northamptonshire

DAVENTRY GB E 119
Daventry Trucks Ltd,
Unit 3, Plant House,
Royal Oakway North,
Daventry NN11 5PQ
Tel 0327 77009

KETTERING GB E 109
John R Billows (Sales) Ltd,
Pytchley Road Industrial Estate,
Kettering NN15 6JJ
Tel 0536 516233

NORTHAMPTON GB E 211
Northampton Diesel & Electrical
Services Ltd,
Holloway Industrial Estate,
Weedon Road,
Northampton NN5 5DG
Tel 0604 55321

NORTHAMPTON GB E 318
Arlington Motor Co Ltd,
Bedford Road,
Northampton NN1 5NS
Tel 0604 250151

NORTHAMPTON GB E 208
Airflow Streamlines plc,
Truck Centre,
Letts Road,
Northampton NN4 9HQ
Tel 0604 581121

WELLINGBOROUGH GB E 101
Brookside Garages (Wellingborough) Ltd,
Finedon Road,
Wellingborough NN8 4BN
Tel 0933 76651

WELLINGBOROUGH GB E 310,
E Ward (Wellingborough) Ltd,
Truck Division,
Northampton Road,
Wellingborough NN8 3PP
Tel 0933 440110

Northumberland

BERWICK UPON TWEED GB A 308
Cochranes Garage (Berwick) Ltd,
Tweedside Trading Estate,
Berwick Upon Tweed TD15 2XF
Tel 0289 305585

CHOPPINGTON GB B 217
Heathline Commercials Ltd,
Stakeford Lane,
Choppington NE62 5QJ
Tel 0670 824006

Nottinghamshire

BEESTON GB E 116
Barton Transport plc,
61 High Road,
Chilwell,
Beeston NG9 4AD
Tel 0602 221441

HOVERINGHAM GB E 110
Tarmac Roadstone Ltd East Midlands,
Hoveringham Tachograph Centre,
Hoveringham,
Lowdham NG14 7JY
Tel 0602 663197

HUCKNALL GB E 107
K & M (Hauliers),
T/A Nevilles Garage Ltd,
The Aerodrome,
Watnall Road,
Hucknall NG15 6EN
Tel 0602 630630

NEWARK GB E 220
C F Parkinson (Notts) Ltd,
Brunel Drive,
Northern Industrial Estate,
Newark NG24 2EG
Tel 0636 72631

NOTTINGHAM GB E 317
Hooley's Garage Ltd,
Abbey Street,
Lenton,
Nottingham NG7 2PP
Tel 0602 786145

NOTTINGHAM GB E 121
Sherwood Leyland DAF Ltd,
522 Derby Road,
Lenton,
Nottingham NG7 2GX
Tel 0602 787274

NOTTINGHAM GB E 225
R H Commercial Vehicles Ltd,
Lenton Lane,
Nottingham NG7 2NR
Tel 0602 866571

NOTTINGHAM GB F 319
Charthire Services,
Boulevard Industrial Estate,
Beacon Road,
Beeston

STAPLEFORD GB E 209
Trent Trucks Sandcliffe Motor Group,
Nottingham Road,
Stapleford NG9 8AU
Tel 0602 395000

SUTTON IN ASHFIELD GB E 312
Evans Halshaw (Sutton) Ltd,
Station Road,
Sutton-in-Ashfield NG17 5FH
Tel 0623 511511

WORKSOP GB E 313
J T Hunt (Workshop) Ltd,
Claylands Avenue,
Worksop S18 7BQ
Tel 0909 475561

Oxfordshire

BANBURY GB E 118
Banbury Trucks Ltd,
Transport Centre,
Unit One, Tuston House,
Station Approach,
Banbury OX16 8MB
Tel 0295 67528

BANBURY GB K 312
Hartford Motors (Banbury) Ltd,
98 Warwick Road,
Banbury OX16 7AH
Tel 0293 67711

KIDLINGTON GB N 112
Hartwells of Oxford Ltd,
Langford Lane,
Kidlington OX5 1RY
Tel 08675 71511

OXFORD GB E 215
Evenlode Truck Centre Ltd,
Eynsham Road,
Cassington,
Oxford OX5 1DD
Tel 0865 881581

OXFORD GB K 311
Hartford Motors (Oxford) Ltd,
Besselsleigh Road,
Nr Wootton,
Abingdon OX13 6TP
Tel 0865 736377

OXFORD GB K 226
Tappins Coach World,
Collett Southmead Industrial Park,
Didcot OX11 7ET
Tel 0235 511115

Shropshire

SHREWSBURY GB D 116
Furrows Commercial Vehicles Ltd,
Emmerdale Road,
Harlescott Industrial Estate,
Shrewsbury SY1 3NP
Tel 0743 57971

SHREWSBURY GB D 212
Lucas Service UK Ltd,
Lancaster Road,
Harlescott,
Shrewsbury SY1 3NJ
Tel 0743 55061

TELFORD GB D 320
Furrows Commercial Vehicles Ltd,
Halesfield,
Telford
Tel 0952 584433

Somerset

FROME GB H 115
J R Harding & Sons (Frome) Ltd,
Whitworth Road,
Marston Trading Estate,
Frome BA11 4BY
Tel 0373 64970

SHEPTON MALLET GB H 215
Tachograph Services
(Shepton Mallet) Ltd,
Crowne Trading Estate,
Shepton Mallet BA4 5QU
Tel 0749 3963

TAUNTON GB H 107
White Bros (Taunton) Ltd,
Commercial Division,
Bathpool,
Taunton TA2 8BA
Tel 0823 74957

TAUNTON GB H 203
H N Hickley & Co Ltd,
Castle Street,
Tangier,
Taunton TA1 4AU
Tel 0823 276041

TAUNTON GB H 307
National Carriers Fleetcare,
Canal Road,
Taunton TA1 1PL
Tel 0823 331151

WINCANTON GB H 219
Wincanton Truck Centre,
Aldermeads,
Wincanton BA9 9EB
Tel 0963 33800

YEOVIL GB H 101
Douglas Seaton Ltd,
West Hendford,
Yeovil BA20 2AG
Tel 0935 27421

YEOVIL GB H 309
Abbey Hill Vehicle Service,
Boundary Road,
Lufton Trading Estate,
Yeovil BA22 8SS
Tel 0935 29111

Staffordshire

BURTON UPON TRENT GB D 108
Marley Transport Ltd,
Lichfield Road,
Branston,
Burton upon Trent DE14 3HG
Tel 0283 712264

BURTON UPON TRENT GB D 317
BRS Midlands Ltd,
Derby Street,
Burton upon Trent DE14 2LN
Tel 0283 63702

CANNOCK GB D 124
Cannock Tachograph Centre Ltd,
Units 2 & 3 Cannock Industrial Centre,
Walk Mill Lane,
Bridgetown

LICHFIELD GB D 114
TRS (Transport) Ltd,
Freeford Bridge,
Tamworth Road,
Lichfield
Tel 0543 480798

NEWCASTLE UNDER LYME GB D 314
Hartshorne (Potteries) Ltd,
Rosevale Road,
Parkhouse Industrial Estate,
Newcastle under Lyme ST5 7EF
Tel 0782 566400

STAFFORD GB D 200
Lloyds Garage Ltd,
Stone Road,
Stafford ST16 2RA
Tel 0785 51331

STOKE-ON-TRENT GB D 101
Beeches Garage (1983) Ltd,
Leek Road,
Hanley,
Stoke-on-Trent ST1 6AD
Tel 0782 13836

STOKE-ON-TRENT GB D 500
Chatfields of Stoke,
Commercial Vehicle Division,
Clough Street,
Hanley,
Stoke-on-Trent ST1 4AR
Tel 0782 202591

STOKE-ON-TRENT GB D 315
Kay's Ltd,
Leek New Road,
Cobridge,
Stoke-on-Trent ST6 2DE
Tel 0782 264121

STOKE-ON-TRENT GB D 120
Mainline Trucks,
High Street,
Sandyford,
Tunstall,
Stoke-on-Trent ST6 5PD
Tel 0782 575222

STOKE-ON-TRENT GB D 219
BRS Midlands Ltd,
Repair Centre,
Vernon Road,
Stoke-on-Trent ST4 2QF
Tel 0782 48281

Suffolk

BECCLES GB F 214
Gales Garages Ltd,
Common Lane North,
Beccles NR34 9QD
Tel 0502 717023

BURY ST EDMUNDS GB F 115
Chassis-Cabs Ltd,
Northern Way,
Bury St Edmunds IP52 6NL
Tel 0284 68570

FELIXSTOWE GB F 311
Crossways (European) Ltd,
Sub-Station Road,
The Dock,
Felixstowe IP11 8QU
Tel 0394 673272

IPSWICH GB F 114
Marshall (Cambridge) Ltd,
Goddard Road,
Whitehouse Industrial Estate,
Ipswich
Tel 0437 240200

IPSWICH GB F 210
Lucas Service UK Ltd,
Hadleigh Road Industrial Estate,
Ipswich IP2 0HB
Tel 0473 215931

IPSWICH GB F 320
Duffields of East Anglia,
Foxtail Road,
Ransomes Park,
Ipswich IP3 9RT

LOWESTOFT GB F 101
Days Garage Ltd,
Whapload Road,
Lowestoft NR32 1UR
Tel 0502 565353

STOWMARKET GB F 316
Robinson Truck Ltd,
Violet Hill Road,
Stowmarket IP14 1NN
Tel 0449 613553

SUDBURY GB F 113
Solar Garage (Ipswich),
Co-operative Society Ltd,
Cornard Road,
Sudbury CO10 6XA
Tel 0953 72301

WOODBRIDGE GB F 104
A G Potter,
New Road,
Framlingham,
Woodbridge IP13 9AI
Tel 0728 723215

Surrey

EPSOM GB N 500
Cummings & Foster Ltd,
T/A Benhill Motors,
London Road,
Ewell-by-pass,
Epsom KT17 2PT
Tel 081-394 2196

GUILDFORD GB N 307
Grays Truck Centre Ltd,
Slyfield Industrial Estate,
Woking Road,
Guildford GU1 1RY
Tel 0483 571012

GUILDFORD GB N 207
F G Barnes & Sons Ltd,
Slyfield Industrial Estate,
Woking Road,
Guildford GU1 1RT
Tel 0483 37731

HORLEY GB N 107
Horley Services Ltd,
Salfords Industrial Estate,
Horley,
Nr Redhill RH1 5ES
Tel 0297 771481

Sussex

CHICHESTER GB K 308
Francis Transport Ltd,
Portfield Quarry,
Shopwyke Road,
Chichester PO20 6AD
Tel 0243 780011

EASTBOURNE GB K 211
Panda Diesels (Newhaven) Ltd,
Eastbourne Road,
Pevency,
Westham,
North Eastbourne BN24 5NH
Tel 0323 767626

HORSHAM GB K 205
Evans Halshaw (Sussex) Ltd,
78 Billingshurst Road,
Broadbridge Heath,
Horsham RH12 3LP
Tel 0403 56464

HORSHAM GB N 303
Hancocks of Horsham Ltd,
53-55 Bishopric,
Horsham RH12 1QJ
Tel 0403 60465

PORTSLADE GB K 115,
Endeavour Motor Co Ltd,
Truck Division,
Ellen Street,
Portslade BN4 1DY
Tel 0273 418231

SHOREHAM-BY-SEA GB K 207
Evans Halshaw (Sussex) Ltd,
44 Dolphin Road,
Shoreham by Sea BN4 1DY
Tel 0273 454887

WORTHING GB K 117
I G Bacon Commercials Ltd,
Meadow Road Industrial Estate,
Worthing BN11 2RU
Tel 0903 204127

Tyne & Wear

BLAYDON GB B 318
North East DAF Trucks Ltd,
Chainbridge Road,
Blaydon NE21 5TR
Tel 091-414 3333

GATESHEAD GB A 109
BRS Northern Ltd,
Eastern Avenue,
Team Valley Trading Estate,
Gateshead NE11 0UU
Tel 091-487 8844

GATESHEAD GB A 200
Lucas Service UK Ltd,
Saltmeadows Road,
Gateshead NE8 3BS
Tel 091-477 3851

NEWCASTLE UPON TYNE GB A 103
Union Trucks Ltd,
Mylord Crescent,
Killingworth,
Newcastle upon Tyne NE12 0UW
Tel 091-268 3141

NEWCASTLE UPON TYNE GB A 211
Henly's (Newcastle) Ltd,
Melbourne Street,
Newcastle upon Tyne NE1 2ER
Tel 091-261 471

NEWCASTLE UPON TYNE GB A 306
R H Patterson & Co Ltd,
Forth Street Works,
Newcastle upon Tyne NE1 3PP
Tel 091-261 2661

SUNDERLAND GB A 307
Cowies of Sunderland,
North Hylton Road,
Southwick,
Sunderland SR5 3HQ
Tel 091-549 1111

Warwickshire

ALCESTER GB D 105
Smiths Coaches (Sherington) Ltd,
Tything Road,
Arden Forest Industrial Estate,
Alcester B49 6EX
Tel 0789 764401

BARFORD GB D 117
Oldhams of Barford,
Wellesbourne Road,
Barford CV35 8DS
Tel 0926 624333

RUGBY GB D 123
Noden Truck Centre,
3 Avon Industrial Estate,
Butlers Leap,
Rugby CV21 3UY
Tel 0788 79535

West Midlands

BIRMINGHAM GB D 122
Evans Halsham Leyland,
31 Shefford Road,
Aston B6 4PQ
Tel 021-359 8261

BIRMINGHAM GB D 110
Gerard Mann,
115-117 Charles Henry Street,
Birmingham B12 0SN
Tel 021-622 3031

BIRMINGHAM GB D 216
Birmingham Trucks Ltd,
292 Wharfdale Road,
Tyseley B11 2DT
Tel 021-707 9700

BIRMINGHAM GB D 220
Lucas Service UK Ltd,
171 Lichfield Road,
Aston B6 5SN
Tel 021-327 1525

BIRMINGHAM GB D 501
Bristol Street Motors Ltd,
Beacon House,
Long Acre,
Nechells B7 5JJ
Tel 021-322 2222

BIRMINGHAM GB D 309
Transfleet Services Ltd,
Bannerly Street,
Garretts Green Industrial Estate,
Birmingham B33 0SL
Tel 021-784 4000

BIRMINGHAM GB D 318
Midlands BRS Ltd,
Bromford Mills Branch,
Erdington B24 8DP
Tel 021-328 2200

BRIERLEY HILL GB D 119
Dudley Tachograph Centre Ltd,
Thorns Road Trading Estate,
Quarry Bank,
Brierley Hill DY5 2JS
Tel 0384 70301

BROWNHILLS GB D 322
Brownhills Tachograph Centre,
Lindon Road,
Brownhills WS8 7BW
Tel 05433 372528

COVENTRY GB D 319
Dawson Freight Commercials Ltd,
Unit 1,
Eden Street,
Coventry CV6 5HE
Tel 0203 683221

COVENTRY GB D 221
Carwood Motor Units Ltd,
Herald Way,
Binley,
Coventry CV3 2RQ
Tel 0203 449533

HALESOWEN GB D 209
Lex Tillotson Birmingham,
Park Road,
Halesowen B63 2RL
Tel 0384 424500

WALSALL GB D 111
Maybrook Trucks Ltd,
Coppice Lane,
Aldridge WS9 9AA
Tel 0922 56356

WALSALL GB D 206
Tildesley Ford,
Northgate,
Aldridge WS9 8TH
Tel 0922 743031

WALSALL GB D 305
Hartshorne Motor Services Ltd,
Bentley Mill Close,
Walsall WS2 0BN
Tel 0922 720941

WALSALL GB D 306
S Jones (Garages) Ltd,
Truck Centre,
Westgate,
Aldridge WS9 8ET
Tel 0922 743783

WARLEY GB D 312
Charthire Services Ltd,
Pearsall Drive,
Oldbury B69 2RA
Tel 021-544 5125

WEDNESBURY GB D 213
Wincanton Transport Ltd,
Heath Estate,
Whitworth Close,
Darlaston,
Wednesbury WS10 8LJ
Tel 021-526 3833

WEST BROMWICH GB D 118
Browns Electro-Diesel Co,
Vicarage Road,
West Bromwich B71 1AL
Tel 021-588 3101

WEST BROMWICH GB D 307
Guest Motors Ltd,
Truck Service Department,
Old Meeting Street,
West Bromwich B70 9SQ
Tel 021-553 2737

WOLVERHAMPTON GB D 103
Don Everall Motor Sales Ltd,
Bilston Road,
Wolverhampton WV2 2QE
Tel 0902 51515

WOLVERHAMPTON GB D 316
A F Glaze Ltd,
Dixon Street,
Wolverhampton
Tel 0902 55434

Wiltshire

CALNE GB H 121
Syms Engineering (Calne) Ltd,
Port Marsh Industrial Estate,
Calne SN11 9PZ
Tel 0249 814333

CALNE GB H 123
HDL Engineering,
Unit 4-5 Bumpers Farm Industrial Estate,
Chippenham
Tel 0249 443523

SWINDON GB H 109
Howard Tenens (Swindon) Ltd,
'D' Building,
Parsonage Road,
Stratton St Margaret SN3 4RL
Tel 0793 827050

SWINDON GB H 220
Gardiners Auto Electrical Services Ltd,
Hawksworth Trading Estate,
Swindon SN2 1EE
Tel 0793 29254

SWINDON GB H 312
BRS Western Ltd,
Green Bridge Industrial Estate,
Stratton St Margaret
Tel 0793 29281

WESTBURY GB H 312
Rygor Commercials Ltd,
The Broadway,
West Wilts Trading Estate,
Westbury BA13 4HU
Tel 0373 864334

North Yorkshire

BOROUGHBRIDGE GB B 117
Boroughbridge Motors Ltd,
Bar Lane,
Boroughbridge YO5 9NN
Tel 0423 322741

MALTON GB B 212
Slaters Transport Ltd,
Kirby Misperton,
Malton YO17 0UE
Tel 065 386 275

THIRSK GB B 128
Crossroads Commercials Ltd,
Stockton Road,
Thirsk YO7 1AY
Tel 0845 22057

YORK GB B 207
York Autoelectrics Ltd,
58 Layerthorpe,
York YO3 7YN
Tel 0904 54513

YORK GB B 307
Polar Motor Co (York) Ltd,
Fulford Way,
Fulford,
York YO1 1YF
Tel 0904 625371

YORK GB B 126
BRS Northern Ltd,
7 James Street,
York YO1 3DW
Tel 0904 410955

South Yorkshire

BARNSLEY GB B 112
BRS Northern Ltd,
Shawfield Road,
Carlton Industrial Estate,
Barnsley S71 3HS
Tel 0226 298321

BARNSLEY GB B 305
The Polar Truck Centre,
Wombwell Lane,
Stairfoot,
Barnsley S70 3NX
Tel 0226 732732

BARNSLEY GB B 205
Cameron Motor Service Centre,
Barrowfield Road,
Platts Common Trading Estate,
Hoyland,
Barnsley S74 9SF
Tel 0226 742654

DONCASTER GB B 114
Trailer Supermarket (Bawtry) Ltd,
Doncaster Road,
Bawtry,
Doncaster DN10 6NX
Tel 0302 710711

DONCASTER GB B 310
E G Charlesworth Ltd,
Truck Service Department,
Decoy Bank North,
Carr Orange Industrial Estate,
Doncaster DN4 5JE
Tel 0302 327111

DONCASTER GB B 311
BRS Northern Ltd,
Barnsley Road,
Doncaster DN5 8RD
Tel 0302 390066

SHEFFIELD GB B 312
Oughtibridge Tachograph Centre,
Station Lane,
Oughtibridge,
Sheffield S30 3HS
Tel 0742 863881

SHEFFIELD GB B 316
Sherwood Leyland DAF (Sheffield) Ltd,
Highfield Lane,
Sheffield S13 9DB
Tel 0742 693230

SHEFFIELD GB B 120
Charles Clark,
1 Saville Street,
Sheffield S4 7TF
Tel 0742 766600

SHEFFIELD GB B 201
T C Harrison Group Ltd,
Sheffield Truck Operations,
Shepcote Lane,
Sheffield S9 1TX
Tel 0742 440051

SHEFFIELD GB B 211
Plaxton Parts & Services,
Ryton Road,
South Anston,
Sheffield S31 7ES
Tel 0909 551155

SHEFFIELD GB B 214
Lucas Service UK Ltd,
300 Savile Street,
Sheffield S4 7UD
Tel 0742 752522

West Yorkshire

BATLEY GB B 210
Lucas Service UK Ltd,
232 Bradford Road,
Batley WF17 6LF
Tel 0924 472415

BRADFORD GB B 125
Long Truck Services Ltd,
T/A Northern Coachworks Ltd,
Northside Road,
Bradford BD7 2BA
Tel 0274 579262

BRADFORD GB B 300
C D Bramall (Bradford) Ltd,
Truck Workshops,
Dagenham Road,
Dudley Hill,
Bradford BD4 9LS
Tel 0274 682224

BRIGHOUSE GB B 122
Reliance Commercial Vehicles Ltd,
Wakefield Road,
Brighouse HD6 1QQ
Tel 0484 712611

CLECKHEATON GB B 115
Crossroads Commercials Ltd,
Bradford Road,
Gomersal,
Cleckheaton BD19 4BE
Tel 0274 851111

HUDDERSFIELD GB B 309
Brockholes Ltd,
Leeds Road,
Huddersfield HD2 7UW
Tel 0484 28111

LEEDS GB B 102
Archbold Truck Sales & Service Ltd,
Albert Road,
Morley LS27 8TT
Tel 0532 538511

LEEDS GB B 302
Trimoco Motor Group Ltd,
Trimoco Trucks,
54 Dolly Lane,
Leeds LS9 7NE
Tel 0532 421222

LEEDS GB B 308
Transfleet Services Ltd,
Howley Park Trading Estate,
Morley LS27 0BS
Tel 0532 524422

LEEDS GB B 104
WASS Ltd,
123 Hunslett Road,
Leeds LS10 1LD
Tel 0532 439911

LEEDS GB B 202
Sewell of Leeds Ltd,
49 Marshall Street,
Leeds LS11 9SU
Tel 0532 435101

LEEDS GB B 127
Charthire Services plc,
Parkside Lane,
Dewsbury Road,
Leeds LS11 5TD
Tel 0532 773377

LEEDS GB B 180
Knottingley Truck Ltd,
Common Lane,
Knottingley WF11 8BG

PUDSEY GB B 100
Chatfields of Leeds,
Grangefield Industrial Estate,
Richardshaw Lane,
Pudsey LS28 6SO
Tel 0532 571701

ROTHERHAM GB B 129
Crossroads Commercials Ltd,
Canklow Meadows Industrial Estate,
West Bawtry Road,
Rotherham
Tel 0709 365566

WAKEFIELD GB B 118
Chalderford Motor Co Ltd,
Barnsley Road,
Wakefield WF1 5JS
Tel 0924 290290

Scotland

Borders Region

GALASHIELS GB M 207*
Chalmers McQueen Ltd,
Albert Place,
Galashiels TD1 3DL
Tel 0896 2729

Central

FALKIRK GB M 111
Scottish Road Services Ltd,
Burnbank Road,
Bainsford,
Falkirk FK2 7PD
Tel 0324 22805

FALKIRK GB M 209
Millar's of Falkirk Ltd,
Millar's Truck Centre,
North Main Street,
Carronshore,
Falkirk FK2 8HZ
Tel 0324 556211

STIRLING GB M 113
Charthire Service plc,
Whitehouse Road,
Springkerse Industrial Estate,
Stirling FK7 7SP
Tel 0786 51761

Dumfries & Galloway

DUMFRIES GB M 108
Gateside Commercials (DFS) Ltd,
Brownrigg Loaning,
Dumfries DG1 3JT
Tel 0387 61146/7

DUMFRIES GB M 307
Scottish Road Services Ltd,
Glasgow Road,
Dumfries DG2 ONY
Tel 0387 53171

STRANRAER GB M 211*
Western SMT Co Ltd,
Lewis Street,
Stranraer
Tel 0776 5174

Fife

KIRKCALDY GB L 306
Laidlaw (Fife) Ltd,
Forth Avenue,
Kirkcaldy KY2 5PS
Tel 0592 261199

Grampian

ABERDEEN GB L 204
The Harper Motor Co Ltd,
218 Auchmill Road,
Bucksburn,
Aberdeen AB2 9NB
Tel 0224 714741

ABERDEEN GB L 302
Scotman Truck & Van Centre,
Greenwell Road,
Tullos,
Aberdeen
Tel 0224 873641

ABERDEEN GB L 213
McPhersons Transport,
Units 3 & 4,
Girdleness Road,
Aberdeen AB1 4DQ
Tel 0224 895050

ABERDEEN GB L 107
Grampian Regional Transport Ltd,
395 King Street,
Aberdeen AB19 1SP
Tel 0224 637047

ABERLOUR GB L 206*
McPherson Transport (Aberlour) Ltd,
Fisherton Garage,
Aberlour AB2 9LB
Tel 03405 401

ELGIN GB M 116
Scottish Road Services Ltd,
Grampian Road,
Elgin,
Morayshire
Tel 0343 542171

HUNTLY GB L 304*
Woodside Garage,
Knock,
Huntly AB5 5LJ
Tel 046 686 245

THE TRANSPORT MANAGER'S AND OPERATOR'S HANDBOOK

Highland

INVERNESS GB L 201
Macrea & Dick Ltd,
36 Academy Street,
Inverness
Tel 0463 238036

INVERNESS GB L 310
Scottish Bus Group Engineering Ltd,
64 Seafield Road,
Longman Industrial Estate,
Inverness IV1 1TN
Tel 0463 231404

TAIN GB L 103*
G Bannerham (Tain) Ltd,
Shore Road,
Tain,
Rosshire N19 1EH
Tel 0862 2480

Lothian

BROXBURN GB M 216
Beaverbank Motor Co Ltd,
East Mains Industrial Estate,
Broxburn EH52 5AU
Tel 0506 854834

DUNBAR GB M 219
Lowland Scottish Omnibus,
Countless Road,
Dunbar EH42 1JH

EDINBURGH GB M 315
Fulton Auto Electric Ltd,
Bowling Green Street,
Leith,
Edinburgh EH6 5PR
Tel 031-554 1571

EDINBURGH GB M 118
James Bowen & Son Ltd,
Newbridge Industrial Estate,
Newbridge,
Edinburgh EH28 8PJ
Tel 031-333 5333

EDINBURGH GB M 200
SMT Sales & Service Co Ltd,
2 Westfield Avenue,
Edinburgh EH11 2RE
Tel 031-337 9300

LOANHEAD GB M 314
Lothian Leyland DAF Ltd,
Straiton,
Loanhead EH20 9HQ
Tel 031-440 4100

Strathclyde

AIRDRIE GB M 213
Central Motors (Calderbank) Ltd,
Carlisle Road,
Airdrie ML6 8RD
Tel 023 64 62881

BARRHILL GB M 305*
W & J Barr & Sons (Scotland) Ltd,
Braehead,
Barrhill KA26 0QR
Tel 0465 82253/82279

BELLSHILL GB M 312
Laidlaw Trucks (Strathclyde) Ltd,
Rigghead Industrial Estate,
Bellshill ML4 3LG
Tel 0698 747015

BLANTYRE GB M 120
Ailsa Trucks (Northern) Ltd,
Whistleberry Road,
Blantyre ML3 0ED
Tel 0698 823300

CAMPBELTOWN GB M 212*
Martin Maintenance Campbeltown Ltd,
Ben Mhor Garage,
Saddell Street,
Cambeltown,
Argyll
Tel 0586 53155

CUMBERNAULD GB M 301
Scotia DAF Trucks Ltd,
8 South Wordpark Court,
Wordpark South,
Cumbernauld G67 3HE
Tel 0236 727771

CUMNOCK GB M 103
Kerr & Smith (Cumnock) Ltd,
Riverside Garage,
Ayr Road,
Cumnock KA18 1BJ
Tel 0290 22440

GLASGOW GB M 115
Charthire Services plc,
23 Moss Road,
Ayr Road,
Glasgow G51 4JT
Tel 041-440 1889

GLASGOW GB M 201
Lex-Tillotson Glasgow,
131 Bogmore Road,
Glasgow G51 4TH
Tel 041-425 1530

GLASGOW GB M 204
Lucas Service Ltd,
200-210 Garscube Road,
Glasgow G4 9RR
Tel 041-332 6591

GLASGOW GB M 206
Wylies Ltd,
149 Kilbirnie Street,
Glasgow G5 8JH
Tel 041-429 6262

GLASGOW GB M 210
Leyland Bus,
Scottish Service Centre,
2121 London Road,
Glasgow G32 8XJ
Tel 041-778 3491

GLASGOW GB M 215
Ailsa Trucks (Northern) Ltd,
101 Kelburn Street,
Barrhead,
Glasgow G78 2LB
Tel 041-881 5851

GLASGOW GB M 303
Transfleet Services Ltd,
79 Hardgate,
Govan,
Glasgow G51 4SX
Tel 041-445 3913

GLASGOW GB M 218
Reliable Vehicles Ltd,
Clyde Street,
Renfrew,
Glasgow PA4 8SL
Tel 041-886 5633

GLASGOW GB M 110
Callenders Engineering Co Ltd,
47 Kirklee Road,
Kelvinside,
Glasgow G12 OSR
Tel 041-334 8155

KILMARNOCK GB M 313
Johnston & Drynan,
1 Fullarton Street,
Kilmarnock KA1 2RB
Tel 0563 2300

KILMARNOCK GB M 217
SBG (Engineering) Ltd,
Nursery Avenue,
Kilmarnock KA1 3JD
Tel 0563 23084

PAISLEY GB M 306
Clanford Motors Ltd,
37-41 Lonead,
Paisley PA1 1SY
Tel 041-887 0191

Tayside

DUNDEE GB L 101
Dundee Plant Co Ltd,
T/A Dundee Truck Centre,
411 Clepington Road,
Dundee DD3 8ED
Tel 0382 813644

DUNDEE GB L 108
Camperdown Motor Co Ltd,
Kingway West,
Dundee DD2 4TD
Tel 0282 623111

DUNDEE GB L 300
Tayscot Truck Ltd,
Smeaton Road,
Western Gourdee,
Dundee
Tel 0382 623263

DUNDEE GB L 212
Dundee Leyland DAF Ltd,
Bett Trucks Ltd,
Faraday Street,
Dundee DD2 3QQ
Tel 0382 817002

FORFAR GB L 214
A M Phillips Ltd,
Muiry Faulds Garage,
Angus,
By Forfar DD8 1XP
Tel 030 782 255

PERTH GB L 307
G Mutch Mechanical Services,
Shore Road,
Perth
Tel 0738 30291

PERTH GB L 500
Frews Cars Ltd,
Riggs Road,
Perth PH2 0NT
Tel 0738 25121

Western Isles

STORNOWAY GB L 309*
Galston (Stornoway) Motor Services Ltd,
Ness Road,
Barvas PA86 0QS
Tel 0851 84269

Wales

Clwyd

CLWYD GB C 132
Deeside Truck Services,
Pinfold Lane,
Alltami,
Mold CH7 6NY
Tel 0244 547202

COLWYN BAY GB C 107
Gordon Ford,
The Trading Estate,
Mochdre,
Colwyn Bay LL28 3HA
Tel 0492 46756

DEESIDE GB C 326
Thomas Hardie Commercials (North Wales),
Chester Road East,
Deeside CH5 1QA
Tel 0244 822707

HOLYWELL GB C 117
Ellis Davies & Son Ltd,
Crown Chert Quarry,
Trelogan,
Holywell CH8 9 BD
Tel 0745 560320

WREXHAM GB C 231
Unigate plc,
Kays Wrexham Ltd,
Wrexham Road,
Rhostyllan,
Nr Wrexham LL14 4DP
Tel 0978 291915

WREXHAM GB C 312
Border Tachograph Services Ltd,
Pentybont Industrial Estate,
Penybont Works,
Chirk,
Wrexham LL14 JAW
Tel 0978 823434

Dyfed

CARMARTHEN GB G 303
Western BRS Ltd (West Wales Branch),
Heol Alltycrap,
Johnstown,
Carmarthen SA31 3NE
Tel 0267 230650

HAVERFORDWEST GB G 105
Merlin Motor Co Ltd,
Fishguard Road Industrial Estate,
Haverfordwest SA62 4BT
Tel 0437 2468

LLANFYRNACH GB G 206*
Mansel Davies & Son Ltd,
Taffyale Garage,
Station Yard,
Llanfyrnach SA35 OBZ
Tel 0239 831631

LLANRHYSTUD GB G 212*
Lewis' Coaches,
Bryneithin,
Llanrhystud
Tel 09748 495

Mid Glamorgan

BRIDGEND GB G 210
BRS Western Ltd,
Westerton Road,
Bridgend CF31 3YS
Tel 0656 653331

CAERPHILLY GB G 104
R J Brown Ltd,
The Truck Centre,
Pontygwindy Industrial Estate,
Caerphilly CF8 3HU
Tel 0222 852222

TREFOREST GB G 301
Griffin Mill Garages Ltd,
Upper Boat,
Treforest,
Nr Pontypridd
Tel 044385 2216

South Glamorgan

CARDIFF GB G 109
Tanner Tachograph Centre Ltd,
c/o W T Davies (Transport) Ltd,
232 Penarth Road,
Cardiff CF1 7XJ
Tel 0222 225580

CARDIFF GB G 214
Lucas Service UK Ltd,
Unit 2c,
Glynstell Close,
off Hadfield Road,
Cardiff CF1 8TR
Tel 0222 28361

CARDIFF GB G 307
Cardiff Truck Centre,
Whittle Road,
Leckwith Industrial Estate,
Cardiff CF1 8AT

West Glamorgan

SWANSEA GB G 108
City Electro Diesel Services,
Site F3,
Nantyffin Road South,
Llansamlet,
Swansea
Tel 0792 792010

SWANSEA GB G 209
Shorts Auto Electrical Services Ltd,
43-49 Station Road,
Landore,
Swansea SA1 2JE
Tel 0792 469595

SWANSEA GB G 300
Bevan Commercial Vehicles Ltd,
18-20 Morfa Road,
Hafod,
Swansea SA1 2EH
Tel 0792 650646

Gwent

NEWPORT GB G 103
South Wales Commercials Ltd,
Leeway,
Spytty Road,
Newport NPT OUQ
Tel 0633 271005

NEWPORT GB G 211
BRS Western Ltd,
Watch House Parade,
Alexandra Dock,
Newport NP9 5YG
Tel 0633 840083

NEWPORT GB G 306
Newport Ford,
T/A Newport Truck Centre,
Leeway Industrial Estate,
Newport NP1 OQU
Tel 0633 278020

Gwynedd

ANGLESEY GB C 320*
Maelog Farm Services,
Elim Garage Ltd,
Llanfachraeth,
Anglesey LL65 4UP
Tel 0407 740261

CAERNARFON GB C 222*
J T Jones & Sons,
Dulyn Motors,
Penygroes,
Caernarfon
Tel 0286 880218

Powys

BRECON GB G 207*
Brecon Motors (DIS) Ltd,
The Walton,
Rich Way,
Brecon LD3 4EG
Tel 0874 2223

NEWTOWN GB C 216*
Grooms Industries,
Pool Road,
Newtown SY16 1DL
Tel 0686 26731

477

DIRECTORY OF TRANSPORT SUPPORT SERVICES

1 Accessories and components

2 Bodybuilders

3 Ferries and container terminal operators

4 Driver agencies

5 Heavy haulage contractors

6 Light freight and express services

7 Recovery and repair services

8 Tachograph analysis

9 Training services

10 Vehicle and trailer manufacturers, dealers and distributors

1 ACCESSORIES AND COMPONENTS

Aerodyne Equipment
3 Aintree Road,
Perivale,
Greenford,
Middlesex UB6 7LA

Tel 081-998 5042
Contact: A Kingston (Marketing Manager)

Air deflectors, truck styling/streamlining kits, spray suppression, reversing bleepers.

Garphyttan Ltd
Hilton Road,
Aycliffe Industrial Estate,
Newton Aycliffe,
Co. Durham DL5 6SX

Tel 0325 310110
Fax 0325 311834

Hawkes Truck Supplies
Sherwood Road,
Aston Fields Ind. Estate,
Bromsgrove,
Worcs B60 3DR

Tel 0527 70749/70849
Fax 0527 70774
Contact: M Hawkes (Director)

Suppliers of commercial vehicle body fittings, sleeper cabs, deflectors, sheetracks.

Perkins Engines Ltd
Eastfield,
Peterborough PE1 5NA

Tel 0743 52262
Fax 0743 69911

Voith Engineering Ltd
6 Beddington Farm Road,
Croydon,
Surrey CR0 4XB

Tel 081-667 0333
Fax 081-667 0403

2 BODYBUILDERS

J C Bennett & Co (Coachbuilders) Ltd
240 Petershill Road,
Springburn,
Glasgow G21 4AP

Tel 041-558 6044
Contact: Bill Ritchie (Director)

Mechanical electrical respray and repair facilities available, quotations free.

Bodystyle Limited
'Little Tanyard',
Petworth Road,
Wisborough Green,
Billingshurst,
West Sussex RH14 0BH

Tel 0403 700222
Contact: R G Ellis (Director)

Bodybuilding specialists – commercial vehicles, trailers, horseboxes. New, repairs, conversions, hire.

McComb Coachwork
22 Market Place,
Tattershall,
Lincs LN4 4LJ

Tel 0526 42292
Fax 0526 44411
Contact: W Limb (Partner)

Vehicle body building, accident repairs, painting in 50ft low bake.

Olivers (Coachbuilders) Limited
Wharncliffe Road,
Shipley,
West Yorkshire BD18 2AD

Tel 0274 582594
Contact: Tony Lee (Managing Director)

Manufacturers of curtainsided bodies, van/aluminium and GRP dropsides, pantechnicons, platforms, plant vehicles and glass carrying vehicles. Complete painting and lettering service. Accident and general repairers.

Scarab Sales Ltd
Underlyn Farm,
Maidstone Road,
Marden,
Tonbridge,
Kent TN12 9BQ

Tel 0622 831006
Fax 0622 832417
Contact: R L Hoadley (Managing Director)

Manufacturers of suction road sweepers, Scarab Major and Scarab Minor.

3 FERRIES AND CONTAINER TERMINAL OPERATORS

Railfreight Distribution
Freightliner Terminal,
Trunk Road,
Grangetown,
Middlesbrough,
Cleveland TS6 7SD

Tel 0642 455575
Fax 0642 457935
Telex 58478
Contact: E E Parsons (Terminal Manager)

Specialists in intermodal transport and storage and repair of containers.

Sally Freight
York Street,
Ramsgate,
Kent CT11 9OS

Tel 0843 585496

4 DRIVER AGENCIES

Drake International
14/16 Powis Street,
Woolwich,
London SE18

Tel 081-854 7705
Contact: Karen Meekums (Branch Manager)

Through numerous locations around Greater London, Drake can meet all your temporary and permanent industrial and driving staffing requirements.

5 HEAVY HAULAGE CONTRACTORS

W E Haselden (Midlands) A Division of HND
573 Stoney Stanton Road,
Coventry,
West Midlands CV6 5ED

Tel 0203 682122
Fax 0203 637065
Contact: T Fox (Manager)

General haulage. Short notice, urgent work, anywhere. Clearing house specialists.

Heavy Transport Association
c/o Aaron and Partners,
Grosvenor Court,
Foregate Street,
Chester,
Cheshire CH1 1HG

Tel 0244 315366
Fax 0244 350660
Contact: John Dyne (Secretary)

Promotion of the professional and trading interests of heavy hauliers.

R C Robinson Haulage Ltd

1 Warrengate Road,
North Mymms,
Hatfield,
Hertfordshire AL9 7TT

Tel 0707 53200
Fax 0707 52508
Telex 893650
Contact: Daphne Dean (Director)

General haulage, UK specialising construction, industry and heavy haulage.

6 LIGHT FREIGHT AND EXPRESS SERVICES

C & C Transport Services

The White House,
Winterbourne Monkton,
Swindon,
Wiltshire SN4 9NW

Tel 06723 375
Fax 06723 448
Contact: Stefan Foster (Senior Director)

Finearts and furniture distribution, computer handling, weekly London multi-drop

7 RECOVERY AND REPAIR SERVICES

AA BRS Fleet Rescue

Monaco House,
Bristol Street,
Birmingham B5 7AS

Tel 021-622 6841
Fax 021-622 6768

Pirelli Ltd

Derby Road,
Burton on Trent DE13 0BH

Tel 0283 66301
Fax 0283 32042

Sellers & Batty Peterborough

Fengate,
Peterborough,
Cambs PE1 5XG

Tel 0733 60591/60594
Fax 0733 891122
Contact: D Wright (After Sales Manager)

ERF Distributors covering Bedfordshire, Cambridgeshire, Lincolnshire, Huntingdonshire. Recognised Cummins, Rolls Royce, Gardner engine repair specialists. Lucas Kienzle tachograph testing station. 24-hour recovery repair service. Members of RAC Octagon RRAS. Van delivery service covering above areas. A new truck, a new part or repair. We can help. Phone 0733 60591.

8 TACHOGRAPH ANALYSIS

Sellers & Batty Peterborough

Fengate,
Peterborough,
Cambs PE1 5XG

Tel 0733 60591/60594
Fax 0733 891122
Contact: D Wright (After Sales Manager)

ERF Distributors covering Bedfordshire, Cambridgeshire, Lincolnshire, Huntingdonshire. Recognised Cummins, Rolls Royce, Gardner engine repair specialists. Lucas Kienzle tachograph testing station. 24-hour recovery repair service. Members of RAC Octagon RRAS. Van delivery service covering above areas. A new truck, a new part or repair. We can help. Phone 0733 60591.

9 TRAINING SERVICES

Management Development Associates
134 Wood End Road,
Erdington,
Birmingham
Tel 021-382 5036
Contact: Professor John Hibbs (Managing Partner)

Short courses developing management skills and competences in your staff.

10 VEHICLE AND TRAILER MANUFACTURERS, DEALERS AND DISTRIBUTORS

Bodystyle Limited
'Little Tanyard',
Petworth Road,
Wisborough Green,
Billingshurst,
West Sussex RH14 0BH

Tel 0403 700222
Contact: R G Ellis (Director)

Bodybuilding specialists – commercial vehicles, trailers, horseboxes. New, repairs, conversions, hire.

Contract Hire (Commercial Vehicles) Ltd
Severnside Trading Estate,
Avonmouth,
Bristol BS11 8AG

Tel 0272 825571
Fax 0272 235141

H & L Garages Ltd
Lealand Way,
Riverside Industrial Estate,
Boston,
Lincolnshire PE21 7FW

Tel 0205 311288
Fax 0205 311277
Contact: A Graham (Director)

Iveco Ford Trucks
Station Road,
Watford,
Hertfordshire WD1 1SR

Tel 0923 246400
Fax 0923 240574

Renault Trucks
37/43 Gorst Road,
London NW10

Tel 081-965 9181
Fax 081-961 8590

Index of Advertisers

AA BRS Fleet Rescue	4
Charnwood Publishing Co Ltd	58
Contract Hire (Commercial Vehicles) Ltd	423
Garphyttan Ltd	183
Iveco Ford Trucks	Outside front cover
National Breakdown Recovery Services	48
Perkins Engines Ltd	Outside back cover
Pirelli Limited	429
Renault Trucks	Facing inside front cover
Sally Line Ltd	392
S P Tyres Ltd	Inside front cover
Voith Engineering Ltd	232
Wabco Automotive	ii

Index

AA (Automobile Association) 109, 412, 433, Appendix IV
abandoned motor vehicles 363
abnormal loads 281-9
 see also dangerous and explosive
accident, notification of 263-5, 367
Action Volvo 248
ADI (Approved Driving Instructors) 126
ADR (international carriage of dangerous goods) 294, 404
AETR (*European Agreement Concerning the Work of Crews of Vehicles Engaged in International Road Transport 1971*) Rules 70, 413
agency cards 432-3
agency drivers and 'O' licences 18-19
AILs (Abnormal Indivisible Loads) 281-9
ALLMI (Association of Lorry Loader Manufacturers and Importers of Great Britain) 271
anti-spray devices 175-82
Applications and Decisions (As & Ds) 34, 36, 38, 44
Approved Substance Identification Numbers, Emergency Action Codes and Classifications for Dangerous Substances Conveyed in Road Tankers and Tank Containers (HMSO) 291, 296-7
Arrangements in GB for the Approval of Containers (HSE) 270
articulated vehicles
 'O' licence exemptions 16
 weights and dimensions 139-53
ATP (*Agreement on the International Carriage of Perishable Foodstuffs*) 277
autoguide, London 369
automatic bunkering 433

band 3 radio 439-40
bilateral permits 394-5
brakes 156-8, 375
 braking standards 157-8, 284
Braking Connections for Goods Vehicles and Trailers (DOE/DTp booklet) 158
breakdowns *see* recovery services
breath tests 361-2
BRS (British Road Services) Rescue 248
BT (British Telecom) 287, 440-2
builders' skips 206, 362-3
 Northern Ireland 391
bulk tankers 292-6

cabotage 47, 387, 395-6

carnets de passage 397-9
CB radio 436-8
CEFIC (*Conseil Européen des Fédérations de l'Industrie Chimique*) 295
CEGB (Central Electricity Generating Board) *see* National Grid Company
Cellnet (BT) 440-1
cellular telephone 440-2
Chemfreight Training 313
Chemical Industries Association 302
CIA voluntary code 307
CIM (*International Convention for the Conveyance of Goods by Rail*) 294
Classification and Labelling of Explosives Regulations 1983 309-10
Classification, Packaging and Labelling of Dangerous Substances Regulations 1984 (CPL Regs.) 291-2
A Guide to (HMSO) 292
CMR convention 407-10
communications, mobile 435-42
Community Drivers' Hours (Harmonisation with Community Rules) Regulations 1986 60
Community Drivers' Hours and Recording Equipment (Exemptions and Supplementary Provisions) Regulations 1986 60
Community Drivers' Hours and Recording Equipment Regulations 1985 60
Community licences *see* unified driver licensing scheme, new
company cars 374-5
conditions of carriage, RHA 334, 335-41
Construction and Use Regulations
 constructural requirements 155-82
 anti-spray 175-82
 brakes 156-8
 fuel tanks 163
 ground clearance, trailer 173-82
 horn 161-2
 lifting axles 158-9
 mirrors 161
 power-to-weight ratio 163
 safety glass 163
 seat belts 162
 sideguards 165-73
 silencer 163
 speedometer 162
 tyres 159-60
 underrun bumpers 164-5, 166
 windscreen wipers/washers 160-1
 wings 163

491

definitions, vehicle 155-6
loads 273-9
   abnormal and projecting 281-9
   dangerous and explosive 291-314
plating/testing inspections 207-31
safety 255-71
use of 18, 182-7
   exhaust emissions (Stages II/III) 185
   gas powered vehicles 185
   noise 183-4
   reversing alarms 187
   smoke 184-5
   television 186-7
   towing 185-6
   see also maintenance; records
weights and dimensions 139-53
Contracts of Employment Act 1972 131
Control of Pollution Act 1974 308
Control of Pollution (Special Waste) Regulations 1980 308, 309
COSHH (Control of Substances Hazardous to Health) Regulations 263
CPC (Certificate of Professional Competence) 49-57, 50
   classes of 50-1
   examinations 53-7
     dates/fees 53-4
     new syllabus 55-7
   exemptions 52-3
   Northern Ireland 56, 382
   qualifications 51-3
   'Grandfather Rights' 51-2
cranes
   lorry mounted 271
   mobile 221, 319
Criminal Justice Act 1988 279, 308
Customs Convention on the International Transport of Goods by Road (TIR Carnets) 1959 397-9
Customs and Excise, HM *see* excise duty
Customs Notices 750/A/B and 755 400

DAF Aid 248
dangerous and explosive loads 291-314
   bulk tankers 292-6
   CIA voluntary code
   driver training 302, 305, 313
   explosives 309-14
   in packages 202, 303-6
   restrictions/exemptions 302-3
   see also COSHH Regulations
Dangerous Substances (Conveyance by Road in Road Tankers and Tank Containers) Regulations 1981 292, 307
Data Protection Act 322
declaration of intent ('O' licence)
defect notices and prohibitions 224-31
Department of the Environment 309
   Belfast 382, 386, 388
Department of Transport 191, 402
derogation, temporary 41, 42
diamonds *see* hazard warning signs
Diesel Engines for Road Vehicles, the Performance of (DE) 184-5
diesel fuel (rebated heavy oil) 325-6
dimensions, vehicle *see* weights and dimensions

Disposal of Poisonous Waste Act 1972 308
Docks Regulations 1988 (SI 1655/88) 271
driver training 129
   dangerous goods 302, 305, 313
   on motorways 354-7
   Young Driver Scheme 129-35
drivers' hours 59-73
   AETR Rules 69-71
   British domestic rules 67-9, 375-6
     keeping records 31, 75-9
   EC rules 59-67
     break/rest periods 63-6
     exemptions 60-2
     summary 66-7
   mixed EC/British driving 69
   tax relief 71-3
Drivers' Hours (Harmonisation with Community Rules) Regulations 1986
drivers' records 31, 75-9, 238-9, 375-6
driving licences
   Euro-Licence 47, 97, 100, 107-8, 111, 121-3
   exchange of 108-9
   HGV 111-23
     classes of 113-14
     exemptions 114-15
     licence application 115-16
     licence renewal 117-18
     medical requirements 116-17
     new unified licensing scheme 121-3
     notional gross weights 120-1
     provisional licences 119-20
     suspension, revocation and disqualification 118-19
   ordinary 97-109
     age of drivers 98-100
     examination/endorsement codes 101-4
     international permits 109, 412
     licence application 100-1
     new unified licensing scheme 107-8
     penalty points/disqualification 104-5, 359-61
driving tests 125-37
   Advanced Commercial Vehicle 135-7
   HGV 126-9
     new procedures 129
   ordinary 125-6
   Young Driver Training Scheme 129-35
DSA (Driving Standards Agency) 125-6
DTI (Department of Trade and Industry)
   CB specifications 437
dual purpose vehicles 17
dump trucks 286
DVLA (Driver and Vehicle Licensing Agency) 97, 100, 321
DVLC *see* DVLA
dynamic weighers 153, 367

EC regulations
   brakes 156-8, 284, 375
   drivers' hours 59-67, 69, 71, 412-13
     summary of 66-7
   drivers' records (ICBs) 75-9
   EC/ECMT permits 18
   exhaust emissions 184-5

INDEX

fuel tanks 163
insurance cover 327-47
international plates 219
lighting/marking 193-206, 375
mirrors 161
noise 183-4
operators' licence 49
seat belts 162, 368-9, 370
tachographs 81, 89-91, 93-4
EC vehicle categories, new 122-3
electric vehicles 319
emergency action codes (dangerous loads) 202, 298-301
endorsement codes, driving licence 101-4
Energy Act 1976 377-8
environmental matters 27-8, 47
Environmental Protection Bill 278-9, 308
Euro-Licence 47, 97, 100, 107-8, 111, 121-3
European Agreement concerning the International Carriage of Dangerous Goods by Road (ADR) 294, 404
European Agreement on the International Carriage of Perishable Foodstuffs (ATP) 277
European Insurance Committee (CPA) 331
excise duty 315-26, 371-2
   excise licences 315-22
      exemptions 315-16
      payment 316-19
      registration/renewal 319-21
   rebated heavy oil 325-6
   recovery vehicles 324-5
   trade licences (plates) 322-4
exhaust emissions 184-5
   Stages II/III 185
explosives *see* dangerous and explosive loads
Explosives Act 1875 309, 313
Explosives Act 1875 (Exemptions) Regulations 1979 313

farmers' vehicles/'F' licences 40, 319
Finance Act 1987 325
Financing the Acquisition of Commercial Vehicles (NFC) 426
first aid 265-8
First Aid at Work (HS(R) 11) (HMSO booklet) 266
fixed penalty system, extended 359-61
   endorsable offences 360-1
fleet car/light vehicles 371-9
   C and U regulations 375
   drivers' hours/records 31, 60-2, 375-6
   excise duty 371-2
   fuel consumption 377-9, 431-3
   insurance 372-5
   'O' licence exemptions
   seat belts 377
   speed limits 376-7
   testing
'fly tipping' 278-9
Food Hygiene (Markets, Stalls and Delivery Vehicles) Regulations 1966 276
Food Hygiene Regulations 1970 277

fork-lift trucks 269
forms
   benefit, industrial injury (B176) 265
   Customs clearance 400
   HGV licence/test applications
      D1 100
      DLG1/(R) 115, 117
      DLG 26/X/Y/Z 126-7
      DTP 20003 116
   medical (F2508/A/9) 265
   'O' licence forms
      GV3 224
      GV9/A/B/C *see* PG9
      GV10 *see* PG10
      GV79/A/E/F 25, 27-8, 40, 249, 252
      GV80 36, 37
      GV81 37-8, 39
      GV160 152
      GV203 (CPCs) 50-2
      GV243 (NI) 385
      GV251A 45
      OL1/(R)/(S) 42
   police licence examination HO/RT1 101
   'prohibition goods' PG9/10 224-31, 241, 244
   RFOs (NI)
      RFL3 384-5
      RFL58 386
      see also GV243
   T-forms 397-401
   taxing (excise duty)
      V1 321
      V10 316, 320
      V11 320, 321
      V55 192, 320
      V112G 223, 322
      V205 320
      VE 55/1/5 316, 319
   testing/plating
      VT 17 236
      VT 20 236
      VT 29 236
      VT 30 235
      VTG4A/B/C/D 211
      VTG5/A/B 213
      VTG6 218
      VTG7 217
      VTG8 215
      VTG10 219-20
      VTG33 220-1
      VTG59 214
Foster Committee Report 248
'four-way flashers' 197-8, 375
Freight Containers (Safety Convention) Regulations 1984 270, 278
FTA (Freight Transport Association) 130, 245, 394, 416, 447
   Maintenance Services 241-4
   in Northern Ireland 382
   Regional Offices Appendix II
fuel economy 95, 427-34
   consumption tests 378-9
   vehicle 427-30
      checklist 434
      driving techniques 430-1
      fleet management 377-9, 431-3

mechanical considerations 163, 427-8
tyres 430

Gas Installations in Motor Vehicles and Trailers (DTp guide) 185
gas powered vehicles 185
GIT (Goods in Transit), insurance of 333-5
'good repute' 30-1, 56-7
Goods Vehicle (Certification) Regulations (Northern Ireland) 1982 387-8
Goods Vehicle (Operators' Licences, Qualifications and Fees) Regulations 1984/6/7 15, 49
Goods Vehicle (Operators' Licences) Regulations 1977 15
Goods Vehicle Testers' Manual (HMSO) 211, 238, 246, 250
Goods Vehicles (Plating and Testing) Regulations 1982/3/4/5/6 207, 220
'Grandfather Rights' 51-2
GTAs (Group Training Associations) 129, 133
Guide to Goods Vehicle Operators' Licensing, A (GV 74) (DTp) 26, 237, 242-3, 244, 251
Guidelines on the Responsible Disposal of Wastes (CBI booklet) 308

hazard warning lamps 197-8, 375
hazard warning signs (dangerous loads) 202, 298-301
Hazchem labels 293, 296, 297
Health and Safety at Work Act 1974 259-63, 271, 309, 313
  Docks Regulations 1988 271
  employees' duties 261-2
  employers' duties 259-61
  improvement/prohibition notices 262-3
  see also COSHH Regulations
Health and Safety (First Aid) Regulations 1981 265
Heavy Commercial Vehicles (Controls and Regulations) Act 1973
Heavy Goods Vehicle (Drivers' Licences) Regulations 1977 114
HGV (Heavy Goods Vehicle)
  annual testing 207-31
  defect notices/prohibitions 224-31
  driving licences 111-23
  driving tests 125-37
  inspections, DTp 223-4
  plating vehicles and trailers 215-23
  standard lists 216-19
Highways Act 1971 362
hiring, vehicle 239, 422-4
Hydrocarbon Oil Regulations 1973 326

IAM (Institute of Advanced Motorists) 135-6
ICBs (EC drivers' records) 75-9
IDS (International Diesel Service) 433
IMDG (*International Maritime Dangerous Goods) Code* 300
IMO (International Maritime Organisation) 300

Information Approved for the Classification, Packaging and Labelling of Dangerous Substances (HMSO) 304
inspections, DTp 223-31
  defect/prohibition notices 224-31
  on premises 223-4
  roadside 223
insurance 327-47
  business and premises 342-7
    employers' liabilities 342
    fire and special perils 344
    motor contingencies 345-6
    public liability 342-3
  claims, making 346-7
  company cars 372-5
  MIB 327, 367, 406
  obtaining best cover 346
  vehicles 327-31
    additional cover 331-3
    certificate of 328-9
    fleet/light vehicles 331, 372-5
    GIT (Goods in Transit) 333-6
      RHA conditions of carriage 336, 337-41
    international cover 330-1, 336-41
    invalidation/cancellation 329-30
    passenger liability 327-8
    property cover 328
    security 341-2
    third party 327
International Carriage of Dangerous Goods by Road (ADR) 294, 404
International Carriage of Perishable Foodstuffs Act 1976 404
International Convention for the Conveyance of Goods by Rail (CIM) 294
International Convention for Safe Containers - Geneva 1972 270, 278
International Road Freight Office
International Road Haulage Permits Act 1975 397
international transport operations 393-419
  bans on goods vehicles 415
  CIM 294
  CMR convention 407-10
  CPC 55-7
  customs procedures 397-401
    carnets de passage 401-2
    dangerous goods (adr) 402-4
    perishable foodstuffs (atp) 404-5
    T-forms 397-401
    taxes 405-6
    TIR convention 397-400
  documentation 410-12
  drivers' hours/work records 59-67, 69, 75-9, 412-13
    see also tachographs
  insurance 406-7
  Middle East journeys 416-19
  permits 394-7
    ECMT 18, 395-7
  proof of compliance plates
  weighing for ferry crossings 414
Ionising Radiations (Unsealed Radioactive Substances) Regulations 1968 294

INDEX

IoTA (Institute of Transport Administration) Appendix IV
IRFO (International Road Freight Office) 387, 416

journals, motoring Appendix IV

LA's (Licensing Authorities) 15-16, 445-6
  areas covered Appendix I
  'O' licences 30-5
  reorganisation of 46-7
leasing, vehicle 424-6
'Les Routiers' organisation 415
licences see driving licences; operators'
lifting axles (draft regulations) 158-9
light vehicle and fleet car operations 371-9
  C and U regulations 375
  drivers' hours/records 31, 60-2, 69, 375-6
  excise duty 371-2
  fuel consumption 377-9
  insurance 372-5
  'O' licence exemptions 45-6
  seat belts 377
  speed limits 376-7
  testing 231, 233-6
lighting and marking, vehicle 193-206
  beacons (rotating lamps) 199-200
  builders' skips 206
  dangerous loads 202, 288
  lamps 193-200
    auxiliary/optional 195-6
    direction indicators 197-8
    hazard warning 197-8, 375
    headlamps 194-5
      dim-dip lighting 195
    rear fog 198-9, 375
    rear (position) 196, 288
    reversing 196
    side (front position) 195, 288
    side marker 199, 288
    stop 196-7
  markings 200-6
    dangerous substances in packages 202
    rear reflective 202-6
    retro reflectors 200-1
lighting up times 353
  during daytime 357
loads
  abnormal and projecting 281-9
    projecting 287-8
    special types vehicles 281-7
  dangerous and explosive 291-314
    'Approved Lists' 291
      restrictions/exemptions 302-3
    bulk tankers 292-6
    CIA voluntary code 307
    explosives 309-14
    notification of accidents 263-5, 367
    in packages 303-6
    packaging and labelling 291-2, 296-302
    petroleum 306-7
    poisonous waste 307-9
    see also COSHH Regulations

  general 273-9
    animals 275-6
    container carrying 278
    distribution of 273
    'fly tipping' 278-9
    food 276-7
    length and width 274-5
      in London 275
    sand and ballast 277-8
    solid fuel 278
  safety of 255-6
'log books' see drivers' records
lorry loaders 271

MAC (Minister's Approval Certificate) 320
maintenance records 249-54
  defect repair sheets 250-2
  driver reports 249-50
  inspection reports 250
  retention of records 252-3
  vehicle history files 253-4
  wall planning charts 253
maintenance, vehicle 237-48
  contract maintenance 240-5
    FTA Maintenance Services 241-4
    sample agreement 242-3
  DTp advice/code of practice 237-9, 246, 249, 253
  in-house repairs 245
  inspections 245-7
  recovery services 248
  servicing/cleaning 247-8
Manual Handling Framework Guidance (HSE notes) 270
Merchant Shipping (Weighing of Goods Vehicles and other Cargo) Regulations 1988 414
MIB (Motor Insurers' Bureau) 327, 367, 406
mobile communications 435-42
  CB radio 436-8
  cellular telephone 440-2
  PMR (Private Mobile Radio) 439-40
  radio pagers 438-9
MOT Testers' Manual (HMSO) 234, 235
MOTECs (Multi-Occupational Training and Education Centres) 129
Motor Vehicles (Authorisation of Special Types) General Order 1979/81/ Amendment Order 1987 281
Motor Vehicles (Driving Licence) (Amendment) Regulations 1990 107-8
Motor Vehicles (Type Approval for Goods Vehicles) (Great Britain) Regulations 1982 189
motoring journals Appendix IV
motorway driving 354-7
Movement and Sale of Pigs Order 1975 275-6
multilateral permits 395
multipliers (notional weights) 120-1

National Breakdown Recovery Service 109, 248
National (Dangerous Substances) Driver Training Scheme (NDSDTS) 302, 305
National Grid Company 286

495

National Power 287
NFC (National Freight Consortium) 426
NJTC (National Joint Training Committee) *see* Young Driver Training Scheme
noise 183-4
North Review, the 349
Northern Ireland operations 45, 381-91
  builders' skips 391
  'O' licensing 381-5
  own-account operators 385
  period permits 385-7
  plating and testing 387-91
notional gross weight (multipliers) 120-1

'O' licences *see* operators' licensing
oil, rebated heavy 325-6
Operational Code of Practice
  dangerous bulk loads (HMSO) 292
  dangerous substances in packages (HMSO) 303
operators' licensing 15-47
  additional vehicles 36-7
  exemptions 16-18
  farmers' 'O' licences 40
  Foster Committee Report 248
  LA's considerations 30-5
    good repute 30-1
    local resident representation 32-3
    statutory objections 34-5
    suitability of premises 33
  licence applications 25-30
    declaration of intent 26-7
    fees and discs 30
    interim licences 29
  licence variation 37-8
  licensing courts/transport tribunal 42-5
    appeals 43-5
  light goods/foreign vehicles 45-6
  Northern Ireland 45, 381-5
  notification of changes 39
  penalties against 'O' licences 40-2
  proposed changes/1992 46-7
  recovery vehicles 221, 248, 324-5
  renewals 40
  requirements for 'O' licensing 20-5
    good repute 21-2
  restricted and standard licences 19-20
  subsidiary companies 39-40
  temporary derogation 42
  transfer of vehicles 38-9
  vehicle user, the 18-19, 421
organisations connected with transport Appendix IV
overloaded vehicles 31, 151-3, 364-7

Passenger Car Fuel Consumption Order 1977 378
penalty points/disqualification, licence 104-5, 359-61
permits, period 394-7
  Northern Ireland 386
petroleum, carriage of 306-7
PGR (dangerous packages regulations) 303, 309
plating, goods vehicles and trailers 215-23

DTp (Ministry)
  alterations, notifiable 192, 219-20
  articulated vehicle matching 216
  exemptions 220-3
  international plates 219
  standard lists 216-19
  manufacturers' 215
  Northern Ireland 387-91
  type approval certificate 191-2
PMR (Private Mobile Radio) 439-40
poisonous waste 307-9
power-to-weight ratio 163
professional competence 49-57, 50
  classes of 50-1
  examinations 53-7
  dates/fees 53-4
  syllabus 55-7
  exemptions 52-3
  Northern Ireland 56, 382
  qualifications 51-3
    'Grandfather Rights' 51-2
prohibition notices 224-31, 262-3

RAC (Royal Automobile Club) 109, 412 Appendix IV
Racal (Vodafone) 440-1
radio pagers (bleepers) 438-9
rebated heavy oil 325-6
records, driver 31, 75-9, 238-9, 375-6
records, maintenance 238
recovery services 248
  vehicles (licensing of) 221, 324-5
reefer (refrigerated) vehicles 145
Refuse Disposal (Amenity) Act 1978 363
Rehabilitation of Offenders Act 1974 22, 25
rental, vehicle 239, 421-2
reversing alarms 187, 269
RFO (Road Freight Operator's) Licence (NI) 381
RHA (Road Haulage Association) 130, 245, 448
  conditions of carriage 334, 335-41
  Hazfreight scheme 302
  journal *Roadway* Appendix IV
  in Northern Ireland 382
  Regional Offices Appendix III
RIDDOR (*Reporting of Injuries, Diseases and Dangerous Occurrences Regulations 1985*) 263-5
road fund licences *see* excise duty
Road Haulage Permits Act 1975 57
road safety *see* safety
Road Tanker Testing, Code of Practice on (HMSO) 292, 295
Road Traffic Act 1972 99, 118, 245, 250, 364
Road Traffic Act 1974 129-30, 364
Road Traffic Act 1988 152-3, 155-6, 207, 237, 249, 327, 364-6
Road Traffic (Carriage of Dangerous Substances in Packages etc.) Regulations 1985 (PGR) 309
Road Traffic Law Review Report (HMSO) 349
Road Traffic Offenders Act 1988 104
road traffic regulations 349-69

INDEX

abandoned motor vehicles 363
accident reporting 367
breath tests 361-2
builders' skips 362-3
bus lanes 358
fixed penalties 359
    endorsable offences 360-1
hazard warning 357
level crossings 358
lighting up times 353
    during daytime 357
lorry routes/bans 363-4
motorway driving 354-7
overloaded vehicles 364-7
owner liability 359
parking 357-8, 364
pedestrian crossings 362
radios/telephones in vehicles 369, 442
road humps 368
sale of unroadworthy vehicles 368
seat belts 368-9
speed limits 349-52
stopping/loading/unloading 353-4
traffic wardens 361
weight-restricted roads/bridges 358-9
wheel clamps 363
Road Transport of Hazardous Chemicals - A Manual of Principal Safety Requirements (CIA code) 307
Road Transport (Qualification of Operators) Regulations (Northern Ireland) 1977 381
Road User and the Law (DTp white paper) 349
Road Vehicles (Construction and Use) Regulations 1986 see Construction and Use Regulations
Road Vehicles (Construction and Use) Regulations 1990 139, 142-4
Road Vehicles Lighting Regulations 1984 193
RSA (Royal Society of Arts) 31, 53
    examinations Appendix IV
    Northern Ireland 56, 382
    see also Young Driver Training Scheme
RSAC (Royal Scottish Automobile Club) 412
RTITB (Road Transport Industry Training Board) 129-30
    Hazfreight scheme 302
    ITB training grants 133
    Young Driver Training Scheme 134-5 Appendix IV

SAD (Single Administrative Document) 401
Safe Operation of Lorry Loaders, Code of Practice for the (ALLMI) 271
safety 255-71
    dangerous loads 255-6
    dock premises 271
    first aid 265-8
    fork-lift trucks 269
    freight containers 270-1
    HSE report 256-9
    lorry loaders 271

manual handling 269-70
mobile communications 442
notification of accidents (RIDDOR) 263-5
road humps 368
safety signs 268
seat belts
vehicle reversing 268-9
Safety in Docks (HMSO Code of Practice) 271
Safety of Loads on Vehicles, A Code of Practice (DTp) (HMSO) 255-6, 278
SDRs (Special Drawing Rights) 408
seat belts 162, 368-9, 377
security, vehicle 341-2
semaphore arm indicators 197
sideguards 165-73
smoke 184-5
special types vehicles 201, 281-7, 351
speed limits 349-52
    fleet car/light vehicles 376-7
    special types vehicles 284
'spent' convictions 22
SSAP21 (*Statement of Accounting Practice*) 425
standard lists, HGV plating 216-19
STGO (Special Types General Order) 351
Study Manual of Professional Competence in Road Transport Management (Lowe) 55
subsidiary companies 39-40

T-forms 397-401
TAC (Type Approval Certificate) *see* type approval
tachographs 81-95, 452-77
    breakdown 85-6
    calibration, sealing and inspection 83-5
        BSI approved repairers Appendix V
    chart analysis 94-5
    drivers' responsibilities 82-3
    employers' responsibilities 81-2
    exemptions 89-91
    the instrument 91-4
    offences 89
    testing 223
    use of 86-9
TACS (Total Access Communications System) 440-2
tankers, bulk load 292-6
testing
    driver *see* driving tests
    vehicles
        HGV 207-15
            applications 208-10
            dates 208
            pass/failure-tests 213-15
            procedure 211-13
            refusal to test 210-11
            types of test 207-8
        light vehicles (MoT) 231, 233-6
            classes/exemptions 233-4
            the test 234-6
            test certificates 236
            Vehicle Defect Rectification Scheme 236
            Northern Ireland 387-91

497

TGWU 130
Three into Two Can Go (DoT leaflet) 158
TIR convention 397-9
trade plates 322-4
Traffic Areas 15-16,
  Appendix I
  reorganisation of 46-7
trailers, construction and use 173-82
training, driver *see* driver training
transfer of vehicles 38-9
Transfrigoroute (UK) 277
Transport Act 1968 19, 21, 27, 43, 49, 67, 75, 237, 293
Transport Act (Northern Ireland) 1967 381, 384
Transport of Dangerous Substances in Tank Containers (HSE booklet) (HSMO) 292-3
transport journals Appendix IV
Transport Kills (HSE report) (HMSO 1982) 256-9
Transport Tribunal 42-5
'Tremcards' (transport emergency cards) 295, 305
  multi-load Tremcards 305
Trucking International journal Appendix IV
type approval 189-92
  certificate of 320
tyres 159-60
Tyres and the Law (leaflet) 160

UICR (Union International des Chauffeurs Routiers) 415
underrun bumpers 164-5, 166
unified driver licensing scheme, new 47, 97, 100, 107-8, 111, 121-3
  dangerous goods tankers 302, 305, 313
  test procedures 129

VDRS (Vehicle Defect Rectification Scheme) 236
Vehicles (Excise) Act 1971 114, 234, 294, 315, 325
VOC (Vehicle Observer Corps) 341
vocational driving licences *see* unified driver licensing scheme

Waste Management Paper No 23 *Special Wastes: A Technical Memorandum* (DoE/HMSO) 309
Weighing of Motor Vehicles (Use of Dynamic Axle Weighing Machines) Regulations 1978 367
weight-restricted roads/bridges 358-9
weights and dimensions, vehicle 139-53
  height 145-6
  length 139-44
  special types
  weight 146-53
  width 144-5
Weights and Measures Act 1985 278

Young Driver Training Scheme 111, 129-35
  RTITB notes for employers
  training programme

see also EC vehicle categories, new
Your Driving Test and How to Pass (DL68) (DpT) 128
Your Lorry Abroad (RFO guide) 394

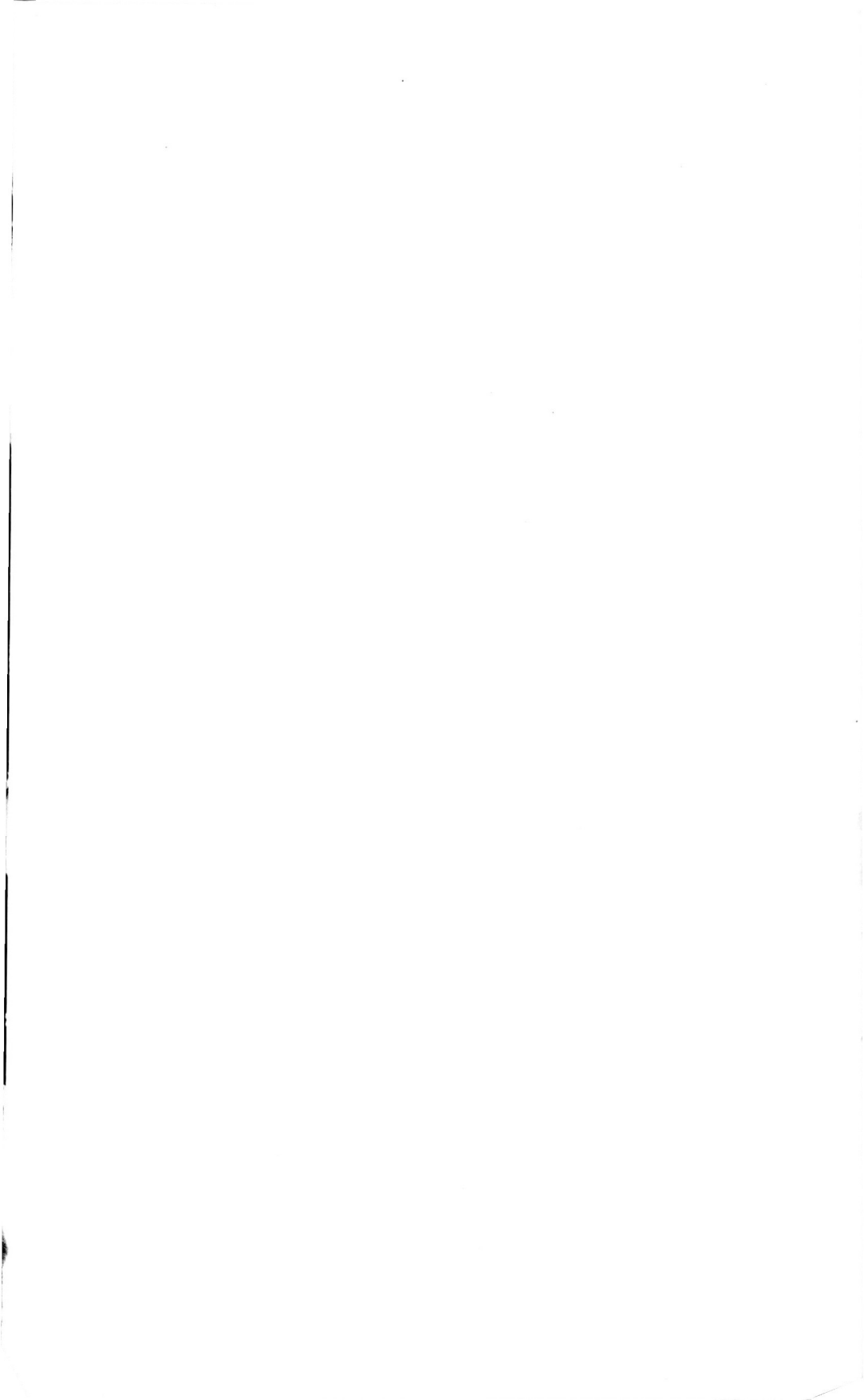

MR CORDY   INFORCEMENT
        0255-503792.
        0255-240586.

GOODS VICH
TESTING STATION
PURFLEET.   0708 866 389

INFORCEMENT
        081 518 0785.